THE POOR MAN'S MORNING AND EVENING PORTIONS

THE

POOR MAN'S MORNING AND EVENING PORTIONS;

BEING

A SELECTION OF A VERSE OF SCRIPTURE,

WITH

SHORT OBSERVATIONS FOR EVERY DAY IN THE YEAR,

INTENDED

FOR THE USE OF THE POOR IN SPIRIT, WHO ARE RICH IN FAITH, AND HEIRS OF THE KINGDOM.

"I have esteemed the words of his mouth more than my necessary food." — Job 23:12

"Thy words were found and I did eat them; and thy word was unto me the joy and rejoicing of mine heart." — Jer. 15:16

"The law of thy mouth is dearer unto me than thousands of gold and silver." — Ps. 119:72

by
Rev. Robert Hawker

REFORMATION HERITAGE BOOKS
Grand Rapids, Michigan

Reformation Heritage Books
2965 Leonard St. NE
Grand Rapids, Michigan 49525
(616) 977-0889 • Fax (616) 285-3246
e-mail: orders@heritagebooks.org
website: www.heritagebooks.org

ISBN # 978-1-89277-705-8

First Printing 1995
Second Printing 2001
Third Printing 2004
Fourth Printing 2011
Fifth Printing 2021

This edition of *The Poor Man's Morning and Evening Portions* was taken from Volume 8 of *The Works of the Rev. Robert Hawker, D.D.* (London: Printed for Ebenezer Palmer, 1831)

For additional volumes of Reformed persuasion both new and used, request a free book list from Reformation Heritage Books.

INTRODUCTION

With heartfelt joy we recommend the reprint of *The Poor Man's Morning and Evening Portions* by Dr. Robert Hawker (1753-1827), a prolific author and experiential, Calvinist preacher in the Church of England. Like Samuel Rutherford, he became well-known for his relish of Christ, exemplified most vividly in his book of daily devotions, reprinted here for the first time in more than a century.

This book received its unique name because it was originally published in small "penny" portions so as to be affordable to the poor. The morning portions were then gathered and re-published in 1809, followed in 1810 by a second volume of evening portions. The first American edition of the morning portions, taken from the fifth London edition, was published in New York by R. Wauchope in 1819. Ten years later, shortly after Hawker had passed on to glory, the morning and evening portions were combined in one volume according to his previous instructions, and printed in London. In 1831, the combined morning and evening portions were reprinted as volume 8 of the ten volume set of *The Works of the Rev. Robert Hawker, D.D.* (London: Printed for Ebenezer Palmer by E. Justins & Son). The present reprint is taken from this 1831 edition.

Hawker's writings — most notably his daily "portions" which went through numerous editions in the nineteenth century — have been spiritual food and drink for the God-fearing. Hawker excels in Christ-centered, practical divinity. He has been taught by the Spirit how to find Christ in the Scriptures, as well as how to present Him amiably to hungry sinners in search of daily communion with a personal

Redeemer. For the genuine Christian, here is daily devotional writing at its best — warmly Christ-centered, eminently practical, personally searching.

Unlike most other daily devotional books of Reformed persuasion which consist of fragmented extracts, *The Poor Man's Morning and Evening Portions* was composed expressly for such use. You will feel the difference immediately. Each devotion is complete in itself and speaks directly to you, compelling you to hold soliloquy with your own soul.

The only definitive biography of Hawker is that of Dr. John Williams (who sat under Hawker's ministry before becoming vicar of Stroud, Gloucestershire), which prefaces volume 1 of his *Works*, and was first published in 1831. Of these daily portions, Williams notes, "His remarks exhibit a great warmth of affection, a lively energy of expression, a graceful flow of language, and an affluent store of scriptural sentiments.... There is a lovely simplicity in his sublimest thoughts, and in his humblest themes a becoming dignity."

As popular as his writings were, Hawker was even more popular as an extemporaneous preacher in his own day. He was both spiritually and naturally gifted for the pulpit.

Robert Hawker was born to God-fearing parents on April 13, 1753 at Exeter, England. His father, a reputable surgeon, died when he was an infant. He was reared by his mother with the assistance of two aunts, one of whom taught him to memorize numerous portions of Scripture before he went to school. This storehouse of memorized Scripture served him well throughout his long ministry and persuaded him that the early education of children should be taken as much as possible directly from the Word of God. Out of this conviction, he compiled *The Child's First and Second Books*, consisting of simple lessons from Scripture or illustrative of Scripture.

As a child, he attended Exeter's grammar school, where he

gained some proficiency in Greek and Latin. Subsequently, his mother, who desired him to follow his father's profession, had him study surgery and medicine under Dr. White, a surgeon from Plymouth.

At the age of eighteen, he married Anne Rains, with whom he had eight children. After forty-five years of marriage, she died, leaving him a widower for the last ten years of his life.

After his marriage, Hawker pursued further training in the hospitals of London, prior to spending three years as assistant surgeon in the royal marines. Against this background, he would later write *Zion's Warrior, or the Christian Soldier's Manual, in which the duties and occupations of the military life are spiritualized and improved.* While in the royal marines, he came under some religious impressions and decided to pursue the ministry. Notwithstanding his indistinct and sometimes erroneous views of the doctrines of grace at that time, he entered Oxford University as a member of Magdalen Hall in 1778. He took holy orders and became curate of St. Martin for three months prior to becoming curate to Rev. John Bedford, vicar of Charles, near Plymouth. Upon Bedford's death in 1784, Hawker succeeded his mentor as vicar of Charles, where he enjoyed the love and respect of his congregation for forty-three years until his death. He was buried on his seventy-fourth birthday, Good Friday, 1827.

It was in his early years at Charles that Hawker came to clear views on the doctrines of grace both in his preaching and in his own experience. He finally was persuaded to abandon his former conviction that a sinner's salvation depended upon an act of free will, and embraced the doctrine of salvation by Christ alone, through gracious Spirit-wrought faith.

Dr. Hawker reached out beyond the boundaries of Charles through his prolific writing and a variety of religious activities. In 1792 he was awarded a doctorate of divinity by

Edinburgh University for his *Sermons on the Divinity of Christ*. In 1797 he accepted the deputy-chaplaincy of the garrison at Plymouth. In 1802 he founded The Great Western Society for Dispersing Religious Tracts among the Poor. In 1813 he established the *Corpus Christi Society*, which aimed to provide spiritual and financial relief to "the body of Christ." Meanwhile, he increased in fame and popularity as a powerful high Calvinist preacher. For many years, he annually visited London where he preached to crowded churches from some of the city's most renowned pulpits.

All of Dr. Hawker's major writings are included in the ten volumes of his works except *The Poor Man's Commentary on the Old and New Testaments*, which is itself an additional ten volumes. Other principal works include *Sermons on the Divinity and Operations of the Holy Spirit; Paraclesis, or Consolations for a Dying Hour; Zion's Pilgrim; The Sailor Pilgrim; Visits to and from Jesus upon the most interesting occasions; Lectures on the Person, Godhead, and Ministry of the Holy Ghost; The Poor Man's Concordance and Dictionary to the Sacred Scriptures; Catechisms and Books for the Use of Children.* His works also contain nearly a hundred additional articles on various subjects, two volumes of sermons, and a volume of expositions called *Scripture Extracts.*

Hawker's ministry has been largely overlooked by modern scholarship. It is our hope that the reprinting of Hawker's daily portions will stimulate desire for the reprinting of more of these significant writings.

Hawker lived and died by the doctrines of free grace of which he preached and wrote. On the day after his seventieth birthday, he wrote:

> From the first dawn of the day-spring which from on high visited me, when the Lord was pleased to bring me into acquaintance with myself, and to make me know the plague of my own heart, I have been unlearning what I had before

> been studying with so much care — how to recommend myself by human merit to divine favour. But when the Lord in mercy took me under his pupilage, he inverted this order of teaching. I was then led to see more of *his* ways, and to think less of my *own*. And from that hour of matriculation in his school to the present, I have been learning to get daily out of love with myself, and in love with Christ. And so it hath proved, that in the exact ratio in which I have advanced in the knowledge and love of the Lord, and in the ways of grace, I have been going back in my estimation of all creature excellency and creature attainments.

Read this volume daily; let Hawker bring the Word of God close to your conscience. May the Spirit apply these short, savory devotions to our daily and eternal gain, that for us also Christ may increase and we may decrease (John 3:30) more and more.

— Joel R. Beeke

PREFACE

TO THE

POOR MAN'S MORNING PORTION.

The title-page of this humble work sufficiently explains itself. It is designed as a means, in the divine hand, to promote the Redeemer's glory, and his people's happiness. It hath often struck me, that such a method, under the blessing of the Lord, might prove eminently useful. By publishing in this way, in little penny books, some sweet portion of scripture for every day in the year, it might come within the reach of all pockets, be within the reach of all hands, and bid fair to be read when larger books are laid aside and forgotten.

It was, indeed, with the same view, that some few years since I sent forth a Diary of this kind. But, in that work, the selection was confined wholly to the promises. Experience hath since shewn, that reference may be occasionally had, with great advantage, to other parts of the word of God. In this, therefore, I have enlarged the plan. And besides making extracts from the whole scripture, I have ventured to add, under each passage, such thoughts as passed over my own mind in the perusal, hoping that the Lord might render them profitable to others.

It will be scarcely necessary to go over the same ground, by way of preface, as was then done. But it cannot be too often said, by way of reminding the believer, that the promises of God in Christ are evidently meant by the gracious Giver of them for the daily comfort of his people. And what is said of the promises, may be equally applied to the whole tenor of covenant love which runs through the bible. Indeed, if the truly awakened soul did but consider the word of God in this point of view, and make use of it upon every occasion, as his own circumstances are found to require, it could not fail of opening to his mind a perpetual source of joy and consolation all the day.

For what are the promises, but so many bonds and engagements of a covenant God in Christ? In them, the Lord hath pledged himself to his people, as they stand related to Christ; and by the fulfilment of them, they prove his faithfulness. So that, strictly and properly speaking, God's promises are our charter; his word our security; his verily and amen the breasts of consolation whence God's little ones are nourished. And if the Lord's people would seek from the Holy Ghost the testimony he gives in them concerning Jesus, and from general promises make application of them to their own particular state and circumstances, as they may require, they would find, upon numberless occasions, that the Lord is speaking in them, and by them, to the souls of his people, and in the sweetest and most endearing language. 'I would rather have God's amen, and his yea, and verily, (said a tried soul of old) than the promises or oath of all the men upon earth.' And so would every believer, when from long experience of God's fulfilment of his word and promises, he could "set to his seal that God is true." But, if we never make use of God's promises, never exercise faith upon them, never bring them before the throne for payment, nor make memorandums when they are paid, how shall we know their value, or God's love and faithfulness in their accomplishment?

Convinced of the importance of the thing itself, and with a view to direct the minds of God's people to the daily exercise of this grace of faith upon the word and promises of our covenant God in Christ, I have here gathered out of the holy treasury some sweet portion for gracious souls to feed on from day to day. And so fully persuaded am I of the preciousness of this employment, that I am confident to say, if the people of God would make it their uniform custom, morning by morning, with the first return of day, and if possible, before the world hath power to break in upon the mind, thus to have recourse to God's word, and (as David said he did) "to hearken what the Lord God would say concerning him," they would find, and perhaps frequently before night, sufficient cause to bless God for his faithfulness in the accomplishmeut. Nay, sometimes indeed, they would discover the word to be so immediate and direct to the present moment, as if the Lord had left for a while the whole world, to draw nigh to them in those visits of his love. Like the patriarch at Bethel, they would be constrained to say, "Surely the Lord is in this place, (or in this word) and I knew it not!"

It was thus holy men of old walked with God. They communed with the Lord, and the Lord with them through the medium of his word. They made known their wants, and the Lord made known his grace. Prayers went up, and answers came down; and he "made all his goodness to pass before them." In a more special manner they considered all the promises as their own. And they accepted of them as given of the Lord, with this express design, as if the Lord pledged himself by them to his people, that they might bring them before the mercy-seat whenever they needed, and plead for payment. Hence they kept house, feasted, and lived joyfully upon them, when they had nothing else to live upon. And from this cause it was, that after a succession of many generations from father to son, they could, and did appeal to the uninterrupted experience of every preceding history, and left it upon record for the assurance and comfort of all that should come after, that "Not one thing had failed of all the good things which the Lord had promised, but all was come to pass as it is this day."

I cannot therefore but earnestly recommend to the gracious souls for whom this little work is intended, similar conduct, that we may be the patient "followers of them who now through faith and patience inherit the promises." And a method so short, so easy, and so practicable as is here set forth, and which the most busy life, even among the labouring poor of our people, cannot find much difficulty in performing, will, I trust, be abundantly blessed of our gracious God. The labourer who is straitened for time, and obliged sometimes to hasten to his work without falling upon his knees in family prayer, may yet, even while putting on his clothes, look at the Morning Portion; and if unable to run through the observations which follow the scripture, may yet take with him the scripture itself, and gather matter from it, under divine teaching, for prayer and praise as he hastens on. And if this plan be constantly and invariably followed up, without the omission of a single morning, I venture to believe his diligence will be abundantly recompensed, upon numberless occasions through life.

There is one advantage more, from the use of this little work, which I detain the reader to mention, which will be, I conceive, of no small importance in making it blessed, if so be the Lord should dispose the minds of many gracious souls to the daily use of it; I mean the communion of saints. This privilege of God's people is much spoken of; but I rather fear, not so much attained to or regarded as it ought. And yet, next to the rapture arising from communion with our glorious head, what can open to more enjoyment than communion through him, with the members of his mystical body? I cannot help telling, in this short way, many precious souls, whom I love in the faith, and who I know love me, that I am looking forward to much spiritual enjoyment on this account, from our use of this little work, humble as it is; not from my poor labours in the observations which follow the scripture, but from God's blessing on the scripture itself. Let it be supposed (what is very possible) that many a true believer in Jesus, in different places be led in one and the same moment of the morning, to the perusal of the Morning Portion. Now, as the scripture is the same; as the Almighty Spirit, who is the author of that scripture, the quickener in prayer, and the helper of the infirmities of his people in prayer, is the same; and as he who leads out the minds of his people at all times and in all places is the same; and his blessed work in glorifying the Lord Jesus is always the same; what can be more animating or delightful than the thought, that all so engaged, in one and the same scripture, being under the same gracious influence, must necessarily be all looking up to the Lord Jesus in one and the same moment; and having fellowship with the Father, and with his Son Jesus Christ, have spiritual union also one with another, "as members of his body, of his flesh, and of his bones." Hence, though far asunder from each other in the body, and in numberless instances having never seen each other's face in the flesh, yet by virtue of connection with our spiritual head, we truly participate in one and the same divine life, and enjoy the very sweet and distinguishing felicity of the communion of saints.

I stop the reader no longer than just to say, I humbly hope every truly gracious and awakened soul who makes use of this Morning Portion, will not fail to connect with the use of it a constant application to, and dependance upon the Holy Ghost as the glorifier of the Father and of the Son; without whose work upon the heart, not a promise can we plead; not an argument can we use; not a grace can we exercise; even to the knowledge of our wants, or of the fulness of the Lord Jesus to supply them. But, my brother, let me add, if your soul be warmed under the influence of the Holy Ghost, and while you read God's promise you find grace to convert that promise into a prayer, and when you have thus done, act faith upon it; this will be to realize the mercy, and to make every promise your own. And Oh! how truly blessed is it, when the believer thus proves that "all the promises of God in Christ Jesus are yea and amen, unto the glory of God by us."

CHARLES VICARAGE, PLYMOUTH.

PREFACE

TO THE

POOR MAN'S EVENING PORTION.

A New edition of the Poor Man's Evening Portion being called for, I beg to introduce it with a short preface.

The smallest attention to the work itself, will, it is hoped, be sufficient to manifest to every reader, that in this little volume there is nothing spoken of with an eye to salvation, but Jesus only. Christ is the all in all. Indeed the very title implies as much. For unless Jesus be the portion of his people, they can have none.

The reader is therefore particularly requested to have this in view through every part of this work; that, as the holding forth the Lord Jesus, the one glorious portion of the church, is the only design the author had in writing; so it may be the only expectation of the reader in the perusal. Christ is here made, what the scriptures of God every where make him, the Alpha and Omega; the first and the last; the author and finisher of salvation. That foundation stone which Jehovah laid in Zion, is here shewn to be the only bottom on which the believer can rest the whole spiritual building. Isa. xxviii. 16. That vine the Lord planted in his vineyard, the only root from whence can be derived life, support, and fruitfulness to the branches. John xv. 1. That head of his body, the church, the sole source from whom "all the members having nourishment, ministered and knit together, increase with the increase of God," Col. ii. 19. In a word, Jesus is here set forth as substantially the whole of the believer's portion, to live upon in time and to all eternity.

Moreover, the reader is yet further desired to observe, that as in this little volume the Christ of God is considered as the whole of salvation in Jehovah's appointment, so the believer, who really and truly knows and accepts the Lord Jesus in this comprehensive character, is supposed to be thus using Christ in his whole dependance upon him, to the divine glory and his own happiness. I make a nice distinction in my creed (and yet not more nice than important) between the actings of my faith, and the almighty object of that faith; between what I feel, or say, or do, and what the Lord Jesus Christ hath done in accomplishing redemption; between what Jesus is in God the Father's view and what in mine. Were I to substitute any thing of my own by way of recommendation, or what is to the same effect, mingle any thing of my own, as a procuring cause to the divine favour; this were to lessen the infinite dignity and merit of the Redeemer's person and righteousness, and render the covenant of grace uncertain and nugatory. In every mingling of this kind, it might with truth be said, "O thou man of God, there is death in the pot!" 2 Kings iv. 40. Moral virtues, pious dispositions, holiness of life and conversation, yea, faith itself, as an act of man, form no part in the justification of a sinner before God. All these are highly proper in their place, accompany a work of grace wrought in the heart, and become precious evidences of the renewed life. But all the while, these are effects only, not causes; streams, not the fountain. Jesus is the whole in redemption; for "there is salvation in no other." And the glorious inscription over the very gate of heaven must be read to this effect: "To the praise of the glory of his grace wherein he hath made us accepted in the beloved," Eph. i. 6.

If it were not for swelling this preface beyond the limit, I must observe, I should humbly beg to add another observation on this important point, and say, that I am every day more and more convinced that the want of thus living wholly upon Christ, is the sole cause why so many of God's children go so lean from day to day. For if he who is the Father's glory, was made the believer's confidence; and while we know (as we do know) that "in him are hid all the treasures of wisdom and knowledge;" from him we seek for all we need; "wisdom, righteousness, sanctification, and redemption;" there would be nothing fluctuating in our happiness, while there was found nothing wavering and unsteady in our faith. This would be to enter into the sweet retirings of Jesus, and to realize that blessed promise, "Thou wilt keep him in perfect peace whose mind is stayed on thee; because he trusteth in thee," Isa. xxvi. 4.

I send forth this feeble labour, under an humble hope, that he, with whom is the residue of the Spirit, will own it to the comfort of his people. In the reading of it, may they hear the love-calls of Jesus, and receive the love-tokens of Jesus, and find that self-invitation of the Lord in every evening portion of their retirement. "Behold I stand at the door and knock; if any man hear my voice and open the door, I will come in to him, and will sup with him and he with me," Rev. iii. 20.

CHARLES VICARAGE, PLYMOUTH.

THE POOR MAN'S

MORNING AND EVENING PORTIONS.

JANUARY 1.

MORNING.—" Jesus Christ; the same yesterday, and to-day, and for ever."—Heb. xiii. 8.

Precious truth to open the year with, and to keep constantly in view amidst all the fluctuating and changeable circumstances arising both within and without, and all around! My soul, meditate upon it: fold it up in thy bosom to have recourse to as may be required. Contemplate thy Redeemer as he is here described. He is Jesus, thy Jesus; a Saviour, for he shall save his people from their sins. He is Christ also; God thy Father's Christ, and thy Christ: the Anointed, the Sent, the Sealed of Jehovah. He is the same in his glorious Person, the same in his great salvation:— "Yesterday;" looking back to everlasting: "To-day;" equally so through all the periods of time: "For ever;" looking forward to the eternity to come. And, blessed thought, he is the same in his love, in the efficacy of his redemption; his blood to cleanse, his righteousness to justify, his fulness to supply grace here and glory hereafter. And what sums up the precious thought; amidst all thy variableness, thy frames, thy fears, doubts, and unbelievings, he abideth faithful. He is, he will be, he must be, Jesus. Hallelujah!

EVENING.—" And He that sat upon the throne said, Behold, I make all things new."—Rev. xxi. 5.

My soul! thou hast been engaged in the morning of the new year, with contemplating the eternal and unchanging glory of thy Jesus, in his person, work, offices, character, and relations, as in covenant engagements for thy welfare: and thou hast found him to be an everlasting and secure foundation to rest upon, and dwell in, for time and for eternity.—Come now, in the evening of the day, and look up to thy Redeemer in another precious point of view, and behold him as creating all things new, while he himself, in the eternity of his nature, remains for ever and unchangeably the same. Behold him on his throne; and remember that one and the same throne belongs to God and the Lamb, to intimate the unity of the Father and the Son in nature and dignity; in will, worship, and power. When thou hast duly pondered this view of Jesus, next listen to the important words he proclaims: "Behold, I make all things new." Pause.—Hath he made thee a new creature? Yes! if, as the Holy Ghost saith, "old things are passed away, and all things are become new." The new creature is a thoroughly changed creature. It is a new nature, not a new name. "A new heart will I give you," is the blessed promise; "and a new spirit will I put within you." So that "if any man be in Christ, he is a new creature." When this grand point is fully and clearly ascertained, then, my soul, let the next consideration from this scripture be, the blessed assurance here given, that Jesus himself hath wrought it. This indeed cannot but follow; for surely the same power that created the world out of nothing, must be necessary to create a new spirit in the sinner's heart. In the old creation of nature, though there was nothing to work upon, yet there was nothing to oppose it: but in the unrenewed heart of a sinner there is every thing to rise up against it; for "the carnal mind is enmity against God." Mark it down then, my soul, that no power less than God's could have done this, and thy Jesus from his throne declares it. Is there any thing more to be gathered from this proclamation from the throne? Yes! He that first creates the heart anew, ever lives to send forth the renewings of the Holy Ghost: for creating grace, and renewing grace, are both alike his. Hence, therefore, let thy morning and evening visits be to Him that sitteth upon the throne, and maketh all things new. The same that hath made new heavens, and the new earth, wherein righteousness dwelleth; that hath made his tabernacle with men, and dwelleth in them; that sitteth upon the throne, making all things new; the same is He, yesterday, to-day, and for ever, that giveth power to the weak, and to them that have no might he increaseth strength. Hither, my soul, come, under all thy weakness, fears, doubts, tremblings, and the like: Jesus can, and will renew thy strength. When I want a heart to pray, to praise, to love, to believe; yea, when my heart and my flesh faint, and hope fails: Oh! let me hear thy voice, thou that sittest upon the throne, and makest all things new: for then wilt thou be the strength of my heart, and my portion for ever.

JANUARY 2.

MORNING.—"Lord! let it alone this year also, till I shall dig about it, and dung it: and if it bear fruit, well; and if not, then after that thou shalt cut it down."—Luke xiii. 8, 9.

Do I not behold the Lord Jesus here represented in his glorious office of our High Priest and Intercessor? And is it thus that he so mercifully pleads for the unawakened and unprofitable among his people? Pause, my soul! Was it not from the effects of his intercession, that the world itself was spared from instant destruction, when Adam first brake through the fence of God's law? Is it not now by the same rich grace that thousands are spared from year to year in Christ Jesus, before that they are called to the knowledge of Christ Jesus? Nay, my soul! pause once more over the view of this wonderful subject, and ask thyself—was it not from the same almighty interposition that thou was kept from going down to the pit during the long, long period of thy unregeneracy, while thou wert wholly unconscious of it? And was it from thy gracious intercession, blessed Jesus, that I then lived, that I am now spared, and, after all my barrenness, that another year of grace is opening before me? Oh, precious, precious Jesus! suffer me to be no longer unfruitful in thy garden! Do, Lord, as thou hast said. Dig about me, and pour upon me all the sweet influences of thy Holy Spirit, which, like the rain, and the sun, and the dew of heaven, may cause me to bring forth fruit unto God. And, Lord, if so unworthy a creature may drop a petition at thy mercy seat for others, let the coming year be productive of the same blessings to all thy redeemed; even to my poor unawakened relations among them; and to thousands of those who are yet in nature's darkness. Oh that this may be to them the acceptable year of the Lord!

EVENING.—"Now when the even was come, he sat down with the twelve."—Matt. xxvi. 20.

And now the even is again come, will Jesus graciously sit down with me? Wherefore, my soul, shouldest thou doubt the kindness of thy condescending Lord? It may be allowed, that in many of the tenderest incidents which passed between Jesus and his disciples while upon earth, there were some peculiarly suited, and designed to have a personal respect to them alone. But in many things they were the representatives of Jesus's whole family; and hence every child of God may invite Jesus to sit down with him, and enjoy communion with him; that while Jesus speaks by his word to his people, and they to him; as his whole heart and soul is theirs, so their whole hearts and souls may go forth, in all the sweet exercises of love and faith to him, and a holy familiarity may take place between them. Come, then, thou gracious Lord, and sit down with me, after all the toils of the day, and close the evening with some blessed token of thy favour. I remember somewhat of thy past kindness, and therefore I feel encouraged to seek a renewal of thy love. Do I not know thee, O thou dear Lord! as a tried, a sure, an unchanging friend; a brother born for adversity? And shall not this knowledge make me confident for all that I have now to ask? Shall I go to the Lamb of God, who hath died for me, as one under doubts and fears that he will not own me, nor regard the purchase of his blood? No! precious Jesus, never will I so dishonour thee, while thou hast given me, not the spirit of bondage, but the spirit of adoption. Never will I lose sight of thee in this endearing part of thy character; for thine own love, and not our desert, is the rule of thy grace to thy people. Come, then, Lord Jesus, in the stillness of this evening, and manifest thyself to my heart otherwise than thou dost to the world. If Jesus will but speak, yea, whisper in the words of his holy scripture, I shall feel all the power, sweetness, and energy of its saving truths. One view of Jesus's heart, and the love in it to poor sinners, will bear down all the cries of unbelief, all the clamours of the world, and all the temptations of the enemy. Yea, Lord, I shall for a while forget every sorrow, every pain, every difficulty and trial. And will not the tempter flee, when he beholds my poor feeble soul upheld in Jesus's arms, and lying in Jesus's bosom? Blessed be my God and Saviour, I feel a sense of thy strengthening and refreshing presence. My faith lays hold of thee, neither will I let thee go, O thou, the hope of Israel, and the Saviour thereof! "And why shouldest thou be as a stranger in the land, and as a wayfaring man that tu[illegible] aside to tarry but for a night?"

JANUARY 3.

MORNING.—" The year of my redeemed is come."—Isa. lxiii. 4.

Yes! from everlasting the precise period of redemption was determined, and the appointed time of the vision could not tarry. Every intermediate event ministered to this one glorious æra—redemption by Jesus. The church was in Egypt four hundred and thirty years, and in Babylon seventy. But we are told in the former instance, ' the self-same night' the Lord brought them forth with their armies; and the latter did not outstay the hour of their promised deliverance. So when the fulness of time was come, the Son of God came for the redemption of his people. And observe how graciously Jesus speaks of them; he calls them his redeemed. They were so in the covenant from everlasting; and when the time arrives for calling them by his grace, he claims them as the gift of his Father, and the purchase of his blood. My soul, is this thy jubilee year? Art thou living as the redeemed of the Lord? If so, plead with thy Redeemer for the holy renewed visits of his love to thee, and for the year of redemption to all his unawakened.

EVENING. — " He shewed unto them his hands and his side."—John xx. 20.

My Lord and my God! I would say, while thou openest to me such a view, and while I would look into and read thine heart in it. And what was such a display designed for, dearest Lord? I think thou hast taught me to discover. Was it not as if Jesus had said, ' See here the marks of your sure redemption. From hence issued the blood that hath cleansed you from all sin. And this blood hath a voice. It is a speaking blood, which speaketh better things than that of Abel. For his blood cried for vengeance, mine for pardon. It speaketh for thee to my Father of his covenant promises. And it speaketh to thee from my Father of thy sure acceptance in my salvation.'— Neither was this all. For surely, dearest Jesus, when thou shewedst thine hands and thy side, it was also as if thou hadst said, 'See here an opening to my heart. Here put in all you wish to tell my Father, and I will bear it to him with all my warmest affections. And let all my disciples, in every age of my church do this. I will be the bearer of all their suits. And sure they may be both of my love and of my success for them ; for I will carry all that concerns them in this opening to my heart.' Precious Lord! cause me often to view with the eye of faith this gracious interview of thine with thy disciples. And as in the evening of the day the disciples were thus favoured with thy presence, and so rich a manifestation of thy love ; so, Lord, make me to realize the scene afresh, and very often in the silence of the night may my soul be going forth in the full enjoyment of this spiritual blessing! Yea, Jesus! let me behold thine hands and thy side, and learn day by day to put therein all I would tell my God and Father of thy great salvation, and my firm reliance upon it; until from a life of faith I come to enter upon a life of absolute enjoyment, and behold thee still as the Lamb that hath been slain for the redemption of thy people, in the midst of the throne, leading the church to the living fountains of waters, where all tears are wiped away from all eyes.

JANUARY 4.

MORNING.—"And when Abram was ninety years old and nine, the LORD appeared to Abram, and said unto him, I am the Almighty God; walk before me, and be thou perfect."—Gen. xvii. 1.

Our old bibles, in their margin, have retained the original *El Shaddai*, which we now read God Almighty, and marked it also *God All-sufficient*, meaning that Jehovah in covenant with Jesus, as the head of his people, is all-sufficient in himself, and all-sufficient for all their need in time and to eternity. He is God All-sufficient, or of many paps, many breasts of consolation, (as some derive the word) for his faithful ones to suck at and draw from, in an endless supply. Here then, my soul, take this sweet title of thy covenant God and Father in Christ Jesus for thy daily meditation, both at the opening, and through all the periods of the coming year. And as even at old age the Lord still opened to Abraham this precious source for his comfort, so look up in Jesus and behold it as thine. And Oh, my soul! do thou walk before him in the perfect righteousness of God thy Saviour, and thus daily keep up fellowship with the Father, and with his Son Jesus Christ.

EVENING.—" And David said, seemeth it to you a light thing to be a king's son-in-law, seeing that I am a poor man and lightly esteemed?" —1 Sam. xviii. 23.

Did David indeed set by so high an honour in being allied to the family of an earthly prince; what then must be the dignity to which believers are called, in being heirs of God and joint-heirs with Christ? The apostle was so lost in the contemplation of this unspeakable mercy, that he cried out with holy rapture, " Behold! what manner of love the Father hath bestowed upon us, that we should be called the sons of God!" My soul, art thou begotten to this immense privilege? Ponder well thy vast inheritance. Not a barren title, not an empty name; this relationship brings with it a rich revenue of all temporal, spiritual, and eternal blessings. Sons in law and in grace to God in Christ, believers are born to an inheritance incorruptible and undefiled, and that fadeth not away. They have the spirit of adoption and of grace; and " because they are sons, God hath sent forth the Spirit of his Son into their hearts, whereby they cry, Abba, Father." Are they poor in outward circumstances? bread shall be given, and water shall be sure; and their defence shall be the munitions of rocks. Are they afflicted in body or in mind? their back shall be proportioned to their burden; and as their day is so shall their strength be. Every child shall have his own portion, and the Father's blessing sanctifying all. Yea, death itself is in the inventory of the inheritance of a child of God; for so far is death from separating from God, that it brings to God. What sayest thou, O my soul! to these things? Art thou, like David, a poor man and lightly esteemed? Look up and enjoy thy relationship in Jesus, and from this time do thou cry out, in the words of the prophet, and say unto God, " My Father! thou art the guide of my youth."

JANUARY 5.

MORNING.—" I am my beloved's, and his desire is towards me."—Song vii. 10.

Yes, dearest Jesus! I am truly thine, by every tie which can make me thine. I am thine by the gift of GOD the FATHER; by thine own betrothing me to thyself; by the HOLY GHOST anointing me in thee, and making me one with thee, and in thee, before the world. And I am thine in the recovery of the church from Adam's fall and transgression by the sacrifice of thyself: for thou hast bought me with thy blood, and made me thereby the conquest of thine HOLY SPIRIT. And now through thy divine teaching I can and do discover, that from everlasting thy desire was towards thy redeemed ones, and even when dead in trespasses and sins, it was thy desire to quicken them into life, and bring them to thyself. And even now, notwithstanding all my backwardness to thee, thou restest in thy love, and thou art calling me by thy grace, and seeking continual fellowship in ordinances, and by thy word and providences; all which prove that thy desire is towards me. And as to the everlasting enjoyment of all thy church above, thy prayer to thy Father manifested thy desire, when thou saidst, "Father, I will that they whom thou hast given me be with me to behold my glory!" Are these then the desires of my God and Saviour, my Husband, my Brother, my Friend? And shall my heart be thus cold towards thee? Oh for the reviving influences of thy Spirit; that I may cry out with the church, "Let him kiss me with the kisses of his mouth; for thy love is better than wine."

EVENING. — "And Melchizedeck, king of Salem, brought forth bread and wine: and he was the priest of the Most High God." — Gen. xiv. 18.

Was it not in the evening of the day, when Abraham, returning from the slaughter of the kings, met this illustrious person? And will Jesus, my Melchizedeck, meet and bless me in the evening of this day, after my return from conflicts, trials, and exercises? — I would fain indulge the sweet thought. Surely this Melchizedeck could be no other than Jesus. And did he love his people then — and doth he not love them now? Did Jesus witness their battles, and come forth and refresh them? And is he not Jesus still? — Sit down, my soul, and attend to what the Holy Ghost saith of this Melchizedeck; and see whether, through his teaching, thou canst make no discoveries of Jesus. Was this Melchizedeck priest of the Most High God? And who but the Son of God was ever sworn into this office with an oath? Was Melchizedeck a priest for ever? Who but Jesus was this? Had Melchizedeck neither beginning of days nor end of life? And who but Jesus is the first and the last? Was Melchizedeck without father, without mother? And who of Jesus shall declare his generation? Did Melchizedeck bless the great father of the faithful? And hath not God the Father sent his Son to bless us, in turning away every one of us from our iniquities? Did the king of Salem bring forth bread and wine to refresh the patriarch and his people? And doth not our King of righteousness bring forth at his supper the same, as memorials of his love: yea, his own precious body, which is meat indeed, and his blood, which is drink indeed? Precious Jesus, thou great Melchizedeck! bring forth anew, this night, these tokens of thy love. Make thyself known to me in breaking of bread and prayer. And whilst thou art imparting to me most blessed views of thyself, give me to apprehend and know thee, and richly enjoy thy soul-strengthening, soul-comforting presence. And Oh! for grace from thee, Lord, and the sweet influences of thine Holy Spirit, that, like the patriarch Abraham, I may give thee tythes of all I possess! It is true, I have nothing, and am nothing, yea, in myself am worse than nothing. But of thine own would I give thee. Like the poor widow in the gospel, I would cast all my living into thy treasury. The two mites, which make a farthing, my soul and body, do I give unto thee. And those are both thine, by creation, by gift, by purchase, and by the conquest of thy grace. Take, therefore, all; and enable me to present my soul and body a living sacrifice, holy, acceptable unto the Lord, which is my reasonable service.

JANUARY 6.

MORNING.—"For verily he took not on him the nature of angels." —Heb. ii. 16.

Contemplate, my soul, the peculiar sweetness of that grace which was in thy Jesus, when, for the accomplishment of thy salvation, he passed by the nature of angels to take upon him thy nature. There were but two sorts of transgressors in the creation of God; angels and men. But angels are left in everlasting chains, under darkness, to the judgment of the great day. And fallen, sinful, rebellious man, finds the grace of redemption. Had Jesus taken their nature, would not this have been nearer to his own? Would not their services have been vastly superior to ours? Would not the redemption of beings so much higher in rank and intellect, have opened a far larger revenue of praise to our adorable Redeemer? Pause over these thoughts, my soul, and then consider therefrom how our Jesus, in his unequalled condescension, hath thereby the more endeared himself to thy love. And learn hence, that if Jesus needs not the service of angels, how is it possible that man can be profitable to God! And the simple act of faith of a poor fellow sinner, in believing the record that God hath given of his dear Son, gives more honour to God than all the services of men or angels for ever. Mark this down as a blessed truth; Jehovah is more glorified by thy faith and trust in him, than by all thy works. Lord, give me this faith, that I may cleave to thee, hang upon thee, follow thee, and never give over looking unto thee, until mine eye-strings break and my heart-strings fail, and then as now, be thou "the strength of mine heart, and my portion for ever!"

EVENING.—"When my heart is overwhelmed, lead me to the Rock that is higher than I."—Ps. lxi. 2.

Yes, Lord! I would make this my morning, noon, and evening petition, that the great glorifier of Jesus would gently lead me to him who is a rock, and whose work is perfect. I know, dearest Lord, in theory, and can even reason upon it in seasons of coolness, that thy strength and thy security never fail; the failure is in me and my unbelief. And it is only when I lose sight of thee and thy promise, that I am tossed about with doubts and misgivings. If Jesus be out of sight, and thwarting dispensations arise, Oh! how soon is my poor forgetful heart ready to exclaim with the church of old, "I said, my strength and my hope is perished from the Lord." Then come on the reasonings of flesh and blood. And then the question, whether my interest in Jesus and his salvation be sure? And then my poor heart goes forth, like the dove of Noah from the ark, having lost sight of Jesus, and can find no resting-place for the sole of my foot. Oh! Lord the Spirit, in all such seasons, do thou "lead me to the Rock that is higher than I." If thou, blessed leader of the Lord's distressed ones, wouldest be my pilot when those storms are beating upon me, I should soon be blown upon the firm landing-place of Jesus's security. Oh! how should I ride out the storm even when the tempest was highest, as long as God the Holy Ghost enabled me to cast the anchor of faith upon this eternal rock of Jesus. Oh! lead me then, thou sovereign Lord, continually to my all-precious Jesus. Open the port of communication, and keep it constantly open, between Christ and my soul. Faith will find a soft and quiet bed to sleep on, in the arms of Jesus, and no noise of wars shall break the soul's rest while reposing on him; for so the promise runs: "Thou wilt keep him in perfect peace, whose mind is stayed on thee, because he trusteth in thee." Oh! then once again, I send up the earnest cry of my soul, let it be continually answered in mercy! "When my heart is overwhelmed, lead me to the Rock that is higher than I."

JANUARY 7.

MORNING.—" One pearl of great price."—Matt. xiii. 46.

Great indeed, and but one! for salvation is in no other; neither is there any other name under heaven given among men whereby we can be saved. My soul, hast thou considered Jesus in this precious point of view? Hast thou beheld him both in his divine and human nature, how unspeakably glorious in himself, and how enriching to the souls of his people? Art thou a spiritual merchantman, seeking goodly pearls?

And is Jesus the one, the only one, costly, precious, and so infinitely desirable in thine eye, that thou art willing to sell all, that thou wouldest part with millions of worlds, rather than lose Christ? Hast thou found him in the field of his scripture, and dost thou ask how shall I buy? Listen to his own most gracious words: —" I counsel thee to buy of me gold tried in the fire, that thou mayest be rich." Yes, thou generous Lord! I am come to buy of thee without money and without price. For well I know, through thy teaching, that neither the obedience of men or angels can purchase the least title to thee, but thine own precious merits and thine atoning blood. And now, Lord, possessing thee, I possess all things; and will give up all beside, and part with all, and forget all, since Jesus is mine, and I am his, in time and to all eternity.

EVENING.—" Is it nothing to you, all ye that pass by? Behold and see if there be any sorrow like unto my sorrow, which is done unto me, wherewith the Lord hath afflicted me in the day of his fierce anger."—Lamentations i. 12.

Dearest Jesus! I would sit down this evening, and looking up to thee, ask the instructions of thy blessed Spirit, to unfold some of the many tender inquiries wrapped up in this question of my Lord's. Whatever the mournful prophet's views were of the church's sorrow, when he wrote his book of Lamentations, surely sorrow never had its full potion poured out, but in the cup of trembling which thou didst drink. And as in all the afflictions of thy people, thou wert afflicted, added to all thine own personal sufferings, their's also thou didst sustain. And where shall I begin, dear Lord, to mark down the amazing history of thy sorrow? From the manger to the cross, every path was suffering. Indeed thou art, by way of emphasis, called " the man of sorrows and acquainted with grief." Thorns and thistles the earth is made to bring forth to human nature at large; but as in taking away this curse, thou becamest a curse for thy people, none but thyself, dearest Jesus, was ever crowned with thorns; as if to testify the supremacy of thy sufferings. And did all our curses indeed fall upon thee? Was all the Father's wrath in the full vials of his anger against sin, made to light upon thee? Didst thou wade through all, and sustain all, and bear all, on purpose that thy redeemed might be delivered? Did great drops of blood in a cold night (when a fire of coals became needful to warm thy disciples) fall from thy sacred body, from the agony of thy soul's suffering? Did the Son of God, who from all eternity lay in his bosom, the only begotten and dearly beloved of his affection, indeed die under amazement and exceeding sorrow, and the cry of his soul issue forth of his Father's desertion? Were these among the sorrows of Jesus? And is it nothing to you, all ye that pass by? Is it nothing to you, Oh! ye that by disregard and indifference would crucify the Son of God afresh and put him to an open shame? Come hither, ye careless and unconcerned; come hither, ye fools, that make a mock of sin; come hither, ye drunkards and defiled of every description and character, whose cups of licentiousness and mirth have mingled for him the wormwood and the gall; behold Jesus, and say, "is it nothing to you, all ye that pass by?" My soul, bring the question home to thine own heart, and never give over the solemn meditation. It is indeed to thee every thing that is momentous and eternally interesting. Yes! precious Jesus! every wound of thine speaks; every feature, every groan, every cry pleads *for* me, and *with* me. If I forget thee, O thou bleeding Lamb! let my right hand forget her cunning. If I do not remember thee, let my tongue cleave to the roof of my mouth; yea, if I prefer not the solemn meditation of Gethsemane and Calvary above my chief joy!

JANUARY 8.

MORNING.—"Thou hast kept the good wine until now."—John ii. 10.

The good wine of the gospel must be Jesus himself; for He, and He alone, trod the wine-press of his Father's wrath, when the Lord bruised him and put him to grief. This is the wine which, in scripture, is said to cheer both God and men; for when God's justice took the full draught of it for the sins of the redeemed, the Lord declared himself well pleased. And when the poor sinner, by sovereign grace, is first made to drink of the blood of the Lamb, he feels constrained to say, the Lord had kept the good wine until now; for never before had his soul been so satisfied. Oh, precious Jesus! how sweet is the thought! Thy first miracle converted water into wine. Moses' ministry, under thy commission, was first manifested in turning water into blood. Yes, dear Lord! when once thy grace hath wrought upon the heart of a sinner, thou makest his most common mercies, like water, to become richer than wine. Whereas the law, which is the ministration of death, as long as the poor sinner continues under its power, makes all its enjoyments to partake of the curse. O for continued manifestations of thy glory, dearest Lord! Give me to drink of thy best wine, my beloved, which goeth down sweetly, causing the lips of those that sleep to speak.

EVENING.—"A pool, which is called in the Hebrew tongue, Bethesda."—John v. 2.

Go down, my soul, this evening, to the pool and cloisters of Bethesda, as the prophet was commanded to go down to the potter's house. Peradventure thy Lord may do by thee as he graciously did by him; cause thee to hear his words. The pool of Bethesda was the place or house of mercy. It was so to the bodies of those whom the Lord healed there. It becomes so now to the souls of those who behold Jesus in the representation. In the cloisters around the pool, lay a great multitude of sick, waiting for a cure. Ponder over the miseries of our fallen nature. It is always profitable to note distinguishing blessings. Are hospitals numerous, frequently filled, numbers sick, numbers dying, numbers dead? Am I in health? And will not the voice of praise go forth to the bountiful Author in a consciousness of the distinguishing mercy? The waters of this pool were blessed with a miraculous quality. One poor creature, and but one, at that season when the waters were moved by the descent of an angel into the pool, (most probably discovered by the agitation of the water) was cured of whatsoever disease he had. Sweet testimony, before the coming of Christ, that the Lord had not left his people, notwithstanding the very languishing state in which the church then was. But, my soul, attend to the spiritual beauty of this interesting record. The pool of Bethesda, no doubt, was intended as a typical representation of the fountain opened to the house of David, and to the inhabitants of Jerusalem, for sin and for uncleanness. And the Son of God, by visiting the pool, and healing a poor paralytic by the sovereign word of his own power, without the means, seemed very plainly to intimate the inexpediency of the type, when the person signified was present. Behold in this pool then, the house of mercy always open. In a world like the present, full of misery because full of sin, multitudes of folk, impotent in soul, should be found in the cloisters of ordinances, and under the means of grace. Jesus loves those places. These are his favourite haunts. Here he comes to heal and to impart blessings; and that not to one only at a season. In his blood a sovereign efficacy is found for all who are washed in it. He cures the guilt of sin, destroys its dominion, roots out its sting, and raises from the death of sin. And he doth all in so gracious, so condescending, so sovereign a manner, as cannot but endear him to every heart. Blessed be the Lord that hath led me to his pool at Bethesda, and hath healed my soul in his blood. "The Lord is my strength and my song, and he is become my salvation."

JANUARY 9.

MORNING.—" That will by no means clear the guilty,"—Exod. xxxiv. 7.

Pause, my soul, over these solemn words! Will not Jehovah clear the guilty? And art thou not guilty? How then wilt thou come before God, either now or hereafter? Hearken, my soul, to what thy God hath also said; " deliver him from going down to the pit; I have found a ransom." Oh! soul-reviving, soul-comforting words! yes, Jesus became my surety, took my guilt, and bought me out of the hands of law and justice. God hath not therefore cleared the guilty, without taking ample satisfaction on the person of the sinner's surety. Hence now the double claim of justice and grace demands the sinner's pardon. Here then, my soul, rest thy present and thine everlasting plea. Keep up a daily and hourly remembrance of it at the mercy seat. While Jesus lives, and lives there as thine advocate, never doubt thy acceptance in the beloved: guilty as thou art in thyself, yet spotless in him. The same God which made thy Jesus to be sin for thee, who knew no sin, makes thee the righteousness of God in him.

EVENING.—" And think not to say within yourselves, we have Abraham to our Father; for I say unto you, that God is able of these stones to raise up children unto Abraham."—Matt. iii. 9.

Precious are the doctrines contained in the bosom of this most blessed scripture! May the almighty Author of his own holy word, open to me, this evening, some of the many divine things contained in it. And first, my soul, remark that the blessing to Abraham and to his seed was not through the law. He is not a jew that is one outwardly. The blood of nature which ran through Abraham's veins, had no respect to the grace which was planted in Abraham's heart. If ye be Christ's, is the relationship, for then the Holy Ghost beareth witness ye are Abraham's seed, and heirs according to the promise. No Ishmaels, no sons of Keturah, not of the bond-women, but of the free. And what a sweet thought it is also to consider, that as God called Abraham when an idolater, so now the gifts and callings of God are the same. And in every call doth he not say, "look unto the rock whence ye are hewn, and to the hole of the pit whence ye are digged? Look unto Abraham your father, and unto Sarah that bare you, for I called him alone, and blessed him, and increased him." Do not overlook this, my soul, it will always tend to exalt and endear thy Jesus. But let us not stop here. Supposing, as some have thought, that the Baptist was standing on the banks of Jordan, and referring to the twelve stones which Joshua formerly placed there for a memorial (Josh. iv. 9.) of the twelve tribes of Israel; the allusion to the creating souls from such unpromising, and unheard-of means, becomes a most delightful thought to a child of God, to comfort him concerning the sovereignty of God's grace. Pause, my soul, and let the thought fill up thine evening's meditation, lie down with thee, and form thy songs of the night. Had it pleased thy covenant God in Christ so to have wrought his salvation, no doubt, nothing could have been more easy to his Omnipotency than to have raised heirs of glory from the stones. When the human soul, which came out of the Almighty Maker's hand at first pure and holy, had by apostacy lost all its beauty and loveliness, how quickly might Jehovah have reduced it to its orignal nothingness, and from the stones of the earth raised up a seed to praise him! But here, as in a thousand instances, God's ways are not our ways, nor his thoughts our thoughts. To glorify his dear Son, the soul, though polluted and defiled, shall be made infinitely more precious by redemption, than it was by creation when unpolluted. Beautiful as it was before it fell, yet it is vastly more beautiful now, when washed in the Redeemer's blood. Had it continued in its uprightness, it would have been but the uprightness of the creature, still liable to fall at any time from its integrity, as Adam did. But now united to Jesus, the righteousness and purity of the redeemed is the righteousness and holiness of the Redeemer, and cannot possibly be lost or forfeited any more. "Thy Maker is thine husband, the Lord of Hosts is his name; and thy Redeemer, the Holy One of Israel, the God of the whole earth shall he be called." Pause, my soul! Hast thou a part, an interest in this blessedness? Art thou a poor gentile by nature and practice, an alien to the commonwealth of Israel, a stranger to the covenants of promise, and once without hope, without God, and without Christ in the world; and art thou now brought nigh by the blood of Christ? Surely had God raised a seed from the stones of the earth to Abraham to bless him, the act would not have been more sovereign, neither the mercy more gracious! Hath Jehovah raised thee from death, sin, and hell; washed thee in the blood of the Lamb; regenerated thee by his blessed Spirit; made thee a temple for himself, and formed thee for his glory? O then join the prophet's song, and cry out in his words, "Sing, O ye heavens! for the Lord hath done it; shout, ye lower parts of the earth: break forth into singing, ye mountains: O forest, and every tree therein: for the Lord hath redeemed Jacob, and glorified himself in Israel."

JANUARY 10.

MORNING.—" My beloved is gone down into his garden, to the beds of spices, to feed in the gardens, and to gather lilies."—Song vi. 2.

Wonderful condescension! Jesus, the beloved of all his people, is indeed come down into his garden, the church; for he loves the sacred walks of a spot so near and so dear to him, which is at once the gift of his Father, and the purchase of his own most precious blood. Moreover, he hath gathered it out of the world's wide wilderness, and separated it as a sacred inclosure by his distinguishing grace. Surely then he will visit it. Yes, here he constantly walks; here he comes to observe the souls of his people as trees of his own right-hand planting. He is said to feed here; for the graces of his Spirit, which he calls forth into exercise, are more fragrant to him than all the spices of the east. And all the beauty and whiteness of the lily is not to be compared to the glory, loveliness, and sweet-smelling savour of the righteousness of Jesus, in which he beholds the souls of his redeemed as clad. And Oh! here Jesus is gathering them to himself in all the different degrees of their growth, from the first moment of planting them in his garden, until he transplants them into the paradise of God. Art thou, my soul, in this garden of Jesus? Art thou rejoicing under his gracious hand? Are the dews of his ordinances, in this inclosure of thy Lord, dropping upon thee!

EVENING.—" Whose I am, and whom I serve."—Acts xxvii. 23.

Here is a delightful subject for an evening meditation, if, like the apostle, who thus expressed himself, a child of God can take up the same words, and from the same well-grounded authority. Paul was in the midst of a storm, with not only the prospect, but the certainty of shipwreck before him, when he thus reposed himself in his covenant relations. An angel had informed him of what would happen; and had bidden him to be of good courage. But Paul's chief confidence arose from the consideration of whose property he was, and whose service he was engaged in. See to it, my soul, that thy assurance be the same; then thy security in every dark night will be the same also. For if thou art Jesus' property, depend upon it, thou wilt be Jesus' care. Hath Jesus bought thee with his blood; made thee his by grace; and hast thou voluntarily given up thyself to him in a covenant not to be broken? Hath the Lord spoken to thee by the sweet voice of his word, brought home to the heart in the gracious application of his Spirit? Doth he say to thee, as to Jacob of old; "Fear not, for I have redeemed thee; I have called thee by thy name, thou art mine?" Oh! then how sure will be the promise that follows; "When thou passest through the waters I will be with thee, and through the rivers they shall not overflow thee: when thou walkest through the fire thou shalt not be burned, neither shall the flame kindle upon thee: for I am the Lord thy God, the Holy One of Israel, thy Saviour." If, in a view of covenant relationship, thou canst say with Paul, concerning Jesus, "whose I am;" do thou next search after the love-tokens of thine own heart, in covenant engagements also, and see whether thou canst adopt Paul's language in the other particular, and say as he did, "whom I serve." Is Jesus the one only object of thy love? Did he give himself for thee; and hath he by his Holy Spirit enabled thee to give thyself unto him? Hast thou given thyself *to* him, and given thyself *for* him, and art thou willing to part with every thing for the promotion of his glory? Depend upon it, the real confidence of the soul can only be found in faith's enjoyment of these things. My soul! drop not into the arms of sleep before thou hast brought this point to a decision. No storm of the night, no tempest without, will alarm, while Jesus, by his Holy Spirit, speaks peace within. If Jesus be thine, then all is thine; and as thou art his, every promise is made over to thee with him, whose thou art, and whom thou dost serve. Sweet promise to lie down with on the bed of night, or the bed of death: "My people shall dwell in a peaceable habitation, and in sure dwellings, and in quiet resting places." Isa. xxxii. 18.

JANUARY 11.

MORNING.—"I am the bright and morning Star."—Rev. xxii. 16.

How oft, in some dark wintry morning, like the present, have I beheld the morning star shining with loveliness, when all the other lights of heaven were put out! But how little did I think of thee, thou precious light and life of men! Thou art indeed the bright and morning Star in the firmament of thy church, in thy word, and in the souls of thy redeemed. Henceforth, dearest Jesus, let the morning visit of this sweet planet to our darkened earth remind me of thee, amidst all the gross darkness by which in nature we are surrounded. Sure pledge of day as this beneficial star is, yet not more sure than thou in the day-dawn and day-star of prophecy, which ministered to thy coming; and in the twilight of grace upon the soul, the forerunner of a glorious day. Be thou my morning song, my noontide joy, my evening meditation, and midnight light. Through all the wintry seasons of my pilgrimage, shine forth, sweet Jesus, upon my soul. Oh! ye sons of sloth, ye children of darkness, and of night, rouse from your beds of drowsiness, before the sleep of death seal up your eyes in everlasting darkness. Jesus, the Morning Star, now shines; and ere long, Jesus, the Sun of Righteousness, will appear, no more to go down, and all the sons of God will shout for joy.

EVENING.—" Thou that dwellest in the gardens, the companions hearken to thy voice; cause me to hear it."—Song viii. 13.

Hark, my soul! Is not this Jesus speaking to thee? Listen to thy Lord, for sweet is his voice, and his countenance is comely. But how know I that Jesus is speaking to me in these words of the Song? Search, and see if it be so. What are these gardens, the Lord speaks of? Surely the special congregations of his churches. Is not Jesus's church, one universal church, of jew and gentile, made up of the several assemblies of the faithful throughout the earth? And art thou, my soul, brought into the church of Jesus, by regeneration, by adoption, by the special call of God the Father, the purchase of Christ's blood, the conquest of the Spirit, and the voluntary surrender of thine heart to God? And dost thou dwell in those gardens? Are Jesus's ordinances thy delight; his holy days thy beloved days; his presence thy joy; his tabernacles amiable to thee? And is it the uniform desire of thine heart, to dwell in the house of the Lord all the days of thy life; to behold the beauty of the Lord, and to inquire in his temple? Oh! the blessedness of such a dwelling! the felicity of the souls who dwell in it! Is it not to all such who keep his sabbaths, and join themselves to the Lord to serve him, that the Lord Jehovah speaketh in that most gracious promise, " Even unto them will I give in mine house, and within my walls, a place and a name better than of sons and of daughters, I will give them an everlasting name that shall not be cut off," Isa. lvi. 5. My soul! when thou hast answered this inquiry, go on, and make a farther search concerning " the companions." But what a large door of examination will open on this ground! The holy Lord himself, in his threefold character of Persons, has condescended to reveal himself according to the church's faith in Christ. And every individual believer, even thou, my soul, poor and worthless, and insignificant as thou art in thyself, yet considered in relation to Jesus, even thou, in common with all true followers of Jesus, carriest about with thee evident tokens of the grace of the Lord Jesus Christ, the love of God the Father, and the fellowship of the Holy Ghost. Pause, and determine here again: Are these sacred Persons companions of thine? Do they walk with thee, and thou with them? Do they hear thy voice speaking of the love of each, the grace, the mercy, the goodness of covenant compassion to poor sinners, in and through the rich salvation of the blood and righteousness of Jesus? But are there not other companions, even fellow saints and fellow citizens of the household of God, which may be implied in these words? And do they hear thy testimony concerning Jesus? Can they witness for thee, that thy lips drop as the honeycomb concerning thy Lord, and that his name, his love, his full, free, finished salvation, are the one constant, unceasing subject of thy whole conversation? Dost thou so speak, so live, and dwell upon the precious name of thy Lord, and not only talk of Jesus, but walk with Jesus? And doth Jesus hear thee, and take pleasure in thy edifying conversation, ministering grace to the hearers? Is a book of remembrance written before him, concerning those that fear the Lord, and speak often one to another, and think upon his name? And doth Jesus, while he graciously looks on and hearkens, bid thee come to him, and say, "Cause me to hear thy voice?" What! are thy praises of Jesus, and thy praises to Jesus, pleasant to my Lord? Doth he indeed love to hear thy poor lisping stammering tongue? If, while I speak to others of my companions of his blood and righteousness, and of my soul's joy in him, my adherence to him, my dependence upon him, and my expectation from him, Jesus not only favours the sweet employment, but bids me come to him, and tell himself of all that passeth in my heart concerning him; surely henceforth I will hasten to my Lord, pour out my whole soul before him, and tell him that he is a thousand times more precious to me than thousands of gold and silver. Yea, blessed Lord! night and morning, and seven times a day, will I praise thee, and thou shalt hear my voice. Witness for me, ye my companions, angels of light, yea, my Lord himself, if aught but his love and his praise occupy my soul. Thy name, thy love, thy grace, all, all that belongs to Jesus, shall dwell in my heart, and wholly fill it; shall hang upon my tongue in endless commendation of his beauty, and my soul's delight in him. And even in death, may the last trembling sound the companions gather from my lips be of Jesus, the altogether lovely, and the chiefest among ten thousand!

JANUARY 12.

MORNING.—"If thy brother be waxen poor, and hath sold away some of his possession, and if any of his kin come to redeem it, then shall he redeem that which his brother sold."—Levit. xxv. 25.

How poor was I and wretched before I knew Jesus! I had not only sold, as far as I had power to sell, some of my possession, but all. Indeed, dear Lord, I could not sell thee, nor my oneness and union with thee; for that was not saleable, since Christ had from everlasting betrothed me to himself for ever. But in the Adam nature in which I was born, I was utterly insolvent, helpless, and ruined: one like the Son of man redeemed me. But what a double blessedness was it to my soul, when I discovered that this Redeemer was so very near of kin to me, that he was my brother. Hail, thou precious, precious Jesus! thou art indeed, a "brother born for adversity." Yes, blessed Jesus! thou art he whom thy brethren shall praise; and all thy Father's children shall bow down to thee. My soul, see to it that thou make the most of this relationship. Never, Oh never, will thy brother suffer his poor indigent relation to want any more, after that he hath thus redeemed both thyself and thy possession. Now do I see why it was that the church so passionately longed for Jesus under this tender character. "Oh! (said she) that thou wert as my brother, that sucked the breasts of my mother; when I should find thee without I would kiss thee; yea, I should not be despised."

EVENING.—"Then went Boaz up to the gate, and sat him down there. And, behold, the kinsman of whom Boaz spake, came by; unto whom he said, Ho! such an one! turn aside; sit down here. And he turned aside, and sat down."—Ruth iv. 1.

It is blessed to see, when from *general* calls in the gospel, the call becomes *personal*. The *general* invitation is, "Ho! every one that thirsteth, come ye to the waters." The *personal* call is, "Ho! such an one." Jesus calleth his own sheep by *name;* how is this done? When at any time the Lord speaketh by the ministry of his word to their particular state and circumstances: as for example, when Jesus saith, "I came not to call the righteous, but *sinners* to repentance." Faith saith in answer, then it is for me; for I am a sinner. So again when it is said, "God commendeth his love to us, in that while we were yet sinners Christ died for us!" Faith replieth, then is that love suited to my case and circumstances, for I am both by nature and by practice a sinner before God. So again, when Jesus ascended up on high, he is said to have received gifts for men: yea, for the rebellious, that the Lord God might dwell among them. Faith again finds similar encouragement to go upon, in order to make the thing personal; for the believer saith, I have been a rebel from the womb. In short, faith always discovers ground to rest for assurance, when, from general rules, there is found sufficient scope for special application; and in the suitableness of Christ to the sinner's necessity, and the suitableness of the sinner for the Redeemer's glory, the word comes with power to the heart, and with an energy not unlike the application of the apostle's sermon: "to you is the word of this salvation sent." For then, like the kinsman of Boaz, the call becomes personal, changing the appellation from every one, to such an one; and the believing soul comes at the call, turns aside, and sits down, as the very one with whom the business is to be transacted. My soul! hast thou heard the gospel invitation, and found it personal? The answer will not be far to obtain, if such evidences be discoverable in thyself. Faith is a precious grace, which never rests until it hath acquired all it stands in need of. As the invitation comes from Christ, so where it is personally received and accepted, it leads to Christ. Faith is never satisfied with general views, its whole aim is at personal enjoyments. There is a selfishness to appropriate and bring home all that is offered. Salvation is proclaimed from heaven for sinners. God the Father gives it; God the Son purchaseth it; God the Spirit sends it to the heart with an "Ho! such an one, turn aside, sit down." See to it, my soul, that thou hast this personal interest in it, and that Christ is formed in thy heart the hope of glory.

JANUARY 13.

MORNING.—"Master! where dwellest thou?"—John i. 38.

Is this the earnest inquiry of my soul? Hear then the answer: "Thus saith the high and lofty One, whose name is Holy, I dwell in the high and holy place; with him also that is of a contrite and humble spirit, to revive the spirit of the humble, and to revive the heart of the contrite ones." Pause, my soul. Are these qualities produced by grace in thine heart? Jesus, Master, make me what thou wouldest have me to be; and then come, Lord, agreeably to thy promises. Thou hast said, my Father will come, and I will come, and make our abode with him. And thou hast said, the Holy Ghost shall come and abide with us for ever. What, my soul, shall I indeed have such glorious personages for my companions? Behold, Lord, the heaven, and the heaven of heavens, cannot contain thee! Oh for grace and a sanctity of thought corresponding to such mercies, since our bodies are the temple of the Holy Ghost, which dwelleth in us!

EVENING.—"And Enoch walked with God."—Gen. v. 24.

I have often considered, and as often found pleasure in the consideration of the very honourable testimony which the Holy Ghost hath given to the faith of the patriarchs, both in the old and new testaments. What wonders were wrought by faith! "They walked with God! They endured (saith the sacred writer) as seeing him who is invisible." They communed with God, and were as conscious of his spiritual presence, and spiritual society, as we are of sensible objects. Hence, by these acts of frequent communion, their souls found a growing likeness. The more they loved God, the more their minds were led by grace into an increasing conformity to what they loved. This assimilation is a natural consequence, even among natural things. He that walketh with wise men will be wise. We naturally imbibe the manners, the sentiments, yea, the very habits of those with whom we like to associate. How much more must a frequent intercourse and communion with the Lord, and under his spiritual teaching, induce a conformity to the most fair, most lovely, and most beloved object of the soul! "Beholding (saith the apostle) as in a glass, the glory of the Lord, we are changed into the same image, from glory to glory, even as by the Spirit of the Lord." Are these things so? Then it is explained to thee, my soul, wherefore it is that thou goest so lean, and art yet so poor in the divine life. Thou dost not, as Enoch did, keep up a continual communion with Jesus. Pause this evening, over the subject, and see if this be not the case. All the days of thine unregeneracy, before thou wert first brought acquainted with God in Christ, were spent in a total ignorance of God. There was then no communion with him; yea, not even the desire of communion. But when God, who commanded the light to shine out of darkness, shined into thine heart, then was first given to thee the light of the knowledge of the glory of God, in the face of Jesus Christ. Recollect then, what were thy feelings when the day-spring from on high first visited thee. Didst thou not flee to Jesus, as the man-slayer hastening for his life to the city of refuge? Oh! how feelingly wert thou made to value the very name of a Saviour! How earnestly didst thou seek him above thy necessary food! And if thou hast since intermitted those visits to Jesus, and lost a sense of thy daily want of him; can it be a subject of wonder that this leanness of soul is induced in thee. Will not a distance from, and a shyness of Jesus produce a poverty in spiritual things, as much as the want of food to the body will bring on a leanness and a decline in corporeal things? Learn then, this evening, an unanswerable reply to all thy complaints, and the complaints of the church at large. Wherefore is it that believers live so much below their privileges, but because they live so much below the enjoyment of sweet communion with Jesus? If worldly concerns swallow up our time, as the earth did Korah and his company; if we are satisfied with a mere form of prayer in our morning and evening retirement, and in our family worship before God, while destitute of the power of godliness; if we are still but little acquainted with the Lord, and seldom go to court, to behold the King in his beauty, and to be favoured with his smiles; it is no longer a matter of surprize, that from keeping so poor an house, we are so poor in enjoyment. Oh! for grace to walk with God, as Enoch walked! Make me, thou dear Lord, jealous above all things of my own heart.

Let every morning, with the first dawn of day, call me up to holy communion with thee. And let every night toll the bell of reflection, to examine what visits I have had *from* thee, and what visits I have made *to* thee; and let nothing satisfy my soul but the continual walk of faith with thee; that from an increasing knowledge *of* thee, increasing communion *with* thee, and increasing confidence *in* thee, my soul may be growing up into such lively actings of grace upon thy person, blood, and righteousness, that a daily walk of communion with my Lord, may be gradually preparing my soul for the everlasting enjoyment of him; and when death comes, though it make a change of place, yet will it make no change of company; but "awaking up after thy likeness, I shall be fully satisfied with it."

JANUARY 14.

MORNING.—"And she said to the king, it was a true report that I heard in mine own land, of thy acts, and of thy wisdom. Howbeit, I believed not the words until I came, and mine eyes had seen it: and behold, the half was not told me!"—1 Kings x. 6, 7.

If the queen of the South was so astonished in the view of Solomon's wisdom, what ought to be thy surprize, my soul, in the contemplation of Jesus, in whom are hid all the treasures of wisdom and knowledge! When thou didst first hear of Jesus, and when constrained by necessity to come to him, a poor blind ignorant sinner, how little didst thou conceive either of thyself or him. He told thee, indeed, all that was in thine heart, and made thy very spirit, like her's, to faint within thee, when he shewed thee thy sin and his salvation. Surely then, and often since, even now, hast thou been constrained to say, as she did, the half was not told thee by others, of what sweet discoveries he hath made to thee of himself. Think then, my soul, what holy surprize and joy will burst in upon thee in the day when, at the fountain-head of glory in his courts above, he will unfold all his beauty, love, and wisdom; when thou shalt see him as he is, and know even as thou art known!

EVENING.—" A certain beggar, named Lazarus."—Luke xvi. 20.

What an affecting representation hath the Holy Ghost here made of a poor, but gracious man! He was not only poor in the mere wants of life, but exposed in person to great misery; full of bruises, sores, and griefs. His lot was not to be taken into the house of the rich man, but to lie at his gate. He had the sorrow to behold every day some pampered at the tables of the great, caressed and entertained; but for himself, the crumbs which fell from their over-abundance appear to have been denied him. At length his sorrows are ended, and death removes him to the upper world. " The rich man also died, and was buried; and in hell he lifteth up his eyes, being in torments, and beholdeth Abraham afar off, and Lazarus in his bosom." My soul! this is no parable, but a reality; and in the general view of it, may serve to teach how very widely we err in our estimate of men and things. Who that looked on, but would have concluded that Lazarus was the most miserable of creatures? And who but would have thought the rich man to have been the most happy? Yet it was the aggravation of even hell itself, in the torments of the damned, to behold the felicity of the righteous. Jesus himself hath so marked it: " There shall be weeping, and gnashing of teeth, (saith Christ) when ye shall see Abraham, and Isaac, and Jacob, and all the prophets, in the kingdom of God, and ye yourselves thrust out," Luke xiii. 28. But were these the principal points our Lord had in view in this representation? I think not. My soul! turn the whole over again in solemn consideration this evening, and see whether, in this " certain beggar," there are not to be discovered features of thy Lord? Though he was rich, yet we know for our sakes he became poor, that we through his poverty might be made rich. Though he was in the form of God, and with him it was no robbery to be equal with God, yet he made himself of no reputation, and not merely humbled himself to the condition of a poor man, and one that had not where to lay his head, but he humbled himself to the cursed death of the cross. Was Lazarus poor, full of sores and maladies? And was not Jesus "the man of sorrows and acquainted with grief?" Who, like the Son of God, was ever so wounded? Of whom but Jesus could it ever be said, the Father of mercies, and God of all grace, was pleased to bruise him, and put him to grief? Did the beggar lie unregarded at the gate? And who can overlook the neglect and scorn, the cruelty and ill usage exercised upon the person of Jesus, when he lay at the door of the rich scribes and pharisees, when arraigned at the bar of Pilate, and when nailed to the cross? Precious Lord Jesus! thy death closed thy sufferings, and angels attended thy triumph unto thy kingdom in heaven! Oh! the blessedness of beholding thee at the right hand of the Majesty on high! Oh! the hell upon earth in refusing to hear Moses and the prophets, in their persuasions concerning thee! And what a tremendous close will it be—everlasting torments in the hell to come—when thou shalt "come with ten thousands of thy saints, to execute judgment upon all, and to convince all that are ungodly among men, of all their unrighteous deeds which they have committed, and of all their hard speeches which unregenerate sinners have spoken against thee!" Then, blessed Lord! every eye shall see thee, and they also which pierced thee; and all kindreds of the earth shall wail because of thee. Even so! Amen.

JANUARY 15.

MORNING.—"I was brought low, and he helped me."—Ps. cxvi. 6.

It is blessed sometimes that the streams of creature comforts should be dry, in order to compel us to go to the fountain head. When the fig-tree doth not blossom, and the field yields no meat, then a covenant God is precious to fly to. My soul, say, was not that assault of Satan sanctified, when it brought Jesus thereby to thy rescue? Was not that cross sweetly timed, when it tended to wean thee from the world? And wouldest thou have been without that sickness, when Jesus sat up by thee, soothed thee in thy languor, and made all thy bed in thy sickness? Well was it for me that I was brought low, or I should never have known, in a thousand instances, the help of my God. Oh then, my soul, like Paul, learn to glory in thy infirmities, that the power of Jesus may rest upon thee.

EVENING.—"At evening-time it shall be light."—Zech. xiv. 7.

Then must it be miraculous; for nothing short of a supernatural work could produce such an effect. Sunrise at even-tide is contrary to nature; and the rising of the Sun of righteousness is a work of grace. Pause then, my soul, over the promise, and see whether such an event hath taken place in thy circumstances. As every thing in Jesus, and his salvation, in respect to his church and people, is the sole result of grace, not nature; so all the Lord's dispensations carry with them the same evidences. It is even-time in the soul, yea, midnight darkness, ere first the Lord shines in upon it; it is so in all the after dispensations, when some more than ordinary manifestation is made; it is among the blessed methods of grace, when the Lord surprizeth his people with some rich visits of his love and mercy. "I said, (cried the church, at a time when the waters of the sanctuary ran low) my way is hidden from the Lord, and my judgment is passed over from my God." But it is in creature weakness that Creator strength is manifested; and when we are most weak in ourselves, then is the time to be most strong in the Lord. We have a lovely example of this in the case of the patriarch Jacob. His beloved Joseph was torn in pieces, as the poor patriarch thought, by wild beasts; a famine compelled him to send his sons into Egypt to buy corn, and there Simeon, another son, was detained; and the governor of Egypt declared, that until Benjamin, Jacob's youngest son, was sent, Simeon should not return. Under these discouraging circumstances, the poor father cried out, "Joseph is not, and Simeon is not, and will you take Benjamin also? All these things are against me." But the sequel proved that all these things were *for him*, and all working out a deliverance for him and his household, in which the church of Jesus (which was to be formed from the house of Jacob) should triumph for ever. "At evening-time it shall be light." The Lord sometimes, and perhaps not unfrequently, induces darkness, that his light may be more striking. He hedges up his people's way with thorns, that the almighty hand, which removes them, may be more plainly seen. Oh! it is blessed to be brought low, to be surrounded sometimes with difficulties, to see no way of escape, and all human resources fail, purposely that our extremity may be the Lord's opportunity, and when we are most low, Jesus may be most exalted. My soul! is it now even-tide in the soul, as it is even-tide in the day? Art thou stripped, humbled, convinced of thy nothingness? Oh! look to all-precious, all-suitable Jesus. Hear what the Lord saith: "When the poor and the needy seek for water, and there is none, and their tongue faileth for thirst, I, the Lord, will hear them; I, the God of Israel, will not forsake them. I will open rivers in dry places, and fountains in the midst of vallies." "At evening-time it shall be light."

JANUARY 16.

MORNING.—"And Hezekiah rejoiced, and all the people, that God had prepared the people; for the thing was done suddenly."—2 Chron. xxix. 36.

Sweet thought, ever to keep in view, that it is the Lord that prepares the heart, and gives answers to the tongue. And Oh! how sudden, how unexpected, how unlooked-for, sometimes, are the visits of his grace! "Or ever I was aware (saith the church) my soul made me like the chariots of Amminadab." Is my heart cold, my mind barren, my frame lifeless? Do thou, then, dearest Lord, make me to rejoice, in warming my frozen affection, making fruitful my poor estate, and putting new life into my soul. All I want is a frame of mind best suited to thy glory. And what is that? Truly, that when I have nothing, feel nothing, can do nothing, am worse than nothing, that then, even then, I may be rich in thee amidst all my own bankruptcy. This, dear Lord, is what I covet. And if thou withholdest all frames which might melt, or warm, or rejoice my own feelings; yet if my soul still hangs upon thee notwithstanding all, as the vessel upon the nail, my God and Jesus will be my rock, that feels nothing of the ebbings and flowings of the sea around, whatever be the tide of my fluctuating affections.

EVENING.—"A certain man made a great supper, and bade many." Luke xiv. 16.

Is not this *certain man* designed to represent the Father of mercies, and God of all grace? And is not the great supper intended to set forth the full, generous, free, and plentiful feast made for poor sinners by Jesus Christ in his gospel? My soul! thou art invited, for the message of grace is to the poor, and the maimed, and the halt, and the blind. Jesus keeps a *noble* house, and it is an *open* house. The evening is come —the hour of supper is arrived: arise then, and accept the invitation. Behold, Lord, I am come! And now what are the spiritual delicacies of thy table? First, methinks I hear the generous Lord proclaim a hearty welcome. And it is a sweet thought for my poor soul to cherish, that in whatever heart Jesus is welcome, that heart is welcome to Jesus; for as a poor hungry sinner needs a full Saviour, so a full Saviour needs a poor empty sinner to give out of his fulness upon, and grace for grace. Neither is a poor sinner more happy in receiving Jesus, than Jesus is glorified in receiving a poor sinner. "The Lord waits to be gracious." And what are the viands at his table? "The kingdom of God is not meat and drink; but righteousness, and peace, and joy in the Holy Ghost." Here then, I find the whole of the blessed feast. Here is Jesus himself, the bread of life, and the water of life, whose flesh is meat indeed, and his blood drink indeed. Here are pardon, and mercy, and peace; here is strength to help in every time of need; all grace treasured up for his people in himself, and now to be imparted as their several circumstances require. Moreover, the King himself is to come to his table. I could not be mistaken in his voice. He saith, "I am come into my garden, my sister, my spouse. I have gathered my myrrh with my spice. I have eaten my honeycomb with my honey. I have drunk my wine with my milk. Eat, O friends! drink, yea, drink abundantly, O beloved!" What doth our Jesus mean by "his myrrh with his spices?" Doth he mean the preparing the souls of his guests for this banquet, by enduing them with the spirit of repentance and faith? or is it to set before them his own sufferings and death, "by whose stripes they are healed?" In either sense, blessed be my bountiful Lord! he is himself the provider; it is his table, and he himself furnisheth the whole of it. He is the substance, the life, the way, the means, the end, the first and the last of all; it is all his own, and of his fulness do we all receive. And, dearest Lord! art thou pleased with thy guests, when they come at thine invitation, under a deep sense of want, earnestly desiring to partake of thy bounty, approaching under the sweet leadings of thy Holy Spirit, and clothed in the wedding-garment of thine own righteousness?

Oh, thou bountiful Lord! how blessed are they that sit in thine house, they will be continually praising thee! Now, my soul, thou hast eaten, and art full; arise from the holy table as one fed and filled with the Spirit; bless the kind master of the feast, and give thanks, crying out with holy Simeon, "Lord, now lettest thou thy servant depart in peace, according to thy word, for mine eyes have seen thy salvation."

JANUARY 17.

MORNING.—"My beloved standeth behind our wall. He looketh forth at the windows, shewing himself through the lattice"—Song ii. 9.

It might be truly said, that it was behind the wall of our nature the Lord Jesus stood, when, by taking a body of flesh, he veiled the glories of his Godhead, during the days of his humanity. And may it not be as truly said, that it is still, as from behind a wall, all the gracious discoveries he now makes of himself are manifested to his people? For what from the dulness of our perception, the unbelief, and the sins and infirmities of our nature, the most we see of our Jesus is but as through a glass darkly. But yet, my soul, how sweet are even these visits of his love, when we can get though but a glimpse of the King in his beauty, through the windows of ordinances, or the lattices of his blessed word. Oh, precious Jesus! let thy visits be frequent, increasingly lovely, and increasingly glorious, that the souls of thy people may increasingly delight in thee! Methinks I would lay about the doors, and windows, and courts of thy house, and be sending in a wish, and the fervent prayer of a poor beggar who is living on thy bounty, that thou wouldest come forth to my view and bless me with thy presence, until that all intervening mediums of walls and windows are thrown down, and Jesus manifests himself to my longing eyes in all his glory.

EVENING.—"Behold, I stand at the door, and knock; if any man hear my voice, and open the door, I will come in to him, and will sup with him, and he with me."—Rev. iii. 20.

See, my soul, what condescension there is in Jesus! It was but on the last evening that thou wert feasted by his own gracious invitation at his table; and now the Lord invites himself at thine. So earnest is Jesus to keep up the closest acquaintance and holy familiarity with his redeemed, that if they are at any time backward in inviting him, he will invite himself. Jesus is come then this evening, before thou art prepared for him; yea, not only before thou hast invited him, but even before thy poor timid and unbelieving heart could have had the idea or expectation of such a guest. And hear what the gracious, kind, affectionate Lord saith; Behold! In which he not only desires to have it heard and known by thee, but all the church shall know his love in this particular, and be witness of his great grace and condescension. And where is the Lord? "Behold! I stand," he saith, "at the door and knock!" And wilt thou not, my soul, instantly cry out, as Laban of old did to the messenger of Abraham, "Come in thou blessed of the Lord; wherefore standest thou without?" Oh! the grace that is in the heart of Jesus; that he, who is the sovereign Lord of all, who hath made us, redeemed us, bought us with such a price as his blood, should nevertheless stand without, and beg admittance into the hearts of his people, which he hath made, and new made, and over whom he hath all power to kill and to make alive, to heal and to destroy! Precious, precious Jesus! I bless thy name that I hear thy voice. Thy loud and powerful knocks, by thy word and by thy Spirit, have made me earnest for thy admission. Put in thine hand, Lord, by the hole of the door, and open my heart, as thou didst Lydia's, and give me all-suited grace to receive thee, to embrace thee, to love thee, to delight in thee, and give thee a most hearty welcome. I would say, in the warmth and desire of my soul, and in the language of thine own most sacred words; "Lift up your heads, O ye gates, and be ye lift up, ye everlasting doors, and the King of glory shall come in!" And what hath my Lord promised, when the door of my poor heart is opened? Yea, thou hast said, I will come in to him, and sup with him, and he with me. Bountiful Lord! wilt thou indeed give me the precious privilege of an union with thee, and communion with thyself and thy graces? Wilt thou feed and feast me at my poor house, as on the last night thou didst at thine own? I have nothing to set before thee; I can bring forth nothing worthy thy acceptance. But methinks I hear my Lord say, "I am the bread of life, and the bread of God which cometh down from heaven." I am all, and provide all, and will give the true relish and enjoyment for all! Lord, I fall down under a deep sense of my vileness and thy glory; my emptiness and thine all-sufficiency. Yea, blessed master! be thou all in all, and let my poor soul feast upon thy fulness; and do thou "stay me with flagons, comfort me with apples, for I am sick of love."

JANUARY 18.

MORNING.—"Therefore doth my Father love me, because I lay down my life that I might take it again."—John x. 17.

Mark, my soul, the precious cause which thy Jesus here assigns for the love of his Father. God the Father not only loves God the Son, as God, one with him in nature and in all divine perfections; but he loves him peculiarly because he voluntarily undertook and accomplished by his death the salvation of his people. Now then, my soul, make these two sweet improvements from what Jesus hath here said. First, think what must have been, and now is, the love of thy God and Father to thee and every poor sinner, when he truly loves his dear Son because he became the Saviour of poor sinners. And, secondly, think what love Jesus hath shewn to poor sinners in thus manifesting his mercy in such a way, and how dear they must be to the heart of Jesus, which have made him dear in the sight of God. My soul, never lose sight of this argument, when thou goest to the mercy-seat. Tell thy God and Father thou art come to ask mercies in his name, and for his righteousness' sake, whom the Father loveth on this very account. And Oh, how very dear should Jesus be to thee for his blood and righteousness, who is dear to the Father for the same cause!

EVENING.—"And thou shalt say unto them, this is the offering made by fire, which ye shall offer unto the Lord; two lambs of the first year, without spot, day by day, for a continual burnt-offering. The one lamb shalt thou offer in the morning, and the other lamb shalt thou offer at even."—Numb. xxviii. 3, 4.

Pause, my soul, over the scriptural account of this solemn transaction! Think how infinitely important in the sight of Jehovah, was, and is, that vast sacrifice of the Lamb of God "slain from the foundation of the world," which every day, morning and evening, the Lord commanded to be set forth in an offering made by fire. With what exactness did the church observe this daily rite of oblation! How scrupulous were all true Israelites in this service! and how fully did it proclaim to them the doctrine that "without shedding of blood there was no remission!" Who that reads the solemn precept, and remarks the strictness of Israel in their obedience to it, but must be struck with this conviction? And who can for a moment doubt but that the whole was performed by faith in the Lamb of God, who, in after ages, did away all the penal effects of sin by the sacrifice of himself? Pause again, my soul. Hath this daily sacrifice ceased, as the prophet Daniel declared it should? (Dan. ix. 27.) Are the lamb of the morning and the lamb of the evening now no more? And wherefore? Because the thing signified being accomplished, the sign is needed to minister no longer; the substance being come, the shadow is for ever done away. And shall not thy morning and thine evening act of faith be expressly exercised upon this one Lamb of God which taketh away the sin of the world? Did the faithful Israelite at nine in the morning, and three in the evening, (the hours of those daily sacrifices) offer the lamb by faith in the promised Redeemer; and shall not the believing followers of the blessed Jesus have their hours of commemoration in spiritual acts of praise and faith upon the bleeding body of him, who by the one offering of himself, once offered, hath for ever perfected them that are sanctified? Yes, thou precious Lamb of God! I would pray for grace to behold thee in every act of faith, in every offering of prayer, every ordinance, every means of grace, and all the rites of religious worship. I would see thee through the whole of the bible as the one thing, the only thing signified. I would trace the sweet, the blessed, the soul-comforting, soul-strengthening, soul-transforming subject, until, from the Lamb slain from the foundation of the world, I followed the Lamb whithersoever he went; until I beheld thee, as the beloved apostle saw thee, "the Lamb as it had been slain, in the midst of the throne," still wearing on thy glorified body the marks of our redemption. And there, precious Jesus, should my eyes fix, and my heart centre all her joys, because also in this exalted state thou art still the Lamb. Thy glory and thy power have made no change of nature, though of place. Thou art the Lamb of God, and the brother of thy people still. The eternal efficacy of thy blood and righteousness, and the everlasting love in thine heart towards thy redeemed are the same. As in person, so in office, thou art "Jesus Christ, the same yesterday, and to-day, and for ever." Amen.

JANUARY 19.

MORNING.—"As the new wine is found in the cluster, and one saith, destroy it not, for a blessing is in it; so will I do for my servants' sakes, that I may not destroy them all."—Isa. lxv. 8.

It is blessed to trace our mercies to the fountain-head, and to find them all folded up from everlasting in Jesus. What was it that preserved our whole nature when blasted and withered by the fall? Was it not because Jesus, the promised seed, was in it? And what is it that preserves every individual among the children of God during the dark season of their unregeneracy, but the same precious cause? He that looks on (and who is this but Christ himself?) amidst all our perishing circumstances, by his powerful and all-prevailing intercession, commands the destroyer not to touch his people; for though in themselves loathsome, yet in Jesus they are fair and lovely. My soul, learn hence thy security. The whole cause for which thou wert preserved until called, and, when called, preserved through grace unto glory, both in conversion and in every after-act of God's dealings with thee, all refers itself into this one source. Destroy it not, there is a blessing *in* thee, though not *from* thee: Jesus is in thee, as the new wine is found in the cluster!

EVENING.—"And grieve not the Holy Spirit of God, whereby ye are sealed unto the day of redemption."—Eph. iv. 30.

Methinks I would make this scripture the motto of my daily walk, to keep in remembrance more than the dearest friend that wears the ring of love upon his finger, and bears it about with him whithersoever he goeth. And is the Holy Spirit grieved whenever a child of God forgetteth Jesus, and by indulgence in any sin, loses sight of those sufferings which he endured on account of sin? Yes, God the Holy Ghost is grieved, communion with God the Father is interrupted, and all the agonies and bloody sweats of Jesus forgotten, if there be a loose and careless life. And shall I ever grieve the Holy Ghost by any one allowed transgression? Would not my soul feel shame at the consciousness of it, even if no eye but his had seen the foul act? Wouldest thou grieve for me, O Lord, at such a sight? Can it be possible that a poor worm of the earth, such as I am, should excite such regard and attention? And shall not the consideration have its constant unceasing influence upon my soul? Shall I grieve the holy Lord by an unholy conduct? Shall I quench those sweet influences which first quickened me, and recompense the kindness, which, had it not been called forth to my spiritual life, would have left me to this hour as it first found me, dead in trespasses and sins? Oh! thou holy, blessed, gracious Lord God! withdraw not, I beseech thee, thy restraining influences; leave me not for a moment to myself? Thou knowest that I shall grieve thee, if unassisted by thy grace. Self-will and confidence, sloth and forgetfulness, pride and presumption, will afford an opportunity to the great enemy of souls to betray me into sin, if thou do not keep me; but if thou, Lord, wilt keep me, I shall be well kept. Thou wilt lead me to the all-precious Jesus, thou wilt take of his, and so effectually shew it to me, that I shall be prepared for, guided in, and carried through all acts of holy obedience; and by thy sweet influences, and the sprinkling of the blood of Jesus, I shall be enabled to mortify the deeds of the body, so as to live. My soul! be thou constantly looking to Jesus, seeking communion with the Holy Ghost, and crying out to God the Father, with David, "Take not thine Holy Spirit from me;" that I may not grieve that Holy Lord, by whom I am sealed unto the day of redemption.

JANUARY 20.

MORNING.—"What shall be done unto the man whom the king delighteth to honour?"—Esther vi. 6.

Nay, my soul, ask thine own heart what shall be done to the God-man whom Jehovah, the King of kings, delighteth to honour? Oh, for the view of what John saw, and to hear what John heard, when he beheld the heaven opened, and heard the innumerable multitude chanting salvation to God and the Lamb! Lord, I would say, "let every knee bow before him, and every tongue confess that Jesus Christ is Lord, to the glory of God the Father." And Oh, most gracious Father! dost thou take delight that Jesus should be honoured? Is it thine honour when Jesus is honoured; thy glory when Jesus is glorified? Oh, what wonderful encouragement is this to the faith and belief of a poor sinner! that I not only praise my adorable Redeemer when I come to him for all things, and trust him for all things; but when also my poverty and emptiness afford occasion to him to get glory by me, in giving to me all things, and blessing me in all things. And these exercises of grace are acceptable to God my Father, as they are honourable to God the Son. And this is the only way, and a blessed way it is indeed, by which a poor sinner can give glory to the Father, in believing the record which he hath given of his Son. Here then, my soul, do thou daily be found in honouring the glory-man, the God-man, Christ Jesus, whom God the Father delighteth to honour.

EVENING.—" And not only they, but ourselves also, which have the first fruits of the Spirit, even we ourselves, groan within ourselves, waiting for the adoption, to wit, the redempton of our body."—Rom. viii. 23.

It is blessed to receive from the Holy Ghost such gracious interpretations of his own most holy word as bear a correspondence with what we feel in a life of grace. We know that our adorable Jesus is the Saviour of the body as well as the soul; but we know also that these vile bodies of ours are not regenerated, as the souls of his redeemed are. In this tabernacle, therefore, we groan, being burthened. "I know," saith Paul, "that in me, that is, in my flesh, dwelleth no good thing." And

I too often know, to my sorrow, the same. Pause, my soul, this evening, over this solemn scripture, and look up to the great author of it, to unfold its sacred truth to thy comfort. I hope I can humbly adopt the language, and say, that I "have the first fruits of the Spirit." I know what it is to enjoy the first dawnings and leadings of grace. I know what it is to have been once afar off, living without God and Christ in the world, an enemy to God by wicked works. And I know what it is to have been brought nigh by the blood of Christ: Jesus, by his Holy Spirit, hath come nigh to me, and brought my soul nigh to God. I know also what it is at times to have sweet seasons of communion. I am as sensible of the reviving, comforting, strengthening, refreshing graces of the Spirit, as the earth is of the falling showers, or the sweet return of light. I know no less what it is to have an enlargement of soul, in the going forth of the exercises of faith and grace upon the person and work of the Lord Jesus. When the Redeemer is pleased to call forth into lively actings upon himself the graces he hath planted, I can then find a blessed season in contemplating his glories, his beauties, his fulness, his suitableness, and all-sufficiency. I then sit down as the church of old did, "under his shadow with great delight, and his fruit is sweet to my taste." The Lord hath then "brought me into his banqueting house," and my whole soul, under his banner of love, is delighted in fatness. But amidst these "first fruits of the Spirit," these blessed earnests and pledges of the glory that shall be revealed, I know no less also what it is to groan within myself, waiting for the adoption, to wit, the redemption of my poor polluted, sinful body. I find this partner of my heart, this earthly half of myself, at times the greatest opposer of my better dispositions. "The flesh lusteth against the Spirit;" the soul is straitened, shut up, so as to say nothing, and do nothing, when appearing before the

Lord. I dare not neglect prayer; I dare not absent myself from going to court! The king will know and mark my neglect. But if I go, I am cold, dead, and lifeless: I hear as though I heard not; I pray as though I prayed not. Can I do otherwise than groan? Can I help at times being deeply affected, although I have "the first fruits of the Spirit?" Lord Jesus, undertake for me, and let all the sanctified blessings, intended by thy love and wisdom to be derived from these painful exercises of the soul, be accomplished. Let this thorn in the flesh make me humble: root out the very existence of spiritual pride; reconcile my whole heart to the humiliation of the grave; and, above all, endear thee, thou precious Immanuel, the Lord our righteousness, more and more to my affections, since it is thou, and thou alone, that canst be our peace here and our salvation for ever!

JANUARY 21.

MORNING.—"But for Adam there was not found an help meet for him."—Gen. ii. 20.

My soul, mark what is here said, for sure it is a sweet scripture. Amidst all the works of God, "there was not one that could be found an help meet for man." The inferior creatures could indeed minister to his bodily comfort, but not to his soul. Eve herself, with all her loveliness, must have failed in this particular. Both the woman and her husband alike needed this help to the soul. How refreshing is the thought, and what a lovely view doth it give us of God's grace and mercy, that in the seed of the woman an help, in the fullest sense of the word, was found both for time and eternity. Jesus in our nature needed the church for his partner: and the church needed Jesus, and he was, and is, the very Adam of whom our first father in nature, was but the shadow, and Christ the substance. Yes, blessed Jesus! in thee we trace this wondrous gift of God. Pause then, my soul, and add this thought to the vast account: The same love which fitted thee with an help meet in a Saviour, hath fitted thee, and will continue to fit thee, with the supply of all thy need. It were to be wished, that every child of God would never lose sight of this certain truth—that he must have the fittest station in life, the fittest frame of mind and of body, the fittest yoke-fellow, the fittest circumstances; in short, the fittest mercies and the fittest trials; because every thing is made subservient to the divine glory in Jesus. Sweet thought! "He that spared not his own Son, will with him also freely give us all things."

EVENING.—" In deaths oft."—2 Cor. xi. 23.

What did the apostle mean by this expression, but that from *living* in Christ, he was always on the look-out for *dying* in Christ; so that death could make no change of state, whatever change it made of worlds; for that living or dying, he was still in Christ? Paul seems to be speaking out his whole soul in the thought. It seems as if the conscious sense of his union and interest with Jesus was so inwrought in his very nature, that he was " in deaths oft," hoping that this providence, or that appointment, would be found the messenger to call him home to his Redeemer, to be with him for ever. My soul! as every night the bed of sleep to thy wearied body becomes a representation of the night of death, and the chamber of the grave, sit down this evening, and look over the memorandums of thine heart, whether there are some of the same sweet testimonies, and arising out of the same blessed source, as the apostle's, thou art " in deaths oft," and canst protest, as he did, by the rejoicing which thou hast in

Christ Jesus, that "thou diest daily?"—If the apostle's state is thine, the habitual frame of thine heart, from a well-grounded interest in Jesus, must be such as to leave a constant impression on thy mind, that the change of death, come when it may, and coming, as it must, from thy Lord's own appointment, must be to thy happy account. It is to die and be with Christ, which is far better. Here we live, we walk, we enjoy Jesus, but by faith; there we shall ever be with the Lord; we shall see him as he is, we shall be like him. As here Jesus imparts all the grace the souls of his redeemed need in life to carry them on, and bring them home, so there he imparts glory: as he shines in one glorious fulness as the sun, so they as the stars of heaven for multitude and brightness. He that is the source and fountain of all grace in this life, is the source also of glory and happiness in the world to come. If then, my soul, thou art "in deaths oft," as one on the look-out for the coming of thy friend to call thee home to himself, is not the prospect delightful? Wouldest thou shrink back, if his chariot-wheels were now at the door?—Pause. Are you daily pleading his blood and righteousness before God? Are you most firmly, and most satisfactorily convinced of his conquest over sin, death, hell, and the grave? Do you heartily, cordially, fully approve of God's rich covenant mercy in Christ? Can you, do you, will you take God at his word, and give him the credit due to him, in believing the record which he hath given of his dear Son? And are you *living* daily upon these precious, blessed things, and under his grace, determined to *die* in the faith of them? What sayest thou to these solemn, but precious soul-transactions? Can a throne of grace witness for thee, that thou art constantly pleading them there, as the only means, the only security thou art looking to for thy acceptance? If so, and should the messenger of Jesus come, and find you upon your knees, would you say, not yet, Lord? Would any thing make you linger here, when Jesus stood above, calling to thee, 'Come up hither?' Oh! dearest Jesus, for more of that grace, for more of that faith, to overcome all fears, doubts, and misgivings. Oh! for some sweet increasing manifestations from thyself, dear Lord, day by day, that the nearer I am drawing to the period of my departure, the closer I may cling to thy embraces, and the more sensibly I may hang my soul upon thee; that when death comes thou mayest impart such strength to my poor dying frame, that like the patriarch I may cry out: "Into thine arms, Lord Jesus, do I commit my spirit; for thou hast redeemed me, O Lord, thou God of truth!"

JANUARY 22.

MORNING.—"They shall cry unto the Lord because of the oppressors, and he shall send them a Saviour, and a great one, and he shall deliver them."—Isa. xix. 20.

Mark, my soul, the sweet encouragement contained in these words. Here is a cry, and it is the cry of the soul; for it is directed unto the Lord. There is (as Elihu tells us) a cry of nature under oppression; but as this is not *to* God, it is evident that it never came *from* God; for he tells us, that none of them saith, "Where is God my Maker, who giveth songs in the night?" Job xxv. 9. But when the Holy Ghost convinceth of sin, and puts a cry in the heart by reason of it, he convinceth also of the righteousness of Jesus. Hence the difference of those cries is as wide as the east is from the west. Mark, therefore, my soul, this distinguishing feature of grace, and see whether thy cries are *praying* cries, and not *complaining* ones. And now observe what follows. When poor sinners thus cry unto the Lord, "he shall send them a Saviour, and a great one." Who but God the Father, sent his Son to be the Saviour of poor lost sinners? Was not Jesus a Saviour indeed, and a great one! Who, but he, could deliver the sinner from destruction? And remark, further, the absolute certainty of the promise; for it is said, " he *shall* deliver them." Yes, blessed Jesus, thy deliverance is sure, thy salvation certain. Thou hast said, thy " sheep shall never perish, neither shall any pluck them out of thine hand." Pause, now, my soul, over this sweet verse. Surely in its bosom is folded up the sum and substance of all the gospel. Here are all the Persons of the Godhead engaged for the salvation of every poor crying sinner. Here is God the Holy Ghost, agreeably to his blessed office, causing the sinner to feel the oppressions of sin, and putting a cry in his heart to the Lord, to be delivered from them. Here is God the Father, answering that cry in mercy, and sending his almighty Son to be the Saviour of the poor sinner. And here is Jesus the Saviour, and a great one, saving the poor sinner with an everlasting salvation. Shout then, my soul, and begin the song of salvation to God and the Lamb!

EVENING. — " And their nobles shall be of themselves, and their governor shall proceed from the midst of them; and I will cause him to draw near, and he shall approach unto me; for who is this that engaged his heart to approach unto me? saith the Lord."—Jer. xxx. 21.

When the patriarch Jacob was dying, he pronounced, under the spirit of prophecy, that " the sceptre should not depart from Judah, nor a lawgiver from between his feet, until Shiloh come," Gen. xlix. 10. And here in the prospect of the Babylonish captivity, now on the eve of its arrival, the prophet is commissioned by the Lord to tell the church, that notwithstanding all present appearances, no foreigners should judge or rule over them; but one should proceed from the midst of them, to be their governor, even David their king, whom I (saith Jehovah, verse 9.) will raise up unto them. One like unto themselves, such as our Jesus was, like unto his brethren. Sweet confirmation of our faith! And that no doubt might arise concerning the justness of the application, the Lord by another prophet (Micah v. 2.) mentioned the place of his birth, and marked at the same time, the features of his eternal power and Godhead. "But thou, Bethlehem-Ephratah, though thou be little among the thousands of Judah, yet out of thee shall he come forth unto me that is to be ruler in Israel, whose goings forth have been from of old, from everlasting." But we must not stop here in our views of this precious scripture. He that is to come forth from among his brethren as their governor, Jehovah engageth for him, that he will cause him to approach unto him. Blessed thought! No son or daughter of Adam could ever have drawn nigh to God, but for this gracious interposition. The holiness of the divine nature, the holiness of the divine law, and the enmity of the heart of man by sin, totally precluded it. None but he who is holy, harmless, undefiled, separate from sinners, and made higher than the heavens, could have engaged his heart to this service. And indeed he graciously undertook it, and as completely accomplished it. Jesus was peculiarly suited for this vast undertaking. For as God he was one with the Father, to whom he approached; and as man, he was the person for whom, and by whom the reconciliation was to be accomplished; and as both God and Man in one Person, he could (as Job calls it) be a proper Day's-man, to act between both parties, and restore to God his glory, and to man his happiness. And what a blessed addition to these delightful things respecting Jesus, is it to see, that God the Father's hand was with Jesus in all! "I will cause him to draw near, and he shall approach unto me." Pause, my soul, over this blessed scripture, and behold in all the vast work of thy Redeemer's salvation, the name and authority of God thy Father confirming it. And wilt thou not then, in all thy approaches to God in Christ, have respect to this sovereign act of Jehovah? Is it indeed God the Father who hath given his dear Son, called him, appointed him, solemnly introduced him into his high priest's office, *by an oath*, and in all his offices as Mediator, caused him to draw near in the accomplishment of redemption: and wilt thou not in all thy approaches, look unto Jesus as the Father hath respect unto him? Oh! for grace, in all the lively exercises of it, to draw nigh to the footstool of the mercy-seat, and unceasingly to remind God our Father of his own gracious appointment and acceptance of the church in the person of his dear Son. Yea! holy Father, I would say, in every act of worship, love, and praise, "Behold, O God, our shield, and look upon the face of thine anointed!"

JANUARY 23.

MORNING.—"That as sin hath reigned unto death, even so might grace reign through righteousness unto eternal life, by Jesus Christ our Lord."—Rom. v. 21.

Pause, my soul, and put forth thy fullest thoughts in the contemplation of those two united sources of thy felicity, marked in this verse: the Father's eternal purpose, in the reign of grace; and the everlasting efficacy and infinite value of thy Jesus's righteousness, to eternal life. None but God himself can know the fulness and extent of either. I am persuaded, that angels of light can never entertain adequate conceptions of either. The eternal purpose of God hath bounded the reign of sin; it is but unto death. But those purposes give a further extent to the redemption from death and sin, by Jesus; for the glory of Christ's person, and the worth of his salvation, possess in both a vast overplus, a redundancy of merit, which brings the redeemed into favour and acceptance in Jesus, and with such a title to everlasting felicity, as eternity itself can never exhaust—no, nor fully recompense nor pay. Oh for grace to contemplate the love of the Father, and of the Son, by this standard; and the love of God the Holy Ghost, through whose gracious influence we enjoy both. Lord, I would be lost, I would be swallowed up, day by day, in the unceasing meditation! Dearest, blessed, precious Jesus! give me to think of nothing else, to speak of nothing else; but by faith to possess in anticipation, the joys of thy redeemed, until I come, through thee, and in thee, to the everlasting enjoyment of them, in thy kingdom of glory.

EVENING.—"Now when Jesus was risen early, the first day of the week, he appeared first to Mary Magdalene, out of whom he had cast seven devils."—Mark xvi. 9.

My Lord! I have often found occasion to stand amazed at the wonders of thy grace, as set forth in thy blessed word. Every thing manifests that it is altogether free and undeserved; nothing, in the objects of it, having the least tendency to call it forth into exercise; no, not even our misery: for though our misery afforded an opportunity for the greater display of it, yet thy grace was long before our misery, originating as it did in thine own everlasting love. Every circumstance connected with the manifestation of thy grace calls forth astonishment. The greatness, the continuance, the unceasing nature of it, notwithstanding all the undeservings of the objects of thy rich bounty; all tend to excite astonishment in my soul. But, Lord! when at any time I behold abounding grace shewn, where there have been abounding transgressions; and, as the apostle expresseth it, "where sin hath reigned unto death, that there more eminently grace should reign unto eternal life;" my soul is overwhelmed in the contemplation; for here I discover, as upon numberless other occasions, that "thy thoughts are not my thoughts, nor thy ways my ways." Will Jesus, this evening, graciously tell me, why the poor Mary Magdalene was first blessed, before any of the disciples, with the sight of her risen Saviour? Was it to teach her, and all poor sinners like her, that "where sin hath abounded, grace shall much more abound?" Was it indeed to encourage every poor broken-hearted sinner, long exercised with the power and temptations of Satan, that it is to such more especially that Jesus hath an eye, that he knows their sorrows, and will assuredly relieve them? Did my honoured Lord mean, by this wonderful act of grace, to shew that he will take yet more delight to inhabit that precious soul out of which he hath cast seven devils, than where legions of evil spirits have not been suffered so long, and so powerfully to triumph? Am I, blessed Lord, authorized by this gracious act of thine, so to construe thy wonderful love? Shall a poor Magdalene, who only ventured, while thou wast upon earth, to fall at thy feet, behind thee, weeping, be first blessed with a sight of thy Person after redemption-work was finished, before the beloved apostle who lay in thy bosom at thy table? Oh! thou dear, thou gracious, thou condescending Lord! what am I to interpret of this kind act of thine, but that the heart of Jesus yearns over poor sinners, and can and will administer consolation to them in their most desperate circumstances? Yes! thou dear Lord! such hath been thy mercy, love, and grace, in every act. Rebellious angels are passed by, and fallen man calls forth thy pity! And among men, thy grace is shewn, not to the wise, and noble, and self-sufficient; but to the poor, the needy, the maimed, the halt, the blind. Yea, Lord! thy grace is frequently manifested to tempers the most unpromising, to stubborn and rebellious persons; whilst those who are wise in their own eyes, and prudent in their own conceit, starched in the ceremonies and forms of religion, live, and it is to be feared die, without the knowledge of salvation by Jesus. Hence the young man in the gospel, who thought himself from his own goodness just ripe for heaven, shall go from thee sorrowful, while Jesus will take up his abode in the heart of a Magdalene, which had before been occupied by seven devils! Oh! for grace "to comprehend with all saints, what is the breadth and length, and depth and height; and to know the love of Christ, which passeth knowledge, that I may be filled with all the fulness of God."

JANUARY 24.

MORNING.—"And he shewed me Joshua, the high priest, standing before the angel of the Lord, and Satan standing at his right hand to resist him. And the Lord said unto Satan, the Lord rebuke thee, O Satan; even the Lord that hath chosen Jerusalem, rebuke thee. Is not this a brand plucked out of the fire?"—Zech. iii. 1, 2.

Who shall say, how many such transactions as these are continually going on, for and against the people of God, in the court of heaven, while we upon earth are unconscious either of our misery or mercy? The Holy Ghost was graciously pleased to have this made known to the church. And John was again directed to tell the church, that a song in heaven was sung at the expulsion of the devil from heaven, because the accuser of the brethren was cast down. My soul, doth he that first tempts thee, then become thine accuser? Is he carrying on this practice day and night before God? And while Satan is thine accuser, is Jesus thine advocate? Oh precious, precious Lord! how little hath my poor ignorant and unthinking soul been meditating on thee, in this thy merciful, sweet, and gracious office. Oh glorious thought! Now I see a blessedness in that scripture which I have often read with indifference in times past; "If any man sin, we have an advocate with the Father, Jesus Christ the righteous; and he is (for God my Father hath set him forth so) the propitiation for our sins." Hail, holy, wonderful Counsellor! condescend, thou mighty Pleader, still to take up my cause! Oh may I behold thee often in this high office! Oh may I often hear thee with the ear of faith, and my whole soul going forth in love towards thee, while thou art pointing to my poor soul, and saying, "Hath not God the Father chosen this brand plucked from the fire? Take away the filthy garments from him. I have caused thine iniquity to pass from thee."

EVENING.—"Who now rejoice in my sufferings for you, and fill up that which is behind of the afflictions of Christ in my flesh, for his body's sake, which is the church."—Col. i. 24.

What can the apostle mean from these expressions? Not, surely, that the sufferings of Jesus were incomplete, or that the sufferings of his people were to make up a deficiency: for in treading the wine-press of the wrath of God against sin, Jesus trod it alone, and of the people there was none with him. And so perfectly finished and complete was the whole work of redemption by Jesus, that by the one offering of himself, once offered, "he hath perfected for ever them that are sanctified." But what a sweet scripture is this of the apostle's, when it is interpreted with reference to Jesus, that in all the sufferings of his people Jesus takes a part! Jesus suffered in his own person fully and completely, when as an expiatory sacrifice for sin he died, the just for the unjust, to bring his people to God. These sufferings as a sacrifice were full, and have fully satisfied: they cease for ever, and can be known no more. But the sympathy of Jesus with his people gives him to bear a part in all their concerns. And the consciousness of this made the apostle tell the church that he rejoiced in all his exercises, because Jesus took part, and thereby endeared the affliction. My soul! cherish the thought also. Thy Jesus knows all, measures out all, bears part with thee in all, and will carry thee through all, and finally crown all with his love and blessing. The same interest that Jesus felt in the persecution of Saul over his afflicted ones, when he called from heaven to restrain Saul's rage, and said, "Saul, Saul, why persecutest thou me?"—the same interest he feels in every minute event, with which his redeemed are exercised now. " Whosoever toucheth you, toucheth the apple of his eye." Blessed Lord! may my soul keep in remembrance those endearing views of thy love. Give me to keep alive the recollection of the oneness between the glorious head, and all his exercised members. I see that a child of thine cannot mourn, but Jesus marks it down, and puts the tears in his bottle. He notes his sorrows in his book. So that by this fellow-feeling, Lord! our interest in thee is most fully proved. And while thy people partake in thy righteousness, thou takest part in their sorrows. As it was in the days of thy flesh, so is it now in the fulness of thy glory: " in all their affliction he was afflicted, and the angel of his presence saved them: in his love and in his pity he redeemed them, and he bare them and carried them all the days of old."

JANUARY 25.

MORNING.—" This is a faithful saying, and worthy of all acceptation, that Christ Jesus came into the world to save sinners."—1 Tim. i. 15.

Hearken, my soul, to the proclamation from heaven! Is this the faithful saying of a faithful God? Surely, then, thou mayest well regard it, for it is for thy life. And if it be worthy of *all* acceptation, it must be eminently so of *thine;* for thou hast been a transgressor from the womb. But did Jesus indeed come to save sinners? Yes, so the proclamation runs. Sinners, enemies to God. Jesus, it is said, " received gifts for the rebellious, that the Lord God might dwell among them;" and with that tenderness which distinguished his character, he said himself, that he " came not to call the righteous, but sinners to repentance." Well, then, my soul, upon this warrant of the faithful word of a faithful God, wilt thou not so fully rely as to believe unto salvation? If any inquiries arise contrary to this belief, let this be thine answer:—Christ came to save sinners; that is enough for me; for I am one. God's salvation is said to be for enemies; that is my name by nature. Jesus received gifts for the rebellious; to this character I plead also guilty. If men or devils would endeavour to work unbelief in my heart, this is my answer:—"Christ came to save sinners." Let those that never felt sin, and consequently know not the need of a Saviour, stay and argue the point as they may; my soul's eternal welfare is concerned, and I will not lose a moment to close with the heavenly proposal. Lord Jesus, thou waitest to be gracious! The faithful saying of my God I accept on my bended knees. It is indeed worthy of all acceptation, and above all, of mine. Here while upon earth will I proclaim thy praise; and in heaven, the loudest of all voices must be mine, that "Christ came to save sinners, of whom I am chief."

EVENING.—"As the apple-tree among the trees of the wood, so is my beloved among the sons."—Song ii. 3.

My soul! if the church found so much blessedness in making comparisons between her Lord and any of the beautiful objects of nature around her; see if thou canst raise a subject for thy meditation, this evening, from the statement she hath made in this lovely verse. Why should not Jesus be in thy view as in her's? Doth he not infinitely transcend all sons, of whatever description or character that can be found? Angels, no doubt, by creation may be called "the sons of God;" and when God had finished the works of his hands, we are told that "the morning stars sang together, and all the sons of God shouted for joy." But Jesus as far excels all angels of light, as the apple-tree the trees of the wood: for "he hath by inheritance obtained a more excellent name than they." Neither did God at any time say unto the angels, "Sit thou on my right hand until I make thine enemies thy footstool." But to our Jesus he said, "Thy throne, O God! is for ever and ever, a sceptre of righteousness is the sceptre of thy kingdom." And to shew at once the infinite superiority of the Lord Jesus, when he bringeth in the first-begotten into the world, he saith, "And let all the angels of God worship him." Therefore if by the term *sons*, it could be supposed that angels are meant, well might the church declare Jesus her beloved, to be above them. And if by *sons*, the sons of men be meant, what is the whole church of saints compared to Jesus? Though the church, by the comeliness her Lord hath put upon her, shines like a beautiful constellation among the heavenly bodies, yet all her glory and lustre are derived from Jesus, the Sun of righteousness. Pause, my soul, over this view of thy Lord. And when thou hast feasted thyself with the sweet subject, go on, and mark some of the many beauties contained in this comparison between the apple-tree and the trees of the wood. In our cold country, the apple-tree, in its best appearance, affords but a poor resemblance, to what naturalists relate of the pomecitron, as it is called, of the warm eastern climates. It is said of the apple-tree of those countries, that it is a lofty, majestic, stately tree, abundantly fruitful, and yielding both shade and fruit to the traveller. Some assert that it continues bearing fruit the whole year, and is never without blossom. If so, without going farther, we may discover enough by which to understand the beautiful allusion the church hath made of it in this verse to her Lord. Jesus is all this, and infinitely more. He is indeed the tree of life in the midst of the paradise of God, and he bears fruit every month, and the leaves of this tree are for the healing of the nations. Precious Jesus! thou art the fairest and the chiefest among ten thousand! Be thou to me, Lord, as the fruitful bough which the dying patriarch blessed by the well, whose branches ran over the wall. And Oh! do thou give strength to my poor feeble faith, to gather all the rich fruits of thy righteousness for the healing of my soul, that I may daily sit down under thy shadow with great delight, and thy fruit be sweet to my taste!

JANUARY 26.

MORNING.—"And they said one to another, did not our heart burn within us, while he talked with us by the way, and while he opened to us the scriptures?"—Luke xxiv. 32.

Ought not the disciples of Jesus to do now, as the disciples of Jesus did then? What but of Jesus should we speak of by the way? Methinks the Lord's people, and especially when coming from the Lord's house, should be distinguished from the frothy conversation of mere carnal worshippers. I would, by talking of Jesus, invite him to mingle with us, and open to our understandings the scriptures. I would therefore sometimes ask one and another, when returning from the house or the table of the Lord, how went the matter with your soul to-day? I pray you tell me; was the King at court? Did he receive petitions? Did he answer prayers? Were you refreshed? were any healed? any comforted? any made joyful in his house of prayer? Surely we might hope, by such edifying inquiries, each would help his fellow. And he of whom it is said the Lord hearkened and heard, when of old the people of God were often talking one to another, would again draw nigh, and make the heart burn with the sweet manifestations of his love. But chiefly, blessed master! if I meet with none to ask whether they have seen the King in his beauty, give me to taste of the sweet savour of thy grace myself. Come to me, Lord, in the refreshing, strengthening, heart-warming, soul-rejoicing manifestations of thy presence; for thy love is better than wine, and the very crumb from under thy table is more delicious than the honey and the honey-comb.

EVENING.—"And they took knowledge of them, that they had been with Jesus."—Acts iv. 13.

Oh! for the same grace to rest upon me, as upon those faithful servants of my Lord; that, like them, I may manifest the sweet savour of Jesus's name in every place; wherever I am, with whomsoever I converse, in every state, and upon every occasion, that all may witness *for* me, and every thing bear witness *to* me, that I have been with Jesus! I would entreat thee, my honoured Lord, that I may honour thee so before men, that after my morning visits to thy throne of grace, my mid-day communion, my evening and nightly fellowship, my return to the society of men might so be distinguished as one that had just been with Jesus. And as it might be supposed, if an angel was to come from heaven that had seen thy face, and heard thy voice, and been an eye witness of thy glory; so, Lord, having by faith enjoyed such views, I might delight to tell, as he would relate to the inhabitants of the earth, the grace, and beauty, and love of Jesus. And surely, Lord, if I have been with thee, and thou with me; if I know any thing of thy grace and salvation; will not, out of the abundance of the heart, the mouth speak? Shall I not delight to tell every one I meet what my Lord is in himself, and what he is to his people? Shall I not speak with rapture of the glories of thy Person, and the infinite value and worth of thy blood and righteousness? Surely in the circle of my acquaintance, I shall be daily speaking of thy grace and salvation, for I know no end thereof. And especially in a day like the present, where the name of my Lord and his cross are banished from all conversation. Oh! that it may be shewn that I have been *with* Jesus, in speaking *for* Jesus. Yes! thou dear Lord! thy truths I would espouse, thy doctrines profess, salvation alone by thy righteousness and cross would I bear before a whole world, with earnestness and with zeal; and if this brought upon me the laugh and derision, yea, the persecution of the proud; like thy servants of old, "I would rejoice in being counted worthy to suffer shame for thy name." And chiefly, and above all, let it not only be noticed that I have been with Jesus, in speaking *of* Christ and *for* Christ; but let the sweet unction of thy Holy Spirit be so abiding upon me, from continual intercourse and communion with thee, that my whole life and conversation may be such as becometh the gospel of Christ. Oh! for the same blessed effect as Moses, whose face shone when he came down from the holy mount, that every one with whom I have to do may see the light of thy grace, in all my transactions with the world, so shine before men, that they may glorify my Father which is in heaven. Precious Lord! grant me these unanswerable testimonies of vital godliness; then will it be proved indeed and in truth, that, like thy servants of old, I have been with Jesus.

JANUARY 27.

MORNING.—"He shall glorify me; for he shall receive of mine, and shall shew it unto you."—John xvi. 14.

Some precious souls are at a loss to apprehend how the Holy Ghost makes application of Jesus and his benefits to his people. Hence they ask, how am I to know that the righteousness of Jesus, and the blood of Jesus, are applied to me. But be not thou, my soul, ignorant of so important a matter, on the clear apprehension of which thy daily comfort depends. Attend, my soul, to what thy Jesus saith in those precious words; and, under the blessed Spirit's teaching, the matter will appear abundantly plain. He shall glorify me, saith Jesus. And doth not the Holy Ghost do this in every believer's view, when he gives the soul to see that all that vast extent of redemption-blessings which the Father treasured up in his dear Son for poor sinners, flow immediately from Jesus? And observe, the Holy Ghost doth not at first shew the sinner that all result from the everlasting love, and grace, and purpose of God the Father; but he leads the sinner to view them, and receive them, as the blessed fruits and effects of Jesu's mediation; and then opens more fully the glory of the Father in the original design of them, in this precious way, from everlasting. This is needed to glorify Jesus, and to glorify the Father in him. And how are these blessings applied? The scriptural answer is the best answer:—"He shall receive of mine," saith Jesus, "and shew it unto you." And doth not that almighty Teacher do all this most sweetly and effectually, when at any time he so holds up the Lord Jesus, in all the glories of his person, and in all the beauties of his finished work, as to incline the sinner's heart so to behold the Saviour as to believe in him, and firmly to rely upon him? Is not the righteousness of Jesus received, and his precious blood applied, when the soul is led to the hearty and cordial assurance that that righteousness is effectual to justify, and that blood to cleanse from all sin? Yes, precious Jesus! I praise thee for these blessings in thee. I adore thee, thou Holy Spirit, for thy divine teaching concerning them; and I glorify thee, thou Almighty Father, for thine abundant grace and mercy in the gift of thy dear Son.

EVENING.—"And on his head were many crowns."—Rev. xix. 12.

Every view of Jesus is blessed. But there are some views which the heart of a believer finds a peculiar gratification in contemplating. The Holy Ghost hath in this scripture given a very interesting representation of Jesus. Heaven is opened; Jesus appears in his well-known characters, "faithful and true." A "white horse" he rides on, to manifest his equity and justice. His vesture is "dipped in blood," to intimate that by blood he hath purchased his kingdom. And his glorious name, "the Word of God," is also mentioned to testify the greatness and almightiness of his person. But amidst these distinguishing characteristics, the coronation of the Lord Jesus is particularly striking. "On his head were many crowns." The crown of Godhead is his by right, in common with the Father. And the crown of God-man mediator is his also, being his by gift, by purchase, and by conquest. Having conquered death, hell, and the grave, God the Father hath set "a crown of pure gold upon his head." "For his honour is great in his salvation; glory and majesty hath he laid upon him." But there is another crown put upon the head of our Jesus, and which every poor believing soul delighteth to see, amidst the many crowns on the head of Jesus; namely, the very crown which that poor precious believer puts by faith upon the glorious head of Jesus, when ascribing his own personal salvation to the alone merits of his blood and righteousness. This is a coronation day indeed of the Lord Jesus; and ever after, most blessed to the review of every believer. And as the Son of God was crowned "Lord of all," in the day when he ascended to the right hand of his Father in heaven, having finished redemption's work, when the whole assembly of heaven cast their crowns at his feet; so is the adorable Redeemer again crowned, when, descending in the power of his Spirit, he takes the throne of a poor sinner's heart, and rules and reigns there, the Lord of life and glory. My soul! pause and ask thine heart what knowest thou of this coronation? Amidst the many crowns discoverable upon the head of the blessed Jesus, canst thou with rapture discern the one, the very one, he wears as thy Redeemer and Lord? It is very easy to discover it, if thine hand of faith hath placed it there. Art thou his subject? "Know ye not," saith the apostle, "to whom ye yield yourselves servants to obey, his servants ye are to whom ye obey, whether of sin unto death, or of obedience unto righteousness?" Hast thou been translated out of darkness into the kingdom of God's dear Son? Is Jesus thy King, as the acknowledged and adored head of the church, which is his body? And art thou living upon him, and from him, as this glorious head, from whence is conveyed to thee, in common with all his members, life, light, grace, strength, and every thing in a way of communion, by which thou provest that thou art among the members of his body, of his flesh, and of his bones; and he the glorious source and fulness that filleth all in all? These are precious views and soul-comforting evidences to this grand truth. And if these be found in thy experience, then art thou so beholding him, on whose head are many crowns, as to venture all thy salvation wholly upon him, and every renewed act of faith is but a renewal of thy coronation of the Lord Jesus: for in every one thou bowest the knee of thine heart before him, and confessest that "Jesus Christ is Lord, to the glory of God the Father."

JANUARY 28.

MORNING.—"As having nothing, and yet possessing all things."—2 Cor. vi. 10.

My soul, hast thou learnt this holy science? There are three blessed lessons the Holy Ghost teacheth on this ground. As, *first*, the believer is thoroughly emptied of himself. Art thou thus taught of God? Hast thou been led to see, to feel, to know, to be convinced that, after all thine attainments, after all thy long standing in the school of Jesus, thou hast nothing, canst do nothing, art worse than nothing, and, literally, hast no more in thyself now to recommend thee to

Jesus, than the first moment thou didst hear of his name? This is to have nothing; this is to be poor in spirit. *Secondly,* dost thou possess all things in Jesus? Yes, if so be thou art living out of thyself wholly upon him; and how is this known? Nothing more evident. When a sense of my emptiness endears to me his fulness; my poverty, his riches; my weakness, his strength; my sins, his righteousness; my guilt, his blood; I truly possess all things, as far as I improve what Jesus is to his people, and rest upon him and the blessed fruits of his salvation, as God the Father designed him, who hath made him wisdom, righteousness, sanctification, and redemption to his people. And there is a *third* precious lesson the Holy Ghost teacheth to the poor that have nothing, and yet possess all things; namely, so to possess Jesus himself that he may not only make his poor ones rich in his riches, but be himself their treasure; so to supply them not only with what they need, but to be himself their fulness; not only to open to them light and life, but to be himself both their light and life; so to impart to them salvation as to shew them that he is himself their salvation; and, in short, so to give them present peace, and the assurance of everlasting happiness in his blood and righteousness, as to give them the perfect enjoyment that he is himself both their present and everlasting happiness, and their portion for ever. My soul, hast thou learnt, and art thou every day more and more learning, these precious truths? Oh, then, look up to thy Jesus, and say with one of old, "Whom have I in heaven but thee, and there is none upon earth I desire besides thee. My flesh and my heart faileth; but thou art the strength of my heart, and my portion for ever."

EVENING.—"I knew that thou wouldest deal very treacherously, and wast called a transgressor from the womb."—Isa. xlviii. 8.

Humbling as the view is, it is profitable to look back, and trace all the way the Lord our God hath brought us, through many a year in the wilderness, to humble us, and to prove us, and to shew us what is in our heart; and this perhaps is the sweetest of all subjects, when the Holy Ghost takes us by the hand, and leads the heart back. Even from the first moment of conversion, to the very moment when taking the review, every step serves to prove what this scripture sets forth, that the Lord knew that his people would deal very treacherously, and be transgressors from the womb. My soul! let thy meditation, this evening, as it concerns thyself, be to this amount: Where wert thou, when in a state of unawakened nature, and as all other carnal persons, intent only upon the best means of fulfilling to the desires of the flesh; living without God, and without Christ in the world; a child of wrath, deserving wrath even as others? The Lord, who knew this, and also what undeservings would follow, still was pleased to visit thee with his great salvation. He manifested the riches of his grace in calling thee, justifying thee, adopting thee into his family, and putting thee among his sons: and he gave thee the Spirit of his Son in thine heart, whereby thou wert enabled to cry, "Abba, Father." And what hath it been since, but the same rich display of free and unmerited mercy? Doth he not know, that thou art still a transgressor? Doth he not continually wait to be gracious, when thy unthinking wandering heart is forgetful of him? Doth Jesus withhold or suspend his grace, and the manifestations of his favour, because thou art forgetful of him? Oh! not so. He deals by thee, as he did by Israel of old! When Israel remembered not the multitude of his mercies, but were disobedient at the sea, yea, even at the Red Sea, nevertheless, it is said, "he saved them for his name's sake," that he might make his mighty power to be known. So doth thy Jesus deal by thee. Though thou art a "transgressor from the womb;" yet Jesus is Jesus still.

The covenant promises of God the Father are the same; and the efficacy of Jesus's blood and righteousness the same: therefore Jesus deals by thee, not according to thy deserts, but according to his own free and sovereign grace. His love, and not thy merit, becomes the standard of his dealings with his people. Oh! how blessed is it to trace mercies to their fountain-head, and to behold God in Christ, dispensing pardon, love, and favour, from his own free and sovereign will and pleasure; and every renewed mercy carrying with it this divine signature: " Not for your sakes do I this, saith the Lord God, be it known unto you: be ashamed and confounded for your own ways, O house of Israel."

JANUARY 29.

MORNING.—" If the servant shall plainly say, I love my master' my wife, and my children, I will not go out free. Then his master shall bring him unto the judges; he shall also bring him to the door, or unto the door posts; and his master shall bore his ear through with an awl, and he shall serve him for ever."—Exod. xxi. 5, 6.

How sweet is scripture explained by scripture! Jesus saith, when sacrifice and offering under the law were both unprofitable, " Mine ears hast thou opened;" or, as it might have been rendered, " Mine ears hast thou digged." Ps. xl. 6. And elsewhere, " The Lord God hath opened mine ear, and I was not rebellious." Isa. l. 5. The apostle to the Hebrews decidedly explains this in reference to Christ, Heb. x. 5. And what was all this but to shew the voluntary service of Jesus to the office and work of the Redeemer. Was not Jesus, in all that high work, the servant of Jehovah? Though he was in the form of God, and with him it was no robbery to be equal with God, yet he made himself of no reputation, and took upon him the form of a servant. And for whom did he this? Was it not, in effect, saying, like the jewish servant, which was typical of him, " I love my master, my father, in the work of redemption?" John xiv. 31. "I love my wife, my church, my spouse." Song iv. 10. "I love my children: behold I, and the children thou hast given me." Isa. viii. 18. "I will not go out free." Oh, precious Lord Jesus! well might the apostle say, "Husbands, love your wives, even as Christ loved the church, and gave himself for it!" Surely it was thy love, dearest Lord, to thy church, that moved thee to serve Jehovah, "as Israel served for a wife, and for a wife kept sheep." Hosea xii. 12. Oh for grace to love thee, and to serve thee for ever!

EVENING.—"He shall not speak of himself."—John xvi. 13.

I have found, in time past, a very great blessedness in this short but sweet account, which Jesus gives of the gracious office of the Holy Ghost; and therefore I would make it the subject of my present evening meditation. I find what the Lord Jesus said concerning the blessed Spirit, in this most delightful part of his divine ministry, to be true. For look wherever I may, through the bible, it is of Jesus only the Holy Ghost is continually speaking, and not of himself. And hence, by the way, I learn how to form a most decided testimony of the faithful preachers of the word. For, if God the Holy Ghost, in his glorifying the Lord Jesus, is never found to be speaking but of Jesus; surely all his faithful servants, who act by his authority, and are commissioned and ordained by him to the work, will never preach themselves, but Christ Jesus the Lord. And how blessed is it to be taught of Jesus, by the Holy Ghost! It is astonishing, when we take into one mass of particulars the agency of the Holy Ghost in his glorifying the Lord Jesus, to observe the patience, the compassion, the tenderness, and love, which that blessed Spirit manifests to the church of Jesus, in holding up to their view, and in bringing home to their heart, the person, work, character and relations of Jesus! How sweetly and effectually doth he speak *of* him, plead *for* him, and win over the affections *to* him, by his saving light, his illuminating grace, and persuasive arguments in the heart! It is the Holy Ghost that takes of Christ, and the things of Christ, and makes both appear lovely and desirable in our eyes. It is his blessed work to bring about the gracious union, when, as the bridegroom of his church, God the Spirit represents him in his beauty, and persuades the soul of the sinner to receive him and accept him as her Maker and her husband, to whom she is betrothed for ever! And from whom, but the Holy Ghost, do those sweet influences arise from day to day, and from one degree of grace to another, by which the life of the believer in Christ is kept up, maintained, and carried on in the soul, from the first beginning of the spiritual life, until grace is consummated in eternal glory. Oh! Lord the Spirit! I beseech thee, glorify my adorable Redeemer in my poor cold and lifeless heart, and sweetly lead over the whole of my affections to all-precious Jesus, that I may live upon his glorious person, and feel my interest in his great salvation increasingly precious. And Oh, thou holy Lord! keep alive, I beseech thee, thine own saving and powerful influences in my heart, that I may never, never by sin, quench thy divine flame, nor "grieve the Holy Spirit, whereby I am sealed unto the day of redemption."

JANUARY 30.

MORNING.—"That in the ages to come he might shew the exceeding riches of his grace, in his kindness towards us through Christ Jesus."—Eph. ii 7.

Pause, my soul, and gather in all the powers of arithmetic, and try if thou art able to count what the exceeding riches of God's grace amount to. Think how great, how free, how sovereign, how inexhaustible, how everlasting! All that a poor sinner hath in time, all that we can enjoy to all eternity, all is of grace. And what a title hath thy God chosen to be known by among his people, when, to make himself known more fully in Jesus, he styles himself "the God of all grace!" All grace? Yes, all grace, and all sorts and degrees of grace: pardoning grace, renewing grace, quickening grace, strengthening grace, comforting grace; in short, all grace. And is all this treasured up in Jesus? Oh then, my soul, see that Jesus be thine, and all is thine. And mark this down as a sure unerring rule—as grace hath no source but in the Father's love, so the exalting that grace, in Jesus, is the Father's design in salvation. The brightest pearl in the Redeemer's crown is that which shines with this inscription: "To the praise of the glory of his grace, wherein he hath made us accepted in the beloved." Here, my soul, seek thy daily grace more earnestly than thy daily bread.

EVENING.—"Thou art fairer than the children of men: grace is poured into thy lips: therefore God hath blessed thee for ever."—Ps. xlv. 2.

I admire this blessed portion, as well as the method in which the sacred writer hath introduced it. He opens the psalm, professing his design of speaking of the King: but in a moment, as if beholding him, he breaks off, and speaks to him. The verse now quoted contains but three short sentences: but indeed within its bosom, there are folded up as many volumes. For who so fair, so lovely, so engaging, as Jesus? "He is the brightness of his Father's glory, and the express image of his person:' and if all the accomplishments and perfections which can constitute excellency, be among the recommendations of beauty and loveliness; then it will be found, that in the person of Jesus they all centre and shine in one full constellation. Well might the prophet therefore speak of him in this character: for he is a perfection of loveliness. Every thing in him is lovely, nor can there be any loveliness but what is derived from him. " Thou art comely, (saith Jesus to the church), from the comeliness that I have put upon thee." My soul! never lose sight of this view of thy Jesus. And let it be everlastingly impressed upon thy mind, that whatever is fair, or amiable, or lovely, in the church of Jesus, or in any individual member of it, ordinances, or means of grace, all are so only as beheld in him. Nothing can endear or recommend them to God, but as they are accepted in Him, the beloved. This is the first volume of beauty contained in the bosom of this verse of scripture. And the second is like unto it. For, next to the glory of Christ's person, we are called upon to admire the glories of his work and office. " Grace is poured into his lips." Not a fulness of grace in his heart only, or in the purity and holiness of his nature: but it is " poured into his lips," to give out to his people. And no wonder, therefore, that the church, under this view of her Lord, cried out with an earnestness of holy longings and desires, " Let him kiss me with the kisses of his mouth," as if conscious, that by those means, grace would be communicated in fulness and abundance. Let those who know the blessedness of these communications, explain the justness of the church's breathings for those tokens of the love of Christ; for such only can fully explain their meaning. But, my soul, do thou judge for thyself, whether thou hast so tasted of the Lord's graciousness, from the fulness " poured into his lips," as to have received those frequent manifestations of his love. There is one word more in this delightful verse to be noticed, and which indeed gives a finishing beauty to the whole, namely, " God hath blessed him for ever." Yes, Jesus, as the glorious Head and Mediator, is blessed for ever, and is

Jehovah's salvation to the ends of the earth. "Men shall be blessed in him," is the sovereign decree, and "all nations shall call him blessed." My soul! behold what a blessed subject for endless delight, the Holy Ghost hath opened to thee, in this one short verse of scripture. Take it with thee to thy bed; let it lie down with thee, and arise with thee; for it will give thee songs in the night, and under the Holy Spirit's teaching, it will so open to thy view the glories of thy Jesus, as to make thy constant "meditation of him sweet."

JANUARY 31.

MORNING.—"What, think ye that he will not come to the feast?" —John xi. 56.

Is this thy inquiry, my soul, when at any time thou art seeking Jesus in his word, in his ordinances, at his table? Will he not come? Will Jesus not be there? Think how he hath dealt in times past. Did not Jesus rejoice when the hour arrived for coming into the world for salvation? Doth he not rejoice, when coming to the heart of the poor sinner for conversion? and will he not come with joy in all the renewed visits of his love? Besides, doth not Jesus know that it is a time of need to thee? And hath he not opened a way to the throne of grace, on purpose that his poor helpless children might come boldly to a throne of grace to obtain help, and find grace in every time of need? Oh then, mark it down as a sure thing, thy Jesus will be there. He spreads the feast, and he will be present. He waits to be gracious; waits to be kind to thee. Love is in his heart, and salvation in his hands. Hasten then to his house, to his table, to his bosom, to his heart; and say, with the church, "Come, my beloved, and be thou like a roe, or a young hart, upon the mountains of Bether."

EVENING.—" And above the firmament, that was over their heads, was the likeness of a throne, as the appearance of a sapphire stone, and upon the likeness of the throne was the likeness as the appearance of a man above upon it."—Ezek. i. 26.

It forms the most satisfying consideration to the breast of the faithful, that every event and every providence concerning the people of God is as much directed, arranged, and determined, as the purposes of redemption themselves. The covenant is " a covenant ordered in all things and sure." He who hath undertaken and completed salvation for them, hath no less secured the means that shall infallibly accomplish the end; and all things, how unpromising soever on the first view, shall work together for good to them that love God. When the Holy Ghost would graciously lead the church into the proper apprehension of this great truth, the prophet is directed to the contemplation of a vision by the river Chebar, which opened before him. There were living creatures moving in a straight direction upon wheels, wheel within wheel, attended with a noise and a voice; hereby intimating, as it should seem, that the government of every thing, in the kingdom of providence and grace, was regulated by an unerring standard; and that the prophet's mind might farther understand the vision, he was led to see above the whole, " the likeness of a throne, and the appearance of the likeness of a man upon it." Nothing could be more gracious, by way of teaching the church that the government of all things is in the hand of Jesus, and the most minute circumstance of his people subject to his controul. Amidst numberless improvements to be made of this doctrine, there is one, my soul, which, in the exercises of thy warfare, thou wilt find perpetual occasion to apply; for what can be more blessed than to contemplate this government of thy Jesus, as continually exercised in his sin-preventing providences, whereby the Lord keeps back his people from presumptuous transgressions? How often, how very often, might a child of God discover those sweet restraints of the Lord, when he is at any time hedging up his way with thorns, that he may not find his paths? How often hath some outward affliction, or inward sorrow; sickness in ourselves, or death in our houses, acted in a way of prevention to this end? There are a great variety of ways, by which the remains of indwelling corruption would manifest themselves, and break forth in their several disorders, but for restraining grace. What a beautiful instance was that of David, in the case of Nabal, and what a gracious sentiment to this amount the psalmist expressed upon it! When Abigail came, in the seasonable moment to check his anger, David discerned the divine hand in the appointment, and brake out in a devout acknowledgment: "Blessed be the Lord, and blessed be thy advice, and blessed be thou, that hast kept me this day from shedding blood," 1 Sam. xxv. 32. And who shall say, amidst the ten thousand occurrences of life, what multitudes of instances to the same purport are going on, to restrain the children of God from the commission of evil? Oh! how blessed it is to view Jesus as well in providence as grace, and, like the prophet, to keep an eye to that throne, and to see one like the Son of man sitting upon it, regulating and ordering all things for his own glory, and the salvation of his people. Precious Jesus! keep me in the hour, and from the power of temptation. Do thou order my steps by thy word, so shall no iniquity have dominion over me.

FEBRUARY 1.

MORNING.—"And they shall call his name Emanuel, which, being interpreted, is God with us."—Matt. i. 23.

My soul, hast thou never remarked what a peculiar beauty and sweetness there is in every name by which thy God and Saviour is made known to thee in his holy word? Surely, if nothing more had been intended by it, than to identify and prove his sacred person, one name would have answered this purpose: evidently, therefore, somewhat of great importance is designed from his many names. And depend upon it, my soul, so much loveliness is there in every individual name of thy Jesus; and at one time or other, in thy walk of faith, so very much wilt thou need every one, and find the preciousness of every one, that thou wouldest not part with one of thy Redeemer's names — no, not for the world. This of Emanuel, by which thou art commanded to call him, is a sweet one to endear him to thee. Had he not been Emanuel, he could not have been Jesus, for none but God can save a sinner: and therefore he is called Emanuel, which signifies, "God with us." Hence, therefore, he is God. Put this down as a glorious truth in thy esteem. God in our nature: God tabernacling in our flesh. God in us; and God in our hearts, the hope of glory. It is the Godhead of thy Jesus which gives efficacy and value to every act of redemption. As God, his righteousness is the righteousness of God to justify thee. Mark that! his sacrifice to atone—his blood to cleanse — his grace to bless. All these blessed acts of thy Jesus derive efficacy to answer all their glorious purposes, because they are the acts of God. And remark, my soul, yet further, that all that yet remains to be fulfilled, in what he hath promised concerning salvation, in now pleading thy cause, and hereafter taking thee to glory; these cannot fail—because he who hath promised is Emanuel. Go on, my soul, one step further, and remember that He, whom thou art to call Emanuel, is also God in thy nature. Hence he is so very near and dear, in all tender alliances, as to be bone of thy bone, and flesh of thy flesh. My soul, never, never lose sight of this most sweet and precious name of thy Jesus. Call him as thou art commanded, call his name Emanuel.

EVENING.—"In that day shall the Lord defend the inhabitants of Jerusalem, and he that is feeble among them at that day, shall be as David; and the house of David shall be as God, as the angel of the Lord before them."—Zech. xii. 8.

My soul! in the calculation of times and seasons, thou art entering this day upon a new month; stand still and consider what progress thou art making in the spiritual path. Here is a sweet promise for the gospel dispensation. It is an old testament promise to be fulfilled in a new testament day. The weak and feeble, in our spiritual David, being really and truly *in David*, shall be as David, that is, strong in the grace and strength that are in Christ Jesus. And the whole house of David, every true believer in Jesus, shall be as Jesus; that is, so accounted before God, as one in Christ, and accepted in him the beloved; for in the eye of God, and of his holy law, they are one and the same. But what a sad consideration is it, that the progress in the divine life, here set forth, is so seldom sought after by the people of God! We are, for the most part, satisfied to have made our calling and election sure, and do not seem to feel it much at heart, that frequently the soul goes lean, and is feeble in spiritual attainments. My soul! let me impress it upon thy most serious consideration, this evening, how needful it is to have this sweet promise brought home, and proved in thy daily experience. Is not Jesus, in his person, work, and righteousness, to be continually improved in soul-acquaintance and communion? Should I not seek to preserve a constant communication with my Lord? Whenever I consider his fulness, which is all for his people, surely I ought to send forth a desire for a renewed token of his love. And yet when I come to sit down in the evening, and to look back upon what hath passed between my Lord and me, through the day, alas! how little hath my soul been going forth in desires after him, and in enjoying communion with him! Come, blessed Jesus! come, I pray thee, and let my awakened faculties be exercised upon thy person, blood, and righteousness, until this sweet promise be mine, and I find my feebleness becoming strength in my Lord. Let the growing acquaintance with thee, of one day, be made the step for desiring greater knowledge, and greater enjoyment of thee, for the next day; and let my earnest soul be pressing after fresh discoveries of thee, and for sweet manifestations from thee every day, in greater frequency, and in more enlarged views of thy glory. Oh! for grace from my Lord, for the liveliest actings of faith, and love, and praise, and every longing desire upon and towards him whose name is "the Lord our righteousness;" that the grace and good-will, the mercy and kindness of God my Saviour, may be my daily song, and evening delight, in this house of my pilgrimage!

FEBRUARY 2.

MORNING.—"Seest thou this woman?"—Luke vii. 44.

My soul, look at this woman at the feet of Jesus; for thy Jesus bids thee look, and gather instruction from the view, as well as the pharisee. Behold how she wept, how she washed the feet of Jesus, and anointed them with ointment. These were sweet tokens of her love and adoration. But were these the causes for which she obtained forgiveness? Oh, no. Read what the Lord said to her: "Thy faith hath saved thee." Learn, then, my soul, in what salvation lies. Love may bring ointment to Jesus. Sorrow for sin, when grace is in the heart, will cause tears to fall. But faith brings nothing, for it hath nothing: it casts itself wholly upon Jesus. Amidst all its guilt, and fears, and tears, it is Jesus only to whom faith looks; it is Jesus upon whom alone it depends. It hath nothing to do with self; neither our own feelings, nor the exercise of our graces. These are blessed *evidences* of the work of the Lord upon the heart; but they are not salvation. It is Jesus, all precious, all glorious, all suitable Jesus! He is the One blessed object of faith's joy and hope, and pursuit and desire. And, depend upon it, thy God and Father in Christ Jesus, is more pleased, more honoured, by this simple act of faith upon Jesu's glorious person and righteousness, than by all the tears in the world; when those tears lead us to place a stress upon the *effects* of faith, instead of hanging wholly upon the *cause*, in the glorious object, Jesus. Pause, my soul, over this nice but proper distinction; and this will be to find comfort always in Jesus, "Seest thou this woman?"

EVENING.—"If I have told you earthly things, and ye believe not, how shall ye believe if I tell you of heavenly things?"—John iii. 12.

Was there ever condescension like that of Jesus, to accommodate himself to the dull and senseless capacities of his people? Kind, compassionate, indulgent Teacher, I would say, how shall I sufficiently admire or adore thy love? Oh! that a consciousness of my ignorance would endear to me thy wisdom! And Oh! that a sense of the deep things of God would induce in me a temper and frame of mind suited to the docility and humbleness of a weaned child! Now, my soul! mark from these words of thy Jesus to that master in Israel, Nicodemus, that so sublime are the wonders of redemption, even in that part of it which is connected with earthly things, that our capacities, until opened and fitted for the apprehension of divine truths by grace, cannot enter into the enjoyment or belief of them. And how then shall the glories of eternity, which are reserved for unfolding on the other side of Jordan, be brought within the grasp of our intellect? And yet there are some, yea, many, who with the incredulity of Thomas, refuse conviction, unless they receive what, in the present state of things, cannot be granted. Blessed Master, I desire to praise thee for that proportion of faith thou hast given me, to "believe the things which are freely given to me of God;" and I beseech thee, Lord, to grant me increasing proportions of faith and grace, that I may both believe the earthly things of salvation, and the heavenly things to be revealed. I would pray for grace and faith in lively exercise, to connect and bring into the same view, both worlds, as they concern thee and thy great salvation. Yea, Lord, I would pray for increasing knowledge of, and delight in all the great things of salvation, among the transactions of earth here below; such as the momentous truths of regeneration, justification by thy blood and righteousness, and the eternal acceptance of thy people in thee, and in thee only, the beloved. And I would pray also for the most enlarged and enlarging views of faith, concerning the glories which shall be revealed, which "eye hath not seen, nor ear heard, neither hath entered into the heart of man to conceive." Lord, increase my faith, and prepare me for the everlasting enjoyment of thyself in glory, when faith "shall be swallowed up in sight; when I shall see thee as thou art, and know even as I am known."

FEBRUARY 3.

MORNING. — "Who loved me, and gave himself for me." — Gal. ii. 20.

See, my soul, how Paul is for ever using Jesus, and feasting for ever upon him. Oh! seek grace to do the same. He saith, Jesus loved him; Jesus, the Son of God, loved Paul. Now love from any object is valuable, but from the first, and best, and greatest of all Beings, what invaluable love is this? And who did Christ love? "Why me," saith Paul: "who was a blasphemer, a persecutor, and injurious." And how do you know, Paul, that Jesus loved you? "He gave himself for me," saith Paul. "Gave himself?" Yes, himself. Not his gifts only, not his grace, not his mercies, though all creation is his. And whatever he gave must have been an undeserved mercy; for I merited hell, when he bestowed upon me heaven. But even heaven, with all its glories, is nothing, saith Paul, to what Jesus gave me; for he gave " himself for me." Oh! my soul, wilt thou not look up, wilt thou not be encouraged to hope, to believe, to hang upon Jesus, for the same. Oh! for faith to believe. Precious Jesus! thou author and finisher of faith, grant me this mercy! And while I read these sweet words concerning thee, who loved and who gave thyself for poor lost sinners—Oh! like Paul, and with the same assurance of faith, cause me to add —me, me: Jesus " loved me, and gave himself for me."

EVENING.—" None of them can by any means redeem his brother, nor give to God a ransom for him. (For the redemption of their soul is precious, and it ceaseth for ever.)"—Psalm xlix. 7, 8.

How very striking is the former of these verses! And Oh! how justly true! If it were possible for the rich worldling to keep back from the grave, by purchase, his worldly friend, would he do it? Yes, indeed, it is possible he might, under the presumption, that when it came to his turn, he should himself be redeemed. It is, however, of little consequence to estimate human friendships, when they are altogether helpless in the most important of all concerns. But, my soul, doth not this scripture point to him, and tend to endear him to thy warmest affections, who was indeed " a brother born for adversity;" and who, " though rich, yet for our sakes became poor, that through his poverty we might be made rich?" Jesus was, and is, the brother (mentioned in that scripture, Lev. xxv. 25.) who, when our whole nature was waxen poor, and we had sold our possession, and had no power to redeem it, came and proved his relationship by ransoming our lost inheritance.

But mark, my soul, what is said in the latter of

these verses; "the redemption of their soul is precious." Precious indeed! since none but Christ could redeem it; and he only by his blood; yea, not his blood only, but his soul. For it was expressly agreed upon, and so the tenor of the everlasting covenant ran; "when thou shalt make his soul an offering for sin," (Isa. liii. 10.) then "he should see his seed." But remark yet further, that this latter verse is enclosed in parenthesis. I have often thought wherefore the Holy Ghost was pleased so to enclose it? Not surely, that, like other parenthesis, it might be read or left out; not so, I venture to believe. But rather, I should conceive, that hereby its total unconnection with what was said before of the rich worldling having no power to redeem his brother, the preciousness of Christ's redemption might be more strikingly conspicuous. And so it doth indeed. And how precious, blessed Jesus, was, and is, thy redemption! Not purchased with corruptible things, as of silver and gold, and therefore not liable to perish and become corruptible like them. And being so richly purchased, and so fully and completely bought with a full value, and infinitely more than value, even with the soul of Christ, it ceaseth for ever. It is impossible ever to need again redemption, for it is impossible ever more to be lost. Oh! precious salvation! Oh! precious, precious, Redeemer!

FEBRUARY 4.

MORNING.—"The Comforter that should relieve my soul is far from me."—Lam. i. 16.

Whence is it, my soul, that those distressing thoughts arise? Pause, and inquire. Is the Holy Ghost, the Comforter, indeed withdrawn, when Jesus, thy Jesus, sweetly and graciously promised that he should abide for ever? This cannot be. Is the righteousness of Jesus less; or hath his blood to atone and cleanse, lost its efficacy? Oh no! Jesus' righteousness, and Jesus' all-atoning propitiation, like the almighty Author of both, must be eternally and everlastingly the same; "yesterday, and to-day, and for ever." Hath God thy Father forgotten to be gracious? Oh no! God thy Father proclaimed from heaven that he is well pleased for his dear Son's righteousness' sake; and never, never, shall a word gone out of the Lord's mouth be altered. From whence then, my soul, is thy leanness, thy fears, and despondency? Canst thou not discover? Oh yes! It is all in thyself, and thy unbelieving frame; thou art looking to thyself, and not to all-precious Jesus! Thou wantest to feel some new frame of thy own; some melting of heart, or the like; and if thou couldest be gratified in this, then thou wouldest go to Jesus with confidence, and then plead as thou thinkest, Jesus' name, and blood, and righteousness for acceptance. And doth the want of these feelings keep thee back? Oh, fie! my soul, is this thy love, thy kindness to thy friend? Can any thing be more plain, than that thou art making a part saviour of thy feelings, and not a whole Saviour of thy Jesus? No wonder thou criest out, "the Comforter is far from me;" for the Holy Ghost will teach thee, that all comfort is only in Jesus. And mark this, my soul, for all future occasions.—If thou wilt seek comfort in any thing out of Jesus, though it be in the sweetest frames, as thou mayest think of thine, Jesus, in mercy and love, will put thy comforts out of thy reach. Oh then, come to Jesus, poor and needy, with or without frames. Make him all, and in all; and he will be thy joy, thy comfort, and thy portion for ever!

EVENING.—"And Jesus himself began to be about thirty years of age."—Luke iii. 23.

How marvellous in all things are the ways of God to us! Was Jesus indeed in the world, and the world made by him, and the world knew him not? And did he remain hid away, and unknown for the first thirty years of his life? Did the Son of God come on earth to do away sin by the sacrifice of himself, and yet enter not upon the full purpose of his mission until so large a portion of his life upon earth had passed away? Oh! wonder-working God! how true is it, that thy ways are not our ways, nor thy thoughts our thoughts! Yet, my soul, though thy Jesus did not engage in his public ministry, in the more open display of it by his miracles and preaching, yet surely those thirty years were of vast importance on the score of redemption. No doubt Jesus spent them in obedience to his Father's law, manifesting a life of holiness and purity, suited and corresponding to the immaculate perfection of his nature, "who did no sin, neither was guile found in his mouth." Convinced as I am, my honoured Lord, that the body which thy Father gave thee, and the human nature which thou didst assume for the purpose of salvation, was not produced in the ordinary method of generation, but by the miraculous influence of the Holy Ghost, so am I equally convinced that during the whole of thy life, from the manger to the cross, every act, and word, and thought of thine, manifested that thou wast holy, harmless, undefiled, separate from sinners, and made higher than the heavens. And shall I not also believe, that these thirty years were of some sweet, though to us secret importance, in thy covenant engagements as our surety? Can I suppose, that the thirty years of my Redeemer's life, before his being publicly made known to Israel, were spent in doing nothing with relation to the great work which he came purposely to do? Did not those seasons minister also to the cancelling the sin of his people, taking away the curse by bearing it, and by dying for it; and may we not suppose that God the Father had an eye to every minute act in the life of his dear Son, whom he had called to the work of salvation; and given as a covenant to his people, to be their head and mediator; their law-fulfiller and sin-offering? Precious Lord! silent as the scriptures are on this great portion of thy life, yet is not their silence a call upon thy people to meditate on the subject? Give me grace, then, my honoured Lord, to be often contemplating the infinite condescension of Jesus in this part, as well as in others, in which thou must have "endured such a contradiction of sinners against thyself." And let not this be the smallest improvement of this sweet and interesting view of my Lord, that when I call to mind how thy holy soul must have felt, during the thirty years, from the open displays of sin, in the blasphemies and daring defiances of God, the reproaches of the ungodly, and the torrent of evil all around; yet nothing stopped the gracious purposes of thine heart, in executing the errand on which thy whole mind was bent, "in dying, the just for the unjust, to bring sinners unto God!"

FEBRUARY 5.

MORNING.—"In the hand of a Mediator."—Gal. iii. 19.

The hand of a Mediator was the great blessing every enlightened son of Adam, from the fall, sighed after, and looked for, in every approach to God. Hence the first transgressor, for the want of it, hid himself from the presence of God, amidst the trees of the garden. Hence Israel cried out to Moses, "Go thou near, and hear all that the Lord our God shall say; but let not God speak with us, lest we die." And Job longed for a day's man, that is, a Mediator, that might lay his hand upon both parties. See then, my soul, thy privileges; for thou hast a Mediator, and a glorious one indeed, in whose almighty hand all thy concerns are eternally secured. "Ye are come," saith the apostle; he doth not say, ye are *coming*; but, ye are *come*, "to Jesus, the Mediator of the new covenant, and to the blood of sprinkling." Oh then, in all thy approaches, have an eye to Jesus. Put all thine affairs into this glorious Mediator's hand. Remember, he wears thy nature, pleads thy cause, takes up all thy concerns, and ever liveth to make intercession for sinners; and therefore, cast all thy care upon him, for he careth for thee. And look to this one grand thing—that all thy confidence, and all thy joy, ariseth wholly from Jesus' person and righteousness; not from any supposed graces, tears, repentance—nor even from faith itself, if viewed as an act of thine. Cast aside, as filthy rags, all that is thine; and never, no not for a moment, look at any thing as a procuring cause; but let Jesus have all thy confidence, all the glory, and thou wilt have all the comfort. Though Satan accuse, though conscience pleads guilty, God's broken law pronounceth condemnation, and justice demands the penalty, Jesus hath answered all, and is on the throne to see the issue. Oh, the blessedness of having all in the hands of a Mediator!

EVENING.—"For the Father judgeth no man, but hath committed all judgment unto the Son. And hath given him authority to execute judgment also, because he is the Son of Man."—John v. 22, 27.

Here, my soul! here is a sweet and blessed portion to take with thee, night by night, as a sleeping draught, to lie down with in holy composure; or if thou lie watchful, to give thee songs in the night. Every night is a new watch-word of the night of death; and none can tell thee when thou droppest asleep, whether, in the next opening of thine eyes, thou mayest not open them in eternity, and find thyself standing before the judgment-seat of Christ! Dost thou not wish to be prepared for such an event, and not to leave so infinitely momentous a concern to a peradventure? Read then, again and again, this sweet scripture. I take for granted, that thou knowest Jesus; and art acquainted, yea, savingly acquainted with his glorious person, as thy surety; and the merits of his blood and righteousness, as thy salvation! See then what this blessed scripture saith, that all judgment is committed unto thy Jesus, because he is the Son of man. Mark that, my soul! not because he is the Son of God; for in that case, judgment could not have been *committed* to him; for it was his before, in common with the Father and the Holy Ghost; the whole Three Persons constituting the one eternal Jehovah. But judgment is committed to Christ, and is peculiarly his, "because he is the Son of man." Cherish the sweet, the soul-transporting, the soul-supporting truth. Thy Jesus, who is now thy surety, is then to be thy Judge. He that hath died for thy sins, is then to be thy advocate. And he that hath paid the ransom with his blood in this life, is then to see the reward of it in another. Now then behold where alone thy confidence is to be found. Bring forward to thy view the solemn, the awful day. Realize it, as if the archangel's trumpet were now sounding, and thou beheld Jesus coming to be glorified in his saints, and admired in all that believe. Let others, who now boast of their good works, and hope allowance will be made for human frailty, and the like; or all that troop of half disciples, who partly to Christ, and partly to themselves, look for salvation; let such do as they will; there is but this one thing left for thee to do, and this one thing well done, will do for all; remember, Jesus is thy Judge; and all judgment is committed unto him, "because he is the Son of man." Humbly, my soul, but with the boldness of faith through his blood, draw near to his gracious seat; and against all law charges, and the divine demands of justice, hold up the blessed testament of Jesus's blood. Here, Lord, I would say, are the Father's promises of redemption, in thy name and righteousness; and this is the record God hath given of his dear Son. And here, Lord, is the new testament of thy blood, which thou hast given for sinners. Thou, blessed Lord, wilt know thine hand, and own thy word. Thou therefore shalt answer for me, O Lord my God!

FEBRUARY 6.

MORNING.—"The rich shall not give more, and the poor shall not give less than half a shekel, when they give an offering unto the LORD, to make an atonement for your souls."—Exod. xxx. 15.

Pause, my soul, over this sweet scripture, and mark the graciousness of thy God and Father in the blessed truth conveyed in it. What, were all the souls of the redeemed charged equally alike in the account of God? Did God thy Father rate them thus? And did Jesus, thy precious Jesus, purchase all his redeemed with an equal price, when he bought them with his blood? If this be so, my soul, it must follow, that thou, a poor unworthy creature as thou art, overlooked as thou art by the great ones of the earth, and too frequently overlooking in thyself how precious every redeemed soul must be in Jesus's sight, cost as much to Jesus as the soul of Peter, or of Paul, or of any of the patriarchs, apostles, or prophets. Oh, think of this; write it down in the tablets of thy remembrance. Will not this tend to endear Jesus yet more to thee, and bring home thy Father's love in the strongest affection? Add one thought more to this precious relation. If to Jesus thy redemption cost as much as any one of the redeemed in glory, think, my soul, after such a purchase, such a price, will he lose his property? will he forego what cost him so dear, and suffer one pearl of his mediatorial crown to be wanting? Add another sweet thought, my soul, to this delightful meditation. If, amidst the various inequalities of life, some poor and some rich, yet whatever difference was allowed, or even expected in other offerings, according to the abilities of God's people; yet here, as a representation of the offering of the soul in Jesus' purchase, no one distinction was to be made. Is it not plain that the redemption by Jesus is in him, and him only; and "his righteousness is unto all, and upon all, that believe; for there is no difference." Dearest Lord! may my soul never lose sight of this blessed equality. Here thou art, indeed, no respecter of persons.

EVENING.—"And he, bearing his cross."—John xix. 17.

Were grace always in lively exercise, how would every incident in the life of Jesus lead out the souls of his redeemed in endless contemplation! Alas! my honoured Lord! how little do I think of thee, and of thy sufferings! Will Jesus, this evening, awaken me to the solemn subject? The bell of the neighbouring church is now tolling the curfew of the day. I hear it from my window. Ah! why should I want such a call to think on my Lord! Awake, awake my soul, and let thy meditation take wing, and flee to Gethsemane, and from the garden, and the hall, behold the Lamb of God bearing his cross towards the place of execution. Oh! Pilate! thou unjust jùdge! is this thy pretended innocency, to suffer him whom thou didst declare to be innocent, in the moment thou didst pass sentence for his death, to bear his cross also? See what long furrows the ploughers have ploughed upon his sacred back; and wilt thou compel him to bear the heavy weight upon a part so tender? See! Jesus faints under it! Will none of those whose souls he hath redeemed, and whose bodies he hath healed, help the Lord of life and glory? Where are his disciples? Are there none to aid? Not one to be found that dares assist him? Pause, my soul, over the sad contemplation! Christ is here, as his type represents him, the gospel Isaac, carrying the wood for his own burnt-offering. "In all things it behoved him to be made like unto his brethren." It was his office to be "led as a lamb to the slaughter, and as a sheep before his shearers is dumb, so he opened not his mouth." "It pleased the Father to bruise him, and to put him to grief." The cross was ponderous. The body fainted under its pressure. But the sins of his redeemed made it heavier to his soul; and the weight of the Father's wrath against sin, aggravated the dreadful load. Precious Redeemer, dying Lamb of God! were my sins adding to thy sorrow? Have I been reproaching Pilate, and all the while forgetting that every transgression of mine became more painful to thy soul than the cross, or the thorns, or the soldier's spear that pierced thine heart? Oh! for grace to crucify those sins which nailed thee to the cursed tree! Oh! for grace to take up the cross and follow thee, day by day. Lord Jesus, I would pray thee to give me grace, to go forth unto thee, "without the camp, bearing thy reproach."

FEBRUARY 7.

MORNING.—"Behold the Lamb of God!"—John i. 36.

Who is it calls upon thee, my soul, to this most gratifying and enriching of all employments? Is it not God the Holy Ghost, by the ministry of his servant John? And doth not God thy Father do the same by the ministry of his servant Isaiah, when he bids thee behold him in whom his soul delighteth? And is not Jesus himself calling, again and again, in the ministry of his word and ordinances, upon thy poor forgetful heart, when he saith, "Behold me! behold me! look unto me, and be ye saved!" And wilt thou not obey the sweet and gracious calls, on which all thy present peace and everlasting happiness depend? Precious, precious Jesus! Yes, my Lord! I would, methinks, so look unto thee, and so behold thee, until my whole heart, and all its affections, followed my eyes, and left not a thought behind for a single object besides thee. I would eye thee, thou dear Redeemer, as the Lamb of God; both where thou once wast, and where thou now art, and follow thee whithersoever thou goest. I would behold thee, as the Lamb of God, set up in the decrees of eternity, from everlasting; for thou art "the Lamb slain from the foundation of the world." I would behold thee, set forth in all the representations of thy redeeming blood, in the innumerable sacrifices of the law, and in the lamb of the morning, and the lamb of the evening, through the intermediate ages, to thy coming. I would behold thee, Oh thou unequalled pattern of excelling meekness! when, in the days of thy flesh, thou walkedst through the streets of Jerusalem; and when, as a lamb, thou wast led to the slaughter. I would eye thee, Oh thou Lamb of God, until my eye-strings could hold no longer, when as the Lamb of God, and my soul's surety, thou didst hang upon the tree, putting away sin, and satisfying divine justice by the sacrifice of thyself. And never would I take off my eyes from thy cross, until called by thee to behold thee as a Lamb in the midst of the throne, where thou art feeding thy church above, and dispensing blessings to all thy church below. Yes, yes, blessed triumphant Lamb of God, thou art the Lamb still. Change of place hath made no change in thy nature, or thy love, or the efficacy of thy redemption. Thou still appearest as a Lamb that hath been slain. And still thou bearest on thy glorified body, the marks of my redemption. Shall I not behold thee, then, dearest Jesus? Shall I not unceasingly behold thee, thus called upon by the Father, Son, and Spirit, and thus finding every thing that can satisfy my most unbounded desires for time and for eternity? Help me, blessed Jesus, so to look, and so to live upon thee; and Oh, do thou behold me, and bid me live, and make me thine for ever."

EVENING. — " And they sent the coat of many colours, and they brought it to their father; and said, this have we found; know now, whether it be thy son's coat, or no. And he knew it, and said, it is my son's coat."—Gen. xxxvii. 32, 33.

The life of the patriarch Joseph is very beautiful and interesting, as an history only; and the several incidents arising out of it are such as cannot but more or less affect every heart. But when we have gone through the whole relation, in the mere letter of the word, we are constrained to believe, that in the spiritual sense and meaning of it, almost every thing in the life of Joseph was typical of Jesus! I would not strain scripture upon any account. Neither would I frame to myself any thing fanciful of Jesus and his blessed offices; so as to see him where he is not. Yet I cannot but think, that since in so many instances, as is universally allowed, Joseph is a lively type of Christ, the Holy Ghost, in his glorifying the Lord Jesus, was, in many cases, pleased to shadow forth, somewhat of the Redeemer, where he is not at first so immediately discovered. Whether in the passage I have just read, for the present evening's meditation, there be any thing typical of Jesus, I know not; but to those who, like Philip, have " found him of whom Moses in the law and the prophets did write, Jesus of Nazareth;" the coat of the patriarch, dipped in the blood of the kid, may minister in leading the heart to the contemplation of Jesus, who appeareth unceasingly in his priestly garments, in the presence of God our Father, for us. And may not a believer humbly take up the language of faith, when drawing nigh to our God and Father in Christ Jesus; and when we enter, as it were, into his retirings, with earnest prayer, and earnest pleadings, seeking favour in and through Jesus; may we not, in the arms of our faith, bring the vesture of Jesus dipped in blood, and say, this have we found; know now, whether it be Jesus's, thy dear and ever beloved Son's vesture, or no? Oh! for faith to behold Christ, as the Father beheld him, when he set him forth to the church, and to love him as God our Father loved him. And how surely will God confirm his own gracious testimony concerning him, and say with the patriarch, or in words to the same effect; "This is my beloved Son, in whom I am well pleased!"

FEBRUARY 8.

MORNING.—"Who shall lay any thing to the charge of God's elect? It is God that justifieth. Who is he that condemneth? It is Christ that died; yea, rather, that is risen again; who is even at the right hand of God, who also maketh intercession for us."—Rom. viii. 33, 34.

See, my soul, what a blessed security thou hast. Here is God justifying; Christ dying; the Holy Ghost raising the sinner's surety from the grave, as an evidence that the debt of sin is cancelled; and Jesus ever living to see the travail of his soul, and be satisfied in the redemption of his people. What, then, shall rob thee of thy comfort, while thou art triumphing in thy Jesus? Sin shall not; for Jesus hath put it away by the sacrifice of himself. The law cannot; for thy Jesus hath answered all its just demands. Divine justice cannot; for God himself justifieth. Death and hell cannot; for Jesus hath conquered both. In short, all that stood in thy way, the Son of God hath removed. And wilt thou not, my soul, triumph in the great salvation of thy Jesus? Surely the poor debtor may walk as boldly before the prison door, as the king in his palace, when his debts are paid. No bailiff can touch him; no mittimus again confine him. "If the Son shall make you free, you shall be free indeed." Triumph then, my soul, in the liberty wherewith thy Jesus hath made thee free; only be sure that all thy triumphs are in him. Let him have all the glory, who hath wrought the whole redemption. Make thy Jesus all; for he hath done all for thee; and then sweetly repose thyself upon the person and work of thy beloved. Let the adversary accuse, or opposition arise from without or within, yet, saith an apostle, here is the answer:— "God justifieth; for Christ died." Oh, how precious it is, after all the storms, and winds, and boisterous tossings, of law and conscience, to enter into that harbour, which is, Jesus. "We which have believed," saith the apostle, "do enter into rest." He is indeed the rest, wherewith he causeth the weary to rest; and he is the refreshing.

EVENING.—"I am the rose of Sharon, and the lily of the valleys." —Song ii. 1.

Yes! dearest Lord Jesus, thou art all this, and infinitely more to my soul; more fragrant than both, and more precious than all the flowers of the field. Help me, this evening, to contemplate my Lord under those sweet similitudes. Do I not, and shall I not henceforth, in the red blushing beauty of the rose, behold thy human nature, which thou hast assumed for the redemption of thy people? Are not thy bloody sufferings, and thy red apparel, strikingly set forth by the image of the rose; as thy spotless purity is shewn under the loveliness of the white lily? Can the sweet-scented rose, even of Sharon, vie with the perfume of the incense of thy righteousness, to a poor sinner's soul? Or can the beauty of the lily be as grateful to the eye, as the purity of Jesus to a mind conscious of its own pollution, and beholding itself complete in his salvation, who is "holy, harmless, undefiled, separate from sinners, and made higher than the heavens?" But wherefore Sharon's rose, and the valley's lily, unless it be to speak thine infinite greatness in the excellency of Sharon, and thine infinite humbleness, in the lowest part of the earth, as the valley. And indeed, Lord, in thine own wonderful person, thou comprehendest all things, in the length, and breadth, and depth, and heighth! Thou art both "Alpha and Omega; the first and the last." And though Lord of all, thou didst condescend to become servant of all; be thou to me, my Lord, every thing that is precious and lovely, as the rose of Sharon, and as the lily of the valley. And Oh! give a sweet conformity to thyself, and thy loveliness. And though my sins be red as scarlet, do thou make them whiter than the snow; though they be as the crimson, do thou make them as the wool! Cause me to be washed in that fountain, which thou hast opened for sin and for uncleanness; and bring me to join that happy multitude, before thy throne, "who have washed their robes, and made them white in the blood of the Lamb!"

FEBRUARY 9.

MORNING.—"The Lamb which is in the midst of the throne shall feed them."—Rev. vii. 17.

My soul thou hast not forgotten what thou wert so lately engaged in, a day or two since, at the call of God the Holy Ghost, to behold the Lamb of God. And art thou not still looking at him, gazing upon him, feasting thine eyes, thine heart, all thy affections, upon him, and following him, in the sweet contemplation, from his cross to his crown. Come then, my soul, harp again and again upon this blessed string; for sure it is most blessed. And remember, my soul, as thou lookest, thy Jesus is in the midst of the throne—that is, the very centre of it. "In Him dwelleth all the fulness of the Godhead bodily." For what is the Lamb of God, but GOD revealing himself in him, to thee, my soul, and all his people? And remember also, that the throne, in the midst of which thy Jesus is, in scripture, is called "the throne of God and the Lamb," on purpose to shew thee that it is one and the same. And what is that throne, my soul, but a throne of grace—a mercy-seat, a place for the poor and the needy to approach, "to obtain mercy, and find grace to help in time of need?" Flee to it, my soul; haste! stay not; and remember, as Jesus is in the midst of it, it is accessible every way, and all around. The poor timid believer, that fears to go in front, may, like the woman in the gospel, who came behind, touch but Jesus' garment: efficacy from the Lamb is in every direction. If Jesus was not there, it might be alarming to approach; but, remember the Lamb is there—and he is the Lamb of God. Sweet encouraging thought! Come then, my soul, look to the Lamb. See, by faith, how he feeds the church which is above. And will he not feed the church below? Oh, yes. "His flesh is meat indeed, and his blood is drink indeed." He is the heavenly pelican, that feeds his young with his blood. And Oh, what spiritual food, what divine food, what suitable food, what soul-satisfying, soul-ravishing, soul-strengthening food! Precious Lamb of God! every thing in thee is food. Feed my hungry soul, Oh thou that art in the midst of the throne, and send me not empty away.

EVENING.—"Thus saith the Lord: set thine house in order, for thou shalt die, and not live."—Isa. xxxviii. 1.

My soul! whether or not the decree be as yet gone forth for an early day for thy removal, as here to Hezekiah, it must shortly arrive; and as thou knowest not how soon, it is good to set both thine house and thine heart in order; for he that is best fitted to live, is best prepared to die. How stands thy great account? This body of thine must go down to the chambers of the grave. And surely if the soul be safe in union with Jesus, such an event as the dissolution of the body, is more to be desired than dreaded. If the pearl be safe, no matter though the casket be broken. Pause over the view; for though it be solemn, it is profitable. If a voice from heaven declared the dead to be blessed, who die in the Lord; then will thy death be blessed, if thou art living in union with Christ. See to it this night, this very night, whether this be thy case; all is well if this be well. Hath not the Holy Ghost, in times long since passed, led thee to all-precious Jesus? And from his sweet teachings, and constraining influences, hast thou not ventured thyself upon him? Convinced that there is salvation in no other, "neither any other name under heaven given among men, whereby thou mightest be saved;" didst thou not cast thyself upon his blood and righteousness, and at a time when under the deepest sense of thy sin, and his all-sufficiency to save? And hast thou not many a time since, when the false reasoning of men, the temptations of hell, and a host of foes, from within and without, would have turned thee aside from thy Lord; hast thou not, by this sweet, constraining, and supporting grace, been kept leaning upon Jesus? Yea, moreover, hath not that dear Redeemer, the Lord God of the Hebrews, who first met thee by the way, brought thee acquainted with himself, and caused thee to believe in him; hath he not since, in a thousand, and ten thousand renewed manifestations of his love, comforted thee, strengthened thee, and made thee sensible of his gracious presence? Surely then, if he saith to thee, "Set thine house in order, for thou shalt die, and not live!" it is but the call of Jesus to the exercise of the last act of faith, and indeed to die to this world only, that thou mayest live with him in glory in a better. And wouldest thou now draw back? Didst thou first venture upon Christ, when thou hadst known but little of his faithfulness; and shall it be said now, that the shadow of a doubt remains, when multitudes of evidences upon evidences have been given thee, that he is, he must, he will ever be Jesus? Precious, precious Redeemer! Oh! for a full tide of thy grace to be poured in upon my soul, when thou shalt be pleased to send forth a messenger with, " Set thine house in order, for thou shalt die, and not live;" that I may then gather all into one, of the many tokens of thy redeeming love to a poor worthless worm, such as I am; and all the many goings forth of my soul after thee, through a life of grace, since thou wast pleased to quicken me to the knowledge and desire after thee; that finally, fully, and completely, I may, once for all, cast my soul into thy blessed arms, with a " Lord Jesus, receive my spirit."

FEBRUARY 10.

MORNING.—" Unto you, therefore, which believe, he is precious." 1 Pet. ii. 7.

My soul, art thou anxious to know whether thou art a true believer in Jesus? Try it, then, by this mark, which the Holy Ghost hath given by his servant the apostle. Do you believe in Jesus for life and salvation? Yes, truly; if so be he is precious. Look at him, then. Is Jesus precious in his person, precious in his work, precious in his offices, precious in his relations, precious in his whole character? Do you know him, so as to love him, to live to him, to rejoice in him, and to cast your whole soul upon him, for life and salvation? Do you accept him as the Father's gift, the Sent, the Sealed, the Anointed, the Christ, of the Father? Is he so precious, that there is nothing in him but what you love—nothing that you would part with? His cross is dear, as well as his crown! Afflictions with Jesus, sweeter than prosperity without him! Pause over these questions. Recollect that there is nothing out of Jesus that can be truly satisfying. Thy dearest earthly friend, however sweet, hath yet some tinge, some alloy of what is not sweet. But there is no mixture in thy Jesus; all is pure, and lovely, and transcendantly glorious. He is, as one of old described him, a sea of sweetness, without a single drop of gall. And now, my soul, what sayest thou concerning Jesus? Is he precious to thee under all these, and a thousand more distinguishing excellencies? Say, if Jesus were to be bought, wouldest thou not sell all thou hast to buy? Were he to be sold, wouldest thou not rather lose thy life than part with him? Surely, then, he must be precious to thee: and, as such, thou art a believer; for the apostle has commanded us to say, that "unto them which believe he is precious." Take comfort, then, my soul: he that is precious now, will be so for ever. Yes, precious Lord, there is none in heaven or earth I desire besides thee!

EVENING.—"And David spake unto the Lord when he saw the angel that smote the people, and said, lo! I have sinned, and I have done wickedly; but these sheep, what have they done?"—2 Sam. xxiv. 17.

My soul! here is a subject of an heart-searching nature opened to thee this evening, in those expostulating words of the man after God's own heart. Summon up all thy faculties to the meditation; and yet, infinitely more than this, seek the teaching of the Holy Ghost, that thou mayest profit by them. The apostle was commissioned by the Holy Ghost to tell the church, that for man's sin the whole creation groaneth and travaileth in pain together until now. The slaughter of every beast, the sacrifice of every lamb, proclaimeth with a louder voice than words can declare, the baleful malignity of human transgression. And if David, when he saw the destroying angel brandishing his dreadful sword over Jerusalem, felt remorse in the recollection of his own sin, and the punishment falling on the harmless sheep; what views ought the contemplation of the unequalled sorrows and sufferings of the Lamb of God to occasion, when it is recollected that "he died the just for the unjust, to bring us to God?" To see sin as exceeding sinful, we may get some idea, from beholding apostate spirits cast out of heaven; or from the curse of Jehovah upon the earth, and all the children of Adam involved in it; the destruction of the old world by water; or the burning of Sodom and Gomorrah by fire; and the everlasting torments of the damned in hell: these form awful views of the dreadful nature of sin, as it appears in the sight of God. But all these are nothing, in comparison to one remaining to be mentioned. Wouldest thou see sin in all its tremendous consequences, thou must go to Golgotha. There behold the Lamb of God, taking away sin by the sacrifice of himself. Here take up the words of David, and ask thine own heart, while confessing that thou hast sinned, and done wickedly, what had this Lamb of God done? — But do not stop here. Go on in the contemplation. If "he who knew no sin became sin" —if he who in his sacred person "was holy, harmless, undefiled, separate from sinners, and made higher than the heaven, yet became both sin and a curse for his redeemed, that they might be made the righteousness of God in him;" wilt thou not think it the first, the last, the highest, the best, the most momentous of all points, to know whether thou, even thou thyself, art made the righteousness of God in him? Oh! thou holy, blessed, and eternal Spirit! give me to see in the Lord Jesus, my almighty Surety, that in all he did, in all he sustained, and all he suffered, he bore my sins in his own body on the tree, and that not a single sin of omission or commission was left out. Oh! for grace to believe, and to plead, now and for ever, before the throne, that then all mine iniquities and all my transgressions, in all my sins, the Lord Jehovah laid (as Aaron typified on the great day of atonement, Lev. xvi. 21.) upon the person of his dear Son! Help me, Lord, with increasing confidence of faith, and holy hope, and ardent joy, thus to view Jesus as my Surety, and thus to answer the account given of it in that blessed scripture: "Surely shall one say, in the Lord have I righteousness and strength: even to him shall men come, and all that are incensed aginst him shall be ashamed. In the Lord shall all the seed of Israel be justified, and shall glory."

FEBRUARY 11.

MORNING.—"Let mine outcasts dwell with thee, Moab; be thou a covert to them from the face of the spoiler."—Isa. xvi. 4.

"When a man's ways please the Lord, he maketh even his enemies to be at peace with him." Moab was the sworn foe of Israel, but yet Moab shall be overruled to shelter and feed Israel. The world, like Moab, dislikes God's people: but as God's people must sojourn in the world, until the time comes for God to take them home, they shall be taken care of. "Let mine outcasts dwell with thee, Moab;" house them as travellers in an inn. See that they have a lodging. Let their bread be given, and their water sure. "They are poor; but they are my poor," saith our God. "They are outcasts; but they are mine outcasts." Oh! precious Jesus, I see thou wilt still own thy people. And wherefore is it, dearest Lord? Not for their worth, not for their deservings, not for their adherence to thee; but because thou hast loved them; because the Father hath given them to thee, and thou hast purchased their persons, redeemed them, and washed them, and made them thine. Grant, dearest Lord, that though we are constrained to dwell with Mesech, and to have our habitation among the tents of Kedar; though we "are made as the filth of the earth, and the offscouring of all things," yet never, never may we forget our relationship to thee. Though outcasts, yet Jesus's outcasts. Be thou, Lord, our hiding-place, our covert, in the midst of Moab; and so shall we be free from every spoiler; thou wilt be to us all we need — "rivers of water in a dry place, and as the shadow of a great rock in a weary land."

EVENING.—"And the angels which kept not their first estate, but left their own habitation, he hath reserved in everlasting chains, under darkness, unto the judgment of the great day."—Jude 6.

This scripture, concerning the rebellion, and consequent punishment of apostate spirits, will form a solemn meditation, my soul, for thy evening thoughts to be exercised upon. And perhaps, under grace, it may lead thee to some sweet improvements in the contemplation of the distinguishing grace manifested to our rebellious nature; while judgment the most awful, and everlasting, overtook the higher nature of angels. If we humbly inquire what was the nature of their sin, all we can gather of information concerning it, was, that it was rebellion against God. One part of scripture indeed tells us, that "there was war in heaven: Michael (by which we understand, Michael our Prince, the Lord Jesus Christ, Dan. x. 21.) and his angels fought against the dragon; and the dragon fought and his angels, and prevailed not, neither was their place found any more in heaven," Rev. xii. 7, &c. By which it should seem, that the cause of this contest of the devil with Christ, was personal, and on account of the kingdom which Jehovah gave him as God-Mediator over angels and men. And hence, when these apostate spirits left their own habitation, and were cast out, they set up a kingdom in opposition to the Lord's. And from their bitter hatred to Christ and his kingdom, they wreaked all their malice in corrupting and seducing our nature to join in rebellion against God. Hence "that old serpent, called the devil, and Satan, which deceiveth the whole world," beguiled our first parents, and introduced sin and death into this our world; which hath passed, and must pass upon all their posterity, because "all have sinned, and come short of God's glory."—Pause, my soul, over the solemn account. Think, duly think, of the fallen state, into which, by nature and by practics, thou art brought by this apostacy. And when thou hast had thy mind thoroughly impressed with the awfulness of such a situation, turn thy thoughts to the due contemplation also of the love, and grace, and mercy of God, in thy recovery. Sweetly dwell on the love of God thy Father, in the gift of his dear Son, for the purposes of redemption. Mark well the blessed features of the Son in his work of mercy, in this great accomplishment. And do not overlook, but delight evermore to contemplate the love of God the Holy Ghost, in condescending both to bring thee acquainted with the grace of the Father, and of the Son, and to incline thine heart to the thankful belief of it, and love of both! And that the whole subject may have its full influence upon thee, to induce in thee all the suitable and becoming affections of love, thanksgiving, holy obedience, and praise to the Author of such mercy; mark well the distinguishing nature of that grace, which hath left fallen angels in their ruin and misery, reserved in everlasting chains under darkness, unto the judgment of the great day, while bestowing pardon, reconciliation, and favour, upon fallen men, amidst all our unworthiness, sin, and rebellion. And, Oh, Lamb of God! give me the continued grace to meditate for ever on the unequalled love of thine heart, who passedst by "the nature of angels, to take on thee the seed of Abraham; that in all things thou mightest be made like unto thy brethren, in being a merciful and faithful High Priest in things pertaining to God, to make reconciliation for the sins of thy people!"

FEBRUARY 12.

MORNING.—"And the Lord shut him in."—Gen. vii. 16.

It was a sweet invitation to the patriarch Noah, when the Lord called him to the ark. Jehovah did not say, go thou into the ark; but, "Come." So saith Jesus to his people: "Come with me, from Lebanon, my spouse; with me, from Lebanon." Yes, precious Jesus, to be with thee is heaven; for thou thyself art the heaven of the soul. But observe further, my soul: when Noah had entered the ark, what kept him there? "The Lord shut him in." Yes, neither bolts nor bars were his security; but God himself, in his covenant engagements, kept him. The patriarch could no more get out, than the unbelieving carnal throng (who perhaps hung about the ark when they saw the flood arise, and felt its power) could get in. Precious Jesus! and what is it keeps thy people now? Is it not thyself? Are not thy redeemed eternally secure in thee, and thy blood and righteousness, as Noah in the ark? Yes, thou who hast the key of all things; "thou openest, and none shutteth; thou shuttest, and none openeth." In thee my soul is kept secure; for the Lord Jehovah hath shut me in: and I shall ride out all the storms, and floods, of sin and Satan; and, Noah-like, rise above the fountains of the greatest deeps, being shut in in the ark Christ Jesus.

EVENING.—"And he was sore athirst, and called on the Lord, and said, thou hast given this great deliverance into the hand of thy servant: and now shall I die for thirst, and fall into the hand of the uncircumcised."—Judges xv. 18.

Here is a sweet thought, my soul, suggested in these words of Samson, and wilt thou not hope that the Holy Ghost may make it blessed to thy evening meditation? The Lord had wrought a great deliverance for Samson, in the discomfiture of his enemies: and now on a renewed pressing occasion, he makes this the plea of looking up for being again delivered. "Thou hast given," saith he, "this great deliverance into the hand of thy servant, and shall I now die for thirst, and fall into the hand of the uncircumcised?" As if he had said, 'Shall my God cease to be God; or shall I now want his help, who hath always helped me in what has passed? Hath he begun to deliver; and will he now cease to do so ?'— Pause, my soul ! — And when thou hast duly made thine observations upon the blessedness of faith, which, when in lively exercise, always finds unanswerable arguments for future blessings, in the recollection of those that are passed, take the same plea to thy Jesus for every event which thou meetest with in thine exercises. Hath one like the Son of Man redeemed thee, brought thee out of the hands of infinite justice ; given thee this great deliverance, from both the guilt and dominion of sin ; taken thee into covenant relations with himself ; opened a new and living way for thee in his blood ; and doth he ever live to keep it open by his intercession ? Hath Jesus indeed saved thee, loved thee, blessed thee, given himself for thee, and treasured up for thee a fulness of all needed supplies of grace for thy sojourning here ; and is he gone before, to prepare an everlasting fulness of glory for thy enjoyment of himself to all eternity hereafter ? And shall any circumstance now befal thee in the way, to cast down thy hopes, and to lessen thy faith in such a Saviour ? Shall any thing arise to frustrate his designs, or ruin thy cause? Is it possible, that any new evil, for which Jesus hath made no provision, can happen ; or any unthought of, unexpected calamity arise, which shall counteract the covenant of redemption, " ordered in all things and sure ?" Precious Lord Jesus ! help me ever to keep thee in view, and then all the springs of dependence on thee will be sure to flow.

FEBRUARY 13.

MORNING.—" Christ hath redeemed us from the curse of the law, being made a curse for us."—Gal. iii. 13.

Pause, my soul, and contemplate the unspeakable mercies contained in those precious words. However little thou hast regarded them, yet they contain in their bosom the whole blessings of the gospel. It is to

Jesus in this one glorious act of his faith, should the sinner be continually looking. There, the believer should say, there hangs my hope, my joy, my confidence. "Christ hath redeemed me from the curse of the law, being made a curse for me." Now, my soul, observe how Jesus accomplished this great mercy for thee. Whatever Christ redeemed the sinner from, he became *that* for him. In the act of redemption, by substituting himself in the sinner's place and room, he redeemed him from that place and room, by standing there himself. Hence, as the sinner stood before God, accursed by reason of sin; so Christ, by taking the sinner's sin upon himself, and standing in his stead to answer for it, was made a curse also. If, therefore, Christ will come under the law for sinners, that law will have as much to demand of him, as of sinners. If Jesus, from his boundless love and mercy, will take the sinner's curse upon himself, the law will speak as harsh to him as the sinner that is under the curse: and not only speak, but exact from him all that could be demanded from the sinner. Pause, my soul! And did Jesus, thy Jesus, thus stand; thus be considered, and was he made a curse for thee? Did he really, truly, suffer the cursed sinner's punishment, "and die, the just for the unjust, to bring sinners to God?" Look to it then, my soul; he hath bought thee out, paid the full ransom, and taken away both sin and the curse of sin, by the sacrifice of himself. Shout, my soul, shout salvation to God and the Lamb! Say, as Paul, "Christ hath redeemed us from the curse of the law, being made a curse for us."

EVENING.—"If I forget thee, O Jerusalem, let my right hand forget her cunning. If I do not remember thee, let my tongue cleave to the roof of my mouth: if I prefer not Jerusalem above my chief joy." Ps. cxxxvii. 5, 6.

My soul! sit down this evening, and contemplate the languishing state of Zion. Did ever the church of

Christ lie in more desolate circumstances than now? Amidst a great profession of zeal for religion, how little possession of the divine life is to be met with among men! And who is there that seriously lays it to heart? For whom doth a throne of grace witness, that they are holy mourners for Zion, and are earnestly wrestling, night and day, with the Lord, that he would visit Zion, and make his glory to appear? Where is the priest, the minister of the Lord, that is weeping between the porch and the altar, and saying, "Spare thy people, O Lord! and give not thine heritage to reproach?" Joel ii. 17. And where are the people that seriously lay it to heart? My soul! what sayest thou of these things, personally considered? Dost thou really love Jesus? Surely then, thou canst not be indifferent to his interests? Is not Zion the purchase of his blood? Are not her walls, in all her ruined state, constantly before him? Yea, is not her name engraven on the palms of his hands? And shall her name be on Jesus's hand, and no concern for Zion in thy heart? Moreover, look and see, in the tribulations of the present day; are not God's judgments abroad in the earth? And is not his jealousy for his church the sole cause? And if the nations of the earth are under the frowns of thy God, canst thou rejoice in aught but the church's prosperity? Are thousands dying in sin, and shall not the children of God mourn? Where are the trophies of the Redeemer's precious death and salvation? When shall Jesus see, agreeably to the promise, the travail of his soul, and be satisfied? Oh! for a portion of that holy zeal with which the Lord inspired the prophet, when he cried out, "Oh! that my head were waters, and mine eyes a fountain of tears, that I might weep day and night for the slain of the daughter of my people!" Oh! holy Lord! give my soul from henceforth a more earnest concern for the prosperity of thy Zion! Oh! for grace to enter, through the blood of Jesus, into the retirings of the Lord, and to plead with him, as the patriarch did, with an importunity not to be resisted, that he would turn the captivity of his people. Oh! take away the rebuke of thy chosen, and let it be no longer said, of any of thine, who know Jesus, and have been made partakers of salvation by him: "There is none to guide her, among all the sons whom she hath brought forth; neither is there any that taketh her by the hand, of all the sons that she hath brought up." Isa. li. 18.

FEBRUARY 14.

MORNING.—" For where two or three are gathered together in my name, there am I in the midst of them."—Matt. xviii. 20.

What an encouraging declaration is this of our Jesus, to prompt the faithful to meet together on the Lord's day; or in short, any day, at all times, and all places. Observe, my soul, how sweet the Lord speaks; 'There am I in the midst of my people; not by my word only, not as represented in ordinances, not by the ministry of my servants, but I myself spiritually. The calls, the motions of grace felt in the heart, the tender tokens, the manifestations of my suitableness, fulness, and all-sufficiency; these are all truly mine, which, by the influences of my Spirit, I communicate among you.' Oh, precious, condescending Lord, now we see what it is that constitutes a true gospel church—even thy presence. Thou art the beauty and glory of it; and from thee alone all power and efficacy is derived. Thy churches are, indeed, as thou hast taught, the golden candlesticks; and thy ministers are as stars in thy right hand. But the candlesticks have no light, until thou, by thy presence, enlighten them; neither do thy servants, the ministers, hold forth the light of thy word profitably, until thou openest the heart, as thou didst poor Lydia's, to receive the things delivered, to the salvation of the soul. Ye ministers of my God! draw all your comfort and encouragement, amidst all the difficulties you meet with, both from within and without, in your sacred service, from this sweet assurance of Jesus. Whenever you go up to the assemblies of God's people, hear the footsteps of your Master behind you. And ye, who pant after sweet fellowship and communion with Jesus, seek it by the footsteps of the flock, beside the shepherd's tents, where Jesus feeds his sheep. Who would be absent from that blessed place where Jesus comes to bless? And Oh, what encouragement to the faithful to bring with them their unawakened friends and relations to the assemblies which Jesus honours with his presence. Surely he who wrought salvation in our hearts, can work the same in theirs. No wonder, when such mercies Jesus brings with him to his people, that the heart of David fainted to go up to the house of the Lord, that he might see the power and glory of Jesus, as he had seen it in the sanctuary.

EVENING.—" Unto the pure, all things are pure; but unto them that are defiled and unbelieving, is nothing pure."—Titus i. 15.

An union with Christ brings with it the sweet and sanctified use and enjoyment of all things. My soul, ponder, this evening, what the apostle here saith, with an eye to this, and behold thy blessedness in Jesus. Every thing which comes into the account of what may be called *real good,* can be so no farther than as it is found and enjoyed in Christ. Creature comforts have nothing in them of good, but what is derived from the blessedness of the covenant in them. To the pure in Christ, all things are pure. His gracious leaven in them, leaveneth the whole lump. And wherefore is it, that to them that are in a state of unrenewed nature, being defiled and unbelieving, there is nothing pure; but because there is nothing of Christ in them? They, and all they have, are under the curse; for every thing is so out of Christ. It is Jesus which must put a blessing and a relish into even the most common providences; or, instead of mercy, they will bring forth evil. See to it then, my soul, that Christ be the foundation of all thine enjoyments. Be very jealous over thyself, and thine own heart, when thou art most happy, that it be on Christ's account; or that when exercised with difficulties, thou still see Jesus in them, and receive them as coming from his appointment. And learn never to put a value upon any thing but on his account, and from their connexion with him. This will confirm what the apostle saith, to thy experience; "To the pure, all things are pure." For Jesus seen in all, will be enjoyed in all; and will sweeten, sanctify, bless, and render profitable all. For as there is infinitely more blessedness in the most common of our mercies, from their relationship to Jesus, and their coming from him than we are aware of; so we ought to have the greater regard to him, in all that we enjoy. And if we consider nothing as a blessing, but what is received *in* Jesus, we shall learn to set a value upon nothing but what is brought home to the heart *by* Jesus.

FEBRUARY 15.

MORNING.—"With purpose of heart they would cleave unto the Lord."—Acts xi. 23.

My soul, art thou cleaving to thy Jesus? It is a grand thing so to do; and it must be from continued supplies of grace in Jesus, if thou art really doing it. A few points will shew. Is Jesus thy all? Is he uppermost in all things? Faith hath for its one object, Jesus. Let a true believer be wheresoever he may—at home, or abroad; alone, or in company; the closet, or the church—it is all the same, if he really, truly, cleaves to the Lord with purpose of heart; there is a looking unto Jesus *for* all things, and *in* all things. Again; if I cleave to the Lord, I shall do no one thing but in his strength, and deliberately desire nothing but for his glory. The graces of the Holy Spirit, implanted in the souls of the faithful, are fed and kept alive, and brought forth into exercise by the communications of Jesus. My joy then is in Jesus; not in myself, not in what I feel. These feelings of mine may languish, but while I cleave to the Lord, my spiritual joy will always be the same. "From me," saith that sweet Lord, "from me is thy fruit found." Once more—if I cleave unto Jesus, shall I not find an increasing love for him, an increasing desire for him, and an increasing communion with him, from increasing knowledge of him, and of his love and preciousness? To be sure I shall. Well then, my soul, art thou indeed cleaving to him? Think how precious Jesus was, when first thou wast brought so savingly acquainted with him as to see thy need of him, and his suitableness and disposition to save thee. Dost thou think of these blessings less now? Oh no! You love him more because you know your need of him more, and therefore cleave to him the closer. Lastly, to add no more, doth my soul truly cleave to Jesus? Why then, I am loosening more and more from every thing beside. If Jesus hath my whole heart, then is the world and all creature idols thrown down. One Lord Jesus Christ is portion enough for a whole ransomed church of God to live upon to all eternity. In him there is portion enough for me. Oh! then, precious Lamb of God, be thou my portion; for in thee I have all things.

EVENING.—" A door opened in heaven."—Rev. iv. 1.

Lord! give me, as thou didst to thy servant John, a call to "come up hither," and by faith behold the glories which shall be revealed; and immediately I shall be in the spirit as he was, and so substantiate and realize, in present enjoyment, those felicities in Jesus, that this evening my soul will be, by happy faith, in the very suburbs of that blessed city, "which hath foundations, whose builder and maker is God!" Is it not true, Lord, that all thy possessions are mine? And shall I not take the map of them from scripture, and look over them with holy rapture and delight? Do men of the earth take pride in their lands and manors; the very holding of which is precarious, even in the moment of possession, and which begin to slide from under their feet, as soon as they enter upon them; and shall not an heir of God, a joint-heir with Christ, rejoice in having a kingdom which cannot be moved? Come, my soul, look within the veil, whither thy forerunner is for thee entered, and now that God the Holy Ghost hath opened a door in heaven, behold what felicities are presenting themselves to thy view. Behold, amidst all the glories of the palace, how eminently Jesus, even thy Jesus, appears as a Lamb in the midst of the throne; and still as a Lamb that hath been slain; as if to testify the eternal unceasing efficacy of his blood and righteousness. But what an innumerable host are these, which stand around the throne, and encircle the Redeemer! "These are they which came out of great tribulation, and have washed their robes, and made them white in the blood of the Lamb!" Mark that, my soul! They were once in the tribulated path that thou art now in; they were once sinners here below, as thou art now; and they owe all their advancement, not to their merit, but to divine bounty; not to works of righteousness which they have done, but to the same source as thou art now seeking acceptance from—the blood of the Lamb. Oh! precious soul-satisfying testimony, on a point of such infinite importance! Blessed, for ever blessed, be God the Holy Ghost, for first opening to the beloved apostle, this door in heaven, and for all the after-revelations of Jesus made by this condescending discovery to the church in all ages. Often, my soul, look up, and behold the door still open; and often by faith look in, and behold thy Redeemer, and his redeemed, in "the spirits of just men made perfect." Realize these blessed things, and seek from thy Jesus, a strength of faith (for such a faith hath been given to some, and why not to thee?) as shall absolutely bring down the present enjoyment of heaven into thy soul, before the Lord shall finally and fully call thee up to the everlasting enjoyment of him in glory. Blessed be God (my soul, do thou cry out with the apostle) "who hath blessed us with all spiritual blessings, and hath raised us up together, and made us sit together in heavenly places, in Christ Jesus!"

FEBRUARY 16.

MORNING.—"Help, LORD! for the godly man ceaseth; for the faithful fail from among the children of men."—Ps. xii. 1.

My soul, art thou sometimes distressed in the recollection of the languishing state of Zion—are faithful men, faithful ministers, taken away from the evil to come! And dost thou sometimes, at a mercy-seat, feel thyself drawn out in fervent prayer, that the Lord would fill up the vacancies he is making by death, and raise up pastors after his own heart, and believers who love Zion, to supply their place? Take comfort, my soul; thy Jesus loves Zion; and she is still engraven on the palms of his hands, and her walls are continually before him. Jesus must have a church in the earth as long as the sun and moon endure. Remember, the reins of government are in Jesus' hands; and however the enemies of Zion, like wild horses, would ride over the children of Zion, Jesus puts his bridle in their jaws, and will turn them back by the way they came. Remember, also, that the care of the church is with Jesus. He saith himself concerning it, "I the Lord do keep it, I will water it every moment: lest any hurt it, I will keep it night and day." Blessed Jesus, I would say then, Zion is, and must be safe. Die who may, Jesus lives; and to his church he saith, "Because I live, ye shall live also." Here then is enough for me, for the church, and for every child of God. My seed, saith Jesus, shall serve him. Hallelujah.

EVENING.—"And Peter said unto him, Lord! dost thou wash my feet?"—John xiii. 6.

My soul! dost thou want some sweet, some tender, some more than ordinarily interesting view of thy Jesus, this evening, to draw out all the finer feelings in love and adoration of thy Redeemer? Look at him then in the moment in which this scripture represents him, in his lowliness and meekness, washing the disciples' feet. Had I the power of drawing the most endearing portrait, Jesus should be my one and only object; and for a subject of the most finished kind, the humbleness and tenderness of Jesus, the Lord of life and glory, washing poor fishermen's feet, should be the picture. And what, my soul, tends if possible, infinitely more to endear and bring home to the heart this unparalleled condescension and grace of Jesus, is, that it was, as the evangelist relates it, at a time when Jesus knew that all things were given by his Father into his hands: that is, all things relating to his mediatorial kingdom; that he should give eternal life to as many as the Father had given him; and in due time take out of his kingdom all things that did offend. Was there ever a more lovely, a more engaging instance shewn, than by the great Redeemer of the world, in this condescending act? Well might the astonished apostle cry out, in the contemplation of it, "Lord! dost thou wash my feet?"—My soul! pause over the subject, and consider it well; and when thou hast duly weighed the matter, let it be asked, what condescension, what grace, what love, what mercy, will Jesus think too great for the salvation of poor sinners? Oh! that I had the power of persuasion, with any poor broken-hearted transgressor, to convince him that there is nothing to keep a soul from Jesus but unbelief. I would say to such an one, my brother, Oh! make trial only of Jesus's love. The greater your unworthiness, the greater will be the grace of Jesus, in his mercy towards you. And the lower the Son of God bends down to wash a sinner, the higher surely will he be in the sinner's love and esteem. Let it be asked, through the whole church of Christ upon earth, who loves Jesus most, but the sinner to whom Jesus hath forgiven most? Let it be inquired, through the realms of heaven, whose song of redemption is the loudest and the best? and the reply must be, the song of those who were most low upon earth when Jesus first stooped to wash them. Oh! thou blessed Immanuel! thou, the Lord our righteousness! never let me forget this instance of thy grace to poor sinners, but do thou cause it to be my daily encouragement to come to thee, and under the same conviction as the apostle, to cry out, " Lord, wash not my feet only, but also my hands and my head."

FEBRUARY 17.

MORNING.—" Knowing that whilst we are at home in the body, we are absent from the Lord: we are confident, I say, and willing rather to be absent from the body, and to be present with the Lord."—2 Cor. v. 6, 8.

My soul, is this thy real language? Pause, while thou art at home in the body, how dark and dim, how few and short, are all the glimpses thou hast by faith of Jesus. What from the workings of corruption, the claims of the body, the concerns of the world, and the numberless, nameless, obstructions which surround thee, how little dost thou know of Jesus! And wouldest thou desire for ever to live at this distance? Think what the first view only of Jesus will be, when thou art once absent from the body, and present with the Lord! —What holy transports will break in upon the soul, when all the lines of love meet in one centre, to manifest the Lord Jesus to thy view in his redeeming fulness! If here below a single hour's enjoyment of thy Jesus, through the medium of his word or ordinances, be so precious that no felicity on earth are equal; what must a whole eternity be, in the full uninterrupted vision of God and the Lamb! If, through the influences of thy blessed Spirit, dearest Jesus, the tear of joy, and love, and praise, will fall in the contemplation of thy person and work; surely all the flood-gates of the soul will open, when I see thee as thou art, and come to dwell with thee for ever. Oh! for grace, then, to long for that blessed hour, when, absent from the body, I shall be present with the Lord;—" when I shall behold thy face in righteousness, and shall be satisfied when I awake with thy likeness."

EVENING.—" Thus saith the Lord, the God of Israel, unto thee, O Baruch! Thou didst say, woe is me now! for the Lord hath added grief to my sorrow; I fainted in my sighing, and I find no rest. Thus shalt thou say unto him: the Lord saith thus: behold, that which I have built, will I break down; and that which I have planted, I will pluck up, even this whole land. And seekest thou great things for thyself? Seek them not."—Jer. xlv. 2—5.

Here, my soul! take an instruction, and a blessed one it is, when applied by the Holy Ghost, suited for God's people in all ages of the church, and in all generations. At all seasons, it is unbecoming in a believer in Jesus to have a mind hankering after things of the world, which the carnal seek; but the evil is increased in times of general calamity. Baruch, though the Lord's servant, yet felt too much desire of the world's ease. My soul, learn to avoid every thing which may lead to an attachment to things below; that when thou art called upon to leave them, their hold may be too little to be felt. And in a day like the present, doth not thy Lord speak to thee, in the same language as to the prophet: "Seekest thou great things for thyself? Seek them not. If I have been with Jesus, and given in my name to him, "what have I to do any more with idols?" It is remarkable, that after the Lord Jesus had instituted his holy supper, and put the cup into his disciples' hands, he observed, "I will not drink henceforth of the fruit of the vine, until that day when I drink it new with you in my Father's kingdom;" hereby teaching us, that in the dedication of the soul to him, an exchange is then made of earth for heaven. And as from that hour, Jesus's cup was the cup of trembling, and of wormwood and the gall; so the disciple is not above his master, nor the servant above his lord. And they that are Christ's, are said to have "crucified the flesh, with its affections and lusts."

FEBRUARY 18.

MORNING.—"And I will make an everlasting covenant with them, that I will not turn away from them to do them good; but I will put my fear in their hearts, that they shall not depart from me."—Jer. xxxii. 40.

Precious consideration to a poor exercised soul, that a covenant God in Christ, hath not only engaged for himself, but undertaken for his people also. God *will* not, and his people *shall* not. My soul, take a short view of the foundation of this precious, precious promise. It is God's everlasting love, everlasting grace, everlasting covenant. And remember, the Author of it is not changeable as thou art: "with Him is no variableness, neither shadow of turning." Moreover, it is purchased by the blood, sealed in the blood, and made eternally firm and sure in the blood and righteousness of Christ; the everlasting efficacy of which is as eternal as the Author of it. Neither is this all. There is an union with the person of thy Jesus. The head without a body would be incomplete; and, united to his Person, the believer is interested in all his graces, fulness, suitableness, all-sufficiency: so that this preserves grace from perishing, because it is an everlasting spring. And Jesus lives to see it all complete. His intercession answers every want, and supplies every necessity. Neither is this all; for God the Holy Ghost sets to his seal, in the heart, that God is true. His quickening, convincing, converting, manifesting grace in the soul, in taking of the things of Jesus, and shewing to the heart, becomes an earnest and pledge in assurance; and all tending to confirm, that God *will* not, and his redeemed ones, *shall* not turn away, but his covenant remain everlasting.

EVENING.—" A citizen of no mean city."—Acts xxi. 39.

It certainly was very laudable in Paul, in a moment of danger, to avail himself of the common privileges of his freedom, in the common rights of men. But it would have been a sad thing for the apostle, had he not, at the same time, been also " a fellow citizen with the saints, and of the household of God." He, like the patriarchs, knew his right in that city " which hath foundations, whose builder and maker is God." My soul! see to it, this evening, that thy name is enrolled among the citizens of those who are built upon the " foundation of the apostles and prophets, Jesus Christ himself being the chief corner-stone." And if thou canst find evidences of this high calling, thou wilt know also, as well as Paul, that thou art " a citizen of no mean city." Now a city that hath " foundations, and whose builder and maker is God," differs totally from all the cities founded among men. All these have their rise, their increase, and fall. Where are the vast monarchies of past generations? Alas! time hath passed over them as a flood, and swept them all away. And what the sacred writer hath said of one, may be equally applied to all: " Babylon, the great, is fallen, is fallen; in one hour is thy judgment come!" But the citizenship of a believer is firm, eternal, and secure. God the Father is the founder of it: he hath laid the foundation-stone in Zion. God the Son is the Rock on which it is built. And God the Holy Ghost is the eternal source of life and strength, and all the immutable privileges of it. This city is everlastingly and eternally secure, for "salvation hath the Lord appointed for walls and bulwarks." And the peace and happiness of its inhabitants must ever remain the same; for the citizens are of one body, and one spirit, even as they are called, in one hope of their calling. For the Son of God hath made them free by his blood and righteousness, and they are free indeed. Such, my soul, among numberless other distinguishing characters, are the outlines of the history of that city which hath foundations, and of which we may say, with the psalmist, "Glorious things are spoken of thee, O city of God!" If thou art a citizen of it, the enrolment of thy name among the freemen may be easily seen, for Jesus, the King of Zion, must have signed it with his blood. And then art thou come, as the apostle describes, not to the mount that might be touched, and that burned with fire: not unto blackness and darkness, and tempest; but unto Mount Zion, and unto the city of the living God, the heavenly Jerusalem, and to an innumerable company of angels; to the general assembly and church of the first-born, which are written in heaven; and to God, the Judge of all; and to the "spirits of just men made perfect;" and to Jesus, the Mediator of the new covenant, and to the blood of sprinkling. Then, have you found also the blessedness of the place, and the immense privileges of its inhabitants? In the freedom of this city is found peace with God, through the blood of the cross; and access at all times, through him, by one Spirit, unto the Father. And as among other citizens there are certain marks and characters, by which the privileges of one city are distinguished from another; so in this, the language, the dress, the manners, and customs, are wholly foreign to all the rest of the world. A citizen of God's house, talks the language of God; he is dressed in the garment of salvation, and the robes of Jesus's righteousness. His manners and customs are altogether peculiar to a child of God and an heir of heaven; for all is in conformity to the gospel of Christ. My soul! what sayest thou to these characters? Are they thine? If so, thou mayest assume Paul's account of himself; for, like him, thou art "a citizen of no mean city."

FEBRUARY 19.

MORNING.—"The prisoner of Jesus Christ."—Eph. iii. 1.

My soul! art thou a prisoner of Jesus Christ? See to it, if so, that, like the apostle, thou art bound with Jesu's chains for "the hope of Israel." They are golden chains. When Paul and Silas were fast bound in the prison, the consciousness of this made them sing for joy. Men have *their* prisons, and God hath *his*. But here lies the vast difference: no bars or grates, among the closest prisons of men, can shut God out from comforting his prisoners; and, on the contrary, nothing can come in to afflict Jesu's prisoners, when he keeps them by the sovereignty of his grace, and love, and power. Blessed Lord! look upon thy poor prisoner; and come in, dear Lord, with thy wonderful condescension, and do as thou hast said: sup with him, and cause him to sup with thee.

EVENING.—"Surely he hath borne our griefs, and carried our sorrows."—Isa. liii. 3.

My soul! call up, this evening, all thy most earnest and most solemn thoughts, to the meditation of a subject, which the Holy Ghost opens to thy view in these words. And if the Lord the Spirit, that proposeth to thy soul the solemn consideration, will graciously instruct thee through it, perhaps it will lead to such views of Jesus as may not before so fully have struck thine attention. Oh, Lord! guide thy servant in it! Now here it is said, "He hath borne our griefs, and carried our sorrows." By which, it may be supposed, is meant, both the curse and the punishment. And certain it is, that unless Christ bore both, the sinner is not freed. From the sinner, or his surety, God's justice must exact full payment. But if it be found that in the surety that exaction hath been made, and fully paid, then is the sinner free; for from both it would be unjust to exact. Now behold, my soul, in the person of thy surety, how in the most minute points, even as the sinner himself, thy Jesus stood for thee. And then see, from beholding thy Redeemer in this most endearing point of view, whether thou art not constrained to cry out, with the prophet, "Surely he hath borne our griefs, and carried our sorrows!" A few of the most prominent features in the griefs and sorrows of Jesus, will be sufficient in point, by way of illustration. And first, every sinner, by virtue of being a transgressor, is exposed to the curse of God; and that curse is upon every thing belonging to him, as Moses told Israel; "Thou art cursed in thy basket, and in thy store; in lying down and rising up; in going out and coming home." Deut. xxviii. 16, &c. Now Jesus, as the sinner's surety, is, by way of peculiar emphasis, called "the man of sorrows, and acquainted with grief." He endured, in his person, the very curse denounced upon the sinner. All was poured upon Jesus, through every part of his life: and as the curse, but for Jesus's interposition, would follow the sinner in death; so Christ was followed by it to the cross. The sinner's dying chamber would open to him the horrors of divine wrath on sin; such as Jesus, for the sinner, sustained in the garden of Gethsemane. And as no by-standers, no earthly friends, could mitigate the horrors of the sinner's soul in such a season; so we find Christ, when going through these conflicts for the sinner, could gain no help from any of his disciples—" they all forsook him and fled." And doth the sinner's conscience then betray and aggravate the load of woe? And did not Judas, Christ's bosom friend, come boldly forward to aggravate the Redeemer's sorrow? And as every sinner, out of Christ, for whom he, as the surety, hath paid no ransom, would in the moment of death, be seized, bound hand and foot, and carried away by an armed band to utter darkness, where there is weeping and gnashing of teeth; so Christ was taken, as the sinner's surety, by an armed band, from the high priest to the judgment-hall, where he lay all night, suffering the punishment of stripes and mocking. And as, in the morning of the resurrection, sinners out of Christ, must arise to all the horrors of judgment; and the irreversible sentence be pronounced in the presence of all beholders, which consigns them to everlasting punishment; so Christ, the surety for his sinful people, in the morning was brought from the hall of Pilate to the hill of Calvary, and there received the sentence of death, executed upon his sacred person, in the view of all that passed by.—Pause, my soul, over the representation of truths so awful! Surely thou mayest say, if Jesus had not sustained the curse and punishment, then must I have borne it for ever. But if, as the prophet hath marked it in this most blessed scripture, " Surely he hath borne our griefs, and carried our sorrows," then is the principal debtor free, when the surety hath paid the debt! Oh! the preciousness, the suitableness, the completeness of Jesus, in the whole purpose of his redemption. Blessed, blessed, blessed for ever, be Jehovah, for Jesus Christ!

FEBRUARY 20.

MORNING.—"I will say unto God, do not condemn me; shew me wherefore thou contendest with me."—Job x. 2.

My soul, art thou at any time exercised with any trying dispensations? Doth thy God, thy Jesus, seem to hide his face from thee? Are his providences afflicting? Art thou brought under bereaving visitations? Is thy earthly tabernacle shaken by sickness? Are the pins of it loosening? Are thy worldly circumstances pinching? Is prayer restrained? Oh, refer thy state, my soul, be it what it may, to Jesus. Tell thy Lord, that of all things, thy greatest dread and fear is, lest thou shouldest be mistaken concerning his love to thee. Say, as Job did, "Shew me wherefore thou contendest with me." There is an Achan in the heart. Thy Jesus doth not withdraw for nothing. Love is in his lips. Salvation fills the whole soul of Jesus. Fly to him, then, my soul! Say to him, Lord, make me what thou wouldest have me to be. Oh! for a word, a whisper of Jesus. I cannot live without it. I dare not let thee go, except thou bless me. Not all the past enjoyments, experiences, manifestations, will do me good, until thou again shine in upon my soul. Oh! come then, Lord Jesus! I fly to thee as my God, my Saviour, my portion, my all!" Never, surely wilt thou say to the praying seed of Jacob, "Seek ye my face in vain!

EVENING.—"Now thou art commanded, this do ye: take your waggons out of the land of Egypt, for your little ones, and for your wives, and bring your father, and come. Also regard not your stuff; for the good of all the land of Egypt is yours."—Gen. xlv. 19, 20.

What effect must the first news of Joseph's being alive, and his exaltation at the right hand of Pharaoh, have had upon the mind of the patriarch Jacob! And what a flood of overwhelming joy must have broke in upon the poor old man, when convinced of the certainty of the account! But what are all these feelings of nature, compared to the triumphs of grace, when the poor sinner is first made acquainted with the wonders of redemption, wrought out and accomplished by one that is his brother, even our spiritual Joseph, the Lord Jesus Christ? Yes! thou risen and exalted Saviour! by faith I behold thee on the right hand of the Majesty on high; and all power is thine in heaven and on earth. I hear thee giving commandment to thy servants, to take the ordinances, and the several means of grace, in thy sacred word, and, like the conveyances of the waggons of Egypt, to bring all thy kindred, thy redeemed ones, to thee. Yea, Lord! I would do as thou hast said, "regard not the stuff," for gladly would I leave it all behind; for it hath already too long and too powerfully occupied my poor heart, and robbed my soul of thee. I would hasten to thy presence; for sure I am, the good of all the land of heaven itself is thy brethren's, and, what is infinitely more than even heaven, thou, even thou thyself, blessed Jesus, art thy people's. But, Lord! how shall I look thee in the face? How shall I dare to draw nigh, conscious of my having, like the sons of Jacob, sold thee, parted with thee, denied thee, left thee, and as the Jews of old, preferred every Barabbas, every robber before thee? And wilt thou, dearest Lord, still own me, still love me, and still speak kindly to me? Oh! what praises will the realms of heaven resound with, when Jesus shall have brought home all his brethren, into his Father's house, around himself in glory! How will then every knee (and my poor soul among the glorious number) bow before thee, and every tongue confess, that Jesus Christ is Lord, to the glory of God the Father. Amen and Amen!

FEBRUARY 21.

MORNING.—"*Saw ye him whom my soul loveth.*"—Song iii. 3.

Is Jesus still the object of my soul's warmest affection; the subject of all my thoughts, all my discourse, all my inquiry? Oh, yes, my soul; whom else, in heaven or in earth, wilt thou seek after but him? Tell me, ye ministers of Jesus, ye watchmen upon the walls of Zion—"Saw ye him whom my soul loveth?" Ye followers of the Lamb, can ye shew me where Jesus feedeth his flock at noon? Or rather, ye in the upper regions, where the Son of God manifesteth himself in the full glories of his Person; "ye spirits of just men made perfect," ye who have known, while sojourning here below, what feeling of the soul that is, which, in the absence of Jesus, is longing for his appearance. Ye angels of light also—ye who see him without an intervening medium—tell him, I beseech you, how my soul panteth for his visits: tell him, that a poor pensioner, well known to my Lord, is waiting this morning alms: nay, tell him that I am sick of love, longing for a renewed view of his person,—his pardoning love,—the renewals of his grace. Jesus knoweth it all before you tell him, and he will send his gifts and mercies—nay, he will come himself; for he hath assured me of this. He hath said,—"If a man love me, my Father will love him, and we will come and make our abode with him." Behold my soul, thy Jesus is come! I hear his well-known voice: he saith,—"I am come into my garden." Now will I hold him, and not let him go, and pray him not to be as a wayfaring man that turneth in to tarry for a night, but abide with me until the breaking of the everlasting day.

EVENING.—"Being not without law to God, but under the law to Christ."—1 Cor. ix. 21.

Sit down my soul, this evening, and ponder over this blessed distinction which the apostle makes between the lawless conduct of those, who, from a mere conviction of the truth in the head, but who never felt the influences of it in their heart, hold the truth in unrighteousness; and those who, while conscious of being under the law to Christ, are not without law to God. To thee, my soul, who hast been brought under the condemnation of God's holy law, and hast been enabled, through sovereign grace, to take refuge in the person, blood, and righteousness of the Lord Jesus Christ; to thee, justification by faith, so far from relaxing thine obedience to the law of God, has proved the best of all motives to the practice of it. Thou knowest thyself to be bought with a price; and therefore, as the Lord's property, both by his purchase, and thy voluntary surrender, it is thy desire above all things, "to glorify God in thy body and in thy spirit, which are his." It is thy glory, thy delight, thy joy, that thy God and Father hath accepted a righteousness for thee in Jesus, thy Surety; and to him, and him only, the Lord hath respect for thy acceptation. But while thou art taught, and thy heart delights in the soul-reviving truth, that thou art never to seek justification by the deeds of the law; thy heart delights also, that thou art "not without law to God, but under the law to Christ." For though the law of the Spirit of life in Christ Jesus hath made thee free from the law of sin and death; yet while through the law, thou art dead to the law, the blessedness of it is, that thou mightest live unto Christ. And it is by the Spirit of Him that raised up Jesus from the dead dwelling in thee, that the deeds of the body are mortified, and the soul lives. Sweet consideration, my soul, to cherish, and ever to keep in view. Thou art not working for life, but from life. Not seeking to be justified by the deeds of the law; but from Christ's justification, daily shewing forth that "thou art not without law to God, but under the law to Christ."

FEBRUARY 22.

MORNING.—"Where the Spirit of the Lord is, there is liberty."—2 Cor. iii. 17.

What liberty, my soul! art thou brought into by thine adoption into the family of God in Christ? Not from the assaults of sin; for thou still carriest about with thee a body of sin, under which thou groanest. Not from the temptations of Satan; for he is still levelling at thee many a fiery dart. Not from outward troubles; for the world thou art still in, thou findest it a wilderness state. Not from inward fears; for thine unbelief begets many. Not from the chastisement of thy wise and kind Father: for then many a sweet visit of his love, under the rod, would be unknown. Not from death; for the stroke of it thou must one day feel—though, blessed be Jesus, he hath taken out the sting in his blood and righteousness. What liberty then is it, my soul, thou enjoyest? What hath the Spirit of the Lord, as a spirit of revelation, discovering to thee the glory of Jesus, and thy interest in him, brought thee into? Oh, who shall write down the vast, the extensive account of thy freedom? Say, my soul, hath not the sight of God's glory in Christ freed thee from the curse of the law,—from the guilt of the law, —from the dominion of sin,—from the power of Satan, —from the evil of unbelief in thine own heart,—from the terrors of justice,—from the alarms of conscience, from the second death? Say, my soul, doth not the sight of Jesus dying for thee, rising for thee, pleading for thee, enlarge thine heart, and lose thy bonds, and shake off all thy fetters and all thy fears? Doth not Jesus in the throne give thee liberty to come to him, to call upon him, to unbosom thyself unto him, to tell him all thy wants, all thy necessities, and to lean upon his kind arm in every hour of need? Shout, my soul! and echo to the apostle's words,—"Where the Spirit of the Lord is there is liberty:" liberty to approach, liberty to plead, liberty to pray, liberty to praise and to adore the whole persons of the Godhead, for having opened the prison-doors, and given thee freedom in Christ Jesus!

EVENING.—"And he said unto them, say now unto her, behold, thou hast been careful for us with all this care; what is to be done for thee? wouldest thou be spoken for to the king, or to the captain of the host? And she answered, I dwell among mine own people."—2 Kings iv. 13.

What an interesting account, though short, is here given of the Shunamite. The sacred historian calls her "a great woman," and certainly, she here manifests that she had a great mind. What she had done for the prophet, she sought no recompence for. Neither the favours of the king, nor the captain of his host, were of any value to her and her husband. Dwelling with content in what she had, and "among her own people," was in her view enough of earthly enjoyment. But is there not a spiritual improvement to be made of the passage? Do not the people of our God "dwell alone?" And have they not been from everlasting so appointed, in the purposes of God their Father, and chosen in Christ, and called? They may, and indeed they ought to desire to be spoken for to the King, the Captain of the Lord's host, as a people near to himself. Yes! I would say, let me be spoken for, that I may always live under an abiding sense of my Lord's presence and his love; and that my constant views of him, and his gracious tokens of kindness to me, may be my daily enjoyment. Methinks I would always be spoken for to him, in this point of view, and always myself be speaking to him; and tell my Lord that one smile of his, one whisper to assure me of my interest in him, and my love for him, and his love for me, will be more grateful than all the revenues of the earth. Here, like the Shunamite, would I centre all my desires. And while living upon Jesus, it will be my happiness also to "dwell among mine own people," who are also the Lord's people, and who, like myself, keep aloof from all unnecessary acquaintance and connection with the world, to "enjoy fellowship with the Father, and with his Son Jesus Christ!"

FEBRUARY 23.

MORNING.—" Hath a nation changed their gods, which are yet no gods? But my people have changed their glory for that which doth not profit."—Jer. ii. 11.

Pause, my soul, over these words! Was it ever known that any nation changed their dunghill gods for others? Such regard had they for whatever ignorance had set up, that the veneration never after ceased. But Israel, above every other nation of the earth, manifested folly, and even exceeded the most senseless and stupid of men. My soul! dost thou not in Israel's folly behold thy own? Was there ever one, when the Lord first called thee, less deserving? A transgressor, as the Lord knew thee, from the womb! And yet this did not prevent the Lord from calling thee. He loved thee because he would love thee; gave thee his Christ,—gave thee his Holy Spirit—gave thee the name, the privilege, the adoption of a son. What returns hast thou made? How often since hath thy backslidings, thy coldness, thy departures, been like Israel? What vanity, what pursuit, what unprofitable employment, hath not at times been preferred to thy God? Oh how do I see my daily, hourly, continual need of thee, thou that art the hope of Israel, and the Saviour thereof! Keep me, Lord, near thyself; for without thee I am nothing.

EVENING.—" The hidden manna."—Rev. ii. 17.

We have an authority from Jesus himself, to say, that He, and He alone, is the manna of the gospel; for in his discourse with the Jews, he called himself, in allusion to the manna of the wilderness, " the living bread," and " the bread of God which came from heaven," of which, he said, " whosoever should eat, should live for ever." But when Jesus imparts this blessed food to his people, it is *hidden*. And, indeed, many of the properties of it are made more blessed, from the very nature of its secresy. My soul, ponder over the subject a few moments, this evening, and behold in it, how truly gracious it is in the Lord, to hand to his people in secret, those enjoyments of himself, of which the world is altogether unconscious. Mark the outlines of it, and trace it in its effects in thine own experience. Though Jesus was preached to the world, both by the law and the prophets; and when appearing in substance of our flesh manifested forth his glory; yet was he known only to his disciples: the great mass of men neither knew him, nor regarded him. If he was preached in types and sacrifices, under the old testament dispensation, or in open gospel under the new, few believed the report; the cry still went forth, "is not this the carpenter's son?" But say, my soul, is not Jesus still "the hidden manna?" Dost thou discover him in his holy word? still is the word hidden: for though it is read openly by all, yet the mystery of it is known but to few. Doth the Holy Ghost testify to thee of Jesus, in thy desires *after* him; in thy communions *with* him; in the actings of thy faith *upon* him; and in thy enjoyments *from* him? Nevertheless in all these, however certain and refreshing to thee, thy pleasures are *hidden* from the world. This is mercy, personal and peculiar; strangers do not, cannot, intermeddle with this joy. Precious Lord Jesus! give me larger and fuller enjoyments of thee day by day; and night by night let my secret and retired meditations of thee be sweet! Oh! for grace to live more and more upon those hidden privileges, and more and more to prize them. Come to me, dear Lord! and give me such rich participations of thyself, in the fulness of thy person, blood, and righteousness, that receiving from thee "the hidden manna," I may say in thine own precious words, "I have meat to eat which the world knows not of."

FEBRUARY 24.

MORNING.—"He that had gathered much had nothing over; and he that had gathered little had no lack."—2 Cor. viii. 15.

My soul! here is a delightful morsel for thee to feed

upon this morning. Thou art come out to gather thy daily food, as Israel did in the wilderness. Faith had no hoards. Thou wantest Jesus now as much as thou didst yesterday. Well then, look at what is here said of Israel. They went out to gather—what? Why, in the morning bread—God's gift. Such is Jesus, the bread of God, the bread of life. And as Israel would have been satisfied with nothing short of this, so neither be thou. And as Israel was never disappointed, so neither wilt thou, if thou seek it in faith, as Israel did. And observe, "they that gathered most had nothing over;" so "he that gathered least had no lack." Yea, my soul, no follower of Jesus can have too much of Jesus; nothing more than he wants — nothing to spare. So the poorest child of God, that hath the least of Jesus, can never want. The very touch of his garment, the very crumb from his table, is his, and is precious. Dearest Lord, give me a large portion, even a Benjamin's portion. But even a look of thy love is heaven to my soul,

EVENING.—"Behold, I will bring them from the north country, and gather them from the coasts of the earth, and with them the blind, and the lame, the woman with child, and her that travaileth with child together, a great company shall return thither. They shall come with weeping, and with supplications will I lead them: I will cause them to walk by the rivers of waters, in a straight way wherein they shall not stumble; for I am a father to Israel, and Ephraim is my first-born."—Jer. xxxi. 8, 9.

It is blessed at all times to be refreshed with God's promises concerning the latter-day glory; but more especially at a time when things are most unpromising. The present hour is eminently so. Therefore, my soul, see what a cluster of mercies are folded up on this one branch of them; and let thine evening meditations be sweet of Jesus and his sure work, in whom, "All the promises are yea and amen, to the glory of God the Father, by us." Observe, in this blessed scripture, the certainty of the divine promises being all fulfilled, from the foundation on which they rest. If God be the

God of all the families of Israel, and if Israel be his son, and Ephraim his first-born, how can the right of inheritance fail? Surely God is engaged by this covenant and relationship, and he will fulfil his promises. And what are they? Why, that he will bring them not only from Babylon, but from all their places of captivity. Jesus, the Son of his love, is commissioned as the covenant of Jehovah, "to bring the prisoners out of the prison, and them that sit in darkness out of the prison-house." There shall be a day when a nation shall be born at once. They shall be gathered to Shiloh, and shall come from the east, and from the west, and from the north, and from the south. Pause, my soul, over these blessed promises. Thou art frequently put to it for thyself; and art frequently exercised with fears and apprehensions for the welfare of Zion. But what saith this blessed scripture? "Behold, I will bring them from the north country, and gather them from the coasts of the earth." Do not overlook that it is God who undertakes for them, and not themselves: and what God undertakes, he will surely perform. Well, but they are much scattered. Yes! but God will gather them. But they are diminishing. No! a great company shall return. But they are blind, and do not know the way: they are lame, and when they know, have no power to walk in it. Yes! but, saith he that made the eye, and he that giveth strength to the lame, both "the blind and the lame," yea, even the woman in pregnancy, and her that is in travail, all shall come. "I will be eyes," saith God, "to the blind, and feet to the lame; I will lead them in a way they know not; I will undertake for them." And the sole reason is, God's free grace and covenant mercy in Christ. God is a father in this relationship, to all the families in Israel; and in him all the families of the earth are blessed. Pause, my soul, again and again, over this sweet and precious scripture; and see that these covenant marks and impressions be upon thee, as a sure unerring token of thy being in Christ, and gathered from the coasts of the earth; that thou art following Jesus, as Mary Magdalene did, with tears and supplications. Prayers are quickened by tears; and tears flowing from the view of a crucified Saviour, must give energy to prayers. The eye that is looking unto Jesus, will affect the heart; and the heart that is wounded with the view of Jesus dying for our sins, will cause tears to fall from the eye; and both will follow Christ by the waters of ordinances, under the Spirit's teaching and gracious influences. Lord! give to my soul these tokens for good; and lead me in the way of salvation for thy name's sake.

FEBRUARY 25.

MORNING.—"Who of God is made unto us wisdom, and righteousness, and sanctification, and redemption."—1 Cor. i. 30.

What a sweet subject for my morning meditation is here! Who is it, my soul, is made of God to thee these precious things but Jesus? And mark how they are made so. I am a poor ignorant creature, grossly ignorant by reason of the fall. I knew not my lost estate, much less the way of recovery. Here Jesus became to me wisdom. By his illuminating the darkness of my mind, he led me to see my ruin and my misery. But this would never have brought me out of it; for though I saw my lost estate, yet still I had no consciousness by what means I could be recovered. Here again Jesus came to my aid, and taught me, that as I needed righteousness, he would be my righteousness, and undertake for me to God. But even after this was done, I felt my soul still the subject of sin; and how to subdue a single sin I knew not. Here Jesus came again, and gave me to see, that as he was wisdom to cure my ignorance, and righteousness to answer for my guilt, so he would be my sanctification also; purging, as well as pardoning and renewing, by his Spirit, my poor nature, when he had removed the guilt of it. Still I sighed for complete deliverance, and to make my happiness sure; and therefore Jesus came again, that by his full redemption from all the evils of the fall, I might be made free; and therefore he became the whole together—"wisdom, righteousness, sanctification, and redemption." And to stamp and seal the whole with the impression of God my Father, all that Jesus did, he did by God's gracious appointment; for he was made of God to me all these, that all my glorying might be in the Lord. See to it, my soul, then, that this be all thy glory.

EVENING.—"And the rest, some on boards, and some on broken pieces of the ship; and so it came to pass, that they escaped all safe to land."—Acts xxvii. 44.

This is the beautiful conclusion of a history, which, during the providence wherein Paul the apostle and his companions were in shipwreck, afforded large opportunity for the exercise of faith. The issue, it appears, was not doubtful from the first; for an angel of God had assured Paul, that God had given unto him the lives of all that sailed with him. And so it proved; yea, the very wreck of the ship furnished out means for the people's safety. Now, my soul, here is a very precious instruction for thee. In the exercises of thy life, learn from hence to abide firmly by the promise, when every thing leading to its accomplishment seems to fail. God hath said, that eternal life, with all its preliminaries, is in his Son; and that "he that hath the Son, hath life, and shall not come into condemnation." Now let what will arise, after this declaration of God, like the storm and shipwreck of the apostle, these are intervening circumstances with which thou hast nothing to do. Do thou take hold of the promise; for the promise hath its claim upon God. This cannot fail, whatever else may fail. And though, like Paul in this voyage, neither sun nor stars in many days may appear, and no small tempest be upon thee; Jesus is still at the helm, and thou shalt assuredly escape to land. Yea, the very wreck of all things around thee, shall but the better minister to this great end. And thou shalt at length write down the same conclusion to thy history, which Joshua, the man of God, made of the whole history of Israel:—"Not one thing hath failed, of all the good things which the Lord your God spake concerning you; all are come to pass unto this very day."

FEBRUARY 26.

MORNING.—"As for me, I will behold thy face in righteousness. I shall be satisfied when I awake with thy likeness."—Ps. xvii. 15.

Is it refreshing to thee now, my soul, the least glimpse of Jesus's face; the smallest manifestation of the glories of his Person and of his work; and the very sound of his voice, in his word or ordinances? Think, then, what will be thy felicity in that morning of the eternal world, when, dropping thy vail of flesh, he whom thou seest now by faith only, will then appear as open to thee as to the church above in glory! Pause, my soul, over the vast thought! What will be thy first sight of Jesus? What will be thy feelings, when, without any intervening medium, thou shalt see him face to face, and know even as thou art known? Precious Lamb of God! grant me grace to feel the blessedness of this first interview. Appearing, as I trust I shall, in thine own garments, and the robes of thy righteousness, and which thou hast not only provided for me, but put on, what will be the burstings forth of my heart, in the full view of the glories of thy Person, and the perfection of thy righteousness! Surely, Lord, when I thus behold thy face in righteousness, I shall be so fully satisfied, that the rest after which my poor soul, through a whole life of grace, since thou wert pleased to quicken me, hath been pursuing, will pursue no more. My immortal faculties will seek no more—will need no more. In thee, the whole is attained. In thee, I shall eternally rest. Thou art the everlasting centre of all happiness, glory, and joy. I shall be so fully satisfied when I awake to this view, that here, in thee, I shall be at home. And what is more, it will be an everlasting duration, not only in happiness, but in likeness. And as the coldest iron, put into the fire, partakes of the properties of the fire, until it becomes altogether heated and fiery like it, so in thee, and with thee, thou blessed Jesus, cold as my soul now is, I shall be warmed with thy love; and from thee, and thy likeness imparted, become lovely from thy loveliness, and glorious from thy glory. Precious, precious Jesus! Is the hour near? Are thy chariot wheels approaching? Dost thou say, "Behold, I come quickly." Oh! for grace to answer, "Even so, come, Lord Jesus!"

EVENING.—"Who is she that looketh forth as the morning; fair as the moon, clear as the sun, and terrible as an army with banners?" Song vi. 10.

By whomsoever this question is asked, there can be no question of whom it is said; for the church of Jesus, made comely by the comeliness which her Lord hath put upon her, is all this, and more, in every eye that can admire true loveliness; and will be a perfection of beauty, in the upper and brighter world for ever. The first openings of grace upon the soul, after a dark night of the fall, may be compared to the beauty of the morning. But though fair as the moon, it is but a borrowed light, as the moon, and subject to changes in its increasings, and in its wanings also. As long as the sun's influences are upon this planet, its shinings will be fair. But when objects intervene from the earth, and the sun shines not, there will be an eclipse of all its borrowed lustre. Just so the church; and Oh! how often on my soul. While Jesus, the Sun of righteousness, shines upon me, all is fair and lovely; but if he withdraws, the night immediately follows. But Oh! my soul, when grace is perfected in glory; when, as John in a vision saw, that wonder of wonders in heaven, "a woman clothed with the sun, and the moon under *her* feet," (Rev. xii. 1.) then shall the whole church of God shine forth "as the sun, in the kingdom of their Father." Precious Jesus! give me to see my clear interest in thee, from my union with thee! And do thou, dear Lord, so make me strong in thy strength, that during the whole period of my present warfare, I may be "terrible as an army with banners," to all that would oppose my way to thee, and in thee. Yea, Lord! let sin, and Satan, and the world, be ever so united against me; yet do thou put on me the whole armour of my God, that I may "fight the good fight of faith, lay hold of eternal life, and be made more than conqueror through him that loveth me."

FEBRUARY 27.

MORNING.—"He will be very gracious unto thee; at the voice of thy cry, when he shall hear it, he will answer thee."—Isa. xxx. 19.

Mark, my soul, what is here said; for every word in this sweet scripture tells. Thy God, thy Saviour, thy Jesus, knows thy voice, hears thy cry, and will assuredly answer. He will not only be gracious, but *very* gracious. He waits to be gracious; waits the most suited time, the best time, the praying time, the crying time; for he times his grace, his mercy, to thy need. And though thou knowest it not, yet so it is; when his time is near at hand, which is always the best time, he puts a cry in thine heart; so that the time of thy cry, and the time for the manifestation of his glory, shall come together. Is not this to be gracious; yea, very gracious? So that, while thou art looking after him, he is looking upon thee. And before thou callest upon him, he is coming forth to bless thee. Is not this very gracious? Now then, my soul, make a memorandum of this for any occasions which may hereafter occur. Put it down as a sure, unnering truth; thy Jesus will be very gracious unto thee. Never allow this promise to be called in question any more. Next, bring it constantly into use. Faith, well-grounded faith in Jesus, should always bring down general rules to particular cases and circumstances, as the soul's experience may require. Hence, when God saith he will be very gracious unto thee, it is the act of faith to answer—if God hath said it, so it shall certainly be. And therefore, as that gracious God, who giveth the promise, giveth also the grace of faith to depend upon the promise, the mercy is already done, and faith enters upon the enjoyment of it. God's faithfulness and truth become the believer's shield and buckler.

EVENING.—"But none saith, where is God my Maker, who giveth songs in the night?"—Job xxxv. 10.

Ah, Lord! is it so, that among men of the world, though they are oppressed by the world, and the evils of it, and some are compelled to cry out under the bitterness of their sorrows, yet are there no hearts, no voices directed to thee? When death entereth into their window, and taketh away the desire of their eyes with a stroke; or when pains and chastenings of the body chain them to their beds; do they lament the earthly bereavements, and groan under the consequences of sin, by which death and sickness came; and yet in all these things, will nothing lead their unthinking minds "to hear the rod, and who hath appointed it?" Will they turn from one creature comfort to another, and strive to fill up the vacancies made by distressing providences, in their fancied happiness with any thing, or even nothing, rather than look to thee for comfort and support under their trouble? Oh! how great are my privileges, if this be the case, compared to those of the carnal! And Oh! how distinguishing thy grace to my poor soul, that when sleepless on the bed, or when pains keep me awake, I can and do look to Jesus, and say, "Thou art God, my Maker, who giveth songs in the night!" Yea, Lord! thou hast refreshed my soul with many a sweet song, when all the world was to me asleep, and could not interrupt my happiness. Oh! how often have I been blessed with the harmony of the songs of redemption, and run over in some of the blessed verses of it, how Jesus hath loved me, and given himself for me. Yea, Lord! may I not say, as the prophet, "Thou hast wakened me morning by morning; he hath wakened mine ear to hear as the learned." For methinks I have been often wakened in the night by thee, and I have found my soul instantly led out by thy grace, to a sense of thy presence, and to a desire after thee; and was not this, my Lord, calling, as upon the church of old, "Let us get up early to the vineyards, for there will I give thee my loves!" Oh! precious Redeemer! grant me such frequent visits, and such sweet communications of thy grace; and if in thy wise and kind providences, sickness, or pain, or afflictions, be at any time appointed me, do thou sit up by me, Lord, and keep my heart in sweet recollection of thee; that in the multitude of the sorrows of my heart, thy comforts may refresh my soul; and frequently may the earnest petition for thy presence and thy love, go forth in the inquiry, "Where is God, my Maker, who giveth songs in the night?"

FEBRUARY 28.

MORNING.—"Leaning on Jesus' bosom."—John xiii. 23.

Methinks I would contemplate for a while the privilege of this highly-favoured disciple John. Surely to sit at the feet of Jesus, to look up at his face, to behold the Lamb of God, and to hear the gracious words which proceeded out of his mouth, what should I have thought of this but a happiness unspeakable and full of glory! But the beloved apostle leaned on Jesus's bosom. Oh, thou condescending Saviour! didst thou mean to manifest, by this endearing token, how dear and precious all thy redeemed ones are in thy esteem? But stop, my soul. If John lay on Jesus's breast, where was it Jesus himself lay, when he left all for thy salvation? The disciple whom Jesus loved lay upon Jesus's bosom; but he, whom the Father loved, lay in the bosom of the Father—nay, was embosomed there; was wrapt up in the very soul of the Father from eternity. Who shall undertake to speak of the most glorious state of the Son of God, before he condescended to come forth from the bosom of God for the salvation of his people? Who shall describe the blessedness of the Father and the Son in their mutual enjoyment of each other? Jesus, when he was in the bosom of the Father, had not emptied himself of his glory. Jesus had not been made in the likeness of sinful flesh. Jesus had not put himself under the law. He was not then a man of sorrows. He was not then acquainted with grief. He had not then exposed his face to shame and spitting; neither to poverty, temptation, the bloody sweat, and the cross. And did Jesus go through all these, and more? Did Jesus leave the Father's bosom; and did the Father take this only-begotten, only-beloved Son from his bosom; that John might lean on Jesus's bosom, and all the redeemed, like him, one day, dwell with Jesus, and lean and rest in his embraces for ever? Oh, for hearts to love both the FATHER and the SON, who have so loved us; that we may be ready to part with all, and forsake all, and die to all, that we may live in Jesus, and to Jesus, and rest in his bosom for ever.

EVENING.—"Having loved his own, which were in the world, he loved them unto the end."—John xiii. 1.

Sweet thought, my soul, for thee everlastingly to cherish; thy Jesus is the same, and his love the same, amidst all thy changings: yet he abideth faithful. His love, and not thy merit, was the first cause of thy salvation; and the same love, and not thy undeservings, is the final cause wherefore thou art not lost. But mark in this blessed scripture, how many sweet and lovely things are said. Jesus hath a people, and that people are in the world, and that people are his own. What! had he not a people in the other world? Yes! by creation all are his, in common with the Father. But by redemption he had none, until he had redeemed them from this present evil world. And observe how very graciously they are spoken of. They are his own, his peculiar people, his treasure, his *Segullah,* his jewels. And how dearly doth he prize them! They were first given to him by his Father; that made them dear. They are the purchase of his blood; this made them dear also. He hath conquered them by his grace; this endears them to himself as his own. And though they are in this world, too much engaged in the affairs of the world, and too much in love with the world, yet Jesus's love is not abated: their persons are still dear to Jesus, though their sins he hates. The same love which prompted his infinite mind to stand up for their redemption; the same love is going forth unceasingly, and without change or lessening, to accomplish and render effectual that redemption. Precious Lord Jesus! Oh for grace to love thee, who hast so loved us! And while thou condescendest to call such poor sinful worms thine own, and to love them as thine own, and consider every thing done for them and done to them as to thyself; shall not a portion of such love be communicated to my poor heart, that I may love thee as my own and only Saviour, and learn to love thee to the end, as thou hast loved me and given thyself for me, an offering and a sacrifice to God for a sweet-smelling savour?

MARCH 1.

MORNING.—"And his name shall be called Wonderful."—Isa. ix. 6.

'In the opening of the last month, the fragrancy of Jesus's name, as Emanuel, gave a sweet savour to my soul. May He, whose name is as ointment poured forth, give a new refreshment to my spiritual senses this morning, in this name also as Wonderful; for surely every thing in him, and concerning him, of whom the prophet speaks, is eminently so. But who shall speak of thy wonders, dearest Lord! the wonders of thy Godhead, the wonders of thy manhood, the wonders of both natures united and centered in one Person?—Who shall talk of the wonders of thy work, the wonders of thine offices, characters, relations; thy miraculous birth, thy wonderful death, resurrection, ascension?—Who shall follow thee, thou risen and exalted Saviour, at the right hand of power, and tell of the exercise of thine everlasting priesthood? Who shall speak of the wonders of thy righteousness, the wonders of thy sin-atoning blood? What angel shall be found competent to proclaim the wonders of the Father's love, in giving thee for poor sinners? What archangel to write down the wonders of thy love, in undertaking and accomplishing redemption? And who but God the Spirit can manifest both in the height, and depth, and breadth, and length, of a love that passeth knowledge? Is there, my soul, a wonder yet, that, as it concerns thee, and thine interest in him, whose name is wonderful, is still more marvellous to thy view? Yes, Oh thou wonderful Lord, for sure all wonders seem lost in the contemplation compared to that, that Jesus should look on me in my lost, ruined, and undone estate; for his mercy endureth for ever. Well might Jesus say, "Behold, I and the children whom thou hast given me, are for signs and wonders!" Isa. viii. 18. Well might the Lord, concerning Jesus and his people, declare them to be as men wondered at. Zech. iii. 8. And blessed Lord, the more love thou hast shewn to thy people, the more are they the world's wonder and their own. Precious Lord, continue to suprise my soul with the tokens of thy love. All the tendencies of thy grace, all the manifestations of thy favour, thy visits, thy love-tokens, thy pardons, thy renewings, thy morning-call, thy mid-day feedings, thy noon, thy evening, thy midnight grace—all, all are among thy wonderful ways of salvation; and all testify to my soul, that thy name, as well as thy work, is, and must be, wonderful.

EVENING.—" For by one offering, he hath perfected for ever them that are sanctified."—Heb. x. 14.

I hope, my soul, thou hast still upon thee the sweet savour of his name, whom in the *morning* portion thou didst contemplate as wonderful. And if so, here is another view of Jesus, presented to thine *evening* meditation, to keep alive the blessed fragrancy, and under the Spirit's influence, to preserve both, not only through the night, but to the morning; and every night, and every morning that follows, until the night of death be passed, and that everlasting morning break in upon thee, in which thy sun shall no more go down, but Jesus himself be thine everlasting light, and thy God thy glory. Look, my soul, this evening, at thy Jesus, as this sweet scripture sets him forth, and behold him, in his high priestly office, at once the sacrifice, the sacrificer, and the altar, on which he hath offered up that one offering, by which he " hath perfected for ever them that are sanctified." And mark both the preciousness of thy Jesus, and the preciousness of his work. It is but *one* offering, and that one but once offered. For, from its eternal value and efficacy, an everlasting perfection is given to all them that are sanctified, and set apart for himself. "For Christ (as the apostle in his delightful manner expresseth it) being raised from the dead, dieth no more: death hath no more dominion over him. For in that he died, he died unto sin once; but in that he liveth, he liveth unto God," Rom. vi. 9, 10. And what abundant precious things are contained in this view of the one offering of the Lord Jesus, which the Holy Ghost is continually holding forth to the church! It is blessed to behold them, blessed to believe them, and doubly blessed to be living in the constant enjoyment of them. So vast and comprehensive is this one offering of Jesus, that it hath not merely procured the hopes of pardon, but the certainty of it; not only brought poor sinners into a capability of being saved, but absolutely saved them; and not only saved them, but qualified them for happiness: yea, "hath perfected, and that for ever, them that are sanctified." And who are they? Surely all are sanctified who were set apart from everlasting, in the council of peace, between the persons of the Godhead, and given unto the Son, in an everlasting covenant, that cannot be broken: for to this purport are those blessed words of Jesus himself, in his prayer to his Father, John xvii. 2. "That I should give eternal life to as many as thou hast given me." And, my soul, take one observation more, from this sweet scripture; this perfection, given to his people, by his one offering, is *for ever;* "he hath perfected for ever them that are sanctified." So that the blessing runs through all eternity. The efficacy of Jesus's blood and righteousness is eternally the same. In point of merit, it blows as fresh and pure, and sovereign, in its pleadings now, as ever. Hallelujah! Fold up, my soul, this blessed verse, in thy bosom, and carry it about with thee in thine heart. Let it be among the first and last of thy thoughts, when thou liest down, and when thou risest up. Jesus will own it, and prove it to the full, when thou bringest it before his throne.

MARCH 2.

MORNING. — "For if there be first a willing mind, it is accepted according to that a man hath, and not according to that he hath not."— 2 Cor. viii. 12.

Sweet thought this to comfort the soul under small attainments, "If there be first a willing mind." Surely, Lord, thou hast given me this; for thou hast made me willing in the day of thy power. I feel as such, my soul going forth in desires after thee, as my chief and only good; though, alas! how continually do I fall short of the enjoyment of thee. I can truly say, "whom is there in heaven, or upon earth, that I desire in comparison of thee?" When thou art present, I am at once in heaven; it makes a very heaven in my soul: thou art the God of my exceeding joy. When thou art absent my soul pines after thee. And truly, "I count all things but dung and dross to win thee;" for whatever gifts thou hast graciously bestowed upon me, in the kindness of friends, in the affections and charities of life, yet all these are secondary considerations with my soul. They are more or less lovely, as I see thy gracious hand in them; but all are nothing to my Lord. Is not this, dearest Jesus, a willing mind? Is it not made so in the day of thy power? But in the midst of this, though I feel this rooted desire in me after thee, yet how often is my heart wandering from thee. Though there is at the bottom of my heart a constant longing for thy presence, and the sweet visits of thy love; yet through the mass of unbelief, and the remains of indwelling corruption in my nature, which are keeping down the soul; how doth the day pass, and how often doth the enemy tempt me to question my interest in thee. Dearest Jesus! undertake for me. I do cry out, "When wilt thou come to me," though I am thus kept back from coming to thee? When wilt thou manifest thyself to my soul, and come over all these mountains of sin and unbelief, and fill me with a joy unspeakable and full of glory? And doth Jesus indeed accept from the willing mind, he hath himself given, according to what a man hath, and not according to what he hath not?—Doth my Redeemer behold, amidst the rubbish, the spark of grace he himself hath kindled? Will he despise the day of small things? No, he will not. It was said of thee, that "thou shouldest not break the bruised reed, neither quench the smoaking flax." Mine, indeed, is no more. But yet Jesus will bear up the one, and kindle the other, until he send forth judgment unto victory. Peace, then, my soul! weak as thou art in thyself, yet art thou strong in the Lord, and in the power of his might.

EVENING.—"The waters of Marah."—Exod. xv. 23.

My soul! let thine imagination take wing, and flee thou, this evening, beside "the waters of Marah;" and while thou sittest down by the stream, see whether thou wilt be able to gather some of the many improving lessons the Holy Ghost brings before the church, concerning that memorable transaction wrought there for Israel. We read in the history of that people, that they had just before sung the song of salvation, on the borders of the Red Sea, when Israel saw that great sight, themselves redeemed, and the enemy swallowed up; and they were now on their march toward the promised land. Three days they had travelled into the wilderness, and found no water; and when they came to Marah, though water was there in abundance, yet they could not drink of it, for it was bitter. In this situation they cried unto the Lord; and the Lord shewed the people a tree, which when cast into the waters made them sweet. Such are the outlines of the history. Pause, now, my soul, and see what improving reflections thou canst gather from it. The Lord thy God hath brought thee also out of spiritual Egypt, he hath led thee through a new and living way, even the red sea of Christ's blood; and thou hast begun thy song of salvation also, to God and the Lamb. But when, like Israel, he is bringing thee through the wilderness, where dispensations suited to a wilderness may be supposed to abound; how art thou manifesting thy faith and submission? Reader, what is your answer to such a question? Methinks I would hope better things of *you*, than I dare say of myself. But I too often find, when the waters of life are like the waters of Marah; when what I proposed for my comfort turns out to my sorrow, and I discover a worm in the very bud of some sweet flower I have been rearing up for myself with great care; I feel rebellion rising within. I blush even now in the recollection of how often I have been tempted to call in question the divine faithfulness, and, like Israel, have taken offence, at some little difficulty I have met with, which afterwards I have discovered, was purposely put there by the Lord himself, to manifest his watchfulness over me, and how sure my dependence upon him might have been placed. Reader! doth your heart find but too much correspondence to this state of mine? Let us both then do as Israel did, when at any time our waters are like the waters of Marah, cry unto the Lord. Let us put the cross of Jesus into the stream, be it what it may, (for that is the tree which the Lord sheweth his people,) and never doubt, but Jesus's cross, though to him more bitter than gall, yet to us will prove the sweetener of all our crosses. Yes! thou dear Lord! thou didst drink the cup of trembling even to the dregs, that in the view of it, thy redeemed might take the cup of salvation, and call upon the name of the Lord. Thy cross, if cast into a sea of trouble, will alter the very properties of affliction to all thy tried ones. In every place, and in every state, while my soul is enabled to keep thee in remembrance, and " thy wormwood, and thy gall;" the wilderness of all my dispensations will smile, and blossom as the rose. I shall then learn to bless a taking God, as well as a giving God, for both are alike from the overflowings of thy mercy; and, like the apostle, I shall then have learnt the blessedness of that state, " to glory in tribulation, that the power of Christ may rest upon me."

MARCH 3.

MORNING.—" That ye may be able to comprehend with all saints, what is the breadth, and length, and depth, and height; and to know the love of Christ, which passeth knowledge."—Eph. iii. 18, 19.

Did Paul pray that the church might be thus blessed? So should all faithful pastors. And there is enough in Jesus to call up the everlasting contemplation of his people. All the dimensions of divine glory are in Jesus. Who, indeed, shall describe the extent of that love which passeth knowledge? But, my soul, pause over the account. What is the breadth of it? Jesus's death reaches in efficacy to all his seed—all his children: to thee, my soul; for thou art the seed of Jesus. And though that death took place at Jerusalem near two thousand years since, yet the efficacy of his blood, as from an high altar, as effectually washes away sin now, as in the moment it was shed. Remember, Jesus still wears the vesture dipped in blood. Remember, Jesus still appears as the Lamb slain before God. Indeed, indeed, Jesus was the Lamb slain from the foundation of the world. So that, in *breadth*, it is broader than the sea, taking in all the seed of Jesus, through all ages, all dispensations, all the various orders of his people. Neither is the *length* of it less proportioned. Who shall circumscribe the Father's love, which is from everlasting to everlasting? Who shall limit Jesus's grace? Is he not made of God, wisdom, righteousness, sanctification, and redemption? Is he not all this, in every office, every character, every relation? " Jesus Christ; the same yesterday, and to-day, and for ever!" And what is the *depth* of this love, but reaching down to hell, to lift up our poor fallen nature. And what is the *height*, but Jesus in our nature, exalted far above all principalities, and powers, and might, and dominion, and every name that is named, not only in this world, but also in that which is to come! Precious God of my salvation! Oh, give me to see, to know, to entertain, and cherish, more enlarged views of this love; which hath no bottom, no bounds, no shore; but, like its Almighty Author, is from everlasting to everlasting. Shall I ever despond? Shall I ever doubt any more, when this Jesus looks upon me, loves me, washes me in his blood, feeds me, clothes me, and hath promised to bring me to glory? Oh, for faith " to comprehend, with all saints, this love of God which passeth knowledge."

EVENING.—" Wherefore the rather, brethren, give diligence to make your calling and election sure: for if ye do these things, ye shall never fall: for so an entrance shall be ministered unto you abundantly, into the everlasting kingdom of our Lord and Saviour Jesus Christ."—2 Pet. i. 10, 11.

What a very affectionate advice is here given by the apostle; and surely as important as it is tender! Sit down, my soul, this evening, and ponder these words of Peter. The apostle saith, and saith it with great clearness of reason, as well as revelation, that an assurance of being a partaker of grace in this life, becomes as sure and certain an evidence of being made a partaker of glory in another.—The question then is, how shall I ascertain, and without the shadow of a doubt, the certainty of my calling and election? Shall I look into the book of life, to see my name there? That is impossible.

"Secret things belong unto the Lord our God; but those that are revealed belong unto us, and unto our children, for ever." Is there nothing revealed on this important point in the scriptures of truth? Yes. The apostle to the Romans, was commissioned to tell the church, that whom God the Father did predestinate to be conformed to the image of his Son, "them he also called: and whom he called, them he also justified: and whom he justified, them he also glorified," Rom. viii. 29, 30. Hence, therefore, it must plainly and undeniably follow, that where a soul can fully prove his having been *called*, his *election* is included in the discovery; for the one is the result and consequence of the other. If I see a stream of water flowing, there must be a source whence it comes, though the fountain itself be out of sight. The fruit of any tree will of itself ascertain the nature and quality of the tree whence it was gathered, whether the tree be seen or not. And if, my soul, thou possessest clear and unquestionable tokens of thy being called by grace, in the true scriptural evidences which the Holy Ghost hath there marked concerning it, thine election will as plainly be implied. See then if this be thy case. If thou hast a conviction of sin, of righteousness, and of judgment; if a sense of thy transgressions hath been so marked in thine heart, as to be followed with a sense of thy utterly lost and ruined state by nature, and a total inability on thy part to accomplish any thing towards thine own recovery; and if thou hast been led by the Holy Ghost, to the view of Jesus, as the only One mighty to save; and thou art come to him, with the awakened cry of the soul, "Lord, save, or I perish!" these are among the first and most striking testimonies of an effectual and saving call by grace. And therefore the *diligence* the apostle so strongly and affectionately recommends, is to look into thy evidences daily, and habitually to live in the enjoyment of them: so that from long and increasing acquaintance with them, all the great and glorious objects connected with our future and eternal state, may be made familiar to the soul. Stedfastly looking to the Lord Jesus by faith, and living by faith upon him, we may be daily growing up to him in all things: so that when life comes to be closed, and faith swallowed up in enjoyment, like a rich and deeply laden vessel in full sail, we may then have "an abundant entrance ministered unto us, into the everlasting kingdom of our Lord and Saviour Jesus Christ."

MARCH 4.

MORNING.—"How shall we sing the Lord's song in a strange land?" —Ps. cxxxvii. 4.

Methinks, my soul, this strange land is the very place to sing the Lord's song in, though the carnal around understand it not. Shall I hang my harp upon the willow, when Jesus is my song, and when he himself hath given me so much cause to sing? Begin, my soul, thy song of redemption: learn it, and let it be sung upon earth; for sure enough thou wilt have it to sing in heaven. Art thou at a loss what to sing? Oh, no. Sing of the Father's mercy in sending a Saviour. Sing of Jesus's love, in not only coming, but dying for thee! Are the redeemed above now singing, "Worthy is the Lamb that was slain?" Join in the chorus, and tell that dear Redeemer in the loudest notes, that he was slain, and hath redeemed *thee* to God by his blood. Strike up thy harp anew to the glories of redeeming grace, in that he not only died for thee, but hath quickened thee to a new and spiritual life. Add a note more to the Lord's song, and tell the Redeemer in thy song of praise, that he hath not only died for thee, and quickened thee, but he hath loved thee, and washed thee from thy sins in his own blood. Go on in thy song, my soul, for it is the Lord's song. Sing not only of redeeming love, but marvellous grace; for both are connected. He that redeemed thee, hath all grace for thee. He hath adopted thee into his family; hath made thee an heir of God, and a joint heir with Christ. He hath undertaken for thee in all troubles, under all difficulties, to be with thee at all times and all places, until he brings thee home to behold his glory, that where he is, there thou mayest be for ever. And are not these causes enough to keep thy harp always strung—always in tune? And wilt thou not sing this song all the way through, and make it the subject of thy continual praise and love, in the house of thy pilgrimage? Moreover, the several properties of the song are, in themselves, matter for keeping it alive every day, and all the day. Think, my soul, how free was this love of God to thee. Surely if a man deserved hell, and found heaven, shall he not sing? If I expected displeasure, and received love — if I was brought low, and one like the Son of Man helped me, shall I not say, as one of old did—"He brought me out of the horrible pit, and out of the miry clay; he hath put a new song into my mouth, even thanksgiving to our God?" If I think of the greatness of the mercy, of the riches of the mercy, of the sweetness of the mercy, of the all-sufficiency of the mercy, of the sureness and firmness, and everlasting nature and efficacy of the mercy — can I refrain to sing? No, blessed, blessed Jesus! I will sing and not be afraid; "for the Lord Jehovah is my strength and my song, and he is become my salvation." I will sing now, I will sing for evermore. In this strange land, in this barren land, in this distant land from my Father's house, I will sing, and Jesus shall be my song. He shall be the Alpha and the Omega of my hymn; and until I come to sing in the louder and sweeter notes of heaven, among the hallelujahs of the blessed, upon the new harp and new stringed chords of my renewed soul, will I sing of Jesus and his blood, Jesus and his righteousness, Jesus and his complete salvation. And when the last song upon my trembling lips, with Jesus's name in full, shall be uttered; as the sound dies away, when death seals up the power of utterance; my departing soul shall catch the parting breath, and, as it enters the presence of the court above, the first notes of my everlasting song will go on with the same blessed note, "to him that hath loved me, and washed me from my sins in his own blood!

EVENING.—"And she called the name of the Lord that spake unto her, thou God seest me: for she said, have I also here looked after him that seeth me? Wherefore the well was called Beer-lahai-roi."—Gen. xvi. 13, 14.

Behold, my soul, what very blessed instructions arise out of this scripture. Beg of God the Holy Ghost to make thy present evening meditation of it sweet. The words themselves are the reflection of Hagar, the handmaid of Sarah, when she fled from her mistress into the wilderness. In a situation of great distress, the Lord manifested himself to her, and the conclusion she drew from it, was, as is expressed, "thou, Lord, seest me." This indeed, was the name she gave unto the Lord, as if henceforth she would know the Lord in all his mercies by this name. Sweet thought! Jesus is known by his name; and in his name his grace is revealed. But Hagar added another delightful reflection, "for she said, have I also here looked after him that seeth me?" As if she had said, 'And hath the grace God looking upon me, wrought grace in me?' But the words may be read differently, and some indeed read them so: 'Have I looked for the Lord, when the Lord looked after me? Alas! I thought not of him, until that he called me by his grace.' Here is another delightful thought of Hagar's, and in perfect harmony with the gospel of Jesus. For "if we love God, it is because he first loved us." And there is another reflection, as interesting as either: "wherefore the well was called Beer-lahai-roi;" that is, "the well of him that liveth and looketh on." This became Hagar's memorial; as if she would for ever perpetuate the name of him that looked on and regarded her sorrow. This well, this place, this sacred spot, shall be Hagar's Bethel; it shall tell every one that passeth by, here the Lord wrought, and here he manifested grace to a poor handmaid. Precious scripture of a precious God! Who but must feel delight in beholding Hagar's faith? And who but must find cause to bless God, both for giving that faith, and affording so favourable an occasion for the exercise of it? And shall I not, and will not you, reader, gather some of the many delightful instructions from it, for our own use, which it is so highly calculated to bring? Did the angel of the Lord look on Hagar; and doth he not look on every child of his? Am I at any time looking after Jesus, and is not Jesus looking after me? Oh! what a volume of encouragement ariseth from this one view, to persevere in looking after him, and in waiting for him; that before I thought of him, or was looking after him, Jesus was both caring and looking upon me! It is impossible to be beforehand with God. Put down then, my soul, this conclusion from this blessed scripture, that in every place, in every state, upon every occasion, thy Jesus liveth, and looketh on. And do thou call the Lord by the same name as Hagar did, that speaketh to thee, in every place, and by every providence, "Thou God seest me." And never, never forget, when thou art hardest put to it, and art seeking Jesus sorrowing; though, to thy blind eye, he doth not so immediately appear; that he is still seeing, and following thee, even when thou art not seeking and following after him. Let this be in thy constant remembrance; and make every spot that is memorable, like the well Beer-lahai-roi, to draw water of salvation from; for in every one it is the well of him that liveth and looketh on. Precious Lord Jesus! henceforth grant me grace, that while thou art looking after me with love and favour, I may be looking unto thee with faith and praise. And through every step of my wilderness state, while going home to my Father's house, let this be my comfort, and the burden of my song in this house of my pilgrimage, "Thou God seest me!"

MARCH 5.

MORNING.—"Faint, yet pursuing."—Judges viii. 4.

Surely what is said here concerning the little army of Gideon, suits my case exactly. I know that in Jesus the victory is certain; but I know also, that I shall have battlings all the way. From the moment that the Lord called me out of darkness into his marvellous light, my whole life hath been but a state of warfare; and I feel what Paul felt, and groan as he groaned, under a body of sin and death; "as sorrowful, yet rejoicing; as dying, but behold I live; as chastened, and not killed." Truly I am faint, under the many heavy assaults I have sustained; and yet, through grace, pursuing as if I had met with no difficulty. Yes, blessed Jesus; I know that there can be no truce in this war; and looking unto thee, I pray to be found faithful unto death, that no man may take my crown. But, dearest Lord! thou seest my day of small things; thou beholdest how faint I am. Thou seest also, how the enemy assaults me! and how the world and the flesh combat against me. While without are fightings, within will be fears. Yet, dearest, blessed Lord, "in the Lord I have strength;" and how sweet is the thought, that though I have nothing, though I am nothing, yet thou hast said, "in me is thy help." Thou hast said, "the righteous shall hold on his way; and he that hath clean hands shall wax stronger and stronger." The worm Jacob thou hast promised shall thresh the mountains. Write these blessed things, my soul, upon the living tablets of thine heart, or rather beg of God the Holy

Ghost, the remembrancer of thy Jesus, to stamp them there for thee. " He giveth power to the faint; and to them which have no might, he increaseth strength. Even the youths shall faint and be weary; and the young men shall utterly fail. But they that wait upon the Lord shall renew their strength; they shall mount up with wings, as eagles; they shall run, and not be weary; and they shall walk, and not faint."

EVENING.—" Having begun in the Spirit, are ye now made perfect by the flesh?"—Gal. iii. 3.

While beholding the church of Galatia, which set out upon true gospel principles, and before whose eyes Jesus Christ had been evidently set forth as crucified among them; yet after this, turning aside to seek justification by works; let thine evening meditation, my soul, be directed to this heart-searching inquiry: upon what art *thou* building thine hopes of salvation? Is it simply on Christ; or art thou mingling with the blood and righteousness of Jesus, somewhat of thine own, by way of justification? The question is exceedingly important; and the clear answer to it, of the first consequence to thy present peace, and everlasting welfare. See to it then, that there be no reserves, no limitations, nothing to qualify the plain and direct answer to the apostle's words; but that having begun in the Spirit, thou mayest truly say, thou dost not seek to be made perfect by the flesh. If this be thy case, thou hast learned to make a nice, but highly proper distinction between the great object of faith, which is Christ alone, and the fruits and effects of that faith, which are the gracious influences that Jesus, by his Holy Spirit, hath wrought in thine heart. It is very blessed, very desirable, to let the world, both of saints and of sinners, see our light so shine before them, that it may be not the subject of doubt, whose we are, and whom we serve. But, if any attainments, which, by grace, my soul is blessed with, be made a part saviour in my views of justification; and I am not looking wholly to Jesus for this great work, as wrought out and completed by him; certain it is, that however I might begin in the Spirit, I am now turning aside to the flesh. Moreover, besides the motley religion I am thus taking up with, if what I feel, and what I enjoy in the *fruits* and *effects* of faith, be made a part of my hopes and confidence; alas! when those feelings, and those enjoyments at any time abate, my hopes and confidence will abate also. And if justification be made a fluctuating principle, is it not plain, that I shall be void of comfort, when I most want it? And is it not, from this very cause, that so many precious souls go in leanness all their days, sometimes feeling hope, but for the most part, exercised with doubts and fears, according to what they *feel*, and not what *Jesus is* in their view; and because in themselves, they are looking for somewhat that may give a greater confidence in Christ? Pause, my soul, and inquire how the case stands with thyself: is Jesus the whole, in the way of a sinner's justification before God? Is he the Alpha and the Omega also? Dost thou regard him as both the Author and the Finisher of salvation? Is he the first and the last; and dost thou venture thine everlasting *all* upon Jesus? Pause once more, and then say, what are thy views in this distinction between the works of the Spirit and of the flesh? Hast thou so learned Christ?

MARCH 6.

MORNING.—"And every one that was in distress, and every one that was in debt, and every one that was discontented, gathered themselves unto him, and he became a captain over them."—1 Sam. xxii. 2.

My soul, was not this thy case when thou first sought after Jesus? Thou wert, indeed, in debt under an heavy load of insolvency. Distress and discontent sadly marked thy whole frame. Unconscious where to go, or to whom to seek, and no man cared for thy soul.

Oh! what a precious thought it was, and which none but God the Holy Ghost could have put into thine heart—Go unto Jesus! And when I came, and thou didst graciously condescend to be my captain, from that hour how hath my soul been revived! My insolvency thou hast taken away; for thou hast more than paid the whole demands of the law; for thou hast magnified it, and made it honourable. My distress under the apprehension of divine justice thou hast removed; for God's justice, by thee, is not only satisfied, but glorified. My discontent can have no further cause for exercise, since thou hast so graciously provided for all my wants, in grace here, and glory hereafter. Hail, thou great and glorious Captain of my salvation! In thee I see that Leader and Commander which Jehovah, thy Father, promised to give to the people. Thou art indeed, blessed Jesus, truly commissioned by thy Father to this very purpose, that every one that is in soul-distress, by reason of sin, and debtors to the broken law of God, may come unto thee, and take thee for their Captain. And truly, Lord, thy little army, like David's, is composed of none originally but distressed souls. None would take thee for his Captain, whose spiritual circumstances are not desperate. None but the man whose heart hath felt distress, by reason of sin, and is sinking under the heavy load of guilt, will come under thy banner. Oh! the condescension of Jesus to receive such, and be gracious unto them. Oh! that I had the power of persuasion, I would say to every poor sinner, every insolvent debtor, every one who feels and knows the plague of his heart—would to God you were with the Captain of my salvation, he would recover you from all your sorrow. Go to him, my brother, as I have done; he will take away your distress by taking away your sin. He will liberate you from all your debt by paying it himself. He will banish all discontent from the mind, in giving you peace with God by his blood. Yes, blessed, Almighty Captain! thou art indeed *over* thy people, as well as Captain to thy people. By the sword of thy Spirit, which is the word of God, thou workest conviction in our hearts; thou makest all thine enemies fall under thee; thou leadest thy people on to victory, and makest them more than conquerors through thy grace supporting them. Lord, put on the military garments of salvation on my soul, and the whole armour of God, that under thy banner I may be found in life, in death, and for evermore!

EVENING.—"She bare a son, and called his name Samuel, saying, because I have asked him of the Lord."—1 Sam. i. 20.

It is really both blessed and profitable to observe, how holy men of old made memorandums of the Lord's kind dealings with them, as well in providence as grace, by way of preserving alive a due sense of divine mercies upon their souls. A night or two since, the evening portion remarked a beautiful instance of this sort in the case of Hagar: and in the scripture I have brought forth for our present meditation, is another, equally beautiful in the instance of Hannah. In the former, the memorial was set up to perpetuate the *place* of the Lord's graciousness; in this latter, the dedication is of the *person* concerning whom divine favour was shewn. But in both, the design is one and the same, to glorify God. I pause by the way, to remark, how much to be lamented it is, that this truly scriptural and pious custom is so little followed by christians, and even believing christians too in the present hour. What a number of unscriptural, and frequently heathenish names, are now given to children of parents professing the great truths of the gospel? Whereas, with those early followers of the Lord, they called their children by somewhat that should be always significant of divine mercies. So that, whenever their children were at any time called upon, or looked to, the very name might bring to remembrance past blessings, and refresh their souls in the recollection of the mercies which occasioned them. This instance of Hannah is beautifully in point, by way of illustration: she called him Samuel, which signifies, "asked of the Lord." For we find in her history, with what earnestness she sought a child from the Lord. Hence, therefore, we may suppose, upon numberless occasions, in after-days, whenever she heard her Samuel mentioned, or she called him herself, the soul of Hannah went forth in faith, and love, and praise, to the Author and Giver of this blessing. And it is but reasonable to suppose, that if the name reminded the mother of her mercy, and she called her son by this name purposely, that she might remember the Lord in his bounty; no doubt, she was not forgetful to instruct her Samuel also in the same thing. We may, indeed, conclude that Hannah betimes made Samuel acquainted with the cause of his name. And from the sequel of the prophet's history, we find that he who was a child of prayer, and asked of the Lord, was a servant to his praise, and given to the Lord. Reader! methinks it is blessed, it is gracious, and sure I am it is right, thus to keep up intercourse with heaven. You and I have our Samuels; I mean our *asked blessings*, whether in children, or in other providences. Oh! for grace, while receiving mercies, to make those mercies the memorandums of the great Giver! If what we ask *from* God in prayer, we give back again *to* God in praise, and in the stream of creature enjoyments, find a tenfold relish in them, from living upon the Creator fulness; then we shall find cause to call many a blessing Samuel, because "it hath been asked," and often given unasked, *of the Lord.*

MARCH 7.

MORNING.—"They shall hunger no more."—Rev. vii. 16.

My soul! contemplate for a moment, before thou enterest upon the concerns of time and sense, in the claims of the world, the blessed state of the redeemed above. They are at the fountain-head of happiness, in their station, in their service, in their society, in their provision, in their everlasting exemption from all want, and above all, in the presence of God and the Lamb. "They shall hunger no more." Sweet thought! Let me this day anticipate as many of the blessed properties of it as my present state in Jesus will admit. If Jesus be my home, my residence, my dwelling-place, will not the hungerings of my soul find supply? Yes, surely. A life of faith on the Son of God, is a satisfying life, under all the changes of the world around. Finding Jesus, I find sustenance in him, and therefore do not hunger for ought besides him. "Thou art my hiding-place," said one of old; and my soul finds occasion to adopt the same language. And He that is my hiding-place, is also my food and my nourishment. In Jesus there is both food and a fence; there is fruit, as well as a shadow; and the fulness of Jesus needs vent in the wants of his people, for the pouring forth of his all-sufficiency. My soul, cherish this thought to the full. If thy hunger be really for Jesus, and him only, then will thy hunger be abundantly supplied in his communication. As long as I look at my wants, without an eye to Jesus, I shall be miserable. But if I consider those wants and that emptiness purposely appointed for the pouring out of his fulness, they will appear as made for the cause of happiness. Jesus keeps up the hungering, that he may have the blessedness of supplying them; he keeps his children empty that he may fill them, and that his fulness may be in request among them. So far, therefore, is my hungering from becoming a source of sorrow, it furnisheth out a source of holy joy. I should never be straitened in myself, when I am not straitened in Jesus. Nay, it would be a sad token of distance from Jesus if a sense of want was lessened. While, on the other hand, the best proof I can have of nearness to Jesus, and living upon him, is, when my enjoyment of Jesus discovers new and increasing wants, and excites an holy hungering for his supplying them. By and by I shall get home, and then at the fountain head of rapture and delight, all hungering and wants will be done away, in the full and everlasting enjoyment of God and the Lamb!

EVENING.—"Because she judged him faithful who had promised." —Heb. xi. 11.

I admire what the Holy Ghost hath here recorded of Sarah's faith. After what we read of the weakness of her faith at first, in the history to which this refers, I cannot but rejoice in the recovery of the great mother in Israel, through grace; and read with very much pleasure, this honourable testimony, which the Holy Ghost himself hath given of her. And I admire yet more, the grace and goodness of the Eternal Spirit, in causing it to be handed down to the church, among the list of such worthies, and desire to bless his holy name for this scripture. And while I bless God for the memorial, I pray him to give me a spirit of wisdom, to improve it to my own furtherance in faith. The faith of Sarah, like that of her husband's, was the more illustrious, from the seeming impossibilities which lay in the way of the accomplishment of God's promise. For what the Lord engaged to do, was contrary to the whole course of nature. But what was that to Sarah? All she had to do, was to consider the promise; and keep an eye upon the Almighty Promiser. 'If there are difficulties in the way, that is God's business, and not mine,' might Sarah say. 'How the Lord will bring it to pass, is with him, and not with me: I have no concern with that. My province is to believe; it is God's to work.' Here was an act of illustrious faith! and the sequel of Sarah's history, shews how well founded it was. But the Holy Ghost explains the subject, and shews how it was accomplished; "because she judged him faithful who had promised." Now, my soul, see to it, that thou make the same grand cause the foundation of thy faith; namely, Jehovah's faithfulness; and, depend upon it, every promise of the gospel, even Jesus, with all his fulness, thou mayest, as well as Sarah, rely upon; and thou wilt be always able to do it, as long as thou makest the same perfection of Jehovah thy confidence: "because she judged him faithful that promised." While I rest upon his faithfulness, I rest upon the Rock of Ages, which can never give way: and every difficulty, or seeming impossibility, which comes between the promise of a faithful God, and the accomplishment of that promise, hath no more to do with the thing itself, than the tide hath with unsettling the rock; but will, like the tide, soon ebb, and withdraw, and leave the ground dry. Oh! the blessedness of judging Him faithful, who hath promised.

MARCH 8.

MORNING.—"From this day will I bless thee."—Hag. ii. 19.

My soul, what day is the memorable day to thee from whence commenced thy blessings? No doubt from everlasting the Lord hath blessed his people in Jesus. But the commencement of thy personal enjoyment of those blessings, was at the time the Lord graciously laid the foundation of his spiritual temple in thee; the blessed, the gracious, the auspicious, the happy day, when the Lord made thee willing in the day of his power? Oh! blessed day, never, never to be forgotten! A day of light; when the light of Jesus first broke in upon me. A day of life; when the Lord Jesus quickened my poor soul, which before was laying dead in trespasses and sins. A day of love; when his love first was made known to my soul, who so loved me as to give his dear and ever-blessed Son for me: and his love was sweetly manifested, who so loved me as to give himself for me. A day of the beginning of victory, over death and hell, and the grave. A day of liberty; when the Lord Jesus opened my prison doors and brought me out. A day of wonder, love and praise; when my eyes first saw the King in his beauty, and my whole soul was overpowered in the contemplation of the grace, the glory, the beauty, the loveliness, the suitableness, the all-sufficiency of his glorious Person and glorious work. A day, Oh what dear name shall I term it to be? A day of grace, a jubilee, a salvation day! the day of my espousals to Jesus, and of the gladness of my Redeemer's heart! And, my soul, did thy God, did thy Jesus say, that from that day he would bless thee? And hath he not done it? Oh, yes, yes; beyond all conception of blessing. He hath blessed thee in thy basket and thy store. All the blessings, even in temporal mercies, which were all forfeited in Adam, are now sweetly restored, and blessed, and sanctified, in Jesus: nay, even thy very crosses have the curse taken out of them by thy Jesus; and thy very tears have the spiced wine of the pomegranate. And as to spiritual blessings, God thy Father hath blessed thee with all in his dear Son. Thy Father hath made over himself, in Jesus, with all his love and favour. And Jesus is thine, with all his fulness, sweetness, all-sufficiency. And God the Spirit, with all his gracious influences and comforts. And the present enjoyment of these unspeakable mercies becomes the sure earnest of blessings which are eternal. Jesus himself hath declared, that it is the Father's own gracious will that he should give eternal life to as many as the Father hath given him; and therefore eternal life must be the sure portion of all his redeemed. "He that believeth in the Son hath indeed everlasting life; and Jesus will raise him up at the last day." Pause, my soul, and view the vast heritage to which thou art begotten from the day of thy new birth in Jesus, Oh! most gracious Father, let me never lose sight of those sweet words, nor the feeling sense of my interest in them, in which thou hast said, "From this day will I bless thee."

EVENING.—"A psalm of David to bring to remembrance."—Ps. xxxviii. in the title.

This psalm, as well as the seventieth, is particularly marked in the title, and distinguished from every other; and it will be worth while to seek into the cause. A great light will be thrown upon it, if we connect with this title, the character of the great author, under whose inspiration David, as the penman, wrote it: I mean, that sweet and blessed office of the Holy Ghost, the Remembrancer of the Lord Jesus. "He shall teach you" (saith the Lord Jesus, when describing the blessed Spirit in his offices) "all things, and bring all things to your remembrance, whatsoever I have said unto you:" John xiv. 26. Now, if this psalm be found, on examination, to be speaking much of the person and character of Christ, ought it not, when read under the divine teaching of its Almighty Author, to act as a psalm to bring to remembrance, how Jesus thus suffered, thus groaned, bled, and died for his people? He it was, as this psalm represents, whose lovers and friends stood aloof from him, in his sorrows; for in the trying hour, all his disciples forsook him and fled: and he was the only person of whom it could be said, that as a deaf man who heard not, and as a dumb man who opened not his mouth, so Jesus stood, as a lamb before her shearers, when in the hall of Pilate, he was accused and condemned without opening his mouth. If then the great design of this psalm is to bring to remembrance the Redeemer, in those solemn seasons; shall we make application of the contents of it to David, king of Israel, and overlook David's Lord? Oh! thou great and divine Remembrancer of the Lord Jesus! I beseech thee, thou matchless Instructor! to cause every thing, and every incident, to call my poor forgetful heart to remember its

Lord! Lord, I blush to think how men of the world feel interested in the most minute concerns of the histories of any characters of supposed eminence, which in former ages have lived among them; every memorandum of them that can be gathered, is treasured up with more avidity than gold: if a letter, or the hand-writing can be found, how they expressed themselves, or how their hours were engaged, with all, or any of the little events which marked their lives; Oh! what attention it gains in the world! But, as if to shew their indifference to him, who, strictly speaking, is the only one worthy regard, what heart is alive to the ever blessed Jesus? Do thou, I beseech thee, thou eternal Spirit, in this gracious office of thine, as the Remembrancer of my Lord, make this psalm, as oft as I read it, a psalm to bring Jesus to remembrance in all his endearments: and also cause all thy sacred word to minister to this one great end! Here let me learn a lesson from men of the world; and while they feel rapture in the memorandums and reliques of poor sinners, whose places know them no more; let my soul delight in the views his sacred word affords concerning Jesus. ‘Thus Jesus spake,’ I would say: and ‘thus he stood;’ and ‘thus he was encircled by the astonished multitude, who witnessed the gracious words which proceeded out of his mouth.’ Every incident then in his divine life, will be as a psalm to bring to remembrance; and I shall enjoy a thousand things, when the Holy Ghost, as his Remembrancer, brings them forth to view, which, without his gracious office and word, would be lost to my poor forgetful mind.

MARCH 9.

MORNING.—“But now in Christ Jesus, ye, who sometimes were afar off, are made nigh by the blood of Christ.”—Eph. ii. 13.

Of all the vast alterations made upon our nature

by grace, that which is from death to life seems to be the greatest. I do not think the change would be as great, if Jesus were to make a child of God, after his conversion, at once an archangel, as when, by his blessed Spirit he quickens the sinner, dead in trespasses and sins, and brings him into grace. My soul, contemplate the sweet thought this morning, that it may lead thee, with thy hymn of praise, to all precious Jesus! First then, my soul, think where you then stood, before this vast act of grace had quickened you. You stood on the very confines of hell—unawakened, unregenerate, uncalled, without God, and without Christ. Supposing the Lord had not saved you; supposing a sickness unto death had, by his command, taken you; supposing that any one cause had been commissioned to sign your death-warrant while in this state; where must have been your portion? And yet consider, my soul, how many nights and days did yuo live in this unconscious, unconcerned state? Oh! who, in this view of the thought, can look back without having the eye brimful of tears, and the heart bursting with love and thankfulness! Go on, my soul, and contemplate the subject in another point of view; and pause in the pleasing thought, "where you now stand." You are now, saith the apostle, "made nigh by the blood of Christ." You that was an enemy to God by wicked works, yet now hath he reconciled in the body of his flesh, through death, to present you holy, and unblamable, and unreprovable, in his sight. And now, my soul, if death should come, it is but the messenger to glory. Precious, blessed thought! And Oh, how much more precious, blessed Jesus, the Author of it! Advance, my soul, one step more in this sweet subject, and pleasingly consider, where you soon shall be. Paul answereth; "So shall we be ever with the Lord." "Ever with the Lord!" Who can write down the full amount of this blessedness? "Ever with the Lord!" Here we are, in Jesus, interested in all that belongs to Jesus; but there, we shall be also with Jesus. Here we see him but as through a glass darkly; but there, face to face. Here, even the views we have of him by faith, are but glimpses only—short and rare, compared to our desires; but there, we shall see him in reality, in substance, and unceasingly, the precious, glorious, God-man Christ Jesus. Here, our sins, though pardoned, yet dim our view, by reason of their effects; there, we shall for ever have lost them, and see, and know, even as we are known. And have these blessed changes taken place in my soul; and all by thee, thou gracious, precious, Holy One of Israel? Oh for grace to love thee, to live to thee, to be looking out for thee, dearest Jesus, that I may be counting every parting breath, every beating pulse, as one the less, to bring me nearer and nearer to Jesus, who is my everlasting home, and will ere long, be my never-ceasing portion and happiness in eternity.—Hallelujah!

EVENING.—" The pool of Siloam."—John ix. 7.

It was a very gracious account given by the Holy Ghost, in the writings of his servants the prophets, that in the last days, meaning gospel days, " living waters should go forth of Jerusalem;" and saith the Lord, " it shall come to pass, that every thing that liveth which moveth, whithersoever the river shall come, shall live;" Ezek. xlvii. 9. And in the day of Christ's flesh, we find Jesus giving life wheresoever he came: and not unfrequently, as if to testify the sovereignty of his power, he communicated his blessing in this life-giving principle of himself, by means altogether, to outward view, unpromising. The clay applied to the eyes of one born blind, and the pool of Siloam, are both directly in point. It is just so, blessed Jesus, that I would have recourse to ordinances and means of grace, and when I attend, I would desire to pass over them to the enjoyment of thyself, and the gracious influences of thy Holy Spirit. Were the pool of Siloam always thus attended, and the several maladies of thy people thus brought before thee, that while using the means, we had an eye to the end, how should we find the diseased that were sent, returning healed. The imagination can hardly conceive any thing more interesting, than to behold souls under their different distresses, thus coming to the pool of Siloam, and thus receiving Jesus in the use of it. Am I faint? "He giveth power to the faint, and to them that have no might, he increaseth strength." Is another walking in darkness and having no light? Jesus saith, "I am the light of the world: he that followeth me shall not walk in darkness." Are our bones dried, like the bones in the valley, "and our hope lost: are we cut off for our parts?" (Ezek. xxxvii. 11.) Behold, saith the Lord God, "I will open your graves, O my people, and cause you to come up out of your graves." And how doth the Lord accomplish it? He saith, "I am the resurrection and the life; he that believeth in me, though he were dead, yet shall he live; and he that liveth and believeth in me shall never die." Are they void of faith? Jesus is the Author and giver of faith. Are they backward to repentance? Jesus is exalted as a Prince and a Saviour, to give repentance to Israel, and remission of sins." Have they backslidden? Jesus saith, "I will heal their backsliding, I will love them freely." In short, at the pool of Siloam, neither the water nor the clay are the objects of faith, but he that sends to the pool: and while we lay our wants over against his fulness, and consider, in our need, the very suitability there is in that need for the display of Christ's grace in the supply, this is the very way of following up the divine appointments. And as every poor sinner is made blessed in receiving from Jesus: so Jesus is made glorious in giving out of his fulness; and the gracious purpose of salvation is answered in the comfort of the sinner, the glory of the Saviour, and the everlasting praise of Jehovah, in the wonders of redemption! My soul! let thine evening meditation be thus sweet in viewing the pool of Siloam!

MARCH 10.

MORNING.—" And hast feared continually every day because of the fury of the oppressor, as if he were ready to destroy; and where is the fury of the oppressor?"—Isa. li. 13.

Pause, my soul, over those sweet expostulating words of thy God. Wherefore should the fear of man bring a snare? How much needless anxiety should I spare myself, could I but live, amidst all my changeable days and changeable circumstances, upon my unchangeable God. Now, mark what thy God saith of thy unreasonable and ill-grounded fears—" Where is the fury of the oppressor?" Can he take from thee thy Jesus? No! Shouldest thou lose all thy earthly comforts, Jesus ever liveth, and Jesus is thine. Can he afflict thee, if God saith no? That is impossible. Neither men nor devils can oppress without his permission. And sure enough thou art, thy God and Saviour will never allow any thing to thy hurt; for all things must work for good. And canst thou lessen the oppressor's fury by anxious fears? Certainly not. Thou mayest, my soul, harrass thyself and waste thy spirits, but never lessen the fury of the enemy thereby. And wherefore, then, shouldest thou crowd the uncertain evils, and the *may be's* of to-morrow, in the circumstances of this day's warfare, when, by only waiting for the morrow, and casting all thy care upon Jesus, who careth for thee, his faithfulness is engaged to be thy shield and buckler? Peace then, my soul, thou shalt be carried through this oppression, as sure as thou hast been through every former; for Jesus is still Jesus, thy God, and will be thy guide even unto death.

EVENING.—"*If one man sin against another, the judge shall judge him. But if a man sin against the Lord, who shall intreat for him?*"—1 Sam. ii. 25.

It is a very solemn thing to behold a trembling convicted malefactor, when standing before an earthly tribunal, although the judge is of the same nature with himself: for every thing is solemn, earnest, and impartial. But what is the awfulness of a court of human judicature, compared to that day, in which a whole world, all found guilty before God, shall stand before the judgment-seat of Christ? In this life, there is, for the most part, somewhat to mitigate, and to excite hope in the worst of cases: some tender-hearted friend, some kind neighbour, some feeling relation, will be found to arise, to soften, if not able to relieve, the guilty man's distress. But at that tribunal, where none can plead, and where all hearts are open, what shall be found to stop the overwhelming horrors of the condemned?—Pause, my soul, over the view, for it is solemn. If one man sin against another, thus breaking the law, the judge shall judge him; and who is the judge but Jesus? Here he that is the Judge, is also the Advocate of his people; yea, their surety, their law-fulfiller; so that, as the apostle was commissioned to tell the church, "If any man sin, we have an advocate with the Father, Jesus Christ the righteous; and he is the propitiation for our sins," 1 John ii. 1, 2. Precious thought! soul-supporting consolation! To all the sins and offences, both against God and man, the believer may plead the blood and righteousness of Jesus, as the law-fulfiller and ransom paid for sin. But if a man sin against the Lord himself, by rejecting this counsel of God against his own soul, who then shall entreat for him? For the only advocate, he slights; the only propitiation, he disclaims; and as there is salvation in no other, and there remaineth no more sacrifice for sin, to whom, in that awful day of God, will he look; or who but Jesus could take up his cause? Oh! ye that know not Christ, or ye that slight him, think, before it be too late, what paleness, dread, and horror, must arrest that soul, which, when weighed in the balances, shall be found wanting! Cherish, my soul, the blessedness of thy hope, which is founded wholly on the Mediator's righteousness; and resteth on what can never fail of acceptance, because founded both on the merit of Christ, and God the Father's own appointment; redemption in the blood of the Lamb, and being made accepted in the beloved.

MARCH 11.

MORNING.—"And behold, there came a leper and worshipped him, saying, Lord! if thou wilt, thou canst make me clean. And Jesus put forth his hand and touched him, saying, I will; be thou clean. And immediately his leprosy was cleansed."—Matt. viii. 2, 3.

Behold, my soul, in the instance of this leper, thine own circumstances. What he was in body, such wert thou in soul. As his leprosy made him loathsome and offensive before men, so thy polluted soul made thee odious in the sight of God! He would not have sought a cure, had he not been conscious of his need of it. Neither wouldest thou ever have looked to Jesus, had he not convinced thee of thy helplessness and misery without him. Moreover, he would not, though convinced how much he needed healing, have sought that mercy from Jesus, had he not been made sensible of Jesus's ability to the cure. Neither wouldest thou ever have come to Jesus, hadst thou not been taught who Jesus is, and how fully competent to deliver thee. The poor leper did not doubt whether Jesus was able: though he rather feared that ability might not be exercised towards him. His prayer was, not if thou art *able*, but, "Lord, if thou *wilt*, thou canst make me clean." Now here, my soul, I hope, thy faith, through grace, exceeds the Jewish leper. Surely thou both knowest Jesus's power and Jesus's disposition to save thee. Unworthy and undeserving as thou art, yet his grace is not restrained by thy undeservings, no more than it was first constrained by thy merit. His love, his own love, his free love, is the sole rule of his mercy towards his children, and not their claims, for they have none, but in his free grace and the Father's everlasting mercy. Cherish these thoughts, my soul, at all times, for they are most sweet and precious. But are these all the blessed things which arise out of the view of the poor leper's case? Oh, no; the most delightful part still remains in the contemplation of Jesus's mercy to the poor petitioner, and the very gracious manner the Son of God manifested in the bestowing of it. He not only healed him, and did it immediately, but with that tenderness which distinguished his character and his love to poor sinners. Jesus put forth his hand and touched him; touched a leper! even so, precious Lord, deal by me. Though polluted and unclean, yet condescend to put forth thine hand and touch me also. Put forth thy blessed Spirit. Come, Lord, and dwell in me, abide in me, and rule and reign over me. Be thou my God, my Jesus, my Holy One, and make me thine for ever.

EVENING.—"Thou art beautiful, O my love, as Tirzah; comely as Jerusalem."—Song vi. 4.

And what was Tirzah? One of the cities in the lot of Manasseh, Joshua xii. 6, 24. and no doubt, as Judea was the glory of all lands, Tirzah, which was a part of it, was lovely. And the comeliness of that highly-favoured spot, Jerusalem, is celebrated in the sacred Song; "In the mountain of his holiness," saith the Psalmist, "beautiful for situation, and the joy of the whole earth, is Mount Zion," Ps. xlviii. 1, 2. And is Christ's church, in her Lord's eye, thus beautiful? Yes! He himself saith she is: and, by consequence, every individual member of her is so, which constitutes her one body. Pause, my soul, over this account, and let thine everlasting meditation dwell upon the pleasing subject. Thou art mourning continually over thine infirmities; thou feelest what Paul felt, and thou groanest under the same burden as he groaned under: and, indeed, the consciousness of the remains of indwelling sin is enough to make the souls of the redeemed go softly all their days. But while thus conscious that in thyself thou hast nothing that is lovely, do not overlook the loveliness which the righteousness of Christ, justifying his people, imparts to all their persons. Zion is said to be the perfection of beauty; and so she is in the eyes of God our Father, being the body of Christ, and made so in his beauty. What Jesus is in God's sight, such must be his people. For Christ, as head of his church, is the fulness that filleth all in all. If, my soul, thou wert looking for any thing in thyself that was amiable or beautiful to recommend thee to Jesus, or to justify thee before God; then, indeed, thou mightest exclaim with the prophet: "Woe is me, for I am undone, because I am a man of unclean lips," Isa. vi. 5. But if Jesus hath touched thy lips, and taken away thine iniquity, and thy sin is purged; then art thou all fair in him, and accepted by God the Father in him, the beloved: and Jesus saith *to* thee, and *of* thee, "Thou art beautiful, O my love, as Tirzah, comely as Jerusalem." See to it henceforth, that thou art never losing sight of thy oneness *with* Christ, thy acceptance *in* Christ, and the loveliness that thou art deriving *from* Christ. And while thou art daily lamenting that a soul united to Jesus should still carry about such a body of sin and death as thou dost, which harrasseth and afflicteth thy soul; yet never, never forget that thou art now looking up to the throne of grace for acceptance as thou art in Jesus, and not as thou art in thyself; and comfort thyself with this pleasing consideration, that ere long thou wilt be openly presented before a throne of glory, "not having spot or wrinkle, or any such thing, but holy and without blemish before him in love."

MARCH 12.

MORNING.—"Followers of them, who through faith and patience, inherit the promises."—Heb. vi. 12.

How gracious is the Holy Ghost, in not only holding forth to the people of Jesus the blessedness and certainty of the promises, but opening to our view multitudes, who are now in glory, in the full enjoyment of them. My soul, dost thou ask how they lived, when upon earth, in the full prospect, before that they were called upon to enter heaven for the full participation of them? Hear what the blessed Spirit saith concerning it in this sweet scripture. "It was through faith and patience." Now observe how these blessed principles manifested themselves. Another part of scripture explains—"they all died in faith, not having received the promises; but having seen them afar off, and were persuaded of them, and embraced them." Now this is the whole sum and substance of the believer's life: he *sees them afar off*, as Abraham did the day of Christ—as David, who had the same enjoyment in a believing view, with which his whole soul was satisfied: for he saith, "it was all his salvation, and all his desire;" a covenant which he rested upon, "as ordered in all things, and sure." Pause, my soul, over this, and ask within, are your views thus firmly founded? What, though the day of Christ's second coming be far off, or nigh, doth thy faith realize the blessed things belonging to it as certain, and as sure as God is truth. Pause, and see that such is thy faith—then go on. The faithful, who now inherit the promises, and which the Holy Ghost bids thee to follow, not only saw with the eye of faith, the things of Jesus afar off, but "were persuaded of them;" that is, were as perfectly satisfied of their existence and reality, as if they were already in actual possession. Pause here again, and say, is this thy faith? Are you perfectly persuaded "that God was, in Christ, reconciling the world to himself, not imputing their trespasses unto them?" Are you convinced that it is God's design, God's plan, God's grace, God's love, God's mercy, in all that concerns Jesus? Art thou convinced that God's glory is concerned in the glory of Jesus, and that every poor sinner gives glory to God in believing the record that God hath given of his Son? Dost thou, my soul, believe heartily, cordially, fully, joyfully, believe these precious things; nay, that in fact, it is the only possible way a poor sinner can give glory to God, in looking up to him as God, in giving him the credit of God, and taking his word as God concerning his dear Son Jesus Christ? Dost thou, my soul, set thy seal to these things? Then art thou "persuaded of the truths of God," as the patriarchs were "who saw them afar off." Once more —the faithful, whom the Holy Ghost calls upon thee to follow, embraced them also, as well as were persuaded of them. They clasped, *by faith,* Jesus in their arms, as really and as truly as Simeon did *in substance.* Their love *to* Jesus, and their interest *in* Jesus, their acquaintance by faith *with* Jesus, were matters of certainty, reality, delight; and their whole souls were, day by day, so familiarized in the unceasing meditation, that they walked by faith with Jesus while here below, as now, by sight, they are with him above in glory. Pause, my soul! Is this thy faith? Then, surely, Jesus is precious, and thou art indeed "the follower of them who now, through faith and patience, inherit the promises." And ere long, like them, thou shalt see him whom thy soul loveth, and dwell with him for ever!

EVENING.—"Surely the wrath of man shall praise thee; the remainder of wrath shalt thou restrain."—Psalm lxxvi. 10.

My soul! thou art returned from the exercises of the day; exercises which sometimes are sharp and trying: come now into the pavilion and retirings of thy God in

Christ, and take with thee this sweet scripture, and under his gracious teachings, see what beauties, by way of comfort, it affords. The Holy Ghost saith, "Surely the wrath of man shall praise the Lord." Pause, and consider in how many ways this blessed scripture proves itself. How often is the wrath of man made to minister to the happiness of God's people! How often do they become the unconscious ministers of producing the very reverse of what they intended: and where they designed evil to the saints of God, there good is found to come! When the Lord makes our friends, in the sweet endearments of society, promote our welfare, and we find blessings spring out of the thousand, and ten thousand charities of life; in providences, in helps, assistances, and the like, in which we minister by his appointment one to another; we do not so often trace the divine hand; and from the commonness of the blessing, lose sight of the direction whence it comes. But when the Lord, at any time, makes our enemies, and the enemies of our God and of his Christ, accomplish the secret purposes of his holy will; and those acts of theirs, which were evidently meant by them to distress, prove the very cause of joy; then we discern how the Lord overrules every thing to his glory, and his people's welfare. Here the Lord speaks in a loud voice, as in that sweet scripture, "In that day sing ye unto her, a vineyard of red wine. I, the Lord, do keep it. I will water it every moment, lest any hurt it; I will keep it night and day." Isaiah xxvii. 2, 3. My soul! learn from henceforth to be on the watch-tower, as the prophet was, looking for the evidences of these things. They will be very blessed, when at any time they are discovered; and, depend upon it, they are more frequent, than with thy poor thoughtless and inattentive mind thou art apt to suppose. Had not the brethren of Joseph sold him for a slave, how would he afterwards have arisen to be governor in Egypt? Had not Pharoah oppressed Israel, how would their cries to God have called Him forth to their rescue? Had not that monster of iniquity pursued the people of God to the Red Sea, how would Israel have seen their foes dead on the shore? Nay, ascending to an infinitely higher and more momentous matter than all these, or every other in history put together, I would ask, had not the wrath of man nailed Jesus to the cross, how, my soul, wouldest thou, and all the ransomed church of Christ, have found redemption in his blood? Oh! for grace, ever to keep this in remembrance. Never, surely, did the wrath of men praise Jehovah in any equal degree, or was so made to minister to the divine glory! Precious, precious Jesus! I beseech thee, gracious Lord, preserve alive in my soul, this contemplation of man's malice ministering to God's praise; that in all my little exercises here below, my soul may be stayed and comforted under them. And when at any time the enemy frowns, bad men afflict, the proud scorn, or the mighty of the earth would trample me under their feet, until in the bitterness of my heart, I cry out, "hath God forgotten to be gracious?" O for grace to cast one look at the cross of my Lord, and there read the whole explained: "Surely the wrath of man shall praise thee; the remainder of wrath shalt thou restrain."

MARCH 13.

MORNING.—"Oh! thou of little faith, wherefore didst thou doubt."—Matt. xiv. 31.

My soul, how sweet is it to eye Jesus in all things, and to be humbled in the recollection of his compassions to thy unaccountable instances of unbelief, after the many, nay, continued and daily experiences, which thou hast had of his love and faithfulness. And doth thy Jesus speak to thee this day, in those expostulating words, "Oh! thou of little faith, wherefore didst thou doubt?" What answer wilt thou return? Is there any thing in thy life to justify, or even to apologize for doubting? Look back—behold thy God and Father's grace, and mercy, and love;—a Saviour so rich, so compassionate, so answering all wants, in spirituals, temporals, and eternals;—a blessed Spirit, so condescending to teach, to lead, and by his influences to be continually with thee! Surely, a life like thine, crowded with mercies, blessings upon blessings, and one miracle of grace followed by another—wherefore shouldest thou doubt? What shall I say to thee, Oh! thou that art the hope of Israel, and the Saviour thereof? Lord, give me to believe, and help thou mine unbelief. I beseech thee, my God and Saviour, give me henceforth faith to trust thee when I cannot trace thee: give me tohang upon thee, when the ground of all sensible comforts seems sinking under my feet. I would cling to the faithfulness of my God in Christ, and throw my poor arms around thee, thou blessed Jesus, when all things appear the most dark and discouraging. And thus, day by day, living a life of faith and whole dependance upon thy glorious Person and thy glorious work, pressing after more sensible communion with thee, and more imparted strength and grace from thee, until at length, when thou shalt call me home from a life of faith to a life of sight—then, precious Jesus, would I say to thee, with my dying breath, 'Oh! present me, washed in thy blood, and clothed in thy righteousness, among the whole body of thy glorious church, not having spot or wrinkle, or any such thing, but that I may be without blame before thee in love.'

EVENING.—"Whose heart the Lord opened."—Acts xvi. 14.

It is always blessed to trace mercies to their source! And blessed when, through grace, we are enabled to give God his glory, and not put down to man's merit what wholly originates in God's grace. The opening of the heart can only be the province of Him that made it. Renewing work, as well as creating work, is his.

He that hath the key of David, is he alone "that openeth, and none shutteth; and shutteth, and none openeth." What a beautiful illustration hath the Holy Ghost given the church of this precious truth, in the instance of this woman, whose heart the Lord opened! We are told in her history, that she was of the city of Thyatira, a place remote from Philippi, where this sovereign act of mercy was shewn towards her. How long she had remained in a state of unrenewed nature, or what predisposing providence it was that brought her to Philippi, with other circumstances which we might have thought interesting to inquire after, we are not informed: the grand feature in her character is summed up in this short, but blessed account, "whose heart the Lord opened." The Holy Ghost hath indeed recorded her name and occupation, by way of making this testimony concerning her:—"a certain woman, named Lydia, a seller of purple." Behold, my soul! what blessed instruction ariseth out of it, for thine evening's meditation. What honourable mention is made of her, from this one blessed act, which the Lord wrought upon her. Poor and inconsiderable as she was in herself; small and of no reputation, yet her name is in the book of life! Pause, and contemplate the rich mercy which the Lord hath also accomplished in thee. Hath not he that opened Lydia's heart, opened thine? And is it not his province also, that first opened it by his grace, to keep it open by the daily influences of his Holy Spirit? Is it not his to renew, to refresh, to comfort, to strengthen, and to confirm unto the end? And wilt thou not, my soul, with the close of day, and the opening of the morning, look up for these precious manifestations? Lord! do thou open mine eyes, mine heart, my whole soul, to the enjoyment of these gracious renewed visits of thy love: and let no night or morning pass, without receiving fresh and increasing evidences from my Lord, that Christ hath both opened my heart, and is "formed in my heart, the hope of glory!"

MARCH 14.

MORNING.—" And for their sakes I sanctify myself."—John xvii. 19.

Let thy morning thoughts, my soul, be directed to this sweet view of thy Saviour. Behold thy Jesus presenting himself as the surety of his people before God and the Father. Having now received the call and authority of God the Father, and being fitted with a body suited to the service of a Redeemer, here see him entering upon the vast work; and in those blessed words, declaring the cause of it—" I sanctify myself." Did Jesus mean that he made himself more holy for the purpose? No, surely: for that was impossible. But by Jesus sanctifying himself, must be understood (as the Nazarite from the womb, consecrated, set apart, dedicated to the service to which the Father had called him), a voluntary offering—an holy unblemished sacrifice. And observe for whom: " for their sakes;" not for himself; for he needed it not. The priests under the law made their offerings, first for themselves, and then for the people. " But such an High Priest became us, who is holy, harmless, undefiled, separate from sinners, and made higher than the heavens; and who needed not daily, as those high priests, so to offer. For the law maketh men high priests which have infirmity; but the Son is consecrated for evermore." My soul, pause over this view of thy Jesus; and when thou hast duly pondered it, go to the mercy-seat, under the Spirit's leadings and influences, and there, by faith, behold thy Jesus, in his vesture dipped in blood, there sanctified, and there appearing in the presence of God for thee. There plead the dedication of Jesus; for it is of the Father's own appointment. There tell thy God and Father, (for it is the Father's glory, when a poor sinner glorifies his dear Son in him) that He, that Holy One, whom the Father consecrated, and with an oath confirmed in his high priestly office for ever, appeareth there for thee. Tell God that thy High Priest's holiness and sacrifice was altogether holy, pure, without a spot; and both his Person, and his nature, and offering, clean as God's own righteous law. Tell, my soul, tell thy God and Father these sacred, solemn truths. And while thou art thus coming to the mercy-seat, under the leadings of the Spirit, and wholly in the name and office-work of thy God and Saviour, look unto Jesus, and call to mind those sweet words, for whose sake that Holy One sanctified himself; and then drop a petition more before thou comest from the heavenly court: beg, and pray, and wrestle with the bountiful Lord for suited strength and grace, that as, for thy sake, among the other poor sinners of his redemption-love, Jesus sanctified himself, so thou mayest be able to be separated from every thing but Jesus; and as thy happiness was Christ's end, so his glory may be thy first and greatest object. Yes, dearest Jesus, methinks I hear thee say, —Thou shalt be for me, and not for another: so will I be for thee. Oh! thou condescending, loving God, "make me thine; that whether I live, I may live unto the Lord; or whether I die, I may die unto the Lord; so that living or dying, I may be thine."

EVENING.—"He shall come to be glorified in his saints, and to be admired in all them that believe."—2 Thess. i. 10.

Among a thousand wonders that will be unfolded before the astonished world, at the great day of God, to call up the unceasing praises of the church of Christ to all eternity, there are *two* very blessed events which will take place, and which this scripture records; the *one* is, how Jesus will be glorified in his own sacred person, in the view of his redeemed, when all his beauties are then displayed; and the *other* is, how Jesus will be glorified *in them*, from the saving change which his grace hath wrought in them. Let thine evening meditation, my soul, be upon both. And first, think how Jesus, thy Jesus, will then appear. He hath indeed been always known to thee, since he was first revealed to thee by grace, as wonderful; and every act of his towards thee, hath fully answered to this name. For in all his perfections, offices, characters, and relations; in all things concerning and relating to him, every view of him is wonderful. But He that is now known by faith, will then become the object of sight; and think, my soul, what an object of sight will it be! Never, but in the person of Jesus, can there be any thing presented to the view of men, or of angels, of equal glory! God and man in one person, can only be found in Christ. And God dwelling in flesh, is only rendered capable by that union, and through that medium, of being seen. And think, if it be possible, how glorious, how unspeakably glorious, the human nature of Christ must be, and is, from its union with the Godhead: such as no excellency of angels can at all, even in the most distant degree, resemble. Pause over this contemplation; for such is thy Jesus! and such will he appear, when he shall come to be glorified in his saints, and admired in all that believe. When thou hast fully feasted thyself, (as far as thy poor unripe faculties can take in the blessedness of it,) by dwelling upon the contemplation of Jesus, as he is, and as he will then appear, in his own glorious person; go on, and consider that glory that shall be revealed of Jesus, in the saving change which he hath wrought in his people, whereby he will be admired in all them that believe. Oh! what a flood of glory will pour in upon the soul, and what endless praises will go forth to the great Author of the unspeakable mercy, when the vast volume comes to be opened and explained, of what Jesus hath wrought *in* them; what he hath communicated *to* them; what everlasting blessings he hath procured *for* them; and what glory, as their great Mediator he will have *by* them, through all the incalculable periods of the eternal world, in their living *upon* him and *to* him, and *from* him deriving all the accessions of light and life, and glory and joy, for ever and ever! My soul! never, never lose sight of these blessed views: but add to that glorious account, that sweet testimony of Jesus, concerning this great day of God to his people: "At that day ye shall know that I am in my Father, and ye in me, and I in you."—John xiv. 20.

MARCH 15.

MORNING.—"Then went king David in, and sat before the LORD. And he said, Who am I, O LORD GOD! and what is my house, that thou hast brought me hitherto? And is this the manner of man, O LORD GOD?"—2 Sam. vii. 18, 19.

The language of David, under the overwhelming views he had of divine goodness, as it concerned himself, is suited to the case of every child of God, as he may trace that goodness in his own history. Surely, every awakened soul may cry out, under the same impression,—"Who am I, O Lord God! and what is my house, that thou hast brought me hitherto?" My soul! ponder over the sweet subject, as it concerns thyself. Behold what manner of love the love of God is from the manner of man. View it in each Person of the Godhead. What is the highest possible conception any man can have of the love of God our Father to us? Was it not, when, as an evidence of the love he had to our nature, he put a robe of that nature, in its pure and holy state, upon the Person of his dear Son, when he gave him a body in all points such as ours, sin only excepted, that he might not only in that body perfect salvation both by his obedience and death, but also, that he might be our everlasting Mediator for drawing nigh to the Godhead, first in grace, and then in glory? Tell me, my soul, what method, in all the stores of Omnipotency, could God thy Father have adopted to convince thee of his love, as in this sweet method of his wisdom. God intimates, by this tender process, that he loveth the human nature which he hath created. And though, to answer the wise measures of his plan of redemption, he hath not as yet taken all the persons of his redeemed up to his heavenly court, yet he will have their glorious Head, their representative there, that he may behold Him, and accept the whole church in Him, and love them, and bless them in Him, now, and for ever. Oh! my soul, if this view of thy Father's love was but always uppermost in thine heart, what a ground of encouragement would it for ever give thee, to come to thy God and Father in him, and his mediation; who, while he is one in the divine nature, is one also with thee in the human, on purpose to bid thee come. And as for thee, thou blessed Jesus, thy love and thy delights were always with thy people. From everlasting, thy tendencies of favour have been towards them; thine whole heart is ours. All thy grace, in being set up as the covenant-head for us, and all the after-actings of the same grace in time; all that thou didst then, and all that thou art doing now,—all, all testify the love of our Jesus. And may I not say to thee, thou dear Redeemer, as David did, "Is this the manner of man, O Lord God?" Yes, it is: but it is of the Glory-man, of the God-man, Christ Jesus. And no less, thou Holy Spirit, whose great work is love and consolation; what a thought is it to warm my soul into the most awakened contemplation and delight in the view of thy love, that though thou art of purer eyes than to behold iniquity, yet dost thou make the very bodies of the redeemed thy temples, for thine indwelling residence. My soul, do as David did: go in before the Divine Presence; fall down and adore in the solemn thought —"Who am I, O Lord God! and what is my Father's house?"

EVENING.—"A man in Christ."—2 Cor. xii. 2.

My soul! thy last evening's meditation was sweet, (was it not?) in contemplating thy Jesus, as glorious in his own person, and as glorified in his people. Wilt thou add to that subject, for it is part of the same, for thy present thoughts, what is suggested in this motto, "a man in Christ?" Dost thou fully enter into the pleasing apprehension of what the phrase implies? Now, who shall fully describe it; or who is competent fully to conceive the whole extent of it? "A man in Christ," must imply every thing connected with a oneness, an union, a part of himself; yea, "a life hid with Christ in God." "A man in Christ" is as much a part in Christ's mystical body, as the head, or hand, or foot, is a part of that body to which those members belong. Hence, (which is indeed a sweet part of the subject) every one who is "a man in Christ," is, to all intents and purposes, interested in all that belongs to Christ, as the Christ of God. Hence also, it must as undeniably follow, that every member of Christ's body, the least, as well as the greatest, the humblest as well as the highest, becomes a part in him, is equally united to him, and participates in what belongs to him. The life of grace here, and the life of glory hereafter, being both derived from Christ, and enjoyed wholly from an union with him, are therefore equally enjoyed; just as the smallest leaf or branch united to a tree becomes a part of that tree, as much as the largest branches. Dost thou enter, my soul, into an apprehension of these outlines of the subject? Art thou "a man in Christ," by regeneration, adoption, justification, and grace? Oh! then, turn over the transporting thought, with holy and unceasing delight, in thy constant meditation. Calculate, if thou art able, the blessed inheritance, to which thou art begotten by it, of grace here, and glory to all eternity. "A man in Christ," is accepted in Christ, justified in Christ, sanctified in Christ, and must assuredly be glorified in Christ. Oh! who that thinks of these things, and through the Holy Ghost is conscious of an interest in them, can suffer the exercises of a dying world to bring affliction into the soul? What a life of dignity, is "a man in Christ" brought into! He is brought nigh unto God, through the blood of the cross. What a state of security is "a man in Christ" placed in! "Because I live," (saith Jesus) "ye shall live also." And what an endless prospect of glory, hath "a man in Christ" opening before him; when Christ hath said, "Father, I will that they also whom thou hast given me, be with me where I am, that they may behold the glory which thou hast given me!" O the unspeakable blessedness of "a man in Christ!"

MARCH 16.

MORNING.—"The man will not be in rest, until he have finished the thing this day."—Ruth iii. 18.

Behold! my soul, in this scripture history, some sweet features by which the disposition of Jesus's love, and the earnestness in his heart to relieve poor sinners, is strikingly set forth. When a poor sinner is made acquainted with the Lord Jesus, hath heard of his grace, goes forth to glean in his fields; at the ordinances of his house, and under the ministration of his word, lays down at his feet, and prays to be covered with the skirt of his mantle; Jesus not only takes notice of that poor seeking sinner, but gives the poor creature to know, by some sweet and secret whispers of his Holy Spirit, that he is not unacquainted with all that is in his heart. And when such have lain long, and earnestly sought, even through the whole night of doubt and fear, until the morning of grace breaks in upon the soul, yet may they be assured, the God-man, Christ Jesus, will not rest until that he hath finished the thing. It is one of the most blessed truths of the gospel, (and do thou, my soul, see to it, that it is written in thy best and strongest remembrance to have recourse to, as may be needed, upon every occasion,) that a seeking sinner is not more earnest to see Jesus, and enjoy him, than Jesus is to reveal himself to that seeking sinner, and form himself in the sinner's heart, the hope of glory. For Jesus will not, cannot cease his love to poor sinners, until the object for which he came to seek and to save them is fully answered. And it is a thought, my soul, enough to warm thy coldest moments, that all the hallelujahs of heaven cannot call off thy Jesus's attention from the necessities of even the poorest of his little ones here upon earth. In every individual instance, and in every case, Jesus will not rest until that he hath finished the thing, as well in the hearts of his people, as in the world, when he finished the work the Father gave him to do. Yes! Jesus will not rest until the last redeemed soul is brought home to glory. Precious consideration, how ought it to endear yet more the preciousness of the Redeemer!

EVENING.—" And it shall come to pass, that he that is left in Zion, and he that remaineth in Jerusalem, shall be called holy; even every one that is written among the living in Jerusalem. When the Lord shall have washed away the filth of the daughters of Zion, and shall have purged the blood of Jerusalem from the midst thereof, by the spirit of judgment, and by the spirit of burning."—Isaiah iv. 3, 4.

What a precious scripture is here! and what vast things are contained in the bosom of it! Mark them down, my soul, one by one, this evening, and see what of thy personal interest thou canst trace in the whole. And first, *who they are*, of whom these things are said, namely, " the living in Jerusalem; even every one that is written: and he that is left, and he that remaineth." By *living*, and being *written*, can only be meant what the beloved apostle saith of being " written in the book of life."—Rev. xiii. 8. And of " him that remaineth," there is, as another apostle saith, " a remnant according to the election of grace."—Rom. xi. 5. Hence the Lord Jesus bids his disciples rejoice, not because the spirits were subject unto them, but because " their names were written in heaven."—Luke x. 20. Secondly, *what they are;* and we find, that they are called *holy*. This is the great object of gospel grace; whence the apostle saith, "We are bound to give thanks always to God for you, brethren, beloved of the Lord, because God hath from the beginning chosen you to salvation, through sanctification of the Spirit."—2 Thess. ii. 13. And when God saith, "Be ye holy, for I am holy,"—Levit. xi. 44; his word works by his divine power, in the new creation of the soul, as he did in the old creation of the earth: the same efficacy is wrought by the one as by the other. "Let there be light, and there was light." Thirdly, *What they shall be.* They shall be cleansed from filth and uncleanness. There shall be cleansing work, and purging work. Zion shall be washed, and Jerusalem shall be purged. Sweet and precious scripture, in proof of that fountain of Jesus's blood, opened in after-days, "to the house of David, and to the inhabitants of Jerusalem, for sin and for uncleanness."—Zech. xiii. 1. Fourthly, *Who shall do all this?*—The Lord! this blessed scripture saith; for He, and he only, can be competent to the great work. The Creator of the soul must also be its Redeemer. None but the Lord can take away the filth of the daughters of Zion, and purge the blood of Jerusalem from the midst thereof. Precious Jesus! it is thy blood only, which cleanseth from all sin. Fifthly, *How will the Lord do it?* By the spirit of judgment, and the spirit of burning! Yea, the Holy Ghost, amidst his manifold gifts and gracious offices, will thus act upon every one that is written among the living in Jerusalem. "As a spirit of judgment," he will plead the cause of an injured God and Saviour, with the sinner's guilty conscience; "convincing of sin, of righteousness, and of judgment." And he will be a "spirit of burning;" for his word will act, (as the prophet describes it, Jer. xx. 9.) "as a burning fire, shut up in the bones," consuming all the day. My soul! what sayest thou to this solemn but sweet scripture? Hath God the Spirit been to thee all these? Hath he convinced thee, enlightened thee, and been to thee a spirit of judgment, and a spirit of burning? Hath he convinced thee of thy sinful heart, enlightened thy dark heart, burnt up the lustful desires of thy corrupt heart, melted thine hard heart, warmed the frozen affections of thy cold heart, and formed a love there towards the person, grace, and righteousness of a dear Redeemer? Canst thou set thy seal to this blessed scripture, that God is true?

MARCH 17.

MORNING.—"Wherein ye greatly rejoice, though now for a season, if need be, ye are in heaviness through manifold temptations."—1 Pet. i. 6.

My soul! it is too difficult a task to flesh and blood, but it is among the most blessed triumphs of grace, to glory in tribulation, that the power of Jesus may rest upon the soul. Pause over the subject, and see whether in the little exercises of thy life, such things are among thine experiences. A soul must be truly taught of God the Father; truly acquainted with Jesus, and living near to him; and truly receiving the sweet and constant influences of the Holy Ghost; when, in the absence of the streams of all creature comforts, he is solacing himself at the fountain-head; and, amidst also the fiery darts of temptations! But, my soul, if this be thy happy portion, thou must have acquired it in the school of grace. There are some precious marks by which thou wilt ascertain these things. As, first—I must see that the manifold temptations, be they of what kind or number they may, are in the permissions of Jesus. I must trace the footsteps of Jesus in them, the hand of Jesus directing me through them, the voice of Jesus I must hear in them; and, in short, his sacred Person regulating and ordering all the several parts of them. If I see his love, his wisdom, his grace, his goodwill, in all the appointment; whatever heaviness the temptations themselves induce, there will still be cause left for joy—yea, for great joy. Moreover, it will be an additional alleviation to soften their pressure, if through the whole of their exercise, the soul be enabled to keep in view, that God's glory, and my soul's happiness, will be the sure issue of them. If I can realize Jesus's presence, as I pass through them, and interpret, with an application to myself that blessed promise, in which the Lord saith, "I know the thoughts I think toward you, saith the Lord; thoughts of peace, and not of evil, to give you an expected end;" these mercies mingled with the trial, will sweeten, and almost take away all its bitter. And, lastly, to add no more—If, my soul, the Holy Ghost should lead out thine whole heart upon the Person of Jesus during the conflict, and by making thee sensible of thy weakness, to take shelter in him, and to lean altogether upon his strength; so that thou art able to believe and to depend upon the fulfilment of his promise, when, to the eye of sense, there doth not seem a way by which that promise may be fulfilled; these are foundations for rejoicing, and of great rejoicing too; because they are all out of thyself, and centered in Him, with whom there is no possibility of change. These are, like the Michtams of David, precious, golden things. For this is to live upon Jesus, to rejoice in Jesus, and to find in him a suited strength for every need. Blessed will be these exercises, my soul, if thou art enabled thus to act under manifold temptations.

EVENING.—"The man which had the withered hand."—Mark iii. 3.

Surely the man in the jewish synagogue, which had a withered hand, will, in the history of his disease and cure, furnish me, this evening, with a very improving meditation. Do thou, blessed Jesus, the great healer both of soul and body, render it profitable, by thy gracious instruction to my heart. This poor man had a withered hand, not only sinew-shrunk, but wasting away. He attended divine worship, for Jesus found him in the synagogue. But we do not read that he asked the mercy from Christ. It was Jesus that first looked upon him; and not he on the Lord Jesus. " Stretch forth thine hand," said the Son of God. Instantly the poor man found the powers of nature restored, the shrunk sinew became lengthened, and the hand which had wasted away, was restored. Pause, my soul! look at the subject as it concerns thyself. How long didst thou attend the means of grace under a withered soul? And to this hour, had not Jesus looked on thee, thou wouldest not have looked on him. Were Jesus to suspend his blessings till sinners had prepared themselves for them, or deserved them, never would blessings come at all. And did Jesus speak, as to this poor man, and bid thee live? Did Jesus command thee to stretch forth thy dead and lifeless soul, and say unto thee, "I am thy salvation?" Surely, then, thy God's commands conveyed with them ability; and the same voice which said, "stretch forth thine hand," gave vigour to the hand to lay hold of his mercy. How sweet is this view of thy impotence, and Jesus's sovereignty! Here we see that scripture most completely fulfilled: " He sent his word, and healed them; and delivered them from their destructions. Oh! that men would praise the Lord for his goodness, and for his wonderful works to the children of men."—Psalm cvii. 20, 21.

MARCH 18.

MORNING.—" And Israel strengthened himself, and sat up on the bed."—Gen. xlviii. 2.

This was an interesting moment in the life, or rather the death, of the patriarch, and may serve, my soul, to shew what ought to be the conduct of the believer in his last expiring hours. The imagination can hardly conceive any situation equally momentous, in every point of view, both as it concerns a faithful God, a man's own heart, and the church the dying saint is going to leave behind. What can form a more lovely sight than a dying saint, sitting up in the bed, (if the Lord permits the opportunity) and recounting, as Jacob did, the gracious dealings of the Lord, all the way along the path of pilgrimage—"The God which fed me," said Jacob, "all my life long unto this day: the angel (and who was this but Jesus?) which redeemed me from all evil." Pause, my soul. Anticipate such a day. Figure to thyself thy friends around thee, and thou thyself strengthened, just to sit up in the bed, to take an everlasting farewell. What hast thou to relate? What hast thou treasured up of God's dealings with thee, to sweeten death in the recital, to bless God in the just acknowledgment, and to leave behind thee a testimony to others of the truth, as it is in Jesus? My soul, what canst thou speak of? What canst thou tell of thy God, thy Jesus? Hast thou known enough of him to commit thyself into his Almighty hands, with an assurance of salvation? Pause! Didst thou not in the act of faith, long since, venture thyself upon Jesus for the whole of thy everlasting welfare? Didst thou not from a perfect conviction of thy need of Jesus, and from as perfect a conviction of the power and grace of Jesus to save thee—didst thou not make a full and complete surrender of thyself, and with the most perfect approbation of this blessed plan of God's mercy in Christ, to be saved wholly by him, and wholly in his own way, and wholly to his own glory? And as such, art thou now afraid, or art thou now shrinking back, when come within sight almost of Jesus's arms to receive thee? Oh, no! blessed be God, this last act of committing thy soul is not as great an act of faith as the first was; for since that time thou hast had thousands of evidences, and thousands of tokens in love and faithfulness, that thy God is true. Sit up then, my soul, and do as the dying patriarch did; recount to all around thee thy confidence in the Son of God, who "hath loved thee, and given himself for thee." Cry out, as he did, "I have waited for thy salvation, O Lord." And as this will be the last opportunity of speaking a word for God, testify of his faithfulness, and encourage all that behold you to be seeking after an interest in Jesus, from seeing how sweetly you close a life of faith before you begin a life of glory, in blessing God, though with dying lips, that the last notes which you utter here below, may be only the momentary interruption to the same subject in the first of your everlasting song—"To him that hath loved you, and washed you, from your sins in his blood."

EVENING.—"Who are kept by the power of God, through faith unto salvation."—1 Peter i. 5.

When I call to mind that in me, "that is, in my flesh, dwelleth no good thing;" when I stand convinced, (as I do most fully, blessed be God the Holy Ghost, for having exercised his gracious office in my soul, to this gracious effect,) that though renewed in the spirit of my mind, yet in that unrenewed part of myself, which is hastening to the grave, every member is virtually all sin; when I know that never did sin break out in acts of open wickedness, in any son or daughter of Adam, but that the seeds of the same sin are in me and my nature; I long not only to know, but always to keep in remembrance by what means, and from what cause it is, that those seeds do not ripen in my heart, as well as in others; that while corrupt nature is the same in all, it is restrained in me, while so many of my fellow-creatures, and fellow-sinners, fall a prey to temptation. Blessed Spirit! the merciful scripture of the evening answers the important question. They who are kept, "are kept by the power of God, through faith unto salvation." Here is the solution of the whole subject. With what humbleness of soul, then, ought every child of God to fall down before the throne of grace, under the deepest sense of distinguishing love, in the consciousness that it is divine restraint, and not creature merit, which maketh all the difference. Help me, Lord, to go humble all my days, in this view, and let it be my morning thought, as well as my mid-day and evening meditation, that I am kept by thy power, through faith unto salvation. Almighty Father, help me to be living upon thy faithfulness in the covenant of grace, established and sealed as it is in the blood of thy dear Son, that "thou wilt not" turn away from me to do me good; and that thou wilt put thy fear in my heart, that I shall not depart from thee.—Jer. xxxii. 40. Precious Lord Jesus! give me to rest also upon an union *with* thee, a communication of grace *from* thee, and a participation *in* thee, in all the blessings of thy redemption. Surely I am the purchase of thy blood, and thou hast said, "thy sheep shall never perish, neither shall any pluck them out of thine hand."—John x. 28. And Oh! thou blessed Spirit of all truth, be thou to me an indwelling security from sin, to keep me from falling, and to preserve me faultless in Jesus, until the day of his coming. Make my body thy temple, and cause me, by thy sweet constraining love, to "glorify God in my body, and in my spirit, which are his."—1 Cor. vi. 20.

MARCH 19.

MORNING.—"Oh that I knew where I might find him, that I might come even to his seat! I would order my cause before him, and fill my mouth with arguments. Will he plead against me with his great power? No; but he would put strength in me."—Job xxiii. 3, 4, 6.

My soul, are these thy breathings? Dost thou really long, and, like David, even pant, to come before the throne of grace? Art thou at a loss how to come, how to draw nigh? Wouldest thou fill thy mouth with arguments, and have thy cause so ordered as to be sure not to fail? Look to Jesus! Seek from him the leadings of the Spirit; and while thine eye is steadily fixed on thy great High Priest within the vail, still wearing a vesture dipped in blood, see to it that thy one great plea is, for a perfect and complete justification before God and thy Father, upon the sole footing of righteousness. Yes, my soul, plead earnestly, heartily, steadily; and, like Jacob, wrestling with God, upon the sole footing of righteousness. Wouldest thou fear on this ground? Yes, thou wouldest have cause enough to fear and tremble, if thy plea was with the least reference to any righteousness of thine. But, my soul, remember it is Jesus's righteousness, and his only, with which, like Job, thy mouth must be filled with arguments. This is the strength thy God and Father will put in thee: and it is a strength of Jehovah's founded in his justice. As a poor guilty sinner, thou couldest have nothing to plead but free grace and rich mercy. But when thou comest in Jesus, thy Surety's righteousness, thou mayest appeal, and art expected so to do, to God's holiness and his justice also. Oh, how sweet the assurance, how unanswerable the plea, how secure the event! Jesus hath fulfilled the law—Jesus hath paid the penalty of justice; and God hath promised to pardon and bless his seed, his redeemed in him. Hence, the apostle Paul, in the contemplation of death and judgment, while looking at his everlasting security in Jesus, cries out, "Henceforth there is laid up for me a crown of righteousness, which the Lord, the righteous Judge, shall give me at that day; and not to me only, but unto all them that love his appearing." Behold then, my soul, thy vast privilege; and when, like Job, thou art desiring to approach a throne of grace now, or looking forward to a throne of judgment hereafter—never, never for a moment forget that this is the way, and the only way, (for a blessed sure way it is,) maintaining communion with God in Christ. Thy God, thy Father, will not plead against a righteousness of his own appointing; but he will put Jesus, his strength, in thee. Hallelujah!

EVENING.—"And he gave them their request, but sent leanness into their soul."—Ps. cvi. 15.

Here is a very solemn subject to exercise the mind of a child of God. My soul, take it for thine own exercise this evening. In the part of the church's history alluded to, it should seem that they were just arrived on the borders of Canaan: they had been all along fed and sustained by God's bounty; and the manna, as usual, came fresh and pure from heaven every morning; but tired and dissatisfied with the table of God's providing, they demanded flesh to eat, and the Lord gave them their request, but sent leanness into their soul. Happy would it have been for the church of God, if such rebellions had been confined to that period of its history. But, alas! in all ages, God's children too often manifest the like temper. My soul! bring the subject home; thy God, thy Jesus, hath appointed thee the very path best suited for thee. Had a synod of angels been convened to choose what would be most conducive to thy present and everlasting welfare, never could they have arranged either thy state or circumstances better than Jesus hath done. Surely, his infinite wisdom and love are manifested in all the appointments by the way, which he hath made for thee as well in providence as in grace. And yet how often hast thou thought, that such an attainment, or such a possession, would have been for thy good! And how often hast thou felt displeased when matters appeared to thee discouraging! and in the fulness of thy thoughts, thou hast at times felt disposed to tell thine heavenly Master that such an exercise might have been spared; or that such a temporal portion might have been given thee! And hast thou not, more than once, afterwards discovered that had Jesus granted what thy wayward heart perversely coveted, evil, and not good, would have followed? If thou wouldest gather improvement from the church's history, in the striking instance before thee, see the sad consequences of having any earthly desire gratified, which for the most part bringeth leanness into the soul. Ask the question from any of the chosen few, whose situations are among the great or affluent, whether their souls do not go lean, from their bodies being better fed than others? Prosperity in this world is too dangerous to God's dear children; which very fully explains why Jesus, for the most part, keeps his people humble. When the Lord made Israel to ride upon the high places of the earth, and caused him to drink of the pure blood of the grape; the next account is, "Jeshurun waxed fat and kicked," Deut. xxxii. 14, 15. Precious Lord Jesus, do thou choose for me, in every thing, and for every state; for then I am sure, I shall be well provided for, and well taken care of. Never, dearest Lord, grant any request of mine, which, in the weakness and perversity of my heart, I might be tempted to put up, lest a state, so truly awful as that of Israel should follow; and while the flesh sought ease and fulness, there should be a leanness of soul!

MARCH 20.

MORNING.—"Thine eyes shall see the King in his beauty."—Isa. xxxiii. 17.

Who, my soul, but Jesus could be intended by this sweet promise? And who is beautiful and lovely in thine eyes but him? There was no beauty in him while thou wert in a state of unrenewed nature, that thou shouldest desire him; neither can any man truly love him, until that a soul is made light in the Lord.

Is Jesus then lovely to thee? Hast thou seen him? Dost thou now know him, love him, behold him, as altogether fair, and the chiefest among ten thousand? Then, surely, this promise hath been, and is continually fulfilled in thy experience. Hast thou so seen him, as to be in love with him, and to have all thine affections drawn forth towards him? Dost thou, my soul, so behold him as to admire him, and love him above all; and so to love him, as never to be satisfied without him? Moreover—hast thou seen this King in his beauty, in his fulness, riches, and suitableness to thee as a Saviour? Surely, blessed Jesus, there are not only glorious, precious excellencies in thee, and thine own divine person, which command the love and affection of every beholder, as thou art in thyself; but there is a beauty indeed in thee, considered as thou art held forth by our God and Father, in all thy suitableness to thy people. In thy beauty, blessed Lord, there is to be seen a fulness of grace, and truth, and righteousness, exactly corresponding to the wants of poor sinners—thy blood to cleanse, thy grace to comfort, thy fulness to supply; in thee there is every thing we can want—life, light, joy, pardon, mercy, peace, happiness here, glory hereafter. And do I not see thee, thou King, in thy beauty indeed, when I behold thee as coming with all these for my supply? So that, under the enjoyment of the whole, I feel constrained to cry out, with one of old, "I will love thee, O Lord, my strength. The Lord is my strength and my song; and he is become my salvation." Neither is this all; for in beholding the King in his beauty, I behold him also in his love. Yes, blessed Lord, thou art indeed most beautiful and lovely; for thou hast so loved poor sinners, as to give thyself for them; and the conscious sense that our love to thee did not first begin, but thine to us was the first cause for exciting ours, and the shedding forth that love in our hearts, by thy blessed

Spirit, first prompted our minds to look unto thee, makes thee lovely indeed. And now, Lord, every day's view of thee increaseth that love, and brings home thy beauty more and more. The more frequent thou condescendest to visit my poor soul, the more beautiful dost thou appear. Every renewed manifestation, every view, every glimpse of Jesus, must tend to make my God and King more gracious and lovely to my soul, and add fresh fervour to my love. Come then, thou blessed, holy, lovely one, and ravish my spiritual senses with thy beauty, that I may daily get out of love with every thing of created excellency, and my whole soul be filled only with the love of Jesus; until, from seeing thee here below, through the medium of ordinances and grace, I come to look upon thee, and live for ever in thy presence, in the full beams of thy glory in thy throne above.

EVENING.—"And they journeyed; and the terror of God was upon the cities that were round about them, and they did not pursue after the sons of Jacob."—Gen. xxxv. 5.

It was the evening before the last, that my soul was led to the contemplation of what is the everlasting security of a child of God, amidst all the corruption, within and without, which he carries about him in a body of sin and death. It will form a very pleasing subject, to a similar effect, to trace also a believer's security from the world at large, in the natural enmity there is in every unawakened heart to a state of grace. And this precious scripture traces every child of God's safety to the same source. The family of Jacob, the praying seed of Jacob, are still journeying; for here we have no continuing city, but we seek one to come. The people of God are but few in number; yea, very few: the scripture saith, "And they are strangers in the land," Ps. cv. 12. The very profession of the cross will always make them strangers; and as men whose manners and pursuits differ from the world, like

Joshua and his people, "they are men wondered at." How are they kept from being run down, oppressed, subdued, and overcome? This text answers: "the terror of God was upon the cities round about them." Pause, and consider the blessed subject, my soul, and never lose sight of it. He that toucheth thee, toucheth the apple of Jesus' eye. The reins of all government, both of men and kings, are in Christ's hand; nothing can take place but by his appointment. Oh! how blessed to live in the full persuasion of this most unquestionable truth. If a thorough sense of an interest in Jesus, and an union and oneness with Christ, were always uppermost in the heart, this filial fear in Jesus would drive out all creature fear, as the fire of the sun puts out the fire on the hearth. The prophet beautifully expresses this in one of his precepts to the church: "Say ye not, a confederacy, to all them to whom this people shall say, a confederacy; neither fear ye their fear, nor be afraid; but sanctify the Lord of Hosts himself, and let him be your fear, and let him be your dread, and he shall be for a sanctuary," Isa. viii. 12, 13, 14.

MARCH 21.

MORNING.—"Truly, our fellowship is with the Father, and with his Son Jesus Christ."—1 John i. 3.

Precious, blessed consideration! Art thou, my soul, at this time in the full enjoyment of it? Pause over the inquiry. Sometimes, for the want of this search of soul, and the neglect of it, deadness, or at least leanness, creeps in. Say then, my soul, how art thou dealing with thy God? and how is thy God dealing with thee? When were his latest manifestations? When did he take thee to his banqueting-house; or when didst thou sit under his shadow? Hast thou very lately heard his voice, saying, "Fear not, I am thy salvation?" The discovery of these things are among the sweetest exercises which flow from the indwelling Spirit. Go on further in the inquiry—how art thou dealing with thy God? When hadst thou fellowship and communion with the Father, and with his Son Jesus Christ? What petitions hast thou now awaiting for answers from the heavenly court? What grateful acknowledgments have lately gone up for mercies received? How is thine acquaintance there advancing? How art thou growing in grace, and in the knowledge of thy Lord and Saviour Jesus Christ? If these things are neglected by thee, will not a strangeness between thy God and thee come on; such as is induced by earthly friendships, when absence and time, where there is no correspondence kept up, wears out remembrance? My soul, rouse up, and consider the vast importance of keeping up constant intercourse with thy God and Saviour. Precious Jesus! do thou keep the flame of love alive; manifest to my soul the certainty and reality of my union with thee, thou sweet Saviour, by causing this blessed communion to be constant, unceasing, and full of divine communications. Let thy Spirit call forth in me the exercise of the graces he hath planted; and do thou come forth in refreshing manifestations of love; so that, while prayers go up, blessings may come down; and while thou art graciously saying, "Seek ye my face," my heart may say unto thee, "Thy face, Lord, will I seek." Oh, the blessedness of such a life to break the power of sin; to revive and strengthen the spirits; to open and to enlarge to my view the discoveries of thy Person, thy glory, thy riches, thy suitableness, thine all-sufficiency. If, dearest Jesus, thou wilt mercifully keep this fellowship, this partnership, alive in my soul, how will my poor soul be living upon thee, and with thee; and how shall I be exchanging with thee all my leanness, poverty, wretchedness, and weakness, for thy fulness, riches, righteousness, and strength? Come, then, Lord Jesus, and "until the day break, and the shadows flee away, turn, my beloved, and be thou like a roe, or a young hart, upon the mountains of Bether."

EVENING.—"A nail in a sure place."—Isaiah xxii. 23.

My soul! through grace, thou hast long been enabled to hang all thy grand concerns for eternity upon the Lord Jesus; and will it not be a very refreshing subject for thine evening meditation, to see how eternally firm and secure all rest, with an unshaken and unchangeable confidence? Behold him as he is in himself, in his person, work, and righteousness; "Jesus Christ, the same yesterday, and to-day, and for ever." Next contemplate him as the source, origin, fountain, and support of all the great things of salvation. There is not a purpose of God, but is founded *on* Christ; not a promise, but is made, confirmed, and fulfilled *in* Christ; and not a dispensation in all the kingdoms of nature, grace, and glory, but comes *from* Christ and his own righteous government. Go on, under a third branch of meditation, and behold Jesus as a nail in a sure place, and that the persons, concerns, and blessings of his people all hang on him; *from* him they derive all their spiritual strength, gifts, graces, authority, order, and appointment; *on* him they all depend for life, ability, power, and disposition to carry it on; and *to* him the whole glory of their services return, in an endless revenue of praise. Lastly, and above all, to crown thine evening meditation, on this nail in a sure place, behold the hand of God thy Father, both fixing him there, and proclaiming it to the souls of his people; "I will fasten him," saith Jehovah, "as a nail in a sure place; and he shall be for a glorious throne to his Father's house." Hail! thou glorious almighty Mediator! founded on such authority, and possessing in thyself such eternal principles, evermore will I hang my soul, and body, and spirit, with all I have, and all

I am or hope to be, in time and to all eternity, on thee; for never can too great a stress be laid upon Jesus, nor too full a confidence be placed in him. How can a soul perish that hangs on God's Christ?

MARCH 22.

MORNING.—" Thus saith the Lord; I remember thee, the kindness of thy youth, the love of thine espousals, when thou wentest after me in the wilderness, in a land that was not sown."—Jer. ii. 2.

Pause, my soul, over this condescending token of God's love to Israel; and see whether it doth not hold forth to thee a blessed portion for thy encouragement. Israel had been most undeserving; but yet the Lord would put Israel in remembrance, by assuring his people that he remembered their love when God first formed Israel into a people. When he led them into the wilderness, and married Israel, they sung the praise of Jehovah in their love-songs, on the day of their espousals. 'Now,' saith the Lord,—'I remember thee in these things; for these were tokens of affection when thou wentest after me in following the pillar of cloud through the desert; in trusting to a harvest, though as yet the land was not sown.' And may I, blessed Lord, sweetly interpret this precious portion with application to myself, as though my God so spake to me of the day of my espousals? Doth my God and Saviour remember me in the first awakenings of his grace, when, at the first mention of his name, my soul made me like the chariots of Amminadab? Well, then, may my soul remember thee, Oh thou God of my salvation! The savour of thy past love and past experiences gives now, at this moment, new delight to my soul, and awakens new desires of communion with my God. The very recollection of what I then was, and how thou calledst me, and made my time a time of love; and how thou passedst by, and didst bid me live, and didst cleanse me, and take me home, and betrothedst me to thyself, and made me thine for ever; the very thoughts refresh my soul now; and these former experiences drive away present distresses and despondency. How is it, my soul, with thee now? Art thou less in frame—less in love? Hast thou not the same earnest liking to Jesus now, as then? Is the strength of thy love, and desires, and delights, abated? Look at this blessed scripture. Hear what God saith to Israel, in a time of Israel's coldness. See how God's love was not changed, though Israel's was so abated. Art thou, my soul, conscious of the same? Art thou lamenting it; desiring, waiting for some renewed token of thy Jesus's love? Is his name, his person, his righteousness still precious? Dost thou wait but for the whispers of his grace? See, here it is—I remember, though thou hast forgotten the day of thine espousals. Oh the wonderful condescension of the Son of God! Behold, my soul, how, in this very way, he is preparing thine heart for the renewings of his love, and his sweet manifestations towards thee. Oh cry out with the church of old, under similar circumstances, "Draw me; we will run after thee." Unless thou drawest, Lord, the distance will remain; but the desire of being drawn, shews the earnestness for union. Lord, I beseech thee, do this; bring me near to thyself, to thine everlasting embraces; then shall I run, nay, even flee to my beloved, and will hang upon thee as the vessel hangeth on the nail, and dwell, and remain with thee for ever.

EVENING.—"This man receiveth sinners, and eateth with them."—Luke xv. 2.

My soul! wouldest thou, by faith, review some more than ordinary representation of the Lord Jesus, to melt the finer feelings of thy heart, in the contemplation of his unequalled condescension and love? Let this be it, which the evangelist hath here drawn of the Son of God. Behold him, encircled with poor publicans and sinners, alluring them to the arms of his mercy; and behold the self-righteous pharisees and scribes withdrawing from the sacred spot, and with all that indignation and scorn, which marked their character, murmuring at the grace of Jesus, saying, "This man receiveth sinners, and eateth with them!" Well is it for thee, my soul, that the Son of God hath received sinners; else how should I have been looked upon by him? And well is it that his table hath been spread for sinners; or how should I have been fed by him? Yea, Lord, is it not the very feature of thy rich dispensation of mercy, that it is for sinners, as sinners, that thou didst come down from heaven, to seek and save them? And who but sinners, should Jesus, the great Saviour of sinners receive, and eat with? Will the Lord allow me, this evening, to dwell upon the sweet subject, and run over some of the blessed thoughts, which arise out of this view of my compassionate and all-loving Lord? Why then, I would say to my soul, remember, when thy Jesus first received thee as a sinner, thou wert hastening on to ruin; and it was then, of all moments the most alarming, when thou didst merit hell, that Jesus received thee, and promised thee heaven. And do not forget how truly seasonable was the mercy; for thou wast then living without hope, without God, and without Christ in the world, when Jesus brought thee nigh by the blood of his cross. And never, surely, was mercy more unexpected, less sought for, or less esteemed, than when Jesus surprised thee with the manifestations of his grace, and made thee willing in the day of his power. Precious Redeemer! the pharisee's reproach shall be my joy; and what they spoke of my Lord in contempt, shall henceforth be the chief note in my evening song to his praise:—'This man, this God-man, receiveth sinners and eateth with them, for he hath received me, the chief of sinners, and eaten with me.' Lord Jesus! ever receive me, the poorest, the most unworthy of all the objects of thy grace. Come in, Lord, to my poor house, to my heart, and bring me to thine house and to thy table; and there let it be noticed, and known to every beholder, while my soul is feasting itself in the rich enjoyment, that "Jesus receiveth sinners, and eateth with them."

MARCH 23.

MORNING.—"By his own blood he entered in once into the holy place, having obtained eternal redemption for us."—Heb. ix. 12.

Ponder, my soul, these solemn expressions concerning thy Jesus. Mark, in them, their vast contents. Jesus, as a prophet, hath revealed his salvation: as a priest, he alone hath procured it, and offered it up to God and the Father; and as a King, he ever lives and reigns to see its efficacy fully accomplished in all his redeemed, being made partakers of it. Behold in this, his priestly office, both as an high priest and as the sacrifice, what he hath wrought, and what he hath accomplished—even eternal redemption. Mark, my soul, the several volumes of mercy comprised in it. First—Of man's revolt from God. Secondly—The deadly breach by reason thereof. Thirdly—The proclamation from heaven, of God's determined purpose to take vengeance of sin. Fourthly—Man's total inability to appease the divine wrath, either by doing or suffering. Fifthly—Divine grace, in the love of the Father, permitting a substitute, competent to do this great act of salvation for men; and appointing and constituting no less a person than his dear Son to the accomplishment of it. Sixthly—Jesus, the Son of God, voluntarily giving himself an offering and a sacrifice for sin, and by that one offering of himself, once offered for ever, perfecting them that are sanctified. Seventhly—Having thus accomplished the purpose of salvation upon earth, Jesus now, by his own blood, entered into the holy place, to make the whole effectual by the exercise of his priestly office in heaven. And, lastly, to add no more—God accepting and confirming his perfect approbation of the whole, and now proclaiming peace on earth, good-will towards men. Ponder over these grand, these glorious, these momentous subjects, my soul, this day. Take them about with thee wheresoever thou goest; fold them in thy bosom; write them on the tablets of thine heart; let them arise with thee, and lay down with thee. And, in all thine approaches to the mercy-seat behold Him, and let him never be lost to the view of the eye of faith, by whom the whole is wrought, and of whom this sweet scripture speaks; who, "by his own blood entered in once into the holy place, having obtained eternal redemption for us."

EVENING.—"And manifested forth his glory; and his disciples believed on him."—John ii. 11.

It forms a very sweet thought to the believer, that, amidst the general darkness and ignorance concerning the person of Jesus, in the days of his flesh, the glory of his Godhead was frequently manifested to his disciples, so that they knew him, and believed on him. And it is equally blessed, that now, amidst the darkness and ignorance of many who call themselves christians, after Christ, (but who denying, or being unconscious of his Godhead, prove that they know him not) the Lord hath not left himself without a witness of who he is, to the minds of his faithful followers; but hath manifested forth his glory; and all true disciples believe on him. My soul! if thou wert called upon to give thy testimony to Jesus, concerning all the grand points which prove the Godhead of his person, and the eternal merits and efficacy of his blood and righteousness; how wouldest thou shew the evidences, that he hath manifested forth his glory to thee, and that thou believest on him? I would answer, Jesus hath fully manifested himself to me, as "One with the Father, over all, God blessed for ever;" and as such, having seen the Son, I believe in him, "in whom dwelleth all the fulness of the Godhead bodily." Hence, therefore, as it is said, "they that know thy name, will put their trust in thee;" so "I know whom I have believed;" and by his blessed Spirit, am persuaded, that "he is able to keep that which I have committed unto him to that day." Now, had not the Lord Jesus, by his Holy Spirit, taught me who he was, and what he was able to perform; had he not manifested forth his glory, never should I have known him, so as to believe on him. But the revelation he hath made of himself, hath induced all those saving effects, which none but the teachings of his Holy Spirit could impart. It hath wrought in me faith and love, humbleness and self-loathing, a regard for his cause, a zeal for his honour, a love to his people, an indifferency to the world; and all those gracious fruits of faith which follow the knowledge of Jesus. Blessed Lord! my soul rejoiceth anew, this evening, in the contemplation of thy glory. And under a sense of the distinguishing mercy, I feel constrained to cry out with the astonishment of the apostle, "Lord! how is it, that thou hast manifested thyself to me, and not unto the world!"

MARCH 24.

MORNING.—"I in them, and thou in me, that they may be made perfect in one."—John xvii. 23.

Think, my soul, to what a transcendant honour, to what a state of unspeakable happiness, the truly regenerated believer in Jesus is begotten. Who shall declare it; what heart shall fully conceive it? Mark, my soul, how graciously thy Redeemer hath pointed it out, in those sweet words. Observe the foundation of the whole, in that glorious mystery of union between the Father and the Son. This is at the bottom of all our mercies, and becomes the source and spring of every other. "Thou in me," saith Jesus; not only as One in the nature and essence of the Godhead, in a sameness of nature, of design, of will, of perfections, and in all the attributes which constitute the distinguishing properties of Jehovah; but peculiarly as Mediator, the head of the church and people, in communicating all the fulness of the Godhead to dwell bodily in Jesus, as the Glory-man, the God-man, the Anointed of God. Thus, being one with Christ, and dwelling in Christ, in such a way and manner as the Godhead never did, and never can, dwell in any other. And as Jesus is thus One with the Father in the essence of the Godhead, and the Father in him, dwelling in him, and being in him, in all the work of redemption, as Mediator—so is Jesus one in the nature of the manhood, with all his mystical members. "I in them," saith Christ, "as thou art in me." Jesus is the Head of his body, the church, and he is their fulness; and they members of his body, of his flesh, and of his bones. Hence result the blessed effects which his redeemed all derive from him, "that they may be made perfect in one." Sweet and precious thought! in Jesus they are made perfect. From him they derive perfection. As one with him, they are counted, and beheld perfect before God; and by him they will be found so to all eternity. And what particularly endears this lovely view of the believer's perfection in Christ Jesus, is this; that every individual member of Jesus's mystical body, is all alike equally interested in this perfection in Jesus. For as it is from the same Spirit dwelling in them all, that they are quickened to this spiritual life in Christ Jesus, and are all of them made living members, and united to Jesus, their one glorious head; so there must be an equally near and dear union to Jesus, and to one another. Delightful consideration! as the apostle reasons upon another consideration—"The eye cannot say to the hand, I have no need of thee; nor the foot say, because I am not the hand, I am not of the body." In Jesus they are all one; neither can any touch the least of his people, no more than the apple of his eye, without touching him. Is it so, my soul? And art thou one with Jesus, one with the glorious Head, one with the precious members? Hast thou communion in all that concerns Christ; communion and interest in his Person; communion in his righteousness; communion in his life, in his death, in his resurrection, in his church, in his people, in his ordinances, in all that concerns Jesus? Oh then, rest assured that thou shalt have an everlasting communion, and nothing shall separate thee from Jesus—neither in time nor to all eternity. Go down, my body, go down to the grave with this perfect confidence—"That if the Spirit of him that raised up Jesus from the dead dwell in you, he that raised up Christ from the dead, shall also quicken your mortal body, by his Spirit that dwelleth in you."

EVENING.—"And it came to pass, when Joshua was by Jericho, that he lift up his eyes, and looked, and behold, there stood a man over against him, with his sword drawn in his hand. And Joshua went unto him, and said unto him, art thou for us, or for our adversaries? And he said, nay, but as Captain of the host of the Lord am I now come. And Joshua fell on his face to the earth, and did worship."—Joshua v. 13, 14.

Behold, my soul, what a most blessed portion here is, for thee to feast upon, in almost endless thought. Who could this be, that appeared to Joshua, but the Lord Jesus Christ? Who ever called himself the Captain of the Lord's host; but he whom the Holy Ghost hath called, "the Captain of our salvation?" Heb ii. 10. Is he not the same who appeared to Adam in the garden, to Abraham in his tent, to Jacob at Bethel, to Moses at the bush? And though he diversified his form, upon these and several other occasions; yet all were only intended to familiarize his people to the knowledge of him. And wherefore, dearest Jesus, was it, that thou didst thus graciously condescend to visit thy chosen, so long before the time appointed for the open display of thyself, when tabernacling in flesh, but to tell thy church, that thy whole heart was towards them in love, and that the thoughts thou hadst towards them, were thoughts of good and not of evil? And although, in this thy appearance to thy servant Joshua, thou didst assume the human form; yet as Captain of the Lord's host, he instantly knew thy glorious character of Mediator, and fell to the earth in adoration. Hail then, thou almighty Lord, thou Captain of the Lord's host, and of my salvation! thou hast indeed, indeed entered the lists of the holy war, and in thine own person, led captivity captive, and fully conquered Satan and sin, and death, and hell, for thy people: and thou wilt assuredly conquer all those tremendous foes of ours, in thy people, and bruise Satan under our feet shortly. Indeed, indeed, dear Lord, thou hast already brought them under; for by thy sovereign grace in the hearts of thy redeemed, thou hast made thy people "willing in the day of thy power." By the sword of thy Spirit, thou hast convinced my soul of sin, and by the arrows of thy quiver, thou hast wounded my heart with deep contrition for sin. Lord, I fall before thee, as thy servant Joshua did, and worship thee; and with all the church of the redeemed, both in heaven and earth, cheerfully confess, "that Jesus Christ is Lord, to the glory of God the Father." Amen.

MARCH 25.

MORNING.—"The mercy promised."—Luke i. 72.

"The mercy promised!" Why, God graciously promised many mercies, and most faithfully and fully performed them. Yes! every thing out of hell may well be called a mercy. Every child of Adam beareth about with him, day by day, tokens of God's mercy. The air we breathe, the garments we put on, the food we eat; all the comforts, conveniences, enjoyments of life; these are all mercies. But none of these are what the sweet portion of the morning points at. It is here a particular, a special, one specific mercy. And who can this mean, my soul, but Jesus, thy Jesus?—He is, indeed, "the mercy promised," the first mercy, the first promise; the first, best, and comprehensive gift of God in the bible. He is indeed the mercy of mercies, the first born, the sum and substance of every other. He is essential to make all other mercies really and truly mercies; for without him, they ultimately prove injurious. He is essential to put a sweetness, to give a relish, a value, an importance, to every other. Where Jesus is, there is mercy; where Jesus is not, what can profit? My soul, hast thou considered this?—Dost thou know it? Is Jesus thine? Is this mercy promised, really, truly given to thee? Hast thou taken him home to thine house, to thine heart? Pause, if it be so, how dost thou value him, know him, use him, live to him, walk with him, hope in him, rejoice in him, and make him thine all? Hast thou received him as a free mercy, an undeserved mercy? Hast thou accepted him as so seasonable a mercy, that, without him, thou wouldest have been undone for ever? Is he now so truly satisfying to thee in all thy desires, for time and for eternity, that thou canst bid adieu to every enjoyment, if needful; and, looking up to Jesus, canst truly say, "Whom have I in heaven but thee, and there is none upon earth that I desire besides thee?" Oh my soul, if this be thy portion, then hast thou a Benjamin's portion indeed! God thy Father hath given thee indeed the mercy promised; and Jesus is, and will be, thy mercy, and the mercy of all mercies, to all eternity. Amen.

EVENING.—"Ye have heard of the patience of Job, and have seen the end of the Lord; that the Lord is very pitiful, and of tender mercy." —James v. 11.

There is something uncommonly soothing and consolatory in these words, concerning the Lord's grace, "that the Lord is very pitiful, and of tender mercy." Very pitiful! Sweet consideration to a child of God, under affliction! For it speaks in the tenderest and most endearing manner, upon all such occasions, that if afflictions abound, while the Lord is very pitiful, and of tender mercy, there must be a needs be for them. My soul, keep this thought always uppermost in thy remembrance; and carry it about with thee in thy bosom for constant use, to have recourse to, as occasion may require. And take another sweet lesson with thee, to help on thy mind to suitable exercises on this account. Hadst thou as much wisdom, and as much love for thyself, and what concerns thy most material interests, as Jesus hath, and is using for thee, the most painful exercises thou art now called to, and which thou art apt to shrink from, would be among the subjects of holy joy. And mark farther what the apostle saith: "Ye have heard of the patience of Job, and have seen the end of the Lord;" that is, in the issue of Job's trials. Who that reads the patriarch's history, can doubt but that the Lord all along intended the whole for his servant's happiness, as well as his own glory? In all thine exercises, my soul, look to the end of them. Some blessed purpose, depend upon it, thy Jesus hath in view in all, and he will accomplish it. In the mean time, never forget, that "the Lord is very pitiful, and of tender mercy:" in all the afflictions of his people he is afflicted. And what a memorable scripture is that: "His soul was grieved for the misery of Israel;" Judges x. 16. Precious Jesus! all is well. In the sorrows of thy children, thou bearest a part; and the largest part is thine; the heaviest end of every cross thou carriest. The cup of our affliction is not bitter like thy cup of trembling: for through thy love in redemption, the gall and wormwood are taken out. There is no bitter wrath in the chastisements of a kind father under sin; for thou hast borne the wrath when made sin and a curse for us, that we might be made the righteousness of God in thee. Often, my soul! let these sweet consoling thoughts refresh thee. Thy Lord, thy Jesus, "is very pitiful and of tender mercy."

MARCH 26.

MORNING.—"Thy lips, O my spouse, drop as the honey-comb." —Song iv. 11.

While Jesus is so precious to his people, that they seek him in every thing that is lovely, and indeed can discover nothing to be lovely until they have found Jesus in it, what an endearment is it to the soul of a believer, when he discovers Jesus looking upon him, eyeing him, and even commending Jesus's own graces, which he hath imparted to the soul, brought out into exercises again by the influences of his own Holy Spirit. My soul, canst thou really be led to believe that Jesus is speaking to his church, to his fair one, his spouse, to every individual soul of his redeemed and regenerated ones, in those sweet words of the song? Doth Jesus, the Son of God, call thee his spouse; and doth he say, thy lips drop as the honey-comb? Pause, my soul, and ponder over these gracious words of thy God. By thy lips, no doubt, Jesus means thy words; of which Solomon saith—"pleasant words are as an honey-comb, sweet to the soul and health to the bones." Prov. xvi. 24. Do thy lips drop in prayer, in praise, in conversation, in christian fellowship, in ordinances, and in all the ordinary intercourse of life? Is Jesus thy one theme; his name, his love, his grace, his work, his salvation; what he hath done, what he hath wrought; how he hath loved, how he hath lived, how he hath died, how he now lives again to appear in the presence of God for his people; and to give out of his fulness, his mercies, his treasures: in visits, in manifestations, and the ten thousand numberless, nameless, ways by which he proves himself to be Jesus? Do thy lips, my soul, drop in these topics when thou walkest by the way, when thou liest down, when thou risest up, and when thou goest in before the presence of God, in the public worship of the temple, or the private closet, where no eye seeth thee but him that seeth in secret? And doth thy Jesus really mark these things? Doth he condescend to notice his poor creature, and to esteem these droppings as the sweetness of the honey? Precious God, precious Jesus! what a love is here. O for grace, for love, for life, for every suited gift of my God and Saviour, that my lips, from the abundance of the heart, may drop indeed as the honey-comb—sweetly, freely, not by constraint, except the constraint of thy love; but constantly, unceasingly, for ever, as the drops of the honey-comb which follow one another; that prayer may follow praise, and praise succeed to prayer; and that there may be a succession in magnifying and adoring the riches of grace; that the name of Jesus may be always in my mouth; and from that one blessed source, that Jesus lives in my heart, and rules, and reigns, and is formed there the hope of glory.

EVENING.—"And Moses said unto God, behold, when I come unto the children of Israel, and shall say unto them, the God of your fathers hath sent me unto you; and they shall say to me, what is his name? what shall I say unto them? And God said unto Moses, I AM THAT I AM. And he said, thus shalt thou say unto the children of Israel, I AM hath sent me unto you."—Exod. iii. 13, 14.

My soul, hast thou fully considered, so as to rest in the full assurance of faith upon it, on what the whole foundation of covenant promises and engagements rest? It is not the greatness of the promise, no, nor the greatness of the deliverance wrought out for poor sinners, by the blood and righteousness of the Lord Jesus Christ, on which faith founds its claim; for, in fact, the more astonishing, and great, and unexpected the mercy is, as in the case of redemption by the Lord Jesus Christ, the more difficult would it be for a poor self-condemned sinner to trust in it, with full assurance of faith; but the great foundation for thee, and for every poor sinner to ground his hopes of redemption by Jesus Christ upon, is the faithfulness of that God which cannot lie, having promised, as appears, from the beautiful instance this precious scripture records. The Lord was going to send Moses, as his minister, to bring out his people Israel from Egyptian bondage; Moses desires the Lord to give him the commission with his name; whence, by the way we may learn, that they who stand up in the Lord's name, ought themselves to know who the Lord is, and from a proper acquaintance with the Lord, to recommend him to those among whom they proclaim him, as one they themselves know and trust in. To the inquiry of Moses concerning the name by which he should hold him forth to his people, the Lord condescends to give this answer; I AM THAT I AM: intimating the self-existence, the eternity, and faithfulness of JEHOVAH. As if God had said, I AM, and therefore by virtue of this underived being, which I possess in myself, I give being to all my promises. My soul! often call to remembrance this grand and glorious truth. Thou hast not only the perfect and covenant redemption of thy Christ's blood and righteousness to confide in; but thou hast this other pillar and ground of the truth to confirm thy faith; I AM hath engaged for it also. So that both the blessedness of the promise, and the faithfulness of the Almighty Promiser, are with thee. Plead both before the throne, for Jehovah will ever be mindful *of*, glory *in*, and prove faithful *to*, all his covenant promises in Christ, to a thousand generations. Hallelujah! Amen.

MARCH 27.

MORNING.—"The trumpet of the jubilee."—Levit. xxv. 9.

My soul, pause over the subject of the jubilee trumpet; for surely much of gospel was proclaimed by it. It should seem that there were four distinct and special sounds of the trumpet in the camp of Israel. The trumpet of memorials, so called, (Levit. xxiii. 24.) was blown on the occasion of the new moon, calling the people to the joyful assembly, Psalm lxxxi. 3. There was also the fast trumpet of which the prophet speaks, Joel ii. 1. Besides these, the war trumpet gave a certain sound to prepare to battle, 1 Cor. xiv. 8. And this of the jubilee, which differed from all. And although the jubilee trumpet was never heard but once in fifty years, yet so sweet and so distinguishing was the sound, that no poor captive among the servants in the camp of Israel, was at a moment's loss to understand its gracious meaning. Say, my soul, is not the gospel sound, when first heard by the ear of faith, precisely the same? When pardon was first proclaimed to thee by the blood of Christ, and the day of his atonement so manifested to thy spiritual senses, that the captivity of sin and Satan lost their power upon thee, was not this indeed the jubilee trumpet, and the acceptable year of the Lord? Hast thou heard this joyful sound? Hath the Son of God made thee free? Hath Jesus caused thee to return to thy long-lost, long-forfeited inheritance? And wilt thou never forget the unspeakable mercy? Hail, thou Almighty Deliverer, thou Redeemer of thy captives! I had sold my possession, sold myself for nought; and thou hast redeemed it for me again without money. I had sold it, indeed, but could not alienate it for ever, because the right of redemption was with thee. Yes, blessed Jesus, thou art he whom thy brethren shall praise. Thou art the next of kin, the nearest of all relations, and the dearest of all brothers. And thou hast redeemed both soul and body, both lands and inheritance by thy blood; and so redeemed the whole, as never more to be lost again, or forfeited for ever. And now, Lord, thy jubilee trumpet sounds; and the proclamation of the everlasting gospel is heard in our land, to give liberty to the captive, sight to the blind, to bring the prisoners out of the prison, and them that sit in darkness out of the prison-house. Oh, cause me to know the joyful sound, and daily to walk in the light of thy countenance. Cause me, by the sweet influences of thy Spirit, to live in the constant expectation of the year of the everlasting jubilee, when the trumpet of the archangel shall finally sound, and all thy redeemed shall then return to Zion with songs, and everlasting joy upon their heads; when they shall obtain joy and gladness, and sorrow and sighing shall flee away. Hallelujah.

EVENING.—" To see thy power and thy glory, so as I have seen thee in the sanctuary."—Ps. lxiii. 2.

My soul! knowest thou what it is, at times, to be sensible of a barrenness of spiritual enjoyments? If at the house of God, to be cold and lifeless there? If at home, or unable to attend the place where God's honour dwelleth, yet there also to be without the Bethel-visits of thy Lord? Behold one of old, in a wilderness state, feeling the same. But do not fail to remark also, in the very breathings of the soul *after* Christ, how plainly his soul was under the sweet influences *of* Christ: David did not so much long for the temple service, as for the presence of the God of the temple. Remark also the peculiarity of expression: he longed to see the Lord's power and glory, so as he had seen *him* in times past. God in Christ is Jehovah's power and glory; and the sanctuary without *him*, would be no better than the wilderness. What a beautiful devout frame of mind was this sacred writer in, when thus going forth in earnest longing after the divine power and glory, as manifested in the person of God in Christ! Now, my soul, canst thou make use of the same language, even when thou art mourning in retirement over the absence of the Lord Jesus? Is Jesus still the one object of desire? And are the power and glory of Jehovah, as manifested in the person of Jesus, the longing of thy heart to enjoy? Be comforted, in still having before thee the great object of faith, and the actings of faith, even when the waters of the sanctuary run low. God is still honoured, still loved, still trusted in, and depended upon, by this humble, though sorrowful frame; and ere long, he whom thou desirest to see in his power and glory will manifest himself in both; and thou shalt yet give him praise, "who is the health of thy countenance and thy God."

MARCH 28.

MORNING.—"For where a testament is, there must also of necessity be the death of the testator; for a testament is of force after men are dead, otherwise it is of no strength at all while the testator liveth."—Heb. ix. 16, 17.

Behold, my soul, how graciously the Holy Ghost hath here represented the necessity of Jesus's death, in order that the testament, or will, he left behind him, might have the intended effect; and all the benefits and blessings he bequeathed in it to his people, might be fully paid and made over to them for their present peace and everlasting happiness. Now, my soul, mark down, for this day's special meditation, the many precious things here contained. Observe how very accommodating the Holy Ghost is to explain to thee divine things, by the similitude of human transactions. As a man makes his will, so Jesus made his. As what a man gives is altogether a free and voluntary act, so Jesus was not constrained by what he gave in his blessed will; but the whole was the result of his own free, gracious, and everlasting love. And as a man must die before his will can be put in force, so Jesus must, and did die, that his testament and will might have the full effect also. But there is one sweet point more to be taken into this account, in which, my soul, thy Jesus hath infinitely surpassed all men in this article of their wills. When a man dies he appoints by will an executor, to whom he must trust the management of all his effects after his decease; and should his executor prove unfaithful, his best designs for those he loved, when living, may all fail of the end when he is dead. Now here lies the sweetness of Jesus's will:—he not only made the will, but he himself will see it fully executed; for as he died once, in order that by his death his will might be confirmed, so he ever liveth to see the whole of his blessed gifts and legacies paid. Precious, precious Jesus! how sure then is thy will, and the certainty of every tittle of it being fulfilled. Now, my soul, there are *two* grand things which concern thee to inquire concerning the will of the Lord Jesus. The *first* is, whether thou hast any interest in it? And the *second* is, what the Lord Jesus hath left behind him? Recollect, my soul, that in this instance, as in the former, when men make their wills, it is to dispose of their effects to their relations, their friends, their families. Jesus also hath his relations, his friends, his family. Yes, thou dear Lord, thou condescendest to call thy people thy spouse, thy brethren, thy children, thy jewels, thy redeemed. My soul, dost thou claim relationship to Jesus? Canst thou prove, or hast thou proved his will? Is Jesus thine husband? Hath he betrothed thee to himself? Again—hast thou the marks of a child in God's family? Art thou born again? Again—if you are his, then hast thou his Spirit: "for he that is joined to the Lord is one Spirit." If you are a child of God, and a joint-heir with Christ, then art thou under his divine leadings; "for as many as are led by the Spirit of

God, they are the sons of God." If thou hast these marks of relationship, thou mayest safely look for his gifts. Surely Jesus hath remembered in his legacies his spouse, his children. And Oh, what an inventory wilt thou find, my soul, under the *second* inquiry, when thou hast fully proved the first. Oh, what legacies, what gifts, what an inheritance, art thou entitled to by the will of Jesus! All temporal blessings, all spiritual blessings, all eternal blessings! Pardon, mercy, peace, in the blood of his cross; the sweet enjoyment of all providences in this life, and the sure possession of everlasting happiness in that which is to come, Oh, how true was it, my God and Saviour, when thou didst say, "I will cause them that love me to inherit substance."

EVENING.—"Who is a God like unto thee, that pardoneth iniquity, and passeth by the transgression of the remnant of his heritage? He retaineth not his anger for ever, because he delighteth in mercy. He will turn again, he will have compassion upon us: he will subdue our iniquities: and thou wilt cast all their sins into the depths of the sea." —Micah vii. 18, 19.

My soul! hast thou ever duly and thoroughly pondered over the several interesting volumes of grace recorded in this glorious scripture? If not, make them the subject of this evening's song. Let every chapter contained in them, pass and re-pass in review before thee, and see whether, in the close of the whole, the astonishment of the man of God is not thine also; crying out, "Who is a God like our God? a God in Christ, gracious and merciful, slow to anger, and of great kindness, forgiving iniquity, transgression, and sin!" And, first, "He pardoneth iniquity, and passeth by the transgression of the remnant of his people." Yes; in Jesus, the Son of his love, he hath done all this, and more than this, for he hath taken the objects of his clemency into favour. Secondly, the cause of all these unspeakable felicities is assigned; "because he delighteth in mercy." It is from himself, and his own free sovereign grace, that these blessings flow. Not what the highly-favoured objects merit, but what grace can do for them. Not what claims they have to his bounty, but how his grace can best be magnified in their salvation. Sweet and precious consideration to the breast of every poor sinner! My soul! I hope that thou canst truly participate in the delightful thought. Thirdly, he that delighteth in mercy, will delight to *turn again* to his people. He will turn their hearts to himself, and then his returns to them will sweetly follow, to their apprehension, and to their joy. " Fourthly, he will not only pardon their iniquity, but " he will subdue their iniquities: not only take away the guilt of sin, but also destroy the dominion of sin; not only cast their sins behind his back, but " cast them into the depths of the sea:" and so effectually shall they be lost, that if the sin of Judah be sought for, it shall not be found. The depths of the sea, that fountain which God hath opened in the Redeemer's blood, shall more completely bury them, than the congregated waters of the ocean cover any mountain or hill cast into them. Say now, my soul! dost thou not look up to a God in Christ, and cry out, with the prophet, in the same holy rapture and astonishment, " Who is a God like unto thee ?"

MARCH 29.

MORNING.—" The precious ointment upon the head, that ran down upon the beard, even Aaron's beard, that went down to the skirts of his garments."—Psalm cxxxiii. 2.

My soul, behold, in the anointing here set forth of the Jewish high priest, a type of His anointing who is a. Priest for ever, and a Priest upon his throne; and while looking at Aaron, say, as the Lord Jesus did upon another occasion concerning Solomon, " A greater than Aaron is here." It is sweet, very sweet, and very profitable, to behold the old church shadowing forth the new, and the law ministering to the gospel. Yes, blessed Jesus, I behold in Aaron, and in the precious ointment poured forth upon his head, thus running down to the skirts of his garments, the beautiful representation of that fulness of the Spirit, which was poured out upon thee without measure; that from thee the communication might flow down to the poorest, the humblest, the lowest of thy members, even to the very skirts of thy clothing. "It pleased the Father that in thee should all fulness dwell:" that of that fulness all thy people might receive, and grace for grace. And by virtue of our interest in thee, and union with thee, all thy people do richly partake of communion in all thy benefits, blessings, mercies. The sun shines not to itself, nor for itself, but to impart light and life to others: so dost thou, the Sun of Righteousness, shine forth in all thy glory, not for thyself, but to bless, and enliven, and give out of all thy grace and fulness, every suited blessing, according to the measure of the gift of Christ. My soul, bring home these precious truths to the conviction of experience. Was Jesus indeed anointed for his people? Was grace poured into his lips? Was he, like Aaron, so installed into the office of the priesthood, and the Holy Spirit so unmeasurably communicated to him, on purpose that all his little ones should partake of this unspeakable gift of God? Did God the Father say to Jesus, "I will pour my Spirit upon thy seed, and my blessing upon thine offspring?" Well then, my soul, hast thou partaken of the Holy Spirit? Hast thou communion with Jesus in all that concerns thy salvation? A child of God, a joint-heir with Christ, and a soul begotten of the Holy Spirit, hath interest and communion in all that belongs to Jesus, as the Great Head and Mediator of his church; interested in his Person, interested in his work, interested in his righteousness, in his life, in his death, in his resurrection, in his everlasting priestly office, and in his everlasting glory. What sayeth my soul to these things? Go, my soul, go this morning, go in the strength of this interest, and look at a throne of grace, within the vail, whither thy forerunner is for thee entered; behold thy glorious Aaron, wearing the priestly vestments still, and having all grace, all fulness; waiting to be gracious, and to impart of that fulness to thy necessities; and having received gifts for men, yea, for thee, the most rebellious, that the Lord God might dwell among them. Lord, proportion thy mercies to my wants; and as the day is, so let the strength be.

EVENING.—"Agree with thine adversary quickly, whiles thou art in the way with him; lest at any time the adversary deliver thee to the judge, and the judge deliver thee to the officer, and thou be cast into prison. Verily, I say unto thee, thou shalt by no means come out thence, till thou hast paid the uttermost farthing."—Matt. v. 25, 26.

My soul! hast thou agreed with thine adversary, and made full payment of all the law charges? If so, it is blessed to review the account, and look over the several particulars, wherein thou wert a debtor, now struck out of God's book, and marked *paid, paid,* in red letters, with Jesus's blood. To thee, as a sinner, born in sin, and an insolvent debtor, both by nature and by practice, the law of God stood forth as thine adversary. To agree with him as quickly as possible, whilst in the way with him, and while life remains, which is every moment subject to be ended, is the first and most momentous of all concerns. Hadst thou not done this, and death had come, both law and justice must have consigned thee over to the Judge of quick and dead; and having rejected him as thy Saviour, and knowing him only as thy Judge, he must have delivered thee to the angels, who are officers in his kingdom, to execute his wrath; and into hell, as the eternal prison, thou must have been cast: and as the debt then could never have been paid, so deliverance could never have been obtained; but unsatisfied justice would have continued to demand, without any possibility on thy part of paying, to all eternity. Now see how thy account stands. It is a solemn thing to deal with God. If thy debt of original and actual sin be not paid by thy surety, it is not cancelled; but if Jesus, thy surety, hath paid it for thee, thy God hath accepted it of him; yea, he himself constituted and appointed him to pay it; and Jesus never gave over, nor did he compound with God, until he had paid the uttermost farthing: then art thou free. Oh! then, be often reviewing the blessed account, in which all thy plea for grace and acceptance here, and glory hereafter, most completely stands. Jesus hath paid the whole, and God the Father graciously saith, "Deliver him from going down into the pit; I have found a ransom."—Job xxxiii. 24.

MARCH 30.

MORNING.—"So then with the mind I myself serve the law of God; but with the flesh the law of sin."—Rom. vii. 25.

Is this thy language, my soul? Hast thou learnt with Paul, with Job, with Isaiah, and all the faithful gone before, to loathe thyself in thine own sight? Dost thou groan, being burthened with a body of sin which drags down the soul? Pause over this view of human nature. In the first place—think, my soul, what humbling thoughts such a state of corruption ought to induce. Though the mind be regenerated, though with the mind the believer serves the law of God, delights in the law of God, loves the law, and would make it the subject of devout meditation all the day; yet such is the body of sin, the flesh with its affections, and appetites, and desires, that it draws away the attention, imperiously puts in its claims, and rises up in rebellion continually. And are the souls of God's children thus exercised, thus afflicted, in the struggles between the different motions of grace and corruption from day to day? Yes, such is the state, such the uniform experience of God's people in all ages. Paul thus complains, though he had been so highly sanctified. Perhaps there never was a child of God brought into a closer and more intimate communion with God. He had been caught up to the third heaven, and heard unspeakable words. He had laboured more than all the apostles. He had been converted by a miracle from heaven, and by the immediate call of the Lord Jesus personally to him. But yet this highly favoured servant of the Lord, this blessed apostle, who was continually flying on the wings of zeal and love in the service of his Master, even he, with his flesh, he tells us, served the law of sin: nay, he felt and discovered "a law of sin in his members, warring against the law of his mind, and bringing him into captivity to the law of sin which was in his members;" and under a deep distress of soul he cried out—"Oh wretched man that I am, who shall deliver me from the body of this death!" Is it so, then, my soul, with thee also! Dost thou discover the same in thy experience? Dost thou feel the rebellions of sin rising up within thee? Dost thou detect thine heart, wandering even in the moment of solemn exercises; and, in short, thine own body, the worst and greatest enemy thou hast to contend with? Oh then, learn from hence, what humbling views oughtest thou to have of thyself, and to lay low in the dust in consequence thereof before God. When thou hast duly contemplated this state of fallen nature, let thy next improvement of this subject be to endear the Lord Jesus to thee, my soul, more and more; to fly out of thyself, to fly to Jesus, to take refuge in him and his great salvation; from even thyself, with all that body of sin and death, under which thou thus continually groanest; and to derive herefrom a daily and hourly conviction, yet more strong and unanswerably conclusive, that nothing but the blood of Jesus can cleanse, nothing but the righteousness of Jesus can save and justify a sinner. Say as Paul did, when from the bottom of his heart that soul-piercing question arose, "Who shall deliver me from the body of this death? I thank God, through Jesus Christ our Lord."

EVENING.—"I would lead thee, and bring thee into my mother's house, who would instruct me."—Song viii. 2.

My soul! hast thou ever noticed the peculiar beauties of this scripture? if not, make it the subject of this evening's meditation; it will amply recompence thine attention. The church is here in great liveliness, and actings of faith upon the person of her Lord; indeed, so much so, that we do not find any thing like this holy familiarity, used by the church towards her Lord, in any other part of the bible. It is the well-known office of Jesus, to lead his people, and to draw them to himself. God the Father hath given him for this blessed purpose, as "a Leader and Commander to his people." Isaiah lv. 4. And Jesus himself declared, that "if he was lifted up, he would draw all to himself." John xii. 32. But here, it is the church leading Christ. Pause, my soul. Dost thou know any thing of this, or like it, in thine own experienee? Shall I not hope thou dost? Look diligently; for if so, it will form a blessed subject, not only for thy present meditation, but for every evening and morning of thy life. And it will have a blessed effect also, in proving the reality of thy faith, and of endearing to thyself the Redeemer's love. Say, then, is not Jesus led by his people, when he is constrained at any time, as the disciples constrained him at Emmaus, to remain with them, until he maketh himself known to them in breaking of bread? Hast thou not thyself been compelled, at times, to say, as they did, that "thine heart hath burned within thee," when Jesus hath made himself known, in the word of his grace; or when he hath manifested himself in the tokens of his love, in softening thine heart when hardened, in warming it when frozen, comforting it when cast down; and thou hast held him in the galleries of his grace, by faith and prayer, and the exercises of the graces of his Holy Spirit, which his own hand first gave thee, and which his own power, in all the after-enjoyments of them, called forth into actings upon his person, work, and righteousness? Luke xxiv. 28—32. What wilt thou call these things, but leading Christ, and bringing Christ into thy mother's house, the church, where Jesus manifests himself to his beloved, otherwise than he doth to the world? Was it not thus that Jacob led the Lord, and constrained him not to depart from him, until he had blessed him? Gen. xxxii. 26. Was it not of the same kind, in the instance of Lot, when, by faith and prayer, the patriarch so led the Lord concerning Zoar, that the Lord said, "I cannot do any thing till thou be come thither?" Gen. xix. 22. Precious, precious Jesus! is it thus thy people have power with thee, and prevail with thee to stay with them; and thou sufferest thyself to be led by them, in all those instances where their furtherance in grace, and the promotion of thy glory will be accomplished by it? Oh! then, thou dear Lord! I beseech thee, give me such a double portion of thy blessed Spirit, that, taking hold of thy strength, I may lead my Lord, by faith and prayer, and all the goings forth of grace upon thy person and righteousness, into such rich enjoyments as the church here had in view, until "I cause thee to drink," also as she did, "of spiced wine of the juice of my pomegranate!"

MARCH 31.

MORNING.—"Having a desire to depart, and to be with Christ."—Phil. i. 23.

My soul, thou hast not, I hope, dismissed the solemn

thoughts opened to thy view by the scripture of yesterday. Surely, since that last morning, thou hast had but too many renewed occasions to feel the truth of it. Sin is not only present *with* thee at all times, but *in* thee, and as inseparable from thy unrenewed part, as the shadow from the substance. Thou knowest this, thou feelest it, thou groanest under it; and the consciousness of it is, in itself, enough to make thee go humbly all thy days. All other afflictions are nothing to this affliction: this, like the ocean compared to rivers, surpasseth and swalloweth up all. It is indeed a soul-supporting thought, (and, blessed be God, thou feelest the sweetness of it,) that under all, and in all, Jesus is thy hope. And while sin is always present with thee, Jesus, thy Advocate and Propitiation, is present for thee with the Father. But though in Him, and his righteousness accepted and secure, yet the consideration how much thy daily short-comings and transgressions dishonour God, and deprive thee of comfort here, is matter sufficient to make thine eyes run down with water, and thine heart continually to mourn before the mercy-seat. And will these things always be the same, whilst thou carriest about with thee this body of sin? Shall this perishing part of thine be always so unfavourable to the sweet and gracious desires of the soul? Shall I never, never truly and uninterruptedly enjoy Jesus until the body is dissolved, and the dust returns to the earth out of which that part of my nature was taken? Pause, my soul, and say—Hast thou not then a desire to depart, and to be with Christ! Is not the grave, in this view, not only made bearable, but even desirable—nay, even pleasant? What, shall I never be wholly free from sin, until that I am wholly freed from the body! Shall I never be secure of sweet enjoyment with Jesus in ordinances, in retirement, in prayer, in praise, until that I drop this body of sin? And wouldest thou not, my soul, gladly part with such a partner, near and dear as it is, if this partner, in its present state, so dreadfully robs thee of thy most precious enjoyments? It is true, death in itself is not desirable: but if only by dying thou canst enjoy Jesus; and if only by dying this body will lose its corruptions; if the grave hath a commission from thy Jesus to destroy that part only of thy body which is corrupt, and at the same time to act as a preserver of that part which Jesus at the last day will raise up to glory; if Jesus hath assured thee that, though worms destroy thy corrupt part, yet thine eyes, even thy bodily eyes, when raised up by Jesus a glorified body, shall see God; and if thy body, thus raised up and re-animated, shall then be not only wholly freed from all corruption, but equally disposed as the soul to praise thy God and Saviour for ever and for ever, and both soul and body unite as dear friends in this blessed service. Oh then, from henceforth never, my soul, look at death any more but as thy kind friend. It is to die to sin; but it is to live to Jesus. It is to be dead to all things but Jesus, that Jesus may be all things in life for ever. Oh then, for this desire to depart and to be with Christ!

EVENING.—" And the desire of all nations shall come."—Haggai ii. 7.

And who could this be, but Jesus? Who, but he alone, could be the object of desire; or able to gratify the desire of all nations? Sit down, my soul, this evening, and consider the subject to the full; and if the result be, as it surely must be, under divine teaching, that none but Jesus can answer to this character, and he most fully and completely comes up to it in every possible point of view; thou wilt find another sweet testimony to the truth as it is in Jesus, that he who alone is thy desire, hath ever been, and still is, to all that need and seek salvation, the desire of all nations. And, *first,* consider how universal the want of Jesus must be. " All the world is become guilty (the scripture saith) before God." Romans iii. 19. Hence, in every nation, kindred, tongue, or clime, every poor awakened and convinced sinner stands in need of a Saviour; and, however diversified by language, customs, or manners, sin is felt exceeding sinful, and the desire of deliverance from its guilt and its consequences, however variously expressed, is the burden and cry of every prayer. Now suppose, that to souls of this description, Jesus and his glorious salvation was revealed, would not the desire of every heart be towards him? Surely every eye would be directed to Jesus, and every tongue call aloud upon his name. Hence it is that Jesus, and he alone, is the desire of all nations. And as all poor sinners, whether conscious of it or not, stand in need of salvation; so, *secondly*, it must be observed, that it is Jesus, and he alone, who can give salvation: for, as the apostle speaks, " there is salvation in no other, neither is there any other name under heaven, given among men, whereby we must be saved." Acts iv. 12. And how extensive and all-sufficient is Jesus, to answer the desire of all nations! As one sun in the heavens becomes a fulness of light, and warmth, and healing to a whole earth; one ocean to supply all the rivers and lakes, and the inhabitants of the world; so one Lord Jesus Christ is both the Sun of righteousness, and the everlasting river of life, which maketh glad the city of God. Every want, and every desire that can be necessary for time and eternity, all temporal, spiritual, and eternal blessings, are in Jesus. He that is the desire of all nations, is in himself sufficient to satisfy the desires of every living soul.—Pause one moment, my soul, over this view of thy Jesus, and say, is He, that is, the desire of all nations, thy one, thine only one desire, to which every other is subordinate, and *in* which every other is swallowed up and lost? See what answer thou canst give to the heart-searching question? And when, through grace, thou hast derived renewed conviction from this view of the subject, that none but Jesus can fully answer the desires of an awakened soul, close the month, as thou hopest to close life, with the blessed hope that he who is thy one desire now, will be thine everlasting portion to all eternity. Amen and Amen.

APRIL 1.

MORNING.—"And this is his name whereby he shall be called—THE LORD OUR RIGHTEOUSNESS."—Jer. xxiii. 6.

Begin this month, my soul, with contemplating thy Jesus in this glorious distinction of character; and beg of God the Holy Ghost, who hath here declared that, under this character, Jesus shall be known and called, that every day through the month, and through the whole of life, thou mayest find grace and strength so to know and so to call Jesus, as to be everlastingly satisfied that thou art made the righteousness of God in him. And first, my soul, consider who and what this Holy One is. He is the Lord Jehovah. In the glories of his *essence,* he is One with the Father. In his *personal* glories, he is the Lord thy Mediator. And in his *relative* glories, he is thy righteousness. For, by virtue of his taking thy nature, what he is as Mediator and as the Surety of his people, he is for them. Pause over this blessed view, and then say, what can be more blessed than thus to behold Jesus as what he is in himself *for* his people. Look at him again, my soul, and take another view of him in his loveliness; in what he is *to* his people. This precious scripture saith, that he is the Lord *our* righteousness; that is, by virtue of his Godhead he is our righteousness, in such a sure way, and with such everlasting value and efficacy, as no creature could be. The righteousness his redeemed possess in him, and have a right in him, and are entitled to in him, is the righteousness of God; and therefore impossible ever to be lost, and impossible ever to be fully recompensed in glory. Sweet and blessed consideration! it seems too great to be believed. And so it would indeed, if the authority of Jehovah had not stamped it, and made the belief of it the first and highest act of a poor sinner's obedience. And observe, my soul, yet further, there is this blessed addition to the account —" he shall be called so." By whom? Nay by every one that knows him. The poor sinner shall call him so, who is led to see and feel that he hath no righteousness of his own; he shall call Jesus his Lord, his righteousness. He shall call him so to *others;* he shall call upon him for *himself*; he shall be that true Israelite, that very one whom the prophet describes— " Surely, shall one say, in the Lord have I righteousness and strength." The redeemed upon earth, the redeemed in heaven, the church of the first-born, shall call him so. The whole army of patriarchs and prophets, and apostles, all shall know Jesus as the Lord our righteousness. Nay, God himself, our Father, shall call his dear Son by this glorious name; for it is He who hath constituted and appointed him as the Lord our righteousness. And that Jesus is our righteousness is from this very cause, " that he is made of God to us wisdom and righteousness, sanctification and redemption, that he that glorieth may glory in the Lord." Now, my soul, what sayest thou to this sweet view of Jesus in this most precious scripture? Is not this name of Jesus most grateful to thee, as ointment of the richest fragrancy poured forth? Can any name be as sweet and delightful to one convinced, as thou art, that all thy righteousness is as dung and dross, as that of Jesus the Lord our righteousness? Witness for me, ye angels of light, that I renounce every other; and from henceforth will make mention of his righteousness, and his only. Yes, blessed Jesus, my mouth shall daily speak of thy righteousness and salvation; for I know no end thereof.

EVENING.—" And this is the name, wherewith she shall be called, the Lord our righteousness.—Jer. xxxiii. 16.

My soul! the subject of thy morning meditation would not be complete, if thy personal interest in it were not taken into the account; and therefore let thy mind be led forth, this evening, in sweet contemplation upon what the Holy Ghost hath said, in this scripture, by his same servant, the prophet, concerning the church of Jesus. If Jesus be called " the Lord our righteousness," and be, as he is well known to be, the husband of his people, surely his wife shall be called by her husband's name. She shall be called so because it is her husband's name; " the Lord our righteousness." And as he became sin for her, when he knew no sin; so she, when she knew no righteousness, shall, by virtue of her union and relationship with him, be righteousness, even " the righteousness of God in him," 2 Cor. v. 21. Now, my soul, seeing that these things are certain, sure, and unquestionable, do thou follow up the transporting meditation in every way, and by every way, and by every consideration, in which the blessedness of it is confirmed and assured. Married to Jesus, thou hast an interest in all he hath as Mediator, as the glorious Head of his body, the church, " the fulness of him that filleth all in all." And indeed, it is such an union and oneness, as nothing in nature can fully represent: " For he that is joined to the Lord is one spirit," 1 Cor. vi. 17. It infinitely transcends the marriage union, which is only in natural things, and at death is dissolved; for this union is spiritual, and continues for ever. Hence Jesus saith, " I will betroth thee to me for ever," Hosea ii. 19. Never lose sight of this high union, and the infinitely precious blessings to which, by virtue of it, thou art entitled: and while thou art called by his name, see that thou hast a conformity to his image. An union of grace should be manifested by an union of heart. What thy Jesus loves, thou shouldest love; and what he hates, do thou hate. Let his people be thy people; and his God and Father thine also. And from being one with him in heart, in mind, in sympathy, and affection; receiving life *from* him, living *on* him, and being *in* him; then will he be every thing to thee, of grace in this life, and of glory in that which is to come. Precious Lord, and husband of thy people, be thou made of God to me, and all thy redeemed, "wisdom, righteousness, sanctification, and redemption; that according as it is written, he that glorieth, may glory in the Lord!"

APRIL 2.

MORNING.—"And Aaron shall lay both his hands upon the head of the live goat, and confess over him all the iniquities of the children of Israel, and all their transgressions in all their sins, putting them upon the head of the goat, and shall send him away by the hand of a fit man into the wilderness. And the goat shall bear upon him all their iniquities, unto a land not inhabited."—Lev. xvi. 21, 22.

Pause, my soul, and behold the tender mercy of thy God, in thus causing to be represented to the church of old, by so striking a service, that grand and most momentous doctrine of the gospel, which, in after-ages of the church was fully set forth and completed, when Jehovah laid upon our Lord Jesus Christ the iniquities of his people. And do, my soul, attend to those several most interesting points here graciously revealed. As first—this was at the express command of God. Yes, who but God could transfer or permit a change of persons in the transferring of sin? This is one of the most blessed parts of the gospel, that when Jesus bore our sins in his own body on the tree, it was by the express will and appointment of Jehovah. The Lord Jesus *took* not those sins on himself; but the Lord *laid* on him the iniquity of us all. Mark this down in strong characters. Then next consider — that as Jesus had a transfer of all the sins of his people, consequently they were no longer upon the people, from whom they were transferred. Here faith finds full scope for exercise, in giving God the credit due to God. The sending away the goat was intended to represent the full remission of sins; and by the goat bearing them away into a land not inhabited, intimated that those sins should never be seen nor known any more; according to that precious scripture of the Holy Ghost by the prophet—"The iniquity of Israel shall be sought for, and there shall be none; and the sins of Judah, and they shall not be found," Jer. l. 20. And there is one sweet thought more, not to be overlooked in this blessed scripture, concerning those sins. Observe, my soul, the particularity of the expression. The confession of Aaron, the great high priest, was not only of all the iniquities of the children of Israel, but all their transgressions *in* all their sins. Pause, my soul, over this view, and recollect that there are many, and sometimes very heinous and aggravated circumstances of transgression in thy sins. Now what a sweet thought of relief to thy mind is it, under particular and galling circumstances of sin, to behold thy Jesus bearing thy sins, and all the transgression of all thy sins. The Lord caused *to meet in him*, as the passage might have been rendered, the iniquities of us all. Isa. liii. 6. Jesus was made as the common receiver, the drain, the sink, into which all the sins, and every minute and particular sin, was emptied. "He shall drink of the brook in the way," said the Holy Ghost. Ps. cx. 7. Was not this the black and filthy brook of Cedron, into which all the filth from the sacrifices of the temple was emptied? Here it was Jesus passed, when, in the night of his entering on his passion, he went into the garden. Look to this, my soul, and see whether it doth not strikingly, though solemnly, at the same time, set forth Jesus bearing all and every particular transgression in all thy sins. One thought more. The goat thus laden with all the sins of the people, was to be sent away by the hand of some fit man into the wilderness. As none but Jesus could be competent to bear sins, so none but Jesus could be fit to bear them away into a land of everlasting forgetfulness. It doth not lessen the beauty of this blessed scripture in the representation here made, in Jesus being set forth under two characters; for he is so in many. None but Jesus can indeed accomplish all: he is the High Priest, the Altar, and the Sacrifice, through all the law; and he is the fit man here represented, as well as the burden-bearer of sin. Hail! thou great High Priest! Blessed for ever be thou who hast borne away all the sins of thy people into a land not inhabited. Thou hast crossed out, in God's book of account, each and every individual sin, and the transgression of all our sins, in the red letters of thy blood; and never shall they appear again to the condemnation of thy people.

EVENING.—" I pray thee let me go over, and see the good land that is beyond Jordan, that goodly mountain, and Lebanon."—Deut. iii. 25.

What a very lovely and interesting view doth this sweet scripture afford of Moses, the man of God! Look at him, my soul, as the Holy Ghost hath here represented him, and pray for grace to gather some of those blessed instructions which this part of his history particularly affords. And what was it that made Moses so anxious to go over and see the good land? It was but a type of heaven, even in its highest glory; and surely the type or representation of any thing cannot be equal to the thing itself; and Moses knew, that if he had not the type, he should have the substance: if debarred Canaan, he should be in heaven. There must have been some other cause, which made Moses long for the sight of it. I venture to think (we may at least conjecture) and this scripture, I confess, leads me to the idea: " Let me see (said Moses) that goodly mountain, and Lebanon." This was the one hallowed spot Moses longed to see, and to feast his eyes upon. He who had conversed with Jesus at the bush, wanted to behold, and with sacred meditation, by faith, converse with him, on the very spot where, in after ages, he knew that Jesus would be crucified. He who by faith walked with Jesus, while in Egypt, so as "to esteem the reproach of Christ greater riches than all its treasures;" would there, by faith, have realized the presence of his Lord in sweet communion: and if, through faith, he kept the passover, and the sprinkling of blood, in the ordinance of the paschal lamb, what may we not suppose the man of God would have felt, as he traversed over the sacred goodly mountain, and Lebanon? 'Here,' he would have said, as he beheld, by faith, the day of Christ afar off, like the patriarch Abraham, 'here is the memorable ground, the holy mountain, on which Jesus, "my dweller in the bush," will one day make his soul an offering for sin? Here will go up before God the Father, that one sacrifice to which all under the law shadowed and ministered, and by which the Lord Jesus will for ever perfect them that are sanctified! Here the Son of God will for ever do away sin by the sacrifice of himself.' Oh, Lebanon! that goodly mountain! for ever sacred to the soul's meditation of all the redeemed of the Lord Jesus! though, like Moses, I have not trodden thine hallowed ground; yet, by faith, I have seen Jesus in his agonies and passion there; and bless and praise God and the Lamb, for the wonders of redemption. Lord, bring me to the everlasting enjoyment of thy person, work, and righteousness, in glory, for this will be indeed the good land that is beyond Jordan; the goodly mountain, and Lebanon: that "when I awake after thy likeness, I may be satisfied with it."

APRIL 3.

MORNING.—"A man of sorrows, and acquainted with grief."—Isa. liii. 3.

My soul, there is one feature in thy Redeemer's

character, which, in the unequalled abasement of his person, demands thy constant contemplation. I fear it hath not been considered by thee as it ought. And yet it is so sweetly accommodating and lovely, that the more thou beholdest thy Jesus in this tender light, the more endeared he must appear to thee. The prophet, under the Holy Ghost, hath here in a few words sketched the outlines of it—"A man of sorrows, and acquainted with grief." It was most essential that Jesus should be all this, because it belonged to the curse which he became for his people, when he offered himself as their surety. You will remember, my soul, the curse which God pronounced upon the earth, and man's passage through it, when he broke the divine law. The ground was cursed; the product of it was to be thorns and thistles; in sorrow, and in the sweat of the brow, was man to eat bread; and, at length, death was to close the life. Now it behoved him who undertook to remove the curse, to bear that curse before the removal of it; and, as such, it behoved Jesus to be "a man of sorrows and acquainted with grief." Hence all these seized on the Lord Jesus in the first moment he assumed our nature. And though he had no sin in his nature; not being born in the ordinary way of our nature, yet, as a Surety, he was at once exposed to all the frailties in the sinless sorrows, and travails, and labours of it. This sentence would not have been fulfilled, had not Jesus eat bread in the sweat of his brow. So interesting a part, therefore, was it in Christ's life, that he should labour in a common occupation, that this part of the curse might not go by, without being accomplished. And how eminently, my soul, was this part indeed fulfilled, when, in the garden, the sweat of his brow was drops of blood! How full of thorns and thistles was the earth to Jesus, may be in some measure considered, when we behold him in the unequalled sorrows of the opposition he met with from the world, the unkindness of friends, the malice of enemies. The thorny crown put upon his sacred head was little considered by those that put it; but yet it was, in reality, crowning him Lord of sorrow and grief, beyond all men that ever were exercised with affliction. So great, indeed, was the continued load he bore of grief, and so much did it tend to waste and wear the spirits, that according to that expression of the Jews to him—"thou art not yet fifty years old," evidently proved, that he had the visage of one of fifty, when only thirty. And it is remarkable, though we are told that Jesus rejoiced in spirit, yet we never read that he was once seen to laugh during his whole life. Precious Jesus, enable me ever to be looking unto thee, thou meek and lowly Lamb of God! And may I never lose sight of this sweet part of thy character also; that whilst thou didst bear our sins, so didst thou carry our sorrows; and in fulfilling the law, didst take away the curse also, when in sorrow thou didst eat bread all the days of thy life.

EVENING.—"For him hath God the Father sealed."—John vi. 27.

My soul, hast thou ever remarked the peculiar glory of those scriptures, which comprise within a small compass all the persons of the Godhead, as concurring and co-operating in the grand business of salvation? No doubt, all scripture is blessed, being given by inspiration of God; but there is a peculiar blessedness in these sweet portions, which at one view, represent the Holy Three in One, unitedly engaged in the sinner's redemption. My soul, ponder over this divine passage, in thy Saviour's discourse, as thus: who is the *Him* here spoken of, but the Lord Jesus? And whom but God the Father could seal Christ? And with whom was Christ sealed and anointed, but by God the Holy Ghost? Would any one have thought, at first view, that in seven words, such a blessed testimony should be given to the glorious foundation-truth of the whole bible? "For him hath God the Father sealed." Precious Jesus! enable me to behold thy divine authority as the warrant of faith in this gracious act of thy Father. And while I view thee as infinitely suited for my poor soul, in every state and under every circumstance, let my soul find confidence in the conviction that the validity of all thy gracious acts of salvation is founded in the seal of the Spirit. Yes, thou dear Lord, it was indeed the Spirit of Jehovah that was upon thee, when thou wast anointed to "preach the gospel to the poor, to heal the broken in heart, to give deliverance to the captive, and the restoring of sight to the blind, to set at liberty them that are bruised, and to proclaim the acceptable year of the Lord." And art thou, dearest Lord, thus held forth, and thus recommended by the grand seal of heaven, to every poor sinner who feels a conscious want of salvation? Oh then help, Lord, by thy blessed Spirit, all and every one of this description, so to receive a sealed Saviour, as to rest in nothing short of being sealed by him; and while every act of love, and every tendency of grace proclaims thee, blessed Jesus, as "Him whom God the Father hath sealed," so let every act of faith, and every tendency of the soul, in the goings forth after thee, be expressive of the same earnest longings as the church, of being sealed and owned by thee, when she cried out, "Set me as a seal upon thy heart, as a seal upon thine arm; for love is strong as death; jealousy is cruel as the grave; the coals thereof are coals of fire, which hath a most vehement flame."

APRIL 4.

MORNING.—"A place called Gethsemane."—Matt. xxvi. 36.

My soul, let thy morning meditation be directed to the garden of Gethsemane, that memorable spot, sacred to the believer, because so much beloved and resorted to by Jesus. Here Jesus oft came with his disciples. And here, my soul, do thou often take the wing of faith, and flee in devout contemplation. Was this place dear to thee, thou precious Redeemer? And was it not because here thou didst enjoy the sweetest refreshing in communion with the Father? Was it not because here thou knewest would begin the conflict and the agony, in which the great business for which thou camest on earth would be accomplished. Didst thou abide here, Lord, a whole night, after a day's constant preaching to the people, the week only before thy crucifixion. (See Luke xxi. 37.) And when the night was past, didst thou again repair to the temple to the same employ? Was Gethsemane dear to Jesus! Was here his favourite haunt? And shall not my soul delight to be oft here in solemn meditation? Will not my Lord lead me there, and go with me there, and sweetly speak to me there; that while, in imagination, I tread the sacred ground, my soul may view the several spots, and say—Here it was, perhaps, my Redeemer was withdrawn a stone's cast from his disciples, that the powers of darkness might more furiously assault his holy soul; and here stood the angel sent from heaven to strengthen him; and here the Lord Jesus was in his agony, when the sweat of his body forced through all the pores great drops of blood, falling down to the ground! Is this Gethsemane? And why Gethsemane? The Jews call it Ge-hennom, or hell; for here it was that Josiah burnt the idol vessels. 2 Kings xxiii. 4—10. And it is the same as Tophet, the only word the Jews used for hell after their return from the Babylonish captivity. The field of Cedron was indeed a dark and gloomy place; and by its side ran the foul and black brook which Jesus passed over when he went into Gethsemane. Here David, of old, went mourning and lamenting, when Ahitophel, like another Judas, betrayed him, and his life was sought after. 2 Sam. xv. 23. And here the Son of David passed also, when the man of whom David by the spirit of prophecy spake, (Ps. xli. 9.) which eat bread with Jesus, lifted up his heel against him. And was this Gethsemane the favoured spot of Jesus, because here he had so sweetly enjoyed communion with his Father, and because he here should encounter the powers of darkness? Learn then, my soul, from thy Jesus where thou oughtest to seek grace in a refreshing hour, to comfort a trying hour. Say, my soul, where should be thy dying place, but where thy God hath most blessed thy living place? There, Jesus, make my seasons (if needs be) of conflict, where thou hast sanctified and made blessed by thy Bethel visits. And was a garden the favoured spot of Jesus? Yes, it was in a garden the first Adam lost himself and his posterity; there, then, Jesus will recover the forfeited inheritance. Did the devil begin in heaven to ruin man? Why, then, in Gethsemane Jesus will begin to conquer hell for man's recovery. Did Satan, from the garden, bind and carry captive the first Adam? Then from a garden also shall he cause to be bound, and carried away to the cross, the second Adam, "that he, by death, might destroy him that had the power of death—that is, the devil; and deliver them who, through fear of death, are all their life-time subject to bondage." Solemn Gethsemane! awful, but hallowed spot! Here would I often come here contemplate Jesus, my blessed Surety, groaning, yet conquering; pressed under all the hellish malice of the devil, yet triumphing over all; deserted by his disciples, sweating a bloody sweet, sustaining the wrath of offended justice, drinking the cup of trembling! Is this Gethsemane? Oh, thou Lamb of God, thou paschal Lamb! here oft bring me; here shew me thy loves: and as thy joys were here turned into sorrows, give me to see how the curses which I deserved, but which thou didst endure, were converted into blessings; and that by thy stripes I am healed. Hail sacred Gethsemane!

EVENING.—" Thy rebuke hath broken my heart."—Psalm lxix. 20.

Hast thou, my soul, still upon thee the solemn savour of thy morning meditation? Surely Gethsemane is not forgotten by thee! Pause over the subject; and from the whole mass of the soul sufferings of thy Lord, behold what crowned the whole: " Thy rebuke, (saith Jesus to the Father,) thy rebuke hath broken my heart." To search into the depths of this mediation is impossible; for who shall describe it? What human, or even angelic intellect can fathom the profound subject? That this was the greatest and heaviest weight in the whole curse, we may venture to suppose: because we read of nothing which bore so hard upon the holy Jesus, amidst all his agonies, as the Father's rebuke. It was this which " broke his heart." My soul! repeat the solemn scripture, as if Jesus was in the moment uttering the words: " Thy rebuke hath broken my heart." Precious Lord! could not this have been spared thee?—Pause, my soul!—Lamb of God! must the rebuke of thy Father be also in the curse?—Pause again, my soul! When Jesus made his soul an offering for sin, would not the Father of mercies, and God of all consolation, shew the least portion of favour to his dear, his beloved, his only begotten Son?—Pause, my soul, yet once again, and ponder over the solemn subject! " It pleased the Father to bruise him, to put him to grief."—But, my soul! though neither thou, nor perhaps angels of light, can explain the extremity of the Redeemer's sufferings, in the rebuke of the Father for sin, which broke his heart; yet in the contemplation of the *lesser* sorrows of the curse which Jesus endured, thou wilt be led to form some faint idea, however small, in comparison of the real state of it, to induce a train of the most solemn meditations. When the Son of

God assumed our nature, though in a holy portion of that nature, untainted by the fall, being not derived by ordinary generation, yet coming as the sinner's surety, he took upon him the curse for sin; he was first made *sin*, (2 Cor. v. 21.) and then a *curse* for us (Gal. iii. 13); as such, he was invested with every thing belonging to the frailties of our nature, which might expose that nature to sorrow, and suffering, and death. The sentence of the fall was, "Dust thou art, and unto dust shalt thou return;" Gen. iii. 19: so that the curse, then seizing the human nature of Christ, at once tended to waste all the animal spirits, and to induce a state of mind peculiarly low and dejected. Agreeably to this, we find, that the holy Jesus, though it is once said of him, that in that hour "he rejoiced in spirit," when the devils were subject to his name (Luke x. 18—21.) yet is it never said of him, that he was once seen to laugh. As the sinner's surety, he sustained every thing of sorrow which belonged to God's curse against sin; and became eminently marked with affliction; and in a way which none but himself ever waded through; yea, to make the horrors of death more tremendous and bitter, the very sun became darkened at mid-day; not so much, I humbly conceive, as some have thought, to intimate, by the miracle, God's displeasure at the act of the Jews in the crucifixion of Christ, as to manifest the Father's rebuke of sin, which Jesus then stood as the sinner's surety to answer for, and which Christ, as if summing up the whole of his misery, declared to be the finishing stroke, which had "broken his heart." My soul! look up, and thus behold the Lamb of God! Oh! thou precious, precious Redeemer! the sons of thy Zion, but for this blessed undertaking of thine, "would have fainted for ever!" They would have lain "at the head of all the streets as a wild bull in a net; they would have been full of the fury of the Lord, the rebuke of thy God." But now, Lord, thou hast swallowed up death in victory: "the Lord God hath wiped away tears from off all faces: and the rebuke of thy people thou hast taken away from off all the earth: for the mouth of the Lord hath spoken it."

APRIL 5.

MORNING.—"Being in an agony."—Luke xxii. 44.

My soul, art thou still in Gethsemane? Look at Jesus once more; behold him in his agony; view him in his bloody sweat, in a night of cold, and in the open air, when we are told the servants, in the high priest's hall, were obliged to make a fire of coals to warm themselves. In such a night was thy Jesus, from the extremity of anguish in his soul, by reason of thy sins, made to sweat great drops of blood. Look at the Lord in this situation; and as the prophet, by vision, beheld him coming up with his dyed garments, as one that had trodden the wine fat; so do thou, by faith, behold him in his bloody sweat; when, from treading the winepress of the wrath of God, under the heavy load of the world's guilt, his whole raiment was stained with blood. Sin first made man to sweat: and Jesus, though he knew no sin, yet taking out the curse of it for his people, is made to sweat blood. Oh thou meek and holy Lamb of God! methinks, I would, day by day, attend the garden of Gethsemane by faith, and contemplate thee in thine agony. But who shall unfold it to my wondering eyes, or explain all its vast concern to my astonished soul! The evangelists, by their different turns of expression to point it out, plainly shew, that nothing within the compass of language can unfold it. Matthew saith, the soul of Jesus was "exceeding sorrowful, even unto death." Matt. xxvi. 38. The sorrows of hell, as is elsewhere mentioned, encompassed him. Ps. xviii. 5. My soul, pause over this. Was Jesus's soul thus sorrowful, even with hell sorrows, when, from the sins of his people charged on him, and the penalty exacted from him as the sinner's surety, the wrath of God against sin, lighting upon him, came as the tremendous vengeance of hell? Mark describes the state of the Lamb of God as "sore amazed." The expression signifies the horror of mind; such a degree of fear and consternation as when the hairs of the head stand upright, through the dread of the mind. And was Jesus thus agonized, and for sins his holy soul had never committed, when standing forth as the surety of others? John's expression of the Redemer's state on this occasion is, that he said, "his soul was troubled." John xii. 27. The original of this word troubled, is the same as the Latins derive their word for hell from. As if the Lord Jesus felt what the prophet had said concerning everlasting burnings. Isa. xxxiii. 14. "My heart," said that patient sufferer, "is like wax; it is melted in the midst of my bowels." Ps. xxii. 14. Hence Moses, and after him Paul, in the view of God's taking vengeance on sin, describe him under that awful account—"our God is a consuming fire." Deut. iv. 24. Heb. xii. 29. Beholding his Father thus coming forth to punish sin in his person, Jesus said—"Mine iniquities have taken hold upon me, therefore my heart faileth me." Ps. xl. 12. And Luke folds up the account of Jesus with "being in an agony;" such a labouring of nature as implies an universal convulsion, as dying men with cold clammy sweats: so Jesus, scorched with the hot wrath of God on sin, sweated, in his angony, clots of blood! My soul, canst thou hold out any longer? Will not thine eye-strings and heart-strings break, thus to look on Jesus in his agony! Oh precious Jesus! were the great objects of insensible, inanimated nature, made to feel as if to take part in thy sufferings; and am I unmoved? Did the very grave yawn at thy death and resurrection; and were the rocks rent, while my tearless eyes thus behold thee? Oh gracious God, fulfil that promise by the prophet, "that I may look on him whom I have pierced, and mourn as one that mourneth for his only son, and be in bitterness as one that is in bitterness for his first-born."

EVENING.—"Then came Jesus forth, wearing the crown of thorns, and the purple robe. And Pilate saith unto them, behold the man." —John xix. 5.

My soul, thou art engaged in solemn subjects at this season, both night and morning; and here is one as solemn as any; thy Jesus coming forth in his coronation robes! Yes! For he, and he alone, is the prince of sufferers, as the prince of his people. Many of his dear children have been beset with thorns; and to many, indeed to all more or less, the Lord hedgeth up their way with thorns. But none but the ever blessed Jesus was *crowned* with thorns. Now, my soul, ponder well the solemn subject. And Oh! that God the Holy Ghost may open all the glories of it to thy view. And *first*, look at thy Jesus, crowned with thorns. None but the Lord Jesus could properly wear this crown; because the curse pronounced by God at the fall, of thorns being brought forth *to the man*, could belong to none but him, the God-man Christ Jesus. This curse contained an abridgment of all the curses in the bible: and which never fell upon any but the person of Christ, so as to *crown* him as having suffered all. He was first made sin, and then a curse for his redeemed. Now the *three* grand branches of this curse were never fulfilled in any but in Christ: as, *first*, a separation from God; *secondly*, a state of unequalled sorrow, subject to all the frailties of nature, in pain and misery; and *thirdly*, death: in dying he died; intimating thereby the *very death*, as comprehensive of all in one. All men in death are exposed to a cold and *clammy* sweat; but it was reserved to the Lord Jesus, in his death, to sweat a *bloody* sweat. My soul! do thou thus look at him, in his purple robe, and crown of thorns, who is here represented to thy view, and never, never forget, that in all this he was and is thy surety; the Lord thy righteousness! But there is another point to be regarded in this solemn scripture, which demands thy closest attention; and let this form a *second* delightful consideration for thy evening's comforts. When Jesus thus came forth, wearing the crown of thorns, and the purple robe, as the translation represents the passage, it is Pilate who saith, "Behold the man!" But this is a mistake, and a sad mistake indeed: for it is not Pilate that speaks, but Christ. The word *Pilate,* if you well observe, is printed in italics, which denotes that it is a word not found in the original, but put in by another hand; and much to be lamented it is, that it should ever have been there. The Lord Jesus Christ had been all along pointed out in the old testament scripture as *the man,* the very man, that should be "a man of sorrows, and acquainted with grief;" who should give his back to the smiters, and his cheek to them that plucked off his hair, and that would not hide his face from shame and spitting. When, therefore, Pilate brought the Lord Jesus to the view of his people, in direct and full testimony as answerable to those characters, Jesus saith unto them, "Behold the man!" He had before, under the spirit of prophecy, cried out, "Behold me! behold me!" (Isaiah lxv. 1.) and now, as if to shew the wonderful and complete agreement of scripture prophecy with his sacred person, he saith, "Behold the man!" Oh! how blessed is it to receive this testimony from Jesus's own mouth! Oh! how refreshing to the soul, to perceive Christ's gracious attention, in such a moment of trial, to the security and comfort of his people! And what a blessed strengthening to the faith of his redeemed, to behold all the persons of the Godhead calling upon the church to the same contemplation! "Behold (saith God the Father) my servant, whom I uphold; mine elect, in whom my soul delighteth?" Isa. xlii. 1. Behold (saith God the Holy Ghost) the Lamb of God, which taketh away the sin of the world!" John i. 29. "Behold the man!" saith Christ himself, as in this most blessed scripture. Lord Jesus! give me to behold thee, with an eye of faith, and so to gaze, with holy joy, and wonder, love, and praise, upon thy glories, that my ravished soul may go forth in longing desires after thee, and thus daily behold thee, until faith be swallowed up in sight, and hope be lost in absolute fruition!

APRIL 6.

MORNING.—"Jesus therefore, knowing all things that should come upon him, went forth, and said unto them, whom seek ye? They answered him, Jesus of Nazareth. Jesus saith unto them, I am he. And Judas also, which betrayed him, stood with them. As soon then as he had said unto them, I am he, they went backward and fell to the ground." —John xviii. 4, 5, 6.

What a glorious scripture is this! Ponder it well, my soul; for of all the miracles of thy Jesus, there is not one more sweet and satisfactory to contemplate. Yesterday thou wast loking at thy Redeemer under a heavy cloud. Look at him as he is here represented, for he is still, in this transaction, in the same garden of Gethsemane; and behold how the Godhead shone forth with a glory surpassing all description. Observe what a willing sacrifice was Jesus. He knew the hour was come, for he had said so. He doth not wait to be taken, and by wicked hands to be crucified and slain: but he goeth forth to surrender himself. Yes! Jesus did not go to the garden of Gethsemane for nothing; he knew Judas would be there; he knew the powers of darkness would be there; he knew his whole soul would be in an agony; but there Jesus would go. He had said at the table of his disciples, "Arise, let us go hence." Precious, precious Jesus! how endearing to my poor soul is this sweet view of thy readiness and earnestness to become a sacrifice for the sins of thy people. Thou hast this baptism, Lord, to be baptised with; and how wast thou straitened until it was accomplished! There was a time, dear Lord, when the multitudes sought for thee to make thee a king; so convinced were they, for the moment, who thou wert; and then thou didst hide thyself from them. But now thine enemies come to make thee king with a crown of thorns, and to nail thy sacred body to the cross, thou didst hasten to meet them. Well might the prophet say, thou wentest forth for the salvation of thy people. Look at this scripture again, my soul. "Whom seek ye?" said Jesus. Did they not know him? It was a light night, most probably; for the moon was then at the full; besides, the seekers of Christ had lanterns and torches. How was it they did not know him? Didst thou for the moment, dearest Lord, do by them as thine angels at the gate of Lot by the Sodomites, so cause their eyes to be holden that they should not know thee? Was there somewhat of a miracle in this also? But, my soul, behold the wonder of wonders that followed: no sooner had Jesus said to their inquiry, (whom seek ye) "I am he," than they went backward and fell to the ground. Was there indeed some sudden overpowering emanation of the Godhead, breaking through the vail of Jesus's flesh, which induced this effect? Was it ever known, ever heard of, in any age or period of the world, of such an effect before? Supposing all the monarchs of the earth, with the mightiest armies of men, could be assembled together, how should such an event be induced by the breath of their mouth? Contemplate this, my soul, again and again Rejoice, my soul, in this view of thy Saviour; for never, surely, was a greater miracle of thy Redeemer's wrought; and remember how soon it took place after his agony. Never go to Gethsemane in meditation, without taking the recollection of it with thee. "Behold the man!" behold the God! Here was nothing exercised by Jesus; no weapon, no threat, no denunciation, no appeal to the Father. Jesus only simply said, " I am he," and they fell to the earth. Precious Jesus, what a volume of instruction doth it afford. If such was the effect in the day of thy flesh, how sure is that scripture concerning the day of thy power, in which it is said, " The Lord shall consume the wicked with the breath of his mouth, and destroy them with the brightness of his coming." 2 Thess. ii. 8. And if, my soul, there was such power in the word of thy Saviour, when he only said to his enemies, " I am he," why shouldest thou not feel all the sweetness and gracious power of his love, when he saith, " Fear not, I am he; behold I am with thee: it is I; be not afraid." Ponder, my soul, in this view also, the awful state of a soul hardened by sin. The enemies of Jesus, though they fell to the ground at his mere word, felt no change, no compunction, at the display of it. Judas also was with them. Yes! he fell also; but Satan had entered into him, and a reprobate mind marked him as the son of perdition. Oh precious Jesus! how fully read to thy people, in every part of thy word, is the solemn truth, that grace makes all the difference between him that serveth God, and him that serveth him not. Oh keep me, Lord, and I shall be well kept; for unto thee do I lift up my soul!

EVENING.—" A place called Golgotha."—Matt. xxvii. 33.

And wherefore called Golgotha? It was " a place of skulls;" not a charnel house; not a sepulchre for the great; but probably where a number of unburied skulls of poor criminals lay together, or scattered here and there, as the feet of those who visited this place of sorrow, might kick them. Luke calls it Calvary, (Luke xxiii. 33,) but both mean one and the same place. And was this a suited place for thee, Oh thou Lord of life and glory? Yes, blessed Jesus! if thou wilt become sin, and a curse for thy redeemed; then, surely, this of all places becomes thee, where thy people must have lain for ever, hadst thou not interposed, and undertaken all that behoved them to suffer, that they might be made "the righteousness of God in thee!" My soul, did Jesus suffer at Golgotha? Go thou forth to him "without the camp, bearing his reproach." And is this Golgotha? And was it here that Jesus "then restored that which he took not away?" Oh! how blessed the review! how memorable, how sacred the spot! Who would have thought that a place so wretched should have produced so much good! Confusion had been introduced into all the works of God, by reason of sin; here Jesus restored perfect order to all. God's glory had been tarnished; God's law had been broken; God's justice despised. At Golgotha, Jesus restored all. And as man had lost the image of God, the favour of God, the acquaintance with God: at this memorable spot, Jesus restored to God his glory, and to man God's favour. My soul! do thou often visit the place called Golgotha; and to endear the sacred haunt still more, look at thy Lord as thou goest thither, and figure to thyself thy Jesus going with thee. Here it was that his person and all his sacred offices were blasphemed. Is Jesus the Lord God of the prophets? Then will the rabble vilify his prophetical office. "Prophecy," say they, "thou Christ, who is he that smote thee!" Is Jesus the great High Priest of Jehovah, after the order of Melchisedec? This also shall be despised. "Save thyself and us," said the scoffing multitude. And is Jesus a king? "Come down then," say they, "from the cross, and we will believe." Yea, and as the most aggravating circumstance of cruelty, and which, as far as I have ever heard, or read, was never practised upon the most abject criminal, his very prayers were turned into ridicule. "My God, my God," said the holy sufferer, "why hast thou forsaken me!" "This man calleth for Elias," said they; "let us see whether Elias will come to take him down!" Pause, my soul! over the solemn view: and as thou takest thine evening stand at Golgotha, ask thine heart, is this Jesus, who is "the brightness of his Father's glory, and the express image of his person?" Is this He, whom angels worship, and at whose name "every knee shall bow, of things in heaven, and things on earth, and things under the earth?" Oh! thou bleeding Lamb, that art now in the midst of the throne! often let my soul ruminate over the affecting scenes of Golgotha. Solemn is the place, but blessed also. Here would I sit down, and as I contemplate Jesus, in this endearing part of his character, I would hear his voice, speaking in the tenderest manner, "Is it nothing to you, all ye that pass by? Behold, and see, if there be any sorrow like unto my sorrow, which is done unto me, wherewith the Lord hath afflicted me in the day of his fierce anger."

APRIL 7.

MORNING.—"He hath poured out his soul unto death."—Isaiah liii. 12.

My soul! from the garden to the cross, follow Jesus. Behold him apprehended and hurried away, both to judgment and to death. He who struck to the ground the band that came to take him, might surely, by the same breath of his mouth, have struck them to hell, and prevented his being apprehended by them. But one of the sweetest and most blessed parts of Jesus's redemption of his people, consisted in the freeness and willingness of his sacrifice. Yes, thou precious Lamb of God! no man (as thou thyself hadst before said) had power to take thy life from thee; but thou didst lay it down thyself: thou hadst power to lay it down, and thou hadst power to take it again. Delightful consideration, to thee, my soul! Now, my soul, let this day's meditation be sacred to the view of thy Redeemer pouring out his *soul* unto death. And to-morrow, if the Lord give thee to see the morrow, let the solemn subject of thy study be the sufferings of Jesus in his *body*. Pause then, my soul, and call up all the powers of thy mind to the contemplation of what the scripture teacheth concerning thy Redeemer's pouring out his soul unto death. Seek the teachings of the Holy Ghost in this solemn and mysterious subject. The original curse pronounced on the fall, which Jesus took upon himself, and came to do away, contained somewhat vastly great. For as the blessing promised to obedience, "Do this, and thou shalt live," certainly meant somewhat much greater than mere animal life, and implied sweet fellowship and communion with God; so the curse to disobedience, "Dying, thou shalt die," as plainly intimated much more than the mere return of the body to the dust out of which it was taken: it meant what in scripture (Rev. xx. 6.) is called the "second death," meaning hell and everlasting misery. Hence, in the recovery of our lost and fallen nature from this awful state, when Jesus undertook the salvation of his people, he was to sustain all that was our due; and, in the accomplishment of this, he not only died in his body, but he poured out his soul unto death. As the sinner's representative, and the sinner's surety, he bore the whole weight and pressure of divine justice due to sin; according to what the Holy Ghost taught —"Indignation and wrath, tribulation and anguish, upon every soul of man that doeth evil."—Rom. ii. 9. Not that the Redeemer needed, in the accomplishment of this, to go down into hell to suffer the miseries of the damned; for when the avenging wrath of God came upon him, he endured it here. The wrath of God may be sustained in earth as well as hell: witness the evil spirit that is called the prince of the power of the air, Ephes. ii. 2; for wherever the apostate angels are, they still endure divine wrath. Hence, when the Lord Christ poured out his soul unto death, by reason of the extremity of his soul sufferings, and soul's travail for his redeemed, he sustained all this as the sinner's surety, in becoming sin and a curse, to feel and suffer all that was the sinner's due. Oh! who shall say, what heart shall conceive, the greatness and extensiveness of thy sufferings, precious, precious Lamb of God! Oh! who shall undertake fully to shew the infinite suitableness of Jesus to every poor humble convinced sinner, in delivering him from the wrath to come! Here, my soul, fix thine eyes; here let all thy powers be employed in the unceasing contemplation, while beholding Jesus, thy Jesus, "pouring out his soul unto death; while numbered with the transgressors, and bearing the sin of many, and making intercession for the transgressors."

EVENING.—"And the scripture was fulfilled, which saith, and he was numbered with the transgressors."—Mark xv. 28.

Look up, my soul, to the cross, and behold thy Lord hanging with two thieves; yea, in the middle of them, as if the greatest malefactor of the three; and, what is the most awful part of the subject, not only was he thus considered by the Jewish rabble, but as the sinner's representative, Jesus was thus beheld in Jehovah's view; "numbered with the transgressors," and virtually, the great surety and sponsor of them all. Pause, my soul, as thou readest this scripture, and as thou beholdest it fulfilled on the cross. Will it not undeniably follow, that if Christ was so reckoned, and so numbered, then must it have been, not for himself, for he had no sin, but for his people; and if made sin and a curse, surely he hath taken away both sin and the curse, by the sacrifice of himself, that they might be made the righteousness of God in him? There is one circumstance in this representation of Jesus being reckoned with the transgressors, as a sin and a curse, yea, sustaining the whole of sin and the curse in his own sacred person, that is particularly striking; I mean, that amidst all the shadowy representations under the law, the only type on this subject, and a most decisive one it was, is that of "the brazen serpent." Of all the creatures of God's creation, it was the serpent only that was pronounced cursed at the fall; and therefore, though the blood of many beasts may be, and indeed was made typical of redemption by the sacrifice of Christ, yet none but the serpent could represent Christ as a curse for his people. There is somewhat very striking in this. Christ, in redeeming us from the curse of the law, must be represented as a curse for us: the serpent therefore, the cursed beast, shall be lifted up in the wilderness; and Jesus himself will graciously explain it: "As Moses lifted up the serpent in the wilderness, so must the Son of man be lifted up, that whosoever believeth in him shall not perish, but have eternal life:" John iii. 14, 15. What a wonderful event! Who, but for the scripture, and the teaching of the Holy Ghost, would have been able to trace the affinity? "My righteous servant," saith Jehovah, "shall justify many, for he shall bear their iniquities." He is therefore *numbered* with the *transgressors*, Isaiah liii. 11, 12. And agreeably to this, all the circumstances attending this sustaining of the curse, shall correspond: a drop of water is denied to none but the cursed in hell; Jesus, therefore, in his thirst, shall be denied it also. If malefactors under the curse have no one to mitigate their sorrows, here again Jesus shall be the same; for in his sufferings, "all his disciples forsook him, and fled." Is the darkness in hell an aggravation of the miseries of the cursed there? Thus also shall it be in the extreme agonies of Jesus; for darkness covered the earth during his crucifixion, from the sixth to the ninth hour. Yea, and above all, the sense of divine manifestation shall be withdrawn, as from those in the regions of everlasting misery, who have no sense of the divine presence, but in his wrath.

So that Jesus needed not to go down into hell to suffer the torments of the damned; for being numbered with the transgressors, and standing forth to the view of Jehovah, as sin and a curse for his people, the waters of the great deep were broken up, to overwhelm his precious soul; and in those tremendous hours, all the cataracts of divine wrath were poured out upon him, until the holy patient sufferer was constrained to cry out in that dolorous cry, "All thy waves and thy billows are gone over me!" Psalm xlii. 7. Lamb of God! is it thus at Golgotha thou wert numbered with the transgressors? And was it thus that the scripture was fulfilled? Oh, for grace so to behold thee, so to fix and feast my soul upon thee, that, while conscious that thy holy soul knew no sin, though made sin for me, I, who know no righteousness, and truly have none, may be made the righteousness of God in thee!

APRIL 8.

MORNING.—"He humbled himself, and became obedient unto death, even the death of the cross."—Philip. ii. 8.

My soul, dost thou not feel, at every step towards Calvary, somewhat of the angel's words when he cried, "One woe is past, and behold there come two woes more hereafter?" Rev. ix. 12. Surely, never was there a manifestation of the holiness of Jehovah, nor the utter detestation of God against sin, as was set forth in the crucifixion of Jesus. Would men, would angels, see what sin really is, let them go to the cross of Jesus. The casting rebellious angels out of heaven, the curse pronounced upon the earth, the drowning the old world by water, the burning of Sodom by fire; nay, the millions of miseries among men, and the unquenchable fire of hell; though all these may make the souls of the awakened exclaim against sin, yet all these are slight and inconsiderable things, compared to the wrath of God poured out upon the person of God's own Son, when he died the accursed death of the cross. My soul, take thy stand this day at the foot of the cross. Behold the Lamb of God! There see divine justice more awfully displayed than would have been in the everlasting ruin of all creation. And Oh may it be thy portion, my soul, while looking unto Jesus, to say as Paul did—"I am crucified with Christ: nevertheless I live, yet not I, but Christ liveth in me; and the life which I now live in the flesh, I live by the faith of the Son of God, who loved me, and gave himself for me." But, my soul, while thou lookest up to Jesus hanging on the painful tree, contemplate the sufferings of the Lord Jesus in his sacred body. The death of the cross was a *violent* death; for as there was no sin in Jesus, there could not have been those seeds of death, which in all the race of Adam, are found to bring forth fruit unto death. Precious thought this, even in the moment of beholding Jesus's life taken by violence. Had Jesus not died by a violent death, he would have been no sacrifice; for that which died of itself naturally, could not by the law have been offered to God. The death of Jesus was also a *cursed* death; for it is written, "Cursed is every one that hangeth on a tree." Behold, my soul, thy Lord thus lifted up a spectacle between heaven and earth, as if cursed and despised both of God and man. The death of Jesus was a *painful* death, in which many deaths were, as it were, contained in one. The nails driven through the most feeling parts of the hands and feet, and the body stretched forth on the transverse timber; in this manner the cross, with the Lord Jesus fastened upon it, was lifted up in the air, until the bottom fell into its socket, which suddenly shook the whole and every part of his sacred body; and thus the whole weight hanging on his pierced nailed hands, the wounds in both hands and feet by degrees widened as he hung, until at length he expired in tortures. Precious, precious Redeemer! was it thus thou didst offer thy soul an offering for sin? Was there no method, in all the stores of Omnipotency, for satisfying divine justice, but by thy holy, harmless, undefiled body dying the violent, cursed, painful death of the cross? Oh by the crimson fountain of thy blood, which issued from thy pierced side, enable me to sit down, day by day, until I find my whole nature crucified with thee in all its affections and lusts. Let there be somewhat, dearest Lord, of an holy conformity between my Lord and me; and if Jesus died *for* sin; may my soul die *to* sin; that by mortifying the deeds of the body I may live; and by carrying about with me always the dying of the Lord Jesus, the life also of Jesus may be made manifest in my mortal body.

EVENING.—" And Pilate marvelled if he were already dead."—Mark xv. 44.

Precious Jesus! had the unjust judge but known thy soul travail and agonies, instead of wondering at the speediness of thy death, all his astonishment would have been that nature, so oppressed, and so suffering, could have held out so long; for what would have crushed in a moment all creation, as well angels as men, in sustaining the wrath of God, due to sin, Jesus endured on the cross for so many hours! In point of suffering, he wrought out a whole eternity due to sin, on the cross: and in point of efficacy, he " for ever perfected them that are sanctified." Jesus therefore accomplished more in that memorable day, than all the creatures of God could have done for ever. Wonderful were the works which God dispatched in creation; but the wonders of redemption far exceed them. The six hours which Jesus hung upon the cross, wrought out a more stupendous display of almighty power and grace, than the six days God was pleased to appoint to himself in making the world. But, indeed, Pilate need not, on another accouut, have marvelled at the quickness of Christ's death, had this unjust judge but reflected on the previous sufferings of the Redeemer. They who have spent sweet hours in tracing Jesus's footsteps through the painful preludes to his death, and especially in the concluding scenes, have been able to mark many a sorrowful part which (besides the soul agonies of Jesus in accomplishing redemption-work) bore hard upon his body also. My soul, if thou wert to trace back the solemn subject, thou wouldest find enough to excite thy astonishment that Jesus lived so long on the cross, rather than that he died not before. His agony evidently began four days before the passover. The evangelist Luke tells us, that he spent the whole night in prayer, and the whole day in preaching to the people in the temple, Luke xxi. 37, 38. Read also Matthew's account four days before his crucifixion, in the prospect of what was coming on, Matt. xx. 18, 19. And again, before a single assault was made upon him in the garden, Matt. xxvi. 38. "My soul is exceeding sorrowful," said the dying Lamb, "even unto death." And the beloved apostle's relation is to the same amount, four days before his crucifixion: "Now is my soul troubled (said the holy sufferer); and what shall I say? Father, save me from this hour! But for this cause came I unto this hour!" John xii. 27. And if to these agonies of soul, before the tremendous season of Gethsemane and Golgotha arrived, be added the exercises of the Redeemer in body; all must have contributed to wear out and exhaust his strength, and hasten on the pains of death. When we call to mind how the Lamb of God was driven to and fro; hurried from one place to another; from Annas to Caiaphas, and from the judgment hall to Calvary; we cannot be surprised at his fainting under the burden of the cross. Many a mile of weariness did he walk, before nine of the o'clock in the morning of the day of his crucifixon; and many a bodily fainting must he have felt from the thorny crown, the soldiers scourging, and their buffetings and smitings with the palms of their hands. Unfeeling Pilate! thy marvellings will be now, and to all eternity, of another kind. As for thee, my soul, take thy stand at the foot of the cross, and do thou marvel, whilst thou art looking up, and beholding Jesus dying, that He who might have commanded twelve legions of angels to his rescue, should in love to his church and people, thus give "his soul an offering for sin," and die, "the just for the unjust, to bring us unto God!"

APRIL 9.

MORNING.—"Then said Jesus, Father, forgive them, for they know not what they do."—Luke xxiii. 34.

My soul, art thou still taking thy stand at the foot of the cross? Art thou still looking up to Jesus? If so, listen now to his voice. There were seven expressions of Jesus, which were his last words, which he uttered on the cross. The last words of dying friends are particularly regarded: how much more the last words of the best of all friends; even the dying friend of poor lost perishing sinners. Those which I have chosen for the portion of the day were the first; and they contain the strong cry of Jesus to his Father for forgiveness to his murderers. And what endears those expressions yet more to the heart are, that they are not only the first upon the cross, but they are wholly, not for himself, but the people. During the whole painful process of suffering, when they scourged him, crowned him with thorns, smote him with their hands, and mocked him, we hear no voice of complaint. "He was led as a lamb to the slaughter; and as a sheep before her shearers is dumb, so he opened not his mouth." Precious, meek Lamb of God! But now, when lifted up on the cross, Jesus broke silence, and cried out, "Father, forgive them, for they know not what they do." Pause, my soul. Look again at the cross. Was not Jesus now entered upon his high priest's office? Was not the cross as the altar from whence the sacrifice was offered? Was not Jesus himself the sacrifice? And was not Jesus the sacrificer? Might not the pale, the dying, whitened visage of Jesus be compared to the white ephod of the high priest; the streaming blood, flowing over his sacred body from the several wounds, as the incense of his censer; and the dying sweat of his holy frame, like the smoke ascending with the sweetest savour before God? As the arms of Jesus, when he thus prayed, were stretched forth on the cross, so the high priest spread forth his hands, when burning the incense for sacrifice, in pleading for the people. Hail, thou glorious high priest! in this the humblest moment, and the most powerful of thine intercessions. Surely every wound of thine, every look, every feature, every groan, pleaded with open mouth this gracious intercession for forgiveness of sinners. Lord, was I not included in the prayer? Was not the eye of Jesus upon me in the moment of this all-prevailing advocacy? Oh ye of every description and character, that still sit unconcerned and unmoved at this cry of the Son of God, "is it nothing to you, all ye that pass by?" Think, my poor unawakened brother, how justly that voice might have been heard for all the enemies of Jesus—"Depart from me, ye cursed;" when the tender language of Jesus was, "Father, forgive them, for they know not what they do." And think, moreover, that the same gracious voice is still heard in heaven, and of the same blessed force and efficacy as ever; for while our sins are calling for judgment, the blood of Jesus calls louder for mercy. Dear Lord, let this first cry of thine upon the cross, be the first and last of all my thoughts, under every exercise and temptation of sin and Satan—"Father, forgive them, for they know not what they do."

EVENING.—" He shall see of the travail of his soul, and shall be satisfied."—Isaiah liii. 11.

Is not this covenant promise of thy faithful God and Father peculiarly suited, my soul, for thine evening meditation, after the subject of the morning, in contemplating the first cry of Jesus upon the cross: " Father, forgive them, for they know not what they do?" And was not the cry answered in the case of the Jerusalem sinners at the day of Pentecost, soon after, when, under the apostle Peter's sermon, they were pricked to the heart, and cried out, " Men and brethren, what shall we do?" Acts ii. 23, 37. Ponder over the solemn expression, ***the travail*** of the Redeemer's soul. Did Jesus really sustain in soul somewhat like those throes of nature with which a woman is exercised in her hour of extremity? Did he travail in birth for his redeemed?—Pause, my soul, and very solemnly consider the subject. If the eighteenth Psalm be supposed to contain prophetical allusions to Christ, we may therein discover somewhat which will be helpful in this study: " The sorrows of hell compassed me about: the snares of death prevented me;" Psalm xviii. 5. We have similar expressions, Psalm cxvi. 3. As therefore these strong terms are very highly descriptive of suffering, and of a peculiar kind, it may be well to inquire farther, whether there be any ground to make application of them in reference to this subject? Now it is worthy remark, that the curses pronounced by God at the fall, upon Adam and his wife, became distinct acts of suffering; and it should seem, that he, who, in after ages, was to take away sin and the curse from both, must do it by suffering for both, in order to deliver them from it. My soul, review them: " Unto the woman he said, I will greatly multiply thy sorrow, and thy conception; in sorrow thou shalt bring forth children: and thy desire shall be to thy husband, and he shall rule over thee. And unto Adam he said, because thou hast hearkened unto the voice of thy wife, and hast eaten of the tree of which I commanded thee, saying, thou shalt not eat of it: cursed is the ground for thy sake; in sorrow shalt thou eat of it all the days of thy life. Thorns also and thistles shall it bring forth to thee; and thou shalt eat the herb of the field. In the sweat of thy face shalt thou eat bread till thou return to the ground; for out of it wast thou taken; for dust thou art, and unto dust shalt thou return;" Gen. iii. 16 to 19. Now, that Jesus, in his own sacred person, literally and truly bore every title of this sentence as it referred to Adam, none, who have read the history of the blessed Jesus in the gospels, can for a moment question. So much in sorrow did Jesus eat his bread, that he, and he alone, by way of emphasis, must be peculiarly called, "The man of sorrows, and acquainted with grief." And he it was that was crowned with thorns, by way of eminency in affliction, and sweat a bloody sweat; and he said himself, "Thou hast brought me into the dust of death," Psalm xxii. 15. But unless we can trace a similarity of Jesus bearing in his own sacred person somewhat in reference to the woman also, how shall we see the curse removed, and the sentence done away? Hence, if the travail of soul spoken of by the Lord, through the prophet, be intended to allude to the Lord Jesus bringing forth his sons to glory (and wherefore it should not, cannot be shewn), then have we a most gracious and beautiful representation folded up in this scripture; and the promise connected with it is equally delightful. And may we not interpret that scripture of another prophet by this illustration: "Ask ye now, and see whether a man doth travail with child? Wherefore do I see every man with his hands on his loins, as a woman in travail, and all faces are turned into paleness? Alas! for that day is great, so that none is like it; it is even the time of Jacob's trouble: but he shall be saved out of it;" Jer. xxx. 6, 7. Precious Jesus! thou art indeed the man, the God-man, that didst travail for thy children; and while all faces are turned into paleness by reason of sin, thou, our glorious Jacob, our Israel, Jehovah's servant, in the day, the great day of thy soul travail, shalt be saved out of it, and shalt see of the travail of thy soul, and be satisfied. Yea, Lord, thou wilt remember no more thine anguish, for joy that the dew of thy birth is as incalculable as the drops of the morning. Hail! Almighty Lord! the trophies of thy redemption shall correspond to the greatness of thy name: "men shall be blessed in thee, and all nations shall call thee blessed." Amen.

APRIL 10.

MORNING—"When Jesus therefore saw his mother, and the disciple standing by, whom he loved, he saith unto his mother, woman, behold thy son. Then saith he to the disciple, behold thy mother."—John xix. 26, 27.

This was the *second* among the dying words of the Lord Jesus; and no doubt, of high importance in their full sense and meaning: not simply to recommend Mary to the care of the beloved apostle, John, but probably of greater moment in reference to the church of Jesus at large. My soul, is it not very certain that the Lord Jesus knew all the events which would take place in all generations of his people? And as such, did not Jesus perfectly well know also that the time would come when divine honours would be offered to Mary? These points cannot be disputed. Well then, is it not worthy the closest observation, that Jesus both in this place, and upon all other occasions, when speaking of Mary, called her woman? Why so? If, as Jesus knew, that there would be some who would pray to her, and call her mother of God, by which name the Holy Ghost never distinguished her, neither the Lord Jesus himself;

could there have been a more decided method adopted than this to discountenance such idolatry, than when Jesus, in his dyiug moments, called Mary only woman? Besides, was it not on another account, that as Jesus was to be the seed of the woman, which was promised to bruise the serpent's head, such a dying testimony might serve instead of a thousand witnesses, in proof of the confirmation of the fact: and Mary's song might be the song of thousands—"My soul doth magnify the Lord, and my spirit hath rejoiced in God *my Saviour!*" But when we have thus attended to the second cry of Christ upon the cross, in reference to those sweet points, do thou, my soul, remember also how tenderly those expressions of thy Lord recommend all the endearing affections of love and regard through all the members of Christ's mystical body. To behold our mother, or to behold our sons, are only different expressions to intimate that all true believers in Jesus are members of one another, and of his body, his flesh, and his bones. And as it was by our Lord himself in this life, so is it with all his redeemed, both in this life and in that which is to come; they who do the will of his Father, which is in heaven, the same are Christ's brethren, and sisters, and mother.

EVENING.—"Awake, O sword, against my shepherd, and against the man that is my fellow, saith the Lord of Hosts: smite the shepherd, and the sheep shall be scattered."—Zech. xiii. 7.

That this blessed scripture points to Christ, and to him only, the Lord Jesus himself fully confirmed in his discourse with his disciples at the Mount of Olives, Matt. xxvi. 31. And indeed of whom could Jehovah thus speak, as "fellow to the Lord of Hosts," but to Him, who, "though in the form of God, and with whom it was no robbery to be equal with God, yet took upon him the form of a servant, and was made in the likeness of men?" But what call is this to the sword? Was it the flaming sword at the gate of Paradise, which was placed there to guard the way to the tree of life? And had the sword been for so many ages sleeping? Could none presume to enter but Jesus? And if he enters, the sword of God's justice must first awake, and be sheathed in his heart? And is it God the Father himself that thus commands the sword to awake, and smite his only begotten Son? Did God indeed so love the world, that he thus gave his only begotten Son, "to the end that all who believe in him should not perish, but have everlasting life?" Pause, my soul, over these solemn, but blessed thoughts. And is he God, on whom these things are to be transacted? Yes; for he is "fellow to the Lord of Hosts." And is he man also? Yes; for "the word was made flesh, and dwelt among us!" Such is the mystery of godliness; "God manifest in the flesh!" And, what! is he both God and man in one person? Yes; for so only could he be Christ. Well might the prophet exclaim, "Wonder, O heavens, and be astonished, O earth!"—My soul! take thy stand, this evening, at the foot of the cross, and contemplate, among the prodigies of that memorable day, that great wonder concerning Him crucified, who was fellow to the Lord of Hosts. View both his natures: He was truly and properly *man*; for it was one express article in the covenant of redemption, that "as by man came death, by man should come also the resurrection of the dead. And as by the disobedience of one many were made sinners, so by the obedience of one should many be made righteous." Moreover, the first promise of the bible, which came in with the fall, was express to this purpose: "The seed of the woman should bruise the serpent's head." The devil had triumphed over the nature of man in the fall; and the same nature of man was promised to conquer death, hell, and the grave: and as both the law and the justice of God were solemnly concerned that the same nature which had rebelled should obey, and the same nature which had sinned should atone; and all the divine perfections were concerned, that he who undertook the purposes of redemption, should be the man that was fellow to the Lord of Hosts, even Christ Jesus. Secondly, as none but man could be suited for a Redeemer, so none but God could be competent to accomplish redemption. Hence he must be fellow to the Lord of Hosts. In point of dignity, in point of merit, the glory due to a Redeemer when redemption should be accomplished, and the adoration, love, and praise to be ascribed to him, could never be suitable to any less than God. Hence by the union of both natures, Jesus, and Jesus only, who thus formed one Christ, became the very person here described, and was, and is, and ever must be, "the man that is my fellow, saith the Lord of Hosts." Now, my soul, whenever thou lookest up to the cross, (let it be daily, hourly, continually, yea, unceasingly) never lose sight of this glorious union of God and man in thy Jesus. Fix thine eyes, thine heart, thy whole affection upon him; and while thou art resting all thine assurance of pardon, mercy, and peace, the joy of this life, and the glory of that which is to come, wholly upon thy Jesus; Oh! let thine ear of faith receive in transports of delight, the proclamation of God thy Father concerning Him, "the man that is my fellow, saith the Lord of Hosts."

APRIL 11.

MORNING.—"And Jesus said unto him, verily I say unto thee, today shalt thou be with me in Paradise."—Luke xxiii. 43.

My soul, hear the gracious words of thy Jesus. This was the *third* cry of the Redeemer on the cross. And Oh! how full of grace, rich, free, unmerited, unexpected, unlooked-for grace, to a poor lost perishing sinner, even in the very moment of death. Let the self-righteous pharisee behold this example of redeeming love, and wonder, and be confounded. Surely no one will venture to suppose that this man's good works were any recommendation, when the poor wretch was dying under the hands of justice. What was it then that saved him but the complete salvation of Jesus? The Son of God was offering his soul on the cross a sacrifice for sin, and being between two notorious sinners, gave a rich display of the sovereignty of his grace, and his love to poor sinners; and in confirmation, snatched this one as a brand from the burning—took him from the very jaws of hell, and that very day led him in triumph to heaven; thereby manifesting to every poor sinner, in whose heart he puts the cry for mercy, that, that cry shall never be put forth in vain. And mark, my soul, how powerful the grace of the Lord Jesus wrought upon this man. He and his companion both knew that before night they would both be in eternity. The thought affected neither; they joined the rabble in insulting Jesus. "Save thyself and us," was the language of the heart of both, until the grace of Jesus wrought on this man's mind, and changed the reviler into an humble suitor. What could there be in Jesus thus to affect him! Jesus hung upon the cross like a poor Jew. Jesus had been always poor, and never more so than now. And yet, in the midst of all these surrounding circumstances, such a ray of light broke in upon this man's mind, that he saw Jesus in all his glory and power, acknowledged him for a King, when all the disciples had forsook him and fled, and prayed to be remembered by him when he came into his kingdom. Precious Lamb of God! bestow upon me such a portion of thy grace as, under all the unpromising circumstances around, may call forth the like conviction of thy power, and my need. And Oh! that this pattern of mercy might be reviewed by thousands of poor perishing dying sinners! Methinks I would have it proclaimed through all the public places of resort, through all the haunts of licentiousness, among the numberless scenes of hardened sinners who fear that they have sinned beyond the possibility of forgiveness. Oh look at this example of Jesus's love, ye that are going down to the grave full of sin and despair! behold the thief! behold the Saviour! And Oh for a cry of grace like that of the dying malefactor—"Lord, remember me when thou comest into thy kingdom;" and Jesus's gracious answer—"To-day shalt thou be with me in paradise."

EVENING.—"And one of the malefactors, which were hanged, railed on him, saying, if thou be Christ, save thyself and us. But the other answering, rebuked him."—Luke xxiii. 39, 40.

My soul! thy morning meditation was directed to that soul-reviving, penitent, encouraging prospect, which the cross of Christ affords, in the recovery of the thief upon the cross, as furnishing the most illustrious example of the sovereignty of grace! Oh! what a trophy was there of the Redeemer's conquest! Now take thy stand again at the foot of the cross, and look on the other side, and behold the dreadful reverse, in the obduracy of the human heart. Here view the sinner dying in all the possibilities of a hardened conscience, railing and blaspheming; while the other departs in the most finished act of faith and repentance, glorifying the Lord. Pause over the contemplation, and then ask, what was it made the mighty difference? Who made thee, my soul, to differ from another? And what hast thou, which thou didst not receive! Blessed Lord Jesus! I do indeed rejoice with trembling, when I consider what I am; yea, what every man is by nature; and how resolutely shut and bolted the hearts of all men are, in our universally fallen state, and cannot but remain so for ever, unless thou, who hast the key of David, dost open, and by thy sweet influences dost enter in! Pause once more, my soul! Perhaps, among the wonders which attended the crucifixion and death of Jesus, this, of a determined obduracy, is not the least. Nothing can be more plain, than that a general suspicion took place, both among the Jews and the Roman soldiers, who attended the crucifixion of Jesus, that he was more than man. Jesus had wrought many miracles, in confirmation of his being the Christ: and, now on the cross, the stupendous events which took place most loudly proclaimed it. The sun became dark at mid-day; the veil of the temple was rent in twain by an invisible hand; the earth did quake, the rocks were rent, and graves were opened! And to such a degree were these portentous sights carried, that the centurion, who presided at the execution, for the moment, felt himself so overcome with a conviction of Christ's real character, that, unable to resist the impulse on his mind, he cried out, and feared greatly, saying, "surely this was the Son of God!" Matt. xxvii. 51—54. But, as if to shew the desperately wicked state of the human heart, even these prodigies, and the renewal of them on the morning of our Lord's resurrection, soon lost their effect, and were considered no more. Though an earthquake ushered in the morning of Christ's triumph over the grave; though for a while, at this, and the presence of an angel, the Roman soldiers became as dead men; though Christ had foretold his resurrection, and the pharisees obtained a guard to watch the sepulchre on this account, and had it sealed with a seal, and a stone; still, both soldiers and pharisees, when recovered from their fright, rather than own Jesus for the Christ, will resolutely persist to their own damnation! My soul! pause over this solemn subject, and learn to have a proper view of the desperately wicked state of every man's heart by nature. Learn also where to ascribe the whole of that difference between one man and another, in the blessed effects of distinguishing grace. But for this, neither wouldest thou have believed in the resurrection of Jesus.

That "Jesus is believed on in the world," is one of the wonders in the apostle's account "of the great mystery of godliness;" 1 Tim. iii. 16. And however astonishingly it strikes the mind, yet the word of God confirms the undeniable truth, that were the devils in hell liberated from their chains, still devils would they remain. This we learn from the solemn account in the book of Revelations. Under the vials of God's wrath, they who have hardened their hearts against God and his Christ, are there given up to be hardened for ever: "In the kingdom of darkness," it is said, "they gnawed their tongues for pain; and blasphemed the God of heaven, because of their pains and their sores, and repented not of their deeds;" Rev. xvi. 8—11. Lord Jesus! give grace to all thy redeemed, in the view of thy distinguishing love, to know our mercies, and to bless thee, as the author of them.

APRIL 12.

MORNING.—"And about the ninth hour Jesus cried with a loud voice, saying, Eli, Eli, lama sabacthani; that is to say, My God, my God, why hast thou forsaken me?"—Matt. xxvii. 46.

Mark, my soul! Jesus had hung upon the cross now for six hours. Think what agonies he sustained both in soul and body. The fury of hell had broke out upon him, and in the cruelties of the men around him, exercised upon his sacred person, manifested how extensive that fury was. But had this been all; had God the Father smiled upon him, had the cup of trembling been taken away, some alleviation would have taken place in Jesus's sufferings; but so far was this from being the case, that the heaviest load of the sorrow his holy soul sustained, was the wrath of the Father due to sin, as the sinner's surety. Angels, no doubt, looked on. All heaven stood amazed. And, at length, overpowered with the fulness of sorrow and anguish of soul, the dying Lamb cried out, "My God, my God, why hast thou forsaken me?" Pause, my soul, while thou hearest in the ear of faith, still vibrating in the air, the dolorous cry; and conceive, if it be possible, what the holy, harmless, undefiled Jesus felt, when such expressions of exquisite terror and distress were forced from his dying lips. What forsaking was this of Jesus by God his Father? Not the dissolving of the union between them: not the withdrawing the arm of his strength; for Jesus still calls him, "Eli, Eli," that is, My strong One. Not that he left him to himself; neither that his love for Jesus was lessened: but it was the withdrawing or withholding those sweet manifestations whereby he had sustained the human nature of Jesus, through the whole of his incarnation. It was beholding Jesus in this solemn season as the sinner's surety; and as such, it was a punishing desertion; implying that as Jesus stood, or rather hung, with all the burden of our sins, he was so deserted for that time as we, out of Jesus, deserve to be forsaken for ever. The cry of Jesus, the shriek of his precious soul, under this desertion, represented the everlasting shrieks of them that are cast out of God's gracious presence to all eternity. Here pause again, my soul. And wouldst thou have howled this endless, pitiable cry for ever, had not Jesus uttered it for thee once? And art thou, by virtue of it, saved from this wrath to come? Hath Jesus both borne thy sins, carried thy sorrows, and been forsaken of his Father, that thou mightest enjoy his presence and favour for ever? My soul, what wilt thou render to the Lord for all his benefits? Wilt thou not take the cup of salvation, and call upon the name of the Lord, now thy Jesus hath for thee taken the cup of trembling, and drank all the dregs of it? Precious, precious Redeemer, may I never, never lose sight of thee in this part of thy sufferings also; and especially eye thee still more when my soul is under the hidings of God's countenance. Let me recollect, dearest Lord! that thou hast been forsaken before thy people, and for thy people; and here, as in all other instances, thou hast the pre-eminence, so as to sanctify even our momentary desertions to our good and to thy glory. Yes, precious Lord! such are the blessed effects of thy desertion, that hence my soul learns, my God still supports, though my God may withhold his comforts. Jesus was forsaken for a season, that my soul might not be forsaken for ever. And grant me, dearest Lord, from thy bright example, to cast myself wholly upon thee, as thou didst upon thy Father, when all sensible comforts fail, convinced that thou "art the strength of my heart, and my portion for ever!"

EVENING.—"And Pilate wrote a title, and put it on the cross. And the writing was, JESUS OF NAZARETH THE KING OF THE JEWS." —John xix. 19.

My soul! thou hast not yet read the inscription over the cross of Christ, in thine evening meditations. Do not withdraw from the sacred spot, until thou hast read it, and also, through divine teaching, understood its blessed design. Pilate meant it in reproach: but Jehovah over-ruled the design, to give his dear Son due honour. It was written in the three learned languages, in Greek, and Latin, and Hebrew. And it is the best of all learning to be able to read it in the light in which the Lord the Spirit caused it to be written. Do thou, almighty Teacher, cause me so to read it! Pilate meant it as Christ's crime; as if to tell the world wherefore he suffered: but, so far is the inscription itself from notifying a crime, that it positively asserts what it was meant to deny. Pilate wished it to be understood that Christ was punished as an usurper: but then he should not have said that he was the king of the Jews, but that he assumed the title; whereas he marks it as a thing perfectly understood; "Jesus of Nazareth, the king of the Jews." Some of Christ's enemies perceived this, and accordingly desired Pilate to alter the words —"write not," say they, "the king of the Jews: but that he said, I am king of the Jews." But he who over-ruled the mind of Pilate to write, over-ruled his mind that he should not alter. "What I have written," said he, "I have written." Yes, Pilate: Jesus was indeed king of the Jews! And now that memorable scripture was fulfilled: "Yet have I set my King upon my holy hill of Zion;" Psalm ii. 6. Precious Lord Jesus! thy title hath been this from everlasting; and will be to everlasting. It is like thyself, "the same yesterday, and to-day, and for ever!" And now, my soul, do not lose sight of the testimony of an enemy to the kingship of thy Lord Jesus. Look at the cross now, where thy Redeemer was publicly proclaimed king upon it; and behold how the offence of the cross is ceased. And Oh! for grace to own Jesus now in glory for my King, as Pilate notified to all the world that he was king, when in the lowest humiliation upon earth. And Oh! what rapture will break in upon the soul, when he, whom Pilate proclaimed king upon his cross, shall come as a King upon his throne. Lift up thine head, O my soul, and contemplate thy King, who once was crowned with thorns, now crowned with glory, Hear what the apostle saith, and let thy whole mind be occupied in contemplating the glory that shall be revealed: "Behold, the Lord cometh with ten thousands of his saints, to execute judgment upon all, and to convince all that are ungodly among them, of all their ungodly deeds, which they have ungodly committed, and of all their hard speeches, which ungodly sinners have spoken against him!" And what is the answer of the church, but "even so; come, Lord Jesus!" Amen.

APRIL 13.

MORNING.—"After this, Jesus knowing that all things were now accomplished, that the scripture might be fulfilled, saith, I thirst."—John xix. 28.

After this, that is, I conceive, (though I do not presume to mark the very order in which the Lord Jesus uttered his loud cries upon the cross,) after his complaint of desertion: for whether this was the fourth or fifth of the seven last words of the Redeemer, I dare not determine: yet the words themselves were highly important, and significant of great things, in reference to Jesus and his people. Jesus thus cried, that the scriptures might be fulfilled, it is said; for it had been prophesied of him, that gall was given him to eat—and, when thirsty, vinegar to drink, Ps. lxix. 21. And the soldiers, unconscious of what they did in fulfilling this very prophecy, gave him sponge dipped in vinegar. But, my soul, was it the thirst of the body thy Jesus complained of? I think not. He had before declared, at his last supper, that he would drink no more of the fruit of the vine, until the day he drank it new in the kingdom of his Father. What could be then the thirst of Jesus, but the thirst of his soul, for the accomplishment of redemption for his people, and the accomplishment of redemption in his people. He thirsted with an holy vehement thirst for the everlasting salvation of his ransomed, and seemed to anticipate the hour by this expression, when he should see the travail of his soul, and be satisfied. But did not Jesus also, in this hour, as bearing the curse and wrath of God for sin, thirst in soul with that kind of thirst which, in hell, those who bear the everlasting torments of condemnation feel, when they are under an everlasting thirst which admits of no relief! That representation the Lord Jesus gives of this state, in the parable of the rich man's thirst, serves to afford a lively but alarming view of such superlative misery. Oh that those who now add drunkenness to thirst, would seriously lay this to heart. Did God suffer his dear Son, to whom sin was but transferred, and not committed by him—did he suffer him to cry out under this thirst? and what may we suppose will be the everlasting cry of such as not only merit his wrath for sin, but merit yet more his everlasting wrath for refusing redemption by Jesus, who thirsted on the cross to redeem sinners from endless thirsting in despair and misery? My soul, did Jesus thirst for thee? Were his dying lips parched, and his soul deeply athirst, for thy salvation? And shall not this thirst of thy Redeemer kindle an holy thirst in thee for him, and his love and his great salvation? Wilt thou not now this morning anew, look up by faith to the cross and to the throne, and catch the flame of love from his holy, loving, longing, and languishing eyes, until all thy powers go forth in vehement desires, like him of old, crying out—"As the hart thirsteth for the water brooks, so longeth my soul after thee, O God. Let him kiss me with the kisses of his mouth; for thy love is better than wine."

EVENING.—"His soul was not left in hell, neither his flesh did see corruption."—Acts ii. 31.

Two sweet, but distinct thoughts, arise out of this scripture: one, concerns the soul of Christ; the other, respects his body; and both are most blessed to the believer in the review. My soul! thou hast attended to the parched state of thy Redeemer, as represented on the cross, and made it the subject of thy morning meditation; do thou now behold what this scripture states, under all his humiliating circumstances, that neither hell nor the grave can have dominion over him. His soul shall not be long in a way of separation from the body, in the invisible state; for very shortly it shall arise from hades, the hell here mentioned. And his body is too holy, harmless, and undefiled, to admit of putrefaction; yea, it must be presented before the Lord for a sweet-smelling savour. Precious thought to the believer! Jesus needed not to lie long under the dominion of death: he had fully paid the debt of sin by death; and therefore there needed no detention to make farther restitution for the sins of his people, when thus fully cancelled. And as the infinite holiness and purity of his nature could not become subject to the power of corruption, he needed not to lie longer in the grave than might clearly and fully ascertain to his people in all ages, the reality of his death, for the better confirmation of the resurrection that followed. Hence Jesus could not be left, as the great representative of his people, in a situation so comfortless, when the work was completed which the Father gave him to do. And as his holy nature could not admit the possibility of corruption; so the covenant of redemption exempted him from it. Add to these, it was needful that, both in soul and body, He who had died for our sins, should rise again for our justification, and not only triumph in our nature over death, hell, and the grave, but return to the right hand of power, " there to appear in the presence of God for us." Hail! thou holy and triumphant Lord! I bow the knee before thee! In thy holiness thy people are considered holy: and as thy spotless soul could not be detained in hell, neither thy flesh see corruption, so all thy redeemed shall be accounted holy before thee, and through thy righteousness, be considered righteous before God and thy Father for ever. Amen.

APRIL 14.

MORNING.—" When Jesus therefore had received the vinegar, he said, it is finished."—John xix. 30.

Perhaps these words formed the sixth cry of the Lord Jesus on the cross. The glorious close of all his sufferings was now arrived; and full of these high ideas which occupied his holy mind, he cried out, "It is finished!" What is finished? Redemption-work is finished. All the long series of prophecies, visions, types, and the shadows of good things to come, which pointed to Jesus and redemption by him, were now finished in their accomplishment. The law was finished in its condemning power; and the gospel commenced its saving influence. Jesus, by that one sacrifice now offered, had for ever perfected them that are sanctified. The separation between Jew and gentile was now finished and done away for ever. Jesus had now "gathered together, in one, all the children of God which are scattered abroad." The iron reign of sin and Satan, of death and hell, were now broken in pieces by this stone cut out of the mountain without hands; and life and immortality, pardon, mercy, and peace, were brought to light, and secured to the faithful, by this finished redemption of the Lord Jesus Christ. The peace, the love, the favour of God the Father, was now obtained; and that spiritual kingdom of the Lord Jesus, which shall have no end, was from this moment set up in the hearts and minds of his people. The sure descent of the Holy Ghost was now confirmed; and the Lord Jesus already, by anticipation, beheld his Israel of old, and his gentile church, as well as Ethiopia and the multitude of the isles, stretching forth their hands unto God. Full of these and the like glorious prospects the mind of Jesus was filled; and having received the vinegar, as the last prophecy remaining then to be completed, he cried out, "It is finished!" My soul, never let these precious, precious words of Jesus depart from thy mind. Do by them as Moses commanded Israel concerning the words he gave them; "let them be in thy heart, and in thy soul; bind them as a sign upon thine hand, and let them be as frontlets between thine eyes." Tell thy God and Father what thy Jesus hath told thee—" It is finished!" He hath finished redemption for thee; and He will finish redemption in thee. He hath destroyed death, both satisfied and glorified the law, taken away the curse, made full restitution for sin, brought in an everlasting righteousness, and opened the glorious mansions of the blessed as the home and rest of all his people. Oh my soul, let these dying words of thy Jesus be made by thee as an answer to all thy prayers, and begin that song to the Lamb, which ere long, thou wilt fully and loudly sing among the church above—" Worthy is the Lamb that was slain; for thou wast slain, and hast redeemed us to God by thy blood."

EVENING.—" And the people stood beholding; and the rulers also with them derided him, saying, He saved others; let him save himself, if he be Christ, the chosen of God. And the soldiers also mocked him, coming to him, and offering him vinegar, and saying, if thou be the king of the Jews, save thyself."—Luke xxiii. 35—37.

My soul! thou art not tired, I hope, of taking thy stand, night by night, and morning by morning, at the foot of the cross. Surely it is blessed to sit down by the fountain, which was opened by the soldier's spear, in the heart of Jesus, and contemplate, one by one, the mercies which flow in it to the souls of his redeemed. There are more to be seen, more to be discovered at every renewed review; for in the death of Christ, is the life of the soul. It is not the smallest part of the excellencies which Jesus discovered in his death, that it was " the death of the cross;" for the apostle joins this with his sufferings. He not only endured the cross, but he despised the shame; and yet that shame, in all the parts of it, forms a wonderful branch in the subject. My soul! look at the cross in this point of view, and see whether thou wilt not draw sweet consolation from it, under the grand consideration, that as thy sins have caused shame before God, so the shame thy blessed Surety endured, has more than made satisfaction to the divine glory. Behold the people, with the rulers, deriding Christ with taunts and reproaches; and even the Roman soldiers mocking Jesus, though they knew him not. Indeed, every thing in Christ became the subject of their resentment. Through his whole life, this had been the case; and now, in the close of it, the whole is summoned up into the most finished contempt. His person most daringly despised: "if he be the Son of God, let God save him if he will have him," say they! His offices blasphemed: "art thou a king then," said Pilate, in the most sovereign contempt. "If thou be the King of Israel," said the rabble, "save thyself and come down from the cross." "Prophecy, thou Christ," said one of them in the hall, "who is he that smote thee." And as a priest, when Jesus was stretched forth on the cross, as in the act of blessing, and truly in the act of dying for them, the taunt was, "He saved others, himself he cannot save." Thus the Lord of life and glory, as the prophet had foretold, hid not his face from shame and spitting! And, as if to crown all with the highest possible instance of shame and disgrace, while the multitude counted him for a deceiver, and all his disciples forsook him and fled, as from a person with whom it was dangerous to be found, he is hung up as a malefactor, and that between two thieves; yea, God himself allowed him, nay, appointed him to be reckoned among the transgressors. Pause, my soul, over this blissful subject; and most blessed it is, when Christ is thus beheld in relation to his people. For surely whatever shame and confusion of face is the sinner's, due by reason of sin, the Lord Jesus hath fully paid it, yea, more than paid it, as the sinner's representative. And herein is that scripture completely explained and applied: "Comfort ye, comfort ye, my people, saith your God. Speak ye comfortably to Jerusalem, and cry unto her, that her warfare is accomplished, that her iniquity is pardoned: for she hath received of the Lord's hand double for all her sins." Surely this was literally and truly the case in the person of her Almighty Surety and Representative, when Jesus endured the cross, and bore the shame for all his people!

APRIL 15.

MORNING.—"And when Jesus had cried with a loud voice, he said, Father, into thy hands I commend my spirit: and having said thus, he gave up the ghost."—Luke xxiii. 46.

My soul, ponder well these last of the last seven words of thy God and Saviour which he uttered on the cross; for surely they are most sweet and precious, and highly interesting, both on thy Saviour's account and thine own. And first remark, the *manner* in which the Lord Jesus thus breathed out his soul; not like a man spent and exhausted, after hanging so many hours on the cross, faint with loss of blood, and such agonies of soul as never one before endured; but it was with a loud voice, thereby proving what he had before declared—"No man taketh my life from me; I have power to lay it down, and I have power to take it again." Precious Jesus, how sweet this assurance to thy people. But wherefore cry with a loud voice? A whisper, nay, a thought of the soul only, if with an eye of communication to God the Father, would have been sufficient, if this had been all that was intended. Wherefore then did Jesus cry with a loud voice? Was it not that all in heaven, and all in hell might hear? Did not angels shout at the cry? Did not the spirits of just men made perfect among the faithful gone to glory in Jesus's name, hear, and sing aloud? Did not all hell tremble when Jesus thus cried aloud, conscious that the keys of the grave, and death, and hell, were now put into his Almighty hand? Oh! precious, precious Jesus! was this among thy gracious designs for which, when thou wert retiring from the bloody field of battle, as a conqueror, thy loud voice shouted victory? And was there not another sweet and gracious design in this loud cry, Oh! thou blessed Jesus? Didst thou not intend thereby that poor sinners, unto the ends of the earth, might, by faith, hear and believe to the salvation of their souls? Didst thou not, dearest Lord! when bowing thy sacred head, as if to take a parting look of the disciple and the Marys, at the foot of the cross, and beholding them as the representatives of all the members of thy mystical body, didst cry with a loud voice, that all with them might behold thy triumphs, and rejoice in thee their glorious Head? Yes, Lamb of God! we adore thee in this glorious act; for we do accept it as it really is, the act of our one glorious head. In this solemn committing of thy spirit to the Father, we consider our spirits also as committed with thee, and by thee. (My soul! mark this down carefully in the inmost tablet of thine heart.) In all this, blessed Jesus! thou wert, and art, our Head. Thou didst, to all intents and purposes, take every individual believer of thine as a part of thyself, and by this act didst commit, with thyself, the whole into thy Father's hands, to be kept until the hour of their dropping their bodies, then to be united to thee for ever. Oh! precious Jesus! O precious mercy of our Jesus, how safe, how eternally safe, and secure, are all thy redeemed! Well might thine apostle say, "No man liveth to himself, and no man dieth to himself; for in Jesus his people ever live, and in Jesus they securely die." Henceforth, dear Lord! let me know myself to be already committed with thee, and by thee, into the hands of my God and Father in Jesus, and when the hour cometh that the casket, in which that precious jewel, my soul, now dwells, is opened for the soul to take her departure, O then for faith in lively, active, earnest faith, to follow the example, and to adopt the very language of my God and Saviour; and to cry out—"Lord Jesus, into thy hands I commend my spirit; for thou hast redeemed me, O Lord, thou God of truth!"

EVENING.—"And every priest standeth daily ministering and offering oftentimes the same sacrifices, which can never take away sins: but this man, after he had offered one sacrifice for sins, for ever sat down on the right hand of God."—Heb. x. 11, 12.

The morning portion was the finishing cry of Jesus on the cross. This, my soul, I hope thou didst, as it were, hear with the ear of faith: beholding with the eye of faith, the Lord of life and glory as retreating from the field of battle, having gotten himself the victory, and by that "one offering of himself, once offered, for ever perfected them that are sanctified." Fold up then the blessed object for thy nightly pillow, as for thy morning meditation, and bring it forth continually for thine unceasing joy and peace in believing, that (as the Holy Ghost hath in this scripture, for thy present enjoyment, sweetly set it forth) when all the priests in their daily ministry could accomplish nothing, this man, this God-man, this thy Jesus, whose name is Wonderful, hath "by his one offering," for ever put away sin, and is "sat down on the right hand of God," to see the purchase of his redemption, by price and by power, fully compensated to all his people. But here lie the blessed effects of thy Jesus's redemption; and do thou mark it, and bring it forward constantly in thy pleadings for acceptance with the Father in the Beloved, that so rich, so precious, so inestimable and invaluable is the redemption of God's dear Son, that it never can be fully compensated to his people. A whole eternity will not be sufficient to pay, nor can all the glories of heaven constitute a sufficient recompence; for after millions of ages are past, and millions of redemption blessings have been given in them, such is the infinite merit, and such is the infinite glory of the Son of God's righteousness, and blood, and sacrifice, that there must still remain a surplus unpaid, a redundancy still unaccounted for. Jesus will have brought in such everlasting revenues of glory to Jehovah, by the redemption of sinners, and in the honour done to his justice, love, and wisdom, by accomplishing the work the Father gave him to do, as will never be fully recompensed; yea, the merit of his cross alone will, to all eternity, shine with such splendour as to fill heaven with songs of endless praise. The sons of God, we are told, shouted for joy, when beholding the six days works of creation. But the six hours which Jesus hung on the cross wrought a more glorious work of redemption to Jehovah's praise, and will call up the unceasing adoration of angels and men to all eternity. What sayest thou, my soul, to this view of the wonderful subject? Let such be thy meditation day by day, and may thine eyes prevent the night watches to be fully occupied in it. Take thy stand at the foot of the cross; there by faith behold Him on whom the eye of Jehovah is unceasingly fixed: and when thou hast followed the Lamb from the cross to the throne, where Jesus is now for ever sat down on the right hand of God, catch the notes of the hymn which the redeemed are now singing in glory before him, and in which, ere long, thou wilt assuredly join: "To him that sitteth upon the throne, and to the Lamb that was slain, be glory and honour for ever and ever. Amen."

APRIL 16.

MORNING.—"There laid they Jesus."—John xix. 42.

My soul, it is usual for the relations and friends of those that are deceased to attend the funeral. Art thou a friend, a relation, of Jesus? Oh yes; I trust thou art. He was, and is, the dearest of all friends, the nearest of all relations. He is at once all and every one—the Father, the Husband, the Brother. The invitation is therefore sent to thee, personally to *thee.* Every voice of affection calls thee to the tomb of Jesus, saying, "Come, see the place where the Lord lay." And if, like Mary Magdalene, from more abundant love, thou art asking, "Where have they laid him ?"—the answer immediately is returned, "Come and see." Yes, thou dear Redeemer! by that faith thou hast graciously given me, I will come and see. Let my faith take wing, and light down in Joseph of Arimethea's garden, and behold the place where the Lord lay. Was this the memorable spot? Did Jesus lay here? Did he here make (according to the ancient prophecy foretold of him) "his grave with the wicked, and with the rich in his death, because he had done no violence, neither was any deceit in his mouth?" Here let me look; here let my soul wander in contemplation. Oh what a marvellous sight to behold Jesus thus lain in the grave. Surely we may cry out, as the church did in the view, "My beloved is white and ruddy." Never did death triumph so before. Never did the grave receive and hold such a prisoner. But, my soul, behold also, in the view, how Jesus triumphed even in death. It was "through death he destroyed him that had the power of death—that is, the devil, that he might deliver them who, through fear of death, are all their life-time subject to bondage." And what saith Jesus to my soul from the grave? Fear not, "I have the keys of death and the grave: fear not to go down to the Egypt of the grave, I will go with thee, and will surely bring thee up again from thence." And observe, my soul, as the grave could not detain thy Lord, thine Head, a prisoner; so neither can the grave, beyond the appointed time, detain any of his members. And as the union between the Godhead and the manhood in Jesus was not broken off by death, so neither can the union between Jesus and his people be interrupted by death. The covenant of redemption, the union of Jesus with his people, the love of God in Christ to the souls and bodies of his redeemed, all these rot not in the grave; nay, where sin is taken out, the very enmity of the grave is slain; and though it acts as a devourer of our corrupt bodies, yet it acts as a preserver also of the refined part, that the dust and ashes of his saints Jesus may visit, and manifest his care over, from day to day. Precious Lord, here then, as in every thing, thou hast the pre-eminence. Thou hast gone before: thou hast sweetly perfumed the grave by having lain there. And where should the dying members be but where their living Head hath been before? Hence then, my soul, take comfort and fear not, when thy partner, the body, is called upon to go down to the grave. When the soul flies to Jesus in heaven, the body will sweetly rest in Jesus till summoned from the grave. Thy God, thy Jesus, hath the appointment for thy departure; both the place *where*, the time *when*, and the manner *how*, are all with him. He hath the keys both to open the door of death, and to open the kingdom of heaven. Leave all then with him. Frequently, by faith, visit his sepulchre, and behold where they laid him. And in the triumphs of thy Jesus, as thine head, already take part, as a member of his body, crying out with the apostle, "Oh death where is thy sting? Oh grave, where is thy victory? God be praised who giveth us the victory, through our Lord Jesus Christ."

EVENING.—"Having loosed the pains of death; because it was not possible that he should be holden of it."—Acts ii. 24.

My soul! thou hast been in contemplation to the tomb of Jesus this morning, and seen the place where the Lord lay; now sit down, and ponder over what this blessed scripture saith, that "the pains of death were loosened, because it was not possible for Jesus to be detained a prisoner by it." And if there were no other scripture, but this one, in proof of Christ's godhead, this in itself would be unanswerable; for it could be nothing but the godhead of his person which made it impossible. It was this which, from the union of the manhood with the godhead, preserved his soul from sin, and his body from corruption; for though the human nature that Christ took was subject to all the sinless infirmities of nature, and to feel hunger, weariness, and the like, to the full, being part of the curse on the fall, which he came to bear and do away; yet was he not left to the infirmities of what we, in our fallen state, are exposed to, and often sink under. Sweet thought, to look to the tomb of Jesus with! Here, as oft as we contemplate the spot, we may say: here Christ hath lain down, to teach his followers to lie down. But here Christ could not be detained; his holy body was not subject to corruption. "Thou wilt not leave his soul in hell, neither wilt thou suffer thine Holy One to see corruption." But may it not be added also, on another account, that the pains of death could not hold Christ; forasmuch as God's justice being fully satisfied by the offering of the body of Jesus Christ, once for all, there could be no detention of the prisoner when the debt was paid? The Lord Jesus did not, for he needed not, go down to hell for the purpose of receiving there the punishment our sins deserve, and which, by suffering in our stead and room, he did away: his sufferings were fully commensurate upon earth: and it is not the *place*, but the *degree* and *nature* of punishment, that makes an equivalent on the score of paying. His capability of suffering, and the extremity of what he endured during his agony in the garden, and on the cross, (not to mention a whole life of sorrows, in being all along acquainted with grief) these were the full cup of trembling which Jesus drank, and completely adequate it was, or he would not have said upon the cross, "it is finished!"

Neither was it necessary that the Redeemer should long endure the sufferings due to sin, as the sinner's surety. Here also his capability of sustaining much, in a little space, plainly proves, that when all the vials of divine wrath were poured out upon his sacred head; being once completely emptied, they could not again be filled. Though had not Jesus died, "the just for the unjust, to bring us to God," the second death (which, out of Christ, is the sinner's due) must be an eternal death, because the vessels of wrath fitted for destruction, are only fitted for, and capable of receiving misery by portions, which never being fully poured out, are consequently never finished. But not so with Him who stood the sinner's surety. He could, and did receive at once, in life and death, the whole of the punishment due to sin: and therefore he it is of whom the Holy Ghost speaks, "All thy waves and thy billows are gone over me," Psalm xlii. 7. Precious Lord! while I think of these things, and my whole soul is going forth in sorrow at the contemplation of those sufferings of thine for my salvation, grant me to feel at the same time the blessedness of thy redemption, and my interest in it, since "by thy stripes I am healed."

APRIL 17.

MORNING.—"The Lord is risen indeed."—Luke xxiv. 34.

Let thy meditations, my soul, this morning, be sweetly exercised upon thy risen and exalted Saviour. For if thy Lord be indeed risen, then will it undeniably follow, that as he died for our sins, so he arose for our justification, and is thereby become the first fruits of them that sleep. Beg of God the Holy Ghost to lead thee into the devout contemplation and enjoyment of this soul-reviving subject. Trace the testimonies of this wonderful event, until, from being overpowered in the vast assemblage of witnesses, thou art prompted to cry out in the same language, "the Lord is risen indeed." And surely never was there any one fact so fully, so clearly, and so circumstantially confirmed. It hath the united testimony of heaven and earth: of angels and men, of the living and the dead, of friends and foes; and God himself confirming it in the midst of his people, by sending down the Holy Ghost agreeably to the promise of Jesus at the day of Pentecost. Review these things in order. *First,* heaven gave in its evidence in those supernatural signs which issued in the morning of Jesus's resurrection; for we are told that "an angel descended from heaven, and rolled back the stone from the door of Jesus's sepulchre, and sat upon it." And, *secondly,* earth gave her testimony also to the same, by the convulsions sustained at his approach—"there was a great earthquake." And then again, as angels came to inform the pious women who waited to embalm the sacred body of Christ, that Jesus was risen; so the testimony of multitudes among men gave equal attestation to this glorious truth. For besides the many separate and distinct appearances Jesus made to numbers, he appeared to above five hundred brethren at once, by way of confirming the undoubted fact. The *living*, who ate and drank with him after he arose from the dead, surely could not be mistaken. And the *dead* which arose from their graves, as if to celebrate the glories of his resurrection, in which they took part, came forth when the sepulchre yawned at the triumph of Jesus, and went into the holy city and appeared unto many. And not only the friends of Jesus, but the foes of Jesus, became undesignedly the witnesses of this great truth: for, by attributing his resurrection to the disciples' stealing away his body, they positively proved that the body of Christ remained not in the sepulchre. And that the poor timid disciples whose meetings were all in secret for fear of the Jews, should project such a scheme as to take away the body, which the Roman soldiers were purposely placed to secure, is not to be equalled in folly in the very idea, unless by that other part of the childish story, that the body was stolen while the guard slept, that so the testimony, it should seem, to this tale, is the testimony of men sleeping. Here then, my soul, in devout contemplation, take thy stand at the door of the sepulchre of thy Jesus, and ponder over such a multitude of witnesses, who all cry out with one voice, as the angels did to the astonished women, "He is not here; for he is risen, as he said. Come, see the place where the Lord lay." And O thou dear Redeemer, do thou, while my soul is pondering these things, do thou draw nigh, as thou didst to the disciples on the morning of thy resurrection, and sweetly commune with me of all these blessed truths concerning thyself; lead me, by faith, through all the precious subject, from the sepulchre to thine house of prayer, to the ordinance and thy table, from thy cross to thy crown; and cause my whole heart to burn within me, while thou art talking to me by the way, and while thou art opening to me the scriptures. Then shall I truly rejoice that my Lord is indeed risen from the dead, and my soul is risen with him, from dead works, to serve thee, the living and true God.

EVENING.—"The same day at evening, being the first day of the week, when the doors were shut where the disciples were assembled for fear of the Jews, came Jesus and stood in the midst, and saith unto them, Peace be unto you."—John xx. 19.

There is a peculiar blessedness in this first visit of the Lord Jesus to the whole college of disciples (at least as many as were present of them) after he arose from the dead: and the manner of relating it is peculiarly striking also. It was the same day at evening; and it was the *first day* also; as if the Lord Jesus would again and again honour the day, as well in the evening as the morning of his resurrection, and make that day for ever memorable to his church, and among his people. My soul! thou hast celebrated thy Lord's triumphs over death, in the morning, both at home and abroad, in his church, at his ordinances, at his table, and among his disciples; but learn hence also, that at evening time Jesus will make it light by the sweet renewed visits of his grace; and when the doors are shut, and in thy retirement the world is shut out, and thou art communing within, Jesus will come and say, "Peace be unto thee." And doth Jesus do this? Hast thou this precious legacy of peace, which he left to his people, administered to thee by his own blessed hand? Is he thy peace, and hath he made thy peace through the blood of his cross? Having purchased it by his death, doth he confirm it to thee by his resurrection, and in the earnest of his Spirit, seal it on thy soul to the day of eternal redemption? Oh! then look up to him, my soul, again this evening, as thy peace, thy surety, thy sponsor; and say with the prophet, "This man shall be our peace, when the Assyrian shall come into our land;" Micah v. 5. Yes, thou dear Redeemer! thou art indeed the peace, the very means and end of all joy and peace in believing, and wilt be the everlasting security of thy people in peace with God through all eternity! Methinks I hear thee say, in the nightly visits of thy love and grace, as to the disciples of old: "Peace I leave with you; my peace I give unto you; not as the world giveth, give I unto you: let not your heart be troubled; neither let it be afraid!"

APRIL 18.

MORNING.—"And declared to be the Son of God with power, according to the Spirit of holiness, by the resurrection from the dead."—Romans i. 4.

Do not, my soul, hastily pass away from this most precious subject of thy Lord's resurrection. It is an inexhaustible theme, and will be among thy felicities in eternity. Yesterday, thou didst but barely consider the fact. Let this day occupy thy thoughts on another sweet portion of it, in beholding how Jesus effected it by his own power and Godhead. He had said before that he had power to lay down his life, and power to take it again. And he had told the Jews to destroy the temple, by which he meant the temple of his body, and he would raise it again in three days. He had proclaimed himself to be the resurrection and the life: and here he proved it, when he was declared to be the Son of God with power, according to the Spirit of holiness, by his resurrection from the dead. Now, then, pause over this glorious view of Him who was thus proved to be one with the Father, and who, at the same time, was one in thy nature, bone of thy bone, and flesh of thy flesh. Beautiful and comprehensive is the expression —"declared to be the Son of God!" for who but God could accomplish such an event? And by the Spirit of holiness he was equally declared to be not liable to corruption; for, as God's Holy One, it was impossible that his flesh should see corruption. Psalm xvi. 10. And the Holy Ghost again, by Peter the apostle, explains it when he saith, "Christ was put to death in the flesh, but quickened by the Spirit." 1 Pet. iii. 18. The flesh here means his human nature; and the quickening by the Spirit (being what is called the antithesis, that is, the opposite to flesh) means his own Spirit, his own power and Godhead; similar to what is said in the Hebrews concerning the offering of Jesus, that through the Eternal Spirit he offered *himself*, Heb. ix. 14.— meaning, that his Godhead gave dignity and value to the offering of his body for the sins of his people. Ponder this blessed truth, my soul; for it is most blessed, and of much greater importance than, at the first view of the words, it may strike you. Behold in it, that it was the Godhead of Jesus by which thy Jesus triumphed over death and the grave. The Father's hand was in it most certain, as it was in all the other acts of redemption; for the Holy Ghost taught the church, by Paul, that God had raised up the Lord. 1 Cor. vi. 14. And manifested by this, saith the Holy Ghost, that he was the God of peace, in bringing again from the dead the Lord Jesus Christ. Heb. xiii. 20. And the Holy Ghost had his almighty hand in the same; for it is the Spirit that quickeneth; and hence Christ is said to have been justified in the Spirit. 1 Tim. iii. 16. But while we are taught by these scriptures, and others to the same purport, to behold both the Father and the Holy Ghost acting in the resurrection of Jesus—by this, and others of the same kind, we are taught to view the Godhead in Christ as the cause of his resurrection. For if Jesus had been raised by the power of the Father and the Holy Ghost only, how would he have been declared to be the Son of God by his resurrection? For, in this case, nothing more would have been manifested in his resurrection than in the resurrection of others; for it is by the power of God that the dead are to be raised. Hence, my soul, behold the vast importance of this great point in the resurrection of thy Lord: and never lose sight of this blessed truth, that thy Jesus, who is thy resurrection and thy life, arose himself by this self-quickening principle. Behold, in this point of view, what a glorious truth is the resurrection of Jesus. And what a lovely promise did the Lord, by the prophet, give to all the people of God concerning this, ages before this glorious event took place—"Thy dead men shall live; together with my dead body shall they arise. Awake and sing, ye that dwell in the dust; for thy dew is as the dew of herbs, and the earth shall cast out her dead." Isaiah xxvi. 19.

EVENING.—" Of one Jesus, which was dead, whom Paul affirmed to be alive."—Acts xxv. 19.

And well might Paul affirm it; for Jesus, after his resurrection, had spoken to Paul from heaven! Well might John, the beloved apostle, give the church his repeated evidence to it; for Jesus not only made his appearance to John, in common with the other apostles, but in the island of Patmos appeared to him alone, and proclaimed himself under those glorious distinctions of character: " Fear not; I am he that liveth, and was dead; and behold, I am alive for evermore!" Rev. i. 17, 18. And well might Peter testify to the same, as he did in the family of Cornelius, when he had such indisputable proofs for himself and the rest of his brethren, the apostles, who were " the chosen witnesses of his resurrection: we did eat and drink with him (saith Peter) after he arose from the dead;" Acts x. 41. But, my soul! mark, in the contempt with which this blessed truth is spoken of, by the Roman governor, how little esteemed, and less regarded by the world, is that doctrine, which is thy life. And are there not thousands in the present hour, like Festus, who, even if they do profess a belief of Jesus's resurrection, are like him, unconscious of its vital effects on their hearts; and as to any of the saving influences resulting from it in the descent of the Spirit upon them, have " never so much as heard whether there be any Holy Ghost!" My soul! how wilt thou prove the resurrection of Jesus in thine own experience, that, like Paul, thou mayest with equal confidence speak of this *One Jesus*, this only One, this blessed One, who was truly and indeed dead, but whom thou affirmest to be alive? Pause over the question, and then look into the real testimonies of it in thine heart. Remember what thy Jesus said as a promise which should take place soon after his resurrection and return to his Father, when redemption-work was finished: "I will send the Holy Ghost the Comforter. He shall teach you all things, and bring all things to your remembrance, whatsoever I have said unto you;" John xiv. 26. Hence therefore, if the Holy Ghost is come, then is Jesus risen and ascended; and then hath the Father also most fully confirmed his perfect approbation of the righteousness and death of Jesus, as the Surety of his people, in raising him from the dead, setting him on his own right hand, and sending down the Holy Ghost, agreeably to Christ's promise. And dost thou know all these things, in thine own experience? Is Jesus thy resurrection and life? Hath he recovered thee by the quickening influences of his Holy Spirit, from death to life, and from the power of sin and Satan to the living God? Is he now the daily life-giving, life-imparting, life-strengthening source of all thy faith, and life, and hope, and joy? Is it Jesus that becomes to thee as the dew unto Israel, reviving, like the dew of herbs, thy dry and unpromising wintry state, where there is no vegetation, and causing thee to put forth the tender bud afresh, when, without his influence, every thing in thee was parched and withered? Oh! then do thou proclaim it far and near, and let every one witness for thee, in every circle in which thou art called to move, that that one glorious Jesus, which was once dead, thou affirmest to be alive, and liveth for evermore. Precious Lord Jesus! how blessed are those sweet words of thine to my soul: "And because I live, ye shall live also!"

APRIL 19.

MORNING.—"Who was delivered for our offences, and was raised again for our justification."—Romans iv. 25.

My soul, thou must not yet dismiss—no, nor ever dismiss, the sweet and precious subject of thy Lord's resurrection. One part of it thou hast not yet scarce glanced at; and yet it is such a one as thine everlasting safety, and thy justification before God depends upon. "For," as the Holy Ghost hath said, by the mouth of his servant the apostle, "if Christ be not risen, then are believers yet in their sins." 1 Cor. xv. 17. See to it then, my soul, that what this sweet scripture of the morning saith be true, that Jesus was delivered for thine offences, and was raised again for thy justification. While Jesus was on the cross, and when Jesus was taken down and laid in the grave, the payment and the ransom for sin was then discharging. Jesus was then truly delivered for our offences. And when he arose from the dead, then the poor sinner, for whom he was delivered, and for whom he died, was truly justified before God; for thereby proof was made that the debt was paid, the receipt given, and God, in confirmation of it, styled himself by a new name, even the God of Peace, in bringing again from the dead our Lord Jesus Christ, as the great Shepherd of his sheep, through the blood of the everlasting covenant. Hence the resurrection of Jesus was like going into the presence of God to cancel the bond, the hand-writing of ordinances, that was against us. It was as if Jesus gave this testimony in his glorious resurrection, that both sin and death had now lost their retaining power; the dominion of both were for ever done away, and all true believers in Christ might join the apostle's song — "Who shall lay any thing to the charge of God's elect? It is God that justifieth; who is he that condemneth? It is Christ that died, yea rather, that is risen again, who is even at the right hand of God, who also maketh intercession for us." My soul, be sure to keep this in constant view, when, at any time, thou art meditating on the death and resurrection of Jesus: and let both be thy daily meditation. Think how truly blessed, how truly happy, how present and everlastingly secure, must those souls be who are interested in the death and in the resurrection of the Lord Jesus. By the one he hath purchased their pardon, and by the other he hath justified their persons; so that, when law and justice present their charge against them, this is the unanswerable plea—Jesus "was delivered for our offences, and raised again for our justification." Oh dearest Lord, grant me daily and hourly to be bringing into all my spiritual enjoyments the sweet sense and consciousness of being thus interested, justified, and secured. Give me a present right and title, that I may live upon it; and by and by, when thou shalt call me home, then, Oh Lord, present me finally and fully, once for all, as made comely in thy comeliness, clothed in thy righteousness, and fully prepared, both in soul and body, for everlasting happiness and glory among them that are sanctified.

EVENING.—"Thy dead men shall live; together with my dead body shall they arise. Awake and sing, ye that dwell in dust: for thy dew is as the dew of herbs, and the earth shall cast out the dead."—Isaiah xxvi. 19.

Thy morning meditation was a blessed portion, to shew thee, my soul, how the justification of the believer is effected by the person of his glorious Head. When Jesus died on the cross, not as a private person, but as the public head of his church, then he paid the full debt of sin: and when he arose from the dead, the full release was given to our whole nature in him. Jesus received the discharge; the bond he had entered into for his people was cancelled, and his resurrection became the proof of their's also. But as the justification of all the persons of his redeemed is *in* Him, and *by* Him, so another sweet confidence is in Him also: Jesus is not only the cause of their being *justified*, but of their being *glorified* also. In these precious words we have, first, God the Father's promise to his dear Son: "Thy dead men shall live:" first in grace, and then in glory. How shall this be effected? Christ then takes up the subject in answer; "Together with my dead body (saith he) shall they arise:" or it is possible the words may be still the words of the Father; for the body of Christ is said to be given of the Father: "A body hast thou prepared me," Heb. x. 15. But in either sense, the doctrine is the same; the resurrection of the believer is assured from its union with Christ. Jesus is the head of his body, the church. "Your life (saith the apostle) is hid with Christ in God;" Col. iii. 3. And so again: "If the Spirit of him that raised up Jesus from the dead, dwell in you; he that raised up Christ from the dead, shall also quicken your mortal bodies, by his Spirit that dwelleth in you;" Rom. viii. 11. Lastly, to crown all, as Jesus is the whole cause, both in *justifying*, and in *glorifying*, so is he the *pattern*, in his resurrection, *how* they shall arise. As the dew of herbs casteth out the same from the earth every year, so shall the earth cast out her dead. Christ's body was in substance the same, and so must be his people. "This corruptible (saith the apostle) this very identical body, must put on incorruption, and this mortal must put on immortality." Not "another body;" for then it would be "another person;" and this, instead of a *resurrection*, would be a *creation*. But the identical person that was buried, shall arise with the same identity. Well might the prophet, when giving this blessed promise, at the command of Jehovah, close it with that delightful injunction: "Awake and sing, ye that dwell in dust." And what a song to God and the Lamb will burst forth at once from millions of the redeemed, when rising to all the wonders of futurity, *in*, and *through*, and *from* a personal union *with* the Lord Jesus Christ!

APRIL 20.

MORNING.—"Now is Christ risen from the dead, and become the first fruits of them that slept."—1 Cor. xv. 20.

One view more, my soul, while thou art meditating upon this delightful subject of thy Redeemer's triumph over death and the grave, and now look at Jesus's resurrection as a sure pledge and confirmation of thine own. Did Jesus's holy body arise? Then so shall thine, sinful and polluted as it now is, but then made a glorified body by virtue of thy union with him. For so saith the Holy Ghost, by his servant the apostle: "He shall change our vile body, that it may be fashioned like unto his glorious body. For if the Spirit of him that raised up Jesus from the dead, dwell in you, he that raised up Christ from the dead, shall also quicken your mortal bodies, by his Spirit that dwelleth in you." Phil. iii. 21. Rom. viii. 11. Pause then, my soul, and rejoice in this glorious and transporting doctrine. As sure as Jesus arose, so sure shall all his people; for Jesus arose as the first fruits. Jesus arose not as a private person, but as the public Head. Never call to mind the resurrection of Jesus, but be sure to connect always with it this blessed view of the subject—every redeemed believer is part of Christ's body. And as we are by nature part of the first Adam, and die, from our union and connection, and being of the same nature with him; so, by grace, being part of Christ's mystical body, who is called in scripture, particularly on this account, the second Adam, his people are interested in all that concerns him; and because he liveth, they must live also. Hence he is called the first fruits, the first-born from the dead. And as all the after fruits of the harvest follow the first fruits; so the saints, born again in God, follow the first-born from the dead to glory. Oh heart-reviving subject! The eyes that now read these lines, and the hand that now writes them, is a part of Christ's mystical body by regeneration, must assuredly be a part in the resurrection. In the eye of the law they are one. Jesus is the head of his body the church: and how incomplete in glory would be that glorious head without the whole and every individual member of his fair one, his spouse, which he hath betrothed to himself for ever. Shout then, my soul, and shout aloud, and say with Job —"Though after my skin worms destroy this body, yet in my flesh shall I see God." My flesh shall moulder indeed in the dust, and see corruption. And so would I have it to be. Vile and polluted as it now is, and fighting as it now doth against my soul's desires and affections, methinks I would not, if it were possible, take it with me to heaven as it now is. But when Jesus shall change this vile body, and have fashioned it like unto his glorious body, then it will be without spot or wrinkle, or any such thing; and then soul and body, united together in love, and both united to the Lord, will form one united object to praise and glorify God, Father, Son, and Holy Ghost, to all eternity! My soul, dwell upon these things; give thyself wholly to them; and as thou believest that Jesus died and rose again, so equally believe also, that all they that sleep in Jesus will God bring with him. For this the apostle had in commission from the Lord to tell all true believers, that when Jesus shall "descend from heaven, with a shout, with the voice of the archangel, and with the trump of God, the dead in Christ shall arise; and then they which remain unto the coming of the Lord, shall be caught up together with them to meet the Lord in the air, and so shall they ever be with the Lord." Oh for grace to comfort one another with these words!

EVENING.—"So man lieth down, and riseth not: till the heavens be no more, they shall not awake, nor be raised out of their sleep. O that thou wouldest hide me in the grave, that thou wouldest keep me in secret, until thy wrath be past, that thou wouldest appoint me a set time and remember me!"—Job xvi. 12, 13.

My soul! thou hast been viewing and reviewing some of the blessed things connected with the glorious doctrine of thy Redeemer's resurrection, for several nights and mornings past; but there is one more point of view in which that heavenly truth demands attention, and which thou hast not even glanced at. Sit down, and ponder over the joy, the gratulations, the unspeakable rapture which will result from the meeting of thyself! I mean thou and thy body meeting together after the long separation made by the grave, and all the humbling circumstances of this flesh of thine having seen corruption. Figure to thyself what an interview that will be of soul and body! In this life, my soul may truly say to the body, Oh! how exceedingly burdened am I, day by day, from an union too dear to be parted from but with pain; and yet too opposed, in all my pursuits and desires, to what I am longing after in spiritual attainments, to wish always to continue! I know, that whilst I am now at home in the body, I am absent from the Lord; and still so much am I allied to thee, so dear art thou, that when the prospect of separation appears, though I know it is but for a season, nature shrinks back, and recoils with terror!—There must be the clammy sweat of death, and, whatever it be, or in whatever it consist, there must be a separation of soul and body. Therefore, like the apostle, "though in this tabernacle I groan, being burthened," yet it is "not to be unclothed, but clothed upon, that mortality might be swallowed up of life." Pause, my soul, and receive comfort from the divine portion of the evening. Job comforted himself with it, and why should not you? Though death separate soul and body, yet it is only to devour that corrupt part of the body which is now so afflictive to the soul. The Lord will "appoint a set time and remember." "He will call, and thou shalt answer him. He will have a desire to the work of his hands." Moreover, thy body, corrupt as it now is, and virtually all sin, yet hath Jesus as much made it his purchase as the soul. And when the *set time* arrives, by virtue of his resurrection, thy body shall arise, and thou shalt be among the first, when Jesus gives the word, to descend, and meet thyself in the body, then no longer disposed to interrupt thy purer joys, but as much alive as thou art to the everlasting service, love, and praise of God and the Lamb. Hail, thou glorious Restorer of all things! In thy light shall I see light: and "when thou, who art my life, shall appear, then shall I appear with thee in glory." Amen.

APRIL 21.

MORNING.—"The glory which thou gavest me I have given them, that they may be one, even as we are one."—John xvii. 22.

Those are sweet views of Jesus which point to our oneness and union with him, by which alone we derive an interest in him, and are made partakers both in his grace and glory. By virtue of this it is, that the glory the Father gave Jesus, as Mediator, all his people are interested in, and truly enjoy. For though like the heir of a kingdom, when an infant, the babe is unconscious of his dignity, yet is not the less entitled to his high birth and rank: so the seed of Jesus, while in this childhood of existence, though they do not live up to their high privileges through the weakness of their faith, yet their claim in Jesus is not the less. Jesus hath given them the glory of being brought within the covenant, the glory of redemption, the glory of the Holy Ghost's gifts and influences; and, in short, all the glory which a state of grace implies, and which is the earnest of the future fulness of glory. And, my soul, dost thou ever pause over this account of present glory as if thou didst not truly know thine interest and the enjoyment of it? Look at it only under these *two* considerations, and then bow down under a sense of it in the dust before God. In the first, put forth thy utmost faculties to calculate that glory which, if thou art one of Jesus's redeemed people, thou now truly hast in having union with Christ! Who shall undertake to describe that glory imparted to a poor worm of the earth, who is brought into union with God's dear Son? Paul speaks of it as an high privilege, when he said, "Ye are come to an innumerable company of angels." But what is the society of angels, compared to an union with Jesus? Moreover, angels have no such privilege: for while Jesus is to them their Lord and Sovereign, and governs them by his supreme command, yet is he not to them as he is to his church, the glorious head of that church, which is his body, and by which he perpetually communicates to all his members a source of gracious and glorious influences, according to what he hath said, "Because I live, ye shall live also." Hence, what the Redeemer said to the Father is explained on this sure testimony — "The glory thou gavest me I have given them, that they may be one even as we are one." Look at the subject under *another* consideration. Hath not Jesus given present glory to all his redeemed in that communication which is perpetually passing and repassing between him and them by virtue of this oneness, and unity, and interest, into which they are actually brought? My soul, what sayeth thy experience to this precious truth? Dost thou really and truly partake of what is Jesus's; and doth he not really and truly partake of what is thine? Is there not an exchange, a barter, a fellowship, carried on between thy glorious head and thyself? Surely thou hast communion in whatever belongs to Christ as Mediator; in his righteousness, in his grace, his redemption, his glory. And doth not Jesus manifest continual tokens that he takes part in all that concerns thee; thy sorrows, thy wants, thine afflictions? Was it not said of him, ages before his incarnation, when speaking of his people, "in all their affliction he was afflicted?" And is it not said now, that "whosoever toucheth his people toucheth the apple of his eye?" Oh unparalleled grace! O matchless love, that the Son of God should thus manifest his affection! What will you call this, my soul, but what thy God and Saviour hath called it — the glory which the Father gave him, he hath given to his people. And all this on purpose to prove that they are one with him. Hallelujah!

EVENING.—" Verily, verily I say unto you, except a corn of wheat fall into the ground, and die, it abideth alone: but if it die, it bringeth forth much fruit."—John xii. 24.

How sweet and lovely is this similitude of the Lord's, in allusion to himself! See to it, my soul, this evening, that thou art able to receive it. Thou hast been attending thy Lord to the tomb: here behold the blessed fruits of his precious death. When Jesus became incarnate, like a pure corn of the finest wheat, he fell to the ground; and when at his death, " he made his grave with the wicked, and with the rich in his death," he fell into the ground: and now what an abundant harvest of glory to God, and salvation to souls, hath that death, and grave of Jesus produced! Had Jesus never died, how would he have seen his seed, and the pleasure of the Lord prosper in his hand? Had Jesus not descended to the grave, how would he have been the life-giving, the soul-quickening root of all his church and people? But now, by this one precious corn of wheat falling into the ground, and dying, how hath the garner of God been filled, and is now continually filling, with his seed! Precious Jesus! give me to see that I am thy seed, in the ever green and flourishing verdure of my soul from thy quickening influence! And let that promise of my covenant Father and God in Christ be my daily portion: " As for me, this is my covenant with them, saith the Lord: my spirit that is upon thee, and my words which I have put into thy mouth, shall not depart out of thy mouth, nor out of the mouth of thy seed, nor out of the mouth of thy seed's seed, saith the Lord, from henceforth and for ever."

APRIL 22.

MORNING.—" Wheresoever the carcase is, there will the eagles be gathered together."—Matt. xxiv. 28.

My soul! these are the words of Jesus, none of which should be suffered to fall to the ground. No doubt much instruction is contained in this passage. An eagle is a bird of prey: and Job saith, that the eagle hasteneth to the prey as the swift ships. Job ix. 26. In all birds of prey there is great sagacity, a vast quickness of scent to smell their proper food afar off; and thus natural instinct, added to a rapacious appetite, compel those creatures to fly swift to their prey, and to devour the carcase. Is there nothing in all this that suits thee, my soul? Oh yes: If Jesus hath given thee a real principle of life in himself, which becomes a spiritual quickening from day to day, and from one hour to another, thy hungering and thirsting for Jesus will be as earnest and as importunate as the instinct of nature in those birds for daily food. Pause, my soul, and say—is it so? Dost thou seek after Jesus in his ordinances, in his word, in retirement, in meditation, in prayer, in providences; and, in short, in all the various ways by which thou mayest enjoy him, as a famished bird would hasten to his prey? If Jesus be indeed the one blessed object of thy desire, will not this be manifested by the earnestness of thy desires? Did David long for the waters of Bethlehem when thirsty? Did he declare, " that as the hart panteth for the water-brooks," so he longed for the enjoyment of God? Here then, my soul, mayest thou learn how to estimate the real standard of thy affections to thy Jesus. Oh for grace to have the soul exercised day and night, and never, never to give over those longings, like pregnant women, until the full desires of the soul in Jesus, and upon Jesus, be fully gratified. Methinks as the eagles gather together unto the carcase, so should believers be found feasting upon Jesus. In Jesus, and his glorious excellencies, every thing is suited to the wants of the believer: his name, his person, his work, his blood, his righteousness; every perfection, every promise, every experience we have had in him in times past, becomes food to the soul. So that the spiritual cravings of the soul, when the soul is in health and strength, like the natural cravings of the bird of prey, act like the same instinct to lead to and to feed upon Jesus. See then, my soul, whether this morning thou art risen with a keen appetite for Jesus. Surely thou hast tasted that the Lord is gracious in times past. And if thou art in health of soul, wilt thou not as much hunger again for this heavenly food, as the body of an healthy man craves for his morning meal? Oh blessed Lord, give me this appetite. Excite an hungering in me for thee. Let it be for thyself; not for thy gifts only, not for thy graces only, sweet as these are; but, blessed Jesus, let it be for thyself. And let this desire be continual: every day, and all the day. And let it be wholly to thee, in all that belongs to thee. I mean, after every thing in Jesus; thy cross, if needful, as well as thy crown; a love to thy precepts, as well as thy promises. And, O let this desire be so insatiable, so earnest, so unceasing, that nothing I have of thee may so satisfy me that I should long no more after thee; but rather provoke my soul's appetite, and tend but to inflame my heart and longings more and more, till, from tasting of thee here below, thou bringest me to the fountain-head of enjoyment above, where my longing eyes and longing soul shall feast upon Jesus and his love for ever and for ever. Amen.

EVENING.—"He shall enter into peace: they shall rest in their beds, each walking in his uprightness."—Isaiah lvii. 2.

Here, my soul, is a sweet portion for thee to lie down with, this night, and every night until the night of death arrives, and thou droppest asleep in the arms of Jesus, to wake no more, till the everlasting morn arise that shall have no night. This is the privilege of the faithful, who enter into the peace of Jesus, and these are the beds they repose in, yea, each of them, for it is the personal enjoyment of each, and of all, to make Jesus their rest. " This is the rest (saith the Holy Ghost, by this same prophet, chap. xxviii. 12.) wherewith ye may cause the weary to rest, and this is the refreshing." And dost thou know it, my soul, that Jesus is all this for thee to rest upon, for peace here, and glory to all eternity ? Behold him in his person; behold him in the fulness of his grace, his righteousness, his blood, and the unceasing efficacy of his atonement and salvation ! Surely thou hast both known him, and rested upon him, under all these endearing views, and therefore cannot now need to inquire, what is the rest of the weary, and the sure dwelling-place of the believer? Look at each sweet character and office of Jesus, and mark how suited they all are for his people, when buffetted by Satan, or fatigued in the world, or tired with the many burdens and interruptions to their peace, which arise from bodily infirmities; look at each, and see what a bosom Jesus opens to receive, and lull to sleep in his arms, every lamb of his fold. If the tempter should hiss from the " lion's den, and from the mountain of the leopards, how quieting is that voice which speaketh pardon and peace in the blood of the cross! And what strength does faith afford in Jesus's righteousness, " to quench all the fiery darts of the wicked!" If the world frown, if family cares and sorrows arise, or if any of those various afflictions which necessarily arise out of a fallen state, abound to make this state wearisome, still the promise holds good : " he shall enter into peace; they shall rest in their beds :" Jesus will here again lull them to sleep with his sweet refreshments. " In the world ye shall have tribulation, but in me ye shall have peace." And if, my soul, thine own manifold frailties, which daily and hourly harass thee, from that body of sin and death thou carriest about with thee; if these induce sorrow, as well they may, Oh! how blessed is it to look up to Jesus under all, and view that blood which speaketh for thee, more than all thy errors plead against thee! Here, thou dearest Lord, wilt thou cause me to find constant support and consolation in thee; and, amidst all, I shall hear thy lovely voice saying, "Come unto me, all ye that are weary and heavy laden, and I will give you rest." Lie down then, my soul, this night, and every night, until thou takest thy last night in the quiet bosom of the grave, upon the covenant promises of thy God, in the sure and safe resting-place of thy Jesus, and his finished salvation. And as the waters of the flood allowed no resting-place for the dove, neither could she find place for the sole of her foot, until she returned to Noah in the ark, so neither will the tribulated waters of sin, and sorrow, and temptation, suffer thee to enjoy rest in any thing short of Jesus, which the ark of Noah signified. "Return then to thy rest, O my soul, return to thy Jesus, thy Noah, thine ark, for the Lord hath dealt bountifully with thee?"

APRIL 23.

MORNING.—"For to this end Christ both died, and rose, and revived, that he might be Lord both of the dead and living."—Rom. xiv. 9.

And was this the cause, dearest Jesus, of all thy sufferings, that thou mightest be the universal monarch on thine eternal throne? Then bend thy knee, my heart, and all the affections of my soul, and hail thy Jesus Lord of all! Now, Lord, I see through thy blessed teaching, though a fool, and slow in heart to believe all that the prophets have spoken—now I see how expedient it was that Christ should suffer, and should enter into his glory. Yes, thou art, indeed, Lord both of dead and living; the dead to raise, even the dead in trespasses and sins; and the living to live in them, and rule, and guide them. And as thou art Lord both of dead and living, so, precious Jesus, wilt thou be Lord over all the dead and lifeless affections of thy redeemed. Surely, Lord Jesus, my soul may well believe this; for if, when upon the cross, thou didst conquer death, now thou art upon the throne, every power must be put beneath thy feet. Shout then, my soul, shout all ye followers of the Lord; never more let dead frames, or dying affections, or unbelief, or all the temptations of Satan, cast us down. Is not Christ upon the throne? And is he not Lord both of dead and living? And hath not this Almighty Lord, both of dead and living, power to save, power to quicken dead sinners, and comfort living saints; to give grace to the weak; and to them that have no might, to increase strength? Hath he not power to kindle anew his own graces that he first planted; to bring back again wanderers, to reclaim the long-lost backsliders, to soften hard hearts, to bind up broken hearts, to justify the guilty, to sanctify the filthy, to adopt orphans, to bless the fatherless, to be gracious, and kind, and merciful—in a word, to be Jesus? For in that one word is summoned up all. Oh blessed Master! Oh for an heart to love thee, to live to thee, to walk with thee, to rejoice in thee, to be always eyeing thee on thy throne; and never, never to lose sight of thee, my glorious, risen, and exalted Saviour, in this sweet and endearing point of view, in which thy servant the apostle hath here represented thee; that it was for this end, as well as a thousand other blessed purposes, that Christ both died, and rose, and revived, that he might be Lord both of dead and living. Hallelujah. Amen.

EVENING.—"A feast is made for laughter, and wine maketh merry: but money answereth all things."—Eccles. x. 19.

What feast is this, which the wise man meant, and the wine which, for true mirth, he would here recommend? He could not mean the laughter of the fool, for that, he tells us elsewhere (chap. vii. 6.) "is as the crackling of thorns under a pot." The drunkard's song is but the mirth of the moment, which, like the burning thorn, may blaze and flash amidst the midnight crew, but suddenly goeth out, and leaves a total darkness. But if Solomon had an eye to the feast which Jesus hath made in the mountain of the Lord's house, "a feast of fat things," where his body broken, and his blood shed, are the food of the table; this indeed is a feast made for real joy of heart, and "wine which cheereth God and man;" Judges ix. 13. When the justice of God drank of this blood of the Lamb, it was satisfied; and when the poor sinner hath tasted of it, his soul is satisfied also. And as "money answereth all things," because all things are procurable by it, so the redemption of Jesus answereth all the wants of a sinner. He is meat to the hungry soul, and drink to the thirsty. He is a garment to the naked, and the medicine of life to the diseased. "I will cause them (saith Jesus) that love me to inherit substance, and I will fill their treasures." Sit down, my soul, this evening, and mark the striking contrast. The pleasures of the carnal are short and unsatisfying; yea, they have nothing more in the enjoyment of them than what is common to the brute that perisheth, and the after effects are all on the side of sorrow. The word of God hath described it in a finished form of misery: "though wickedness be sweet in his mouth; though he hide it under his tongue, though he spare it, and forsake it not, but keep it still within his mouth; yet his meat in his bowels is turned, it is the gall of asps within him," Job xx. 12, 13, 14.

What an awful termination to a life of sensuality and carnal pursuits. Sin and folly lead in the front, and misery and sorrow bring up the rear! But in the sweet feast of Jesus, all is joy and peace in the Holy Ghost; and the believer sits down, as under the everlasting smiles of God, hearing and embracing the blessed invitation: "I have gathered my myrrh with my spice, I have eaten my honeycomb with my honey, I have drunk my wine with my milk: eat, O friends; drink, yea, drink abundantly, O beloved!" Blessed Lord! be it my portion, thus, night by night, and day by day, to hear thy voice, to behold thy countenance! And do thou, Lord, come in and sup with me, and cause me to sup with thee, until thou take me home to thine eternal feast above, whence I shall rise no more; where one everlasting banquet will remain, and the redeemed of the Lord will live for ever "in the presence of God and the Lamb!"

APRIL 24.

MORNING.—"The breaker is come up before them: they have broken up, and have passed through the gate, and are gone out by it: and their king shall pass before them, and the Lord on the head of them." —Micah ii. 13.

Pause, my soul, over this precious scripture, and ask thine own heart who this Almighty Breaker can be, except the Lord Jesus Christ; for he, and he alone, answers to such a divine character. Was it not he which came up as the Breaker from everlasting; when, in the council of peace, the divine decree was broken open, and the Son of God stood forth the sinner's Surety? Was it not he whom John saw by vision, who alone was found worthy in heaven to open the book, and loose the seals thereof? Was it not the same precious Holy One, who, when in the volume of the book it was found written of him, that he should fulfil the law of Jehovah for sinful man, cried out, "Lo, I come?" And was it not Jesus, even thy Jesus, my soul, that in the fulness of time came up as the Breaker, to break down the dreadful bar of separation which sin had made between God and man, and to open a new and living way for the sinner to God by his blood? And when he had broken down the fence sin had made in disobedience to the divine law, the accusations of Satan, the dominion of death and the grave, by sustaining the whole weight and burden of all in his own precious person; did he not, as the Almighty Breaker, burst asunder the bars of death, and prove himself thereby indeed to be this Almighty Breaker in such a palpable evidence, that it was impossible his holy soul could be holden by it? And hath he not broken through all intervening obstacles, ascended up on high, led captivity captive, entered into glory, and there ever liveth and appeareth in the presence of God for us? Is not Jesus then this Almighty Breaker? But, my soul, look yet further. It is said also, in this blessed scripture, that the Breaker is not only come up before them, (that is, his people,) but that "they have broken up, and have passed through the gate, and are gone out by it; and their king shall pass before them, and the Lord on the head of them." And so they are, if so be this Almighty Breaker hath broken down the strong holds of sin and Satan in which they lay bound; broken down the natural hatred and enmity of their own heart against God and his Christ in which they were born, and in which they lived, and must have died, but for his sovereign grace manifested in them and towards them; burst open the prison doors of Satan, and broke off his cursed chains, and brought them out! If these things are wrought and accomplished in the people, may they not be said, in his strength, to have broken up, and have passed through the gate of Satan's dominions, and are gone out by it into the glorious liberty of the sons of God? Is it so, my soul, in thy experience? Dost thou indeed know Jesus for thy Almighty Breaker, by such sweet and precious tokens of his love and power? Hath thy King passed thus before thee, and thy Lord on the head of thee? Oh then, be ever on the look out for all the renewed visits of his grace, in which he still acts as thine Almighty Breaker, in breaking down all the remaining obstacles which thy unbelief, and fears, and doubts, are continually raising up against thy own happiness, in his precious manifestations. Look up to him daily, hourly, minutely, if possible, that he may break down all the remains of indwelling corruption in thy nature, by which these fears and this unbelief gets hold fast in thy soul; and be often on the look out also for that glorious day of God, when this Almighty Breaker shall finally and fully come, and break through the clouds to judgment, to break down every remaining evil that keep thee now from the everlasting enjoyment of thy Lord. Hasten, blessed Jesus! come, my beloved, and, with a glory infinitely surpassing all conception, manifest thyself as the Almighty Breaker, in this full display of thy sovereignty and power. And then, as Samson (the type in this instance) carried with him the gates of his prison, so wilt thou break up and carry away all the gates of thy people's graves, and take all thy redeemed home with thee to glory, that where thou art, there they shall be also. Hail, thou Almighty Breaker! Jesus omnipotent reigneth!

EVENING.—" Because thou sayest, I am rich, and increased with goods, and have need of nothing; and knowest not that thou art wretched, and miserable, and poor, and blind, and naked; I counsel thee to buy of me gold tried in the fire, that thou mayest be rich; and white raiment, that thou mayest be clothed, and that the shame of thy nakedness do not appear; and anoint thine eyes with eye-salve, that thou mayest see."—Rev. iii. 17, 18.

My soul! take a leisurely view of what the Redeemer hath here stated of the church of Laodicea, and gather from it thine evening improvement. What a melancholy representation hath Jesus given! It would have been bad enough to have been in this state, even had the church been seeking deliverance from it; but to fancy herself well when very ill, to have the spots of death upon her when she supposed herself recovered, what can be more awful? See to it, my soul, that this be not thy case; ponder over the several characters here drawn, and mark well, whether, through grace, thou hast happily been better taught? Dost thou fancy thyself "rich, and increased in goods, and having need of nothing?" Alas! thou knowest that thou art as poor as ever the circumstances of original sin and actual transgression could make a sinner; from thy first father, Adam, thou hast derived a nature which is virtually all sin, and that sin is continually breaking out, to manifest that all thine affections and thy desires cleave to the earth, and are altogether earthly. So that, so far from needing nothing, thou art insolvent before God, and in want of every thing. Hence thou knowest thy wretchedness and poverty by nature and by practice: for without a view of Christ, and void of an interest in him, thou art so *wretched,* as to be lost for ever; so *blind,* that thou wouldest not have had even a knowledge of thy miserable state; and so *naked,* that thou wouldest not have sought the covering of Jesus's robe of salvation, to conceal thy shame, either in this world, or in that which is to come. And hath the Lord taught thee these precious truths? Art thou more and more sensible of the utterly lost state of every man by nature? And after all that thou hast attained in thy pursuit of the divine truths, hast thou arrived at the same conclusion as the apostle, "that thou knowest nothing yet as thou oughtest to know?" Oh! then listen to the gracious advice of Jesus, and accept the counsel of that Wonderful Counsellor; buy of him all he recommends, for *in* him, and *with* him, are deposited all graces. "In him dwelleth all the fulness of the Godhead bodily. He hath *gold*, yea, "gold tried in the fire;" all grace, mercy, pardon, strength, faith, hope, love, holiness; yea, every thing that can make a poor sinner rich. And he hath *white raiment* to cover thee, even the spotless robe of his own righteousness, which will not only conceal the shame of thy nakedness, but when he hath washed thee from all thy pollutions in his blood, will make thee appear comely in his comeliness, that thou mayest appear before God and the Father justified and complete in his salvation. And he hath *the eye-salve*, for opening the eyes of the spiritually blind, which will effectually, under the anointing of the Holy Ghost, give thee to see thy nothingness, and the glory, fulness, and suitableness of Jesus! What sayest thou, my soul, to these things? Wilt thou not accept the counsel of thy Jesus? Yea, Lord, I do accept it, on my bended knees, with thanksgiving, love, and praise. And more especially, dear Lord, do I bless thee for thy bounty, that the purchase of these mercies from thee comes from thy free grace, not from my ability; Jesus never proposed to the poor to merit what he freely *gives;* nor to the insolvent, who have nothing to offer, to suspend his riches upon their merits. Thou, Lord, art too rich to need any thing from thy creatures; and the things proposed are too costly to be purchased; yea, Lord, thou hast thyself already bought them with a price no less dear than thine own most precious blood. Hence, therefore, thou wise, gracious, kind, and compassionate Lord, I pray for grace to accept thy counsel, and to buy of thee gold tried in the fire, and the white raiment of thy righteousness, and the anointings of thy blessed Spirit, for I need them all, "without money and without price."

APRIL 25.

MORNING.—"And the apostles said unto the Lord, increase our faith."—Luke xviii. 5.

Did the apostles need so to pray? Then well may I. Oh! thou great author and finisher of our faith! I would look up to thee, with thankfulness, that thou hast granted even the smallest portion of faith to so unworthy a creature as I am. Surely, my soul, it is as great a miracle of grace that my God and Saviour should have kindled belief in thy stony heart, amidst all the surrounding obstructions of sin and Satan which lay there, as when the miraculous fire from heaven, in answer to the prophet's prayer, came down and consumed the wetted sacrifice. I praise thee, my God and King, this day, in the recollection of this unspeakable, unmerited mercy. And though this faith in my heart still be but as a grain of mustard seed; though it be but as a spark in the ocean; though it be but as the drop of the dew, in comparison of the river; yet, blessed, precious Jesus! still this is faith, and it is thy gift. And is it not a token of thy favour? Is it not an earnest of the Holy Spirit, and a pledge of the promised inheritance? Babes in faith, as well as the strong in the Lord, are equally thine; for it is said that "as many as were ordained to eternal life believed;" (Acts xiii. 48.) "and to as many as believed, thou gavest power to become the sons of God." So it is by thyself, blessed Redeemer, and not by the strength or weakness of the faith of thy people, their justification before God the Father is secured. Precious is that scripture which tells us, that by thee all that believe, whether great faith or little faith—"all that believe, are justified from all things." Acts xiii. 39. But, my soul, while the consciousness of thy possessing the smallest evidences of faith in thy beloved, gives thee a joy unspeakable and full of glory, dost thou not blush to think what ungrateful returns thou art making to thy Redeemer in the littleness of thy faith in such a God and Saviour? Whence is it that thine affections are so warm in a thousand lesser things, and so cold towards Jesus? Whence that his holy word thou so often hearest as though thou heardest not? Whence the ordinances of Jesus's house, the promises of his scriptures, the visits of his grace; whence these pass again and again before thee, and thou remainest so cold and lifeless in thy affections? Whence that the temptations of Satan, the corruptions of thine heart, the allurements of the world, gain any influence upon thee? Whence that thou art so anxious about things that perish; about any thing, about nothing, deserving to be called interesting; whence so seldom at the court of the heavenly King, where thou oughtest to be found daily, hourly, waiting; and whence, under trials, or the want of answers at a mercy-seat, fretful, impatient, and misgiving—whence all these, and numberless other evils, but from the weakness and littleness of thy love to Jesus, thy trust in Jesus, thy dependance upon Jesus, and thy communion with Jesus? All, all arise out of this one sad cause, my soul, thine unbelief. Jesus, Master, look upon me, put the cry with earnestness in my heart, that I may unceasingly, with the apostles' prayer, be sending forth this as the first and greatest petition of my whole soul—"Lord, increase my faith."

EVENING.—"But when the morning was now come, Jesus stood on the shore; but the disciples knew not that it was Jesus. Then Jesus saith unto them, children, have ye any meat?"—John xxi. 4, 5.

Every incident in relation to Jesus, and his love to his people, becomes interesting; and here is a very sweet one. Jesus was now risen from the dead. But his disciples had only faint and indistinct notions of the immense importance of this glorious event. They therefore were returned to their employment of fishing, as unconscious of what the resurrection from the dead should mean. All night they had been employed in a fruitless pursuit, and when the morning began to dawn, Jesus stood on the shore; but their eyes were holden, that they did not know him. My soul! learn from hence, that Jesus is often with thee, often looking on thee, and often providing and preparing for thee, while thou art ignorant of his presence and his love. He speaks to them, before they speak to him. Yes; "if we love him, it is because he first loved us." And what doth Jesus say? "children, have ye any meat?" Precious account of Jesus! My soul, turn over the several blessed particulars shewn in it. He calls them children. Yes: his people are his children, for he is the everlasting Father, as well as their Husband and Brother: indeed, he stands in the place of all relations, and fills all. My soul! if thou didst but consider this, and keep the remembrance of it always uppermost in thine heart, how wouldest thou delight to go to Jesus, as to "a brother born for adversity, a friend that loveth at all times, and one that sticketh closer than a brother!" Observe how earnest the Lord is concerning their present state and safety. Oh! that every child of God in Christ would learn from hence how Jesus takes part in all that concerns them. Surely this solicitude of Jesus takes in the whole of a believer's warfare. Are they poor in this world? Do they seek their bread out of desolate places? Like the disciples, do they toil all night, and gain nothing? And shall not He, who providently caters for the sparrow, know it, and provide for them, amidst all their manifold necessities? Look up, my poor afflicted brother (if perchance such an one should read these lines of my Evening Portion); look up, I say, and behold Jesus in this endearing instance of tenderness to the wants of his few faithful disciples. He that caused a miraculous draught of fishes to supply the pressing necessities of his disciples, can, and will equally now regard the state of all his redeemed, under their various temporal straights and difficulties. The promise is absolute, and hath never failed: " thy bread shall be given, and thy waters shall be sure, and thy defence shall be the munitions of rocks," Isa. xxxiii. 16. And as for spiritual famine, when at any time the waters of the sanctuary run low, Jesus is the Almighty Governor, our spiritual Joseph, through all the Egyptian state of his people here below; and he speaks to every one, yea, to thee, my soul, in the number: " children, have ye any meat?" Lamb of God! though thou art now in thine exalted state, yet not all the church in glory above, nor all the hallelujahs of heaven, can detain thee one moment from knowing, and visiting, and supplying all the manifold wants of thy church in grace here below! Doth Jesus say to me, " hast thou any meat?" Lord, I would answer, thou art " the bread of life, and the bread of God; yea, the living bread, which cometh down from heaven, and giveth life to the world!" Precious Jesus! be thou my bread, my life, my hope, my fulness, my joy, and my portion for ever!

APRIL 26.

MORNING.—" Thy teeth are like a flock of sheep that are even shorn, which came up from the washing; whereof every one bear twins, and none is barren among them."—Song iv. 2.

See, my soul, how Jesus sets off the beauties of his church, when made comely in his comeliness, which he hath put upon it. Jesus's whole church forms but one flock; for there shall be one fold and one shepherd. And though it is called a little flock, and a flock of slaughter, yet it is a beautiful flock in the Lord's hand. But wherefore are the teeth of the church said to be like a flock shorn? Probably, from their never being exercised but upon divine things: shorn to all desires in which unshorn and carnal persons delight. The believer feeds on Jesus: his flesh he finds to be meat indeed, his blood drink indeed. To the roof of his mouth this becomes like the best wine, "which goeth down sweetly, causing even the lips of those that sleep to speak." And how do believers, like sheep, come up from the washing, but when from the washing of regeneration, and a renewing of the Holy Ghost shed upon them abundantly, through Jesus Christ, they come up clean and washed in Jesus's blood, and adorned in the robe of Jesus's righteousness, and are presented before God and the Father, and accepted in the Beloved? And Oh how fruitful are they, like sheep which bear twins! None are barren or unfruitful among them, because they shew forth the praises of him who hath called them out of darkness into his marvellous light. The twin graces, if they may be so called, of faith and love, of prayer and praise, mark whose they are, and to whom they belong. The old fleece of nature being taken from them, they are shorn to the world, and the former filthiness and uncleanness of mind, they are washed from to themselves: and hence they come up to mention the loving-kindness of the Lord, and to prove that they are neither barren nor unfruitful in the knowledge of the Lord, and in the power of his might. My soul, is this thy state? Are thy teeth like this flock; and thy knowledge and enjoyment of Jesus a real heartfelt enjoyment of him? Canst thou truly relish nothing of food but what hath Jesus in it? nothing pleasant to thy taste but this bread of God, which came down from heaven? Comfort thyself then, my soul, that by and by the teeth of death will separate, like the sheep that is shorn, the body of corruption under which thou still groanest, being burdened; and thou shalt come up from the washing in the fountain of Jesus's blood, clothed in his garment of salvation, and made a meet partaker of an inheritance with the saints in light!

EVENING.—" Was not Esau Jacob's brother? saith the Lord; yet I loved Jacob, and I hated Esau!"—Malachi i. 2, 3.

My soul! sit down this evening, and ponder over some few particulars of the characteristics of grace, and behold its freeness, fulness, unexpectedness, greatness, sovereignty, and undeservedness; and yet, if possible, more astonishing than either, in its *distinguishing* operations. The Lord himself invites his redeemed people to this blessed study; and when a poor sinner can receive it, and mark his own interest in it, nothing more tends to humble the soul to the dust before God, and compels it to cry out, under a deep sense of its own unworthiness, " Lord, how is it that thou hast manifested thyself to me, and not unto the world?" In this demand of God, the question is decided and answered. " I have loved you, saith the Lord. But ye say, wherein hast thou loved us?" or as some read it, *wherefore* hast thou done so, when we were utterly undeserving of it? How is it, Lord, that thy grace was so personally distinguished? To which the Lord replies, " Was not Esau Jacob's brother? yet I loved Jacob, and hated Esau." As if Jehovah had said, ' I have been pointing out my distinguishing love from the beginning. Was not Esau Jacob's brother; yea, his *elder* brother? And had any right of inheritance arisen by birth, or from my covenant with Abraham, was not Esau before Jacob? Yet, to shew the freeness and sovereignty of my decrees, " before the children were born, or had done either good or evil," it was said by me, " The elder shall serve the younger." '—Lord! help me to bow down under a deep sense of thy sovereignty, and to cry out with the patriarch, " Shall not the Judge of all the earth do right?" or in the precious words of the patriarch's Lord, " Even so, Father, for so it seemed good in thy sight." My soul! sit down, and trace the wonderful subject all the bible through; and when thou hast done that, ponder over thine own experience, and fall low to the dust of the earth, in token that it is, and ever must be, from the same distinguishing grace alone, that one man differs from another; for all that we have is what we first received. And how marvellous is the distinguishing nature of grace, when passing by *some* that we might think more deserving, to single out others apparently the most worthless and undeserving. The *young man* in the gospel, 'full of good deeds, and, as he thought, within a step of heaven, shall go away from Christ very sorrowful; while Paul, in the midst of his hatred of Jesus, and making havoc of his people, shall be called. Nay, my soul! look not at these only, but look at thyself. Where wert thou, when Jesus passed by, and bid thee live? How wast thou engaged, when grace first taught thine eyes to overflow; and he that persuadeth Japheth to dwell in the tents of Shem, persuaded thee, and constrained thee by his love? And what is it now but the same distinguishing love, and grace, and favour, that keeps thee, under all thy wanderings, and coldness, and backslidings, from falling away! Who but Jesus could keep the immortal spark of grace from going out, amidst those floods of corruption which arise within? Who but Jesus could prevent the incorruptible seed from being choked for ever, which at times seems to be wholly encompassed with weeds, or buried in the rubbish of thy sinful nature? Precious Lord Jesus! let others say what they may, or think what they will, be it my portion to lie low in the deepest self-abasement, under the fullest conviction that it is thy free grace, and not creature desert, which makes all the difference between man and man! Oh! for the teachings of the Holy Ghost the Comforter, to accompany all my views of this most wonderful subject! And when at any time pride would arise in my heart, or any supposed excellency in me, compared to others, or when beholding the state of the vain or the carnal, Oh! for grace to hear that voice speaking and explaining all; "Was not Esau Jacob's brother? saith the Lord; yet I loved Jacob, and Esau have I hated."

APRIL 27.

MORNING.—"Behold how he loved him!"—John xi. 36.

The tears of Jesus at the tomb of Lazarus produced that astonishment in the mind of the Jews, that they thus exclaimed! But had they known, or did the whole world know, what I know of thy love to me, thou dear Redeemer of my soul, every one that heard it might with greater wonder cry out, "Behold how he loveth him!" I would for the present pass by, in my contemplation of thy love, all the numberless instances of it, which I possess in common with thy church and people; for though these in every and in all cases carry with them the tokens of a love that passeth knowledge, yet, for the meditation of the morning, I would pause over the view of Jesus's love to me a poor sinner, not as it is displayed in *general* mercies, even the glorious mercies of redemption, but as those mercies come home, in their *personal* direction of them to my own heart, even to mine. Think, my soul, what a huge volume thou wilt have to read over in eternity, of Jesus's love to thee, as *distinguished*, *express*, *personal*, and *particular*. And, amidst all the several chapters of that love, how wilt thou dwell with rapture on those two sweet verses of it, which, like the hymn in one of the psalms, thou wilt have to chaunt aloud, after the review of every blessing noted down; "for his mercy endureth for ever." I mean, *first*, that Jesus should ever look with pity on thee; and *next* to this, that after such distinguishing grace, the floods of sin and corruption in thee should not have quenched that love, and extinguished it for ever. The thought of Jesus's love, if looked at only in these two points of view, will be enough to employ thy immortal faculties in contemplation, and love, and praise to all eternity. Pause, my soul, and take a short view of each. Jesus looked on thee, loved thee, called thee, redeemed thee, manifested himself to thee, otherwise than he doth to the world; and this at a time when thousands and tens of thousands are passed by, of temper, mind, disposition, and understanding, in every point of view vastly thy superiors, and far more promising to glorify him. Bow down, my soul, while thou ponderest over the rich mercy, and refer all the praise and all the glory unto him, whose free grace, not thy deserts, became the sole cause. And when thou hast fully turned this astonishing subject over in thy mind, think again, that after such distinguishing grace, how increasingly astonishing it is that all thy repeated and aggravated transgressions have not extinguished this love towards thee, but that Jesus still loves, though thou hast been, and still continuest, so ungrateful. Oh love unequalled, past all comprehension! When shall this base, this shameful heart of mine so love thee, as to live to thy glory? Lord, I abhor myself in this view of thy grace and my vileness!

EVENING.—" But Mary stood without at the sepulchre, weeping; and as she wept, she stooped down, and looked into the sepulchre."—John xx. 11.

Behold, my soul! in this woman, a delightful instance of what thy love should be to thy Lord. If at any time thou dost miss thy Jesus, and longest for his return, where wouldest thou expect him? Surely at his ordinances, in his word, at his throne of grace, where Jesus " feedeth his kids by the footsteps of the flock, and beside the shepherds' tents." How do men of the world pursue the object of their wishes, but where it is to be found? Are they thirsty? they haste to drink. Are they cold? they seek the fire. Follow this plan. If Jesus be away, seek him where he hath directed thee to come. So Mary waited at the sepulchre; and as she waited, she looked in, while she wept, to see the place where Jesus had lain. Sweet view of a sincere seeker! The heart and eye are both engaged, and all the affections are going forth in desire. The angels addressed Mary; but the sight of angels could not satisfy her, till Jesus himself came. It is worthy of remark, that the first appearance the Lord Jesus made of himself, after he arose from the dead, was to this woman, out of whom he had cast seven devils. And it is yet farther remarkable, that the first words which Jesus spake after the glorious event of his resurrection, was to Mary Magdalene! He passed by the whole of the apostles, to give Mary this distinguished honour. Mary stood at the door of the sepulchre, weeping, but the apostles had returned to their own homes; and the Lord Jesus rewarded that waiting. "Woman," saith Jesus, "why weepest thou?" As if the Son of God had said, "What cause can there be now to weep, since all the ruins of the fall are done away, and sin, death, hell, and the grave, with all their tremendous consequences, are destroyed for ever?" I hope I do not mistake, but I think this feature in the character of the Lord Jesus, is calculated to dry up every tear from every eye of his redeemed. It seems to speak in the language of that precious scripture: "For the people shall dwell in Zion at Jerusalem. Thou shalt weep no more. He will be very gracious unto thee, at the voice of thy cry: when he shall hear it, he will answer thee," Isaiah xxx. 19. My soul! do not fail to take with thee the many blessed improvements, which the waiting of Mary, and the grace of Jesus in thus rewarding that waiting, brings with it. There is no interruption, no pause in Jesus's love. In reading that sweet volume, there are no stops, no, not a comma, but what we ourselves make. And if at any time we find ourselves come to the bottom of a page full of the relations of

Jesus and his love, it is only to turn over the leaf, and there we find the continuation of the same blessed subject. Now, my soul! learn, from Mary, to take thy stand where she stood; not at the sepulchre of Jesus, for he is risen, as he said, and we are commanded not to seek the living among the dead; but we are to follow the Lamb whithersoever he goeth, and to look at Christ upon his throne of glory. Nevertheless, as the angels said to those who sought Christ at the tomb, "Come, see the place where the Lord lay!" so we may by faith often view that memorable sepulchre; and precious will be the meditation, as Mary's was. And, my soul, do not forget who it was that led Mary thither, and gave her those sympathies, and at length converted her sorrow into the most heartfelt joy. Oh! it is blessed, it is precious, to be kept in the way, "the good old way," of waiting upon the Lord. He is always near, and though he may for awhile seem to conceal himself, yet he will be found of them that seek him. He saith himself, "It shall come to pass, before my people call, I will answer; and while they are yet speaking, I will hear. Then shalt thou call, and the Lord shall answer; thou shalt cry, and he shall say, here I am!" Blessed Jesus! do thou by me, do thou by all thy children, who seek thee sorrowing, as thou didst by Mary, and as thou dost by all thy people; "Woman, why weepest thou? whom seekest thou?" And when our souls reply, "It is Jesus alone we seek," Oh, then, to hear our own names called upon, as her's was, Mary! and in such a way as to draw forth every affection of the heart in our answer, "Rabboni! my Lord and my God!"

APRIL 28.

MORNING.—"And the Lord said, Arise, anoint him; for this is he. Then Samuel took the horn of oil, and anointed him in the midst of his brethren."—1 Sam. xvi. 12, 13.

Was David singled out from amidst his brethren, to

be the Lord's anointed; and do I not behold in this the representation of Jesus, that Holy One, concerning whom the Lord spake in vision, and said, I have laid help upon One that is mighty; I have exalted One chosen out of the people? Yes, thou Lord our righteousness, in this I behold thee. And let my soul make this sweet subject the meditation of my morning song, for surely it is a lovely song, to hail thee the chiefest among ten thousand. I behold thee then, thou dear Emanuel, by the eye of faith, as coming up from everlasting, when amidst that immense multitude of those thou disdainest not to call thy brethren, thou stoodest forth, in the eternal view, as the glorious One, to be the Christ, the God-man Mediator, for the salvation of thy church and people. Here, precious Jesus, didst thou appear, to God our Father's view, pre-eminent above thy fellows. And of the whole body, the church, which God our Father in the great decree determined to form as the receivers of grace and mercy, and of eternal life and salvation, thou wert appointed their glorious Head; and *in* thee, and *from* thee, and *through* thee, they might become a glorious church, not having spot or wrinkle, or any such thing, but that thou mightest present it to thyself in love. And surely, dearest, precious Jesus, had every individual of thy redeemed brethren been present, as all the sons of Jesse passed in review before the prophet, to have chosen their glorious head, on none but thee could that choice have fallen. All voices would have echoed to Jehovah's proclamation: "Arise, anoint him; for this is he." Yes! truly, Lord, thou art he whom thy brethren shall praise; and all thy Father's children, with devout rapture and holy joy, shall bow down before thee. Thou art heir of all things, the chiefest and first-born in the womb of mercy. It is thou that art entitled to the most full, honourable, and unchangeable right to all thy Father's inheritance. "Men shall be blessed in thee, and all nations shall call thee blessed." My soul, delight thyself unceasingly in this contemplation of thy Jesus. God thy Father hath chosen him. He hath anointed him with the holy oil for salvation, and the Spirit was given unto him, not by measure. And is not God's chosen thy chosen; the Father's anointed, thine anointed? Is there any in heaven, or upon earth, to whom thou art looking for help, or strength, or comfort, or salvation, but to Jesus? Who but Jesus, my soul, wouldest thou have for a Saviour? What object so desirable as Jesus, to claim thy love? Witness for me, ye sons of light, ye angels that see his face and do his pleasure, that Jesus is my only beloved, my hope, my portion. Shortly I shall join your assembly, and with you bless and adore Jesus in endless song, the fairest and chiefest among ten thousand.

EVENING.—" Jesus himself drew near, and went with them; but their eyes were holden, that they should not know him."—Luke xxiv. 15, 16.

My soul! here is a most interesting subject proposed to thine evening meditation, in this account of an interview between Jesus and two of his disciples, in the interval between his resurrection and ascension. Sit down, and under the divine teaching, ponder it well. Were the eyes of those disciples so holden, that they should not know him, from some supernatural effect wrought on their powers of vision; or was it induced from any alteration wrought upon the person of their Lord? Probably there might be a concurrence of both these causes. The effect accomplished by this interview seems indeed to shew it; but it is profitable, highly profitable, to exercise our meditation upon it, though the point cannot be determined. I think it more than probable, that death had given an aspect to Jesus, which in itself must have induced a change. That face which once, in the days of his flesh, brake forth as the sun when shining in his strength, at the mount of transfiguration, might now have appeared with paleness, from the sweat, and dust, and blood, spread over the countenance. But, however this might have been, so it was, their eyes were holden, that they should not know him. Precious Lord Jesus! cause me to learn from hence, that all the gracious manifestations which thou art pleased to make of thyself to thy people, are of thyself, and depend upon thy sovereign will and pleasure; and cause me to learn also, how very gracious thou art, to condescend at any time, by the sweet influences of thy Spirit, to reveal thyself to thy people, and to manifest thyself to them, otherwise than thou doest to the world. And hence, Lord, I beseech thee, very frequently to draw nigh, and go with me, as thou didst with them; and though mine eyes be holden, so as that I do not discern thee, yet, like them, thy gracious discourse will make mine heart burn within me, while thou art walking with me by the way, and while thou art opening to me thy scriptures. And, especially, do by me as thou didst by them, when at thy table, or in thine house of worship; give me an open communication of thy glory "in breaking of bread, and in prayer."—My soul! do not dismiss this interesting account of the appearance of Jesus, before thou hast taken another view of thy Redeemer. It was a solemn moment in which it took place. The Son of God had finished redemption work; but he was not as yet ascended to his Father. Behold him for a moment, and contemplate his person in that interval! — Jesus in his human nature, though his visage was marred more than any man's, and his form more than the sons of men, is yet said to have been fairer than the children of men, because grace was poured into his lips, and Jehovah had blessed him for ever. And as he was altogether free from sin, so was he "the altogether lovely." And as he was now raised from the dead, though not yet exalted to the right hand of power, yet surely that human nature of Jesus, in union with the Godhead, and worshipped by angels, must have possessed a glory unspeakably blessed and divine. The way to judge of the appearance of thy Jesus, at this time, is from the conduct of the angels towards him. From their ministration to him in the garden, and at the sepulchre, and especially their attendance on him at his return to glory, it is easy to gather in what light they gazed on Christ. Such an assemblage of glory as the human nature of the Lord Jesus possessed, and derived from its personal union with the Godhead, called forth at once the love, and adoration, and delight of all the angels of heaven. They saw holiness in the person of Jesus, in all its perfection; and every grace, in wisdom, truth, and knowledge, in their highest properties. Hence their views of Christ may very safely be made the standard of ours. Hail then, thou blessed Emanuel! Let this interval between thy resurrection and ascension, be ever sacred to my soul. And while I behold thee as lovely, fair, and glorious, in every eye, both of angels and thy redeemed, be thou increasingly lovely and precious in mine also. And let it be my delight to talk of thee by the way, and when lying down or rising up. And Oh! do thou always draw near to me, thou blessed Lord, though my dim-sighted apprehension of thee doth so often prevent me from enjoying thy presence. Yet a little while, and thou wilt call me home, to behold thy glory unveiled with a cloud, or any intervening object, where I shall behold thee as thou art, and dwell with thee for ever. Amen.

APRIL 29.

MORNING.—" The marriage of the Lamb is come, and his wife hath made herself ready. And to her was granted that she should be arrayed in fine linen, clean and white: for the fine linen is the righteousness of saints."—Rev. xix. 7, 8.

Behold, my soul, behold that day, that glorious day,

in which redemption is to be consummated, and in the kingdom of heaven; when the Son of God brings home his bride, the church, the full celebration of God's glory in the happiness of the redeemed in Jesus, everlasting joy will burst forth. See how thy nature is then to be adorned. The whole body, the church, is then to be arrayed in the robes of Jesus's righteousness, having been washed from all their sins in his blood. And these nuptial ornaments are to be granted or given to the church; for she hath no righteousness of her own; but as all along in this world she had professed, so there in the upper world she triumphantly sings, "I will greatly rejoice in the Lord, my soul shall be joyful in my God; for he hath clothed me with the garments of salvation, he hath covered me with the robe of righteousness, as a bridegroom decketh himself with ornaments, and as a bride adorneth herself with her jewels." Isa. lxi. 10. Pause, my soul, over this view. Is this to be thy adorning in glory? See to it then, my soul, that it becomes thy covering now. How suited is it to all thy circumstances! Thou hast no fine linen, nothing clean, nothing white. Think how comely Jesus's robe of righteousness must be to appear in. This is the wedding garment, by faith worn at his supper upon earth, and the same in fruition in which thou art to sit down at his table above. And Oh how suitable a covering to hide all thy deformity, to conceal and take away all thy pollution. And will not this procure thee favour and acceptance with God? Is it not thus that Jesus's followers are distinguished from men of the world? Art thou now clothed with it? Hath God the Spirit put it on? Doth Jesus now send thee his love-tokens as his betrothed; and, in the ordinances of his grace, doth he grant thee many sweet espousals? Oh then, my soul, see to it, that thy righteousness is that of Jesus's own, with which his church is arrayed, and that these robes are always clean and white, which are washed in the blood of the Lamb: for, ere long, the midnight cry will be heard; "Behold the bridegroom cometh, go ye out to meet him!" Oh precious Lord Jesus! give me to hear that voice with joy, that, with holy wings of love, in the last office of faith, to be then swallowed up in sight, I may arise to enter with thee into the marriage, to sit down with thee for ever.

EVENING.—"The ornament of a meek and quiet spirit, which is in the sight of God of great price."—1 Pet. iii. 4.

My soul! where is this to be had? Hast thou considered it in its importance, or in its attainment; whence it cometh, and on whose account it is given? Sit down, this evening, and ponder over it. What is a meek and quiet spirit, but grace, in all its blessed properties and saving effects, keeping the heart and mind through Christ Jesus? Now mark *some* of the many precious things belonging to it. The fountain of it is God; for "every good gift, and every perfect gift is from above, and cometh down from the Father of lights, with whom is no variableness, neither shadow of turning," James i. 17. It is also the purchase of Christ's blood, and the fruit of the Holy Ghost; and so infinitely important in its operation, that believers are said thereby "to be made partakers of the divine nature, having escaped the corruption that is in the world through lust," 2 Pet. i. 4. And what a lustre doth the possession of it impart to the whole man? Being a portion of the same Spirit which was given to the manhood of Jesus *without measure;* it produces a resemblance and similitude in the character of every renewed soul to him. As a fair and beautiful countenance gives a loveliness to the *natural* form, so grace is that which gives the whole that can be called blessed or engaging to the *spiritual.* Hence a poor man with grace in his heart, is infinitely more lovely in the sight of God, than the persons of the great void of it, though the blood of kings were to flow through their veins. It is this which is the source, and it is this which gives the finishing gracefulness to the whole man. And as it flows *from* God, so all its tendencies are *to* God. Next to the *person* of Jesus, the *grace* of Jesus, is, or ought to be, the one earnest object and desire of every soul. Until we have this ornament of a meek and quiet spirit, every man by nature, in the sight of God, is of no esteem. There can be nothing lovely or desirable in the unregenerate. "He that liveth in pleasure, is dead while he liveth," saith the scripture, 1 Tim. v. 6. And however, to our view, the actions of such may carry with them much moral sweetness, yet as those actions are not quickened from the Spirit of grace, they are no other than as flowers strewed over the bodies of the dead. They are of no esteem in the sight of God. The *person* must be first sanctified by grace, and then the *action* follows. The Lord had respect *first* to Abel, and *then* to his offering; but as to Cain, as he had no respect, so neither could his offering be acceptable; Gen. iv. 4, 5. My soul! what saith thy experience to these things? Hast thou this precious grace, this saving grace, this sanctifying grace, which flows at once from God the Father's gift, the blood and righteousness of Jesus Christ, and the regenerating influences of God the Holy Ghost? Are those blessed effects wrought in thee, which saving grace is sure to work? Is God's glory your delight; his Christ your Christ; his salvation your salvation? Hast thou felt the renewing, transforming, confirming, establishing principles of grace, flowing in from the Spirit of Jesus upon thy spirit, so that the new man is "renewed in knowledge, after the image of him that created him?" In a word, hast thou so beheld, as in a glass, "the glory of the Lord, that thou art changed into the same image, from glory to glory, even as by the Spirit of the Lord?" If, my soul, thou hast these blessed tokens, these ornaments of a meek and quiet spirit, which are in the sight of God of great price: then dost thou possess that which all the world can neither give nor take away. "It cannot be gotten for gold, neither shall silver be weighed for the price thereof." Precious Jesus! it is the purchase of thy blood, it comes from the sovereign gift of God the Father, and is the earnest of the Holy Spirit! Lord, seal my soul with it "to the day of eternal redemption!"

APRIL 30.

MORNING.—"Nevertheless, I am continually with thee."—Ps. lxxiii. 23.

Yes, my soul, and well it is for thee that it is so; there is a *nevertheless* in the precious redemption by Jesus, which secures thee, amidst all thy languishing seasons, when to thy view it sometimes appears as though the Lord had forgotten to be gracious, and had shut up his loving-kindness in displeasure. And whence this security but in Jesus, and the covenant engagements of God thy Father in him? The everlasting worth and efficacy of the Redeemer's righteousness and death, are the same amidst all the changeable circumstances of his people's warfare. By the expression of being continually with Jesus, is meant, no doubt, that union with his person, as the sinner's Surety, which gives security and firmness to the everlasting state and happiness of his redeemed. And it is this which constitutes, not only the safety of his people now, but the happiness of his people for ever. Heaven itself, but for Jesus, and the constant flow of righteousness and glory in him, and from him, would cease to be heaven. The souls of just men made perfect could be no longer happy nor righteous, but as those supplies flow in upon their souls from him. So that the everlasting preciousness of Jesus, as the glorious Head of his people, is thus confirmed, and the felicity of the church must be wholly made up from this eternal union with him. Hence how precious the thought, "I am continually with thee!" And is this thy portion, my soul? Art thou alive to this sweet and soul-reviving thought? Is Jesus, thy Jesus, continually with thee, and thou continually with him? See to it, that the nearness of Jesus to thee hath the same effect upon thee, as with things in nature, when the earth and the inhabitants testify their sense of feeling. Doth not the earth, and the plants, and the birds, and every thing look gay when the sun renews the face of the earth, and shines with loveliness to make all nature smile? And shall thy Sun of Righteousness arise unobserved or unenjoyed, who comes with healing in his wings? Oh precious Jesus, cause me so to live upon thee, that I may be always eyeing thee, in dark seasons as well as bright hours; that, from never suffering thy dear image to depart for a moment from my heart, I may be so prepared to behold thy face in open glory, when the veil of this flesh is removed, and I awake up after thy likeness, that, though I change my place, I shall not change my company. In earth, or heaven, yet, if with thee, happiness is begun in the soul; and faith, in lively exercise, is itself an anticipation of glory, by just so much as the soul realizeth thy sweet presence, in being ever with the Lord.

EVENING.—"Only fear the Lord, and serve him in truth, with all your heart; for consider how great things he hath done for you."—1 Sam. xii. 24.

How truly affectionate was this pastoral advice of the prophet to Israel, in the close of recapitulating Israel's history, and God's love over them! My soul! take this portion from Israel's history, and apply it to thine own; for the argument, and the reason upon which the argument is founded, are one and the same; and thou wilt find the same causes, both from interest in Christ, and from received mercies from Christ, to form the same conclusion. But at what part of thine history wilt thou begin, or where wilt thou end, in considering *what great things* thy God, thy Jesus, hath done for thee? Wilt thou open with the consideration of God's mercies towards thee in nature, or providence, or grace? What arithmetic will be competent to score the vast account, even in a thousandth degree, of either of those departments; much more if thou wert to study the subject in all? Who indeed can be sufficient to note them down, or to state in order, as they passed before him, the numberless events which testified divine favour, during the long season of thine *unregeneracy*? What a huge volume might be formed in nature only, of the Lord's watchfulness, providings, preservings, and ordinations, in making all minister and become subservient to our welfare? Oh! it is blessed to consider, even if it were here only, what great things the Lord hath done for us. And while we mark the footsteps of his love, and note our wanderings from him; when we trace back the wonderful subject of distinguishing mercy, and call to mind the graves of some, yea, many, with whom were spent our youthful days, while we remain not only the *spared*, but we hope the *saved* monuments of free sovereign grace and mercy; well may we exclaim, with one of old, "Bless the Lord, O my soul, and forget not all his benefits; who redeemeth thy life from destruction, and crowneth thee with loving-kindness and tender mercies!" And if from the outer court of nature and providence, our souls enter into the inner court of grace, and there mark down, since the day of our *regeneracy* and the Lord's effectual calling, what great things he hath done for us, surely it would tire the arm of an angel to write the whole account. Precious Lord Jesus! in thee, and by thee, and from thee, all our mercies flow. Thou art the first, the last, the best, the comprehensive gift of God; the channel of all blessings temporal, spiritual, and eternal; through whom all the streams come, from

Father, Son, and Holy Ghost; and through whom all love and praise return; not only the channel through whom they come, but the substance in whom they centre. Thou hast purchased them, and they are enjoyed wholly from our union with thee; and their continuation in grace here, and glory to all eternity, must result from thee: all the covenant mercies of God in Christ, are "the sure mercies of David" on thy account! Think, then, my soul! what causes thou art surrounded with, in the great things God hath done for thee, that thou shouldest fear the Lord, and serve him in truth, with all thine heart! Close then the month as thou hopest to close thy life on earth, with this sweet scripture; and as thou didst open the month in contemplating the Lord thy righteousness, as the name whereby thou are enjoined to call him, so now let thy last meditation, before thou droppest to sleep in ending the month, be with the same. "He is (as Moses told Israel) thy praise, and he is thy God, that hath done for thee these great and terrible things, which thine eyes have seen." Be this, therefore, thy daily meditation, and thine evening hymn: "to fear the Lord, and serve him; for consider how great things he hath done for thee." Amen.

MAY 1.

MORNING.—"Thou shalt call his name Jesus."—Matt. i. 21.

This is one more of the Redeemer's names, which is as ointment poured forth. As if the Holy Ghost had been graciously consulting the everlasting comfort and happiness of his people, and therefore commanded the church to know their Lord, by so many different and endearing appellations. As if he had said, are you kept back from approaching him through fear? Oh no;—go to him, for he is Emanuel. So great, as God, that he is able to save; so tender and near, as man, that he is more ready to bestow mercy than you are to ask it. Are you kept back for want of righteousness? Be not so, for he is the Lord our righteousness, and what you need he hath for you. Or, are you depressed by reason of sin? Let not this discourage you, for his name is purposely Jesus, because he, and he alone, "shall save his people from their sins." My soul, what knowest thou practically and personally of this most blessed name of thy Saviour? It is one thing to have heard of him as Jesus, and another to know him to be Jesus. There are multitudes who rest satisfied with the name. The Jews knew him, saw him, conversed with him; but they knew him not as a Saviour. Nay more than this, many have had, and still have, an historical knowledge and belief that Jesus is a Saviour, but yet no apprehension or concern for an interest in him. Thus Balaam, whose eyes were so far opened, but his heart never affected, as to have visions concerning Christ. But what an awful account did this impious creature give of himself! "I shall see him, (said he) but not now; I shall behold him, but not nigh."—Numb. xxiv. 17. What an awful state! O my soul, bless thy God, thy Jesus, that thy knowledge is not of the head only, but of the heart. Thou hast not simply heard of Jesus, but received him as Jesus, to the salvation of thy soul. Thou hast seen God in Christ; the Father's name, the Father's authority in him. Thou hast come to him in that name, and by that authority, as a poor sinner, and found Jesus precious. And is not Jesus precious to thee? Is not the very name of Jesus most precious? As one of old expressed it, so hast thou found it, that in this one name of thy Lord, the whole of the gospel is folded up; it is the light, the food, the medicine, the very jubilee of the soul. Yes, thou blessed, holy, gracious Lord! Yes, thy name is indeed Jesus, for thou art, thou wilt be Jesus. "And they that know thy name will put their trust in thee, for thou shalt save thy people from their sins."

EVENING.—"That thou mayest fear this glorious and fearful name, THE LORD THY GOD."—Deut. xxviii. 58.

My soul! thy *morning* meditation, in the opening of a new month, was directed to that soul-reviving subject, the contemplation of the name of Jesus. Oh! what rich stores of unknown, unexplored treasures of mercies are folded in that one name of thy Lord! It will serve to heighten thy study yet more, and tend to endear Jesus as increasingly precious, by pondering over what the man of God taught Israel in the solemn words here proposed to thine *evening* meditation. Every thing in Jehovah is solemn. His sweetest mercies come to us with great sacredness. It is impossible to receive them but with the lowliest reverence, even when the soul is made blessed in divine favours. We rejoice indeed, but we rejoice with trembling. And the greater the mercies are, the more will the conscious sense of our undeservings humble the soul to the dust before God. The Israelites were taught by this scripture, that the great design of Jehovah, in all his dispensations, was to induce a suitable and becoming reverence for this glorious and fearful name of THE LORD THEIR GOD. And his sacred name is here put in large letters, by way of intimating its immense dignity and importance. His name is glorious, because it sets forth how that glory of Jehovah is manifested in his covenant engagements by CHRIST; and his name is no less fearful, because it is by virtue of those covenant engagements that the Lord is pledged to bring all the foes of Christ and his redemption under his footstool. There seems to be a reference to the oath of Jehovah, when Christ was introduced into his high priestly office, that the Lord, at Messiah's right hand, "would strike through kings in the day of his wrath;" Psalm cx. 4, 5. And it should seem no less evident, that this very name, glorious and fearful as it is, was thus expressly proclaimed to intimate, that, by virtue of this oath, Jehovah is engaged as much, on the one part, to fulfil the threatenings, as, on the other, to make good the promises; both of which were rendered firm and irrevocable by the solemnity of an oath. My soul! ponder over these most sacred things with a reverence suited to them. And in these awful days, in which the church of Jesus is now surrounded with the dreadful delusion of heresy, in those who deny the Lord that bought them, see to it, that thou art strong in the grace which is in Christ Jesus. Oh! the blessedness of "knowing whom thou hast believed, that thou mayest fear this glorious and fearful name, THE LORD THY GOD." Thy Lord, thy God in covenant; in his relation to thee in Christ, thy perfect redemption by Christ, and thy acceptance from Christ, in his finished salvation. Oh! did the sinner of every description and character, but for a moment consider what he is doing, who is looking to this glorious and fearful name of the Lord God, without knowing him as his God, that is, God in Christ, the Mediator, and being accepted in him; what dreadful trembling and apprehension of soul would it induce! Bless thy God, thy Jesus, my soul, who hath thus made a sweet revelation of himself to thee, and not only taught thee, but inclined thee by the teachings and influences of his Holy Spirit, to fear "this glorious and fearful name, the Lord thy God!"

MAY 2.

MORNING.—"And they called Rebekah, and said unto her, Wilt thou go with this man? And she said, I will go."—Gen. xxiv. 58.

See, my soul, with what readiness Rebekah determined to accompany the servant of Abraham to Isaac. And wilt thou not arise and go forth at the invitation of the servants of Jesus, who sends them to call thee to his arms? Hath he not, by the sweet constraining influences of his Holy Spirit, as well as by the outward ministry of his blessed word, made thee willing in the day of his power? Did the servant of Abraham give an earnest of his master's affection in putting the bracelets upon Rebekah's hands, and the ear-rings, and the gold? But what was this to the love-tokens which Jesus himself hath given thee, when he set thee as a seal upon his heart, and as a seal upon his arm, and when all the waters of divine wrath his holy soul had poured upon him for thy sins, and all the floods of corruption, which like a deluge, had overspread thy whole nature, could not quench his love, nor drown it. And if it be demanded, then, from thine own mouth this day, "Wilt thou go with this man," this God-man, this Glory-man, this Jesus? Wilt thou not instantly cry out, "I will go?" Yes! thou altogether lovely Lord, thou chiefest and fairest among ten thousand, I will go with thee. I would forget mine own people and my father's house. For my father's house is an house of bondage. I was born in sin, and shapen in iniquity. A child of wrath, even as others, and by nature dead in trespasses and sins. It is thou, blessed Jesus, who hast delivered me from the wrath to come. It is thou who hast quickened me by thy Holy Spirit to a new and spiritual life. It is thou who hast sent thy servants to call me to thyself, and hast betrothed me to thyself for ever. And is there any that yet asketh me, "wilt thou go with this man?" My whole soul would outrun the question, and, like the apostle, I would answer, "to whom else shall I go?" Witness for me, ye servants of my Lord; ye angels, and ministers of light. I have none in heaven, neither in earth, but him. Yes, thou dearest Redeemer! I will go with thee, follow thee, live with thee, hang upon thee, die with thee, nor even death itself shall part thee and me. Oh let those precious words of thine, concerning thy church, be sweetly felt in my soul. "I will say, it is my people:" and my whole soul will make her responses to the gracious sound, and say, "the Lord is my God."

EVENING.—"Thou sawest till that a stone was cut out without hands, which smote the image upon his feet, that were of iron and clay, and brake them to pieces.—And the stone that smote the image became a great mountain, and filled the whole earth."—Dan. ii. 34, 35.

Ponder well, my soul, this wonderful vision of the heathen king, and mark its several features. If the Lord be about to bless and comfort his people, how often is it done by ways the most opposite and unlikely, according to our apprehension of things! It shall be accomplished, even by their enemies, and they who wish most to afflict them, shall not unfrequently be made the unconscious instruments of doing the very reverse of what they intend; as in the instance before us, to which these words in the writings of the prophet Daniel refer. The church was now in captivity; oppressed, and brought very low: the king, in whose dominions they were in their vassalage, a despotic tyrant, whose word became the chief law. The Lord visits this monarch's mind with a vision of the night: he is troubled with what he had seen in his vision; but when he awakes, the remembrance of what he had seen vanished. Daniel is blessed of the Lord, both to bring to his recollection his thoughts in the night, and to give the interpretation of them. The king's heart is for the time subdued, and Daniel honoured with favour. But the most eminent point of this vision was for the church's comfort, and the Lord caused his people to rejoice in the discovery of it. The image to be destroyed represented the several monarchies of the world, before the coming of the Lord Jesus Christ, and in the order in which they should succeed each other. The Chaldean took the lead, and the Persian followed; to which succeeded the Grecian; and during the fourth, which was the Roman power, the Lord Jesus Christ, "the stone cut out without hands," was to arise, which should destroy the image, become "a mountain, and fill the earth." What a wonderful coincidence of circumstances must it have been, that made every minute point in this representation, to answer so exactly to Jesus, and to him only! The birth of Christ, produced without the intervention of a human father; nothing could more strikingly set forth, than the figure of "a stone cut out without hands." And the triumph of his spiritual kingdom was equally beautiful, in the similitude of breaking in pieces "the image which stood on his feet." And when what is said of Christ is considered, which must finally be fulfilled in him, that "the kingdoms of the world shall become the kingdoms of our Lord, and of his Christ, and he shall reign for ever;" who doth not, or will not, see the striking representation of a mountain springing up from slender beginnings, "and filling the whole earth?" My soul! wilt thou not learn, this evening, from this very precious scripture, to appreciate thy Jesus, and to behold how sweetly scripture testimony confirms every thing concerning him? Teach me, thou dear Lord, to view thee under those delightful characters; and while I trace back the history of thine incarnation, low, humble, and despised, as "a stone cut without hands;" Oh! give me to contemplate thy glory in what most assuredly shall be accomplished, when "like a mountain established on the tops of a mountain, all nations shall flow to thee, and thou shalt fill the earth." Divine Master! fill my whole soul with thyself; and let this our land, and our people, be filled with the knowledge of Jesus and his great salvation, "as the waters cover the sea!"

MAY 3.

MORNING.—" Sitting at the feet of Jesus, clothed, and in his right mind."—Luke viii. 35.

Look at this man, my soul, and see whether thou canst find any resemblance to thyself. Before that he heard the voice of Jesus, he was under the possession of the evil spirit. It is said of him, that he wore no clothes. He dwelt in no house, but abode among the tombs. He was cutting himself with stones. No man could tame him, neither fetters nor chains bind him. Poor miserable creature! And yet, my soul, was not this a true emblem of thy state; and indeed, of every man's state by nature? Had not Satan full possession of thine heart and affections, my soul, before that thou becamest savingly acquainted with the Lord Jesus Christ? Did he not lead thee in the pursuit and gratification of thy lusts and pleasure at his will? Thou mightest truly be said to wear no clothes; for so far from having on the garment of Jesus's righteousness, in those days of thine unregeneracy, thou wert naked to thy shame, in the filth of nature. Thou didst not dwell in the house of God, nor even delight to go thither. And, as this poor creature abode among the dead, so didst thou live and abide with characters like thyself, dead in trespasses and sins. And as this miserable man was wounding himself with stones, so wert thou; for thy daily commission of sin was giving wounds to thy soul, infinitely more alarming than the wounds he gave his body. And could no chains or fetters be found strong enough to bind him? So neither did all the solemn commands and threatening judgments of God's holy law act with the least restraint upon thine ungoverned passions. Pause, my soul, over the representation, and acknowledge how just and striking the similarity. Then ask thyself, art thou now sitting at the feet of Jesus, clothed and in thy right mind? Yes! if so be like this poor man, thou hast heard the voice of Jesus, and felt the power of his grace in thine heart. If one like the Son of God hath set thee free, brought thee to his fold, opened thine ear to discipline, and thine heart, to grace, then art thou free indeed. What sayest thou, my soul, to these things? Is there this change, this blessed change, from dead works to serve the living and true God? Oh then, will not the language of thine heart be like Jesus, and his church of old? "I will greatly rejoice in the Lord, my soul shall be joyful in my God: for he hath clothed me with the garments of salvation, he hath covered me with the robe of righteousness, as a bridegroom decketh himself with ornaments, and as a bride adorneth herself with her jewels."

EVENING.—"The eyes of man, as of all the tribes of Israel, shall be toward the Lord."—Zech. ix. 1.

Precious Jesus! when shall this blessed scripture be accomplished? "The eyes of man!" What man? Surely as the church's glorious head, and as her glorious representative, the eyes of our Lord Jesus himself were always from everlasting directed to Jehovah his Father. But secondarily, and subordinately, the eyes of thy redeemed, blessed Jesus, the eyes of man, the eyes of every man, must ultimately, as the tribes of Israel, be all toward thee for salvation. Thou indeed hast said, "Look unto me, and be ye saved, all the ends of the earth; for I am God, and there is none else," Isa. xlv. 22. Pause, my soul! this evening, over this view of thy Jesus, for it is a very blessed one, and see what improvements under divine teaching, thou canst draw from it. It is said, that as one of the tribes, yea, all the tribes of Israel, every eye shall be upon Jesus. And how suitable is it that it should be so! Is not God the Father unceasingly beholding his dear Son in his engagements, as the Mediator and Surety of his church and people? Oh! who shall be competent to describe with what complacency and delight he beholds him in his glorious person, as the God-man, the Glory-man; and in all his offices, characters, and relations? Somewhat of this we may gather from what Jesus hath himself said concerning the Father's love for his undertaking, and accomplishing redemption by his blood. "Therefore (saith our Jesus) doth my Father love me, because I lay down my life, that I might take it again," John x. 17. But the full apprehension of the love of the Father on this one account, cannot perhaps be brought within the capacity of the human mind. But if God the Father loves Jesus as Mediator, and for his undertaking, and is unceasingly beholding him with rapture on this account, it may serve at least to teach thee, my soul, how exceedingly it becomes thee to look to Jesus for the same, and that thine eyes, as the eyes of all the tribes of Israel, should be towards the Lord. Dearest Lord Jesus! let mine eyes, mine heart, my whole soul be fixed on thee, until every affection be going out in desires after thee. I would trace thee, as the whole testament saints, who saw thy day "afar off, rejoiced, and were glad." I would behold thee as new testament believers, who are looking to thee, and "are enlightened, and their faces are not ashamed." I would see thee with the first dawn of the morning; yea, before the morning light, and "until the day break, and the shadows flee away;" and until my beloved come to me "as a roe, or a young hart, upon the mountains of Bether!" Yes, precious Lord Jesus! I would be sending the earnest longings of my soul through the windows of the eye after thee, and never give rest to my eyes, nor slumber to my eyelids, until that blessed hour arrive, when no medium shall intervene to prevent the full enjoyment of my soul in thee; and when a body of sin and death shall no longer weary my soul in her enjoyment of thee; but I shall then see Jesus as he is, and never more lose sight of his lovely person, but live in his presence, and Jesus in mine, for evermore.

MAY 4.

MORNING.—" The hind of the morning."—Ps. xxii. in the title.

The dying patriarch Jacob, under the influence of the prophetic spirit, pointed to the seed of Naphtali as a hind let loose. But it is the church which points to Jesus as the hind of the morning; for he is, indeed, the loving hind, and the pleasant roe. It is sweet and profitable to observe in what a variety of methods the Holy Ghost hath been pleased to give sketches of Jesus. My soul, look at Jesus for thy present meditation as the hind of the morning. Was he not, from the very morning of eternity, marked under this lovely character? Did not the church speak of him, and desire his appearance, under this same character, when she begged of him, that until the shadows of Jewish ordinances were passed away, and the day of gospel light should break in upon her, that her beloved would be like a young hart, or the roe, upon the mountains of Bether? And was not Jesus, indeed, when he did appear, truly as the hind which the dogs that compassed him about, and the assembly of the wicked inclosed? Did he not say, in those unequalled moments of suffering, " Save me from the lion's mouth, for thou hast heard me from the horns of the unicorn?" Yes, precious Jesus, thou art, indeed, the hind of the morning! In the morning of our salvation, thou camest over the hills and mountains of our sinful nature, with the swiftness of the hind, and the loveliness and gentleness of the roe, to expose thyself to the serpent, and the whole host of foes, for the deliverance of thy people. And, having trod upon the lion, and the adder, and the young lion, and the dragon, trampled under thy feet by thy death, thou " didst overcome death, and him that had the power of death, that is, the devil; and hast delivered them, who, through fear of death, were all their life-time subject to bondage." And now, precious Lord! thou art, as the hind slain, the food of the souls of thy redeemed by faith, until faith itself is done away in sight, and hope swallowed up in absolute fruition. Oh let the language of my heart daily, hourly, correspond to the church of old; and, during the shadows of ordinances, and all the dark clouds of unbelief and temptations with which I am here exercised, let me still, by faith, behold thee as the hind of the morning fleeing swiftly to my assistance, hearing and answering my prayers, leaping over all the mountains of distance which sin and unworthiness would throw up between thee and my soul, opposing all my enemies, and beating them under my feet that would keep me from thee; until that day, that glorious everlasting day which will have no night, shall break in upon my soul, and thou wilt then appear, to my unceasing, uninterrupted joy, the hind, indeed, of the morning. "Make haste, my beloved, and be thou like unto a roe, or to a young hart, upon the mountains of spices."

EVENING.—"And continued all night in prayer to God."—Luke vi. 12.

My soul! contemplate thy Lord in the view here represented of him. "Jesus continued all night in prayer to God." But did Christ need to use prayer? Yes, as Christ, the sent, the anointed, the servant of Jehovah, when he voluntarily stood up as the surety of his people, at the call of God the Father. But as God, "one with the Father, over all, God blessed for ever," he prayed not; for all divine perfections were his in common with the Father and the Holy Spirit, eternally, essentially, and underived. But, my soul, as thy representative, Jesus needed the use of prayer, and hath both endeared it, and recommended it by his bright example. And observe the fervency and earnestness of his prayers, by the length of time. For whereas one short hour is found long by thee, (yea, sometimes in that hour, what coldness and deadness creep in!) thy

Redeemer " continued all night in prayer." And what were the subjects of his prayer, but the salvation of his people? He needed no prayer for himself, had not his love to us, and zeal for his Father's glory, prompted his infinite mind to undertake our redemption. But when the Son of God became man for us, to make us sons of God, then our safety, peace, and welfare, both for this life and that which is to come, occupied his divine mind, and led him out " all night in prayer to God!" What an illustrious proof hath Jesus given of this in his farewell prayer, the night preceding his sufferings and death! As a dying father in the midst of his family, behold how he commended his whole household to God. " Keep, holy Father, (said he) through thine own name, those whom thou hast given me, that they may be one, as we are." My soul! often let thy thoughts revolve on this; and in thy cold and languid moments in prayer contemplate how Jesus was engaged for thee and thy salvation. The sun witnessed to the diligence of his labours by day, and the stars in their courses testified of his earnestness in prayer by night. And what is it now, in his glorious office as Intercessor, but the all-prevailing and unwearied exercises of the same, only with this difference: in his exalted state, his addresses are not by way of prayer or petition, as when upon earth; for all the high offices of his everlasting priesthood and sacrifice are carried on by his " appearing in the presence of God for us." He appears in a vesture dipped in blood, and as a Lamb which hath been slain. And his blood is said to be " a speaking blood;" for it speaketh to God for us, on the ground of his merit, and it speaketh *from* God to us, on the account of God's covenant grace and mercy in Christ. Ponder well, my soul, these things; and in the contemplation of thy Jesus, never lose sight of the everlasting and eternal efficacy of his blood and righteousness; nor of thy interest in both. And when at any time, thy poor, polluted, cold, and lifeless prayers find no ascension, no strength nor energy, direct one look, with faith, to the Lamb that is in the midst of the throne. Behold him, whom the Father heareth alway; and call to remembrance, that it is the efficacy of his merits and intercession which is the sole cause of thine acceptance before God and the Father, and not thy earnestness, or the length of thy prayers. Precious Jesus! help me thus stedfastly and steadily to behold thee in thy holy vestments of the everlasting priesthood of Melchisedec; and then shall I be assured that neither my poor person, nor poor prayers, will ever be forgotten before God.

MAY 5.

MORNING.—"Believest thou not that I am in the Father, and the Father in me?"—John xiv. 10.

My soul, thou wilt never sufficiently contemplate this blessed oneness between the Father and the Son, in the great work and glory of redemption. Pause this morning, and observe for the confirmation of thy faith, that as Jesus is one with the Father in all the essence and attributes of the Godhead, so God the Father is one with Jesus in all the offices of redemption. God was in Christ's human nature; for he is said to have been "God manifest in the flesh." God was in every name of Christ, every work of Christ, every word of Christ, every office of Christ, every attribute of Christ. And hence, in seeing Christ, we truly see God; in all his grace, mercy, love, salvation, and every blessing connected with our present, future, eternal happiness. And what a sweet thought is that, my soul, for thee to dwell upon; that as the Father is in Jesus, and in him dwelleth all the fulness of the Godhead bodily, so, in consequence, there is a fulness of grace and a fulness of glory in Jesus to give out a supply here of the one, and hereafter of the other, to satisfy the most capacious desires of the souls of his redeemed to all eternity. For the human nature being personally united to the Godhead in the person of the Lord Jesus, there must be this fulness everlastingly dwelling. There may be, and for certain purposes sometimes there are, great gifts and graces of the Spirit poured out upon the Lord's servants; but never could the Godhead be found in any but Jesus. "God was in Christ, reconciling the world to himself." Pause once more, my soul, and ask thyself, hast thou Christ? Then hast thou God the Father in him. Where Christ is, God the Father is; and where Christ is not, there God is not. See then, my soul, that this is the standard to ascertain the reality of thy case as it appears before God. Hast thou Jesus for thy portion? Then the Father is in him. Dost thou love Jesus? Then must thou love the Father in him. Dost thou seek Jesus? Then art thou seeking the Father in him. Oh for grace to discover our true interest in all the Father's covenant engagements, and promises, from this very source: that this everlasting oneness between the Father and Son infallibly secures to his people all the blessings of redemption, for in seeing the Son, we literally and truly see the Father, and glorify the Father in Jesus. Amen.

EVENING.—"And when Jesus saw her, he called her to him, and said unto her, Woman, thou art loosed from thine infirmity."—Luke xiii. 12.

My soul! sit down this evening, and let the case of this poor woman open to thy view some sweet subjects of instruction and encouragement. Who knows, but that God the Holy Ghost may graciously make thy meditation on it blessed, in Jesus? The evangelist gives a short but interesting history of her. She was a daughter of Abraham; and yet Satan had bound her; and that not for a little space, but for a very long time, even to *eighteen years*. Hence learn, that they who are *within* the covenant, are not *without* affliction; nay, they become the very grudge and hatred of Satan, on that account; and shall assuredly be made sensible of his enmity. Do not overlook this part of the poor woman's memoir. It forms a distinguishing feature in the children of the kingdom. Jesus himself hath said, " Because ye are not of the world, but I have chosen you out of the world, therefore the world hateth you." John xv. 19. And as to the length of time in which Satan had harassed her, no doubt, there was much mercy mingled with the exercise. Jesus knew all; yea, permitted all, and sanctified all. It were devoutly to be wished, that all the Lord's afflicted ones would ever keep this conviction uppermost in their minds. I have often thought, that we should lose some of our highest enjoyments, if the Lord did not afford occasion for the enemy to make use of some of his deepest cruelties. A child of God can never be a loser by the greatest exercises, while Jesus stands by, regulates, restrains, and ultimately blesseth all. The devil, as in the case of this poor woman, meant nothing but evil; but see, my soul, how Jesus at length overruled it for good. And if the sorrow be lengthened, to *eighteen*, or even *eight and thirty* years, as to the man at the pool of Bethesda, yet, if the issue be glorious, it is the end that crowns the action; and in the mean time, the Lord can, and will minister *eighteen thousand* consolations, to bear his children up under them, and to make them " more than conquerors," through his grace supporting them. He can, like another Samson, make " meat come forth from the eater; and out of the strong, bring forth sweetness." How often have I seen a child of God triumphing in weakness, when the power of Jesus hath been resting upon him! Yea, the very tear, which hath been standing in the eye from the pain of body, hath looked like a pearl for beauty, from the spiritual enjoyments of the soul.—But let me take another view of this poor exercised daughter of

Abraham. Though bowed together by reason of this spirit of infirmity, so as in no wise to be able to lift up herself, yet do not fail to remark, my soul, that she did not absent herself from the house of prayer. What multitudes are there who plead sickness, yea, trifling sickness, to justify their absence from the house of God! And who shall say what blessings may be lost upon those occasions? Had Thomas not withdrawn himself from the meeting of the disciples, at that memorable season when Jesus came to bless them, he would have been spared the dreadful mortification that followed. Had this poor woman not been in the synagogue when Jesus visited it, who shall say how long might the blessing she then found have been withheld, or when might another opportunity have offered? And it doth not appear that this poor woman's attendance on worship was with the most distant view of getting relief to her body, but for the care of the soul. She was indeed a daughter of Abraham, and as such, regarded "the one thing needful." She had at least learned the spiritual truth of that blessed saying of Jesus, whether or not she had heard the Lord's sermon on the mount, and was brought into the practice of it: "Seek ye first the kingdom of God, and his righteousness, and all these things shall be added unto you." When Jesus saw her, he called her to him, and said unto her, "Woman, thou art loosed from thine infirmity!" It doth not appear that she made any application to Jesus to be healed. Sweet thought! "If we love him, it is because he first loved us." Gracious as the Lord is to the cries of his afflicted, he doth not always wait for their petitions. It is *his* love, not *our* prayers; his *free* grace, not our *constrained* necessities, that becomes the rule for Jesus bestowing mercy. Oh! thou dear Lord! art thou not now in the assemblies of thy people? and dost thou not seek and search out the poor of thy fold, wheresoever they have been scattered "in the cloudy and dark day?"

Ezek. xxxiv. 11, 12. Pause, my soul, over this delightful view of thy Jesus, in his grace, to this daughter of Abraham; and gather from it sweet instruction in all the remaining infirmities under which thou art frequently bowed together, and from which, in thyself, or thine own strength, thou art no more able to lift up thyself, than this woman, of the stock of Abraham. Learn from this relation where, and in whom alone, thy strength is found. Oh! for grace to live under the constant enjoyment of strength in Jesus, and to say with that exercised servant of old: "I can do nothing of myself; but I can do all things through Christ, who strengtheneth me." And should the Lord, in his providence, cause these lines to meet the eye of any son or daughter of Abraham, who is still under the same spirit of infirmity, of a natural state in which they were born, I would say, do as this poor woman did, diligently attend the means of grace, and let nothing of soul or body hinder a constant waiting upon the Lord; and, depend upon it, Jesus will be there, and will speak personally to your case and circumstances, and say, "Thou art loosed from thine infirmity!"

MAY 6.

MORNING.—"And he said, I am Joseph your brother, whom ye sold into Egypt."—Gen. xlv. 4.

What an interview was this, in the first manifestation the governor of Egypt made of himself to his brethren! We are told that he wept aloud. His bowels yearned over them. He had long smothered in his own bosom those tender feelings he possessed of the greatest love towards them; and when he had dismissed every looker-on and stranger, he broke out in those kind expressions, "I am Joseph your brother, whom ye sold into Egypt." But what were the feelings of the patriarch, compared to those of the Lord Jesus, when he made himself known to his disciples, after he arose from the dead; and as he now manifests himself to every poor sinner, whom, by his grace, he makes partaker in the first resurrection on whom the second death hath no power? I am Jesus, your brother, saith that adored Lord; but he doth not add, whom ye sold for worse than a slave. There is no upbraiding, nothing of our baseness and sins. And yet we have all not only sold him, but by our transgressions crucified him. What a beautiful feature this is in the Redeemer; and how much even the love of Joseph falls short of Jesus! And what endears it still more, is the peculiar attention the Redeemer manifesteth upon the occasion. If there be one of his brethren more distressed and discouraged by reason of sin than another, to him Jesus directs his manifestation more immediately. Witness the case of Peter after his fall. Jesus will have the account of his resurrection not only communicated to all, but Peter is mentioned by name. "Go, tell his disciples, and Peter." As if knowing the apostle might fear that, having denied Jesus, he might justly be denied by him No, saith Jesus, let Peter be particularly told the joyful news, to make his heart glad. And dost thou, dearest Lord, speak to my soul? Dost thou say to me, I am your brother? Art thou not ashamed to call such sinners brethren? Oh thou unequalled pattern of unexampled love! add one mercy more to the vast account, and let a portion of it kindle a flame of love in my soul. I have, indeed, sold them for a slave; nailed thee, by my sins, to the cross, and put thee to an open shame. But since thou hast redeemed me by thy blood, and bought the pardon of my sins so dear; ard now, by thy triumph over death, art become the first-born among many brethren, and exalted as a Prince and a Saviour to give blessings infinitely superior to those Joseph was exalted to bestow on his brethren; behold, Lord, to thee do I come: manifest thyself still the forgiving brother, and supply all thy wants. Yes, blessed Jesus! thou art he whom thy brethren shall praise; and all thy Father's children shall fall down before thee.

EVENING.—"The top of Pisgah."—Deut. xxxiv. 1.

There is somewhat truly interesting in this account of Pisgah, to which Moses ascended before his death. The relation, no doubt, was intended to convey seasonable instruction, of a spiritual nature, to all true believers in Christ, in their Pisgah contemplations of the promised land. My soul! sit down this evening, and see what, under divine teaching, thou canst make of it. Probably thy Lord, thy Jesus, may grant to thy faith, sights yet more glorious than even Moses beheld in open vision, when he went up to Mount Nebo. "The top of Pisgah" afforded to the man of God, a beautiful prospect of Canaan; and as we are told, that "his natural force was not abated, neither his eye become dim;" he might possibly view the boundaries of Israel's dominions; which, in point of extent, reached but little more than fifty miles in one direction, and about three times that length in another. Indeed, we are informed, that "the Lord shewed him all the land;" and the same power which gave him the prospect, would doubtlessly give him a suited strength of vision for the purpose. But what, my soul, are thy views on Pisgah's heights? The utmost extent of the imagination cannot be sufficient to take in what is opened before thee, of that "length and depth, and breadth and height, of the love of Christ, which passeth knowledge!" And if he, who led Moses to the top of Pisgah, go with thee; if the same Lord that shewed him all the land, shew thee also "the glories to be revealed:" think what blessings will pour in upon thee, of "joy unspeakable and full of glory." It is true, thy Pisgah views are in the distant means of grace, and the ordinances of worship; where, very frequently, clouds arise, and darken thy prospect. Nevertheless the word of God opens a true map of that Judea, which is above, and which is "the glory of all lands;" and God the Holy Ghost can, and will give the seeing eye to see, and the awakened heart "to believe, the glorious things which are spoken of the city of God." And if Moses, from the first moment that the Lord spake to him from the bush, when the visions of God began, had been accustomed to contemplate in every thing the view of Jesus; and, like the other patriarchs, had seen his day afar off, so as to rejoice and be glad; surely, since the Lord first called thee by his grace, and was pleased to reveal his Son in thee, thou hast had increasing desires after Jesus, and increasing knowledg of, and communion with Jesus; and therefore on Pisgah's top, in thy evening meditation, thou mayest find sweet anticipations of the glories of that kingdom above, which, ere long, thou hopest to enter into the full enjoyment of, amidst the heirs of God, and the joint heirs with Christ. One sweet thought more, the top of Pisgah opens to the mind, in beholding the man of God going up to it: I mean in that he went alone, the divine presence only being with him. Here indeed is the very life of communion. The blessings Jesus imparts, in Pisgah views, to his redeemed, are all personal, and alone. They are joys with which a stranger cannot intermeddle. The white stone, and the new name, and the hidden manna, which Jesus gives, are all in secret: "no man knoweth, saving he that receiveth," Rev. ii. 17. My soul! art thou acquainted with these things? Are these among the privileges of the true believer; and dost thou hope, after a few more revolving suns have finished their daily course, and the shades of night are done away, to realize these glories, and enter upon the everlasting possession of them? —Get up then, by faith, in thy evening meditations; yea, hear Jesus calling thee by name, as he did Moses, and saying, get thee up into this mountain, Abarim, and behold the land which I have taken possession of for Israel! Oh! for grace and faith in lively exercise, to look often "within the veil, whither our glorious forerunner is for us entered," and there behold Jesus on his throne, and speaking in the same precious words, as to the church of old: "To him that overcometh, will I grant to sit with me in my throne, even as I also overcame, and am sat down with my Father in his throne," Rev iii. 21. And while these soul-ravishing triumphs of faith are upon the mind, with all the warmth of holy joy, from Pisgah's heights, surely, like Simeon, the soul will then cry out in the same language as he did, when he caught Jesus in his arms: "Lord, let thy servant now depart in peace, according to thy word; for mine eyes have seen thy salvation."

MAY 7.

MORNING.—"They shall revive as the corn."—Hosea xiv. 7.

Sweet promise to comfort a soul like mine, under so many and such frequent languishing graces! How often hath it appeared to my view as if the gracious seed had perished! It was small, indeed, in its first beginning, like the grain of mustard seed; and no sooner had it appeared, than I perceived it almost choked with the tares of corruption, unbelief, and Satan's rubbish. I was soon led to suspect God's work upon my soul. Surely, I said, this is not grace. Presently I could see no more of it. I was ignorant that by thus dying to self, the Holy Ghost was opening to my view the only living in Jesus. In a moment unlooked for, it revived as the corn. Ah, from whence is the source? Not from self, not from labours, not from exertions: can dead roots live? The Holy Ghost taught me this must be Jesus. Your life, he said, is hid with Christ in God. Here are the springs of grace: here, from hence, flow the streams of that river which make glad the city of God. Here then is faith's view of God's glory in Christ. Here is the promise. "They shall revive as the corn." And thus it is fulfilled. "In me," saith that precious Redeemer, "is thy fruit found." Mark this down, my soul. Both root and fruit are in one and the same, even Jesus. Spiritual attainments are in Jesus, not in the greenest buddings or fairest blossoms of our own labours. Live then, my soul, wholly upon Jesus, and then thou wilt revive as the corn. Suppose it trodden down; suppose the tares of the wicked rise to oppose it, yet if Jesus be the root, and the springs of grace in him flow, as they cannot but flow, to keep alive all the branches in him, there shall be, there must be at last, a glorious harvest. Oh what a volume doth the soul sometimes read at once in that short promise, "Because I live, ye shall live also." Hail, hail, thou glorious root out of a dry ground; thou wilt send forth the golden ears for thine own garner. Thou wilt weed out every thing that annoys. Thou wilt water, and by the sweet influences of thy blood, thy word, and Spirit, thou wilt shine upon the standing corn. And when, by all thy gracious husbandry, for the whole work and glory is thine, thou hast caused the plentiful crop to hang down their heads in all the humbleness of self-abasement, as the token of ripeness; thou wilt command thine angel to put in the sickle of death, and take home every stalk and every grain of the precious seed to thy garner in heaven.

EVENING.—" Fear none of those things which thou shalt suffer. Behold, the devil shall cast some of you into prison, that ye may be tried; and ye shall have tribulation ten days. Be thou faithful unto death, and I will give thee a crown of life."—Rev. ii. 10.

My soul! thy last evening meditation, by faith, was on Pisgah's top. This evening, do thou attend to what thy Saviour speaks in this scripture of the prospect of a prison. This forms the state and condition of the believer. The transition he is sometimes, and suddenly, called to make, is from the house of feasting to the house of mourning. He is here but in a wilderness at the best; and whatever accommodations he meets with by the way, the apartments of joy and sorrow are both under the same roof, and very often it is but a step from one to the other: yea, sometimes, and not unfrequently, when Jesus hath been feasting with his people, and they with him, before the cloth hath been taken away, and the blessing offered up, a reverse of circumstances hath followed.—But what saith thy Lord in this sweet scripture, (for it is a sweet one, if well considered)? " Fear none of those things which thou shalt suffer." There is a fear which belongs to our very nature, and impossible wholly to be free from it; it is indeed part of ourselves. No creature of God but one, and that is the Leviathan, that we read of, is wholly free from it, Job. xli. 33. The blessed Jesus himself, when assuming our nature, condescended to take all the sinless infirmities of our nature, and therefore was subject in some degree to it; for we are told, that " he was made in the likeness of sinful flesh," Rom. viii. 3. Hence we read, that his holy soul, when in the garden, was " sore troubled, sore amazed, and very heavy." Listen, my soul, to these complaints of thy Redeemer! And when at any time fear ariseth within at the conflicts of Satan, recollect how Jesus felt during his unequalled agony. One look, by faith, directed to him, as in the garden, will quiet all. " Having himself suffered, being tempted, he knows how to succour them that are tempted." But, besides this *natural* fear, to which our nature is subject, there is a *sinful* fear, which unbelief, doubt, and distrust too often bring into the soul. And it is this, if I mistake not, to which Jesus hath respect in his precept before us. All hell is up in arms, to harass and distress a child of God; and if the devil cannot deprive the believer of his heavenly crown, he will rob him as much as possible of his earthly comfort. Mark, then, my soul, what thy Jesus here proposeth for relief. The devil would cast thee into *hell*, if he could, but his rage can reach no farther than to a *prison*. He would cast the *whole church*, if he could, into it; but it shall be only *some* of the church. He would cause the confinement, if he could, to be *for ever;* but Jesus saith, it shall only be for *ten* days. And the Holy Ghost hath caused it to be left on record, as a thing much to be observed, that when the church was in Egypt, and Pharaoh would have kept the people in vassalage for ever; yet when the Lord's time before appointed was arrived, "the self-same night, the Lord brought them forth with their armies," Exod. xii. 41, 42. Oh! it is a subject worthy to be kept in everlasting remembrance, that "the Lord knoweth how to deliver the godly out of temptation." Now, my soul, ponder well these things; and connect with them what Jesus hath connected with the subject in that sweet promise: "Be thou faithful unto death, and I will give thee a crown of life." Precious Jesus! put *thy* fear in me; and the fear of man, which bringeth a snare, will depart. Be thou with me in trouble, and my trouble will be turned into joy. Should a prison shut *me in;* no prison can shut *thee out.* Every distressing thought will be hushed asleep, while, by faith, I hear my Lord speaking to me in those soul-comforting words: "Fear thou not, for I am with thee; be not dismayed, for I am thy God. I will strengthen thee, yea, I will help thee; yea, I will uphold thee with the right hand of my righteousness," Isa. xli. 10.

MAY 8.

MORNING.—"Jesus said unto her, I am the resurrection and the life: he that believeth in me, though he were dead, yet shall he live. And whosoever liveth, and believeth in me, shall never die. Believest thou this?"—John xi. 25, 26.

Pause my soul, over those divine, those glorious,

those soul-quickening, soul-reviving words of thy Almighty Redeemer! What man, what prophet, what servant of the Lord, what angel but he that is the angel of the covenant, one with the Father, over all, God, blessed for ever, could assume such a language, and prove that assumption as Jesus did, both by his own resurrection and that of Lazarus? And mark, my soul, the many precious things contained in this sweet scripture. Observe the blessing itself, even resurrection and life. Observe the source, the author, the fountain of it. Jesus, thy Jesus. Observe *for* whom this stupendous mercy is designed, and *to* whom conveyed; namely, the dead in trespasses and sins, and for the dying languishing frames of believers. And lastly, observe how absolute the thing itself is; they *shall* live. Oh precious words of a most precious Saviour! And may I not say to thee, my soul, as Jesus did to Mary, after proclaiming himself under this glorious distinction of character; "Believest thou this?" Canst thou answer as she did, "Yea, Lord, I believe that thou art the Christ, the Son of God, which should come into the world?" This is a blessed confession to witness before God. For if I believe that Jesus be indeed the Christ of God, every other difficulty is removed to the firm belief that, as the Father hath life in himself, even so hath the Son life in himself, and whom he will he quickeneth. Witness then for me, every looker on, angels and men, that my soul heartily, cordially, fully subscribes to the same precious truth, and in the same language as Mary. Yea, Lord, I would say to every word of thine concerning thy sovereignty, grace, and love, as thou hast said it, so I accept it; in the very words of thine I take it, and cry out, yea, Lord, even so be it unto me according to thy word. And now, my soul, under all remaining seasons of deadness, coldness, backslidings, wanderings, and the like, never henceforth forget, from whom all revivals can only come. Never look within for them; for there is no power of resurrection in thyself. "Can these dry bones live?" Yes, if Jesus quickens. And is Jesus less able to quicken thee than thy connexion with Adam to have killed thee? Oh how plain is it, that the very wants of the soul correspond to the very fulness of Jesus to answer them. And therefore, when the Lord Jesus saith, "I am the resurrection and the life," he comes to seek employment in this glorious character, to quicken the dead and revive the living. Oh Lord, give me to hear thy blessed voice this day, and my soul shall live, and live to praise thee.

EVENING.—"And he called his name Noah, saying, this same shall comfort us concerning our work, and toil of our hands, because of the ground which the Lord our God hath cursed."—Gen. v. 29.

I still think, and believe that I always shall think, that holy men of old possessed great superiority of faith to new testament believers, in the attention they paid to the choice of names given to their children. Our choice, for the most part, is from caprice, or respect to our relations or earthly connections; they had an eye to heaven. Thus, in the instance before us, Lamech evidently called his son, Noah, which signifies rest, in reference to "the rest which remaineth for the people of God;" and, as such, had an eye to Christ, the promised seed, in whom alone that rest was to be found. I do not presume to suppose that Lamech thought this child to be himself the promised seed, as our first mother Eve did at the birth of Cain, when she said, "I have gotten a man," or, as it might be read, "the man, from the Lord," Gen. iv. 1. No doubt she considered this, her first-born son, to be *the very man*, the *Ishi* promised: and hence, when her *second* son was born, she called him Abel, which means *vanity;* thereby intimating, what is indeed true, that every other man but the God-man is but vanity. Poor woman! how sadly mistaken she found herself! But though Lamech had not such high views of his son, as to suppose him the very Christ; yet in calling him Noah, it should seem probable, that he desired, in the remembrance of this child, to keep up an eye to Christ in him as a *rest,* and his son as a *type* of Christ, which Noah eminently was. And indeed the latter part of Lamech's observation seems to confirm it: "This same shall comfort us concerning our work and toil, because of the ground which the Lord hath cursed." It would be a strange, not to say an unnatural thought in a tender parent, to take comfort in the prospect of a son's arriving to manhood, to take off all toil and labour from his parents, that they might enjoy ease; which would be the case, had Lamech meant nothing more than the rest of this mortal life. In this sense, indeed, what is the *curse* here spoken of, and how could the labour of Noah take it away? But on the supposition that Lamech was so well taught of God, as to be looking forward to the day of "Christ afar off," and under the believing expectation of Christ's coming in the fulness of time, who would take away the *curse,* by being made both "sin and a curse" for his redeemed, he called his son Noah, that he might, as often as he should look upon the child, remember Christ. There is somewhat very sweet and striking in this circumstance, which may serve to explain why the Holy Ghost hath thus caused it to be so particularly recorded. My soul! gather a sweet improvement from this scripture, and do not fail to observe how graciously God the Holy Ghost dealt with the patriarchs, in causing, by so many ways, the one glorious event of Jesus and his salvation to be kept alive, in ages so remote from the accomplishment of redemption. And what hast thou to comfort thyself with, concerning thy work, and the toil of thine hands? What is thy rest, because of the ground which the Lord hath cursed? Hast thou thy Noah, thy Jesus, who is thy hope, thy rest, thy righteousness? Precious, precious Noah! I would look up to thee, my Lord

Jesus, and say, Thou hast comforted me, thou dost comfort me, under all the toil and sweat of brow in which I eat my daily bread! Thou hast taken away the curse of the ground, and art indeed thyself the whole blessing of it. Thou, blessed Jesus, art the rest, "wherewith the Lord causeth the weary to rest; and thou art the refreshing!" Isaiah xxviii. 12. "Return then to thy rest, (thy Noah) my soul, for the Lord hath dealt bountifully with thee," Psalm cxvi. 7.

MAY 9.

MORNING.—"A certain Samaritan."—Luke x. 33.

Look, my soul, beyond the letter of the parable, and see if thou canst not instantly discover who it is that is here meant. Mark how he is described: "A certain Samaritan." Not any indifferent undetermined one among the whole mass of men called Samaritans, but an identical certain one: and who but Jesus answers to this character? "Said we not well, (said the Jews) that thou art a Samaritan?" Yes, truly, thus far ye said right; for our Jesus is the true Samaritan, that came a blissful stranger from his blessed abode, to deliver us from our lost estate, for his mercy endureth for ever. And, my soul, observe how exactly corresponding to all that is said of this certain Samaritan in the parable, thy Jesus proves to have been. Our nature, universally speaking, was going down from Jerusalem to Jericho, when it fell among thieves, and when it was left more than half dead by the great enemy of souls; for we had all miserably departed from the Lord, when Jesus came from heaven to the Jericho of this world, to "seek and save that which was lost." And what could the priest or levite do by law or sacrifice, to help our ruined nature? But when Jesus came and bound up the wounds which sin and Satan had made, by pouring in the balsam of his own precious blood, then he proved himself to be this certain Samaritan; for none but Jesus could have done this, since there is salvation in no other; "neither is there any other name under heaven, given among men, whereby we must be saved." And what is it now, but the same gracious mercy carrying on the same blessed purpose in completing the perfect recovery of our nature. It is Jesus, Samaritan-like, which hath brought us to the inn of his church, hath appointed his servants and angels, who are ministering spirits, to minister in all divine things to the heirs of salvation. He hath commissioned the whole train of ordinances, and providences, and promises, to minister to our good. His holy word, his Holy Spirit, are unceasingly engaged to the same blessed end. And what crowns all, and makes our state and circumstances most safe and blessed indeed, is, that Jesus hath commanded all the remaining costs and expences of our cure to be put down to his account. He saith himself to me, a poor worthless sinner as I am, and to every individual of his redeemed, "Whatsoever thou spendest more, when I come again, I will repay." And is it so, my soul? Is not the blessing too great to be bestowed, and thou too worthless to receive it? Oh no! for it is Jesus who promiseth: that is enough. Hail, then, thou certain Samaritan, thou Almighty Traveller through our miserable world! Since the first day that thou didst pass by, and didst behold me in my blood, cast out to perish, and didst bid me live, how hath my soul hailed thee, and now and unceasingly will hail thee, as my life, my hope, my joy, my portion for ever!

EVENING.—"Ye know the heart of a stranger."—Exod. xxiii. 9.

True, Lord, I do indeed! for I was once a stranger in a strange land, even in the land of spiritual Egypt. My soul! wilt thou not find it profitable to look back, and call to remembrance thy original nothingness; yea, worse than nothing, when Jesus passed by, and bade thee live? It is among the gracious precepts of the Lord, "to look to the rock whence thou wert hewn, and to the hole of the pit whence thou wert digged," Isaiah li. 1. And never surely was mercy more seasonable, more abundant, more unexpected, unlooked for, and unmerited, than when bestowed upon me! And doth my Lord say, "Ye know the heart of a stranger? Oh! for grace rightly to apprehend that state out of which the Lord brought me, when living as a stranger to the commonwealth of Israel, "without hope, and without God in the world!" Thou knowest the heart of a stranger, my soul; say then what it was. A stranger to any knowledge of God the Father; ignorant, blind, senseless, unconscious of sin, and unconscious of danger. And what a stranger to thee, thou blessed Lord Jesus! I knew thee not, I loved thee not, I desired thee not. Thy love, thy grace, thy pity, thy mercy, these were thoughts which never entered my breast. Neither thy person, nor thy salvation, the merits of thy blood, nor of thy righteousness, were ever in my view or regard; yea, contempt of thee, and of thy people, thy sabbaths, thy word and ordinances, would have been more the pursuit of my heart, than of thy love. And so total a stranger was I to the idea of any saving change to be wrought upon the heart by regeneration, that, concerning the Eternal Spirit, and his divine agency upon the soul, never had I so much as heard "whether there was any Holy Ghost!" My soul! was this indeed thy case, as thou once didst stand before God? "Dead in trespasses and sins;" and every moment exposed to the tremendous horrors of "the second death," where thou wouldest have been a stranger to any lovely view of God in Christ to all eternity. "Dost thou know the heart of a stranger?"—Pause, and describe, if it be possible, what must be such a state! And then look round, and behold the multitude of souls that are so now; and say, dost thou not feel for the stranger, since thou wert once a stranger in the land of Egypt? Oh! ye that are yet in nature's darkness, fast bound in misery and iron; strangers and aliens; afar off, and enemies to God by wicked works; "Oh! consider this, all ye that forget God, lest he pluck you away, and there be none to deliver you!" Lord! I desire to be humbled to the dust before thee, to ascribe all to distinguishing grace, and everlastingly to be crying out, with the astonishment of the apostle, "Lord, how is it that thou dost manifest thyself to me, and not unto the world?"

MAY 10.

MORNING.—"By the high-way side begging."—Mark x. 46.

My soul, learn a lesson from the beggar this morning. And Oh thou blessed friend of beggars, do thou sweetly make the view gracious to my soul. What was it led this poor man to the high-way side to seek alms? Surely his poverty, wretchedness, and a sense of want. And art thou come forth, my soul, from the same cause, and on the same errand? I presume this poor creature came forth empty; for had he been full he would never have come. And art thou so, my soul! for otherwise it is certain, they that are full in themselves never seek Jesus. But amidst his want and poverty, had this poor beggar hopes that the passers by would commiserate his case and relieve him? Yes, no doubt: though some might overlook and disregard him, all would not. But, my soul, thy case far exceeds his. Though all disregard, Jesus will not: and thou art sure he will pass by, and not only behold thy misery, but give thee needed relief. Jesus, Master, have mercy upon me! Behold, I am come out this morning as poor, as wretched, as empty, and as needy, as though I never before had heard of thy dear name, or been living upon thy fulness. But thou knowest that I cannot live upon the alms of yesterday, no more than my body can keep in health from the food received in the many days that are past, without a new supply, Lord, I know that I am thine, and that thou art mine. I therefore come to thee for a suited supply; and surely, thou wilt not send me empty away. Indeed, Lord, I rejoice that I feel my poverty; for I am thereby, as an empty vessel, better suited for receiving of thy fulness. Give in, blessed Jesus, to my poor hungry soul, and then I shall find cause to rejoice that my emptiness and beggary constrained me to seek thee; and that my need afforded an opportunity for the display of thy grace. Yes, yes, blessed Lord, I am not only content to be poor and to be needy, but to be nothing, to be worse than nothing, so that if thereby my blessed Jesus gets glory in the manifestation of his love and the giving out of his riches, "I will glory even in my infirmities, that the power of Christ may rest upon me." A beggar still I wish to be, and to lay at thy gate, if but to glimpse at thy face, and to receive one token from thy fair hand. Indeed, indeed, then am I most full, when most empty, to be filled with Jesus.

EVENING.—"The transgressions of the wicked saith within my heart, that there is no fear of God before his eyes."—Psalm xxxvi. 1.

How striking is this scripture, and how true! Yes, my soul; thou needest not to look abroad into another's heart to see iniquity; for at home, in thine own, a voice may be heard continually proclaiming it. Renewed as thou art by grace, still thou feelest the workings of corrupt nature: and though, as the apostle said, "with thy mind thou thyself servest the law of God, yet with thy flesh the law of sin," Romans vii. 25. Pause over the solemn subject, and observe the working of a body of sin and death, which is virtually all sin: "the carnal mind, (the apostle saith) is enmity against God," Rom. viii. 7.; not only an enemy, but in enmity: so that the very nature is so; it is averse, naturally averse to God, and is everlastingly rising in opposition to his holy law. And this not only (as some have supposed, but all men, if they would confess the truth, find to the contrary) before a work of grace hath passed upon the soul, but after. Else wherefore doth the apostle say, "the flesh lusteth against the Spirit, and the Spirit against the flesh; and these are contrary the one to the other, so that ye cannot do the things that ye would?" Gal. v. 17. He saith this to the regenerate, to the church at large. And consequently this conflict is after grace hath been manifested to the soul, and not before. A sinner unawakened may indeed feel at times compunctions of conscience, and be alarmed at what will be the consequence of his sins: but these are only the alarms of conscience, not the workings of grace: and for the most part, these alarms are but momentary. His affections are all on the side of sin. His soul still remains "dead in trespasses and sins;" and he himself, like a dead fish, swims down the stream of sin uninterrupted, without resistance, and without concern. But when a child of God is renewed, and the soul, that was before dead in trespasses and sins, becomes quickened and regenerated; then it is that the conflict between the renewed part in grace, and the unrenewed part in nature, begins, and never ends but with life. My soul, hath the Lord taught thee this, made thee sensible of it, and caused thee to groan under it? Dost thou find this heart of thine rebelling against God; cold to divine things, but warm to natural enjoyments; framing excuses to keep thee from sweet communion with the Lord; and even in the moment of communion, running with a swarm of vain thoughts, that "like the flies in the ointment of the apothecary causeth it to send forth an ill savour?" Are these in thy daily, hourly, experience? Why then the transgressions of the wicked saith within thine heart, and not another's for thee, this solemn truth, there is no fear of God at such seasons before the eyes of thy sinful body: "for by the fear of the Lord, men depart from evil," Prov. xvi. 6. Oh! precious, precious Jesus! how increasingly dear, under this view of a nature so totally corrupt, art thou to my poor soul! What but the eternal and unceasing efficacy of thy blood and righteousness could give my soul the smallest confidence, when I find that I still carry about with me such a body of sin and death? Let those who know not the plague of their own heart, talk of natural goodness; sure I am, there is nothing of the kind in me. "I know that in me, that is, in my flesh, dwelleth no good thing." And were it not, dearest Lord, for the holiness of thy person, blood, and righteousness, the very sins which mingle up with all I say or do, yea, even in prayer, would seal my condemnation. Lamb of God! it is the everlasting merit of thy atonement and intercession, thy blood sprinkled upon my person and offering, by which alone the justice of God is restrained and satisfied, and that it breaks not forth in devouring fire, as upon the sacrifice of old, to consume me upon my very knees! Blessed, blessed for ever be God for Jesus Christ!

MAY 11.

MORNING.—"Let him alone, and let him curse; for the Lord hath bidden him. It may be that the Lord will look on mine affliction, and that the Lord will requite me good for his cursing this day."—2 Sam. xvi. 11, 12.

My soul, see here a believer in his best frame. To be sure, it is not always thus with a child of God; but it were to be devoutly desired always thus to be. But while we admire the faith, let us yet more admire and adore him, and his grace and mercy who gives it. Oh what a blessed state it is to eye the hand of the Lord in every thing. When Shimei thus cursed David, he passeth by the instrument, and recognizeth the hand of the Lord in the appointment. "Let him alone, for the

Lord hath bidden him." Sin is at the bottom. The Lord doth not correct for nought. How unjust soever on the part of man, it is both just and right on the part of God. And observe, moreover, the comfort he takes to himself out of it. If my God bid my enemy distress me, is it not that my Almighty Friend may more sweetly comfort me? There is not only a *may be*, but a certainty there *shall be*, in God's requiting evil with good to his people My soul, never overlook this in any, and in all of thine exercises. Behold his hand in it, be it what it may, and then thou wilt never faint under any burden. Jesus not only looks on, but he it is that permits, that appoints. Oh he is tender even in rebukes. By those means he makes his children more like himself; and moreover, it is his gracious plan to extract pleasure from pain, and by impoverishing the soul in self, and in creature love, to turn curses into blessings, and convert loss into gain. Doth the enemy curse you? Doth he come out against you? Oh then depend upon it, Jesus is going to confer some special blessing upon you. Thou art to be advanced to great honour, to be made more conformable to his blessed image. Jesus is hereby giving you not only to believe in him, but to suffer for his sake. Precious Lord! grant me then this grace which thy servant David was enabled to exercise; and when the Shimeis of the day come forth to curse, let them curse, so thou do but bless. And Oh for sweet influences from thee, dearest Lord! "that I may know thee and the power of thy resurrection, and the fellowship of thy sufferings, being made conformable unto thy death."

EVENING.—"And by him all that believe are justified from all things, from which ye could not be justified by the law of Moses."—Acts xiii. 39.

What can be more blessed to a poor conscious sinner, such, my soul, as thou art from day to day, than the glad tidings the Holy Ghost hath here proclaimed, by the ministry of his servant the apostle, in these gracious words. Sit down, this evening, and, under his divine teaching, ponder them duly over. A poor guilty sinner needs a rich and holy Saviour. That he cannot justify himself in the sight of God, is most evident, for the least guilt left upon the conscience would condemn him for ever. He cannot be justified by the deeds of the law; for by the law is the knowledge of sin, and in the law we learn that we have all sinned, and come short of God's glory. He cannot be justified by the offerings and sacrifices made under the law of Moses; for how can the blood of bulls and of goats take away sin? By what then, or by whom, my soul, canst thou be justified? Hear what this sweet scripture saith: "By him, that is, by the Lord Jesus Christ, all that believe are justified from all things." Oh! how blessed is the view! how completely satisfying to the conscience, is the redemption by Christ Jesus, "whom God hath set forth as a propitiation, through faith in his blood!" And do not fail to observe the *extensiveness* of the blessing: it is *all* that believe, yea, every individual believer; for the blood of Christ cleanseth from *all* sin; and the righteousness of Christ, in a way of justification, is *to all* and *upon all* that *believe, for there is no difference.* And do not fail also to observe the *equality* of the mercy in justification; it is *to all the same.* So that though believers differ in the strength of their faith, and in the different degrees of that faith, yet respecting their interest *in* Christ, and their union *with* Christ, the weakest, as well as the strongest, is equally justified, and equally secure. And for this plain reason: because the object of faith, which is Jesus, is one and the same, and justification is *in* and *by* Christ, and doth not arise from the degree of apprehension the believer hath of it. Sweet thought to a poor timid believer! Hence the everlasting safety, both for acceptance in grace here, and the enjoyment of glory hereafter, is to all the same. And however the Lord, in his infinite wisdom, may think fit to appoint different paths for believers departures out of life; though some, like the apostles, shall be called to seal the testimony of their faith in Christ in blood, and wade through this red sea (if it may so be called) to join the multitude on the opposite shore, who are shouting the song of Moses and of the Lamb, whilst others sweetly fall asleep in Jesus on their beds, quiet and composed, amidst surrounding friends; yet, in the act of justification, all are alike. Jesus taketh the lambs of his fold in his arms, and they shall lie in his bosom, while he leads the strong. In short, all that are in union with Christ, do *live* in Christ, and shall *die* in Christ, whether they be little children, young men, or fathers; for "by him all that believe are justified from all things, from which they could not be justified by the law of Moses." See, my soul, that thou hast this faith which is of the operation of the Spirit of God, and then lie down this night, and every night, with the composure of one that is in a state of justification with God, "having peace with God, through Jesus Christ our Lord."

MAY 12.

MORNING.—"Then saith he to Thomas, reach hither thy finger, and behold my hands; and reach hither thy hand, and thrust it into my side; and be not faithless, but believing."—John xx. 27.

Was Jesus willing to have his wounds searched, than his unbelieving disciple should go unconvinced? Look, then, my soul, at Jesus, and he will grant thee a suitable testimony, to hush all thy remaining doubts, if so be after such manifestations of grace as he hath shewn thee, there be a single doubt left behind. Doth not Jesus, in effect, say, in every renewed ordinance, reach hither thy finger, thrust in thine hand, and the precious blood thou needest shall flow; for the fountain for sin, for uncleanness, for unbelief, and, in short, for every necessity of my people, is still open. Is not this the language of all? Doth unbelief doubt the reality of the thing itself, like Thomas? Doth unbelief tempt the soul to doubt the particular efficacy of it to special cases, such as a man's own? Doth unbelief suggest the circumstances hopeless from delay, from past neglect, from present unworthiness? In answer to all, Jesus speaks, "reach hither thy finger;" and if a touch will not satisfy thee, thrust thy hand deeply into my side. Here is enough to silence all fears: why are those wounds still open? Wherefore did I appear to my servant John as a lamb that had been slain, but to convince, by so palpable a testimony, that I am the same yesterday, to-day, and for ever? Oh for grace to return the grateful answer to Jesus, "my Lord, and my God!" My soul, now thou art commanded, this do. Put forth thine hand, and leave every other consequence with Jesus. While Jesus thus gives himself to thee, my soul, do thou make a complete surrender of thyself to him; for this is the very exercise of faith that Jesus is come after, and therefore let him not go away until he hath taken thine whole affections with him, as thy Lord and thy God.

EVENING.—"For I know the thoughts that I think towards you, saith the Lord; thoughts of peace, and not of evil, to give you an expected end."—Jer. xxix. 11.

My soul! thou art "looking for the mercy of thy Lord Jesus Christ unto eternal life." This is thy one object, and that one object is centered in Jesus. But in the view of this, thou art sadly put to it, at times, by thwarting providences, that seem to come between It would be a blessed help to thee, hadst thou grace always to keep in remembrance what the Lord saith in this blessed scripture: "I know the thoughts that I think towards you; thoughts of peace, and not of evil." And how truly fulfilled are these things in the redemption by Jesus! In him the foundation is laid for the accomplishment; and "He is of one mind, and who can turn him?" Be the outward appearances of things what they may, yet the Lord is everlastingly pursuing one and the same invariable plan of mercy. His providences may vary, but his grace never can. It is the deficiency of our faith, and not a defect in the covenant, which makes a believing soul to stagger, and call in question divine faithfulness. I said, saith the church, (at a time when the streams of that river which makes glad the city of God, ran low,) "I said, my strength and my hope is perished from the Lord." But how did the church correct herself soon after! "The Lord is my portion," saith she; "therefore will I hope in him." Lam. iii. 18—24. It is blessed to rest upon the Lord's own words, and to give credit to what he hath promised, when, according to all appearances of things, there seemeth an impossibility to the performance of them. This indeed is faith, and faith in her best dress and character. It is no longer faith, when the thing promised is come to pass: this is not trusting God, but receiving payment from God. But when God's thoughts towards us, find, through his grace in our hearts, corresponding thoughts towards him, of his truth and faithfulness; then, whatever happens by the way, the soul of the believer is kept in peace, because he knows that he shall have an expected end of peace, and not of evil. Oh! then for grace to be everlastingly hearing the Lord's voice in all his dispensations. See to it, my soul, that under all trials, all exercises, all difficulties, be they what they may; as there can be no trial of which Jesus hath not the appointment, no exercise but what he knows, no difficulty that can for a moment alter or interrupt his plan of salvation; Oh! learn to lean upon him, and to leave all with him, entertaining and cherishing the same good thoughts of him for ever! for he it is that saith,

"I know the thoughts that I think towards you; thoughts of peace, and not of evil, to give you an expected end."

MAY 13.

MORNING.—"And one man among them was clothed with linen, with a writer's inkhorn by his side."—Ezek. ix. 2.

Pause, my soul, over this scripture. Who could this one man be, but Jesus, thy Mediator. Did not his garment of linen mark his righteousness, and the inkhorn to write down his people, his pierced side? Hath he not written in the book of life the names of all his redeemed, that none of them may be lost when he cometh to make up his jewels? And was it not with an eye to this the soldier pierced his side when by his death he had obtained eternal redemption for them, that he might with his precious blood mark his people, as a shepherd doth his sheep? Yes, thou dear Redeemer! surely I behold thee sweetly set forth in this scripture. Surely the Holy Ghost, who all along delighted to set thee forth under various similitudes before the old church, hath graciously represented thee here. Methinks I behold thee now coming forth in the white garment of thy spotless righteousness, with thy pierced side, to mark all thine, before the destroying angels go forth to the everlasting destruction of unawakened, unregenerated sinners. Methinks I hear thy blessed, gracious, compassionate voice, in the same tender tone of words as thou once didst utter to thy servant John: "Him that overcometh will I make a pillar in the temple of my God, and he shall go no more out. And I will write upon him the name of my God, and the name of the city of my God: and I will write upon him my new name." Oh Lamb of God, fulfil these blessed promises in my soul! Mark me as thine, unto the day of redemption. Seal me as a signet in thine image, and give me that new name which no man knoweth saving he that receiveth it. Then, amidst burning worlds, my soul will stand secure, being justified in thy righteousness, and sprinkled with thy blood; and I shall hear, with holy joy, that glorious, but awful voice, " come not near any man upon whom is the mark."

EVENING.—" I sat down under his shadow with great delight, and his fruit was sweet to my taste."—Song ii. 3.

My soul! hear what the church saith concerning her Lord, in those early and distant ages, before thy Redeemer became incarnate, and mark the strength of her faith and love. Did old testament saints thus sit down with a recumbency on the person, work, and finished salvation of Jesus, as those determined to arise no more, when they beheld Christ only through " the shadow of good things to come;" and shall not thy rest in Christ, and thy enjoyment of Christ, be equal, and even greater than their's? For shame, my soul! let it never be said, that their views of Jesus, who was then yet to come, and had all the vast work of redemption to perform, were as lively as thine, or their delight in those fruits of his salvation, which they partook of by anticipation, sweeter to their taste, than they are now enjoyed by thee. Thou hast lived to see the whole completed, and canst, and dost look up, and behold thy Jesus returned to glory, having " finished transgression, made an end of sin," and now for ever seated at the right hand of God. Oh, thou dear Redeemer! give me to sit down under the sweet revelations of thy word, and in the gospel ordinances of thy church, and here by faith realize and substantiate all the blessings contained in the glories of thy person, the infinite and eternal merit and worth of thy righteousness, blood, and salvation; and have my whole soul, and body, and spirit, continually feasted with the rich fellowship and communion which there is to be enjoyed with the Father, and with his Son Jesus Christ! And surely, Lord, thou art all, and infinitely more than is here said of thee by the church. Thou art a shade for protection from every thing which can assault a poor weather-beaten soul, harassed by sin, by sorrow, and temptation. Well might the prophet describe thee as "the man that is as an hiding-place from the wind, and a covert from the tempest; as rivers of water in a dry place, and as the shadow of a great rock in a weary land;" Isa. xxxii. 2. I find thee necessary as an hiding-place to shelter me from the wrath to come. I have sinned, and am justly exposed to the wrath of God. I find the accusations of conscience, the arrests of God's law, the temptations of Satan, the alarms of justice; and, under all these, what but thy blood and righteousness can screen my poor soul, or make me secure in an hour of visitation? But, sheltered by thee, and justified by thy great salvation, I find every thing I need, to protect and secure me from the storm, "when the blast of the terrible ones is as a storm against the wall." But, my soul, this sweet scripture doth not only set before thee thy God and Saviour as a shadow to sit under for protection, but as affording fruit also, to refresh thee in thy want of sustenance. Like some rich, luxuriant, and generous tree, which not only shelters the traveller from the scorching heat, but holds forth on its branches delicious fruit to regale and satisfy for food; so Jesus, by his person, work, and righteousness, protects his people from all evil; and by the fruits of his blood and redemption, supplies them with all good. Yes! blessed, bountiful Lord, thou art here again all these, and infinitely more; for the fruits of thy life, death, resurrection, ascension, and glory, give to thy redeemed, mercy, pardon, and peace, with all the fulness of covenant blessings in this life, and everlasting happiness in the life to come. O Lord! grant me then, day by day, and from night to morn, to sit down under thy shadow, that I may "revive as the corn, and grow as the vine." Yea, Lord, I would so sit down, as one that had determined to rise no more; and having found thee, and in thee all I need to bid adieu to all the world holds dear; and, like Paul, "count all things else but dung and dross, that I might win Christ, and be found in thee, the Lord my righteousness."

MAY 14.

MORNING.—"If we live in the Spirit, let us also walk in the Spirit."—Gal. v. 25.

My soul, take this sweet scripture for thy motto, not only this day, but every day; for every day's walk should be the same with Jesus, by the Spirit. And surely, my soul, if Jesus really, truly, dwells in thee, he will manifest that he is at home, by ruling in thee. It is blessed, and gracious, and edifying, when out of the abundance of the heart the mouth speaketh, and like the spouse, the lips drop as the honey-comb, sweetly of Jesus. But the life of Jesus in the soul, consisteth not in talking only of Jesus, but walking *in* him, and walking *with* him. But, my soul, how wilt thou accomplish these things, carrying about with thee as thou dost daily, a body of sin and death? There is but one plan, and that a simple plan, mortifying, indeed, to the pride of human nature, but giving glory to Jesus. Art thou truly content to be mortified, so that Jesus be glorified? If so, this is the only way the apostle hath marked. They, and they only that live in the Spirit, will walk in the Spirit. The same grace which teacheth thee *of* Jesus, must give to thee power *in* Jesus. As long as Jesus is in view, looked to, and lived upon, all the blessed effects of the grace from Jesus will follow, as sure as the rays of light diffuse their brightness when the sun is risen. If, my soul, thou goest forth in a firm dependance upon Jesus's strength, that strength will be assuredly perfected in thy weakness; but if Jesus be lost sight of, and a fancied strength in thyself supply the place, this defect in faith will bring forth a defect in practice. My soul, learn to exercise an holy jealousy over thyself; for after Jesus is once truly known, all thy danger begins at this place; so that the great secret is, to live out of self, upon his fulness; to do nothing but in his strength; to propose nothing but for his glory; and in every step you take in the whole walk of life, to make Jesus every thing, and depend upon him in every thing; and this is the way to find both security and comfort. Dear Lord, do thou enable a poor worm thus to live, by living in thee; and then, sure I am I shall be happy, by walking in thee.

EVENING.—" He turned their heart to hate his people."—Psalm cv. 25.

Oh! precious scripture! what a blessed discovery is here made! Never should I have known, never thought that the hand of my God was in a dispensation like this. Henceforth, my soul, remember, when at any time the world is oppressing thee, and opposing thee, yea, when even "thy mother's children are angry with thee;" look deeper than the surface, and behold both the Lord's wisdom, and the Lord's appointment in the exercise. And dost thou ask wherefore the Lord should dispose the heart of the believer's foes to hate his people? the answer is at hand: it is to keep his people from "mingling with the heathen, and learning their works." Nature cleaves to nature; and the dispositions of flesh and blood are in all the same. If God, therefore, turn the hearts of those we are too fond of, to treat us with unkindness, and reward our love with hatred, this process will do more to separate the precious from the vile, than all the Lord's precepts; yea, even more than a sense of our own danger. How much disposed art thou, my soul, to seek the favour of the world! how frequently dost thou study to conciliate the affections of those who differ from thee in the great truths of God. Jesus, who knows this, beholds it, and will not suffer it to be. He graciously causeth some secret sorrow to spring out of this root. The heart we wish to be particularly friendly, is led to manifest unprovoked unkindness; and where we are looking for most pleasure, there we find most pain. And in all this, Jesus's love and wisdom are at the foundation. No dispensation would answer the purpose to correct our wayward choice but this; and it is blessed to see how the Lord accomplisheth the secret purposes of his will, by means so opposite to our calculation. Mark down this sweet scripture for the special purpose of improvement, under exercises like these. And when at any time the false reproaches of one, or the unprovoked anger of another, in the carnal world, make thee sad, recognize the hand of Jesus in the dispensation, and read this blessed passage in proof; "He turned their heart to hate his people."

MAY 15.

MORNING.—"Thou shalt also be a crown of glory in the hand of the Lord, and a royal diadem in the hand of thy God."—Isa. lxii. 3.

It is very easy to conceive how the Lord of Hosts in the day of salvation becomes for a crown of glory and for a diadem of beauty unto his people, as a prophet hath said, Isa. xxviii. 5. But that the church, and every individual redeemed of the church, shall be the Lord's crown and diadem. Oh, the wonders of grace! Pause, my soul, over the sweet scripture, and take to thyself the blessedness of it. What a variety of images and similitudes thy God hath made use of to manifest how highly he prizeth his redeemed. "Yea, he loveth the people," said one of old; "all his saints are in thy hand." He calleth them jewels, precious stones, his treasure, his chosen, his inheritance, his portion, his crown, his diadem. And what a thought is it for thee, my soul, to meditate upon, that though in thyself thou art nothing, yet considered in Jesus, thou art all this, and more; polished, made comely and glorious, from the comeliness put upon thee and the glory of Jesus. See then, my soul, the vast mercy in Jesus. A worthless worm made dear to God! How infinitely precious and dear should God in Christ be to thee. Let this encourage thee, then, at all times to come to him. Thou art giving glory to thy God, when thou comest to him, to give out of his fulness to thee. Jesus wanteth needy creatures to be glorified upon, by giving out of his abundance to their necessities; and the more he gives, the more is he glorified. Mark that also, for thy greater encouragement to come to him. The more thou art blessed in his fulness, the more blessed he is in imparting it; so that while thou art his crown of glory, he is glorified in thy redemption. And while thou crownest Jesus's head, in ascribing all the glory of thy salvation unto him, he condescends to make thee a crown of glory in his hand, as a token that thou art his, both by purchase of his blood, the gift of his Father, and the conquest of his grace. Hallelujah.

EVENING.—"An Israelite indeed, in whom is no guile."—John i. 47.

And what are we to understand by our Lord's account, in this short but sweet history of Nathaniel, of an "Israelite indeed, in whom is no guile?" If, my soul, thou wilt do as thou art directed, (1 Cor. ii. 13.) attend "to the words which the Holy Ghost teacheth, comparing spiritual things with spiritual," thou wilt soon arrive at a proper apprehension of the Lord's account, of "an Israelite indeed, in whom is no guile." It is our mercy that, on a point of so much consequence, we are not left to mere conjecture; for the Holy Ghost hath himself pointed out what it is to be without guile, in one of the Psalms of David. (See Psalm xxxii.) And in his comment upon it by the apostle, (Romans iv. 6—12.) he hath followed up the same doctrine more fully; "Blessed (saith he) is he whose transgression is forgiven, whose sin is covered. Blessed is the man unto whom the Lord imputeth not iniquity, and in whose spirit there is no guile." Now here observe, that the blessedness here spoken of, is not said to be a man that *hath no sin*, neither *had* sin, but to whom the Lord *imputeth it not*. And wherefore is this blessedness? It is explained: because "his transgression is forgiven, and his sin covered." And the Holy Ghost is pleased, by his servant the apostle, to give a farther explanation, by tracing it to its source, in the forgiveness of sins "by Jesus Christ." And in the case of Abraham, the great father of the faithful, he most clearly and fully proves the truth of this momentous doctrine: "Cometh this blessedness then (saith he) upon the circumcision only, or upon the uncircumcision also? For we say that faith was reckoned to Abraham. How was it then reckoned? When he was in circumcision, or in uncircumcision? Not in circumcision; but in uncircumcision. And he received the sign of circumcision, a seal of the righteousness of the faith which he had, yet being uncircumcised." Now hence, my soul, thou mayest learn what it is to have "no guile," and, by consequence thereof, to be an "Israelite indeed." If thou wilt consult Abraham's history, thou wilt discover that he was justified by faith: "he believed in the Lord, and it was counted to him for righteousness;" and this was many a year before he was circumcised; see Genesis xv. 6. Some have reckoned it full *twenty years;* very certain it is, that it could not be less than *ten years;* see Gen. xvii. And from the moment of his justification by faith, Abraham might truly be said to be one "in whom was no guile." Apply what is here said by the Holy Ghost of Abraham, to the instance of Nathaniel, and of all the spiritual seed of Christ, and the conclusion will be the same: this it is to be "an Israelite indeed, in whom is no guile!" My soul! what sayest thou of thyself? Art thou "an Israelite indeed?" Is thy guilt taken away by the blood of Christ? Pause; and recollect what the scripture saith: "For he is not a Jew which is one outwardly; neither is that circumcision, which is outward in the flesh. But he is a Jew which is one inwardly; and circumcision is that of the heart, in the spirit, and not in the letter, whose praise is not of men, but of God," Rom. ii. 28, 29. "And if ye be Christ's, then are ye Abraham's seed, and heirs according to the promise." Gal. iii. 29.

MAY 16.

MORNING.—"And he that had been possessed with the devil, prayed him that he might be with him. Howbeit, Jesus suffered him not; but saith unto him, Go home to thy friends, and tell them how great things the Lord hath done for thee."—Mark v. 18, 19.

Mark this, my soul, and especially when at any time thy Jesus is so graciously revealing himself to thee, in a way of love, that thou art longing to be absent from the body, that thou mayest be "present with the Lord:" think then, of what Jesus said to this poor man. The thought of being made instrumental in the hand of the Lord in calling sinners to Jesus, made holy Paul willing to wait in a sinful world, and put off his own happiness. Precious frame of mind! Paul knew also, that if the Lord housed his children from the lion's den, and from the mountains of leopards, as soon as he had brought them to the knowledge of himself, then, in this case, Jesus would have no church in the wilderness. The holy seed would not be found amidst the tares of the earth. Blessed Lord! give grace to every exercised child of thine to think of this; that when, under the various trials with which thy wisdom and love see fit to try their graces, they long to be home with thee, and are sending forth the cry of the soul for dismission, they may hear thy voice speaking, as to this poor man, "Go home to thy friends, and tell them how great things the Lord hath done for thee." But pause, my soul—is this thy case? Hath Jesus done great things for thee, and art thou proclaiming it abroad to call others to partake? Suppose one from the throng was to ask thee, "What is thy Beloved, more than another beloved?" what would be thy answer? Wouldest thou say, how he hath blest thee in health, or wealth, or worldly success, or prosperity; in friends, and relations, and the like? And are these all the things, or the chief of them, that thou couldest speak of? If so, what are these more than carnal men can, and do speak of? The infidel, the Turk, the pagan, can boast as much! But if thou canst say, 'Oh! "come hither and hearken, all ye that fear God, and I will tell you what he hath done for my soul!" I was once darkness, and am now light in the Lord. I was once in Satan's chains, and Jesus hath set me free. I was once, like this poor man, under the possession of sin and Satan; but now I sit down at the feet of Jesus, to hear the gracious words which proceed out of his mouth.' Here, my soul, this is indeed to tell thy friends how great things the Lord hath done for thee. Oh! for grace thus to proclaim his adorable name while on earth, until Jesus comes to take me home to himself, there to sound his praise before the whole redeemed church of God for ever!

EVENING.—"So will I go unto the king, which is not according to the law; and if I perish, I perish."—Esther iv. 16.

What a noble act of the soul is faith! Who, indeed, but the Lord Jesus, can be the author or giver of it? Ponder it well, my soul, and see if thou canst discover the smallest possible degree of it in thee. To have the least portion of it is an evidence of an interest in Christ; for it is said, that "as many as were ordained to eternal life believed," Acts xiii. 48. And Oh! what an honour is it to give credit to God the Father's testimony of his dear Son!—Sit down, my soul, this evening, and pause over the subject. There are more difficulties to the exercise of it than are generally considered. The case of Esther, in the court of the Persian king, will serve, in some measure, to explain it. By the law of Persia, every individual, whether man or woman, who ventured into the inner court of the king's presence uncalled, was condemned to death; neither was there any remission of the punishment, unless the king held out to the offender the golden sceptre. The case, however, for which Esther was constrained to go in, was of that nature, that there remained no alternative, but to go or die. Contrary to the known law of the realm, she therefore ventured, crying out as she went, "If I perish, I perish." Now this is quite the state of the poor sinner. The law of God for ever separates between a holy God and an unholy sinner. "Thou canst not see my face and live." Nothing that is "unholy, can stand in God's sight." These are the solemn declarations of the law of heaven. God hath indeed reserved the grace of pardon, to whom he will hold out the golden sceptre. But even this grace doth not reign but through righteousness. The law admits of nothing by way of pardon, but upon the ground of satisfaction. A righteousness every sinner must have in himself, or in a Redeemer, or he will perish everlastingly. Hast thou then, my soul, that faith, that trust, that sure dependence, upon the Lord Jesus Christ, as to go in unto the King, which is not according to law, but wholly on the blessed authority of the gospel, determined, like Esther, to be saved by this grace of thy King and Saviour, or not at all? Yes, Lord! I come. Precious Emanuel! wilt thou not hold forth the golden sceptre of thy grace, and say to my soul, as thou didst to the poor woman in the gospel, "Great is thy faith, be it unto thee even as thou wilt?"

MAY 17.

MORNING.—"I am poor and needy, yet the Lord thinketh upon me."—Psalm xl. 17.

Precious consideration, my soul! Under all thine exercises, the Lord, thy Lord, thy Jesus, thinketh upon thee. Wherefore should I faint, then, under any burden? Surely I may say, as Hagar did at the well, "Thou, God, seest me." Surely I may give my God, my Saviour, this name, as she did; for she said, "Have I also here looked after him that seeth me?" Yes, however unconscious my poor heart is of the blessed truth, yet a very blessed truth it is, while I am looking after Jesus, he is beforehand, thinking and looking upon me. Precious Lamb of God! I will remember my poverty no more: that is, I will remember it no more, but as it is made the means in thy hand to make me sensible of my need and thy fulness. Art thou thinking upon me? Do I hear thy gracious voice, saying to me, "I know the thoughts that I think towards you, saith the Lord, thoughts of peace, and not of evil, to give you an expected end?" Oh then, herein I will rejoice! Poor and needy as I am, let me be more poor, more needy, so but I see my fulness in Jesus. He is thinking of me, providing for me, blessing me. I would not be full for the world, or fancy myself so; for what room should I then have for Jesus? What it will be in heaven, I know not, in the fulness of happiness that is there, though that fulness can only be in and from Jesus; but here below, a full state, or a supposed full state, would be a wretched state. No, let me be poor and needy, empty and in want, wretched and helpless in myself; for then I am sure my Jesus will be most precious. Mark it down, then, my soul, this day, and wear it about thine heart as a pleasing consideration—when thou feelest thy need and poverty most, the Lord thy Jesus thinketh upon thee.

EVENING.—"Matthew the publican."—Matt. x. 3.

It ought not to be overlooked, in the account of this apostle of Jesus, that in the list given by the other evangelists, of our Lord's disciples, he is placed before Thomas; but in this, of his own, he places Thomas first. And whereas, after his call to the apostleship, the brethren, in making mention of him dropped his former occupation of a *publican*, yet Matthew himself still preserves it. Grace always humbles. The call of this man, the distinguishing nature of that grace, the effects, and blessedness of it, open some sweet thoughts for meditation, which, under divine teaching, cannot fail of being profitable to the saint, and encouraging to the sinner: and it will be well, my soul, for thee to exercise thine evening devotion upon it. He was a *publican;* that is, a tax-gatherer for the Romans. Of such characters we cannot have a more lively idea, than from what our Lord himself said of them. For when Jesus, in his description of a sinner more than ordinarily to be avoided, sets him forth as such, he said, "Let him be to thee as an heathen man and a publican." Such was Matthew when called. And where was he when called? Not in the synagogue, attending the means of grace, or desiring to seek the Lord; but when seeking him not, yea, sitting at the seat of custom, and fully engaged in his pursuit of worldly gain. Pause, my soul, and mark the property of grace! Surely in this man's instance, as well as in thousands of others, the Lord might say, "I am found of them that sought me not!" And Oh! what a surprising, unexpected, unlooked for call, was that of the Lord Jesus to Matthew! What a powerful, gracious, saving, and effectual call was it! Precious Redeemer! are we not authorized to consider all these, and other similar points of view, as purposely intended to tell poor sinners, like Matthew, that thy grace is not the effect of our merit, nor the result of any man's worth? Surely, Lord, every poor sinner may from this learn, that whatever best tends to magnify the riches of thy grace, must be in the purposes of thy holy will and pleasure. Hence it is, that thou makest thy grace to shine on such lost, ruined, and undone sinners as we are. But, my soul, take another short view of this man, and thy Saviour's grace towards him. When the Lord had called him by his grace, he invited the Lord to his home: no sooner did Jesus open Matthew's heart, than Matthew opened his house to receive Jesus. See to it, my soul, that thou art daily manifesting the same proofs of *thy* calling. Oh! for grace to take Jesus home to our hearts, to our houses, to our neighbours, to our families, children, and servants, if we have any, and spread forth the sweet savour of his name, and the efficacy of his blood and righteousness, in every direction. Like the Psalmist, let our language be, "O come hither, and hearken, all ye that fear God: and I will tell you what he hath done for my soul!"

MAY 18.

MORNING.—" The flower of the field."—Ps. ciii. 15.

Do I not behold Jesus here pre-eminently set forth above his fellows? Yes, dear Lord, thy people, planted by thy hand, do indeed flourish as a flower of the field; but never any like thee. Indeed all their loveliness, fragrancy, value, all are only so, as derived from thee. Never did God our Father plant so lovely a flower, so sweet, so fragrant a flower in the field of his garden, in the heavenly paradise, or the earthly Eden, as when he planted thee. Sweet plant of renown! aid my meditations this morning to contemplate thee under this interesting view, as the flower of the field. And first, let me behold thee as truly the flower of the field, because thou art altogether of God's right hand planting, and not of man's. The flower of the field hath no father but God, and no mother but the virgin earth. Precious Jesus! thou wert conceived in thy human nature wholly by the overshadowing of God the Spirit, when thou condescendest, for our salvation, to be born of the virgin's womb. And let me look at thee, Oh Lord, under another beautiful illustration of thy nature, as the flower of the field, when I consider the humbleness and lowliness in which thou didst appear. Was there ever a sweet flower of the field more hid, more obscured, and when brought forward to view, less regarded, than Jesus, of whom it was truly said, "He was despised and rejected of men; without form or comeliness, and having no beauty that we should desire him?" And is there not another thought which ariseth to the mind in the contemplation of Jesus as the flower of the field? Yes, methinks I behold in the exposure of the flower of the field to the merciless treading of the foot of the passenger, and to the plucking up or destroying by wild beasts, a striking representation of Jesus, who, in the days of his flesh, was encompassed by beasts of prey, and trodden down of men. Alas, how many even now in the present hour despise thy person, live regardless of thy righteousness, have trodden under foot the Son of God, and count the blood of the covenant an unholy thing. But, precious Jesus! give me to behold thee as the sweet flower of the field, open to the view of every traveller, and shedding the richness of thy fragrancy, under all the influences of thy Spirit, both in the north wind, and the south wind of thy power. Ye travellers to Zion, come, see this lovely flower in the open field of his word, his church, his ordinances. Behold the freeness of his bloom, his beauty, and odour. He sheds his influences, not in a garden enclosed that ye cannot approach, but in the open field. Here he stands, as the plant of renown, which God hath raised up. Oh come to him as the balm of Gilead, and the Physician there, that the hurt of the daughter of his people may be healed.

EVENING.—" But I fear, lest by any means, as the serpent beguiled Eve through his subtilty, so your minds should be corrupted from the simplicity that is in Christ."—2 Cor. xi. 3.

And what is " the simplicity that is in Christ?" The apostle answers this question in another part of his writings, when he saith, " Christ is all, and in all." Now nothing can be more simple than this: " Christ is all;" then it would be equal folly to seek for happiness in any thing but in Christ. And " Christ is in all;" then it would be equal folly to seek for happiness in any thing but in Christ. So that if our minds are led away to seek a supply from any thing short of Christ, this is the same temptation that the devil played off upon our first parent, and succeeded. This indeed is the grand device of Satan: it is the master-piece of his subtilty. This is what all carnal unawakened men fall into: to fancy somewhat that is left for us to do, to qualify ourselves to be made partakers of grace, and to improve the talent which is given to us. And as these things are very flattering to the pride of our nature, and exactly correspond to the state the devil left our first parents in, when he had ruined them, so it becomes the very method which he still pursues with all their poor children, to lull them on to ruin. " Ye shall be as gods (said the devil to our first mother) knowing good and evil;" and, in like manner, thus flattering the pride of our nature, and shutting out Christ, with his blood and righteousness, does he deceive men now. Now Paul was alarmed and distressed on this account. The serpent beguiled Eve through his subtilty, saith Paul, and I fear lest he should beguile you.—How blessed, then, is the teaching of the Holy Ghost, which strips the sinner, makes him all bare, leaves him nothing, but shews him his whole insolvency, emptiness, and poverty, that he may make room for Jesus! And when he hath thus made the sinner sensible of his nothingness, he makes him equally sensible of Christ's fulness and all sufficiency; and that in bringing nothing *to* Christ, but living wholly *upon* Christ, and drawing all *from* Christ; in this simplicity that is *in* Christ, he teacheth the poor sinner how to live, and how to keep house by faith, wholly upon the fulness that is in Christ Jesus. This is the sweet instruction taught in the school of Jesus. "I fear, (saith Paul) lest the serpent that beguiled Eve, should have corrupted you by his subtilty from this simplicity that is in Christ."

MAY 19.

MORNING.—"Is this thy kindness to thy friend?"—2 Sam. xvi. 17.

My soul, borrow the words of Absalom to Hushai, and make application of them this morning to thyself, as if Jesus, the best of all friends, were thus reasoning with thee. In how many ways hath Jesus manifested his love to thee. Think of his unparalleled love in the various ways by which he hath shewn it. He engaged as thy Surety before that thou knewest any need of one. He took thy nature to fulfil all those engagements. He loved thee so as to die for thee. He loved thee so as to shed his blood for thee. He loved thee so as to wash thee from thy sins in his blood. He loveth thee now, so as to appear in the presence of God for thee. He loveth thee so as to be continually supplying thee with all grace, to visit thee, to smile upon thee, to sanctify to thee all his appointments for thy good; and will never give over until he hath brought thee where he is, to behold his glory, and to partake of it. And hast thou not recompensed this love, this mercy, in a thousand, and ten thousand instances, with ingratitude, with indifference, with forgetfulness, with disobedience? "Is this thy kindness to thy friend?" Precious Jesus!

I do remember my faults this day. Oh gracious Lord! grant me from henceforth to live wholly to thee; to be continually eyeing thee, walking with thee, cleaving to thee, hanging upon thee, and to remember thee and thy love more than wine. Yes, thou dearest Redeemer! I would pray for grace to set thee always before me, to record in my heart thy mercies, and to set up in my heart thy person, to follow thee whithersoever thou goest, to watch the steps of Jesus, to pursue thee in all the haunts of thy paths, at thy table, at thine ordinances, in thy word, in thine house of prayer, in thy providences, in thy promises: every where, and in all things, where Jesus is, there may my soul be; that, having nothing to give my Lord to recompense his bounty, I may at least by his grace follow him, to bless him, and to manifest that all I am, and all I have, is his. My soul, see to it, that this is at least thy kindness to thy friend.

EVENING.—"And the Lord said, I have pardoned according to thy word. But as truly as I live, all the earth shall be filled with the glory of the Lord."—Numb. xiv. 20, 21.

My soul! ponder over this solemn scripture, and observe how truly awful Jehovah is, even in his mercies. Well may it be said to the people of God, "rejoice with trembling." This was a memorable moment in the history of Israel, when the spies returned from searching the promised land. The evil report which the greater number brought back, in denying God's faithfulness, is most solemnly recorded; and the falling carcases in the wilderness, most awfully set forth the divine judgment. And what is unbelief now but the same, aggravated, if possible, to a ten thousand times greater degree of guilt, in denying and disbelieving the record which God hath given of his Son? The apostle saith, "it is making God a liar," 1 John v. 10. and John the Baptist confirms the same; and adds a dreadful event, which must inevitably follow: "He that believeth not, shall not see life; but the wrath of God abideth upon him," John iii. 36. And do observe, my soul, how Jehovah engageth to manifest and fulfil his glory. He confirms it with the most solemn asseveration: "As truly as I live, saith the Lord, all the earth shall be filled with the glory of the Lord." And what is the glory of the Lord, but God manifested in the person of the Lord Jesus Christ? Here all the glory of Jehovah centers. In Jesus all is proclaimed; and in the dispensation of the fulness of times, the one great object of all things in the kingdom of nature, providence, grace, and glory, is "to gather together in one all things in Christ." What sayest thou, my soul, to these things? Art thou now gathered to Christ, to whom, as to the glorious Shiloh, the gathering of the people shall be? Is he that is the Father's glory, thy glory: is the Father's beloved, thy beloved; the Father's chosen, thy chosen? Surely, if so, it must undeniably follow, that God is already glorified in thy view, and in thine heart; if the glory of the Lord Jehovah, which is to fill the earth, hath, in the person of his dear Son filled thy soul and affections, and is formed in thine heart "the hope of glory." Oh! for increasing evidences of this love of God, and glory of the Lord, to be shed abroad in my heart, "to give me the light and knowledge of God in the face of Jesus Christ!"

MAY 20.

MORNING.—"Length of days is in her right hand, and in her left hand riches and honour."—Prov. iii. 16.

What is sweetly said of Jesus in one scripture, as the Glory-wisdom, is as sweetly sung in another scripture, as the husband of his church and people. Yes, Lord, thy right-hand blessings may well be called length of days, for they are life itself, even life everlasting in thee: and thy left-hand mercies, which include all temporal good, may well merit the name of riches and honour, for thou givest to all that love thee to inherit substance, and thou fillest all their treasures. There is no substance in any, nothing satisfying, nothing substantial, where thou art not. Why then, blessed Jesus, if these things be so, I would say to thee, as the church of old did, " Put thy left hand under my head, and let thy right hand embrace me." This will make every thing sweet, and every thing precious. Even thy left-hand blessings, in the sanctified use of afflictions, sorrow, bereaving providences, sickness, and the like, even these, being Jesus's appointments, will bring with them Jesus's blessing; and while thine hand is under my head, how shall these, or aught else, separate me from thee? And concerning thy right-hand blessings, in the pardon of my sins, washing me in thy blood, clothing me with thy righteousness, justifying me with thy salvation, feeding me, sustaining me, leading me, comforting me, bringing me on, and bringing me through, and by and by bringing me home to glory; that, where thou art, there I shall be also. Oh, precious Jesus, grant me in this sweet sense to know thee, and to enjoy thee, in every thing; for sure I am, that " riches and honour are with thee, yea, durable riches and righteousness."

EVENING.—" But he who was of the bond-woman, was born after the flesh; but he of the free-woman was by promise; which things are an allegory."—Gal. iv. 23, 24.

My soul! as thou readest this scripture, do not forget to bless the great Author of it, even God the Holy Ghost, for having condescended to teach the church the sacred truths contained in it. Never would it have entered into the heart of man, untaught of God, to have conceived that the births of Ishmael and Isaac had such divine purposes connected with their history. We might have read for ever the account given of it in the book of Genesis, without once forming a thought of the spiritual tendency of the subject, had not the Holy

Ghost, by his servant the apostle, told the church that it was an allegory. But, blessed with such gracious teaching, see to it, my soul, this evening, what a delightful subject it leads to. "These (saith the apostle) are the two covenants;" meaning the mother of Ishmael, and the mother of Isaac. The "bond-woman," represents the covenant of works; and the "free-woman," the covenant of grace. So that all who seek justification by their own good deeds of the law, are of the children of the *bond-woman.* All who are looking for salvation by the Lord Jesus Christ, without the works of the law, are of the children of the *free.* As the son of the bond-woman was born before the son of the free, so our state of nature in this sense, is before grace. And hence believers, when renewed, are said to be born again. Yet, as the promise concerning the son of the free-woman, was before the birth of the son of the bond-woman, so the promise of the gospel was before the law; and the covenant of grace came in before the covenant of works. And as the son of the bond-woman mocked the son of the free, so is it now; they that are born after the flesh do for ever persecute them that are born after the Spirit. Nevertheless, what saith the scripture?—"Cast out the bond-woman and her son; for the son of the bond-woman shall not be heir with the son of the free-woman." The law can make nothing perfect; justification can never be obtained by the deeds of the law, and therefore it is rejected. Pause now, my soul, over this sweet allegory, explained as it is by the Holy Ghost himself, and ask to which family thou belongest? To both thou canst not, for that is impossible. Whosoever seeketh justification by the deeds of the law, denies the merit and efficacy of Christ's blood and righteousness. "For if righteousness come by the law, then is Christ dead in vain." Oh! for grace to discover, and faith to enjoy, the same blessed assurance as the apostle did, when summing up the whole conclusion of this scriptural allegory; "So then, brethren, we are not children of the bond-woman, but of the free."

MAY 21.

MORNING.—"He found him in a desert land, and in the waste howling wilderness."—Deut. xxxii. 10.

My soul, behold in this view of Israel thy case and circumstances. Where did Jesus find thee, when he passed by and bade thee live, but cast out, loathsome in thy person, and perishing in nature? Remember then, it was Jesus found thee, and not thou him. And where wast thou born, and new-born, and nursed, and educated, and trained? Was it not in a desert land, and in the waste howling wilderness? Can any thing be better suited to represent thy state by nature? Is not the heart of man like the heath upon the desert, that knoweth not when good cometh? Is it not like the ground, dry, parched, and barren? And as a wilderness is a land not inhabited, full of perplexed paths and intricate ways, without food, without sustenance, and no springs of water; can any thing more strikingly resemble the whole of thy spiritual circumstances, when Jesus called thee from darkness to light, and from the power of sin and Satan, to himself, the living God? And as a wilderness is a barren state, so is it dangerous also, by reason of the prowling beasts of prey which inhabit it. And hath Jesus called thee out of it, brought thee to a city of habitation, and made himself known unto thee as thy Redeemer? Oh how sweet is it to trace all our spiritual circumstances, in the mercy, grace, and favour Jesus manifested to Israel, thus beautifully illustrated and explained, and to see, and know, and truly rejoice in our unspeakable mercies in Jesus. My soul, never forget then that it was in the wilderness of nature Jesus found thee. And hath he indeed brought thee out of it? See then that thou art now coming up from it, leaning upon thy beloved; hanging wholly upon him, cleaving wholly to him, and determining for thyself, in every remaining period of time, and to all eternity, to make Jesus thy all, thy life, thy portion, thy shield, and thine exceeding great reward!"

EVENING.—" The golden censer."—Heb. ix. 4.

It is blessed, my soul! to behold the numberless types and shadows of " good things to come," which the church of old contained; and it is blessed to see them all fulfilled in Christ, the substance. Jesus, thy Jesus, in his glorious high priestly office, is at once the censer, the incense, the high priest, and offering, and is now unceasingly engaged in carrying on the glorious purposes of his redemption " by appearing in the presence of God for us." He is the " mighty angel" spoken of, Rev. viii. 3. For upon the " golden censer" of his own merit and righteousness, and by the efficacy of his own glorious person, are all presentations made. " No man cometh to the Father but by him." But coming *by* him, and *in* him, and *through* him, all thy poor offerings come up " for a memorial before God." And what is the much incense here spoken of, but the merits of that finished salvation of the Lord Jesus Christ, which hath indeed a fulness, yea, a redundancy of fulness, infinitely more precious and costly than ever can be compensated in blessings bestowed thereby upon his people, in time, and to all eternity. This was beautifully represented in the Jewish church. The incense was composed of sweet spices, which made a fragrant smell through the whole temple. And what was the offering of Christ, but " an offering and sacrifice to God, for a sweet-smelling savour?" And if the incense in the Jewish temple was always burning, what was this but a representation of the everlasting priesthood of Christ, " who ever liveth to make intercession for his people?" And as the incense was burning *within* in the temple, while all the people were at prayers *without*, what a lively representation was this of our High Priest in heaven, in this great office of a priest upon his throne, to offer upon the golden altar of his divine nature, the prayers of his redeemed upon earth, to give acceptance to their persons and their offerings, by the much incense of his own merits and blood? My soul, look up this evening, look up both night and morning, and, with the eye of faith, behold this almighty Angel of the new covenant thus appearing in the presence of God for thee; into his almighty hands do thou commit and commend thine all; neither thy person nor thy poor offerings can find acceptance but in him, the beloved. He is thine altar, thy priest, thy sacrifice, thine incense, thine all; by virtue of whom, God the Father hath respect to his everlasting covenant, and dispenseth grace in this life, and glory in that which is to come. Hail! thou glorious, gracious, great High Priest of a better covenant, founded upon better promises than that by Aaron! Oh! for faith to apprehend thee, to exercise faith upon thy person, work, and righteousness, and every day, and all the day, both night and morning, to come to God by thee, perfectly assured that all that do come, thou wilt in no wise cast out.

MAY 22.

MORNING.—"Thy daughter is dead; trouble not the Master."—Luke viii. 49.

Mark, my soul, in the exercises of the father of this child, and in the happy issue of his application to Jesus how very precious it is, to wait the Lord's time for deliverance, and always to keep in view that delays are not denials. The poor man's child was nearly dead when he first came to Christ. And had the greatest dispatch been used, there would have been still much occasion for the exercise of faith and patience. But as if this was not enough, another poor sufferer comes in the way to stop the progress of Jesus in the cure of his daughter, and during this loss of time his child dies. My soul, here is a sweet subject for thee. Do thy fears, and unbelief, and doubts, and misgivings, aided by the suggestions of the enemy, too often prompt thee to think thy case hopeless; and every thing joins the cry, "thy daughter is dead, trouble not the Master?" Oh think what a precious opportunity all these afford thee to follow up the patriarch's faith, and against hope to believe in hope. What cannot Jesus accomplish? Though the daughter be dead; though Lazarus be four days in the grave; yet Jesus, who is the resurrection and the life, need only speak the word, and both live. In like manner, when exercises arise to the greatest height, until unbelief suggests all is over; dead frames, a dead heart, deadness to all; then is the very time to believe, in order to see the glory of God. Strickly and properly speaking, Jesus cannot be glorified until the stream of all other resources is dried up. Mark it then, my soul, thy time to trust Jesus is, when nothing in nature, but wholly grace, must trust him. And depend upon it, the greater the difficulty for the keeping faith alive, the greater glory will you give to Jesus in the exercise of it, and the greater glory that blessed Saviour will receive from you in supplying that faith during the dead hour, until the deliverance comes. Hear Jesus's voice in thy instance, be it what it may, as in the case of this distressed father, for the issue will be the same. "Fear not; believe only, and thou shalt live."

EVENING.—"And I will bring the blind by a way that they knew not; I will lead them in paths that they have not known: I will make darkness light before them, and crooked things straight. These things will I do unto them, and not forsake them."—Isa. xlii. 16.

Never, surely, was there a promise of a covenant

God in Christ more strikingly fulfilled as to what is said in the former part of this verse, than in thine instance, my soul. By nature and by practice, thou wert so totally blind to any apprehension of divine things, that not a right thought hadst thou ever conceived of God and Christ, when the Lord first manifested his grace to thy heart! No being in the universe was so near to me as God, but none so little known or understood. No heart was nearer to me than my own, but to all its errors and deceitfulness I remained the most perfect stranger! In the works of providence, as well as of grace, I had no consciousness whatever of any guide, nor even of needing a guide. Self-willed, wayward, and full of confidence, I was hastening on with the multitude, intent but upon one thing, "in making provision for the flesh, to fulfil the lusts thereof." Pause, my soul, and look back! When I take a review of what is past, and trace the hand of the Lord, all the way leading me as have come on, I am lost in astonishment in the contemplation of his mercies, and my undeservings. What a huge volume might be written of both, and in the margin to note down how they have kept pace together. My soul! If thou wert to read them by chapters only, what endless ones would they form under the several sections of the Lord's love, his care, his wisdom, his methods, and his grace, in the freeness and distinguishing nature of that grace; and as I read the Lord's mercies, to note, at the same time, my rebellions! Oh! what a subject would the whole form, in proof of this gracious promise, in facing the wisdom, power, and love of God, in awakening, regenerating, converting, and confirming grace! Surely, Lord, thou hast indeed brought a poor blind creature, such as I am, in a way that I knew not, and led me in paths that I never should have known; and still, Lord, thou art graciously performing the same, in making darkness light, and crooked things straight. And shall I not, from the latter part of this sweet promise, derive a strength of faith, from all that is past, to trust thee for all that is to come? Hath the Lord been gracious when in a state of total blindness, to bring me by a way I knew not; and now, when he hath mercifully opened mine eyes to see his glory, and to love his name, will he not lead me still? Had he mercy upon me, when I asked it not, neither knew that I needed it: and will he refuse me that mercy now, when I so earnestly seek it, and know that without his grace and mercy in Jesus, I shall perish for ever? Precious Lord! give me faith to believe, to trust, and to depend! Thou, who hast done such great things for me already, whereof I rejoice, wilt never leave me, nor forsake me, O Lord God of my salvation!

MAY 23.

MORNING.—" Such an one as Paul the aged."—Philemon i. 9.

And what was Paul in the moment here represented? Verily an aged servant of his Master, but not retired from the scene of action. Paul, though grown old in the Lord's service, was still as hotly engaged as ever in the Lord's battle. Art thou such an one, my soul, as Paul was! Then learn from hence, that however many, or however heavy, former campaigns have been, there is no rest for thee this side Jordan, no more than for Paul: no winter quarters for the true soldiers of Jesus Christ. Until thy captain undress thee for the grave, the holy armour in which he hath clad thee is not to be taken off. Art thou " such an one as Paul the aged?" Then, like Paul, see that thou art strong in the Lord, and in the power of his might. And how sweet the thought! Thy Jesus, who hath borne thee from the womb, and carried thee from the belly, knows well the burden of thy increasing years, and all the infirmities belonging to them, and will carry both thee and them. Yes, my soul, those very infirmities which the tenderest hearted friend sometimes feels impatient at, and even thyself, thou knowest not how to bear, Jesus feels, Jesus commiserates, Jesus will soften! He that hath carried all thy sins, carrieth also all thy sorrows. Doth he not say so? "even to your old age I am he; and even to hoary hairs I will carry you!" I have made, and I will bear: even I will carry and will deliver you. Isa. xlvi. 3, 4. Precious Lamb of God! henceforth I cast all my burdens upon thee. Thou hast never called thyself I Am, for nothing. Thou hast indeed made me, and new made me. Thou hast borne all my sins in thine own body on the tree. Art thou not both the Alpha and the Omega, both the author and finisher of my salvation! Oh yes, thou hast been every thing to me, and for me, from the womb of creation: borne me on eagle's wings; made me, and new made me; redeemed me in a thousand redemptions, and been better to me than all my fears! What, indeed, hast thou not done for me? And now then, being "such an one as Paul the aged," shall I now doubt, or now fear, when every pain, and every cross, and every new assault from sin and Satan, bids me go to Jesus. Oh for grace, ever to keep in view what thou hast said and done, and what thou hast promised. Yes, yes, it is enough; Jesus hath said, "Even to your old age I am he." The same I have been, the same I will ever be. "I will never leave thee, nor forsake thee." Shout, my soul, and cry out, hallelujah. He that hath been my first will be my last; my strength, my song, my salvation for ever.

EVENING.—"There was silence in heaven about the space of half an hour."—Rev. viii. 1.

This is a very striking scripture, and records as striking an event, when took place on the opening of the seventh seal—silence in heaven; not a suspension or interruption to the happiness of the place, but the silent adoration of God and the Lamb. This must be the sense of the passage, if by heaven we are to understand the place where dwell "the spirits of just men made perfect." But as it is more than probable that it refers to the events of the kingdom of Christ upon earth, which are here spoken of under prophetical representations, the silence may rather be supposed to mean, that the church of God, both in heaven and on earth, are waiting in solemn expectation of what events the sounding of the seventh trumpet will bring forth. But there are some sweet instructions to be taken from what is here said, of silence in heaven by the space of half an hour, which in the silence of an evening meditation, it may be highly profitable to attend to. If in heaven such solemn pauses are made, doth it not strike the mind, how very becoming such must be upon earth? Surely it is a sweet frame of the spirit, to ponder in silence over the many solemn things which connect themselves with the very existence of man, in a dying state, and in dying circumstances like the present; more especially, in the solemn seasons of devotion, when we draw nigh to a throne of grace, in and through the ever blessed Jesus, a holy silence in the first approaches, seems highly suitable to await divine visitations. What a lovely view doth the Holy Ghost give of David, 2 Sam. vii. 18. "Then went king David in, and sat before the Lord!" And elsewhere he saith, "truly my soul waiteth upon God:" in the margin of the bible it is, "Truly, my soul is silent before God," Ps. lxii. 1. The prophets were commissioned to enforce this by way of command: "The Lord (saith one of whom) is in his holy temple; let all the earth keep silence before him," Habak. ii. 20. And another saith, "Be silent, O all flesh, before the Lord, for he is raised up out of his holy habitation," Zech. ii. 13. And the Lord himself, having pointed out the blessedness of waiting upon him, accompanied with a promise that his people who did so, should renew their strength, immediately sends forth this precept: "Keep silence before me, O islands, and let the people renew their strength; let them come near; then let them speak," Isa. xli. 1. My soul! learn hence, the beauty of holiness, and the blessedness of waiting in silence before the Lord. For then, when the Holy Ghost comes in the refreshing influences of his grace, and commands the north wind and the south wind to blow, sweet will be the manifestations of the Lord Jesus by the Spirit, until, "while the heart is musing, the holy fire from off the altar will be kindled," and the soul will go forth in all the exercises of faith, love, joy, humility, and desire upon the person, work, and offices of Jesus!

MAY 24.

MORNING—"Then ceased the work of the house of God."—Ezra iv. 24.

Ah, how distressed was Zion, when this decree took place; and yet the history of the church plainly proves that the hand of the Lord was in it. My soul, are thine exercises sometimes similar? Doth it seem to thee, as if the work of God in thee was at a stand? Nay, as if it was totally over? Pause, recollect there is a set time to favour Zion. Thy Jesus is of one mind, and who can turn him? He is everlastingly pursuing the designs of his love. And as Zion was graven upon the palms of his hands, and her walls were continually before him, when she appeared in her most desolate circumstances; so the work of his grace, in the hearts of his people, doth not remit, though, to thy view, all thy promising beginnings seems to be blighted, and, as it seems in thy apprehension, thou findest growing imperfection. And is not Jesus, by this very means, emptying thee of self, and all the pride of self-attainments? Is he not preparing thee for his own glory, by removing in thee the rubbish of all creature confidences? Remember what is said: "When the Lord shall build up Zion, he shall appear in his glory." Mark here, that it is the Lord that is to build Zion: and it is the Lord's glory, and not thine, that is to result from it. The work of the house of God in thee would indeed cease, if the work was thine, or thou hadst any hand in the performance of it. But the same Almighty hands which laid the foundation of this house, those hands shall also finish it. And by this process, the glorious Builder is teaching thee to cease from thine own works, as Jesus, when redemption work was finished, did from his. Precious Lord, is this the cause, and are these the lessons thou art teaching me, in the deadness, emptiness, and the numberless complaints under which I daily groan? Oh then, for grace to cease from self, to cease from all fancied attainments, and to have my whole heart and soul centered in thee, in whom alone is all righteousness, grace, work, and fulness. Yes, Lord, the work is thine, the salvation is thine, the glory is thine, all is thine; and all that remains for me, is to be for ever giving thee the just praise that is due to thy most holy name, content to be nothing, yea, less than nothing, that the power of Jesus may rest upon me; for when most weak in myself, then am I most strong in the Lord, and in the power of his might.

EVENING.—"A Nazarite unto God from the womb."—Judges xiii. 5.

And what, in the language of scripture, was a Nazarite unto God? Certainly what the very term implies; one dedicated to God, set apart, and sanctified. Both the person and character are largely described, Numb. vi. 1—21. And was Samson such? It cannot be doubted, notwithstanding the many strange particularities in his life, which were departures from sanctity of character. But in that part of Samson's life wherein the Nazarite was strongly marked, he was eminently proved to be one; and it is in this feature of the illustrious Danite, that we behold him as a striking type of the Lord Jesus Christ. My soul! as it hath pleased the Holy Ghost to give the church so circumstantial an account of Samson, do thou ponder the subject well, and remark (what was evidently the only design for which it was given) how gracious the Lord the Spirit was, thus to set forth, in type, Jesus of Nazareth, so many ages before his incarnation. Was Samson a Nazarite unto God from the womb? Such was Jesus, who was so named by the angel before he was conceived in the womb. And what was the object for which Samson was separated from his birth as a Nazarite to God? We are told that it was to deliver his brethren out of the hands of their enemies, Judges xiii. 5. The same was declared of Jesus: he shall be called Jesus; for "he shall save his people from their sins," Matt. i. 21. Was holiness unto the Lord the distinguishing feature of the Nazarite? How suitably did it set forth the Lord Jesus, "who sanctified himself for his people," John xvii. 19. The very devil himself saluted Christ with his name, when he said, "Let us alone; what have we to do with thee, thou Jesus of Nazareth? Art thou come to destroy us? I know thee who thou art, the Holy One of God." Mark i. 24. And so very important was it considered by the Holy Ghost, that the church's Lord and Saviour should be known by this name of "the Nazarite unto God from the womb," that it is remarkable how many persons have given their testimony, and some of them plainly without design, to this one character of our Lord. The angel at the annunciation; the devil, as before remarked; the Jews in contempt, John xviii. 5; the Roman governor in his inscription on the cross, John xix. 19; the angels at the sepulchre, Mark xvi. 6; the apostles glorifying in this name after his ascension, Acts ii. 22; and Jesus himself, from heaven, at the conversion of Paul, Acts xxii. 8. Precious Nazarite to God! holy Lord Jesus! thou art indeed the true, the only one; for of thee, and by thee, can it be said, " Her Nazarites were purer than snow, they were whiter than milk, they were more ruddy in body than rubies, their polishing was of sapphire," Lament. iv. 7. Help me, Lord, by thy grace, to keep thee ever in remembrance. And while the cry of the infidel is still heard, " Can any good thing come out of Nazareth?" Oh! may my soul hear thy sweet voice, by faith: " the Lord hath called me from the womb; from the bowels of my mother hath he made mention of my name!" Isa. xlix. 1. Lord, thus it is fulfilled, which was spoken by the prophets: " He shall be called a Nazarene," Matt. ii. 23.

MAY 25.

MORNING.—" And the inhabitant shall not say, I am sick: the people that dwell therein shall be forgiven their iniquity."—Isa. xxxiii. 24.

What is this? What happy climate is there where any of its inhabitants are exempt from sickness? Where is that salubrious air, that is not impregnated with disease? Surely, no where but in heaven. But if the cause of sickness be removed; if the envenomed dart of sin be taken out, and hath lost its poison, the inhabitant no longer complains, for both the evil and the pain are gone. My soul, hast thou found this happy spot? Hath Jesus manifested such views of his pardoning grace in the all-sufficiency of his blood and righteousness, that thou not only art fully convinced and satisfied that his blood cleanseth from all sin; but that thou as fully believest and resteth in it for thy salvation; and art of the happy number of those who believe to the salvation of the soul. Hath Jesus said to thee, as to the poor man in the gospel, "Son, be of good cheer, thy sins be forgiven thee?" Surely, then, thou art the inhabitant the prophet pointed at, and art no longer sick, but dwelling in the faith, and forgiven thine iniquity. Blessed Physician! I am no longer sick of that dreadful sickness which is unto death, in an unrenewed, unpardoned, unregenerated state. But I am sick indeed, and fainting for the fresh manifestations of thy grace. I am languishing, thou dearest Lord, for the renewed visits of thy love, the enjoyment of thy person, the larger, fuller, more constant discoveries of thyself and thy glory. When wilt thou come unto me? When will the day of everlasting light break in upon my soul? When shall I behold thee among the inhabitants of the upper, brighter world? Oh ye spirits of just men made perfect; ye who now dwell for ever under the perpetual smiles of Jesus's face; ye who once knew what it was to live in the unceasing desire of his renewed visits, and how precious all his love tokens are—tell him what longings my soul now hath, and what faintings I feel for his manifestation. Tell him, I charge you, Oh ye daughters of the new Jerusalem, ye that everlastingly behold my beloved, tell him that I am sick of love.

EVENING.—"And he is the head of the body, the church."—Col. i. 18.

Sweet view of Jesus! Ponder well the subject, my soul, and behold thy Lord in this endearing character, and thine own personal union with him. Jesus is indeed, in every point of view, "the head of his body, the church." He is so by the Father's own appointment, as our glorious Surety; in which character he stood up at the call of God the Father, from everlasting; for when, at that call, he put himself in our stead, in our law-room and place, he undertook, as the church's representative, to do all, and to suffer all for her; and what he did and suffered, they, as his body, might truly be said to do and suffer *in* him. Sweet thought! When Jesus obeyed the whole law, then was Jesus their law-fulfiller. When he suffered the death of the cross, they in him were crucified. When he arose from the dead, in that resurrection they partook of the triumph, and, as members of his body, arose with him. And when he ascended up on high, and sat down on the seat of the Conqueror, they ascended virtually by their union with him, and may be said "to sit together in heavenly places in Christ Jesus." But, my soul! glorious as are these views of Jesus, thine husband and thine head, yet are they not all. He is the head of his body, the church, by his assumption of our nature. There is an union also of soul, a oneness, a connection as close and intimate as the natural head of the body with its several members; for as the head of the body is the source of life, which gives energy and action to all the parts of the body, so Christ is to his church and people "the fulness of him that filleth all in all." Here is another sweet thought! When Jesus took thy nature, my soul, in his sinless portion of it, he partook of all that could be said to constitute human nature. "Forasmuch (saith the apostle) as the children are partakers of flesh and blood, he also himself likewise took part of the same," Heb. ii. 14. hence he must have a tenderness, an affection, a fellow-feeling (if I may be allowed so to say) for his own nature, in the several members of his body, the church. This is the very argument the Holy Ghost, by the apostle, urgeth with poor exercised believers, to convince them of their safety and assured comfort in him: "We have not an high priest which cannot be touched with the feeling of our infirmities, but was in all points tempted like as we are, yet without sin," Heb. iv. 15. And as this becomes a source of never-failing comfort, to support the several members of

Christ's body with consolation under all their exercises, (for what can any part feel which the head shall be unconscious of, and not participate in?) so doth it equally afford delight in the recollection, that all the wants of the body must be known and felt by the glorious head, and be by him supplied. Sweet thought again to the believer! Jesus hath a fulness corresponding to all our necessities. "It pleased the Father that in him should all fulness dwell. And of this fulness do we all receive, and grace for grace." Look up, my soul, and contemplate the infinite, inexhaustible, unsearchable riches of thy Christ! All awakening, justifying, sanctifying grace; all life, strength, nourishment, support, are poured upon the members of the church, from this glorious head: and what sums up the account, and endears it to the heart, is, that these blessings are everlasting, unchangeable, and eternal. He hath said, "Because I live, ye shall live also!"—Pause, my soul! And is this Jesus thine? Is he indeed thine head? Art thou a member of his body, of his flesh, and of his bones?—Witness for me, ye angels of light! I renounce all other lords, all other alliances, all other husbands! It is to Jesus alone that I bend the knee of love, adoration, and obedience; for he is my Lord God, and I am his for ever.

MAY 26.

MORNING.—"Thou hast ascended on high, thou hast led captivity captive, thou hast received gifts for men: yea, for the rebellious also, that the Lord God might dwell among them."—Ps. lxviii. 18.

Sweet view of a risen, ascended, and triumphant Saviour. My soul, ponder over these words, and while meditating upon them, see that thou art ascending after thy exalted head, and partaking in his glories. Jesus is he who hath indeed ascended, far above all heavens, that he might fill all things. He hath led captivity captive; and that not only in conquering all the powers of hell, but taking his people that were in captivity out of the prison-house, and causing them to partake in the felicity of his triumphs. And mark, my soul, what follows. " He hath received gifts for men ;" or as the apostle to the church of Ephesus expresseth the same blessed truths, he gave gifts to men, Eph. iv. 8. And sweetly Jesus hath done both ; for he received that he might give. He needed not for himself, but it was all for his people. He said himself, when speaking to the Father, " that I should give eternal life to as many as thou hast given me." And, my soul, mark another sweet expression in these words : " he hath received gifts for men :" or, as the margin of our old bibles hath it, and our old bibles are like old gold, precious things, he hath received gifts *in the man;* that is, in his human nature, as Mediator, to give out to his people. See, then, my soul, all thy blessings are treasured up in him, that is, in one and the same moment, thy God and thy Brother. Oh glorious thought! Oh! soul-comforting truth ! Neither is this all. For this sweet scripture points out also for whom he hath received gifts. It is for men. Not for angels, but for men. Not for holy men neither, but for sinners. Not for Jews only, but for gentiles. " Yea," saith the Holy Ghost, as if the Lord the Spirit would lay an emphasis upon it, that it might be particularly noticed, " for the rebellious also, that the Lord God might dwell among them." Oh matchless grace ! Oh world of wonders ! Fallen angels passed by, and rebels of men taken into favour. Great Father of mercies, what manner of love is this, which thou hast bestowed upon our fallen nature ? Oh thou risen and exalted Jesus, send down, Lord, thine ascension gifts. Nay, blessed Lord, come down thyself and dwell among us. Set up thy church in the earth, and in the hearts and souls of thy people, and reign and rule there, the Lord of life and glory.

EVENING. — "Now that he ascended, what is it but that he also descended first into the lower parts of the earth? He that descended is the same also that ascended up far above all heavens, that he might fill all things."—Ephes. iv. 9, 10.

My soul! thy morning portion led thee to the contemplation of a risen and ascended Saviour; and by faith and love, I hope thou didst find thyself ascending with him, and art now still looking to him on the throne of the Majesty on high. And while thy thoughts are thus occupied in the most blessed of all subjects, listen to this word of God's grace, as of a voice behind thee, to remind thee, that he who is thus gone up, first came down! He that is now in heaven, first came down from heaven; he is only returned, as a rightful Lord, to his own kingdom. He hath, indeed, both by his Father's gift, and his own purchase, obtained a mediatorial crown, to add to his crown of the Godhead, which he had before in common with the Father and the Holy Ghost; but in his ascension, thou art not to lose sight of his descent, which preceded it, when he left the bosom of the Father, to tabernacle in our nature, for our redemption, in these lower parts of the earth. And let this sweet view of Jesus give thee an holy boldness and comfort, in looking to thy risen and exalted Saviour for those ascension gifts which he is gone up purposely to send down! I want, my soul (Oh! that the Holy Ghost would for ever be giving it to me) to keep in constant remembrance who it is that thus "ascended up far above all heavens, that he might fill all things." I charge it upon thee, this evening, that thou never cease to ask this blessing from God the Spirit, that in his glorifying the Lord Jesus, he would keep it continually uppermost in thine heart, that it is Jesus who is thus exalted; Jesus thy Brother, thy Redeemer, thine Husband, thine Head. Surely, while thou bearest in remembrance, that "he is ascended up far above all heavens, that he might fill all things," he would never let thee go empty, didst thou tell him that thou art part of himself! Could Jesus, as the head of his body, the church, suffer that body, or any of its poorest or least members, to go lean, and poor, and wretched, while he is gone up purposely to send down, and to fill all things? To use his own words, "No man ever yet hated his own flesh, but nourisheth and cherisheth it, even as the Lord the church," Ephes. v. 29. Were these things left upon record as a testimony how Jesus nourisheth and cherisheth the church, and shall any poor member be without it? Precious Lord Jesus! henceforth I beseech thee, look on me, and give me, by thy sweet Spirit, to be always looking unto thee! I see, Lord, that thou, who art *ascended*, art the same that *descended:* this is enough for me; for, sure I am, thine heart is not changed, but thy love is the same. And if thy love brought thee down to *save*, thy love hath led thee up to *bless:* and what mercy can my soul want which thy fulness cannot supply? How can a poor member of thine below, long need, while "Jesus is ascended up far above all heavens, that he might fill things?" Oh! for grace to come to thee, to look to thee, to depend upon thee, and to rest, with full assurance of faith, in that dependence, that Jesus, our risen, our ascended, our exalted, and full Saviour, will give to every one of his members, "grace, according to the measure of the fulness of Christ."

MAY 27.

MORNING.—"Thine ears shall hear a word behind thee, saying, this is the way, walk ye in it, when ye turn to the right hand, and when ye turn to the left."—Isa. xxx. 21.

My soul, who is this Almighty Teacher, out of sight, but the Holy Ghost? And to what way doth he point but to Jesus, who is both the way, and the truth, and the life? Art thou ever at a stand? listen to this voice.

Art thou about to turn to the right or left? See how seasonably he is promised to come to direct thee. Condescend, thou gracious, matchless Instructor, to guide me. I shall not fail then to know the wholesomeness of thy teaching, when thou hast opened mine eyes, to see the wondrous things of thy law. I shall indeed know that thou art my Director, because thou hast said, "I the Lord teacheth thee to profit." And when thy word comes not in word only, but in power, and in thee, the Holy Ghost, surely I shall know it, in that it not only reaches my ear, but will influence my heart: not only will instruct and teach me in the way wherein I should go, but will incline my feet to walk in it. Yes, thou infallible Teacher! I shall know thee to be the Spirit of truth, by guiding me into all truth. I shall know the voice of the Spirit of Jesus, because it will prompt me to follow Jesus. Did I hear a voice telling me of a way of salvation in a righteousness of my own: did I sit under a teaching, which sent me to my tears, and repentance, and alms-deeds, by way of recommending me to God: did I listen to the siren song, which told me of safety in myself, and my own best endeavours, and that Christ would do the rest: or did any teach me, that I must not come to Jesus, until that, by some previous acts of soul-cleansing in prayers and fastings, I had made myself fit: in all these cases, and the like, I should know that they could not be the voice behind me, promised to direct; because it is thy one glorious office, thou Holy and Eternal Spirit, to testify of Jesus, and to glorify him. When, therefore, I hear the voice behind me, saying, "This is the way, walk ye in it;" and when it directs me wholly to Jesus; when every thing in this divine teaching enlightens my mind in the knowledge of the person, relation, work, power, grace, righteousness, and love of the Lord Jesus Christ; and when that blessed voice bids me to come unto him, just as I am, a poor, vile, needy, perishing sinner, to venture upon him for life and salvation, and how to receive and improve the Lord Jesus, in his infinite suitableness to all my necessities: Oh how fully verified to my experience is this sweet promise of my God to my soul! Holy Father, cause me to hear this blessed voice, in the daily, hourly paths of my pilgrimage; and grant me the spirit of wisdom and revelation, in the knowledge of thy dear Son.

EVENING.—"For there was a tabernacle made; the first, wherein was the candlestick, and the table, and the shew-bread; which is called the sanctuary."—Heb. ix. 2.

It is blessed to see how Christ was set forth in every thing, and by every way in the ordinances of God, during the first ages of the church. Surely they had the gospel preached to them in type and shadow, as we have now in sum and substance. My soul, take thine evening meditation among the furniture of the outer sanctuary, and see what emblems they afford of Christ. The tabernacle, which Moses made in the wilderness, contained, in the first apartment, the things here spoken of. The *candlestick,* if without a light, strikingly set forth the darkness of that dispensation; and if with a light (which seems the most probable, for the lamps were to be always burning) it shewed that the Lord himself, who walketh in the midst of the golden candlesticks, is the light of his people, and the glory of the temple. The next article noticed is *the table,* which was probably placed in such a direction, that the light of the candlestick might shine upon it; by which we may learn, that in going to the table of the Lord, we must be directed by his light; for none cometh to the Father but by him, who is "the way, and the truth, and the life." The table itself, which was of pure gold, became a most lively type of the ever-blessed Jesus. The infinite worth and glory of his person, and the eternal merit and efficacy of his blood and righteousness, may be supposed to be set forth, by golden representations, as the richest and most valuable treasure we are acquainted with. And when we add to these, that Jesus feeds, entertains, supports, nourisheth, and preserves his church and people, what could so well set forth the royal bounties of his grace, and the fulness and richness of his house, as that of a golden table, around which the poor, and the needy, the hungry, and the faint, might be received and feasted? But the first sanctuary had not only the *candlestick* to guide to the Lord, and the *golden table* to receive the followers of the Lord, but the *shew-bread* also, to supply them. This shew-bread was a beautiful and striking representation of him who is the bread of life. Twelve loaves, in allusion to the twelve tribes of Israel, were to be always standing upon it, to intimate the perpetual appearing of Jesus in the presence of God for his people. They were of the finest flour, mixed with frankincense; thereby shadowing the purity of his nature, and the fragrancy of his sacrifice before God. They were to be renewed every sabbath, to shew that Christ is not only exhibited in the gospel every day, and all the day, but to be renewed every sabbath, when his ministers bring forth to the people, out of his treasury, "things new and old." Those taken away when the new loaves were brought, were to be eaten by the priests alone, under this Jewish dispensation; and the same is observed under the new: for the Lord Jesus hath made all his people "kings and priests to God and the Father;" and if any that are not his, by his Spirit given to them, eat at his table, they make the table of the Lord contemptible. Are these some of the delightful subjects, typified by the furniture of the tabernacle in the first court? Dost thou behold, my soul, these things, and through the veil and covering, discover Jesus? Oh! then consider the vast, the infinite importance of redemption by his blood, whom God the Spirit thus set forth to the church by types and shadows; and see thy privilege, and the happiness to which thou art called, when in reading the old testament, "the veil is done away in Christ."

MAY 28.

MORNING.—"They shall grow as the vine."—Hosea xiv. 7.

And how doth the vine grow? Why, in those soils that are favourable to it, vines are not erect like trees, neither are they fixed, as we do our vines, against walls; but the vine creeps along upon the ground, and rests its tender stalk and branches upon the nearest prop that will stay it. And, my soul, is it not so with the believer that wholly leans upon Jesus, and throws the arms of faith wholly upon him, as the staff, and stay, and support of all confidence. And there is another property of the vine which carries with it a striking resemblance to the believer, namely, the tenderness of its nature, and danger to which it is exposed. How very weak, and poor, and frail, and helpless, is the child of God. What can a believer perform in himself. And what an host of foes is he exposed to; corruption within, and the enemy on every side, makes his case truly like the vine, exposed to the wild beasts, and nipping winds, and storms, which every moment threaten to destroy it. And there is a third particularity by which both are known. While flourishing, to what an extensive length will the vine throw out her branches, and what an abundance of fruit will it bear! And doth not the believer in this sense grow as the vine, when, from being ingrafted in Jesus, and nourished by him, and from him, his fruit being found, sends forth the graces and fruits of the Spirit, and brings forth some thirty, some sixty, some an hundred fold? And, to mention no more, what a likeness is there between the dry unpromising stick of the vine, and the lifeless and unpromising appearance of the believer. As Jesus himself, when upon earth, was like a root out of a dry ground, so all his followers now are men every where wondered at. Precious Jesus, thou glorious Vine of thy church, cause me to be so united to thee, as a branch in thee, the one heavenly plant thy Father hath planted, that in thee my fruit may be found; that I may be perpetually receiving fresh communications from thee, and living upon thee, and to thee, and rejoicing in thee, the source and fountain of all that is gracious here, and the everlasting spring of glory, happiness, and joy, that shall be hereafter.

EVENING.—" And after the second veil, the tabernacle, which is called the holiest of all."—Heb. ix. 3.

The veil of separation between the two tabernacles, no doubt, typified Christ's body, which, in the moment of his death, by an invisible hand, was torn in twain from the top to the bottom, thereby intimating that now all separation was removed, and true believers were permitted to enter, by the blood of Jesus, into the presence of God, he having obtained eternal redemption for them. The second or inner sanctuary, had several very interesting particulars, by way of distinction, belonging to it. The veil of separation, under the Jewish dispensation, intimated, that it was impossible for any to draw nigh to God, but by a mediator. When Jesus threw down the separation, and opened a new and living way by his blood, access was obtained to God in Christ; and Jesus, first for himself, and then for his people, led the way into the holy of holies. The veil of separation set forth how man was separated by sin; by the injury done to God's holiness, and by the natural enmity of his own heart. But when Jesus came, and put away sin by the sacrifice of himself, restored that which he took not away, gave to God his glory, restored to man God's image, and took away the carnal mind, by making the heart of stone a heart of flesh; then it was, that the veil of separation was for ever taken away, and the kingdom of heaven opened to all believers. My soul! what saith thine experience to these things? If the veil be removed, and thou art entered in, through Jesus, thy forerunner; then hast thou seen, and known, and felt, and enjoyed the glory of him, whom those things shadowed; and art rejoicing in him, as the Lord thy righteousness. And art thou entered within the veil? Art thou resting upon Jesus, having cast anchor within the veil? Surely, then, Jesus is precious: his love is precious, his grace is precious; yea, every thing in him is precious. And then, by and by, all remaining clouds will be removed, and him whom thou seest now by faith, thou shalt see, face to face, and know, even as thou art known. Precious Lord Jesus! take away all remaining darkness, ignorance, unbelief, and whatever comes in the way of clear views of thee, and the enjoyment of thee; and let the covering which is cast over all people, and the blackness over all faces, be removed for the full enjoyment of thee, in grace here, and in glory to all eternity! Amen.

MAY 29.

MORNING.—"As by the offence of one, judgment came upon all men to condemnation; even so, by the righteousness of one, the free gift came upon all men unto justification of life."—Rom. v. 18.

Concerning the ruin in which thou art involved in Adam, surely, my soul, thou knowest and feelest it from day to day. No one can persuade thee out of this. Thou art as much concerned in the sin, and consequently implicated in the punishment, of the first man's transgression, as if thou hadst been, and which indeed as thy root and head thou really wert, in the garden with him when he did it. And thou feelest the same disposition to sin, the same rebellion in thy very nature. So that most fully and freely dost thou subscribe to the rights of God's judgment, that condemnation cometh upon all men, because all have sinned.

Now then see, my soul, whether, through the same Almighty Teacher who convinced thee of sin, thou art convinced also of the righteousness of Jesus, and art as fully and as truly interested in all that belongs unto him. Now as Adam and his seed are one in sin and its just consequences, so equally Christ and his seed, in the eye of God's law and justice, are one in Christ's righteousness. Remember, my soul, and it is a great point to remember, Jesus is never spoken of in scripture as a single person, and as the Christ of God, but as the covenant head. He is as much the head, the root, the common stock of all his spiritual seed, as Adam was the head, and root, and stock, of all his natural seed. So then, as Adam's sin is the sin of all his children, because they are his children; even so the righteousness of Christ, the second Adam so called, is the righteousness of all his children, because they are his children. This is so plain a truth, that it can need no further argument. The next point now is, in order to enjoy all the comfort and blessedness which ariseth out of this precious doctrine, that thou shouldest be able, my soul, to prove that thou art of Christ's seed. Very fully thou provest from day to day, by the remains of indwelling corruption that ariseth within, that thou art of the stock of the first Adam: how wilt thou prove thy relationship to the second? For, as upon the presumption, I had not sprung from the stock of Adam, and none of his blood was running in my veins, I should not have partaken of his sin, or been subject to his punishment; so equally evident it is, that if I am not born again and belong to the seed of Christ, I am not interested in him or his righteousness. Blessed be God! the relationship with Jesus, as the glorious Head and Mediator of his people, is as easily to be proved as the relationship with Adam. God promised to pour out of his Spirit upon Christ's seed, Isa. xliv. 3, 4, 5. Hast thou then, my soul, the Spirit of Christ as thou hast the nature of Adam? Is Jesus precious, more precious than gold—his salvation dear—his righteousness thy only confidence? Canst thou, and dost thou say, with one of old, "this is all my salvation, and all my desire?" Is he whom the Father delighteth in, thy delight—he that is the desire of all nations, thy desire? If these and the like testimonies are in thy experience, my soul, what greater evidences dost thou need, to manifest thy relationship to thy Jesus, as thy corruptions prove thee allied to the old nature? See then, my soul, that thou foldest up this soul-reviving truth for thy bosom, and carriest it about with thee daily wherever thou goest; so will Jesus be thy hope and thy portion for ever.

EVENING.—"An old disciple.—Acts xxi. 16.

My soul! of what standing art thou in the church of Christ? If there be any thing of real rank and dignity in human life, to cause one man to differ from another, certainly that age, which consisteth not in a multitude of years, but in fellowship and long acquaintance with Jesus, must be most honourable. But in this, as in all other distinctions, the believer's dignity is the reverse of the world's. He that is highest in grace, is the lowest in humility. How beautiful and engaging to this point are the words of Christ: "Whosoever will be chief among you (saith that divine Teacher), let him be your servant: even as the Son of man came not to be ministered unto, but to minister, and to give his life a ransom for many." Hence the simplicity and lowliness of the weaned child, Jesus, make the character and feature of those that are "greatest in the kingdom of heaven." And wherefore is this? Is it because of our spiritual attainments, or of our improvement in the divine life? Will our title to salvation be at length made out, from our having been such a time, or so long a season with Jesus? Is he "an old disciple," who hath been so many years an attendant on ordinances, sacraments, hearing sermons, and the like? Is this the plan of counting years in the school of Christ; and by so much, as we can number our attendance on the means of grace and improvements under them, as we fancy in ourselves the progress of our own holiness, do we estimate an old disciple? Not so, my soul, is the scripture calculation of age in the divine life. There we read, that "the child shall die a hundred years old, but the sinner being a hundred years old shall be accursed," Isa. lxv. 20. What is it then to be "an old disciple?" Surely he is one that is eldest, in having learned, from the continued teachings of God the Holy Ghost, to think *less* of himself, and *more and more* of Jesus. He advanceth the farthest in this scriptural age, who is growing in grace, by growing in the knowledge of our Lord and Saviour Jesus Christ. His every day's experience brings him more acquainted with his own unworthiness, so as to endear the infinite merit of the Redeemer. He is truly "an old disciple," who is old in this science, of being more out of love with himself, and more in love with Jesus. For it is impossible, in this progress of the divine life, but to make advances in this exact proportion; and as the blessed Spirit exalts Christ to the view, and brings him home to the heart, by so much our self-confidence lessens; and the more glorious he appears, the more lowly we become in our own eyes. This is one rule to ascertain the real age of a disciple. And there is another like it: as those who have long lived in a family, best know its government, and find themselves more at home in it; so the oldest disciples in Jesus's household will best know how to improve a long and growing acquaintance with him, be coming to him for all they want, and making his glory the one great object of all their desire. And it will prove indeed that they are faithful to their Lord's interest, when they not only lay out every thing for his praise, but receive every thing that he lays out that it may be for his glory. My soul! what sayest thou to this statement of things, in respect of the real age of the believer in Jesus? Art thou "an old disciple" of thy Lord?

MAY 30.

MORNING.—"Renewing of the Holy Ghost, which he shed on us abundantly through Jesus Christ our Saviour."—Titus iii. 5, 6.

Precious office of the Spirit! Condescend, great God, to grant it me this morning. Oh, renew my soul with all thy sweet revivals, after a night of sleep, as thou renewest the face of the earth. Oh send forth, I beseech thee, Lord, all thy graces, as suited to my necessities, and the Redeemer's glory, and let it be most abundantly shed abroad, through all the faculties of my soul, through Jesus Christ my Saviour. Pause, my soul, over the blessed prospect, and having now pleaded in Jesus's name for the mercy, act faith upon thy God in his promises. Is not every morning a renewing of the Holy Ghost? Is it not said concerning the productions of the earth, that God "sendeth forth his Spirit, and they are created, and thou renewest the face of the earth?" See what an evidence the earth gives in this lovely season, in the fruits, and plants, and verdure all around. And are the saints of Jesus of a less sweet-smelling savour, when perfumed as they are with the everlasting odour of Jesus's never-failing righteousness? Do the fields, when renewed by the sun of the morning, look gay, and lovely, and after the dew or the refreshing shower, give out their odour, perfuming the air with their fragrancy; and shall not the saints of God, when the Sun of righteousness ariseth upon them, with healing in his wings, send forth all the blessed effects of that presence which revives the grace Jesus hath planted, and calls forth into exercise the faith he hath given? Shall not the showers of his love, when he comes down in them as rain upon the mown grass, and the dews of the Holy Ghost's renewings, revive all the languishing frames of the soul, and cause even the desert to blossom abundantly, and to rejoice with joy and singing? Yes, yes, thou blessed Lord? methinks I feel thy sweet and gracious renewings. My very heart is refreshed in the thought. Under thy influence I will look up and wait the coming of Jesus. He is near. He comes. I hear him say, "Rise up, my beloved, and come away: for lo, the winter is past, the rain is over and gone; the flowers appear on the earth, the time of the singing of birds is come, and the voice of the turtle is heard in our land."

EVENING.—"Therefore his sisters sent unto him, saying, Lord! behold, he whom thou lovest is sick. When Jesus heard that, he said, this sickness is not unto death, but for the glory of God, that the Son of God might be glorified thereby."—John xi. 3, 4.

My soul! ponder these words. It may be said now, as it was then, Lord, behold he whom thou lovest, yea, many our Lord Jesus loveth, are at this present hour sick! Who shall calculate the number? Who shall mark down the tears of the sorrowful of the Lord's people? But Jesus knows them all; yea, appoints all; and he it is, of whom it is said, "he putteth their tears into his bottle: are not these things noted in thy book?" These words suggest another sweet thought. The sorrowful sisters, in their message to the Lord Jesus, did not tell him that one whom they loved was sick, but one whom Jesus loved. There could be no doubt of their love to their brother: but their application to Jesus was on account of his love. My soul! do not overlook this. It is the most blessed and the most powerful of all arguments in prayer, when we come to a throne of grace for those that are near and dear to us, when we can and do tell the Lord, that they for whom we seek his mercy are the objects of his love. The observation of our Lord, on receiving the message, is most delightful. Sit down, this evening, and ponder it well. It is what may with safety be applied to every case, and every exercise of the Lord's people, in all their eventful pilgrimage through life, whether in one trial or another. This sickness, this sorrow, this temptation, be it what it may, " is not unto death, but for the glory of God, that the Son of God might be glorified thereby." Now, my soul, bring it to the proof. Every rod of Jesus hath a voice, and speaks as well as corrects; and when at any time he exerciseth it, this is the invariable language: " As many as I love, I rebuke and chasten." And when the voice is heard, and the soul is thereby brought to listen to the Redeemer, then the close of the dispensation proves that it is not indeed unto death, but for the divine glory. So that let the exercise be what it may, we then see Jesus in it. His wisdom sent it; his love is in it; and his strength will carry the believer through it; yea, so much of the Lord's presence will accompany every step we take during the dark hour, that, dark as things are around, there will be constant daylight in the soul. And so truly blessed are those dispensations, which, in their first view, carry a frowning aspect with them, that, when the sable covering is thus taken off by the hand of faith, on hearing Jesus's voice under all, they have been found to be tenfold more productive of the Redeemer's glory and the soul's happiness, than in the smoother providences, where such exercises have not been given. My soul! what saith thine own experience to this statemeat? Doth the Redeemer lay crosses in thy way? Are they marked with his inscription, " Bring them unto me? Art thou visited with sickness, and doth Jesus perform the part of the tenderest nurse, and sit up by thee? Dost thou hear his well known voice, saying, " As one whom his mother comforteth, so will I comfort you?" Surely, then, thou wilt fully subscribe to the sweet words of Jesus, in his answer to the sorrowful sisters. Every exercise and every trial of the Lord's people, which he sweetens and sanctifies, "is not unto death, but for the glory of God, that the Son of God might be glorified thereby." For if it teach creature weakness, and Creator strength; if the believer is made sensible of his helplessness, and of Jesus's all-sufficiency; if renewed feelings add one testimony more, that there is nothing but sickness, sin, and sorrow, in us, and therefore in Jeus alone all our resources of health, and righteousness, and joy are found: these improvements will always give glory to God, and magnify the riches of his grace, that "the Son of God may be glorified thereby."

MAY 31.

MORNING.—"And Jesus came and spake unto them, saying, all power is given unto me in heaven and in earth."—Matt. xxviii. 18.

Hail, then, thou Sovereign Lord of all! I have lately been following thee in sweet and solemn meditation through the seasons of thy humiliation; now let me behold thee on thy throne. And here I am called upon to contemplate my Lord and my God as possessing universal dominion. Ponder, my soul, the vast extent. Thy Jesus, as God, as one with the Father, possesseth in common with him all power from everlasting. This is his, as God, essentially so; not given to him, for by nature it is his, being "one with the Father, over all, God blessed for ever. Amen," said Paul; so let it be; so shall it be. And so say I, and so saith all the church; amen, amen. But what thy Jesus saith here, in these blessed words, is of a power given to him; and that is a power as the head of his church and people. And although had he not been God, one with the Father, he never could have been suited for the exercise of this power; for unless he had been the mighty God, how should he have been the mighty Redeemer! Yet being God, and both God and man, it is precious to consider the power that is given to the Lord Jesus, as Jesus, " the head over all things to the church, which is his body, the fulness of him that filleth all in all." Here then, my soul, let thy thoughts take wing this morning. Behold thy Jesus, the head over all principality and power. See him, by virtue of his Almighty Godhead, exercising and giving energy to the fulness of his power as Mediator; and in this view conceive, if it be possible, to what an extent thy Jesus is unceasingly exercising his power for the everlasting benefit of his church and people. All power in heaven, not only among the highest order of created beings, angels and archangels, but a power with God the Father to prevail for the eternal salvation of all his redeemed. He left it as a record how he exerciseth this power, when he said before his departure, " Father, I will that they whom thou hast given me, be with me where I am, to behold my glory." And he hath power to send the Holy Ghost to all his people. He said himself, before he went away, " If I go not away, the Comforter will not come; but if I depart I will send him unto you." Here then, my soul, here let thy thoughts be directed, to meditate upon the fulness and extensiveness of that power which thy Jesus possesseth in heaven. Well may it be said that he hath the keys of heaven, when he hath all power with the Father and with the Spirit. And well may it be said that he hath the keys of hell also, when all things in heaven and earth, and under the earth, are subject to his command. And hath he not power then, my soul, suited to answer every want of thine, and of all his church and people? Hath he not power over all flesh, to give eternal life to as many as the Father hath given him? Wilt thou complain, shall the church complain, of any want, while Jesus is upon the throne? Art thou poor, is the church poor, weak, helpless, needy, guilty, polluted, oppressed, exercised? What of all these, and ten thousand other situations, while Jesus lives, and hath all power? Nay, is it not so much the better that the people of Jesus are what they are, that they may be the better suited for his glory, and that their wants may give occasion for the supplies of his grace? Hail, thou Almighty Sovereign! Now methinks I would be always poor, always needy, always feeling my nothingness, that all these may constrain me to come to thee: so that every day's necessities may afford a fresh occasion to crown thee Lord of all in a day of grace, until I come to crown thee, with the whole church, the everlasting Lord of all in heaven, to the glory of God the Father. Amen.

EVENING.—"So Moses the servant of the Lord died."—Deut. xxxiv. 5.

My soul! close the month, in contemplating the death of this highly-favoured servant of the Lord: and mark in him the sure event of all flesh: "Dust thou art, and unto dust shalt thou return." What a blessed account hath the Holy Ghost give of this man. "There arose not a prophet (we are told) like unto Moses, whom Jehovah knew face to face." But, as if to draw an everlasting line of distinction between him and his Master; between the highest prophet, and the Lord God of the prophets; the Holy Ghost was pleased, by the ministry of his servant the apostle, to state the vast distinction: "Moses verily was faithful (saith he) in all his house, as a servant, for a testimony of those things which were to be spoken after: but Christ as a Son over his own house, whose house are we;" Heb. iii. 5, 6. Indeed all the great and distinguishing events in the life of Moses became more or less brilliant, as they set forth, in their typical representations, the person, work, or offices of the Lord Jesus Christ. Was Moses the Lord's minister to bring the people out of Egypt? and what was this but a representation of the Lord Jesus, bringing his people out of the Egypt of sin, death, and hell? If Moses led the people through the Red Sea, and opened a path through the mighty waters; what was this, but a type of the ever blessed Jesus, bringing his redeemed through the red sea of his blood, and opening a new and living way into the presence of God? If Moses kept the passover, and the sprinkling of blood through faith, what was the great object of his faith looked at, but Christ, our passover, and the blood of his sacrifice? Did he bring the people through the wilderness; and is not Jesus bringing all his people through? Did he feed them with manna, and give them water from the rock; and what did the manna prefigure, but Jesus, the bread of life; and what was the rock, but Christ, the water of life, in all ages of the church, to his people? In short, every thing momentous in the church's history, wherein Moses ministered to the people, pointed, both in law and sacrifice, to Jesus, the Lamb of God, and his one all-sufficient sacrifice for the salvation of his redeemed. And even the death of Moses, the servant of the Lord, over and above the event of death, common to all, had this peculiar signification annexed to it, that, as the great lawgiver to the people, it set forth the inefficacy of the law to bring into Canaan: this could only be accomplished by Christ, who "is the end of the law for righteousness to every one that believeth, to the Jew first, and also to the Gentile." Farewell, Moses! thou servant of the Lord! Thou, when thou had served thy generation, wast gathered to thy fathers, and, like all the patriarchs, didst see corruption: but Jesus saw no corruption; he ever liveth, and is the same "yesterday, and to-day, and for ever." Hail, thou glorious Mediator of "a better covenant, established upon better promises!" Be thou the Alpha and Omega of thy word, thine ordinances, thy sanctuary, thy servants! To thee all ministered; from thee all come; in thee all centered; and to thine everlasting praise all terminate, in bringing glory to Jehovah, Father, Son, and Spirit, through Jesus Christ. Amen.

JUNE 1.

MORNING.—" The Lord said unto my Lord."—Psalm. cx. 1.

Some have called this Psalm, *David's creed.* Certain it is, that there is scarce an article of a true believer's faith, but what is in it. My soul, look through it this morning, if thou hast time, and see whether it is *thy* creed. If not, look at this precious portion of it, and ask of the Holy Ghost to teach thee the blessed things contained in it. " The LORD said unto my Lord:" that is, Jehovah said unto my Adonai. Observe, my soul, that here, as in many other parts of the bible, one of these words LORD is in capital letters, the other in small characters. This no doubt was done by the translators, by way of telling the English reader that the two words in the original Hebrew are not the same. They had no better method of explaining the difference. But by using different sized letters, they meant to say that there is a difference, and the difference seems to be this: the word LORD, whenever used in the Bible in capital letters, signifies Jehovah; Father, Son, and Holy Ghost: not as a name of office in the work of redemption, but as intimating his own glorious incommunicable essence. The word Lord in small letters, Adonai, is very frequently (as in this Psalm) applied to Christ in this his gracious office as the Christ of God, and of his people. And a most sweet and precious name it is. It signifies, in a double meaning, *first,* his own personal authority and power; and, *secondly,* that power as exerted and called forth into action for his redeemed. Look at thy Jesus, my soul, as thy Adonai this day, and every day, and a thousand sweet and precious blessings such a view of him, as a *ruler*, and a *support,* and a *sustainer*, will open to thy meditation. Yes, all-lovely, all-powerful, all-gracious Adonai, thou art my Adonai! In this thy name, which is as ointment poured forth, would I contemplate thee. In this thy name would I rejoice all the day, and in thy righteousness would I be exalted.

EVENING.—"Thy people shall be willing in the day of thy power: in the beauties of holiness from the womb of the morning: thou hast the dew of thy youth."—Psalm cx. 3.

There is so much of the Lord Jesus in this sweet Psalm, indeed it is altogether so truly a gospel Psalm, that the morning portion, which was a selection from it, cannot be better followed than by taking another verse of it for the evening portion, that both together may furnish out blessed meditations to my soul, in the contemplation of our precious Jesus. Here are views of Jesus, in all his blessed offices, as the Prophet, Priest, and King of his people; and every verse is more or less descriptive of his glorious person, offices, and character. This precious portion for my evening thoughts, contains the promise of Jehovah the Father, in his covenant engagements, that the Redeemer should see the blessed fruits and effects of his undertaking in the hearts and minds of his elect people. "Thy people (saith the Lord) shall be willing." So then Jesus had a *people* before his incarnation, and that people Jehovah engaged to make *willing*; willing to be saved, willing to receive Christ, and own him for their Redeemer? Sweet thought of encouragement to the poor sinner! The Lord undertakes to give the willing mind; so that this is enough to stir the humblest to attend the means of grace, where Jehovah will make Christ's people willing in the day of Christ's power. And while it furnisheth out encouragement to the *sinner*, it holds forth instruction to the *saint*; the *former* can plead no inability, and the *latter* can make no boasting; the willingness is of the Lord, and it is in the day of Christ's power. My soul! thou canst subscribe to this truth. The first awakenings of grace in thine heart, thou knowest, were not the effect of thy strength, but the willingness there wrought by divine power. But there are in this verse, also, "the beauties of the Lord's holiness" spoken of; "from the womb of the morning." It is indeed to see "the King in his beauty," and to worship in the "beauty of holiness," when the Lord's people are made willing in Christ's power, and worship only in the beauties of Christ's holiness. And such, the promise saith, shall be the fruitfulness of the womb of conversion in Christ's strength, when he seeth the travail of his soul, that, as the dew-drops of the morning are incalculable, so shall be the multitude of redeemed souls that shall "flee as a cloud, and as doves to their windows!" Precious Lord Jesus! rule thou as a King, the rightful Sovereign of Zion; subdue thine enemies to the sceptre of thy grace, and bring every knee of thy people to bend to the rod of thy power. And Oh Almighty Father! ever let my poor soul praise thee, love thee, obey thee, adore thee, that thou hast fulfilled this covenant promise to thy dear Son, in the instance of my soul. Thou hast indeed subdued the natural stubbornness of my nature, and made me willing to be saved in the Lord's own way. And now, blessed Lord, I desire to bend the knee of my heart to Jesus, and daily, hourly ascribe the whole of my salvation "to Him that sitteth upon the throne, and to the Lamb that was slain, for ever!"

JUNE 2.

MORNING.—"Living waters shall go out from Jerusalem; half of them toward the former sea, and half of them toward the hinder sea: in summer and in winter shall it be."—Zech. xiv. 8.

My soul, was not this fulfilled in part when the gospel went forth from Jerusalem? And is it not now fulfilling, while the same blessed gospel is going forth from sea to sea, and from the river even unto the ends of the earth? Surely neither the summer's drought, nor the winter's frost, shall dry up or congeal those living waters. But, my soul, hast thou asked of Jesus, as the woman of Samaria did in the moment of Jesus's promise, for those living waters? Oh if thou knowest, my soul, this gift of God, and wilt daily, hourly, ask of him both in summer and in winter, he will give thee these living waters. Oh contemplate their property, and then, my soul, ask and receive, that thy joy may be full. Jesus himself is this well of living waters; and wherever he comes, like the waters in Ezekiel's vision, he gives life, and quickens sinners dead in trespasses and sins. Also, Jesus in those streams maintains the life he hath first given. Moreover, Jesus not only maintains, but revives and renews them, again and again, when the graces of his people languish. Again, these living waters of thy Jesus are always running: here is nothing stagnant, but always flowing. Lastly, into whatever heart Jesus gives them, they shall be, as he hath promised, a well of water springing up to everlasting life. Are these things so; and have the saints in all ages, and under all dispensations of the church, both in the old testament and in the new, been thus supplied? Is it indeed He, my beloved, who is the same yesterday, and to-day, and for ever, that thus hath supplied, and is supplying, and ever will supply all? Is it thou, Oh thou precious Lamb of God, that art in the midst of the throne, leading the church above to fountains of living waters, and becoming the same to the church below! Wilt thou not give of thy fulness to satisfy my thirsty soul in this dry and barren land, where no water is? Yes, yes, my soul, exult with the church of old, for thy Jesus is the same; a fountain of gardens, a well of living waters, and streams from Lebanon is my beloved.

EVENING.—" But God commendeth his love towards us, in that while we were yet sinners, Christ died for us."—Romans v. 8.

It is a very blessed heightening of divine mercies, when we behold them as not only bestowed upon those that deserved them not, but upon those that deserved the reverse of them. It is not enough, in our account of God's love, to say that God was gracious when we had done nothing to merit his favour, but that God was gracious when we had done every thing to merit his displeasure. This is among the sweet features of the gospel. And the reason is very plain. God himself is an infinite Being, and therefore his love must be an infinite love. All the properties of it are infinite; it must be exercised to suit an infinite power; it must be such as corresponds to infinite wisdom; and its effects must be such as shall be suited to infinite goodness. Hence, therefore, in the display of it, such manifestations must be given as shall set forth, that the love of God, as an infinite Being, totally differs from the love of man, who is but a finite creature. Our love is bounded, like ourselves, by circumstances of a finite, limited, perishing, dying nature, such as ourselves, and all the creatures around us partake of. But in the love of God, there are " breadths and lengths, and depths and heights, passing knowledge!" Now God commendeth his love towards us by those properties; that is, he bids us take notice of it by those special marks and characters. And when the Lord surpriseth the souls of his people by the same astonishing instance of his grace, in those acts of goodness, he speaks as in these solemn words: " If it be marvellous in the eyes of the remnant of this people in these days, should it also be marvellous in mine eyes, saith the Lord of Hosts?" Zech. viii. 6. How sweetly is this shewn to us in the gift of his dear Son Jesus Christ! When was Christ given? When we were enemies. On what account was he given?

Purely on account of God's love. And to whom was he given? Not to his friends; not to those who had never offended him; not to those who, by their affection, or by their services, could make some return of acknowledgment for such blessings; but to poor, helpless, barren, unprofitable sinners. So that the love of God in Christ is particularly recommended, sent home, pressed upon our hearts, by this rich display of it. To have blessed us, or to have loved us, if we had never offended God, would have been a stream too shallow, too trifling, to shew forth divine love. No! "God commendeth his love towards us, in that while we were yet sinners, Christ died for us." Pause, my soul! mark these properties, admire divine goodness, and learn how to put a proper value upon the unparalleled love of God in Jesus Christ. So God commended his love towards us!

JUNE 3.

MORNING.—"In his favour is life."—Ps. xxx. 5.

Oh for grace to keep this always in view, for then, thou dear Lord, I should never consider my dead frames, or dead feelings, since I well know that thou ever bearest favour and good-will towards thy people. For if thy providences frown, or seem to frown, do I not know that behind that aspect thy countenance is the same, always gracious, always favourable, and that thou art invariably pursuing the everlasting happiness of thy people? Let it please thee, my Lord, to grant me this morning such views of thy favour, that I may henceforth trace it in every thing. Was it not this favour that first opened a source of salvation? Was it not this favour that brought me into a participation of it? Was it not this favour that begat me to the knowledge of it—that quickened me to an enjoyment of it—that opened the communication of it, by which thy grace became imparted to my soul? And was it not the same favour that kept alive the incorruptible spark, and maintained it through all the attempts of sin, and the world, and the powers of darkness to extinguish it? Nay, blessed Jesus, what is it now but thy favour that secures me in thy love, and gives me all the inexpressible felicities of mercy, pardon, and peace now, and everlasting glory hereafter? And is not thy favour, then, better than life? Is it not more precious than rubies? Can there be aught desirable like it? Truly, Lord, in thee and thy favour I have life, for thou art both my light and my life; my heart trusteth in thee, and I am helped. "Remember me then, Oh Lord, with the favour that thou bearest unto thy people, Oh visit me with thy salvation."

EVENING.—"Jehovah-nissi."—Exod. xvii. 15.

Jehovah-nissi, is the suitable inscription for every undertaking. The meaning is, "The Lord is my banner." And how blessed is it to set this over us in all the conflicts of our warfare, because it appeals to God, and calls in God to our help in all emergencies. Hence the church cries out, "We will rejoice in thy salvation, and in the name of our God we will set up our banners." Ps. xx. 5. And how lovely is the church described, when strengthened in the Lord her God, "looking forth as the morning, fair as the moon, clear as the sun, and terrible as an army with banners!" Song vi. 10. But this inscription hath a yet more special reference to Jesus. The history to which it belongs, gives us an account of Amalek, with whom the Lord declared "he would have war from generation to generation." Now as Joshua was a type of Christ, so Amalek became a type of the devil. There is nothing neutral in this war; "He that is not for us, is against us;" but what a blessed relief is it to the soul, that the issue is not doubtful! While Christ is our banner, and Jehovah-nissi the glorious name under whom we fight, we shall be more than conquerors through him who helpeth us. The cause is his, the glory of God in salvation his, the everlasting issue of it his, and the whole termination his. Hence we go not forth as to a thing doubtful, but already sure. Sit down, my soul, this evening, and write Jehovah-nissi upon all that concerns thee. The Lord is engaged for thee in this holy warfare. The Lord hath sworn that he will have war with all the enemies of his Christ, from generation to generation. Hence he will have a suited grace, and a suited strength, proportioned to the wants of all his people. The name, the person, the work, the righteousness, the finished salvation of the Lord Jesus, is, and must be a banner for triumph, because of the truth. Therefore, as David, who, long before he had possession of the kingdom, enjoyed it by faith; so in Jesus, our Jehovah-nissi, we may with confidence cry out as he did, "Gilead is mine, Manasseh is mine;" Christ is mine, and heaven is mine; yea, all things are mine; for "Christ is the strength of my life, and my portion for ever."

JUNE 4.

MORNING.—"Awake, O north wind, and come, thou south; blow upon my garden."—Song iv. 16.

Are these the words of my Lord? Yes, surely, they can be no other; for none but Jesus can send the Holy Ghost to his church and people. And besides, none can call the church "my garden," but he that is the rightful owner of it. Surely, Lord, it is thine, both by thy Father's gift, and by thy choice, and by thy purchase, and by the conquests of thy grace, and by the voluntary surrender of thy people, when thou hast made them willing in the day of thy power. And dost thou call then, both the north wind and the south, thou dearest Lord, to blow upon my soul? Dost thou command all suited influences of thy grace to visit me, that one may search, and another warm my affections, and call thine own gifts and graces forth in exercise, upon thy glorious Person, and thy glorious work? Oh come then, thou Holy Spirit, with all thy sweet and precious offices. Come, Lord, to convince and comfort me, to humble and direct me, to chill my affections to the world, and to warm them towards the Lord Jesus. Come, thou holy, gracious, almighty, quickener, reviver, restorer, and glorifier of my God and Saviour! Oh if thou wilt make my soul like the chariots of Amminadib, and cause those graces thou hast planted there to go forth in a way of love, and desire, and faith, and expectation, and hope upon the Person and glory of him whom my soul loveth, then shall I cry out with the church, and say, "Let my beloved come into his garden, and eat of his pleasant fruits."

EVENING.—"Yea, he loved the people; all his saints are in thine hand."—Deut. xxxiii. 3.

My soul, here is a very blessed portion to meditate upon in the night watches, and to lie down with, reposing in the bosom of Jesus. The word *yea,* is a sweet scripture word, and very strong to the purpose. God's "yeas," and "amens," are firmer than all the oaths of creatures; and when Jehovah puts his *yea* to the love that he hath to his people, it ought to give great comfort and confidence to our faith. And Oh! what testimonies hath Jehovah, in his three-fold character of person, manifested, in the Father's love, the Redeemer's grace, and the Holy Ghost's fellowship, in proof of this affection! Blessed Lord! help me to keep it in remembrance. But, my soul, do not stop here. Mark what the Holy Ghost hath said, as a farther testimony of it: "All his saints are in thine hand." In whatever point of view we read these words, they become blessed. Whether the saints of the Lord Jesus, here spoken of, be old testament saints, or new testament believers, the sense is the same. Jesus committed all his people into his Father's hands. "Keep them," cried the Saviour, in that divine prayer, the specimen of his holy intercession, "keep, holy Father, through thine own name, those whom thou hast given me!" John xvii. 11. And hence, the Redeemer elsewhere saith, "My sheep shall never perish; neither shall any pluck them out of my hand. My Father, who gave them me, is greater than all, and none is able to pluck them out of my Father's hand; I and my Father are one." John x. 28, 29, 30. Think, my soul, how eternally safe and secure must the church of Jesus be, thus kept by the mighty power of God, through faith, unto salvation! What shall unclasp the hands of Jehovah? Who shall wrest the weakest, the humblest, the poorest of Christ's little ones, from the holding of his omnipotency? Why then art thou, my soul, so frequently exercised with fears, and doubts, and misgivings? It is the Lord's love that is the foundation of thy assurance, and not the strength of thy graces! His own free mercy, and not thy merit, were the first causes of thy calling; and what is it now, in thy present preservation, but the same which holds thee up, and carries thee through every difficulty? "Yea, he loved the people:" that is, the source, the reason, the sole motive. And their safety he secures: "All his saints are in thy hands!" Precious Lord Jesus! it is enough. How shall a child of thine perish, when secured by such almighty support? Oh! to hear thy voice, in the soft whispers of thy love, comforting my soul, as thou didst the church of old: "Can a woman forget her sucking child, that she should not have compassion on the son of her womb? Yea, they may forget; yet, will I not forget thee. Behold, I have graven thee upon the palms of my hands; thy walls are continually before me."

JUNE 5.

MORNING.—"Have ye received the Holy Ghost?"—Acts xix. 11.

My soul, ponder over the solemn question again and

again, and then see what answer thou canst give to a point so infinitely interesting and important. The Holy Spirit is clearly known by the exercise of his blessed offices in every heart where he abides, and where he is the glorious inhabitant. He comes in Jesus's name as an ambassador, to propose to the sinner a rich and precious Saviour. He comes as an almighty teacher; and this condescending office he graciously exerciseth in convincing of sin, and convincing of the righteousness of Jesus. He comes as an advocate; and by his pleading the cause of a poor sinner's own necessities, and the cause of a rich Saviour's willingness and ability to supply all these necessities, he manifests himself a most powerful advocate, when, by his constraining grace, he makes the poor sinner willing in the day of his power. He comes as an enlightener of the dark and untutored mind of the sinner. And this he doth most effectually, when, by shining in the heart, he gives "the light of the knowledge of the glory of God, in the face of Jesus Christ." Most gloriously he shines upon the soul, when, by the ministry of his blessed word, and by the influences of his divine grace, he leads the mind forth to the contemplation and love of the person, blood, and righteousness of the Lord Jesus Christ. He comes as a witness also to testify of Jesus. And this sweet office is manifested in the conscience when at any time he shews sin to be exceedingly sinful, and that nothing but the blood of Jesus can cleanse from it. And his witness in the soul is proved to the fullest demonstration, when he powerfully brings the guilty conscience under so deep a sense of sin, and so alarmingly concerned for the consequences of it, that nothing will satisfy until Jesus is revealed and brought home to the heart in all the beauties of his Person, and the fulness and suitableness of his salvation, and formed there the hope of glory. He comes also as a Comforter; and Oh how sweetly and fully doth he manifest both the power of his Godhead and the sovereignty and grace of his character, when, by his consolations, as he opens and explains them, and makes application of them as they are in Jesus, he revives the drooping spirit, relieves the depressed spirit, animateth, refresheth, sanctifieth the whole heart, and soul, and mind, and gives a joy and peace in believing, abounding in hope by the power of the Holy Ghost. My soul, what sayest thou now to the question? "Hast thou received the Holy Ghost?" Surely, I do know thee, thou gracious God the Spirit, by these sweet tokens of thy covenant office and character. Lord, I pray thee, be ever with me, and, agreeably to Jesus's gracious promise, abide with me for ever. Oh may I never grieve thee, by whom my soul is sealed in Jesus to the day of eternal redemption.

EVENING.—" Thou wentest forth for the salvation of thy people, even for salvation with thine anointed."—Hab. iii. 13.

Every view of redemption is blessed: but there are some views transcendently so. And when the soul is led out in the contemplation of Jehovah, in his threefold character of person, Father, Son, and Holy Ghost, all engaged, in their goings forth from everlasting, for the accomplishment of it, there is somewhat which overpowers the mind with the greatness, and the surpassing glory of the subject. As the salvation of the Lord's people is from Jehovah, and from all eternity; so it is to Jehovah, and to all eternity. All the springs of it are from this one source, and tend to this one end. The song of heaven, which John heard; so proclaimed it: for while the address was to the Lamb, in ascribing to him all the glory of the work; the great purpose for which it was wrought, was ascribed to the Father: " Thou wert slain, and hast redeemed us to God by thy blood;" Rev. v. 9. My soul! mark the similar expression in this song or prayer of the prophet. Jehovah "went forth for the salvation of his people; even for salvation with his anointed." And was not Christ the anointed of the Father! And did not Jehovah go forth with Christ, upholding, supporting, carrying on, and completing redemption work in, and by, and with Jesus? Yea, did not Jesus go forth from everlasting, when his delights were with the children of men before the world? Is it not of Jesus that it is said, "Then I was by him, as one brought up with him; and I was daily his delight, rejoicing always before him; rejoicing in the habitable part of his earth, and my delights were with the sons of men?" Prov. viii. 30, 31. Oh! the soul-comforting subject! How truly blessed to see the whole Godhead thus engaged in the salvation of poor sinners! Yes! blessed Lord Jesus! it is plain, that in all the goings forth of Jehovah, the redemption of thy church was the one grat object and design. Before time began to be numbered, thou wentest forth. In time, when thou camest in substance of our flesh, still the salvation of thy people was the object. And now in eternity, thou art still going forth, in thy priestly office on thy throne, which thou art carrying on in heaven to the same purpose, to make the salvation of thy people secure. Oh for grace to keep these views always in remembrance, that, while Jehovah is thus, in one eternal act, going forth for the salvation of his redeemed, all his redeemed may go forth in love, and adoration, and praise, in the acknowledgment of the mystery of God, and of the Father, and of Christ: and here on earth begin the song which is never to end in heaven: "To him that loved us, and washed us from our sins in his own blood, and hath made us kings and priests unto God and his Father: to him be glory and dominion, for ever and ever. Amen."

JUNE 6.

MORNING.—" Blessed be the Lord, who daily loadeth us with benefits."—Ps. lxviii. 19.

Behold, my soul, what a sweet portion for thy morning meditation is here. See what thou canst gather out of it to furnish new songs of praise to the bountiful Lord whose mercies it records. Blessed Spirit! I beseech thee open these precious words of thine to my view. Blessed be the Lord, it saith, yea, so say I; blessed be Jehovah; blessed be the Father, Son, and Holy Ghost, for they are the united source of all my blessings. And blessed be the majesty and glory of God for ever, who daily loadeth his people with benefits. Count over, my soul, each of these blessed expressions, for every word is weighty and ponderous. God not only gives blessings, but daily. His mercies are constant as the morning, unceasing, continual; strength suited to the day, and mercies adapted to every moment. Faith needs no hoards, no banking-houses: nay, it is faith's precious property, and her blessedness, to be always empty, in order that the sweetness of being filled by Jesus may be the better known. But this is not all. God not only daily gives out blessings, but loadeth his people with benefits. He openeth the windows of heaven, and poureth out of his grace in such fulness, that there is not room to receive. He makes their souls like the heart of Elihu, as it is said of him, for want of vent, like new bottles he was ready to burst. So Jesus poureth out of his love into the souls of his redeemed, that they are overpowered with his goodness. Knowest thou not, my soul, somewhat of this! Oh yes, I trust I do. Why then, " blessed be God, who daily loadeth me with his benefits." And what endears all this in a ten thousand times greater degree, is the assurance that the whole is in a way of salvation. So saith this sweet scripture.

He that loadeth us with benefits, is the God of our salvation. He that is our God, even he is the God of our salvation. Oh precious, blessed consideration, then are these blessings everlastingly secured; for he that now daily loadeth us with benefits, will unweariedly do the same to all eternity. He is not only the portion of his people now, but will be so for ever. He not only gives strength equal to the day, but will himself be our strength to all eternity. And mark it down, my soul, as the most blessed part of those daily benefits; he that thus loadeth the soul with all the benefits of covenant blessings, in the grace, mercy, favour, love, blood, righteousness, and all the sweet tokens of redemption in Jesus, signs and seals every one of them in his dear name: and as he said to Abraham, so he saith to all Abraham's seed, "Fear not, I am thy shield, and thine exceeding great reward." Shout then, my soul, and henceforth let this be thy morning song: "Blessed be the Lord, who daily loadeth thee with benefits."

EVENING.—"So Christ was once offered to bear the sins of many; and unto them that look for him, shall he appear the second time without sin unto salvation."—Heb. ix. 28.

My soul! pause over this blessed portion, for it is most blessed, and seek from God the Holy Ghost, grace to gather all its sweets for thine evening enjoyment. Every word is big with importance. And, first, who is it that is here said to have been once offered? Even Christ, the sent, the sealed, the anointed of Jehovah. So that when thou goest to a throne of grace, to plead for mercy in the blood and righteousness of Jesus Christ; thou goest in his name, whom thy God and Father hath appointed. Thou then tellest thy God, what thy God first told thee. He, in whose name, blood and righteousness, thou askest redemption, is he whom Jehovah himself "hath set forth as a propitiation, through faith in his blood." Hence it is impossible not to succeed. "I have given him (saith the Lord) for a covenant to the people." Next, consider the fulness, the greatness, the all-sufficiency, of this sacrifice, which thy Jesus hath offered. He was once offered. Yes! it is enough: "For by that one offering, he hath perfected for ever them that are sanctified." There was, and is, more merit in that one offering of the Lord Jesus Christ, to take away sins, than there is demerit in all the sins of his people for ever. Mark this down also, when thou goest to the throne. Thou art seeking redemption, upon the plea and footing of a full and rich equivalent made by thy Surety, under Jehovah's own appointment and authority. Then go on to that other most interesting part of this precious verse: "And unto them that look for him, shall he appear the second time without sin unto salvation." Pause, my soul, over these words. When thy Jesus appeared the first time, he came as the burden-bearer of all the sins of his redeemed. And though in himself "he was holy, harmless, undefiled, separate from sinners, and made higher than the heavens;" yet he was made both "sin and a curse for us, that we might be made the righteousness of God in him." Hence all the sins of his redeemed were charged upon him, and "the Lord Jehovah laid upon him the iniquity of us all." But when he had by himself purged our sins, the whole weight and pressure of sin, with all its tremendous effects, were for ever done away. And therefore unto them that look for him, when he shall appear the second time, it will be without sin unto salvation. He put away sin by his first coming; and by his second, he will put all his redeemed into the complete possession of that salvation which, by his one offering up of himself for sin, he hath eternally secured. What sayest thou, my soul, concerning thyself, and thy personal hope in these glorious things? Art thou one of that blessed happy number who are thus looking for

Jesus? Dost thou believe that Jesus died and rose again? Art thou so well pleased with the merits and efficacy of this one offering of the body of Jesus Christ, once for all, as to seek no other, to desire no other; yea, to renounce and despise every other? Pause, and duly consider. These are solemn soul transactions. A mistake here, is a mistake indeed. Oh! it is blessed to be well pleased with what Jehovah hath declared himself well pleased with: and to be satisfied, yea, well satisfied, with what Jehovah is well satisfied. For then thou wilt be daily on the look out for thy Lord's return, as one that is on the look out for a dearly beloved friend. And thus, if thou art in love with his appearing; loving all that appears to promote thy Redeemer's glory on earth, in the conversion of sinners, and comforting of saints, loving his church, his Zion, his ordinances, his people; shortly the hour will arrive, in which the Master will come, and call for thee; thou shalt hear his chariot-wheels at the door, and his voice will be distinctly heard by the waiting spirit; "Arise, my fair one, and come away!"

JUNE 7.

MORNING.—"If there be a messenger with him, an interpreter, one among a thousand, to shew unto man his uprightness; then he is gracious unto him, and saith, deliver him from going down to the pit, I have found a ransom."—Job xxxiii. 23, 24.

My soul, how precious are those views, in looking back upon where the first discoveries of grace were made. Moses never forgot the first visions of God at the bush; neither did Jacob outlive the remembrance of the first Bethel-visit of a God in Christ to his soul; and why should I? Hast thou not known this messenger, this interpreter, one among a thousand to shew unto thee God's uprightness? Oh yes, Jesus by his Spirit hath shewn to me that my "God is righteous in all his ways, and holy in his works." When by the blessed discoveries which had been made to me in his word, by his ordinances, providences, judgments, mercies, like the poor creature described in this sweet scripture, when reduced to a mere skeleton, by reason of soul sickness, driven out of all resources in myself, and utterly despairing of ever seeing the face of God in glory, by any creature attempts, and by all creature righteousness, Oh then it was, thou blessed, glorious messenger of thine own covenant; thou faithful interpreter of the mind and will of Jehovah; then it was I was led to see the freeness, fulness, suitableness, and all-sufficiency of a Redeemer's righteousness, and to cast my poor defenceless, naked, trembling soul upon the rich, powerful, and altogether-sufficient salvation, of thee, my God and Saviour! Oh how hast thou sweetly and mercifully explained to me the secrets of covenant mercies, the glories of thy person, and the greatness of thy finished work. And now at every step I take, at every portion of thy blessed word I read, when my mind feels the remains of indwelling corruption, and all the lurkings of the enemy's suggestions within; then, then it is I hear the Father's gracious voice, "Deliver him from going down to the pit, I have found a ransom." Yes, precious Jesus, thou art my ransom, and my righteousness for ever!"

EVENING.—"He brought me to the banqueting-house, and his banner over me was love."—Song ii. 4.

In whatever sense thou art led, my soul, to look at the banqueting-house of Jesus, thy joy will be great in the contemplation. And if he who hath prepared the banqueting-house, and well stored it with every thing to afford a spiritual repast, will lead thee thither, and regale thee there with the rich enjoyment of himself, and the fulness of blessings in him, thou wilt have a feast of fat things indeed! Come then, this evening, and take a view of Jesus's banqueting-house, and wait on thy kind and condescending Lord. He hath been known to take home many a poor waiting hungry sinner, that hath been on the look-out for him, to his banqueting-house, and given him a gracious, full, and satisfying entertainment. Come then, my soul, and see this banqueting-house of Jesus. *Some* have looked at it as the *covenant* itself of redemption; for this is indeed a house of banquet, where every thing that can enrich the soul in the love of God the Father, God the Son, and God the Holy Ghost, is found. Oh! the blessedness of this covenant! Well might David, when he was brought into it, exult and say, "This is all my salvation, and all my desire!" And *some* have looked at the banqueting-house, and thought it meant the *church*, the house of God; for here all the blessings of the covenant are given to the guests which Jesus brings into it. And here again we find, that they who are blessed with a place in God's house are so delighted, as to resolve to go out no more. "Here would I dwell (is the language that expresseth the sentiment of all): this is my rest for ever; here will I dwell, for I have a delight therein," Ps. cxxxii. 14. And *some* have looked at the banqueting-house of the Lord Jesus, and considered, that it is the blessed "word of God, the scriptures of truth." And certain it is, that "they contain the words of eternal life;" and open every day, and all the day, an everlasting supply to banquet the hungry soul, and to satiate the sorrowful soul. *One*, who could not be mistaken, said, when he had been feeding upon the rich things contained in it, "Thy words were found, and I did eat them, and thy word was unto me the joy and rejoicing of my heart," Jer. xv. 16. And *another*, not less taught, cried out in a transport, "O how I love thy law! it is my meditation all the day," Ps. cxix. 9. But I see no reason why the *whole* may not be considered as the banqueting-house of Jesus. For when, by the sweet influences of his Spirit, he hath brought his redeemed into a heartfelt enjoyment of an interest in his covenant, his church, and scriptures, every word, ordinance, and means of grace, with all the promises, are the inheritance of his people. Pause, my soul, and inquire, whether the Lord Jesus hath thus brought thee in? Art thou acquainted with his banqueting-house, and convinced that none but Jesus could bring thee in? It is a solemn thought! Man may attend the church, may read the scriptures, follow ordinances; yea, go to the Lord's table; but unless Jesus, by his Holy Spirit, lead the sinner there, meets him there, and blesseth him there, to what purpose will be the going? Look to it, my soul, that thy visits are by the Lord's invitation, and thy welcome from him; yea, that he leads thee by the hand, meets thee, and blesseth thee; sets his banner over thee of love, and bids thee partake largely in the riches of his grace and salvation, in those well known words of thy Lord: "Eat, O friends; drink, yea, drink abundantly, O beloved."

JUNE 8.

MORNING.—" A red heifer without spot, wherein is no blemish, and upon which never came yoke. And ye shall give her unto Eleazar the priest, that he may bring her forth without the camp, and one shall slay her before his face."—Numb. xix. 2, 3.

I remember well it is said of our Lord Jesus, that, in order to sanctify the people with his own blood, he suffered without the gate. But though I clearly apprehend that the law, with all its sacrifices, was but a shadow of good things to come, and the body was Christ, yet, had not the Holy Ghost been graciously pleased to illustrate and explain, by other scriptures somewhat either direct, or by allusion, in reference to Jesus, I should have overlooked how, in many striking points, Jesus is here set forth in this type. Surely, Lord, thy spotless purity was beautifully represented in the spotless heifer here appointed for sacrifice. And the very rare colour of a red heifer plainly testified the singularity of thy sacrifice. Adam himself was so called, as a token of the red earth from whence he was taken. And when Jesus, as the Son of man, came to do away all the effects of Adam's sin and transgression, he manifested, by the redness of his apparel, and the blood sprinkled upon his garments, the gracious purposes which all implied. But I do not recollect, in any other type of my Redeemer, a particularity which pointed to the freeness of thy voluntary sacrifice, Oh thou Lamb of God! as the one here represented, in that this heifer was to be one upon which had never come yoke: nothing, Lord, but thine own free, sovereign love, and at the call of God thy Father, prompted thine infinite mind to be the willing sacrifice for poor sinners. There was no yoke, no obligation, nothing to compel thee. Lo, I come, was thy gracious voice, when neither sacrifice nor offering could ransom thy people. Oh Lord! let the sense of thy freeness in salvation comfort my soul under all heart-straitenings in myself; and the consciousness that there was no yoke upon thee, Lord, but thine own everlasting love, be the sweet constraining yoke on my soul, to bind me to thy love and to thy service for ever.

EVENING.—"Whom having not seen, ye love; in whom, though now ye see him not, yet believing, ye rejoice with joy unspeakable, and full of glory; receiving the end of your faith, even the salvation of your souls."—1 Pet. i. 8, 9.

My soul! mark what a blessed testimony believers of the present hour are here said to give to an unseen, but dearly beloved Redeemer; and behold what blessed effects are induced in the soul by such lively acts of faith upon his person and righteousness! And, indeed, when it is considered who Christ is, what he is to us, what he hath done for us, and what he is for ever doing for us, and will do to all eternity, who but must love him? In his person all divine perfections center;

whatever tends to make any creature lovely, in heaven or on earth, is found in Jesus in the most eminent degree. For there is nothing lovely in creatures of any character, whether angels or men, but it is derived from him: it is Jesus who gives all that excellency and grace which they possess; the whole is found *in* him, and received *from* him. And when to these views of what Christ is in himself, the believer adds the consideration of what he is to him, what he hath wrought, and what he hath accomplished in redemption for him, such thoughts of Jesus, under the teachings of the Holy Ghost, in his glorifying him to the soul, give "a joy unspeakable, and full of glory." My soul! what saith thine own experience to these truths? Surely Christ is a portion full enough, and rich enough for every poor needy sinner to live upon to all eternity. And if thou hast been taught (as I trust thou hast long since been taught, and long proved) that all the fulness in Jesus is for his people; that his grace is magnified in giving out of his fulness to supply their need; yea, that Jesus waits to be gracious, and is as truly glorified, when a poor creature lives by faith and joy upon his bounty, as he is when that poor creature lays himself out in praises for that bounty; surely, though thou hast never seen Christ in the flesh, yet by faith thou hast seen him, and lived upon him, and hast such believing views of him, as giveth thee present peace, and immediate enjoyment of salvation. Oh! the felicity of thus realizing future things by present possession! Oh! the blessedness of substantiating things unseen by the strength of that faith which worketh by love! See to it, my soul, that thy God and Saviour is increasingly precious, and increasingly lovely, day by day. See to it, that he who is lovely to the Father, and to the Holy Ghost; the praise of all his saints in glory; the joy and adoration of angels, and the spirits of just men made perfect; and lovely to all creation, but to devils and poor blind unawakened sinners: see to it, my soul, that this lovely and all-loving Jesus is the first, and best, and completely satisfying object of thy delight; that this blessed testimony, which the Holy Ghost hath here given of the faithful, may be thine; and that though not having seen Jesus, you love him, and though unseen, you believe in him. This will be to "rejoice with a joy unspeakable, and full of glory; receiving the end of your faith, even the salvation of your soul."

JUNE 9.

MORNING.—"I would cause thee to drink of spiced wine, of the juice of my pomegranate."—Song viii. 2.

What, my soul, hast thou aught to offer to thy Jesus? Will he accept a present at thine hand? Yes, Jesus will accept those goings forth of his own grace, his own gifts, in the exercises of faith, and love, and joy, and praise; when, by his own sweet and reviving communications, he hath called to the north wind, and to the south wind, to blow a gracious gale upon my soul, and causeth the very graces he himself hath planted in my heart to send forth all their powers in the enjoyment of his person and righteousness. And do not forget, my soul, for thine encouragement to this lovely and becoming frame, these will be more grateful to thy God and Saviour than all whole burnt-offerings and sacrifices. These will be indeed like spiced wine, and the juice of the pomegranate, when those tears of faith, and love, and repentance drop at the mercy-seat, in the contemplation of that love of Jesus, which is better than wine. Help me then, thou dear Lord, thus to come to thee. Help me, as the poor woman at thy feet did, to shed my tears, and to offer thee this spiced wine: and no longer by sin and unbelief, and rebellion, to give thee wine mingled with myrrh, as the Jews did at thy crucifixion. Oh God, my Saviour! let it never be said of my soul, from neglect and indifferency to thee and thy sufferings, as thou complainest of them, "They gave me also gall for my meat, and in my thirst they gave me vinegar to drink." No, precious Lord! if thou wilt shed abroad the influences of thy Spirit in my heart, so as to lead out my whole soul in love to thee, in living upon thee, in contemplating thy glory, thy suitableness, thine all-sufficiency, then will my soul praise thee with joyful lips; and then will my beloved say, as to his church of old, "Thy lips, Oh my spouse, drop as the honey-comb; honey and milk are under thy tongue."

EVENING.—"Blessed is the man that walketh not in the counsel of the ungodly, nor standeth in the way of sinners, nor sitteth in the seat of the scornful. But his delight is in the law of the Lord, and in his law doth he meditate day and night."—Ps. i. 1, 2.

It is blessed to read every portion of scripture which speaketh of perfection in our nature, as referring to the person of the God-man Christ Jesus; and then, from our union *with* him, and interest *in* him, to mark our connection as his people, and our concern in all that is said or written of him. In the book of Psalms, particularly, there are numberless passages, which say that of holiness, which can be said of none among the fallen sons of men with the smallest shadow of truth. Who is the man, and where to be found, that hath never *walked* in the counsel of the ungodly; nor yet, which is more than walking, hath *stood*, as one not distressed at it, in the way of sinners; nor yet *sat down*, which is worse than all, in the scorner's chair? None of the children of men could ever lay claim to the blessedness of such a conduct from his own personal holiness in it. But if we read the words with reference to the ever blessed and ever holy Jesus, all this, and infinitely more, is true; for such was the spotless purity of the Redeemer, that his whole nature was altogether clean; yea, "the law of Jehovah was in his very bowels." See the margin of the bible, Ps. xl. 8. My soul! behold in this account, the true character of thy Lord; and in it behold the holiness and purity of that nature, in whose holiness and purity alone thou canst ever see the face of God, in grace here by faith, and in glory hereafter by sight, in open fruition. Thus read, and thus accepted, the passage in this Psalm becomes blessed indeed. In his righteousness, his people are made righteous; and by virtue of an union with him, and interest in him, and in all that concerns him, being joined to the Lord by one spirit, the souls of the redeemed walk as he walked, avoid the society of the profane, and sit not in the counsel of the ungodly. Precious Spirit of all truth! do thou thus glorify the Lord Jesus to my view; take of the things of Christ, and shew them to me; and grant me daily fellowship and communion with the Father, and with his Son Jesus Christ!

JUNE 10.

MORNING.—" My voice shalt thou hear in the morning, Oh Lord! in the morning will I direct my prayer unto thee, and will look up."—Ps. v. 3.

Sweet thought, my soul, to encourage thee this morning, that thy God in Christ is a prayer-quickening, a prayer-hearing, and a prayer-answering God. Art thou dull, dead, lifeless? One look from Jesus, one influence of the Spirit, will kindle desire, and lead thee to the mercy-seat, and to the throne of grace. Jesus will do more in one moment, to call off thy wandering thoughts, to open to thy views his glory, and to reveal to thee what thy wants are, and to give thee a spirit of prayer suited to thy wants and his praise, than all thy laboured attempts, without an eye to Jesus, can do for thee for ever. Whence is it, my soul, that prayer is ever a burden, but because we have lost a sight of Jesus? Why is it that thou art at times so little affected with the remains of indwelling corruption, and canst neither rightly value God's mercies, or be humbled under thine own infirmities? Is it not because thou dost not look up, and behold Jesus in his priestly vesture, waiting to be gracious? Oh didst thou but eye thy God and Saviour under this blessed character, how wouldest thou feel the preciousness of his great salvation, and haste to unload thyself upon the Lord Christ, and cast all thy burden of coldness, deadness, and sin upon him who is mighty to save! Come, Lord, then, I pray thee, with all thy sweet influences, fill my mouth with arguments, and my heart do thou warm with love. I know, Lord, I shall surely speed this day, this morning, at the mercy-seat, the moment thou hast loosed my tongue, and enlarged my heart with thy grace. Yes, yes, blessed Jesus, my voice shalt thou hear, my voice wilt thou hear in the morning; at the dawn of day, before cock-crowing, I will direct my prayers to thee, I will send them up to heaven; and through the day, and all the day, and seven times a day, will I praise thee, Oh thou God of my salvation, when thou hast caused me to praise thee with joyful lips.

EVENING.—" And Jesus said, who touched me? When all denied, Peter, and they that were with him, said, Master, the multitude throng thee, and press thee, and sayest thou, who touched me? And Jesus said, somebody hath touched me; for I perceive that virtue is gone out of me.'—Luke viii. 45, 46.

What a most interesting passage is here! What an evidence does it afford of the clear knowledge of the Lord Jesus; and, by an undeniable conclusion from such a proof of his omniscience, what a testimony does it bring with it of the Godhead of Christ! Pause, my soul, over the portion, and mark it well. Next pass on to another sweet improvement of it, and duly consider what a beautiful distinction is here drawn between the violent pressure of the throng, and the gentle touch of faith. Multitudes crowd to churches, and they hear of Jesus; but the personal knowledge and enjoyment of the Lord Jesus, is this touching him. Oh! for grace to have this right discrimination! It is very easy to attend the means of grace, to hear or read the holy scriptures; nay, to have a clear head knowledge of divine things, and even to *press* after information concerning Christ; but all these may be, and perhaps often are void of that life-giving, life-imparting kinowledge and enjoyment of Christ in the soul, which is really touching Christ by faith, and believing in him to the salvation of the soul. Once more, remark yet farther, the knowledge Jesus hath of all the individual cases of his afflicted people. He saw this poor woman amidst the whole crowd. He knew her case, knew all that had passed. In the greatest throng, Jesus's eye is upon each, and upon all. He knoweth what the needy require, and what the secret sighs of his poor people express: and it is Jesus that communicates virtue, grace, strength, comfort, and help, in all their vast varieties. What a sweet thought is it then, my soul, for thee to go in the greatest throng, as well as in the most secret retirement! Jesus encourageth thy faith, bids thee come and touch the hem of his garment, and, depend upon it, as in the instance of this poor woman, however unobserved or unknown by others, his eye is upon thee for good. The language of Jesus to every one of this description is, son! daughter! "be of good cheer, thy faith hath made thee whole; go in peace!"

JUNE 11.

MORNING.—" And my people shall be satisfied with my goodness, saith the Lord."—Jer. xxxi. 14.

Examine thine heart, my soul, this morning, and see whether this blessed promise is really and truly fulfilled in thy experience. Art thou satisfied with Jehovah's goodness? Yes, if so be thou hast so received that goodness as manifested and treasured up in the person and work of Christ, and art so believing as to be living wholly upon it. This is a grand thing to do; and when it comes to be strictly enquired into, few, very few, are living so wholly upon it, and so completely satisfied with it, as to be seeking for no additional satisfaction elsewhere. Now, my soul, as there are but few that are so fully satisfied with the Lord's goodness in every thing that concerns salvation, both in providence and grace, let thy morning thoughts be directed to see whether thou art one of that happy few. I will, for the sake of shortening the inquiry, take up the subject from this ground; that thou art satisfied thou hast an interest in Jesus. Thou hast a long time since been driven by thy necessities to Christ as a complete Saviour; and thou art resting all thy hopes, joys, and expectations, upon his blood and righteousness. I will consider this point as fairly and fully determined. Why then, perhaps, my soul, thou wilt say, is not this to be satisfied with Jehovah's goodness? Alas, here is the great defect of God's people! Though resting on this foundation, how often may they find their hearts exercised with endless perplexities how *this* grace is to be improved, or how *that* gift is to be employed. And according as it appears to their view they have improved the *one*, or employed the *other*, their peace and comfort is proportioned. My soul, do you not see that this is self-satisfaction, and not being satisfied with God's goodness? This is setting up the comforts of Jesus's graces and Jesus's gifts above the glorious author of those gifts and graces. To be really satisfied with God's goodness, implies living upon that goodness; and that is Christ himself. Living upon Jesus, acting faith upon Jesus, perceiving all our fresh springs to be in Jesus, and therefore drawing all from him. And, my soul, if thou art thus satisfied with God's goodness, thou wilt find it is injurious to the comfort and blessedness of this life of faith to be ever looking off Jesus to any thing his grace and goodness worketh in thee, lest in the view of the work itself, be it what it may, the source of that work is overlooked, and self-satisfaction, instead of Christ-exalting, should creep into thy soul. In every act, my soul, see to it then that all thy satisfaction is in Jesus, as the goodness of Jehovah. Lord, fulfil this sweet promise, and make me satisfied with thy goodness!

EVENING.—"And the Lord went before them by day in a pillar of a cloud, to lead them the way; and by night in a pillar of fire, to give them light; to go by day and night. He took not away the pillar of the cloud by day, nor the pillar of fire by night, from before the people." —Exod. xiii. 21, 22.

My soul, look back this evening to the church's history in the wilderness, and behold how Jesus watched over his people then as he doth now. Surely it is sweet, it is blessed, to mark the same evidences of the Redeemer's love, and to observe, that in affection to his people (as in person so in love) he is "the same yesterday, to-day, and for ever." Among many precious testimonies to this effect, that of the pillar of the cloud by day, and of fire by night, in the camp of Israel, is not the least. We are told in this scripture, that the Lord was in this cloud; and another scripture confirms it, saying, that Jehovah "spake unto them out of the cloudy pillar." It is wonderful to conceive what effect must have been wrought on the minds of the people by this constant display of the Lord's goodness. Contrary to all other clouds, it was always stationary, always near the tabernacle, and acted as the reverse of all other clouds, in that it shone bright by night, and was dark as a cloud to obscure the sun's brightness and scorching rays by day. Besides these and other wonderful properties, its movements became the token for the camp of Israel to move, and when it rested, it implied that Israel was to rest also. And thus, not for a short transient march or two, not on any particular emergency, did it become the guide and protection of Israel, for forty years together, until all the people of God arrived in the promised land. Pause my soul, and ponder over the grace of thy covenant God in Christ, in this standing miracle; and when thou hast duly considered the wonderful subject, say, was not Jesus then as much, in type and figure, preached to the church of old, as he is now in sum and substance? Was the Lord veiled in a cloud then, and hath he not since veiled himself in our flesh? Did he go before the people then, and doth he not the same now? Was he stationary then, that is, ever with them, and is he not with his people "always, even unto the end of the world?" Was the cloud in the wilderness the reverse of all other clouds, shining by night, but becoming a grateful screen by day? And is not Jesus all this and more; shining most bright upon his people when they are in darkness, and sheltering them when the heat of persecution or distress is at the height? Did the cloud never depart from the people during their forty years' journey through the wilderness until they arrived at Canaan? And doth not our Lord go before, and follow his redeemed, all the way of their pilgrimage, until he hath brought them home safe to heaven? Oh! thou glorious, gracious, great I AM! be thou, dearest Lord, still the light, the way, the truth, and the life, to all thy redeemed. And as now, since thou hast finished redemption-work by thine open presence upon earth, in substance of our flesh, and "washed away the filth of the daughters of Zion, and purged the blood of Jerusalem from the midst thereof, by the spirit of judgment, and by the spirit of burning:" do thou, Lord, fulfil that sweet promise, and "create upon every dwelling-place of mount Zion, and upon her assemblies, a cloud and a smoke by day, and the shining of a flaming fire by night; for upon all the glory shall be a defence!" Isa. iv. 4, 5.

JUNE 12.

MORNING.—" And confessed that they were strangers and pilgrims on the earth."—Heb. xi. 13.

My soul, hast thou also witnessed this confession before many witnesses? See whether thou hast the same evidences they had. In the first place, they were led to see that here they had no continuing city. Sin, sorrow, sickness, death, inhabited this region. Every thing said to them in that sweet voice of God, " Arise ye, and depart, for this is not your rest, because it is polluted." What sayest thou, my soul, to this first view of the subject? Look at it under another. Hast thou learnt, and so learnt as to prize it, the blessedness of that promise, " there is a rest that remaineth for the people of God?" What sayest thou to this also, my soul? Dost thou see that Jesus is that rest, and is he the object of thy desire in rest? For the prophet saith, " He is the rest wherewith he will cause the weary to rest, and he is their refreshing." Isa. xxviii. 12. Hast thou heard and welcomed his invitation?—" Come unto me, all ye that labour and are heavy laden, and I will give you rest!" Go one step further in the enquiry. Under these convictions of soul art thou travelling the heavenly road, asking the way to Zion with thy face thitherward, as a stranger and a pilgrim upon earth? Go further yet. Art thou guided, as Israel was in the way, by the pillar of cloud by day, and guarded by the pillar of fire by night? Art thou coming up out of the wilderness of this world, leaning upon Jesus? Advance yet further in the enquiry. While the Holy Ghost as the pillar of cloud is going before thee, and thou art resting upon Jesus as thy staff and stay, knowest thou God for thy Father, his word thy guide, his promises thy treasure, his ordinances thine inns, not to dwell in, but like the wayfaring man to tarry but for the night? And dost thou draw water with joy out of those wells of salvation? Pause, my soul, as thou seekest answers to these questions. Knowest thou the difficulties of a wilderness dispensation; and the sweets of those streams from that river which make glad the city of God? Art thou like other travellers, sometimes enjoying fine weather when Jesus's face, his love, his mercy, are all in view; and sometimes walking in darkness, when storms of sin and Satan throw clouds over the gracious prospect? More especially, art thou the scorn and derision of the carnal? Do they make thee their subject of laughter, and art thou the drunkard's song? And, lastly, to mention no more, knowest thou, my soul, what it is sometimes to be discouraged by reason of the way, while Satan would prompt thee to go back; but sweetly constrained by Jesus's love, thou art still the patient follower of them "who through faith and patience inherit the promises?" Hast thou, my soul, these precious marks of the stranger and pilgrim upon earth? Oh then, remember what is said of them to whom the Holy Ghost bears testimony, and by thy covenant interest in Jesus behold thy vast privilege in the same blessed promise; God is not ashamed to be called their God, for he hath prepared for them a city.

EVENING.—"The Lord thy God in the midst of thee is mighty. He will save. He will rejoice over thee with joy. He will rest in his love. He will joy over thee with singing."—Zeph. iii. 17.

My soul! look at this old testament promise, through the medium of the new testament dispensation, and behold what a cluster of rich blessings it contains; and which, like all the other promises of the bible, is "yea and amen in Christ Jesus!" And observe how it opens. The Lord thy God, that is, Jehovah in his threefold character of person, in rich covenant engagements, is "in the midst of thee;" hath set up his throne in Zion, and lives, and reigns, and governs in the hearts of his redeemed. So said Jesus, and so that dear Lord explained it in after ages: "If a man love me, he will keep my words; and my Father will love him, and we will come unto him, and make our abode with him;" John xiv. 23. "I will pray the Father, and he shall give you another Comforter, that he may abide with you for ever, even the Spirit of truth;" John xiv. 16, 17. Mark these blessed, precious truths, my soul, in the most lively characters, on thine heart; and hence learn, that the Lord thy God, in covenant engagements, dwelleth in the midst of his people, and in the hearts of his people; that, like the sun at midday, in the centre of the heavens, he may enlighten, warm, refresh, and give forth all his blessings to bless thee. Next mark what the prophet saith of this covenant Lord God, who is in the midst of his church and people: "He is mighty!" Shout aloud at this, my soul; for if he be mighty, then he will support thy weakness, and subdue thy foes. What can bear down, or destroy the soul, whom this mighty God upholds? What shall arise to distress a child of God, as long as God is almighty? And if he hath engaged to be for thee, who can dare to be against thee? Sweet consideration! What signifies my weakness, while Christ is strong? Yea, his strength will be made perfect in my weakness. Go on farther, my soul, in looking over the many blessed things spoken of in this verse. "He will save." Yea: he hath saved, and doth save, and will save. And this is the very cause, the angel said, for which his name should be called Jesus: for "he shall save his people from their sins." Matt. i. 21. Think of this, when at any time, sin or sorrow, trial or temptation, would cast thee down. Jesus is still Jesus, still on his throne: yea, thy Saviour. Amidst all thy changeableness, there is no change in him. And observe yet farther, how the prophet chimes on those sweet words: "He will rejoice over thee with joy: he will rest in his love: he will joy over thee with singing." Pause, my soul, over this most gracious account. Jesus not only saves, not only pardons, but he doth it as God, as Jesus. It is his joy, his delight, his pleasure, to do so. As he saith in another scripture, "Yea, I will rejoice over them to do them good, and I will plant them in this land assuredly, with my whole heart, and with my whole soul;" Jer. xxxii. 41. And as the poor timid believer, from feeling such coldness and deadness, as at times he doth in himself feel, is but too easily prevailed upon by the enemy, and by his own unbelieving heart, to suppose the same of Jesus: that he might not give way to this temptation, the Lord adds, "he will rest in his love:" will abide in it unmoved, and without change; for, as he saith in another scripture, "the Lord God of Israel hateth putting away:" Mal. ii. 16. Oh! what a multitude of sweet things are folded up in this verse! Jesus rejoiceth over his people; yea, Jesus joys over them with singing. How often have I seen, in some lovely evening, like the present, that sweet bird of the air, called the sky-lark, mount aloft from her nest, still looking at her young as she ascends; and when advanced to her height, warbling in the most delightful notes over her brood; until at length, with all the rapidity of love, she darts down to cover, to feed, and to protect them! Thus, but in an infinitely higher degree, doth Jesus joy over his children with singing, resting in his love; and is ever near, ever mighty to defend, to bless, to keep, and to make happy, those who rest in his strength; while he rests in his love, being their God, and they his people.

JUNE 13.

MORNING.—"The master is come, and calleth for thee."—John xi. 28.

My soul, mark how gracious the Lord is to his people in the special and distinguishing tokens of his grace. Jesus doth not barely send his gospel to the church, or house, or family; but he speaketh by the soft, but powerful whispers of his love, to the individual soul. "To thee is the word of his salvation sent." Hence the soul who feels the sovereignty of his word in the constraining influences with which it is accompanied, cries out, I shall never forget thy word, for by it thou hast quickened me. But besides the calls of his grace in his house of prayer, in how many ways, and by what a variety of methods, is the Lord Jesus calling upon his people. My soul, I hope that thou art always upon the look out, and art getting to thy watch-tower to hear what the Lord thy God hath to say to thee, by his word, by his providences, his chastisements in love, and in all the gracious manifestations of his favour. Behold, he saith, "I stand at the door and knock." So Jesus calleth, and so let my soul hear. Now, Lord, thou art calling me by thy word and providence in a way of grace: by and by I shall hear thy voice in the hour of death and judgment. And who shall say how very powerful, sweet, and gracious, that call is, when Jesus cometh to take his people home to himself, that where he is, there they may be also? 'I hear my Master's voice,' said a highly favoured servant of God in the moment of his departure. Perhaps a loud voice, a glorious distinguishable voice to him that is called, when no stander by is at all conscious of the sound. Hence another said, when he was dying, 'I shall change my place, but not my company.' Jesus, master, in that hour be it my happiness to say, "let me hear thy voice, let me see thy countenance: for sweet is thy voice, and thy countenance is comely."

EVENING.—"The golden pot that had manna."—Heb. ix. 4.

There is somewhat very blessed in the account given concerning the furniture of the second tabernacle. Some few evenings since, my soul, a glance was taken of the candlestick, the table and shew-bread, in the first tabernacle. Perhaps the Lord the Holy Ghost will open to thy meditation some edifying considerations in the view of the contents of the second. The golden pot, which preserved the manna pure, that in itself was soon subject to corruption, was unquestionably a beautiful emblem of the divine nature of Jesus, imparting durableness and dignity to his human nature. We are told concerning the manna, that if the Israelites kept it, though but for a day (except when miraculously preserved pure on the sabbath-day, to remind them of that ordinance) it bred worms, and stank; Exod. xvi. 20. But in this golden pot, an omer full of manna put therein, was laid up before the Lord as a memorial, and preserved pure. Precious Lord Jesus! do I not learn from hence, that it is thou, and thou alone, who givest life, and purity, and sweetness to our poor persons and offerings? Every thing in us, and from us, must, like ourselves, be corrupt, and is indeed part of ourselves, and subject to putrefaction: but in thee, and by thee, as the manna was preserved in the golden pot, we are preserved, made clean and holy, in thy holiness and purity. And surely, Lord, I learn, moreover, from this part of the furniture in the second tabernacle, that as thou art entered into the holy place, there to appear in the presence of God for us; so, by this emblem of the golden pot, is set forth the sweet communion and fellowship, which thy people now are privileged to enjoy, in thee, and from thee, and with thee! Yea, Lord, thou art still the bread of God, the living bread, which that manna represented: and still dost thou feed thy church above, and lead them to fountains of living waters. And surely, Lord, thou wilt no less feed thy church below, which yet remains in this dry and barren wilderness, where no water is. I hear what the Spirit saith unto the churches, and I feel delight: "To him that overcometh, will I give to eat of the hidden manna." Rev. ii. 17.

JUNE 14.

MORNING.—"Who is this that cometh up from the wilderness, leaning upon her beloved."—Song viii. 5.

Who is it that asketh this question, my soul? Is it the holy angels, astonished as they well may, at the gracious condescension of thy Jesus in the grace and favour he hath bestowed upon thee? Or is it the world at large, looking on with amazement at the love of Jesus to his chosen? Is it the Jewish church, amazed that Gentiles should be fellow heirs, and of the same body, and partakers of God's promise in Christ? Or, above all, is it Jesus himself, not because be knoweth not the grace he hath bestowed, but because he admireth the grace he hath given, and as he did the centurion's faith which he himself was the author of, he looketh upon it with pleasure? And art thou, my soul, come up from the wilderness of nature, a dry, barren land, where no water of life is; from the wilderness of the world, and from all the unsatisfying and empty pursuits of it? Art thou leaning upon thy Jesus, cleaving to him, hanging upon him, strengthening thyself upon him, determining, like another Ruth, concerning Naomi, where Jesus goeth thou wilt go, and where he lodgeth thou wilt lodge? Is this thy conduct, and dost thou rest the whole stress of thy present and everlasting happiness upon his glorious person and righteousness? If so, angels may well look on, and cry out, who is this to whom the Father of all mercies hath been so gracious; to whom Jesus hath manifested his love, otherwise than he doth to the world; and on whom the Spirit hath shed his blessed influence to make thee willing in the day of his power? Yes, precious

Jesus, I would come up from every thing near and dear in this wilderness state, forget mine own people, and my father's house; I would lean wholly upon thy glorious person for my acceptance before God: lean wholly upon thy righteousness, as all-sufficient for my justification. I would lean upon thy fulness, day by day, for the supply of all grace here; and I would lean solely upon the divine efficacy and blessedness of thy blood to cleanse my soul for everlasting fitness for happiness hereafter. Witness for me, ye angels of light, that this is my beloved on whom I lean, and in whom I trust, and desire to be found in, for time and for eternity. Amen.

EVENING.—" Aaron's rod that budded."—Heb. ix. 4.

One view more of the tabernacle, and the articles of furniture therein contained, may be rendered profitable, under the Spirit's teaching: and therefore, my soul, look at that standing miracle, which was preserved there, of the rod of Aaron. The history of it is related in the book of Numbers, chap. xvii. It was the method which the Lord was graciously pleased to appoint, for the determining on whom his choice rested for the priesthood. To this end, a rod was taken from every tribe, and laid up before the Lord in the tabernacle; the Lord having declared, that whichsoever of the tribes had the rod to blossom, should be the man. The rod of Aaron, on the morrow, had buds, and blossoms, and fruits. But in all these, Christ, in his everlasting priesthood, was typified. To behold a dry stick bring forth buds, and become green and flourishing, was miraculous, and only to be referred into the sovereign power and will of God. But, my soul, when we see Jesus, as the branch out of the root of Jesse, we behold him, as the prophet, ages before his incarnation, described him, growing up before Jehovah in his tabernacle, as the rod laid up before him, " a tender plant, and as a root out of a dry ground." Isa. liii. 2.

And as the rod of Aaron had in one and the same moment the whole product of the season in buds, and blossoms, and fruits; so in the everlasting priesthood of Christ are suited graces for the several ages of his church, and the several wants of all his people. Precious Jesus! may my soul unceasingly look unto thee, as my faithful, everlasting, and unchangeable High Priest! And do thou, Lord, "send the rod of thy strength out of Zion: rule thou in the midst of thine enemies!" Full sure I am, O Lord, that every thing in me, and from me, like the rods of the different tribes of Israel, will remain dry, and neither give forth bud nor blossom. To thee, and the rod of thy strength, therefore, will I look, that thou mayest give life and grace to my poor soul, to bring forth fruit unto God, by grace here, and glory for ever.

JUNE 15.

MORNING.—"Now we, brethren, as Isaac was, are the children of promise."—Gal. iv. 28.

Mark, my soul, the distinguishing characters of those who are the children of promise, and see whether thou art of this blessed family. For as the law and the gospel are strikingly distinguished from each other, so are the children of nature from those of grace. And how is this to be known? Look at the case Paul hath referred to: Isaac was the son of Abraham. And the apostle saith, "that they which are of faith, the same are children of Abraham. And if ye be Christ's, then are ye Abraham's seed, and heirs according to the promise." And as Isaac was a child of Abraham by promise, not by natural power, so believers in Jesus are born, not of blood, nor of the will of the flesh, nor of the will of man, but of God. Hence Paul saith, "to Abraham and his seed were the promises made. He saith not to seeds as of many, but as of one; and to thy seed, which is Christ." Precious truth! The children of promise are of Jesus; for he himself is the one great promise of the bible. So that from everlasting they are the seed of Christ: their being, their well being, their everlasting being, all are folded up in Jesus, as the oak in all its foliage is contained and folded up in the first and original acorn. Hence they are spiritually begotten, born, nourished, fed, sustained, led, strengthened, and carried on, through all the gradations of grace, until grace is consummated in the ripeness of their full stature in glory. My soul, art thou, as Isaac was, a child of promise? Oh live by faith on Jesus, and in Jesus, and see to it, in all thy daily, hourly exercises and experiences, that all the promises of God in Christ Jesus are yea and amen, unto the glory of God the Father.

EVENING.—"Yet have I set my King upon my holy hill of Zion. I will declare the decree."—Ps. ii. 6, 7.

Here is a subject, my soul, opened for thy meditation, which neither the evening nor day of thy whole life, no, nor eternity itself, will ever be long enough to exhaust. Some of the outlines may be gathered here below, when God the Holy Ghost condescends to teach; but the subject itself will, no doubt, be among the glorious employments of heaven. It should seem, that the divine speakers here are God the Father and God the Son. We find similar instances in the word of God: see Isa. vi. and xlix. John xii. 27, 28. And the beloved apostle was led into an apprehension of the same subject, for the church's instruction, in that vision he saw, Rev. v. 1—9. In this vision, Jesus is represented as taking the book, and opening it, and declaring the contents of it. Hence, therefore, when God the Father saith, as in this Psalm, "I have set my King upon my holy hill of Zion;" Jesus, as King, declares *the decree* of the council of peace, which was between them both, for the salvation of his church and people. And what was the decree, but the decree from all eternity; namely, that Jehovah would give a church to his dear

Son, and his dear Son to the church: that Jesus should take the name of his people, and their nature; become their glorious Head and Representative; redeem them from the ruins of the fall, and make them altogether glorious and lovely, from his comeliness that he would put upon them? Upon Christ's thus undertaking the salvation of his people, "the decree went forth," that all power should be his, as Mediator, in heaven and in earth. It began from everlasting: for from everlasting, by this decree, Jesus was set up as the glorious Head and Mediator before all worlds. The same power became his in time; and the same power is his to all eternity. Hence, therefore, Jesus is no sooner seated on his throne, on his holy hill of Zion, but he sends forth the decree; and God the Father confirms the whole, in giving him "the heathen for his inheritance, and the uttermost parts of the earth for his possession." Hail then, thou sovereign Lord! thou almighty King, upon thy holy hill of Zion! Gladly do I acknowledge thee to be my King and my God; for by Jehovah's appointment, by thy conquest of my heart, and by the voluntary surrender of myself since thou hast brought me under the power of thy grace, am I thine, and no longer my own. Oh! for grace so to acknowledge thee, so to obey thee, so to love thee, that while the Lord Jehovah hath set thee upon thy throne, his grace also may give thee the throne of my heart! And while all thine enemies must bow before thee, may all thy friends and followers rejoice in thy service! Even so, Amen.

JUNE 16.

MORNING.—"He shall gather the lambs with his arm, and carry them in his bosom."—Isa. xl. 11.

My soul, mark in this sweet scripture how Jesus is described, in not only attending to all the various wants of his fold, but to the very method of imparting to their several wants in a way corresponding to his own character and their state. In the fold of Jesus, like the sheepfold among men, some are sheep and some are lambs: some of advanced age, and some of younger standing. Well, where will Jesus put the lambs and the weaklings of his fold? Certainly, if there be one place in the heart of Jesus softer and more tender than another, there the lambs shall lay. And as Jesus himself lay in the bosom of his Father, so the lambs of his flock shall lay in his bosom. Sweet thought to encourage thee, my soul, and all the followers of Christ! Jesus will not thrust out the lambs into the dangers of the wilderness, where the prowling beasts of prey are, nor expose them to over-driving, or the speed with which the more mature sheep can travel. But he will proportion their burden to their back, and their day to their strength. And besides this, he will keep them nearer to himself; his arms shall clasp them; the warmth of his bosom shall nourish them; if they cannot walk they shall be carried; and when they cannot find their way, they shall be led. Oh thou great Shepherd of thy sheep, is it thus thou sweetly dealest with thy little ones? Hence I see then explained why it is that young believers, in the first seasons of their knowledge of thee, find so many blessed refreshings, which they afterwards do not so sensibly enjoy. Yes, Lord, it is thus thou gatherest the lambs and carriest them in thy bosom. And sweetly and seasonably dost thou do all this, and in a way which fully proves thy love and compassion to the necessities of thy flock.

EVENING.—" Yea, the stork in the heaven knoweth her appointed times; and the turtle, and the crane, and the swallow, observe the time of their coming: but my people know not the judgment of the Lord."—Jer. viii. 7.

When the Lord would expostulate with his people, what methods he graciously adopts! There are no creatures in nature so dull, so senseless, and stupid, as

God's people are, by reason of the fall. Every animal hath an instinct, prompting to self-preservation. Are they exposed to danger? how speedily do they endeavour to remove! Are they apprehensive of a storm? they flee to some covering to hide them! The birds of passage, when the first symptoms of winter appear, gather together, to depart to a warmer climate. But man, poor blind improvident man, no winter of death can admonish him; no approach of the departing day of life can prevail, to induce him to flee from the wrath to come. My soul! look round on human life, and mark this, by way of admiring, more and more, distinguishing grace, which enabled thee to estimate thy privileges, and discern that sovereign bountiful mercy, which maketh thee to differ from another. "What hast thou, which thou didst not receive?" But, dearest Lord, is it not to copy after that gracious feeling of thine, which thou hadst in the days of thy flesh, when thou hadst compassion on the multitude, in beholding them famishing, and wast moved in pity towards them; when we behold the great mass of thoughtless sinners, whose concern for self-preservation doth not come up to that of the brute which perisheth? In common life, all are interested, and earnest in the pursuit of the different objects of the world: the traveller is full of thought, in his way home, to see that his path be right; the mariner would not run contrary to the direction of the compass; the man of trade never acts in opposition to the gain of that trade; neither does the man of pleasure lose sight of what will most likely promote that pleasure. But thy people, blessed Jesus, are everlastingly pursuing what they have proved a thousand times to be vain and unsatisfying; yet they pursue it again, and do not learn "to know the judgment of the Lord." Blessed Lord! undertake for me: pity, compassionate, direct, guide, keep me! Oh! for grace to learn, and rightly to value the things of salvation!

And, convinced that Christ is all and in all, may I never seek from the creature what only can be found in the Creator! And having discovered the vanity of every thing out of Christ, may I, where Christ is not, from henceforth learn, with the church to say, "Whom have I in heaven but thee? and there is none upon earth that I desire in comparison of thee: my flesh and my heart faileth: but thou art the strength of my heart and my portion for ever!"

JUNE 17.

MORNING.—"He restoreth my soul."—Ps. xxiii. 3.

Yes, Lord, it is indeed thou that bringest back the strayed sheep; for as no man ever quickened, so none can keep alive his own soul. It was indeed thy promise, and most graciously dost thou fulfil it!—"As a shepherd seeketh out his flock in the day that he is among his sheep, so will I seek out my sheep, and bring again that which was driven away." Ezek. xxxiv. 11—16. My soul, mark this trait of character in thy Jesus for thy morning meditation. It is well for thee that restoring work, reclaiming work, reviving work, all is with Jesus; begins in him, and is carried on and completed by him, and through his grace in thee. And it is well for thee, my soul, that though thou so often failest in all things towards thy Jesus, yet he never faileth in his love to thee in any thing. Sweet consideration! his love, and not thy deserts, become the standard for all his tenderness to his people. And mark it down, my soul, in strong characters, that Jesus's grace is much shewn this way. He doth not wait our return, for then we should never return at all; neither doth he wait our cry for help, but he puts that cry into the soul. Alas, how often have we wandered and gone away, even before that we were sensible of our departure. How blessed is it then to see and know that Jesus's eye is upon us, and that before we return to him, he is coming forth to us. His love, his pity, his compassion, are the security of his people's recovery. Yes, Lord, it is thou that restorest my soul. Praises to thy name, for thou doest it all in such a way as proves it to be for thy great name's sake, that thy grace comes freely and without upbraiding. "He restoreth my soul, and leadeth me in the paths of righteousness for his name's sake."

EVENING.—" I shall behold man no more, with the inhabitants of the world."—Isa. xxxviii. 11.

My soul, though thou art, I trust, prepared for thy great change, and in an *habitual* state for death, whenever the Lord shall come to take thee home; yet there is also an *actual* state of being on the look-out for it, so that it is proper at times to go down to the grave in *imagination*, before thou art carried thither in *reality*; that by earthing thyself, thou mayest consider what will be the immediate consequences of death in those things which are now most about thee, and with which thou art necessarily much occupied. "Thou wilt behold man no more, with the inhabitants of the world:" would it not be proper, therefore, to wean thyself from too great an acquaintance with them now, that the separation may be the less felt? Thou wilt be called upon to enter upon a state altogether new, and a path thou hast never before trodden; and would it not be wise to send forth enquiries concerning them, such as scripture gives the clearest answer to, and study the best way to make preparation in Jesus for thy change? What a blessed example hath the apostle Paul left upon record of his conduct in this particular; "I protest," said he to the Corinthian church, speaking on this subject, "by your rejoicing which I have in Christ Jesus our Lord, I die daily," 1 Cor. xv. 31. Such were both the habitual and actual frames of Paul's mind, that he was every day, and all the day, waiting and looking for his Master's call. The fact was, he knew the certainty of the ground on which he stood; he had no farther questions to ask concerning his safety in Christ; and therefore, he rather wished to bring the hour on, than to put it off. His whole heart, his whole affections, centered in Christ; and as such, though to live was Christ, yet to die was gain. My soul, what sayest thou to this blessed frame? Oh! for the same earnestness, and from the same cause; that whether this night, or at cock-crowing, or in the morning, when the Lord comes, though thou wilt behold man no more with the inhabitants of the world, yet thou wilt behold the face of God in glory; and when thou awakest after his likeness, thou wilt be satisfied with it.

JUNE 18.

MORNING.—"To him whom man despiseth; to him whom the nation abhorreth."—Isa. xlix. 7.

My soul, let thy longing eyes be directed to him this day whom man despiseth, and whom God honoureth, and to whom he hath given a name above every name. Pause, in the contemplation of the wonderful mystery. Was Jesus indeed despised, and by the very creature he came to redeem? Did angels hail his wonderful incarnation, and man despise, hate, and abhor him? "Be astonished, O ye heavens; and wonder, O earth!" But, my soul, go further in the contemplation of this mysterious subject. What man, what individual man, was it that could thus requite the unparalleled love of Jesus? Alas, not an individual only, but a whole nation; nay, the whole nature, both Jew and Gentile abhorred him; for while in a state of unrenewed nature, to the one he is a stumbling-block, and to the other his cross is foolishness. Ah, is it so, my soul? Why then it follows, that thou, even thou, my soul, wert once in the same state of hatred, and wert by nature, as well as others, a child of wrath, despising this wisdom of God in Christ for the salvation of sinners. And art thou then, my soul, recovered by almighty sovereign grace from this deadly hatred of nature, and dost thou look this day with love, with joy, with rapture, and unspeakable delight to him whom man despiseth, to him whom the nation abhorreth? Is Jesus indeed lovely, the altogether lovely to thy view? Is he precious, nay, infinitely more precious than the golden wedge of Ophir? Yes, thou Holy One of God, thou art the all in all to my soul. Witness for me, O ye saints that are now around his throne, that I have none in heaven or in earth that I desire besides him. My whole soul desires to know him, to follow hard after him, to trust in him, to cleave to him, to hang upon him, and to accept and receive him, and to make use of him as the wisdom of God, and the power of God, for salvation to my soul, as he is to every one that believeth. Oh ye sons of men, who are still in the unrenewed hatred of your heart, in your hatred against the precious Christ of God, what will ye do when he whom ye now despise shall come to your everlasting shame? Well might the apostle echo the words of the prophet, for from age to age the astonishing truth remaineth! "Behold, ye despisers, and wonder, and perish; for I work a work in your days, a work which ye shall in no wise believe, though a man declare it unto you."

EVENING.—"Elect, according to the fore-knowledge of God the Father, through sanctification of the Spirit, unto obedience, and sprinkling of the blood of Jesus Christ."—1 Pet. i. 2.

Of all blessings, surely this is the highest, and the best, which holds forth to a poor sinner the assurance of redemption, as the united result of the love, grace, and mercy of all the persons in the Godhead. My soul, pause over the glorious truth, and sweetly mark the testimony of each co-operating and acting together in the great work of salvation. Behold thy God and Father setting apart, from all eternity, the chosen vessels of mercy, foreknowing and fore-appointing every event, in his own counsel, purpose, and will. What a blessed thought, in the mind of the redeemed, is this, to live upon, to cherish, and keep alive in the soul, from day to day, to call up the unceasing fruits of adoration, love, duty, and praise, in grace here, and in glory to all eternity. Go on, my soul, to the contemplation of the second chapter in his holy volume of grace and mercy; and mark what the apostle hath here said of "the sanctification of the Spirit." So that the blessed hand of the Holy Ghost is as much engaged in this beneficent act of redemption, in the existence of every individual, as the foreknowledge and appointment of God the Father, or of the obedience and sprinkling of the blood of Jesus Christ. Yea, all the glory of redemption, in the grace provided by the Father, and the merits of the Son's blood and righteousness, depend, for the personal enjoyment of it, in the case of each believer, upon the Holy Ghost's revelation of it in the soul. Oh! it is blessed to see, to feel, to know, and to enjoy those gracious communications of God's Christ in the soul, which God the Holy Ghost awakens, and excites, and brings home to the mind. And no less, as the meritorious cause of all (the third chapter in this wonderful volume) do thou contemplate, my soul, the two united branches of thy redemption; the obedience, and atonement in the sprinkling of the blood of Jesus Christ. How comprehensive, yet how full and satisfactory! It is Jesus, as God's righteous servant, who, by his perfect obedience hath justified his people. And it is the death of the cross which hath fully atoned for their transgression; "The blood of Jesus Christ cleanseth from all sin." Behold then, my soul, in these three glorious chapters of redemption how all the great charter of grace is summed up and contained. Take it with thee as thine evening portion; let it lie down with thee, and arise with thee; and carry it about with thee, for thine unceasing meditation during the whole of thy day of grace, until grace is swallowed up in eternal glory!

JUNE 19.

MORNING.—"Go thy way, eat thy bread with joy, and drink thy wine with a merry heart; for God now accepteth thy works."—Eccles. ix. 7.

My soul, here is a sweet subject for thy morning thoughts. Art thou accepted in the Beloved? Hast thou accepted Jesus, and God accepted thee in Jesus? Well mayest thou then eat of the bread of common providences, and drink of the sweet of all sanctified mercies, for every thing is blessed in Jesus, and Jesus is blessing thee in every thing. Surely an accepted soul is a blessed soul, for he is blessed in his basket and in his store; blessed in his lying down, and blessed in his rising up; blessed in his going out, and blessed in his coming home; yea, blessed in time, and blessed to all eternity. Yes, thou blessed Source of all my blessedness, thou precious Jesus, I will go my way, for thou art my way; I will eat my bread with joy, for thou art my bread of life; I will drink the wine which thou hast mingled for me, for thy love is better than wine. And as God my Father accepteth me in thee, this forms an everlasting cause of everlasting joy; joy in what I have; joy in what I expect; joy in even what I want, for those very wants will lead me the closer and the nearer to thee; joy in what I fear, for my fear will keep me depending upon thee; joy in what I suffer, for my sufferings are sweetly blessed when they afford a renewed occasion for my Jesus to soothe me under them, and in his time to deliver me out of them; and joy in all I lose, for lose what I may I cannot lose thee, I cannot lose God's Christ; I cannot lose his love, his favour, his grace, his Spirit, the efficacy of his blood, and the merits of his righteousness. Oh precious security, precious salvation in the Lord our Righteousness! Shall I not then live up to this heritage, and live under its influence, in the thankful, joyful use of it from day to day? Go thy way, my soul, go in Jesus as thy way; every day, and all the day, eat thy bread with joy; eye Jesus as the spiritual food, and always present at thy table; drink hourly of his cup of salvation, with a cheerful heart, for thou art accepted in the Beloved.

EVENING.—"My heart is fixed, O God, my heart is fixed; I will sing and give praise."—Psalm lvii. 7.

My soul! here is a delightful subject proposed for thine evening meditation, in the fixedness of the heart. The only possible way of really "singing and giving praise to the Lord" with the heart, is when the Lord hath fixed thine heart to the service. Many rush to ordinances, as the unthinking horse rusheth to the battle: not so, my soul, be thy practice. See to it, that He who alone can give a fixedness to the heart, hath fixed thine; for then, when the view of a God in Christ is brought home by the Holy Ghost to thy warmest and most devout affections, then, and not before, will there be a going forth of those affections, awakened and led by the same Almighty Spirit, upon the glorious person of thy Lord, and faith will be in lively exercise, in a way of praise, and love, and obedience, and joy. Then thou wilt sing and give praise "with the spirit, and with the understanding also." Sit down now, in the coolness of this sweet summer evening, and wait upon thy Jesus in silence and in meditation before him, until the Lord hath given thee this fixedness of affection on his person and righteousness; and then thou wilt find a fitness *for* devotion, and a fitness *in* devotion, from the sweet influences of God the Holy Ghost. Oh! how blessed is it to retire from every eye but his, who seeth in secret; and to remember, that while thine eye is looking upon Him, he is ever looking upon thee! Such a thought as this begins to give a fixedness to the heart; for the whole current and stream of the affections are directed, and therefore pour in to this one channel; so that, like a river not divided, nothing of it runs another way. And when the full tide of thine affections is thus tending to the person of Jesus, shall not such a fixedness of thought make thee cry out, as David, "My heart is fixed, O God, my heart is fixed; I will sing and give praise?" It is this state of the heart which makes all the difference between the gracious and the carnal. Both may use closet duties; both may read, yea, study the word; yea, become proficients in the outer understanding of the word; the meditation may furnish the head, but not feed the heart: but it is the gracious soul that enjoys. It is a solemn consideration, how many are employed from year to year, in *spiritual* things, whose hearts all the while remain *carnal.* But where there is a fixedness of the heart, by the Spirit of the living God, upon the person, offices, and character of the Lord Jesus Christ, the meditation doth not settle for the mere discharge of a duty, but for the joy of the soul. Oh how I love thy law!" is then the language of the fixed heart; "it is my meditation all the day." My soul, dost thou know these things by heartfelt testimony? Doth God the Holy Ghost shine in upon thee with his light, to give thee sweet views, engaging views, soul-arresting views of Jesus? Are thine eyes, I mean the whole affections of thy soul, fixing themselves on Jesus, as a longing woman fixeth upon the one object of her desire, which nothing beside can satisfy? Oh! it is blessed to have this fixedness of mind at all times upon the person of Jesus. For this is to enter into the heart, and to shut to the door, (as Christ expresseth it) by shutting out all thoughts besides, and then looking in every direction for Jesus, and finding him in all, and upon all. His word, his grace, his secret whispers, his communications, are like so many rich cabinets of jewels, which the soul turns over, and finds Jesus in every one. Oh! thou dear Lord Jesus! grant me this happy frame of mind, that I may say, with David, "My heart is fixed, O God, my heart is fixed; I will sing and give praise!"

JUNE 20.

MORNING.—"Grace be with all them that love our Lord Jesus Christ in sincerity. Amen."—Eph. vi. 24.

And dost thou, my soul, with the same affection and love as the apostle, bend thy knee this morning before His throne, of whom the whole family in heaven and earth are named? Dost thou look up, and pray that all grace may abound? Oh what a delightful thought is it, my soul, to warm thy affections, that in the moment thou art waiting at the mercy-seat, thousands are waiting also for the morning blessing. Go then, my soul, and tell thy Redeemer this; tell him that he hath all suited grace, and that the eyes of his redeemed, as the eyes of one man, are all directed towards him. Yes, thou glorious, rich, and gracious Saviour, we do behold thee still as the Lamb in the midst of the throne, leading thy church which is above in glory to fountains of living waters. And, Lord, we know that thou art equally attentive to thy church in the dry and barren wilderness here below, where no waters are. Vouchsafe, blessed Lord, to supply each soul. Thou hast every grace, and all grace, suited to all wants; grace to pardon, grace to save, grace to renew, grace to strengthen, grace to bless. Oh Lord, awaken, convince, humble, comfort, and pour out of thy fulness as our several necessities may be, in calling, cleansing, justifying, adopting, sanctifying, and building up thine household, that all grace may abound, according to God's riches in glory by Christ Jesus. Oh ye attendants at the heavenly gate, see that ye come not empty away. Remember Jesus is on the throne; eye him there. Behold, the very grace you need is in his hand; read the love that is in his heart, and remember that he hath not only the very grace you need, but every grace, and every mercy for all that wait upon him. Tell every poor sinner this, and bid him ask in faith, nothing doubting. Tell all you know, and all you meet, and all you see, that He who is on the throne hath abundant grace, and wants vessels, the empty vessels of his people, to give out into: tell them that his grace exceeds all sense of grace, all thoughts, all prayers, all praises, all desires; nay, that he hath exceeding abundantly above all that they can ask or think. Behold, then, O Lord, thy children, thy redeemed, thy family, and let all grace be with all them, and upon all them that love thee in sincerity. Amen.

EVENING.—"Unto me who am less than the least of all saints, is this grace given."—Ephes. iii. 8.

My soul, hear what the great apostle to the gentiles speaks of himself. He calls himself "less than the least;" a thing almost impossible in itself; but he doth it with a view to magnify the riches, the exceeding great riches of grace. And in the same moment that he views himself so low and abject, he is lost in amazement at beholding the exalted office to which he was called. So that Paul cries out, "Unto me," a poor, sinful, unworthy creature of the earth, "to me was this grace given!" My soul, leave for a moment the view of the apostle, and make the subject personal, by looking to a renewed instance of that grace, most freely given, in a case as far surpassing Paul in the greatness and undeservedness of it, as the imagination can conceive. Perhaps every sinner feels the same; this at least is certain, all may well feel the same. But the subject is not properly improved, either in the apostle's instance, or any other, unless there be connected with it the one great object of the whole, the promotion of the Redeemer's glory. This was and is the first and ultimate design for which grace was given. "This people," saith Jehovah, speaking of the redeemed in Christ, "have I formed for myself, they shall shew forth my praise." Isa. xliii. 21. And how do they shew forth the Lord's praise, but by the gifts of the Lord's grace? When Jesus calleth a poor sinner, and manifests himself to him, this is the display of his grace; for it is on such more especially, that he maketh his grace to shine. It would have been no grace had we merited his favour. But because we merit nothing, yea, are justly entitled to punishment, and yet God gives mercy, grace, and favour; this is what illustrates the exceeding riches of his grace, and demonstrates God's love to be indeed the love of God which passeth knowledge, because it differs altogether from creature love. And what tends yet more to display the riches of grace, that the glory of God in Christ, in following up the blessed plan of redemption, may be great indeed, the crown of Jesus, as Mediator, depends upon bringing to glory the objects of his love, on whom he hath made that grace to shine. And who shall calculate the rich revenue of love, adoration, and praise, in glory, which Jesus will have, and be for ever receiving, from the millions of redeemed souls gathered from sin and Satan, by the alone sovereignty of his grace? My soul, it is truly blessed thus to contemplate the person and work of Jesus, and the sweet effects of his grace. And what an addition to the subject is it, to say, with the apostle, each poor sinner for himself, "Unto me, who am less than the least of all saints, is this grace given!"

JUNE 21.

MORNING.—" Men wondered at."—Zech. iii. 8.

Men wondered at indeed, and every redeemed soul may truly say, I am a wonder unto many, a wonder to myself. Oh thou whose name is Wonderful! both thou and the children the Lord hath given thee, are for signs and wonders. Behold, my soul, how it was fulfilled in him whose name was Wonderful, and then thine astonishment will be the less that it should be fulfilled in his followers. I would contemplate thy person, blessed Jesus, and behold thee, not barely wondered at, but despised and rejected of men. The world gazed at thee, but saw no beauty nor form of comeliness in thee to desire thee. In thine offices also, how did the multitude despise thee as a prophet; when blind-folding thee, and smiting thee on thy sacred head, they tauntingly cried out, " Prophecy, thou Christ, who is he that smote thee!" As a priest, what blasphemy did they utter, when they saw enough to be convinced, and to confess, that thou didst save others, but thyself thou couldst not save. As a King, when having nailed thee to the tree, they demanded a proof of thy power in coming down from the cross. And wert thou not, blessed Jesus, wondered at in thy word, when they acknowledged, " never man spake like this man;" yet charged thy doctrines with blasphemy, and derided thee in them? Wert thou not the wonder and the hatred of the world, when thy miracles astonished them, but were ascribed to the agency of Beelzebub? Wert thou not, O thou spotless Lamb of God, wert thou not charged with immorality and called a wine-bibber, a sabbath-breaker, the friend of publicans and sinners? Did the world thus treat Jesus, and call the Master of the house Beelzebub? Oh then, my soul, well may they so treat them of his household! And must it not be so? Yes. The world knoweth them not, because it knew him not. They are made a spectacle, a gazing-stock, a reproach, a by-word. How unknown in their new birth from God, how little understood in their union with Jesus, how perfectly hidden from the world their life in the Spirit! What an everlasting opposition to carnal men are their pursuits, their pleasures, their happiness, their conversation, their desires—how wondered at their life of faith on the Son of God! They have meat to eat the world knoweth nothing of, for they feed upon the person, body, blood, grace, and righteousness of the Lord Jesus Christ. My soul, hast thou this rarity of character? Hast thou this blessed singularity? Art thou wondered at because thou runnest not to the same excess of riot, but art blameless and harmless among the sons of God, in the midst of a crooked and perverse generation? Oh blessed, for ever blessed, be his name, who hath called thee to this high, this glorious, this distinguishing honour, of being wondered at and reproached for Jesus's sake! Yes, Lord, I will not regard the reproach of men, neither be afraid of their revilings, for "the moth shall eat them up like a garment, and the worm shall eat them like wool; but thy righteousness shall be for ever, and thy salvation from generation to generation."

EVENING.—"Come, see a man, which told me all things that ever I did: is not this the Christ?"—John iv. 29.

Those are sweet and blessed views of the Lord Jesus, which he himself gives, when, by letting the poor sinner see himself, how wretched he is, and at the same time how glorious the Lord is, and how exactly suited to his wants and necessities, he makes the soul cry out, as this woman of Samaria did, "Is not this the Christ?" For who but Christ can read the heart, and tell all that passeth there? And as she found it, so all taught of Jesus find the same, that every true discovery of Christ must end in condemning ourselves, and exalting the

Redeemer. My soul! there are numberless instructions to be gathered from this scripture, and the history connected with it. Sit down, this evening, in the coolness of the shade, and look at a few of them. The Lord the Holy Ghost will open them to thy meditation. Jesus, we are told, " must needs go through Samaria." Yes; there was this poor sinner to be convinced of sin, and to be brought acquainted with her Saviour. Hence the opportunity soon offered; and Jesus as soon accomplished the purpose of his going thither. The Lord opened her heart to her own view, and gave her to see the vileness within. He opened, at the same time, her heart to the knowledge of himself, gave her to see his salvation; and the effects were as might have been expected: she hastened to the city, to tell other poor sinners, who also stood in need of a Saviour, that she had found " him of whom Moses and the prophets did write." Come, said she " see a man, which told me all things that ever I did; is not this the Christ?" My soul! hast thou so learned Christ? Hast thou " met with the Lord God of the Hebrews," and learned from him self-humbling thoughts, and a true conviction of sin? Hath he taught thee who he is, and what need thou hast of him? Hast thou seen him to be indeed the Christ of God; the man, whose name is Wonderful; who, in his divine nature, is " one with the Father over all, God blessed for ever;" and in his human nature, " the man, whose name is the Branch;" and by the union of both natures, the one glorious and true Messiah, " the Lord our righteousness?" And hath such a conviction of the infinite importance of knowing Christ been wrought thereby upon thy mind, that thou hast taken every method of recommending him to others? Surely, my soul, no truly regenerated sinner, who hath known, and seen, and felt that the Lord is gracious, but must be anxious that others should know, and see, and feel it also. And, therefore, like this poor woman, thou wilt be taking every proper opportunity of calling upon all, as far as thy sphere of usefulness can extend, to come and enjoy the same blessings, which the Lord hath imparted to thee. Precious Lord! I would not only invite every poor needy sinner to come to thee, but I would desire to accompany them. I would not say, " Go to Jesus," as if I needed thee no more myself; but I would say, " Come to him," let us go together, for " he will shew us of his ways, and we will walk in his paths." And Oh! that multitudes may come, and find to their soul's joy, as the Samaritans did, on the invitation of this poor woman, and be enabled to say, as they said, " Now we believe, not because of thy saying: for we have heard him ourselves, and know that this is indeed the Christ, the Saviour of the world."

JUNE 22.

MORNING.—" And they came unto the brook of Eshcol, and cut down from thence a branch with a cluster of grapes."—Numb. xiii. 23.

Was not this single cluster of God's earnest to the people of the sure possession of the land where those delicious fruits grew? And was not the size and weight of this one branch a sample how full and extensive all the blessings, both of the covenant and of the promised land, should be to the after possession of God's people? My soul, dost thou not see in it then a precious representation of Jesus, that one branch, and of all that cluster of blessings which are in him? Well might the church cry out concerning the Redeemer, " My beloved is unto me as a cluster of camphire in the vineyards of Engedi." For whether this camphire, this copher, denotes the vine of Cyprus, or the fruit of the palm-tree, in either, or in both, the soul-strengthening, soul-exhilirating, soul-healing virtues of this unnumbered excelleneies, may well be set forth under the beautiful similitude, of the cluster of grapes from the brook of Eshcol. Yes, thou dear Lord! thou hast condescended to compare thyself to the vine; and to thy people thou art indeed a cluster of all that is lovely, sweet, gracious, and endearing. In thee dwelleth, like the berries of the richest cluster, all the fulness of the Godhead bodily. In thee is found all the purity, holiness, harmlessness, and perfection of the human nature, as God manifest in the flesh. In thee, as God-man Mediator, we behold the cluster of all spiritual graces, all spiritual, temporal, eternal blessings, all divine promises, all, all are in thee, to give out to thy people. Neither is there a mercy thy people can want, of grace here, or glory hereafter, but what is treasured up in thee, in a fulness perfectly inexhaustible. Precious Jesus, revive my spirits this day with this view of thee. Give me to see when my soul desireth the first ripe fruit, that thou thyself art all my soul can need. Bring me to the brook of Eshcol, and there let my eyes, my heart, my whole soul, and body, and spirit, feast itself in the contemplation and enjoyment of thy person, thy graces, gifts, and fulness, until, under the full satisfaction my soul findeth, in being eternally filled with thy goodness, I cry out with the church, my beloved is unto me as the richest of all the clusters of copher in the vineyards of Engedi.

EVENING.—" Look when the messenger cometh, shut the door, and hold him fast at the door: is not the sound of his master's feet behind him?"—2 Kings vi. 32.

It is blessed to watch every dispensation of the Lord's providence, as well as his grace; for Jesus is in all. So that when messengers of heaviness come, and with sad tidings, as in this instance of the prophet, if we shut to the door as they enter, and suffer them to open their commission, we shall hear the sound of their master's feet behind them, confirming every one. There are no events which can happen to a child of God, but they ought to be thus dealt with. They are like letters personally directed, and speak, in their whole contents, the causes for which the king's post hath brought them; and they cannot be mistaken, if they are well read, and pondered over; for they point to the individual, as the prophet's servant to Jehu. " To which of all us, (said Jehu) is this errand ?" The answer was, " To thee, O captain !" 2 Kings ix. 5. Now, my soul, learn hence how to receive all the messengers of thy Lord. Shut the door upon them, and detain them, until thou hast well studied, and perfectly understood their commission. Oh! my Lord Jesus! in all thine afflicting providences, cause me to hear my master's feet following every one. " I know, Lord, that thy judgments are right, and that thou in very faithfulness causeth me to be troubled." I know, Lord, also, that they are graciously commissioned, and the issue must be blessed. And I know, Lord, that even during their exercise, however sharp, they will be sweetly sanctified, if, through thy blessing upon them, they cause my poor heart to cleave the closer to thee. So long then, dear Lord, as thou causest me to entertain right conceptions of these soul exercises, let me never shrink from shutting the door, that I may the more earnestly meditate upon thy messages; and if I see Christ in every one, and blessings in every one, sure I am, the issue of no one will ever be doubtful. I shall then learn the same precious lesson that Job did, and through thy grace, like him, make it practical: and bless a taking God, as well as a giving God: for, let the Lord take what else he may from me, never, never will he take Christ from me; and while I have him, in him I shall possess all things. Oh! for grace so to receive all the sable messengers of my Lord, as to hear my master's feet behind them. Sure I am, that when their black covering is removed, I shall behold a fulness of blessings which they have brought with them under their garments. Like the angel to Peter in the prison, they may smite roughly on the side; but the very stroke will cause the chains to fall from my hands, and open the prison doors, to give liberty and joy. Acts. xii. 7.

JUNE 23.

MORNING.—" And he will destroy in this mountain the face of the covering cast over all people, and the vail that is spread over all nations." Isa. xxv. 7.

What a precious promise was this with which the Lord comforted the church under the old testament dispensation, that the faithful might look forward to the new testament dispensation, when Jesus, in the holy mountain, where he finished transgression by his triumphant death, would effectually remove the covering which had blackened all faces, and had separated between God and guilty sinners. And, that the gracious promise might be had in everlasting remembrance by thy people, the evangelists were commissioned to tell the church, that in the moment Christ died, the vail of the temple was rent in twain, by an invisible hand, from the top to the bottom. My soul, see how Jesus, thy Jesus, hath most effectually fulfilled this precious promise. There was a vail of covering spread to separate thee for ever from God, had not Jesus taken it away, even the covenant of perfect obedience. God's injured perfections formed also a total separation. And as if these were not sufficient, the vail of sin would have for ever kept up this distance: " Your iniquities have separated between God and you," saith the prophet. But now by this precious undertaking in fulfilling the whole covenant of works, restoring the honour to God the Father's injured perfections, and opening a new and living way by his blood, which he hath consecrated through the vail of his flesh, he hath opened the kingdom of heaven to all believers. Precious Jesus, how endeared to my heart is this view of thee and of thy great salvation! Yes, thou Lamb of God! I have seen by thy Spirit's teaching, this deadly face of covering, which by sin hath been cast over all people; and I have seen, by the same almighty grace, that vail removed by thee. Now, Lord, in thee, and through thee, and by thee, I am led to behold the glory of God in the face of Jesus Christ. And having fled for refuge to the hope that is set before me, this hope I have in thee, as an anchor of the soul, both sure and stedfast, and have cast it within the vail, whither thou, our forerunner, hast for us entered, even our glorious High Priest for ever, after the order of Melchizedec.

EVENING.—" All that the Father giveth me, shall come to me; and him that cometh to me, I will in no wise cast out. For I came down from heaven, not to do mine own will, but the will of him that sent me. And this is the Father's will which hath sent me, that of all which he hath given me, I should lose nothing, but should raise it up again at the last day. And this is the will of him that sent me, that every one which seeth the Son, and believeth on him, may have everlasting life: and I will raise him up at the last day."—John vi. 37—40.

My soul, commit this blessed portion to thy memory; yea, beg of God the Holy Ghost to commit, and write all the gracious things contained in it, on the inner tablets of thine heart! It is in itself a gospel, yea, a full gospel. Methinks, I would have it proclaimed on the house-tops, and published, day by day, in every place of public concourse throughout the earth, until the saving truths were every one of them known, and felt, and enjoyed, by every poor awakened and needy sinner. Mark, my soul, the several contents of what thy God and Saviour hath here said: take the whole with thee to thy bed, this night, and drop asleep, in faith of the whole, in the arms of Jesus; and if the Lord bring thee to the light of the succeeding morning, let those sweet and gracious words, which proceeded out of Jesus's mouth, salute thee with the first dawn of the morning, arise with thee, and go about with thee, in thy remembrance, until the whole be fulfilled in the kingdom of heaven. Now mark their immense blessings, according to the order in which they stand: "All that the Father giveth me, shall come to me." *All;* not one, or two, or ten, or a million only, but *all.* And observe wherefore? They are the Father's gift to Jesus, and therefore they must come. He saith elsewhere, "that I should give eternal life to as many as thou hast given me," John xvii. 2. Hence, therefore, there is a blessed provision, a blessed security, that they shall come; for they are the Father's gift to Christ, as well as the purchase of Christ's blood; and the promise is absolute in the charter of grace; "Thy people shall be willing in the day of thy power," Ps. cx. 3. And, to give every possible encouragement to the poor coming sinner, whom God the Holy Ghost is leading by the hand to all-precious Jesus, however unconscious that poor soul is of the gracious influence under which he is coming, Jesus adds, "And him that cometh to me, I will in no wise cast out." Observe the tenderness of our Lord's words. He had said, *all* shall come: but Jesus well knew the most humble are the most timid, and the most apt to be discouraged; and therefore he makes each one's case to be expressed by the word *him:* "him that cometh." As if Jesus had said, 'Let that poor creature, who is most afraid, by reason of a conscious sense of his transgressions, take comfort: if he cometh, let him know, that "I will in no wise cast him out."' And to confirm it still more, Jesus adds, 'For this is the very purpose for which I came down from heaven; not only because it was my full purpose to seek and save that which was lost, but it is the will of my Father also, who sent me.' And, as if to impress this grand truth upon every poor sinner's heart, he repeats the gracious words: "And this is the will of him that sent me." He saith it twice, that there might be no mistake. And yet farther: if a poor sinner should say, 'But *how* am I to come, and in *what* am I to come; what are the qualifications for coming?' "This," saith the all-gracious Redeemer, "this is the will of my Father, the will of him that sent me, that every one that seeth the Son, and believeth on him, shall have everlasting life." And what is it to see the Son, but so to behold him by the eye of faith, as to believe in him to the salvation of the soul; to see him as the Christ, the Sent, the Sealed, the Anointed of God; the one, and only one ordinance of heaven, for the redemption of poor sinners; whose blood cleanseth from all sin, and whose righteousness freely and fully justifieth every believing sinner? Pause, my soul, and well ponder these precious, saving truths; and then take comfort in the blessed assurance, that thou hast all these testimonies in thine own experience, from having long since come to Christ, and long found the certainty of these promises. Lie down, my soul, this night, yea, lie down, my body, this, and every night, until the last night, even the night of death shall come; for thou sleepest in Jesus by faith, and his words are thy security: "Of all my Father hath given me, I should lose nothing; I will raise him up at the last day."

JUNE 24.

MORNING.—And another angel came and stood at the altar, having a golden censer; and there was given unto him much incense, that he should offer it with the prayers of all saints, upon the golden altar which was before the throne."—Rev. viii. 3.

My soul, behold this mighty Angel, even thy Jesus, in his priestly office. Look at him with an earnest eye of faith before thou goest this morning to the mercy-seat. See his golden censer, with his much incense, and contemplate both the fulness of merit in his own glorious Person, and the fulness of efficacy in his work and righteousness for the sure acceptance of all his redeemed. Go near, my soul, having boldness to enter now into the holiest by the blood of Jesus. Hear thy great High Priest bidding thee to take shelter under his golden censer, and behold him presenting thy person and thy poor offerings upon the golden altar, even his divine nature, before the throne. Yes, Lord! I would draw nigh in thee, and by thee, convinced that it is wholly from thee, and for thy sake, either my person or my prayers can find acceptance. For thee, and for thy sake, my sins are pardoned, my offerings are accepted, grace is bestowed, communion and fellowship is obtained; peace in this life, and glory in that which is to come, are the portion of thy people. Hail, thou glorious, gracious, all-sufficient, High Priest! To thee be glory in the church, throughout all ages. Amen.

EVENING.—"And they rest not day and night, saying, Holy, holy, holy, Lord God Almighty, which was, and is, and is to come."—Rev. iv. 8.

Make a solemn pause, my soul, over these words; and when thou hast found a fixedness of thought, that every faculty may be engaged in the contemplation, ponder well this divine perfection of Jehovah, the holiness of his nature, by which an eternal distinction is drawn between him and all his creatures. None but Jehovah can be essentially holy. Angels, who have never sinned, have indeed a holiness; but it is derived from Him, it exists not in themselves, and, in point of comparison, is but as the shadow to the substance; moreover, being in their nature mutable creatures, their holiness may be changed also: the fallen angels are proofs in point. But with Jehovah, holiness is in himself, the peculiar glory of his nature, and inseparable from his very existence. Pause over this view, for it is scriptural, and truly blessed. Go on to another observation. Thrice is the ascription of holiness given, in this sublime song of the blessed in heaven, as if to point out the personality of the Father, Son, and Holy Ghost; the Holy undivided Three, "which bear record in heaven, for these three are one," 1 John v. 7. When these glorious truths are suitably impressed upon thee, pause once more, and consider with what distinguishing characters the holiness of Jehovah is set forth in the word of God. The heavenly host are said to rest not day and night in proclaiming their deep sense and adoration of Jehovah in this glorious attribute. Now here is somewhat for the mind to lean upon, in contemplating Jehovah's holiness. Jehovah is *eternal* also, and hath commanded the church to know him as the *faithful* God, Deut. vii. 9. But we never read that the host of worshippers thrice repeat his eternity, or his faithfulness, in their hymns of adoration and praise. Moreover, Jehovah himself seems to have pointed out this divine attribute as among the distinguishing excellencies he will be known by; for he singles it out to swear by: "I have sworn once by my holiness, that I will not lie unto David," Ps. lxxxix. 35. Precious thought for the poor timid believer to keep always in view! For it is as if Jehovah had said, 'I have pledged my holiness, as an attribute essential to my very nature, that what I have promised to David's Lord, even my dear Son, of the redemption of his seed, as sure as I am holy, I will most certainly perform.' Moreover, my soul, holiness is the glory of Jehovah. Hence the song of the church: "Who is like unto thee, O Lord, among the gods! who is like unto thee, glorious in holiness!" Exod. xv. 11. And hence Jehovah is said to be worshipped "in the beauties of holiness;" Ps. cx. 3. My soul! keep this also in remembrance. If the representation of an angel, or a man, were to be made, we should figure to ourselves the most beautiful countenance; and if Jehovah be represented to us, how is it done? Surely in the beauty of holiness; for God the Holy Ghost gives us "the light of the knowledge of the glory of God, in the face of Jesus Christ!" 2 Cor. iv. 6. Pause over these infinitely solemn meditations, and while thou art overawed (as, indeed, it is impossible but to be so) in the contemplation of distinguishing a perfection of the divine nature; and, moreover, as this view of God's holiness is so directly opposed to the unholiness of a poor fallen sinful creature, as thou art, look up for grace from the Holy Ghost the Comforter, and take relief in the sweet and consoling consideration, that to this glorious God thou art permitted, yea, commanded and encouraged, to draw near, in and through the holiness of thy Redeemer. Hail, blessed Jesus! upheld by the right arm of thy righteousness, and washed from all our sins in thy blood, all thy church may here draw nigh by faith, and send forth their feeble breathings in the same strain as the church in thy presence doth above, while in their hymns day and night, they shout aloud, "Holy! holy! holy! Lord God Almighty, which was, and is, and is to come!"

JUNE 25.

MORNING.—"The eyes of the Lord are upon the righteous, and his ears are open unto their cry."—Ps. xxxiv. 15.

My soul, never more allow thyself to suppose that thou art overlooked or forgotten amidst the immensity of God's works. Is it not the province of a father to attend to the wants of his children? And will not God regard his own, that cry night and day unto him, though he bear long with them? This was the very argument of our Redeemer. Do you, saith Jssus, "that are evil, know how to give good gifts unto your children; and shall not your heavenly Father give his Holy Spirit to them that ask him?" But, my soul, while thou art taking comfort from this view of divine love, take with thee another sweet thought from this precious verse of scripture. Whose eyes are thus upon thee, and whose ears are thus open to thy cries, but those of the Lord Jesus? Oh how sweet the thought, that by reason of the Son of God, as Christ, being in our nature, and he having taken upon him our nature, he hath eyes to see, and ears to hear, such as we have. What a blessed light the Holy Ghost hath thrown over all those precious passages in which God is spoken of as having eyes, and ears, and an arm, and the like, describing himself by human powers; that it is indeed the divine nature of the Man Christ Jesus. It is Jesus, the Mediator, the Redeemer, the exalted and triumphant Saviour, who hath all power in heaven and in earth; who "having loved his own which are in the world, hath loved them unto the end." My soul, learn then to behold in all these sweet portions, that it is Jesus, thy Husband and Brother, as well as thy God and Saviour, and both forming one glorious Christ, whose eyes are always upon thee, and whose ears are always attentive to thy cries, and to the cries of all his redeemed.

EVENING.—"Then said I, Woe is me! for I am undone, because I am a man of unclean lips, and I dwell in the midst of a people of unclean lips."—Isa. vi. 5.

My soul! thy last evening was deeply exercised on that glorious subject, the holiness of Jehovah. Let this evening's meditation call thee to what ought immediately to follow; thy unholiness and corruption. What a transition! And yet what more suited for meditation? The prophet Isaiah, who had been admitted to the view of a vision, like that which John the apostle saw in the after ages, beheld the glory of Christ, and heard those who cried, "Holy, holy, holy, is the Lord of Hosts! and the effect was as is here related. His consternation was so great, concluding that he should be struck dead (agreeably to what holy men of old had conceived, that the sight of God would produce death), that he cried out, "Woe is me, I am undone." Pause, my soul! thou art also "a man of unclean lips!" How dost thou hope to see the face of God in glory? How art thou prepared for such an overwhelming sight? Convinced of thy uncleanness, and convinced also that God is of purer eyes than to behold iniquity, neither can any evil dwell with him; how art thou looking for acceptance here by grace, and the everlasting acceptance and admittance of thy person hereafter in glory before God? Ponder the subject well, and consider, under this particular, as in every other, the blessedness of an union with Christ, and an interest in Christ. Here lie all thy hopes, all thy confidence, all thy security! Undone as thou art in thyself, and unclean as thy lips and thy whole nature are, by reason of sin, both from the original state in which thou wast conceived and born, and the actual transgressions which thou hast committed; yet looking up to the throne, in and through Jesus, thy Husband, thy Surety, thy Sponsor; here it is, my soul, and here alone, that thy confidence is well founded, and all thy hopes secure. And dost thou not feel a holy joy, a sweet undescribable delight, in contemplating the divine holiness; while contemplating, at the same time, thine own interest and right in the holiness of the Lord Jesus? Art thou not full of rapture in beholding the glory of God's holiness, for which, rather than an atom of it should be tarnished by the sinner, the Son of God assumed the nature of his people, and died on the cross, to make atonement? And art thou not comforted in the blessed view, that God's holiness hath received more glory, more honour, by the obedience and sacrifice of the Glory-man, Christ Jesus, than could have been given by the everlasting obedience of men and angels to all eternity? And say, moreover, dost thou not at times take delight in drawing nigh to the throne of grace, and offering thy poor feeble praises of "Holy, holy, holy, is the Lord God of Hosts," when thou art approaching, and holding communion with God, in and through the holy Jesus, thy Redeemer? Oh! thou dear Emmanuel, *in* whom alone, and by whom alone, all my hopes and confidences are founded, I fall down at thy feet, and as the prophet cried out, so do I desire unceasingly to exclaim, "I am a man of unclean lips!" But do thou cause the iniquity to be taken away, and my sin to be purged, by the live coal, from thee, who art our new testament altar, and I shall be clean; for thou art the Lord my righteousness.

JUNE 26.

MORNING.—"The Lord possessed me in the beginning of his way: before his works of old, I was set up from everlasting."—Prov. viii. 22, 23.

Pause, my soul, over those most blessed words, and see what glories are contained in them. May God the Spirit glorify Christ to thy view while pondering these words! Who is it that speaks them? Is it not wisdom! Even Christ, the wisdom of God, as the apostle elsewhere calls him? But how was he possessed by the Lord, and how set up from everlasting? Not openly in the human form, that he was in the fulness of time to take upon him for the purpose of redemption; but, as it should seem, secretly, as subsisting in covenant engagements from everlasting. As Mediator, was it not? Not as yet made flesh, but if we may from another scripture draw the conclusion, "as the image of the invisible God, the first-born of every creature," Col. i. 15. What a glory, beheld in this view, doth this precious scripture, with all that follows it in the chapter, hold forth! The Son of God, in covenant engagements from everlasting, was in time to take into himself manhood, and from the union of both God and man become one Christ. Hence, from everlasting, wisdom, one of those natures, is set up and speaks as a person, not separate or distinct from the other nature of the Godhead, but as in union, and from both, forming in covenant settlements the one glorious Mediator. So that it is not wisdom, as a person, speaking, without subsisting in the Son of God, neither is it the Son of God without wisdom subsisting as such in him, but both forming one identical person, and that person the Mediator, whose name was then secret, but afterwards was to be called Wonderful, when by the open appearance of the Son of God, tabernacling in a body of flesh, redemption work from everlasting, covenanted for and agreed upon by the several persons of the Godhead, was to be completed. What a blessed contemplation is here opened, my soul, to thy diligent and humble inquiry. Here direct all thy researches; here let prayer ascend for divine teachings to guide thee; and here behold him, who in the after ages of his love, made an open display of himself, as the God-man, when he manifested forth his glory, and his disciples believed on him; thus, as the wisdom-man, declaring himself as possessed by Jehovah in the beginning of his way, and set up before all worlds as Jehovah's delight, while his delights were with the sons of men. Oh the wisdom of God in a mystery, even the hidden wisdom which God ordained before the world began!

EVENING.—" The Urim and the Thummim."—Exod. xxviii. 30.

There is somewhat very interesting in this account of " the Urim and the Thummim;" though in the present distance of time, we can at the best form nothing more than conjectures as to what it was. But through grace, and the teaching of the Holy Ghost, we can have clear views of what it meant. The general acceptations of the Hebrew words, are, lights and perfections. And as Aaron, as high priest, became a lively type of Christ, so, by bearing on his breast-plate " the Urim and the Thummim," there can be no difficulty in beholding Jesus represented as the light and perfection of his people. And as Aaron bare all the names of the people upon his breast, where " the Urim and Thummim" were worn; how delightful is it to see Jesus thus represented, as bearing all the persons of his redeemed, in his own light and perfection, when he goes in before the presence of God for us! Sweet and precious thought to the believer! And now the church cries out: "Set me as a seal upon thine heart, as a seal upon thine arm;" Song viii. 6. And so important did this appear to Moses, when dying, that he expressly prayed, that "the Thummim and the Urim might be with Jehovah's Holy One;" Deut. xxxiii. 8. Now here we have at once the application of the whole; for who is Jehovah's Holy One, but the Lord Jesus Christ? With him it eminently remained, and with him only. For during the captivity, it was lost with the temple, and was never again restored. But with Jesus, the continuance of it was everlasting, for he hath "an unchangeable priesthood, and is the same yesterday, and to-day, and for ever." Precious Lord Jesus! be thou "the Urim and the Thummim" to my soul; for thou art both the light and perfection of thy people, in grace here, and glory for ever.

JUNE 27.

MORNING.—"I am Alpha and Omega, the first and the last."—Rev. i. 11.

My soul, if the precious meditation of yesterday be not wholly gone off from thy poor forgetful mind this day, here is another blessed view to revive the thought afresh, in looking at the Mediator, as the Alpha and Omega, the first and the last, in the same covenant engagements. Jesus is indeed, as the 8th verse of this same chapter expresses it, the Alpha and Omega, as one with the Father, over all, God blessed for ever. But he is also here the Alpha and Omega, as the Mediator, both God and man. For he is the first and the last of all God's thoughts, and in his covenant engagements, of all Jehovah's work; for every thing in creation begins and concludes in him. From everlasting he was set up. So that though Adam was the first man openly, yet not the first man secretly, and as subsisting in covenant engagements. Here again, as was remarked before, and from an authority not to be disputed, "he is the image of the invisible God, the first-born of every creature, that in all things he might have the preeminence." Precious Jesus, be thou to me the Alpha and Omega. And as it is plain that Jehovah possessed thee as the glorious covenant head of thy people in the beginning of his way, and before his works of old, so cause me to possess thee as the all in all, the first and the last, the author and finisher of my salvation.

EVENING.—" Not as though I had already attained, either were already perfect: but I follow after, if that I may apprehend that for which also I am apprehended of Christ Jesus."—Phil. iii. 12.

My soul! take the apostle for an example in thine evening's meditation. Here he freely and fully confesseth himself, after all his attainments in the life of grace, to be far short of what he longed to attain. And observe the aim of the apostle: all his pursuit, and all his desire was, like an arrow shot at a mark, to apprehend Christ, as Christ had first apprehended him: to grasp Jesus, as the Lord Jesus had held, and did hold him. Happy desire! happy pursuit! and blessed mark of grace! For let the Lord have given out to the soul ever so largely, there is more to give out, more to be received, more to be enjoyed. And the Holy Ghost, who is leading a child of God out of himself, more and more, to lead him more and more to the enjoyment of Jesus, is sweetly training that precious soul, and advancing him to the highest lessons in the school of grace. Paul felt this, when he cried out, "Not that I have already attained, either were already perfect." To be sure not: for if we thought we had enough of Christ, it would be more than half conviction that we had nothing at all. Now, my soul, learn from Paul, in what the life of God in the soul consists: to be always pursuing the person of Jesus, for the farther enjoyment of him; never sitting down satisfied with what is already attained; but " pressing (as the apostle did) towards the mark, for the prize of the high calling of God in Christ Jesus:" in short, to make Christ the sum, the substance, the all of every desire; and ever to keep in remembrance, that the more we receive, the more Jesus hath to impart; the more he gives out, the more he is glorified; and, like some rich spring, the oftener we receive from him, the more rich and full he flows: Oh the blessedness of such a state! What a heaven upon earth would it be, if closely followed! To be always living upon Jesus, coming to Jesus, thirsting after Jesus; and the more we receive out of him, and of him, to have the soul's desires after him the more increased by all we enjoy. Precious Lord! grant me this felicity, that, like Paul, I may say, "Not as though I had already attained:" but all my longings are, so to apprehend and hold fast Christ Jesus, as Christ Jesus hath apprehended and dòth hold me fast.

JUNE 28.

MORNING.—" Carry down the man a present."—Gen. xliii. 11.

Ah, poor Jacob, how unconscious wert thou that this man, the governor of Egypt, was so near and dear to thee, and that his bowels yearned to tell thee how much he loved thee. And O ye sons of Israel, who would have had power to convince you while you were bowing down before Joseph under the dreadful apprehensions which agitated your minds, and he was assuming a voice of displeasure, that this very man was your brother? My soul, and what was all this, heightened to the greatest possible degree in the real love and affection of Joseph towards his family, compared to that love of Jesus which passeth knowledge? Jesus is thy brother, and he is the governor, not of Egypt only, but of heaven and earth. The famine, it is true, is sore in the land, and to him thou must go for sustenance, or thou wilt perish for ever. But wilt thou carry down the man a present? My soul, what hast thou to carry? Not thy duties, nor thy prayers, thine alms, thy righteousness; these are all filthy rags. Besides, he to whom thou goest needeth not the gifts and offerings of his creatures. His terms are, without money and without price. Go then, my soul, poor and wretched as thou art, go to him with a broken and a contrite heart, for that he will not despise. And O what a volume of mercies, blessings, and graces is contained in that one word of his, when he shall say, I am Jesus, your brother! Precious Jesus, I would say, thou art indeed a brother born for adversity. "Thou art he whom thy brethren shall praise, and all thy father's children shall bow down before thee."

EVENING.—"And the Spirit and the bride say, come. And let him that heareth, say, come. And let him that is athirst, come. And whosoever will, let him take the water of life freely."—Rev. xxii. 17.

My soul, doth not the evening bell, which calleth to the ordinance, in all its melodious sounds, seem to express these gracious invitations? Wilt thou not attend? Private meditation is indeed sweet; but public ordinances are of more avail. "The Lord loveth the gates of Zion more than all the dwellings of Jacob!" What a blessed sight is it to see the house of God well filled! What a refreshment to my poor weary sin-sick soul, to hear Jesus in his word saying, "Come unto me, all ye that are weary, and heavy laden, and I will give you rest." And every part and portion of the service proclaims the gospel cry:—"Ho! every one that thirsteth, come ye to the waters, and he that hath no money, come ye, buy and eat; yea, come, buy wine and milk, without money, and without price." Isa. lv. 1. And do observe, my soul, how, in the close of scripture, the invitation is repeated; as if to leave the impression fresh and lasting upon every soul. Yea, the Spirit confirms it; "come," is the call of the Holy Ghost; "come," is the call of the whole church, the bride, the Lamb's wife; yea, every one that heard of the free, and full, and glorious salvation; the angels, the ministering spirits to the heirs of salvation, they join the pressing invitation, and cry, "come." And surely every thirsty soul will not cease to say the same, for whoever the Lord the Spirit hath made "willing in the day of his power," may come in the day of his grace. And if Jesus, with his great salvation, be welcome to his heart, that heart is welcome to come to Jesus. My soul, with what a cloud of witnesses is the church of the living God encompassed; and how many and numerous are the invitations of grace! Wilt thou not then, in return, echo to the cry, and hasten thy Redeemer's coming, in the same earnest language? Come, Lord Jesus! to thy bride, the church, and be thou to all thy redeemed the water of life, and the fountain of life; until thou take home thy church, which is here below, to join thy church above, that they may unitedly dwell together, in the light of thy countenance for evermore!

JUNE 29.

MORNING.—"And they sought him among their kinsfolk and acquaintance, and found him not."—Luke ii. 44, 45.

May we not gather a lesson of sweet instruction from the anxious and fruitless search the parents made for Jesus in the days of his flesh? What kinsfolks and acquaintances shall we now search among for the Saviour? My soul, how little of Jesus is to be found in this Christless generation! What parlour conversation makes mention of his name? Is it not plain and evident, from the general, nay almost universal silence observed in all companies concerning his name, and offices, and characters, and relations, that Christ is not there? Shall we seek him among the professors of the gospel? Who are they that honour Jesus? Not they who deny his Godhead; not they who deny the influences of his Holy Spirit; not they who set up their own righteousness as part, or the whole of their justification before God. Jesus is not in that house, in that family, in that heart, among that people who live in sensuality, profaneness, and impiety. Where shall we seek Jesus? Blessed Lord, mine eyes are unto thee to be taught. I would say unto thee, in the language of the church, "Tell me, O thou whom my soul loveth, where thou feedest, where thou makest thy flock to rest at noon. Oh when I shall find thee without, I would lead thee, and bring thee into my mother's house, who would instruct me; and I would cause thee to drink of spiced wine of the juice of my pomegranate."

EVENING.—"Let us keep the feast, not with old leaven, neither with the leaven of malice and wickedness; but with the unleavened bread of sincerity and truth."—1 Cor. v. 8.

My soul, hast thou duly considered the unsuitableness of all leaven to mix up with the unleavened bread of the gospel of Jesus? Whatever sours, and gives a principle of taint to the mind, is indeed a leaven, carefully to be avoided. And "a little leaven leaveneth the whole lump!" So that it was expressly enjoined, in the divine precept of the law, on the passover, that "there should be no leaven found in their houses; the soul that did eat of it was to be cut off from the congregation." Exod xii. 19. Sweet instruction, couched under the prohibition! With Jesus there is to be no mixture; nothing of creature leaven, of self-will, or self-righteousness to mingle. My soul, thou hast been at the gospel feast, and sat with Jesus at his table. Surely thou hast kept the feast then, as here enjoined, and allowed nothing of leaven, in the old nature or in the new, to be with thee. Oh! the blessedness of thus receiving Christ with "the unleavened bread of sincerity and truth!" Oh! the felicity of receiving a broken Christ into a broken heart; preciously feeding upon his body broken, and his blood shed, as the sole, the only, the all-sufficient means of salvation by faith! Oh! Lamb of God! keep thy table sacred from all leaven, both in the persons approaching it, and the offerings made upon it. Let not the children's bread be received, or given to the leaven of hypocrisy and wickedness; but let all who meet around thy board be of the unleavened bread of sincerity and truth! And do thou, Lord, come into thy house, to thy table, to thy people; and let each for himself hear, and joyfully accept the invitation of the kind Master: "Eat, O friends; drink, yea, drink abundantly, O beloved!

JUNE 30.

MORNING.—"In thee the fatherless findeth mercy."—Hosea xiv. 3.

Sweet thought! In Jesus, and the relationship which he hath condescended to place himself in, all his poor followers may find a supply to fill up every vacancy. My soul, contemplate Jesus in this blessed feature of character. What relation do we need? The fatherless are commanded to look to him whose name is the everlasting Father. The motherless also; for he hath said, "As one whom his mother comforteth, so will I comfort thee." Doth death make a breach between the husband and the wife? Then the scripture saith, "Thy Maker is thine husband, the Lord of Hosts is his name." Are we friendless? "Jesus is the friend that loveth at all times, that sticketh closer than a brother." In short, there is no situation among the affinities of life, the kinder charities of nature, but what Jesus fills and infinitely transcends all. Pause, my soul, over this view of Jesus, and behold how he graciously proposeth himself to supply all wants, and to fill all vacancies. Jesus is both the Father, the Friend, the Brother, the Husband, the whole in one of all relationships and of all connexions. And amidst all the changes, the fluctuating circumstances of human affairs, the frailties, and infirmities of our own hearts and the hearts of others, which sometimes separate chief friends, what a blessed thought it is; "Nothing can separate from the love of Christ!" Precious Lord, give me to cry out with the church, under the full assurance of thine unalterable love; "This is my beloved, and this is my friend, O daughters of Jerusalem."

EVENING.—"With the voice of the archangel, and with the trump of God."—1 Thess. iv. 16.

Before I drop into the arms of sleep, I would call upon my soul to ponder these words. I know not, each night, when retiring to rest, whether my next awakening may not be "with the voice of the archangel, and with the trump of God." As what *may be* my state in this particular, and *hath been* the state of many (for the hour of a man's death is to all intents and purposes the day of judgment) becomes an infinitely momentous concern; how can I better close the day and the month together, than by a few moments' consideration of the solemn event? What is meant by "the voice of the archangel?" I do not recollect the name of the archangel being mentioned any where beside in scripture, except Jude 9. and here, as well as there, the person spoken of is but one. We have no authority to say, archangels; yea, it should seem, from what the apostle Jude hath said concerning the archangel, in calling him Michael (if compared with the vision of Daniel, chap. x. 21. and also with what is said in the book of the Revelations, chap xii. 7.) that it means the person of Christ. Jesus himself hath said, that "the dead shall hear the voice of the Son of God; and all that are in their graves shall come forth." John v. 25—28. At any rate, if the Holy Ghost speak but of one, and there be but the shadow of a probability that that one is Christ, it becomes very faulty to join others in the name, by making the word plural. With respect to "the trump of God," we may understand, that as the law was given with solemn splendour and glory on mount Sinai, so the consummation of all things will testify the divine presence. My soul, meditate on these things; give thyself wholly to the frequent consideration of them. And, by the lively actings of faith upon the person of thy Lord, contemplate thy personal interest in all the blessedness of this great day of God. If this "voice of the archangel," be indeed the voice of Jesus, and thou knowest now by grace thy oneness and union with him, shall not the very thought give thee holy joy? It is true, indeed, the day will be solemn, yea, profoundly solemn. But it is equally true, that it will be glorious to all the redeemed. And if the Lord Jesus commanded his disciples to look up, and lift up their heads with holy joy, when their redemption drew nigh, shall we not suppose that it must be pleasing to the mind of our God and Saviour that we welcome and hail the fulfilment of it? Yea, must it not be pleasing to our God and Father, that we believe in his Son Jesus Christ to this day of eternal salvation? We find the apostles thus encouraging the faithful. Paul tells Titus to be "looking for that blessed hope, and the glorious appearing of the great God and our Saviour Jesus Christ." Titus ii. 13. Surely, if the hope be blessed, and the appearing of Jesus, as the Redeemer of his people, glorious; our souls should triumph in the expectation. Peter goes one step farther, and bids the church not only to be looking but hasting unto the coming of it; as souls well assured of their safety in

Jesus; and therefore to cry out with holy faith, "Come Lord Jesus, come quickly!" 2 Pet. iii. 12. What sayest thou, my soul, to these things? Are they blessed? Are thy hopes thus going forth in desires after Christ's coming? Oh! the blessedness of falling asleep each night, in the sleep of nature, in the perfect assurance of a oneness with Christ? And Oh! the blessedness of falling asleep in Jesus, when the Lord gives the signal for the sleep of death! All the intervening lapse of time, from death to this hour of the "voice of the archangel," is totally lost to the body, like the unconscious lapse of time to the labouring man of health, whose sleep each night is sweet. When the patriarchs, of their different ages, arise at "the trump of God," their bodies will be equally unconscious whether the sleep hath been for one night, or several thousand years. Think, my soul, of these solemn but precious things. Frequently meditate with holy joy and faith, upon this great day of God. Recollect that it is Jesus who comes to take thee home. And having long redeemed thee by his blood, he then will publicly acknowledge thee for his own, and present thee to the Father and himself, as a part of his glorious church, "not having spot, or wrinkle, or any such thing; but to be for ever without blame before him in love."

JULY 1.

MORNING.—"Because of the savour of thy good ointments, thy name is as ointment poured forth."—Song i. 3.

Why, my Lord, is thy name so truly blessed, but because thou hast so endeared it to thy redeemed, by every tie which can gain the affections. Didst thou, even before I had being, enter into suretyship engagements for me, that thou wouldest redeem me when fallen, that thou wouldest take my nature, live for me, die for me, become a sacrifice for me, shed thy blood for me, wash me in thy blood, clothe me with thy righteousness, justify me before God and thy Father, become my Advocate, High Priest, Intercessor, betroth me to thyself here in grace, and everlastingly unite me to thyself in glory hereafter? Didst thou do all this, and art thou still doing it, making my cause thine own, and following me with love, and grace, and mercy, every day, and all day, and wilt never thou leave me nor forsake me? And must not thy name be as ointment poured forth? Can there be a savour as sweet, as fragrant, as full of odour, as the name of Jesus? Precious ointments, it is true, have a smell in them very grateful; but what savour can be like that which to the spiritual senses manifests Jesus in his person, love, grace, and mercy; in whom there is every thing desirable, and nothing but what is lovely; all beauty, power, wisdom, strength, an assemblage of graces more full of odour than all the spices of the east? Precious Lord Jesus, let thy name be written in my heart, and let every thing but Jesus be for ever obliterated there, that nothing may arise from thence, but what speaks of thee; that through life and in death, the first and the last, and all that drops from my lips, even in the separation of soul and body, Jesus may form in the close of grace here, and in the first opening of glory to follow, the one only blessed precious name, as ointment poured forth.

EVENING.—" I saw in the night visions, and behold, one like the Son of man, came with the clouds of heaven, and came to the Ancient of Days, and they brought him near before him. And there was given him dominion, and glory, and a kingdom, that all people, nations, and languages, should serve him: his dominion is an everlasting dominion, which shall not pass away, and his kingdom that which shall not be destroyed."—Dan. vii. 13, 14.

Bless the Lord, my soul, who giveth thee "songs in the night," from the night visions of the prophet. Read this sweet scripture, explained as it is, most fully and completely, by the evangelists, in their account of Jesus, as "the Son of man;" and what a wonderful coincidence and agreement is there between them! It is in the human nature of the Lord Christ, that the glories of this kingdom shine so full and resplendant. "The Ancient of Days can be no other than God the Father, who is truly the Ancient of Days, being self-existent, and from everlasting to everlasting. And the Son of God, as God, one with the Father, is the same from all eternity. But here he is spoken of as the Christ of God, and particularly revealed to Daniel, in the visions of the night, as "the Son of man." Ponder this well, my soul. Contemplate the dominion, glory, and kingdom given to Jesus, in thy nature. Recollect also, in the moment of thy meditation, that it is by virtue of this nature, united to the Godhead, that the exercise of all sovereignty, wisdom, and power, is carried on, and Christ's kingdom established for ever. It saith, in this scripture, that these things were *given* to him. They could not have been given to him as God; for all things were his before: but as Christ, the Son of man; the Son of God having taken into union with the Godhead our nature, became one Christ, and as such, received them. And what endears the subject, in the greatness and everlasting nature of it is, that Jesus is all this in our nature. For here it is that that sweet scripture unfolds all its beauty: "As the Father hath life in himself, so hath he given to the Son to have life in himself; because he is the Son of man!" John v. 26, 27. Mark the peculiar blessedness of the expression, for the meditation is most sweet. Jesus, as Jesus Mediator, hath life in himself. He doth not hold it as at pleasure, or like creatures, which, because once given, may be taken away. It is in himself in the human nature, because that human nature is taken in, united to, and become one with the Godhead, and therefore not liable to be recalled. Pause over this subject, this glorious, blessed, joyful subject! Thy Jesus, my soul, hath life in himself, in his human nature, because he is the Son of man. Think, then, of thine everlasting safety in him; and thine unceasing glory from him: for he saith himself, " Because I live, ye shall live also." Hallelujah. Amen, Amen.

JULY 2.

MORNING.—" And thou shalt not be for another man; so will I also be for thee."—Hosea iii. 3.

My soul, was not God the Holy Ghost representing, by the similitude of his servant the prophet's marriage with an adulteress, the astonishing marriage of Jesus with our nature, and his personal union with every individual of his church and people? Look at this scripture, and see how sweetly it points to Jesus. The prophet was commanded to love this woman beloved of her friend, and yet an adulteress. He was to buy her also to himself: and he was to charge her to abide with him, and not to play the harlot any more, saying unto her: " And thou shalt not be for another man, so will I also be for thee." Precious Jesus, do I not behold thee in all this? Can any thing more strikingly shadow forth thy grace, thy mercy, thy love, to thy people? Was not our whole nature estranged from thee, when thou camest down from heaven to seek and save that which was lost? Were not all in a state of daring adultery, when thou hadst from everlasting betrothed thyself to us, in standing up our glorious Husband and Surety? And how striking the expression: " Then said the Lord unto me, go yet, love a woman beloved of her friend!" Surely at the command of God thy Father, and not uncalled, unsent, unauthorized, didst thou come. Our nature was indeed yet beloved of thee, our best and dearest friend, though in a state of spiritual adultery, and wholly gone away from thee. Yes, blessed Jesus! in defiance of all our multiplied transgressions, it might be truly said, we were yet beloved of thee our Friend and Brother, born for adversity: for thou wert then, as now, unchangeable in thy love, the same Jesus yesterday, to-day, and for ever. And surely, Lord, in another feature the prophet shadowed thee forth; for as he purchased the harlot, so thou, Lord, before we became thine, didst purchase us by thy blood. And dost thou now say to me this day: "Abide with me, and thou shalt not be for another man, so will I also be for thee?" Oh condescending God! Oh precious, lovely, all loving Saviour! Lord, make me thine; yea, altogether thine! Let my whole soul, and body, and spirit be all thine, both by the conquests of thy grace, as they are justly thine, and by the purchase of thy blood, that never, never more, I may depart from thee, but with the same full consent as the church of old, I may exult in this blessed assurance, "My beloved is mine, and I am his."

EVENING.—"But strong meat belongeth to them that are of full age, even those who, by reason of use, have their senses exercised to discern both good and evil."—Heb. v. 14.

My soul! of what age art thou in the divine life? It is high time to inquire: high time to know. And the information is not far to attain, if thou dost wish it. A state of full age not only can receive, and relish the strong meat of the gospel, but really desires it, longs for it, and can be satisfied with nothing else. And what is the strong meat of the gospel? Surely the person, the work, the glory, the grace, the love, the every thing that is in Jesus, which belongs to Jesus, and flows from Jesus. And depend upon it, that if thy spiritual senses are so frequently exercised upon Jesus, as to relish this food, to delight in it, yea, to loath all else, there will be a sweet savour of Jesus in thy whole life and conversation. And in the exact proportion that thou takest a fulness of this spiritual food, so may thine age be estimated. All we hear, all we see, all we read of, or meet with, of Jesus, will be food to the soul. Jesus is as the sweet flower of the field: and faith, like the bee, gathers from it, and brings home, both the golden honey and the wax to the hive, and lives upon it: so that then Christ is in the heart, dwells in the heart, as the apostle terms it, by faith, and is "formed in the heart the hope of glory." Now, where there is no fulness of age, yea, no age at all, not a babe in Christ, nor even born again, the strong meat of the gospel can neither be received, taken in, nor enjoyed. An unawakened heart is not only incapable of strong meat, but is disgusted at it. Persons of this kind may hear of Jesus, and apparently, for the time seem pleased. For as all men, when they die, would desire to go to heaven, so a discourse about it, may amuse, as a subject at a distance. But there is nothing within them, with which the subject can incorporate: no digestive powers to receive such strong meat; and consequently no relish. A shower of rain in a dry season may wet the surface, but if it soak not to the root, the plants find no good. My soul! what saith thine experience to these things? Hath the Lord so manifested himself to thee in all his glory, that nothing short of Jesus can satisfy thee? Hast thou found a transforming power accompanying this view of Jesus, so that, by faith, his glory hath excited thy desires to partake of him? And do the daily hopes which arise from such thoughts and views of thy Lord, so give rest, comfort, and joy to thee, that these refreshments are like "the spiced wine of the pomegranate?" Blessed Redeemer! may I be able to ascertain the real ripeness of my age by testimonies like these; and sure I am, in this view and enjoyment of Jesus, I shall find cause to give thanks, yea, unceasing thanks, to "God and the Father, who thus maketh us meet to be partakers of the inheritance with the saints in light."

JULY 3.

MORNING.—"Now the end of the commandment is charity, out of a pure heart, and of a good conscience, and of faith unfeigned."—1 Tim. i. 5.

See, my soul, what Jesus hath secured for thee by his gracious undertaking and accomplishment, and which his servant was commissioned to tell the church, was the very end of the commandment; namely, charity, or love. And this law of love is given thee, that thou mightest manifest whose thou art, and to whom thou dost belong; not as a rule of acceptance, for then that would be to make thy love a covenant of works; but as a sweet testimony of thy affection in the hand of Jesus. It is a law of love indeed, because the cords of love, by which thou art drawn, prove it to be so. Thy obedience is not from slavish fear, for then this would be bondage; but the love of Christ constrains thee. Thy love to him makes thee long to be like him. Thy love to him makes his commandments not grievous but gracious. Thy love to him makes ordinances precious, because Jesus is the whole of them. And thy love to him makes all that belongs to him dear, and in which Jesus requires thy proofs of affection; not in thy strength, as the poor Israelites were demanded to make brick without straw, but by living in thee, and working in thee, both to will and to do of his good pleasure. Here, my soul, thou truly findest strength and grace equal to thy day. The end of every commandment, as well as the beginning, is love; for it begins in Jesus, is carried on in Jesus, and ends in Jesus, and he is all love. And in him, and by him, the conscience, the heart, faith, all are kept pure, undefiled, and unfeigned, because love in Jesus is at the bottom; like the chariot of Solomon, paved with love. Oh thou glorious pattern of all holiness, make me like thyself!

EVENING.—"The waters of Jordan."—Josh. iv. 23.

The sacred streams of Jordan, so often and so highly

celebrated in the word of God, open a very blessed subject for meditation. Sit down, my soul, by the side of that ancient river, and call to mind the faith exercised on that memorable spot by the multitude of the faithful gone before, who were heirs with thyself of the promises; and see, whether the Holy Ghost will not graciously, this evening, make thy meditation sweet? Recollect, as thou viewest the hallowed ground, that here it was, in this river, Jesus received the first public testimony from God the Father; and the first open display of the descent of God the Holy Ghost. Here Jehovah began to magnify the Lord Christ. And here, in ages before, had the Lord begun to magnify that memorable type of Jesus, his servant Joshua. And as, from the baptism of Jesus at this sacred river, the Lamb of God opened his divine commission, so here Joshua, his type, commenced his ministry. From hence he led the people to the promised land. And from hence Jesus, in the baptism of his Holy Spirit, leads his redeemed to the possession of the everlasting Canaan, in heaven. There is, indeed, a double view of our Lord's ministry, in these waters of Jordan; not only of baptism, as introductory to the wilderness-state of temptation that follows to all his people; but also, as the close of the wilderness-dispensation, in the Jordan of death, when, finally and fully, Jesus leads them through, to their immortal possessions. And as the children of Israel had been exercised for *forty years* together, through a waste and howling wilderness, until they came to Jordan, which opened a passage to them of life and liberty, to a land flowing with milk and honey; so the followers of the Lord Jesus, having passed through the pilgrimage of this world, amidst the various assaults of sin and Satan, pass through the Jordan of death, conducted and secured by their almighty leader, unto the possession of that kingdom of glory and happiness which is above. Pause, my soul, over the review! behold, by faith, the wonderful events which passed here. In this sacred river, once rested the ark of the covenant of the Lord of the whole earth. Here Jesus, whom the ark represented, was baptised. Here Israel passed over. And here, my soul, must thou pass over in the hour of death. Oh! how sweet and blessed, in the swellings of Jordan, to behold Jesus, and hear his well-known voice, " Fear not; for I have redeemed thee; I have called thee by thy name: thou art mine. When thou passest through the waters, I will be with thee; and through the rivers, they shall not overflow thee!"

JULY 4.

MORNING.—" I am among you as he that serveth."—Luke xxii. 27.

Surely there is a blessedness in these words that affords substance to feed upon. My soul, read them again and again; pause over them, pray over them, and look up to him that thus so humbly, graciously, and lovingly, expressed himself. Art thou, blessed Jesus, among thy people as he that serveth? I know, Lord, that thou didst condescend to become the servant of Jehovah, though thou wert Lord of all, when for the salvation of poor sinners thou didst undertake to veil thy Godhead, and in our nature to become our surety. And I know, Lord, also, that thou didst, in a very memorable moment, and at a time when as the evangelist had it to relate to the church, thou knewest that the Father had given all things into thine hands, thou didst condescend to wash thy disciples feet. But art thou still among thy people as one that serveth? Be astonished, O heavens, and wonder, O earth! All power is thine in heaven and in earth. And is Jesus among his people, among his redeemed ones, his exercised ones, as he that serveth? Pause again, my soul—meditate upon the blessed gracious words. Was there not a circumstance of trial, when Christ was upon earth, but what he felt in his human nature, when fulfilling all righteousness? Then will it follow, that there cannot be a circumstance of trial which his members now feel, but what he knows; nay, what he appoints. And if he appoints it, is he not looking on; nay, measuring out suited strength, suited grace, as the circumstances shall require? And if all this be in Jesus, now and every minute event both his ordering, supporting under, carrying through, crowning in all, is he not, though Lord of all, servant of all; and doth he not now say to every poor disciple in the present moment, as fully as he did to them in the garden with him, "I am among you as he that serveth?" My Lord and my God, would I cry out, under the same conscious shame of my dreadful unbelief, as Thomas did under his Yes, Lord, thou art still ministering, still serving! And though I lose sight of thee in a thousand and ten thousand instances, where nothing but thy imparted strength could carry me through; yet plain and most evident it is, that in all the blessings of thy finished redemption, thou thyself art giving out, and serving up, grace to thy people. Thou didst first purchase all blessings with thy blood; and now thou ever livest to see them administered by thy Spirit. Precious Jesus, thou art ever with me. By and by I shall be with thee, I shall see thee as thou art, and shall be satisfied when I awake with thy likeness.

EVENING.—"A wedding garment."—Matt. xxii. 11.

My soul! let this evening's meditations be directed to the subject proposed in these few words: "a wedding garment." Very many are the instructions which the passage contains. The Lord Jesus is representing, under the similitude of a wedding feast, the rich provision God the Father had made in the gospel, on account of the marriage of his dear Son with our nature. And most beautiful, indeed, is the representation. For what feast, in point of fulness, richness, and satisfaction, can come up to that which is furnished for the poor, needy, and perishing circumstances of famished and dying sinners? This feast of fat things (as the scripture calls it) is indeed a rich feast, a royal feast, and a true wedding feast: for as Jesus, on whose account it is made, hath united our nature in general to himself, so hath he united each individual of that nature in particular to himself, who is truly, and in reality, made a partaker of it. But the parable supposes (which, though not said, is implied) that the rich and bountiful Donor not only provides a feast for the hungry, but a covering for the naked; and that the very entrance to his table is inadmissible without this wedding garment being accepted, put on, and worn by every individual who partakes of the supper. The case is here stated of one unworthy creature (and that one is a representative of all in like circumstances) who, when the King came in to see the guests, was found deficient of this covering. My soul! pause over this part. This man, it should seem, was not observed by any around him. He had come in with the crowd, and gained admittance with the rest. It was only when the King came in, that he was discovered, and that by the King himself. What a volume of instruction is contained in this short representation? So Jesus comes in the midst of his churches. He presides at his table. Every individual is seen, is known by him, with every secret motive for which each cometh. It should seem, that at this supper there were great multitudes present, and but one without a wedding garment. And yet that one could not be hidden from the King's eye. My soul! while this furnisheth a subject for awful consideration, so doth it no less for joyful thought. Hast thou been at this gospel feast? Wert thou clothed in this wedding garment? Surely, if so, thou art not at a loss to know. If the feast and the garment were both of the King's providing, thou must know whether thou camest to be clothed as well as fed; and whether the Lord, that provided the food, gave thee also raiment? Say then, when Jesus invited thee to his supper, didst thou go to it, as those in the highway, poor, and maimed, and halt, and blind? And while he bade thee come, didst thou regard his counsel; and buy of him, as he had said, without money, and without price, " white raiment, that thou mightest be clothed, and that the shame of thy nakedness should not appear?" Rev. iii. 18. Oh it is blessed, very blessed, to go hungry to such a feast, and clothed in the wedding garment of Jesu's righteousness, and have the robe put on by God the Holy Ghost. Sure will be the acceptance, and gracious the reception, to every poor, famishing, naked, sinner, that thus comes to the gospel feast. Do remark, my soul, one circumstance more in this man's case. It doth not appear that he was naked; for then it would have been said so; and, if conscious of it, the bountiful Lord that made the feast would have clothed him. He had a garment, but not a wedding garment. One of his own providing; like those who have a righteousness of their own, of whom the Lord elsewhere speaks: " Woe to the rebellious children, saith the Lord, that take counsel, but not of me; and that cover with a covering, but not of my Spirit, that they may add sin to sin;" Isa. xxx. 1. Precious Lord Jesus! clothe me with the wedding garment of thy righteousness; and feed me with the rich food of thy body and blood; yea, Lord! be thou my covering, my joy, my all; that when at thy church, at thy table, at thine house of prayer below, and at thine kingdom of glory above, the King cometh in to see his guests, my soul may cry out, in thine own blessed words, and with a joy unspeakable and full of glory: " I will greatly rejoice in the Lord, my soul shall be joyful in my God; for he hath clothed me with the garments of salvation, he hath covered me with a robe of righteousness, as a bridegroom decketh himself with ornaments, and as a bride adorneth herself with her jewels;" Isa. lxi. 10.

JULY 5.

MORNING.—"Thou shalt not wear a garment of divers sorts, as of woollen and linen together."—Deut xxii. 11.

Though the true believer, who like the king's daughter is all glorious within, cannot but know, that as meat commendeth us not to God, so neither doth the necessary dress, which, since the fall, is become suited to cover our sinful bodies, make a part of our holy faith; yet it is highly proper, that persons professing godliness should use great plainness of apparel. The ornament of a meek and quiet spirit, we are told, is of great price in the sight of God. But who should have thought that such a precept as this of Moses had a gospel signification! And yet as Christ was preached under types and figure through the whole law, we may reasonably suppose that not a single command was then given but what had an eye to him and his great salvation. But if we find the Lord so strict respecting the outward dress of the body, what may we conclude the Lord would enjoin respecting the inward clothing of the soul? If wollen and linen were offensive to be worn together, surely, we cannot appear before God in the motley dress of Jesus's righteousness and our own. The fine linen, scripture saith, is the righteousness of saints. With this, which Jesus puts on his people, nothing of our own wollen garments must be worn. The righteousness of a creature, had we any, which in fact we have none, cannot be suited to mix with the righteousness of the Creator. And no man that is wise for salvation, would put the old piece of our corrupt and worn out nature upon the new garment of the renewed nature in Christ Jesus. When therefore the Lord saith, "thou shalt not wear a garment of divers sorts;" my heart replies, no, Lord! let me be clothed with the robe of thy righteousness, and the garment of thy salvation; then shall I be found suited for the marriage supper, when the King comes in to see his guests at his table.

EVENING.—" Though he were a Son, yet learned he obedience, by the things which he suffered."—Heb. v. 8.

My soul! behold what a precious verse of scripture is here! How blessedly doth it set forth thy Redeemer! See here what an example Jesus shews to all his people, and how sweetly accommodating is that example to every case and circumstance, into which any of them can be brought! Surely, if any might have done without going into such a school of suffering, for the purpose of learning, it must have been Jesus; but yet even Jesus would not. And wouldest thou, my soul, after such an illustrious pattern, desire to be excused? Hath not Jesus dignified it, and made it blessed? Oh! the honour of following his steps. There is another beauty in this scripture. The apostle, in a verse or two preceding, took notice of Jesus in his human nature, that he sought not, as such, the high priest's office uncalled. " Christ (saith he) glorified not himself, to be made an high priest, but was called of God, as was Aaron." And by reading this verse in connection with that, it is as if the apostle had said, 'Yea, such was the wonderful condescension of the Son of God, in his divine nature, that, though of the same nature and essence with the Father, yet would he have his human nature trained up in all the exercises of suffering; that, by a fellow feeling, his people might know how he understood their exercises by his own.' Oh! thou gracious, condescending Lord! Surely nothing can soften sorrow like the consciousness that thou hast known it in our nature for thy people; and nothing can more effectually reconcile all thine afflicted members, humbly and patiently to learn obedience in the school of suffering, as that Jesus, though a Son, and the Son of God, in the eternity of his nature, was pleased, in his human nature, "to learn obedience by the things which he suffered."

JULY 6.

MORNING.—"Nay, in all these things we are more than conquerors, through him that loved us."—Rom. viii. 37.

"More than conquerors!" mark that, my soul. Conquerors all the soldiers of Jesus must be, for in his strength they fight, and he has himself subdued all our foes, even death, the last enemy, and Satan, whom the God of peace will bruise under our feet shortly. So that victory is sure. For we overcome by the blood of the Lamb, by the sword of the Spirit, and by the shield of faith, whereby we subdue all the fiery darts of the wicked. But though conquerors, how are we more than conquerors? Yes, through him that loved us, believers absolutely conquer him that is himself unconquerable. For, by union with Jesus, we may be said to have power with God, and to prevail. I will not let thee go," said the praying Jacob, "except thou bless me." A blessing he came for, and a blessing he would have. So all the praying seed of Jacob have power through the blood and righteousness of Jesus, in like manner. Hence Jesus saith to his church: "Turn away thine eyes from me, for they have overcome me." Sweet and precious thought, my soul, never lose sight of it. Through him that loved thee, and gave himself for thee, thou art more than conqueror: nay, thy present victories are more than the victories of the church in heaven. For they have now no more conflicts with tribulation, or distress, or persecution, or famine, or nakedness, or peril, or sword; but, by him that loved us, we arise above the midst of them now, and while troubled on every side, we are not distressed; while perplexed, are not in despair. The love of Jesus is seen in these very exercises, and that in very love, and very faithfulness, the Lord causeth us to be afflicted. Hence, through him we conquer them; nay, we are more than conquerors. We love him that sends the affliction, because we discover his love in it; and as without that affliction, the love of our Jesus in sending it would in that instance not have been known, therefore here we have a blessed victory the church above cannot know. Precious Jesus! to thy love, however, and thy grace, be all the praise and all the glory; for under thy banner of love alone it is that we are more than conquerors.

EVENING.—" A sheaf of the first-fruits."—Levit. xxiii. 10.

This was a most interesting service in the Jewish church, and full of gospel mercies; when the Lord appointed " a sheaf of the first-fruits" of their harvest to be brought before him, and waved towards heaven, as a token that all fruits were of the Lord, and that he was both the giver and proprietor of all. And it hath reference to the person of Christ, both in his death and resurrection. For " a lamb of the first year, without blemish," was to be offered as a burnt-offering with it, to testify that the death of Jesus sanctifies and sweetens all; and Christ himself, in his resurrection, is the " first-fruits of them that sleep." My soul! dost thou observe this Jewish service in a gospel dress? Surely, the service is a reasonable service, and, if possible, more heightened now than then. When this law was given, the Israelite had no power to perform it; neither indeed was it intended to be observed, until the people arrived in Canaan. There was neither tilling of land, nor sowing of seed, in the wilderness; for the people were victualled by the immediate bounty of heaven; and we are told, that they ate the manna until that they came to Canaan. But when they were settled in the land which the Lord had promised them, and God gave them " fruitful seasons, filling their hearts with food and gladness," surely it was meet thus to acknowledge God in his providences, as the providence of God had owned and blessed them. What sayest thou to it, my soul? Here was Jesus in the sheaf of the first-fruits. Here was the Father's blessing, acknowledged in the gift of Jesus. Here was Jesus represented in the lamb, which accompanied the service. Here was the waving it towards heaven, and a prohibition not to eat bread, nor parched corn, nor green ears, until God's portion had been first offered! Oh! my soul, wilt thou not learn hence, to trace Jesus in every one of thy blessings, and to bless thy God and Father for a sanctified use of every thing in Jesus! Help me, Lord, I pray thee, in my heart, in my house, in the field, in the city, in the church, in the closet, in the world, in the family, to be for ever waving before my God, "the sheaf of the first-fruits" in all his bounties. In Jesus I have all; in Jesus would I enjoy all; and then shall I most assuredly have that sweet promise for ever fulfilling in my heart: "Honour the Lord with thy substance, and with the first-fruits of all thine increase: so shall thy barns be filled with plenty, and thy presses shall burst out with new wine;" Prov. iii. 9, 10.

JULY 7.

MORNING.—"Hope deferred, maketh the heart sick: but when the desire cometh, it is a tree of life."—Prov. xiii. 12.

Surely, my Lord and Saviour is the sum and substance of this sweet verse! For art thou not the hope of Israel, and the Saviour thereof? And if thou deferrest giving to my soul renewed views of thy pardoning love, or withholdest the renewed visits and manifestations of thy grace, will not my soul languish and my whole heart be sick? Can I, dear Lord, continue for a moment in health of soul without thee? And art thou not my desire, when thou art the desire of all nations? And when thou comest to my soul in all thy freeness, fulness, suitableness, and all-sufficiency, art thou not the very tree of life in the paradise of God? Precious, precious Jesus! give me to sit down under thy shadow with great delight, for surely thy fruit is sweet to my taste. Do not defer thy blessed visit to my soul this morning, for thou knowest, Lord, that though, through thy grace, that sickness of sin which is unto death, thou hast already cured by the application of thy blood and righteousness; yet there is a sickness not unto death, and which my soul will pine and languish under, unless thou renewest me from day to day. Oh, blessed Jesus, I want every moment fresh manifestations, renewed discoveries of thy presence, grace, and favour. I want to know thee more, to love thee more, to live to thee more; and the deferring these precious mercies maketh my heart sick. Come then, thou blessed Lord, with all thy fulness; my desires are to thee, and to the remembrance of thy name. With my soul have I desired thee in the night; and now, with the first dawn of day, would I seek thee early. And surely, when thou comest, as I know thou wilt come, thou wilt be in deed and in truth the tree of life. Methinks my soul is now opened by thee for thy reception; and therefore, Lord, do thou now make such rich discoveries of thy person, glory, grace, and love, as may fill every portion of my heart; nay, Lord, I pray to feel such goings forth of my poor soul, in waiting for thy coming, that, like the queen of Sheba, overpowered in the view of the riches and wisdom of Solomon, my views of thy condescending grace, and a sense of my unworthiness to be so blessed of my God, may melt my whole soul before thee; and, like her, there may be no more spirit in me from such ravishing enjoyments of thy presence.

EVENING.—" Jesus wept."—John xi. 35.

My soul! look at thy Redeemer in this account of him. Was there ever a more interesting portrait than what the evangelist hath here drawn of the Son of God? If the imagination were to be employed for ever in forming an interesting scene of the miseries of human nature, what could furnish so complete a picture as these two words give of Christ, at the sight of them? " Jesus wept." Here we have at once the evidence how much the miseries of our nature affected the heart of Jesus; and here we have the most convincing testimony, that he partook of all the sinless infirmities of our nature, and was truly, and in all points, man, as well as God. We are told by one of the ancient writers (as well as I recollect, it was St. Chrysostom) that some weak but injudicious christians in his days, were so rash as to strike this verse out of their bibles, from an idea, that it was unsuitable and unbecoming in the Son of God to weep. But we have cause to bless the over-ruling providence of God, that though they struck it out from their bibles, they did it not from ours. It is blessed to us to have it preserved, for it affords one of the most delightful views we can possibly have of the affectionate heart of Jesus, in feeling for the sorrows of his people. And methinks, had they judged aright, they would have thought, that if it were unsuitable or unbecoming in Jesus to weep, it would have been more so to put on the appearance of it. And why those groans at the grave of Lazarus, if tears were improper? Precious Lord! how refreshing is it to my soul the consideration, that, " Forasmuch as the children were partakers of flesh and blood, thou likewise didst take part of the same; that in all things it behoved thee to be made like to thy brethren!" Hence, when my poor heart is afflicted, when Satan storms, or the world frowns, when sickness in myself, or when under bereaving providences for my friends, "all thy waves and storms seem to go over me;" Oh, what relief is it, to know that Jesus looks on, and sympathizes! Then do I say to myself, will not Jesus, who wept at the grave of Lazarus, feel for me? Shall I look up to him, and look up in vain? Did Jesus, when upon earth, know what those exercises were; and was his precious soul made sensible of distresses even to tears; and will he be regardless of what I feel, and the sorrows under which I groan? Oh no! the sigh that bursts in secret from my heart, is not secret to him; the tear that on my night couch, drops unperceived and unknown to the world, is known and numbered by him. Though now exalted at the right hand of power, where he hath wiped away all tears from off all faces, yet he himself still retains the feelings and the character of "the man of sorrows, and of one well acquainted with grief." Help me, Lord, thus to look up to thee, and thus to remember thee! Oh! that blessed scripture; "In all their afflictions, he was afflicted; and the angel of his presence saved them; in his love, and in his pity, he redeemed them, and he bare them, and carried them all the days of old," Isa. lxiii. 9.

JULY 8.

MORNING.—"Ye are my witnesses, saith the Lord, and my servant whom I have chosen."—Isa. xliii. 10.

Doth God indeed appeal to the souls of his people for the truth of his covenant love! Oh the gracious condescension! It is sweet, it is blessed, and a testimony enough to make the heart of every child of God that possesseth it to leap for joy, when the Spirit witnesseth to our spirits that we are the children of God. But it is still carrying on that blessedness with increasing delight, when the people of God themselves become witnesses of covenant love and faithfulness; and, from numberless experiences in themselves, can, and do set to their seals that God is true. See then, my soul, this morning, whether thou art one of thy God's witnesses, and thy Redeemer, as the servant of Jehovah, witnesseth *for* thee, and by his sweet influences *in* thee, all that thine heart can wish concerning the word of his grace, and thy fellowship and communion with him. Run over a few leading points in which thou canst, and dost bear witness for thy God. Did he not remember thee in thy low estate, when he passed by, and bid thee live? Did he not convince thee of sin, and put a cry in thine heart of salvation? Did not God the Holy Ghost convincingly prove to thee, both the infinite glories and perfections of Jesus, and by his gracious leadings constrain thee to a love towards him, dependence upon him, and a perfect approbation of having him for thy Saviour? Did not Jesus so graciously visit thee, shew thee his love, his tenderness, his power, his suitableness, his all-sufficiency, as to warm all thy frozen affections into a warmth for him and attachment to him. And did not thy God and Father, again and again, manifest to thee his covenant love, in accepting thee in Jesus, blessing thee with all spiritual blessings in him, hearing and answering prayer, and proving by all these tokens that he is thy God, and that thou art one of his people? And art thou, my soul, day by day looking up for salvation only in Jesus, and renouncing all other saviours? Dost thou know all these precious things, my soul, and a thousand more of the like nature, in which thou art bearing daily testimony to the word of his grace? Then surely thou art one of those to whom Jehovah appeals in the blessed scripture of the morning. Think then, my soul, what an honour thou art called to! What a privilege is thine! See to it, my soul, that thou witness for Jesus, whom God hath given for a witness to the people.

And while Jesus takes up thy cause before the throne in heaven, do thou plead his cause, and be valiant for his truth here upon earth. And do ye, angels of light, and ye spirits of just men made perfect, witness for me that this Lord is my God.

EVENING.—"By faith the walls of Jericho fell down, after they were compassed about seven days."—Heb. xi. 30.

Never, in the annals of mankind, in the history of all wars, is there a parallel instance to be found, of exploits like what the Holy Ghost hath recorded here, of faith. The walls of a city actually fell down at the blasting of rams' horns; and yet not from the blasting of horns, but from faith in the almighty power of God. My soul! let thy meditation, this evening, be directed to the subject, to see whether it will or not, under divine teaching, give strength to the exercises of thy faith? We find, in the relation given of this memorable siege, that no ramparts were thrown up, no mounds raised, nothing of any human attempt made, either to sap the foundations, or to harass the enemy. The simple process adopted to intimate to the besieged the appearance of war, was an army marching round the walls, once every day, for seven days together. I have often thought how the despisers of God and his army, in the city of Jericho, ridiculed the Israelites in their daily exercise. And what an apt resemblance were they of the despisers, in the present day, of God and his Christ! But what an effect must have been induced, when on the seventh day, and after seven times marching round (perhaps in honour of the sabbath) at the shout of Joshua and his army, the whole of the walls fell flat to the ground! My soul! such, but in an infinitely higher degree, will be the consternation of all the enemies of Jesus, when "he shall come to be glorified in his saints, and admired in all that believe!" Do not overlook the testimony the Holy Ghost hath given to this memorable event, that it was wrought "by faith!" And what cannot faith in Jesus accomplish? Hadst thou been present at this siege, and beheld the stupendous event, when, at the command of Joshua, the Israelites shouted, and the walls fell, thou wouldest have seen a sight not more wonderful and supernatural, than when, at the command of our new testament Joshua, the Lord Jesus Christ, the weapons of sin fall out of the hands of the sinner, and the strong holds of Satan give way in the heart, to the victorious grace of the Spirit. Lord! I would say, in the review of this subject, increase my faith, and make my soul strong in the grace that is in Christ Jesus!

JULY 9.

MORNING.—"But he answered her not a word."—Matt. xv. 23.

Mark, my soul, this feature in thy Redeemer's conduct towards the poor woman that so long and so earnestly entreated him—"Jesus answered her not a word." And yet, from the close of the subject, nothing can be more evident, than that the Lord had determined, not only to grant her petition, but to throw the reins of government, concerning herself, into her hands so completely, that it should be as she would. Learn then from hence how to interpret silence at the throne upon every occasion of thine. In every dark providence, under every dispensation of grace, never forget that Jesus's love is the same. What though he answereth not a word; yet his whole heart is towards his redeemed. Whatever frowns there may be in outward things, there can be none in what concerns the real happiness of his people. Jesus may try, as in the instance of this poor woman, the graces he gives. Faith may be hard put to it, and silence at the throne may make temptation and exercises of every kind more sharp and painful. But Jesus is the same, his love the same, the merits and efficacy of his blood and righteousness the same. These speak *for* thee, my soul, when they may not speak *to* thee. That is a precious thought; never forget it. And remember, moreover, covenant mercies are not suspended upon our deserts. The free grace of God in Christ depends not upon the will or the worth of man; according to the beautiful account by the prophet of the rain or dew of heaven, which waiteth not for man, neither tarrieth for the sons of men. Henceforth, therefore, my soul, do thou learn to wait at the mercy-seat as cheerful, and with as lively actings of faith, when Jesus answereth not a word, as when thy petitions are all complied with. " Men ought always to pray, and not to faint," saith one that could not be mistaken. Oh for grace and faith to take God at his word, and like Job to say, " Though he slay me, yet will I trust in him."

EVENING.—" By faith, the harlot Rahab perished not with them that believed not, when she had received the spies with peace."—Heb. xi. 31.

It were a pity to disconnect what the Holy Ghost hath joined; and as the relation of the destruction accomplished by faith on the walls of Jericho, is followed in the scripture history, with an account of a deliverance, from the same principle, in this wonderful woman, who was an harlot, do thou, my soul, let thy last evening's meditation on the *one*, be followed up in this, by the exercise of thy devout thoughts on the *other;* for both are expressly intended to one and the same purpose, which is to encourage the Lord's people to be " followers of them, who now, through faith and patience, inherit the promises." What extraordinary events are there in the scripture account of Rahab, the harlot; that such a woman, and an harlot, should be distinguished with such grace! That in such a city, even an accursed city, the Lord should have so illustrious an instance of faith! That faith so illustrious should be found in the heart of an harlot! And that the eminency and greatness of it should be such, that God the Holy Ghost hath thought proper to have it recorded, both in its principle and effects, by the apostle Paul, in one epistle, and by the apostle James in another. Yea, and what is more marvellous still, that our Lord, after the flesh, should arise out of such a stock! Oh! what a world of wonders is folded up in the great plan of salvation! But while thou art beholding the wonders of grace in the instance of this woman, and admiring the triumph of faith wrought in her, do not fail to connect with it the still more blessed view of Him who is the author and finisher of faith, and from whom, and in whom, and by whom, the whole is accomplished. Precious Jesus! it is all by thee, and thy glorious undertaking, that Rahab, the gentile, found faith to believe, while the spies of Israel doubted. It was thou, and thy grace, O Lord, that wrought so effectually, and therefore be thou eternally loved and adored in this rich dispensation of thy mercy, that Rahab the harlot perished not with them that believed not. Oh! thou bountiful Lord! publicans and harlots, thou hast said, go into the kingdom of God, before the self-righteous pharisees!

JULY 10.

MORNING.—"And he is before all things, and by him all things consist."—Col. i. 17.

How doth the apostle mean that Jesus is before all things? Not as God only, for then the observation would have been needless; and not as man only, for then how could all things consist by him? What is it then, my soul? Is it not as Mediator, both God and man? And was not Christ thus set up from everlasting? Not openly revealed indeed, neither openly manifested in a body of flesh, until the fulness of time; but secretly, and in the divine counsels. What a blessed thought for the redeemed to exercise their rapturous meditations upon! And is it not this which the apostle hath said; " He is the image of the invisible God?" The image! Yes, that representation of what is in itself invisible; that identical image concerning which Jehovah when calling Adam into existence, said, " Let us make man in our image, after our likeness." So then Adam was the first man indeed *openly*, but not so *secretly;* for it is plain that Adam was made after this likeness which was set up from everlasting. Hence this union of natures, subsisting in one person, formed the one glorious Mediator, who is, and was, before all things, and by whom all things consist. Here is the foundation then of the church, and that from everlasting: without this, the church, and indeed all things beside, had wanted foundation. For there is nothing created that can stand *out* of God; and there was nothing created that could stand *in* God, by a personal union, but him. What a glorious thought! Cherish it, my soul! Never lose sight of it. In Christ the Mediator, all things consist. The church is preserved, redeemed, sanctified, glorified: and how are all his redeemed ones personally and individually secured, but by the same? By him all things consist. Hence their consisting is in him; they are living in him, feeding on him, made righteous in his righteousness, and hereafter will be glorified in his glory. My soul, think what a world of mysteries thou art in; think what an unspeakable life, is a life of grace here; think what a world of glory in Jesus hereafter. Now see if thou canst better enter into an apprehension of those divine words of Jesus: " Because I live, ye shall live also." And again: " At that day ye shall know that I am in my Father, and you in me, and I in you."

EVENING.—" How fair and how pleasant art thou, O love, for delights!"—Song vii. 6.

My soul! thou hast been refreshed, many an evening,

through grace, in beholding thy Lord, both in his person, and in his comprehensive fulness for his redeemed; nor wilt thou be without refreshment this evening, if thy Lord, in his sweet influences, be with thee, to make what is said in this lovely scripture, life and spirit in thine heart. They are the words of Jesus; and they express the love and complacency of delight which Jesus takes in his church. Surely nothing can be more blessed, than to see the high value the Son of God puts upon the church, which the Father gave him, endeared as it is yet more in being the purchase of his blood! But what astonishment is it to the soul of a poor sinner, to be told, and by the lip of truth, that sinners are fair in Jesus's eyes! "Thou art fair, O love, yea, pleasant." Now remember, my soul, and in that remembrance let Jesus have all the glory, that this loveliness and beauty in the sinner, of every degree, that is regenerated, and made anew in Christ, is from Jesus. It is wholly from his righteousness, in which he beholds her clothed: "I washed thee with water, (saith the Lord) and I decked thee also with ornaments; and thy renown went forth among the heathen for thy beauty: for it was perfect through my comeliness which I had put upon thee, saith the Lord God," Ezek. xvi. 5—14. My soul! bow down under the conviction of all that remains of indwelling inbred sin; and, in language like that of the astonished apostle, cry out, 'Lord! how is it that thou hast set thy love upon creatures so polluted and unworthy; and dost "manifest thyself to them otherwise than thou dost to the world?"'

JULY 11.

MORNING.—"If thou knewest the gift of God, and who it is that saith to thee, Give me to drink, thou wouldest have asked of him, and he would have given thee living water."—John iv. 10.

Amidst a thousand precious things concerning Jesus, there are two views of him which are peculiarly so, and which those words of his to the woman of Samaria bring home to the heart in the plainest and most blessed manner. The one is, who, and what, Christ is in himself; and the other is, the Father's authority in him, so as to give faith in him a divine warrant to act by, when a poor sinner comes to make use of Christ. It is our ignorance in those two grand points concerning salvation, which is the sad cause of all our miseries and the little enjoyment even gracious souls, for the most part, have in Jesus. Now, my soul, do thou meditate upon both these things this morning, and from these sweet words of thy Saviour see if thou dost not prove what he so graciously saith to be true. First, consider who, and what Jesus is, as he is in himself. Let thy faith have for its object of meditation, the Person, and the work of God thy Saviour. In all he wrought, in all he did, in all he accomplished, it was as the Surety of his people. And in all the fulness, by virtue of it, which is treasured up in him; it is not for himself, for he cannot need it, but it is for his people. So that a poor sinner is as much suited to Jesus for him to give out of his fulness, as Jesus is suited for a poor sinner to supply his emptiness. And therefore, if we did but thus know him, and thus come to him, we should find that he is as earnest to receive every poor sinner, and to give out of his fulness, as that poor sinner can be to come and take. Now, my soul, when thou hast duly pondered over this, look at Jesus in the other point of view also as the gift of God. Here thou hast a warrant, an authority; nay, a command, to come to Jesus, and to make use of him, for every want which poverty, ignorance, and sin have occasioned in the circumstances of our fallen nature. Christ is the one blessed ordinance of heaven; Christ is the one, and the only one, appointed way, for a poor sinner's acceptance with God. And therefore, did a poor sinner always keep in view that Christ is the gift of God; and that God is honoured, when that poor sinner honours his dear Son, by believing the record God hath given of him; would not this make every poor sinner happy, in thus glorifying God? And therefore, my soul, look to it, that this is thy daily exercise; for then thy thirst for Jesus will not be supplied, as from a pool, which depends upon dry or wet seasons; but Jesus himself will give thee living water: nay, Jesus will himself be that everlasting living spring in thee, which springeth up into everlasting life.

EVENING.—"Thou, O God, didst send a plentiful rain, whereby thou didst confirm thine inheritance when it was weary."—Ps. lxviii. 3.

How truly grateful are the falling showers upon the thirsty earth, after a hot summer's day, such as this season of the year abounds with! Such, my soul, (and thou knowest it, I hope, in the many refreshments thou hast had) is Jesus, in the visits of his grace! "He shall come like rain," was the sweet promise given to old testament saints, "upon the mown grass, as showers that water the earth," Ps. lxxii. 6. And every new testament believer hath, more or less, a real personal enjoyment of it. Sometimes the Lord comes as the tender dew, for he saith himself, "I will be as the dew unto Israel," Hosea xiv. 5. And hast thou not found thy Lord, not unfrequently, so to come? silent and unperceived for a while; yea, at times, when wholly unlooked for, unasked, unsought! Yes! thou dearest Jesus, thou tarriest not for man's desert, neither waitest thou for their prepared state to receive thee! Micah v. 7. And sometimes, as this blessed portion for the evening expresseth it, the Lord comes in a "plentiful rain;" even showers of his love, washing away "the filth of the daughter of Zion," and cleansing every thing that is polluted; as the natural clouds pour their fulness, which wash off the insects from the vegetable creation, and purify the air from noxious vapours. And when my God and Saviour thus comes to his people, how doth he make the wilderness-frames of their dry and languishing minds to blossom as the rose! So come, Lord Jesus, I beseech thee, on my soul, and not on mine only, but on thy churches, thy ministers, thy people! But, my soul, do not dismiss this charming scripture, until thou hast first gathered another blessed instruction from it, for it is most blessed. The words say, that Jehovah sends this plentiful rain, whereby he "confirmed his inheritance when it was weary." And doth not this most abundantly prove, that Christ, with all his fulness, and all his graces, is the *sent* of God the Father? "We have seen and do testify (said John, the beloved apostle) that the Father sent the Son to be the Saviour of the world," 1 John iv. 14. Oh! precious, precious scripture! Do I not read in it the grace, and love, and mercy of all the persons of the Godhead? Surely, Almighty Father! thou dost confirm all thy covenant faithfulness, when thou dost send thy dear Son to the souls of thy people! Thou dost, indeed, both confirm thy truth, and refresh their weary, dry, and thirsty souls, when Jesus comes to bless them, in the dew of his grace, and in the showers of his love and mercy!

JULY 12.

MORNING.—"And they began to pray him to depart out of their coasts."—Mark v. 17.

And was this Jesus whom they desired to depart? Yes: and what had the Redeemer done to merit this treatment? He had dispossessed the evil spirit from the mind of a poor creature, and caused the whole country to be freed from the fury of one whom no chains could bind: was this the cause? Yes. And is it possible that so divine an act could have had such an effect upon the minds of a whole body of people? What, would these Gadarenes rather have the devil ranging among them, in the person of this poor creature, than the Son of God in the kindness of our nature? Pause, my soul: is it not the same now? Do not men still prefer the raging uncontrolled lusts of their own hearts, the dominion of Satan, and the customs, pursuits, and follies, of the world; to the grace, mercy, and sweet dominion of Jesus? Do they not in deed, if not in words, say, "Depart from us, we desire not the knowledge of thy ways?" Pause again, my soul. Was there not a time when the same was thy case? Indeed there was. And is not every one so by nature? And what but an act of grace, like the miracle Jesus wrought on this poor man, can bring any one out of it? Art thou, my soul, brought out of it? Yes, if so be, like him, thou art now sitting at the feet of Jesus, clothed, and in thy right mind. Surely, Lord, thou hast wrought this blessed change upon me! Could I desire thee to depart out of our coasts? Nay, is it not the daily, hourly desire of my heart, that thou wouldest be with me, dwell in me, reign and rule in me, and be my portion, my God, my Saviour, and make me thine for ever? Sweet testimony, in the midst of all my wanderings, coldness, undeservings! Cherish it, my soul! Jesus will not depart from thee. That love which brought him down from heaven to save a world, led him over the lake of Genesareth to save one poor sinner. And he who came in love unsent for, departed not until he was sent away. Oh ye poor blind, deluded, Gadarenes! Oh my poor, equally blind and deluded countrymen and fellow-sinners, who know not, nor desire to know Christ Jesus! Who are ye that thus reject the Lord of life and glory, and desire him to depart out of your coasts?

EVENING.—"And they called the name of that place Bochim."—Judges ii. 5.

Surely it was enough to induce such an effect, when the preaching of an angel informed the people, that the Lord, for their sins, would not drive out their enemies before them. The place might well be called Bochim, and they themselves might hear the name

Bochim, weepers. But, my soul, thou hast lately been to a place which is yet more calculated to make it memorable, by weeping, when thou didst attend Jesus at the ordinance of his supper. For there Jesus himself was, and is, the everlasting preacher, who sheweth thee his hands and his side, pierced and streaming with blood, for thy sins. Didst thou not hear him speak to thee himself, in his own words, "They shall look upon me whom they have pierced: and they shall mourn for him, as one mourneth for his only son, and shall be in bitterness for him, as one that is in bitterness for his first-born?" Zech. xii. 10. Didst thou not weep in beholding such a sight, in hearing such words, and in meditating on such things? Alas! Lord, my heart is harder than the adamant. But if the eye wept not; say, was not my heart broken? Did I not desire to feel, to mourn, and, with the prophet, to cry out: "Oh! that mine head were waters, and mine eyes a fountain of tears, that I might weep day and night," in the recollection of my Redeemer's sufferings, and my sins, the dreadful cause of them? Did Jesus die for *me*! Did the Son of God offer up his precious soul and offering for *me?* Was his body broken, and his blood shed for *me?* For me! a poor, wretched, polluted, hell-deserving sinner? Oh! for grace to make every place a Bochim in the recollection; and especially at the table of Jesus, may my soul always find these ordinance-seasons heart-melting seasons. Here would I frequently attend, to have my soul thoroughly awakened, and my stony heart made flesh. Here would I go, to gather a holy hatred to my sins, which brought Jesus to the cross. Here would I be found waiting, that when any new temptation may arise, I may cry out, with a vehement indignation, "How can I do this great wickedness, and sin against God?" How can I "crucify the Son of God afresh, and put him to an open shame?" Precious Lord Jesus! do thou help me to keep the eye of my soul stedfastly fixed on thee, and all the affections of my soul to be going out in desires after thee; to be "always bearing about in my body the dying of the Lord Jesus, that the life also of the Lord Jesus may he made manifest in my body!"

JULY 13.

MORNING.—"This year thou shalt die."—Jer. xxviii. 16.

I have often thought this passage, pronounced on the lying prophet, a most suitable sermon for a birth-day portion, to be sounded in the ears of the sinner: and if qualified with the possibility and probability which arise out of our dying circumstances, it might, when commissioned by the Lord, have a blessed effect. My soul, take it for the meditation of thy birth-day. It *may be* fulfilled this year; it *must be* fulfilled some year; it *cannot be* a very distant year; and there is a birth-day when it *shall be* passed upon thee in the year. And why not the present? Pause, my soul, and meditate upon it, as if this were the very year. And what though carnal men celebrate the anniversary of their birth-day, as best suited to their carnal minds, let thine be wholly spiritual. If indeed a man came into the world laughing, there might be a suitable correspondence in commemorating the annual return of such a birth with laughing. But if cries first indicated the birth of a poor helpless creature, born to want, and the subject of sin and misery; can rioting and folly be the proper celebration of such an event? And is there no joy suitable on the return of a man's birth-day? Oh yes, there is, and ought to be, real heart-felt joy with every child of God. When a man begins to count birth-days in grace, every return calls for holy joy in the Holy Ghost. Not for that he was born an intelligent immortal creature only, but for that he was made a new creature in Christ Jesus. Not for that he came into the world in a state of nature only, but that he was brought also into a state of grace. Not for that he was of the stock and lineage of Adam only, but of the seed of Christ. Here is an alliance royal, holy, heavenly, divine! My soul, how many moons or years in the new life canst thou mark down? Let this be the arithmetic in thy calculation. And if, like the herald of the morning, the voice should say, "This year thou shalt die:" Oh how sweet to answer, Lord, my times are in thine hands! Can they be in a wiser, or more tender, or more loving hand than Jesus's? Precious Lord, wean me from every thing here below, that I may be living nearer with thee, and in thee, and to thee; that as the last year of my pilgrimage lessens to the month, and the month to the week, and the week to the day, nay to the very hour and moment of my departure from a body of sin and death, the last expiring words on my trembling lips may be of Jesus; and thine, Oh Lord, come home with power and sweetness to my soul, like thine to him upon the cross: "To-day shalt thou be with me in paradise."

EVENING.—"I will both lay me down in peace, and sleep: for thou, Lord, only makest me dwell in safety."—Ps. iv. 8.

My soul! it is blessed, indeed, to lie down, or arise, when Jesus is thy rest and refreshment! But, void of security and safety in him, both the day-light and the darkness have their horrors. And how unsatisfying is every thing where Jesus is not? This is strikingly exemplified, day by day, among all carnal characters. "There be many," saith the Psalmist (in this divine psalm), "there be many that say, who will shew us any good?" Yea, the whole world, who know not the blessedness of Jesus, will thus say! What a busy life some men make of it? And what is it for? Be their pursuits what they may; let them be ever so much diversified, one object is the aim of all. The apostle hath said what it is; "to make provision for the flesh, to fulfil the lusts thereof," Rom. xiii. 14. My soul! what is the first and last, the greatest and most momentous desire of thine affections? Canst thou, and dost thou, adopt the words of the Psalmist, in this sweet psalm: "Lord! lift thou up the light of thy countenance upon me: and it shall put more gladness in my heart than in the time that corn and wine increase?" Oh! the blessedness of such a state! May it be mine! Dearest Lord Jesus! grant it me, day by day; and in the evening and night watches, let thy sweet visits be unceasingly renewing: and then will I take this precious portion for my song, both when undressing for the bed of sleep, and the bed of death: "I will lay me down in peace, and sleep; for thou, Lord, only makest me dwell in safety!"

JULY 14.

MORNING.—"And I only am escaped alone to tell thee."—Job i. 19.

My soul, is there nothing in this account which the messenger to Job gave concerning himself which suits thy case and circumstances? Nay, mayest thou not in a great variety of ways, both in providence and grace, adopt similar language, in which thou art escaped alone to tell? Pause! look back to thy boyish days. Nay, look further back, even to the birth, and to the womb; for had not the Lord carried thee from thence, surely from the womb wouldest thou have died and given up the ghost. And what was thy childhood, but years of perils and dangers, in which multitudes dropped all around thee, so that thou mightest say, while contemplating them, "and I only am escaped alone to tell thee?" And where are numbers with whom the stages of thy youth, and years at school were spent? Where are they? May it not here again be said, "And I only am escaped alone to tell thee?" Go on, and trace the wonderful history in the eventful path of riper years: through what sicknesses, pains and deaths hast thou passed; and mayest thou not, my soul, here again cry out, " And I only am escaped alone to tell?" Oh the wonders of distinguishing love, even in common providences, towards his people, before that the highly-favoured objects have any consciousness how that love is watching over them, and whereby they are preserved to the day of their calling! Who shall count the sum of distinguishing mercy, in preserving and upholding providences, during the whole of an unconverted state! My soul, hadst thou died in any one of these perilous seasons, and how very near sometimes hath death seemed, the language of Job's messenger would not then have been thine as it is now; " And I only am escaped alone to tell thee." Pause once more. Art thou now, my soul, indeed escaped to tell of converting grace? Canst thou now look round, and amidst the dying and the dead in trespasses and sins, unawakened, unconcerned, unregenerated; canst thou indeed say, " And I only am escaped alone to tell thee!" Oh then, my soul, proclaim with earnestness the glorious truth. Invite all, as far as thy sphere of information can reach, as if thou, and thou alone, wert escaped to tell of the wonders of redeeming love; and let thy daily language be: " Oh come hither, and hearken, all ye that fear God, and I will tell you what he hath done for my soul."

EVENING.—" For as often as ye eat this bread, and drink this cup, ye do shew the Lord's death till he come."—1 Cor. xi. 26.

An evening or two since, my mind was led out to the contemplation of the supper of the Lord, as a heart-affecting ordinance, to make the Lord's table a Bochim. I hope, my soul, that in this view, thou didst find it profitable. Here is another proposed to thy meditation, which, under grace, will prove equally so, in which it comes home to thy affections as a subject of holy joy. Look at it in this light, and remark what the apostle saith upon it. The Lord's death, which is thy life, is set forth by every renewed celebration. And what a delightful thought is that. As the body needs its constant regular meals, so doth the soul. And as Jesus is the whole of life, and strength, and happiness to his people; as oft as we receive the holy supper, we testify to the world of men and angels, that he is all this; and we glory in setting him forth as such at his table. And what a blessed addition is that little phrase at the end of this verse; "till he come:" yea, that "when he comes," he may find his people at his table, and in their death celebrating his. Oh the blessedness of being so found! Surely every lover of Jesus would desire to be found there, when the master comes, and calleth personally for each, to take him home: to be, in one and the same moment, in the valley of vision, and the valley of the shadow of death! My soul! from henceforth, among the other glories of the ordinance, do not forget this. The oftener it is attended, the more delightful it will be. For the service keeps the remembrance of Jesus alive in the soul, until he comes to take the soul home to the everlasting enjoyment of himself in glory. And as there, all his redeemed, who feast their souls with the view of his person, unceasingly behold some new glories in him, and, after millions of ages, will find him still increasingly lovely, and increasingly precious; so here below, the more we see him, and know him, and enjoy him by faith, the more we shall long to see him, and know him, and enjoy him by sight: and the glories of his person, and the wonders of his blood and righteousness, will be unfolding more and more to our ravished souls. And while every other object lessens in its value by time and use, and all created excellencies, like the planet under which they are found, have their growing and their waning seasons; Jesus is the same, "yesterday, and to-day, and for ever." Yea, though in reality always the same, yet from the increasing manifestations of love and glory which he makes of himself to us, as our capacities are capable of bearing, he will be in our view more and more blessed, from day to day, from one ordinance to another, and through all the unknown periods of eternity! Oh! the blessedness of setting forth Jesus, "in breaking bread and in prayer!"

JULY 15.

MORNING.—"Rivers of waters run down mine eyes, because they keep not thy law."—Ps. cxix. 136.

Who is there of whom this may be said? Jesus, and Jesus only. He wept indeed over his beloved Jerusalem, for he was a man of sorrows and acquainted with grief. And the love he had to his redeemed, induced a bloody sweat through all the pores of his sacred body. But of every other may it not be said, "All seek their own, not the things which are Jesus Christ's." Did we truly love Zion, would not rivers of tears run down at the present languishing state of Zion? Did we feel the full sense of distinguishing grace, would not every heart mourn over the ruins of our common nature? Think, my soul, what a mass of sin ascends as a cloud before the view of the Lord every day from a single heart of the desperately wicked transgressor? Think what an accumulation in a town, a province, an empire, the world! Might not rivers of waters run down at the contemplation? And worse, if possible! Think of that higher source of sorrow, in that the only possible remedy for this evil is slighted, and Christ, which is God's one gracious ordinance for the recovery of our ruined nature, is so little esteemed among men. Oh how might the people of God be supposed to have their very souls melted in the contemplation! This, this is indeed the condemnation; this is the soul-destroying sin; "that light is come into the world, and men love darkness rather than light, because their deeds are evil." Oh for grace to mourn over a Christ-despising generation! Oh for the "Deliverer to arise out of Zion, and turn away ungodliness from Jacob."

EVENING.—"And Abraham called the name of that place Jehovah-jireh; as it is said to this day, in the mount of the Lord it shall be seen."—Gen. xxii. 14.

My soul! how many Jehovah-jirehs hast thou erected? At least, how many occasions hath thy bountiful Lord afforded thee for erecting them? Oh what cause have I to blush in the recollection! Had I done by my God, as Abraham did by his, what blessed helps would they have afforded me, in the same moment that they became monuments to the Lord's praise! Surely I know all this, in theory, very plainly and fully: but how do I fall short in the practice of it! To set up the *Jehovah-jireh* for all that is past, is the best help to a soul in exercises for all that is to come. When I can, and do put down, after any sharp trial, any *Jehovah-jireh*, and say, here it was "the Lord did provide;" will it not, in any future exercise, enable me to say, 'If the Lord helped me then, may I not hope that he will help me now?' It would be a very sad requital for past mercies, in the moment of receiving them, to say, 'Alas! the Lord did once help, but he will not, I fear, do it again.' This would be to read the inscription of the *Jehovah-jireh* backward. Whereas the very sight of our *Jehovah-jirehs* should teach us to say, "Here the Lord helped me: here he manifested his free unmerited grace to me: and will he not again? Is he less Jehovah than he was? Is he not God all-sufficient, all-gracious still?" O it is blessed to have such stones set up as Abraham's *Jehovah-jireh*. There was nothing in the patriarch's of his own providing. His was simply an act of faith; and neither the result of his asking by prayer, or providing by his wisdom. And, my soul, do not overlook a most interesting mark which the Holy Ghost hath put upon Abraham's Jehovah-jireh, in adding, "As it is said to this day, in the mount of the Lord it shall be seen." As if he had said, 'all the ages and generations yet to come shall profit by the great father of the faithful's testimony to this place; and they shall see it to the latest day of Jesus's church upon earth? Oh! how blessed, when our personal experience bears an exact correspondence to that of the faithful gone before; when we can and do set up the same. All blessings, all provisions are in Jesus. He is the Lamb, which, from everlasting, Jehovah hath provided, and whom his people shall see in all their wants, temporal, spiritual, and eternal. And let their extremities be what they may, yea, though the exercises of their faith abound, yet let them wait but the Lord's time, which is always the best time, and they shall most assuredly, like Abraham, find cause to call the name of every place of trial, Jehovah-jireh; concerning which, in proof and in reality it shall be said, every day and to the last day, "In the mount of the Lord it shall be seen!"

JULY 16.

MORNING.—"I say unto you, there is joy in the presence of the angels of God over one sinner that repenteth."—Luke xv. 10.

What a precious information is this which the Son of God hath given of heaven's joy over every individual instance of the recovery of our poor fallen nature! Surely if angels of light thus participate in the triumphs of our Jesus; well may sinners rejoice over sinners, whenever a single one is awakened from darkness to light, and converted from the power of sin and Satan unto God. Think, ye ministers of my God, what motives arise out of this thought to stir up your most earnest exertions in labouring in the word and doctrine! Ought it not to be the first and most importunate petition at the mercy-seat whenever entering upon your labours, that, by the Lord's blessing upon you, new causes might arise to call forth this joy in heaven? Nay, ought it not to be the fervent prayer and hope of faith, at the close of those labours, and especially every Lord's day, that some souls may have been awakened, and angels may have rejoiced through your instrumentality? Can there be a prayer more interesting upon earth, than when the servant of Jesus saith, 'Lord, crown my labours this day with success?' And can there be a subject to call forth more animated praise than when at the close of a sabbath, you look up and say, 'Lord, have angels rejoiced this day over the conversion of any poor sinner in this congregation?' And no less, ye parents and guardians of the rising generation, should the same hope prompt you to wrestle in prayer with God for the sanctification of your household. Go on, and hope that answers are coming down to your earnest requests. Perhaps the next joy in heaven may be over one for whom you have now prayed! Precious Jesus, it is enough. I bless thee, Lord, for this, among a thousand other proofs of thy care over us, that the salvation of poor sinners adds new joy to the felicity of heaven, and that there is joy in the presence of the angels of God over one sinner that repenteth.

EVENING.—"He shall drink of the brook in the way; therefore shall he lift up the head."—Ps. cx. 7.

The brook of Kedron was a black brook (for so the word Kedron signifies) into which all the filth from the sacrifices was thrown; it was the brook over which the Son of God passed in the night that he entered the garden of Gethsemane. Now, as the whole Psalm from which this portion is taken, refers to the person of Jesus, nothing can be more plain than that David, by the spirit of prophecy, is here describing the deep sufferings of Christ, and the glory that should follow.

By the expression, drinking of this black brook, it is intended to convey an idea of the "cup of trembling" put into the Lord Jesus's hands, when he sustained all the sins and filth of his people, and in consequence as their surety, all the Father's wrath against sin. Hence the Lord said, "The cup that my Father giveth me, shall I not drink it?" My soul! pause, and ask thyself, doth not this sweet but solemn verse give thee precious instruction, when thou considerest that all thy filth, and all thy defilements, were imputed, by the Father himself, unto the person of thy glorious surety? Is it not blessed thus to see, that by Christ's drinking "of the brook in the way," he took all thy transgressions, and was made both "sin and a curse for thee, that thou mightest be made the righteousness of God in him?" And though, in himself, he was "holy, harmless, undefiled, separate from sinners, and made higher than the heavens," yet, as the surety of his people, he was made black with sin and suffering; "his visage was marred more than any man, and his form more than the sons of men." Precious Jesus! may I never lose sight of Gethsemane, the mount of Olives, and the brook Kedron! Here, by faith, let my soul frequently take her evening station, and behold thee "pouring out thy soul unto death, numbered with the transgressors," drinking "of the brook in the way," that thy sacred head might be lifted up, first on the cross in suffering, and then with thy crown in glory!

JULY 17.

MORNING.—"I go to prepare a place for you. And if I go and prepare a place for you, I will come again and receive you unto myself, that where I am, there ye may be also."—John xiv. 2, 3.

How shall I ever sufficiently enter into an apprehension of the love of Jesus? Much less, how shall I ever sufficiently love thee, and adore thee, thou unequalled pattern of excelling love, blessed, precious Jesus? Was it not enough to have given such palpable evidences of thy love in dying for poor sinners; but must thou tell them also before thy departure the cause for which thou art gone away, and to give them an assurance, at the same time, that thou wouldest come again, and take them home with thee to glory? Oh help me, Lord, to love thee, to live to thee, to be always on the look out for thee, and to rejoice with a joy unspeakable in the promise of thy coming. And, my soul, while thou art taking all the sweetness of those precious words of thy Jesus to thyself, in the prospect of his shortly coming to take thee to himself, let them also have their full comfort under any bereaving providences of thy friends. Wouldest thou regret if an earthly king had conceived such a love to any friend of thine, that he had sent for him to advance him to some high dignity, to make him his favourite, and to load him with honours? Considered as to earthly accommodations, would this advancement of some near and dear friend of thine be distressing to thee, because thou wert to see him no more? Nay, would not the generosity of the prince be highly extolled by thee; and more especially if the messengers which came to fetch thy friend, brought with them a promise, that, ere long, a royal guard would be sent to take thee also, to live with thy friend for ever, in the king's palace, and under the king's eye, both enjoying the royal favour? But what would all this fading, dying, perishing, and uncertain grandeur be, to that which Jesus promiseth in these blessed words of the morning? And hath Jesus taken any of thine home to his glory? Are they now at the fountain head of blessedness, and art thou weeping over their breathless remains? Raise up, my soul, thy thoughts from earth to heaven. Hear the voice that speaks, "Blessed are the dead which die in the Lord." Keep up the constant expectation of thine own call. Walk as on the borders of the invisible world. And above all, so watch the daily, hourly, visits of Jesus, by his grace, and enjoy the sweet communion and fellowship in spirit, by which he now speaks to his people, and they to him, that when Jesus draws back the curtain of thy bed at death, and appears to thy ravished view in all his glory, thou mayest leave the trembling body, and run to his embraces, crying out, "My Lord, and my God."

EVENING.—"And as he reasoned of righteousness, temperance, and judgment to come, Felix trembled."—Acts xxiv. 25.

And wherefore did Felix tremble? Did Paul, who was then preaching to him, charge him with any particular sins? It doth not appear that he did. Neither is it probable that a poor prisoner would have been permitted so to have done. But the truth is, God's holy word, by Paul's preaching, and the man's own guilty conscience, which Felix himself applied, so met together, that the conscious sinner could not refrain. The very thought of a future judgment, and a day of account, crossing the mind of a guilty conscience, will be enough to damp the mirth of the sinner in the midst of his jollity. Every man, more or less, must have thoughts now and then of an hereafter. Man, by nature, is a creature compelled to look forward. He is for ever proposing to himself prospects that are to arise. Hence, men of the world are sending out into the highways and lanes of the city, to invite men like themselves to kill time, and to gild the passing hour; and while they can do this, fill up the moment, and drown thought, it is all very well. But when the idea of a judgment to come riseth within, and the very apprehension that things will not always be as they now are, starts up; the alarm, like the hand-writing upon the wall of the impious monarch, instantly takes effect, and a trembling follows. Dan. v. 5. My soul! learn hence (and if well learned, it will be a blessed improvement of thine evening's meditation) that outward circumstances, be they what they may, go but a little way to give inward comfort. It matters not what men possess, if those possessions have not the sanctifying blessing of the Lord upon them. Where Jesus is not, there can be no real enjoyment. All the world of creature comforts are not sufficient to afford real happiness. Hence Felix, a governor, trembled, while Paul, a prisoner, rejoiced. Hence, many an aching heart, in a noble house. Shall not such views endear Jesus to thee, my soul, still more? Shall they not make thee very cheery over thy comforts; and make thee truly jealous that thou wilt not allow thyself one enjoyment where Jesus is not first seen in that enjoyment, and where he doth not sweeten and form the whole of it? Make him the sum and substance of all blessedness, and then thou wilt find that godliness indeed is profitable to all things; "it hath the promise of the life that now is, and of that which is to come!"

JULY 18.

MORNING.—"Take us the foxes, the little foxes that spoil the vines, for our vines have tender grapes."—Song ii. 15.

My soul, mark the sweetness and tenderness of this precept. Foxes no doubt resemble, in this scripture, the subtle, less open, less discovered sins and corruptions which lurk in us, like these cunning creatures, under a covering, and perhaps sometimes under a fair covering. Moreover, they may mean also false but fair teachers. "Oh Israel," said the Lord, "thy prophets are like the foxes in the deserts;" crafty, designing, malignant, and filthy. And in proportion as they put on a more fair and specious appearance, the more are they to be dreaded. Satan never more artfully, nor perhaps more effectually deceives, than when he is transformed into an angel of light. Moreover, the precept is enforced by that important consideration, that vines, by which no doubt are meant believers, have tender grapes. What more tender than a weak conscience? And what more liable to be wounded than the tender principles of young beginners in a life of grace? My soul, look up to Jesus, the Lord of the vineyard, for grace to be on the look out against these destructive enemies to thy welfare. And, conscious that all thy vigilance, without his watchful eye over thee, would never protect thee from foes so shrewd and artful, beg of Jesus himself to take these foxes for thee, and destroy them before thine eyes. Lord, I would say, keep me from every enemy which doth evil in thy sanctuary, and preserve alive, in flourishing circumstances, all those tender graces of thy Spirit bestowed upon me, that I may bring forth fruit to the praise of thy holy name, and may flourish and spread abroad as the cedar in Lebanon."

EVENING.—" And he said unto them, with desire I have desired to eat this passover with you, before I suffer."—Luke xxii. 15.

My soul! thy Jesus holds a feast of the ordinance of his supper; that most interesting service, which he hath appointed in his church as a standing memorial of his death, until his second coming. Surely, thou canst need nothing more endearing, to prompt thee to attend it, than what the Lord himself expressed of his own pleasure in it, in these words. There is somewhat uncommonly affectionate in them: they seem to open and unfold the whole heart of the Redeemer upon the occasion. And do not forget, that what Jesus then said to his disciples, he saith now to thee, and to all his redeemed; they were the representatives of his whole body, the church. Listen to what Jesus here saith, and regard every word in this most tender and affectionate request, as if Jesus in person were now speaking to thee, in prospect of the coming supper: " With desire I have desired to eat this passover with you, now I have suffered, and have accomplished redemption by my blood!" Pause over the blessed view, and trace the wonderful desires of Jesus from everlasting, which he all along manifested towards his people. His goings forth for the salvation of his people have been from everlasting. He saith himself, that "while as yet Jehovah had not made the earth, nor the fields, nor the highest part of the dust of the world; that then his delights were with the sons of men!" Prov. viii. 22—31. And how did the Lord Jesus manifest his desires towards his people, as soon as creation-work took place, in all those appearances he made of himself to them, from the garden of Eden, to his openly tabernacling among them in the substance of our flesh? What were all those manifestations we read of, sometimes in the form of man, and sometimes of an angel, but to tell his church, his redeemed, that with desire he desired for the fulness of time to arrive, when he would become their passover, and suffer for them? And is not the desire of Jesus after the conversion of every poor sinner, whom the Father hath given to him, now as earnest, and as affectionate as ever? Doth he not wait to be gracious? Doth he not long for their recovery from sin and Satan, and to bring his prisoners out of the prison-house? And when they are brought, by his Holy Spirit, which he puts within them, into the liberty wherewith he makes his people free, doth he not delight in their company, seek to allure them to ordinances, call upon them by his word, by his providences, by all his dispensations, to manifest himself to them otherwise than he doth to the world? Dost thou not know somewhat of those precious things, my soul? And if so, shall Jesus say, as he doth in those blessed words to his disciples, in the evening of his agonies in the garden, "With desire I have desired to eat this passover with you, before I suffer?" And wilt thou not be among the first to attend thy Jesus at his table? Oh! bountiful Lord! I beseech thee, let this view of *thy* desires quicken *mine*, and let my whole soul, with all her affections, be earnestly going forth after thee, that I may say with one of old, "O send out thy light, and thy truth; let them lead me, let them bring me unto thy holy hill, and to thy tabernacles; then will I go unto the new testament altar of my God, even unto Jesus, my God, my exceeding joy; yea, upon the harp of my warmest affections will I praise thee, O God, my God," Ps. xliii. 3, 4.

JULY 19.

MORNING.—"Without me ye can do nothing."—John xv. 5.

Dearest Jesus, I know this in theory, from thy gracious teachings, as well as I know that I am by nature a sinner; but I am for ever failing in this knowledge, when I come to put it into practice. Teach me, Lord, how to preserve the constant remembrance of it upon my mind, that I may never go forth to the holy warfare to subdue a single foe but in thy strength, and never make mention of any thing but thy righteousness, and thine only. Be convinced, my soul, every day, more and more, of this most precious truth, and behold it proved from all the circumstances around thee. See and remark the total inability either of God's judgments or God's mercies to induce the least alteration upon the heart of man, without his grace. Behold the prosperous sinner bathing in a full river of blessings, himself in health, his circumstances flourishing, his children like olive-branches round his table, wealth pouring in upon him from every quarter; and yet he lives without God, and without Christ in the world; and as he lives, so he dies, in the vanity of his mind. See him amidst distinguishing preservations, in battles by sea or land, still preserved, while floating carcasses, or opened graves, are all around him: do these things bring his heart to God? Not in the least.

The sum total of his character may be comprised in a few words; "neither God is not in all his thoughts." Look at him in the opposite side of the representation; let such an one be visited with chastisements, in his own person sickness, in his family misery, in his substance want; in short, in all that concerns him, a life of sorrow, care, anxiety, disappointment, ruin. Perhaps to all these, a body long the dwelling-place of some loathsome disease, under which he groans, and at length dies, and dies the same unawakened sinner as he had lived. And suppose these accumulated evils had been distinguished also with some more peculiar maladies, in perils in the sea, in perils in the war, in perils among men; nay, let him be maimed in his limbs, let him be rotting in a prison, let him be worn out with misery from evil upon evil, like waves of the sea following each other; yet still he continues the hardened, unsubdued sinner under all, and as unconscious of God's rods as the prosperous sinner before described is of God's blessings. Are these things so, my soul, and hast thou seen them? Yes, in numberless instances. Oh then, learn, that without Jesus thou canst do nothing. Outward circumstances, unaccompanied with inward grace, leave men just where they found them; and plain it is, that grace alone can change the heart. Lord Jesus, let these loud and crying truths, day by day lead my soul to thee! Be thou all in all, my hope, my guide, my strength, my portion; for "without thee I can do nothing."

EVENING.—"And it shall come to pass, when your children shall say unto you, what mean ye by this service? that ye shall say, it is the sacrifice of the Lord's passover."—Exod. xii. 26, 27.

My soul! thou hast lately been at the table of the Lord, to celebrate Christ as thy passover. If thy children ask of thee, as the Jewish children were here supposed to ask of their fathers, "What mean ye by the Lord's supper?" wouldest thou not catch at the favoured opportunity to inform them? yea, wouldest thou wait to be asked? Can there be a duty, or a pleasure upon earth, like that of a tender father instructing his household in the things which accompany salvation? Can the imagination figure to itself any sight equally lovely to that of a parent, or a master of a family, encircled by his little ones, and answering to their interesting questions; yea, anticipating their inquiries, by speaking of Jesus, his person, his grace, his love, and all the wonders of his work, in the accomplishment of our salvation? And, indeed, these were among the precepts under the old testament dispensation. "Ye shall lay up (said Moses) these my words in your heart, and in your soul, and bind them for a sign upon your hand, that they may be as frontlets between your eyes. And ye shall teach them your children, speaking of them when thou sittest in thine house, and when thou walkest by the way; when thou liest down, and when thou risest up," Deut. xi. 18, 19. And if the subject of redemption was so interesting then, though but in type and figure, what ought it to be now, when Jesus, the whole sum and substance of it, hath come and finished it by his blood? My soul! what sayest thou to these things? Hast thou children, a family, a household, a charge of souls about thee? And wilt thou not, at thy return from the Lord's table, or from the Lord's house to thine own, season thy conversation with speaking of Jesus? Wilt thou not begin the sweet subject of redemption, by way of calling up their inquiries, and exciting their attention? Wilt thou not tell them *where* thou hast been, and *what* thou hast been to the table of Jesus for; what thou hast seen there, and what thou hast felt, and known, and enjoyed of the Lord's presence, in holy communion? Surely their minds, how young soever, will long to know more and more of a service so truly interesting; and they will be looking forward to the time of life when a ripeness of understanding, under the awakening influence of the Holy Ghost, may prepare them to join the Lord at his table also, that they, with all the ransomed of the Lord, may celebrate the Lord's passover. Methinks I hear the earnest question of such, like the Jewish children, "What mean you by this service?" and that, when opened and explained, followed up by a thousand more: hath Christ been *your* passover? Hath he been *with you* at the feast? Hath he manifested himself to *your* soul "otherwise than he doth to the world?" Have you seen "the goings of your God and king in his sanctuary?" And hath Jesus made your heart "burn within you, while talking with you by the way, and in making himself known to you, in breaking of bread, and in prayer."

JULY 20.

MORNING.—"Arise, and go down to the potter's house; and there I will cause thee to hear my words."—Jer. xviii. 2.

Yes, Lord, with the first of the morning will I arise, and go down at thy command, where, by the secret and silent whispers of thy divine teaching, I may gather suitable instructions for interpreting all thy dispensations, both in providence and grace, towards me. Mark, my soul, the vessel marred in the hand of the potter. Alas, how hath our nature been marred since it came out of the hand of our Almighty Potter! Will the potter cast his vessel away? No, he will new make it. Oh thou glorious Lord! methinks I hear thy words in this, for thou hast not thrown us away, but hast new made us, and more blessedly made us in Christ Jesus. My soul, art thou indeed thus new made, a vessel unto honour, sanctified and meet for the master's use? Attend then to thy proper character, and never lose sight of it. Refer every act of mercy and favour in thy original creation, in thy new creation, when marred by sin, and in all the appointments and dispensations, both in nature, providence and grace, in which thou art placed, to the sovereign will and pleasure of Jehovah, thine Almighty Potter. All the different forms, and the different ends, for which the whole is appointed, result from his sovereignty, in which the richest display of wisdom and of love is shewn. "Shall the thing formed say unto him that formed it, why hast thou *made* me thus?" Much less in any of the dispensations, either in providence or grace, shall any say, why dost thou *use* me thus? Precious Jesus, it is enough to be new made in thee; to be new formed in thy blessed likeness; to be taken into thy service; and to be made a meet vessel for the master's use in thy family. Thy church is as a great and well-furnished house, where there are not only vessels of gold and of silver, but also of wood and of earth. And if my Lord condescend to look on me, to use me, nay, to bring me into his house and family, that I may be always under his own gracious eye; how humble soever the place or lowly the station, to belong to Jesus is the supreme honour of all his saints. My soul, make frequent visits to the potter's house, and never fail to go down there whenever any temptation from the enemy, or thine own heart, causeth thee to forget thy creatureship, and the wonders of a marred creature, being new made in Christ Jesus.

EVENING.—"Christ, our passover, is sacrificed for us."—1 Cor. v. 7.

Thou art not wearied, my soul, I hope, with the subject of thy last evening's meditation; and if not, the subject itself of the passover is so abundantly interesting, that it furnisheth endless matter for the sweetest thought. Every thing in the Jewish passover was typical and figurative of Jesus; and therefore, that we might not err on so important a point, the Holy Ghost, by his servant the apostle, calls him by this very name; "Christ, our passover," and adds, "was sacrificed for us." A lamb of the first year, without blemish and without spot, was set apart, in the Jewish church, for the observance of this service; and Christ, the Lamb of God, who was "holy, harmless, undefiled, and separate from sinners," was set apart, in the christian church, for the redemption of his people, from all eternity. The lamb was slain, in the Jewish church, and roasted with fire; and when Christ was slain on the cross, in the christian church, the agonies of his soul were such as one sustaining the fire of wrath against sin: he was made both *sin* and a *curse*, that his people might be made "the righteousness of God in him." The lamb, in the Jewish passover, was to be roasted whole, and not a bone of him was to be broken; and one of the principal features of the Lamb of God, in the christian passover, is, that we are to receive a whole Christ for salvation, whose bones, when on the cross, as if to prove the allusion of the type to him, by a divine providence, were not broken. The blood of the lamb, in the Jewish passover, was to be sprinkled on the lintels and posts of the houses of the Israelites, to preserve the inhabitants from destruction; and in the christian passover, it is not the blood shed only, but the blood applied, by sprinkling on the sinner's conscience, that delivers him from the wrath to come. Neither the bolts nor bars of the Israelites' houses, no, nor all the prayers offered up within, became the least cause of their safety; but the blood on the door. So, in like manner, it is neither the prayers, nor repentance, no, nor faith, as an act of our own, that can preserve from destruction: it is "the blood of Christ alone, that "cleanseth from all sin." Oh! how blessed is it to see the great work of redemption thus shadowed forth in the scriptures from the beginning, and that the whole, and every part of the Jewish service referred to the christian sacrifice of Jesus on the cross. "Christ, our passover, is sacrificed for us." Oh! for grace to keep the feast at the Lord's table, a feast upon that sacrifice, and to remember what the Holy Ghost saith: "Christ being come an High Priest of good things to come, by a greater and more perfect tabernacle, not made with hands, that is to say, not of this building; neither by the blood of goats and calves, but by his own blood, he entered in once into the holy place, having obtained eternal redemption for us," Heb. ix. 11, 12.

JULY 21.

MORNING.—"The righteous shall flourish like the palm-tree."—Ps. xcii. 12.

It forms a beautiful illustration, which the Holy Ghost condescends to give of a true believer's state, as it stands before God, in the allusion not unfrequently made in scripture to that of the palm-tree. The direct tendency of the palm-tree is upward: it lifts its head, in defiance of all impediments, towards the clouds. Now a true believer in Jesus is always looking upward, and directing all his pursuits after Jesus. His person, blood and righteousness are the objects of his desire. And as the palm-tree is said to flourish the more when trodden upon and attempted to be crushed; so the believer most oppressed for Jesus's sake, will flourish in the graces of the Spirit more abundantly. How fruitful also is the palm-tree: and how much the people of God bring forth fruit in their old age, when, after long experience, they have found that in Jesus alone their fruit is found. How much the palm-tree likes sunny places! How precious the Sun of Righteousness is to his people! And as the branches of palm-trees are worn in tokens of victory, so the church above are beheld with palms in their hands: and the church below carry the palm of rejoicing, when, from the atoning blood and righteousness of Jesus, they are made more than conquerors through him that loved them. My soul, art thou flourishing like the palm-tree? Yes; if so be thou art planted in Jesus, and watered from the streams of that river which maketh glad the city of God. Yes, if directing all thy views, all thy hopes, all thy desires to Jesus, thou art living in him, acting faith upon him, making him the alpha and omega of hope here, and happiness hereafter. Blessed Sun of Righteousness, shine with such warm, life-giving, fruit-imparting beams of thy rich grace upon my soul, that I may flourish indeed under thy divine influence, and shew that "the Lord, who is my rock, is upright, and that there is no unrighteousness in him."

EVENING.—"I know that my Redeemer liveth, and that he shall stand at the latter day upon the earth. And though after my skin, worms destroy this body, yet in my flesh shall I see God: whom I shall see for myself, and mine eyes shall behold, and not another."—Job xix. 25, 26, 27.

What sublimity is in these words! and what blessed glorious truths do they contain! Here is Job's creed. My soul, see if it be thine. Job did not say, that he had heard of a Redeemer, and that he hoped it was true, and he gave credit to it; but he saith, he *knoweth it*. And observe who this Redeemer is. Job calls him his Goel, his Kinsman-Redeemer. For the right of redemption belonged to the nearest of kin, and he might redeem; Levit. xxv. 25. We have lost our inheritance, forfeited our possession, and are poor indeed, both in person and in substance. Now as Christ, by virtue of his being our nearest of kin, is the one, the blessed one, the only one to whom the right of redemption belongs, and may redeem both our persons and our mortgaged inheritance; so we find Christ hath done both. Job therefore exults: "I know, (saith he) that my Kinsman, my Redeemer liveth." Oh, how blessed the thought! how precious the assurance! But we must not stop here. This Kinsman-Redeemer "will stand at the latter day upon the earth." Yes, saith the scripture, Jehovah hath given assurance to all men of this, "in that he hath raised him from the dead," Acts xvii. 31. Neither is this all. Job's creed goes on. "Though (saith he) this body of mine be destroyed by worms, yet in this flesh shall I see God; whom I shall see for myself, and mine eyes shall behold *for myself,* and not another *for me.*" Sweet thought! Jesus hath secured the resurrection of his people, and, by his own, hath confirmed theirs. As sure as he arose, so sure must they; for he is the first fruits, and, by their union with him, they are the after harvest. As Jesus arose perfectly and substantially the very same body that died on the cross, so must their redeemed bodies arise the very same. The hand that now writes, and the eye that now reads, if a part of Christ's mystical body by regeneration, must be interested in his resurrection also, and must arise not only precisely the same identical body, but every member of that body must be the same; for this is essential to identity. Were God to raise another body, it would make another person. This might indeed be done by God's power; but then it would be a new creation, and not a resurrection of the old body. I must be the *who I am* now, and the *same* as I am now, as to identity, in order to constitute a resurrection. "This corruptible (saith Paul) must put on incorruption, and this mortal must put on immortality." Pause, my soul, over these sweet, but solemn truths, and say, are they blessed to thy meditation? Dost thou feel a joy, an interest in them? Oh! the unspeakable felicity of knowing that we have a Kinsman-Redeemer, and that he liveth, and that we live in him? Precious, precious Jesus! though all nations die, Jesus liveth; and because he liveth, I shall live also! Lie down, my soul, this night, with this blessed assurance, saying, hallelujah! Amen.

JULY 22.

MORNING.—"These shall make war with the Lamb, and the Lamb shall overcome them : for he is Lord of lords, and King of kings; and they that are with him are called, and chosen, and faithful."—Rev. xvii. 14.

What an awful thing must sin, in its own nature be, which hath introduced such evil into the whole creation of God, in its consequences. One might have hoped, however, that the meek and gentle Lamb of God would have been exempt from the daring rebellion, and that sin would not have bid defiance and waged war against the peaceable, and holy, and harmless Jesus! But so far is this from being the case, that, in all probability, war first broke out in heaven against the person of God's dear Son, as man's glorious Head and Mediator, even before the deadly malignity manifested itself against God and his Christ upon earth, in tempting the first man and his wife in the garden of Eden, to rebel against God. Pause, my soul, over this scripture. Who are they here described that make war with the Lamb? Nay, rather, who are they not? All the powers of darkness, all the varieties of the earth, all the inhabitants of hell, all that are under the influence of that evil spirit, which now worketh in the children of disobedience. Under this dreadful banner of open rebellion against heaven, every man by nature is enlisted; and until an act of sovereign grace and power is past, that he that is Lord of lords, and King of kings, overcomes and brings them under his blessed dominion, all ranks and orders of men are found. My soul, are the weapons of sin fallen out of thine hands? Art thou brought under the conquest of Christ's grace? Hast thou bent the knee of willing homage to the Lamb, who hath bought thee with his blood, and made thee his by his grace? Read thy character, if so, in these sweet words: "And they that are with the Lamb are called, and chosen, and faithful." Art thou *called* with an holy calling? Art thou *chosen,* and fully convinced of this, that had not Jesus first chosen thee, thou wouldest never have chosen him? Art thou *faithful,* in seeking and desiring no other salvation, convinced that there is salvation in no other? Take with thee, then, my soul, these precious marks of thy high calling and fellowship, and see that thou follow the Lamb whithersoever he goeth.

EVENING.—"The wilderness of Zin."—Exod. xvi. 1.

My soul! thou art still in a wilderness state, not yet arrived home to thy Father's house; and thou art frequently exercised with wilderness dispensations. Perhaps, under the Spirit's teaching, an evening's meditation on the wilderness of Zin, where Israel sojourned, will be profitable to thee. Let faith lead thee thither, and see what subjects are there opened before thee. Was there ever an instance like Israel, which was brought out with a high hand, and stretched-out arm, from the tyranny of Egypt? Did the sea open a path for them to march through; and that memorable spot, which to them became the way of salvation, become to their enemies that pursued them, the pit of destruction? Did the Lord go before them in a pillar of cloud by day, and cover them from danger by the pillar of fire by night? After such miracles, yea, in the moment of receiving the same continuance of divine favour, while on their way to Canaan, what was there in the people's passing through the wilderness of Zin, that should have discomposed their minds, or made them call in question God's faithfulness, and his love? Thou knowest, my soul, what the scripture hath recorded of the events of the wilderness to Israel. Though their history furnisheth a continued series of the Lord's mercies over them, yet, on their part, little else can be found but rebellion, unthankfulness, and sin. Pause, and let the apostle's question have its full weight upon thee. "What then? (saith he) are we better than they? No, in no wise; for we have before proved, both Jews and Gentiles, that they are all under sin." Was there ever an instance of grace like this, my soul, so great, so distinguishing, so abounding, when the Lord found thee in the Egypt of thy fallen nature, and when he brought thee out with a sovereign hand? Did Jesus open to thee a new and living way through his blood? And dost thou not know, that his cross, which is thy glory, and thy salvation, will be the condemnation of all the enemies who despise it? Is thy Lord leading thee, going before thee, and following thee, in grace, and goodness, and mercy, all the days of thy life, like the pillar of cloud, and the pillar of fire, to Israel, and bringing thee by a "right way, to a city of habitation?" Are these among the daily manifestations of thy Lord? And shall thy passage (for thou knowest that it is but a passage) through the wilderness of Zin, make thee for a moment lose sight of Jesus? True, thou art exercised; and thine exercises appear to thee so peculiarly distressing, as if no one of God's people before had ever been so circumstanced. But in them thou shouldest mark the wisdom, as well as the love of him that appoints them. Didst thou trace Jesus in all, thou wouldest find a sanctified blessing in all; and the issue of thy heaviest trials would then bring in an exact proportion of the sweetest comforts. It is because they are peculiar, that they are suited to thee. There are numberless things which occur in the exercises of thy brethren, which to thee would be no exercises at all. They feel them, and know their pressure, and the love of Jesus in sending them, and the tenderness of Jesus in helping them under them, and bringing them out of them: all these things thou seest and knowest in others, and findest cause both to admire and to adore the divine faithfulness in the dispensations. But in the study and improvement of the exercises in thine own heart, which, of all others, is the most important, here thou failest. And yet thou art convinced, in a cool hour, when grace is alive, that if a synod of angels were to arrange the circumstances of thy state, they could not order them with the wisdom and love that they are now ordered with. Go then, my soul, go by faith, frequently to the wilderness of Zin. Look at Israel's history, and look up for wisdom to gather suitable instruction. Behold Jesus in every dispensation. Whatever tends to lead thee to him, must be blessed. It is impossible that any trial, be it what it may, can be otherwise than blessed, which opens to the view Jesus therein, and endears and makes Jesus precious thereby. And, my soul! while I wish thee frequently to go by solemn meditation to the wilderness of Zin, let each renewed visit remind thee that thou art getting through it. Like children at school, every day brings on the festival which will take us home to our Father's house. A few steps more, a few exercises more, and Jesus will send his chariot for us; yea, he will come himself to fetch us; and we shall take an everlasting farewell both of the wilderness of Zin and this world of sorrow together. "Haste, haste, my beloved, and be thou like to a roe, or to a young hart, upon the mountain of spices!"

JULY 23.

MORNING.—"One like unto the Son of Man, clothed with a garment down to the foot, and girt about the paps with a golden girdle."—Rev. i. 13.

My soul, thou art going this morning to the throne of grace, art thou not? Pause then, and behold Jesus as John saw him, for the church's joy, in his priestly vestments; for remember he is still a priest upon his throne, and by the oath of Jehovah, abideth a priest for ever. Nay, my soul, be not afraid, draw nigh; hark, surely he calls. Methinks he speaks to thee—'Behold me! behold me! See, I am thine intercessor.

For this cause I wear these priestly garments; and as the high priest of old represented me, I appear in them down to the foot, and the golden girdle round and beneath the breast. What is thy cause? What blessings and praises hast thou to offer for past grace? And what supplications for present and future favours? Behold my vesture dipped in blood. Think of the everlasting efficacy of my righteousness: and for whom should I make intercession but for transgressors?' Fall down, my soul, with holy reverence and godly fear. Jesus will do by thee as he did by John. He will lay his right hand upon thee, and say, "Fear not." Oh precious, precious Lord, thou art, indeed, he that was dead, and now livest for evermore. And thou livest to see the fruits of thy great salvation faithfully and fully applied to every one of thy redeemed. Thy priesthood is for ever. Thy intercession unceasing. I do behold thee, Lord, by faith, even now standing with the blood of the covenant in thine hand, and presenting me, even me, poor, wretched, worthless me, as one of the purchase of this blood. Do I not hear thy voice in those soul-reviving words, "Father, keep through thine own name those whom thou hast given me? Father, I will that they also whom thou hast given me be with where I am?" Oh glorious, gracious, Almighty High Priest! thou art, indeed, "a priest for ever, after the order of Melchisedec." Oh ye trembling souls! ye who have any cause this day to bring before the court of heaven, look unto Jesus, look within the veil, see Jesus there; look steadily, though humbly, and behold his hands, his side; Zion is still engraven on his palms. Nay, do we not see, may we not read our very names, as the high priest bore the names of Israel on his breast, while his hands are lifted up to bless! Yes, Jesus takes up our cause, bears our persons, and all our concerns. And how shall either fail, while he "is able to save to the uttermost, all that come to God by him, seeing he ever liveth to make intercession."

EVENING.—"Perfect in Christ Jesus."—Coloss. i. 28.

Sweet thought! And where should perfection be found, but in Christ Jesus! My soul! turn the subject over and over again; look at it in every point of view; consider it as it relates to the life that now is, and that which is to come; and where wilt thou find any perfection for grace here, or glory hereafter, but in Christ Jesus? Oh! what heart-aches would it have saved me, had I but learned this sweet lesson when the Lord first took me into his school. Had I but thought aright when the Lord passed by, and saw me in my blood, and bid me live, that a creature so polluted, and so poor, could never recompense such riches of grace, it would have tended to hide pride from mine eyes. But I was delighted with myself, and the supposed improvement I should make; all my views were directed how to requite the Lord's goodness, and how to shine above others in the attainments I should make in the divine life: and according to my views then, it would have been no difficult matter to have persuaded me (had the adulation been offered to the pride of my vanity in a guarded manner) that, what from labours and services, in attending ordinances, and prayers, and the like, I was hastening on to perfection, and possessed a good stock of inherent holiness.—Precious Jesus! I bless thee, in the moment of recollection, for thine unspeakable mercy in breaking this snare of the enemy, and bringing me humbly to thy feet! And now, Lord, I again and again, and for ever, desire to praise thee for keeping me still at thy feet, in the same humble frame, convinced "that in me, that is, in my flesh, dwelleth no good thing!" Oh, Lord! how should a creature such as man, who would not for a moment, did his salvation depend upon it, form one good thought, or prevent a train of evil thoughts from rushing in upon his mind; how should such an one ever be led to the presumptuous hope of finding perfection in himself? Precious Jesus! be thou increasingly precious from the increasing wants of my soul for thee. Give me, Lord, yet more and more to see that every thing in me, and from me, must be, like myself, but dung and dross. Accept, Lord, I beseech thee, both my person and my poor offerings, and let both be sweetly sanctified and perfumed with the incense of thy blood and righteousness! Be thou, Lord, my whole and sole perfection for righteousness here below, and may I be found "perfect in Christ Jesus" in a life of grace, that I may everlastingly enjoy thee in a life of glory hereafter. Amen.

JULY 24.

MORNING.—"The stranger did not lodge in the street; but I opened my doors to the traveller."—Job xxxi. 32.

Though Job was thus hospitable, yet we know that angels would have lodged in the street, if Lot had not taken them in. Nay, the Lord of angels, when he came a stranger upon earth, had not where to lay his head. He came indeed "unto his own, but his own received him not." My soul, pause! Hast thou done better by thy Lord? Nay, thou hast not. And though thou knowest the precept the apostle had it in commission to tell the church, "not to be forgetful to entertain strangers, for thereby," as in the instance of the patriarch, and others, "some have entertained angels unawares;" yet, my soul, how long did the Lord of life and glory stand without, knocking at the door of thine heart, by the ministry of his word and ordinances, saying—open to me; yea, and would have stood to this hour, had he not, by his own sovereign grace, put in his hand by the hole of the door, and opened to himself. Oh thou blissful stranger, didst thou indeed come from a far country, on this gracious, blessed errand, to seek and save that which was lost; and didst thou find every heart resolutely shut against thee? Didst thou, blessed Jesus, when travelling in the greatness of thy strength, open to thyself an entrance into the souls of thy people, by the sweet and constraining influences of thy Holy Spirit? Do thou, then, Almighty Lord, throw open the street doors of my heart for thy constant reception! Make them like the gates of that blessed city which are never shut day nor night. And cause my soul, like the prophet on the watch-tower, or Abraham in the tent door, to be always on the look out for my Lord's approach, that I may invite thee; yea, constrain thee to come in, and abide with me, and to make thyself known unto me, by the heart-burning discourses of thy word, and in breaking of bread and of prayer. Yes, yes, thou glorious Traveller! who art perpetually on the visits of thy love, I do know thee, I do sometimes catch a sweet glimpse of thee, and trace the footsteps of thy grace, in thy word, in thy ordinances, and in the various ways by which thy presence is discoverable. Indeed, indeed, thou heavenly Stranger, thou shalt not lodge in the street; but I will take thee home to my house, to my heart and soul; and thou shalt sup with me, and I with thee, according to thine own most gracious promise, and I will cause thee to drink of spiced wine of the juice of my pomegranate.

EVENING.—“ There they made him a supper.”—John xii. 2.

We are very apt to suppose the blessedness of those hallowed seasons in which the Lord Jesus ate and drank familiarly with his disciples, as peculiarly given to the followers of our Lord in the days of his flesh. And, no doubt, there was a precious savour which Jesus manifested upon those occasions. He that laid aside his garments, and condescended to wash his disciples' feet, may well be supposed to have said and shewn a thousand gracious things in those seasons, which are not recorded. But, my soul, depend upon it, if we make Jesus a supper, or if Jesus invites us to his own, which is the same thing, there will be always a blessed savour of his person, work, and righteousness, when his person is the subject of discourse, and his work and righteousness the rich food of the soul. Our ordinary meals would be truly sanctified, if the love, and grace, and favour of the bountiful giver of them, became the chief conversation at our table. But is it to be wondered at, if carnal company mingle at our entertainments, that carnal discourse, and not that which tendeth to edification, should follow? And if Jesus be thus forbidden, how shall it otherwise be, but that every thing connected with Jesus is banished? How often, my soul, hast thou been at such tables, and in such society where thy master is not honoured; but where, at thy departure, thou mightest with truth have taken up the observation, and said, 'Alas! I have neither said ought which might benefit another, nor heard ought to be benefited by myself?' Blessed Lord, while I sit down at the refreshments of thy bounties, give me always to recollect from whom they come; and while I eat of the fat, and drink of the sweet, do thou, Lord, send portions to them for whom nothing is prepared. And cause me and mine, at every supper, to make thee a supper in a true spiritual enjoyment of thee. Oh! for thy presence to be always in view, and the savour of thy name to be as "ointment poured forth!" And do thou, Lord, by the sweet influences of thy Spirit, direct our conversation to the use of edifying, that we may talk of Jesus, while Jesus draweth nigh to us; and at every supper, think of the supper of the Lord; and by faith, enjoy that marriage-supper of the Lamb in heaven, at which we hope, ere long, to sit down for ever!

JULY 25.

MORNING.—" Thou art my hiding-place.—Ps. xxxii. 7.

Yes, dearest Jesus, thou art indeed my hiding-place. In every point of view, I desire grace so to behold thee. Surely, from everlasting, in thee, and thy person and righteousness, were all thy redeemed hid in the councils of peace and salvation. And is not every individual hid in thee also, Oh thou glorious head of thy church; while in a state of unrenewed nature, to be secured from death and the grave, and from the unpardonable sin; and as one of the apostles terms it, " preserved in Christ Jesus, and called." And when called, and quickened by grace, what, but from having our lives hid with Christ in God, could keep alive the incorruptible seed, or preserve unextinguished the immortal spark? Whence is it, my soul, that the smoking flax, which Satan and thine own remaining indwelling lusts strive to blow out, is not quenched; or the bruised reed, which appears so continually falling, is not broken —but because Jesus is thy security, through whom, and in whom thy languishing graces revive as the corn, and grow as the vine? Oh what springs of grace must there be for ever flowing from Jesus, though hidden from mortal view! Surely, Lord, thou art my hiding-place, and therefore, with thy leave, I will consider thee as a strong tower, into which the righteous runneth and is safe. Yes, both my person and life, both my safety and happiness, both my present peace and everlasting joy, all, all are in thee. Doth any then, ask thee, my soul, where dwellest thou? Tell them, in Jesus, in the clefts of the rock, in the secret places of the stairs, even in Christ himself and his justifying righteousness; secret and hidden indeed from mere men of the world, but revealed from faith to faith to all his redeemed; and into which, tell them thou hast found shelter from the broken law of God, from the dreadful effects of sin, from death, from hell, and all the powers of darkness. And all these, and numberless other unknown blessings, because Christ is my hiding-place, who hath both preserved me from trouble, and hath compassed me about with songs of deliverance.

EVENING.—" And when the time of the fruit drew near, he sent his servants to the husbandmen, that they might receive the fruits of it."—Matt. xxi. 34.

The very lovely season of the year, and the fulness of fruits which appear on all the productions of God's providence around, open to the mind some of the most delightful meditations. My soul! sit down this evening, and give scope to the subject; and see, while contemplating thy Lord's bounties in nature, whether thy Lord himself will not lead thee by the hand into the inner department of contemplating his yet greater bounties in grace. Methinks every thing seems to have a voice, and speaks of Jesus. By the fall, our poor ruined nature is entitled to nothing from the earth, but thorns and briers; therefore the numberless sweets of the divine mercy preach Jesus, and his cross. It is as if they all said, 'Are we lovely to the eye, pleasant to the taste, and healthful in the enjoyment; then are we so by Jesus's appointment, and by Jesus's blessing.' My soul! there is more of him, than thy unthinking heart is conscious of, in every blessing and favour around thee. Oh! for grace to keep this always in remembrance, that from henceforth thou mayest find a double enjoyment in all; first, in beholding Him, and then his gift, be it what it may, as his, and which he giveth thee liberally to enjoy. And there is still another blessedness in thus sitting down to the contemplation and enjoyment of divine bounties; I mean, that the soul not only beholds Jesus in all, and enjoys Jesus in all, but it beholds Jesus as looking on, and rejoicing over his people, in their sanctified use of his bounties. How truly blessed is that scripture in point; "Yea, I will rejoice over them, saith the Lord, to do them good, and I will plant them in this land, assuredly with my whole heart, and with my whole soul!" Jer. xxxii. 41. My soul, sweetly meditate on these things; and when thou beholdest, as in the present time of the year, every thing around furnishing the witness of God's love and faithfulness, "in giving rain from heaven, and fruitful seasons, filling our hearts with food and gladness;" let all lead to Him. Jesus himself is in all. It is he who gives all, crowns all, sanctifies and sweetens all. And never did any husbandman among men, wait for the precious fruits of the earth with equal diligence and delight, as Jesus, in beholding the fruits of his own graces, which by his Holy Spirit he first plants, and then calls forth into exercise upon his own person and righteousness. Say, my soul, as the church did, and let this be thine evening song to the same lovely and all-loving Saviour: "My beloved is come down into his garden, (the church) to the beds of spices; to feed in the gardens, and to gather lilies." Song vi. 2.

JULY 26.

MORNING.—"And there wrestled a man with him until the breaking of the day."—Gen. xxxii. 24.

My soul, here is a lovely portion for the morning. For the morning, did I say? Yea, both for night and morning, and, indeed, until the everlasting morning break in upon thee, and all the shadows of the night flee away. For are not all the seed of Jacob like their father, wrestlers in the actings of faith, and the fervour of prayer, until they come off, like him, prevailing Israels? And who was this man which wrestled with the patriarch? Let scripture explain scripture, and give the answer. By his strength, said the prophet

Hosea, chap. xii. 3, &c. "he had power with God; yea, he had power over the angel, and prevailed; he wept and made supplication unto him; he found him in Bethel, and there he spake with us; even the Lord God of Hosts, the Lord is his memorial." Here then light is thrown upon the subject. He that is called a man in one scripture, is called an angel in this other. And that we might not overlook nor forget the identity of his person as the very man whose name was then secret, Judges xiii. 18. but hereafter to be made known, and himself appear openly, the prophet was commissioned to tell the church, that he that spake with us, in the person of Jacob, our father, was the same that found Jacob in Bethel, even the Lord God of Hosts; for that was his memorial. Gen. xxviii. 10—19. And was it then He, whose name is Wonderful, which wrestled with Jacob? And when the poor patriarch was hard put to it, full of fears, doubts, and distresses, on account of his brother Esau, and was stirring up himself to take hold of God's strength, by way of strengthening himself against Esau, did he that came to strengthen him, first take hold of him, and seem to contend with him, until the breaking of the day? Oh then, my soul, here learn a sweet and precious lesson against the hour of the many contentions with the Esaus of thy warfare; for thou wrestlest not only against flesh and blood, but "against principalities and powers, against the rulers of the darkness of this world, against spiritual wickedness in high places." See, my soul, where thy strength is—even in Jesus. See what a blessed example of prevailing in prayer the Holy Ghost hath here set before thee. Look to this God-man with whom Jacob wrestled, and come off successful; and say with Job, "Will he plead against me with his great strength? no; but he will put strength in me." Job xxiii. 2—7. Fill thy mouth with arguments, as Job did. Tell Jesus of thy wants, tell him of his riches, tell him of thy guilt, tell him of his precious blood and righteousness, and tell him that thy misery, and weakness, and unworthiness, renders thee a suitable sinner for so gracious a Saviour to get glory by in saving. Go to him, my soul, with these strong, these unanswerable pleas. Jesus will love to hear, and to receive them. And while he wrestles with thee, do thou wrestle with him, all the night, in which thou art contending with thy sins within, and temptations without; with the errors of the infidel, and the crying sins of the profane. And do as Jacob did, wrestle, plead, supplicate, cry, and take hold of his strength, his blood, his righteousness, and God the Father's covenant promises in him; and never give over, nor let him go, until the day break, and he blesseth thee.

EVENING.—" An altar of earth."—Exod. xx. 24.

Every thing, and every service, in the old testament dispensation, as well as in the gospel church, points to Christ. Behold, my soul, in the Lord's appointment of " an altar of earth," how jealous the Lord is of his honour. If the altar dedicated to the Lord's service, be of earth, or if it be of stone, there was not to be the least mixture. Nothing hewn, nothing polished by man's art, or man's device; " for if," saith Jehovah, " thou lift up thy tool upon it, thou hast polluted it." Behold, how fully Jesus was preached here! There can be nothing offered to the Lord for his acceptance, but what is the Lord's. Jesus is the Father's gift to poor sinners; and when a poor sinner presents before the Father, the Lord Jesus as his whole altar, sacrifice, and offering, he presents to the Father what the Father first presented to him. If the sinner were to join any thing of his own with this offering, this were to pollute it. Sweet thought! my soul, cherish it in the warmest of thine affections; carry it about with thee for thy daily exercise of faith upon the person of Jesus, that nothing of thine may mingle with the pure and perfect salvation, which is alone in him. And, depend upon it, thy God and Father is more honoured, more glorified, and will be more beloved, by such a perfect reliance upon Him in whom his soul delighteth, than he would be by the greatest and most costly sacrifices of thine own providing. The infinite and eternal worth and efficacy of Jesus's blood and righteousness, is upon everlasting record. God is well pleased with him, and his people in him; and a voice from heaven hath proclaimed it to the earth. To offer any thing of our own, by way of making it pleadable, is to pollute it; yea, it is to make it questionable, as if we thought it not complete. And by thus doing, we declare that our hearts are not thoroughly pleased with what Jehovah hath declared himself well pleased, but are seeking to rest our souls, not upon the altar, which is wholly the Lord's, but adding to it of our own. Oh! for grace to make Jesus what the Father hath made him, the all in all of man's salvation; and be ever ready to let him have all the glory, who alone hath accomplished it, "in believing the record that God hath given of his dear Son."

JULY 27.

MORNING.—"That thy trust may be in the Lord, I have made known to thee this day, even to thee."—Prov. xxii. 19.

My soul, mark for thy morning meditation, what is here said. Observe, in the first place, the *general* knowledge the Lord hath given of his saving truth and mercies in Christ Jesus, and which becomes a sufficient warrant and authority for all the world to believe in Christ, and to accept of Christ, to the salvation of the soul. Christ in the word is the Father's authority for every sinner to believe the record God hath given of his Son; and the rejection of this command will be the condemning sin to every one who despises this plan of salvation, because he hath heard and then turned his back upon this love of God in Christ Jesus the Lord. My soul, ponder over this view of the subject, and then turn to another sweet and distinguishing property of God's revelation which he makes by his blessed Spirit, in the *particular* apprehension of it. And this is done in every heart that is made willing in the day of God's power, when the same grace which reveals Christ in the word, reveals Christ also in the heart, the hope of glory. Here the verse of the morning is confirmed in what God saith, that in order to every child of God putting his trust in the Lord, he hath made known to thee, even to thee, this day. Observe, my soul, the personal application of the divine truth. God, by his Spirit, makes it known to thee. It comes like a letter sent down from heaven. Who is it for? Read the direction. It is for thee, my soul. Thus faith takes home the contents to the heart, and finding how exactly every thing in Jesus and his salvation suits his own case and circumstances, he lives upon it, feeds upon it, takes it for his portion, trusts in God for the truth of it, and rejoiceth evermore. My soul, hast thou marked these distinct things? and dost thou know how to distinguish rightly between *general* proclamations of mercy, and *special*, personal enjoyments of it? Oh then, live up to the full enjoyment of God's rich mercy in Christ; accept Christ, and use Christ, daily, hourly, to the glory of Father, Son, and Spirit; as the redemption by Christ was intended; and bless God more and more for his unspeakable gift.

EVENING.—" Woe is me, for I am as when they have gathered the summer fruits, as the grape gleanings of the vintage; there is no cluster to eat; my soul desired the first ripe fruit. The good man is perished out of the earth, and there is none upright among men."—Micah vii. 1, 2.

Is not this lamentation as suited to the present times, as when the prophet delivered it? Were the interests of Zion ever at a lower ebb than now? Did the waters of the sanctuary run less in a stream in any period of the church than the present? Surely it is like the in-gathering of the fruits of the earth at this season of the year; the choicest are gone; the trees are unladen. It is only here and there, as "the shaking of an olive-tree; two or three berries in the top of the uppermost bough." Isa. xvii. 6. The Lord hath been calling home his chosen. Death hath been housing the servants of the Lord. And even those that remain, alas! are they not more like the gleanings, than like the first ripe fruits. Who is there interested for Zion? Who layeth it to heart, that she languisheth in all her borders? My soul! can a throne of grace witness for thee, that many a petition thou art lodging there, that "the Lord would do good in his pleasure unto Zion?" Is it known to the great searcher of hearts, that thou preferrest "her prosperity above thy chief joy?" Dost thou tell the king that thou lovest him, in loving his people; and knowing the preciousness of thine own salvation, art thou seeking by prayer, and by every means in thy power to form and promote the salvation of others? Oh Lord! give me grace "for Zion's sake never to hold my peace, nor for Jerusalem's sake to rest, till the righteousness thereof go forth as brightness, and the salvation thereof as a lamp that burneth!"

JULY 28.

MORNING.—"As an eagle stirreth up her nest, fluttereth over her young, spreadeth abroad her wings, taketh them, beareth them on her wings; so the Lord alone did lead them."—Deut. xxxii. 11, 12.

Here learn a lesson, to form some faint idea how the Lord is unceasingly engaged in taking care of his people. If thy God condescends to represent it by such a similitude, is it not both thy privilege and thy duty to mark the several particulars of such grace and tenderness?

The eagle not only possesseth in common with other creatures, the greatest affection for her young, but manifests a vast superiority over every other of the winged tribe in her management of her brood. She provides for them and protects them, as other birds of the air do; but in educating them, and the method by which she shelters them from danger, here is displayed such superior wisdom and power, as far exceeds whatever we meet with in other creatures. "She stirreth up her nest:" by which we may understand, she suffers not her young eagles to lay sleeping, but calls them forth to life and exercise. She "fluttereth over them," as if to show them how they are to use their wings, and fly. And when she taketh them from the nest, this is not done like other birds, who carry their young in their talons, and in their haste or flight may drop them —or when pursued, or fired at by an enemy, may have them killed and herself not hurt; but the eagle beareth her young on her wings, so that no arrow from beneath can touch the young, until it hath first pierced through the heart of the old bird. What a sweet thought do these views afford; and what a blessed instruction do they bring! My soul, do they not teach thee, since the similitude is the Lord's own, that he that hath stirred up the nest of thine old nature, in which thou wast born, because he would not suffer thee to sleep there for ever in the unawakened state of sin, and hath brought thee out, and brought thee abroad, and taught thee how to fly up, in devout aspirations after him, is the Lord? Is it not he that fed thee and sustained thee from thy youth, even until now; taught thee, and hovered over thee, and caused thee to "mount up as upon the wings of eagles; to run and not be weary; to walk, and not faint?" Yes, yes, blessed Jesus, it is thou that hast indeed borne me, as thou hast said, upon eagles' wings, and brought me to thyself: so that I see, by this delightful comparison, that thou wilt not suffer any of thy little ones to perish; for "he that toucheth them, toucheth the apple of thine eye;"—nay, while on thy wings, he that destroyeth them, must first destroy thee. Oh Lord, give me grace rightly to enjoy and use such marvellous blessings. And since, to the wisdom and strength of the eagle, thou hast now added the tenderness and solicitude of the hen, do thou, Lord, gather me under thy wings, and nourish me with thy love and favour, that I may be thine for ever, and live here by faith, as hereafter I hope to live with thee in glory.

EVENING.—"And Peter said unto him, Eneas, Jesus Christ maketh thee whole."—Acts ix. 34.

My soul! look at this man, Eneas: consider his circumstances of *bodily* sickness, and the long period of *eight years,* in which he had been bed-ridden. And when thou hast duly pondered the subject, behold the sovereignty of that all-powerful, all-prevailing name of Jesus Christ, though pronounced only by a servant, and see the blessed effects of it. And wilt thou, after such an instance, go lean under any *spiritual* sickness? Shall it be said that Jesus Christ *cannot* make thee whole? Surely, thou wouldest tremble at harbouring such a thought, even for a moment! And if thou darest not think such hard things of Christ's *ability,* why shouldest thou not equally shudder at supposing thy Lord's want of *inclination?* Hast thou not found him gracious in times past? And was that grace the result of thy desert? Was it not the pure effect of his own free love? And ought not *past* experience to beget *future* hope? Is not every believer's life, a life of trust and dependence? Go to him, my soul, under every new ailment, as thou wert led to him at first. "Jesus Christ is the same, yesterday, and to-day, and for ever." Let faith have her full exercise. "Jesus Christ maketh thee whole." Here rest thy whole confidence. Never go to him in any attempts of thine own; but by a direct act of faith upon his glorious person, power, grace, and compassion; in his strength, and not thy feeling, rest wholly upon him, and plead thy necessities and his glory: and, depend upon it, this plan, which is of the Lord's own appointing, will bring comfort under all the leanness with which thou art exercised. Remember his own most gracious words: "Verily, verily, I say unto you, whatsoever ye shall ask the Father in my name, he will give it to you. Hitherto have ye asked nothing in my name: ask, and ye shall receive, that your joy may be full," John xvi. 23, 24.

JULY 29.

MORNING.—"We, being many, are one body in Christ."—Rom. xii. 5.

One of the most delightful of all thoughts, and which when fully enjoyed under the influence of the Holy Ghost, gives an unspeakable felicity in the heart, is that union and fellowship of Christ with his church. Ponder it, my soul, this morning. All the members of Christ's body are but one body, the apostle saith, in Christ; "and he is the head over all things to the church, which is his body, the fulness of him that filleth all in all." I would never, if possible, lose sight of this, because in the perfect conviction and assurance of it must be found all our security and joy. And the way by which this blessed truth, under divine teaching, will be kept alive in the soul, is this: I would behold myself, what I am by nature and practice in Adam, and connect with this view what I am by grace and faith in Christ. Now, as Adam was the common head of all his seed in nature, equally so is Christ the common head of all his seed in grace. Do I consider that, when Adam sinned in the garden, I as one of his children, and then, as scripture saith of Levi, in respect to his connection with Abraham, was in his loins, part of himself, and consequently implicated and involved in all the good or bad belonging to him? Then it will follow, that in Adam's sin I sinned, and in Adam's condemnation I was included. So then, as Adam did not transgress only for himself, but for all his seed, by nature, that should come from him; equally so when Christ fulfilled all righteousness, and when Christ expiated all sin by the sacrifice of himself, his seed were considered righteous in him; and his expiatory sacrifice, as the head of his people, must be, to all intents and purposes, the same as if they had been sacrificed with him. Cherish this thought, my soul, and never allow thyself to behold Christ as the Christ of God, in the capacity of a private or single person, but as the covenant Head, the Father's Chosen, the Sent, the Sealed, the Anointed of God, in whom all his members are one body in Christ. See that thou hast the Spirit of Christ, by which thou art proved to be one of his. And for the full enjoyment of all the blessings contained in this union and communion with thy glorious head, daily and hourly remind God thy Father of all his covenant promises made to Christ as the head of his church and people, in which the Lord hath said, "I will pour my Spirit upon thy seed, and my blessing upon thine offspring."

EVENING.—"But I am like a green olive-tree in the house of God." —Ps. lii. 8.

My soul! canst thou humbly take up this language? See, and mark the particulars, one by one, and then determine the important point. Here the church at large is represented as a green olive-tree: and, by a just conclusion, every member is a part; for, "we, being many, are one body in Christ." Now the apostle saith, that by nature this was not the case, for we were of the wild olive-tree, and were grafted, contrary to nature, into the good olive-tree; Rom. xi. 24. Hence, if thou art taken from nature to grace, it must have been by conversion. The work is not of man, but of God. And, so far is any man from contributing to it, that it is altogether contrary to nature. Hast thou felt the cutting work of conviction, when taken from the old stock of nature; and the healing work of conversion, when brought into the new stock of grace, by an union with Christ? And, when there is an union formed on the new stock, there will be a communication from the root to the branch. "He that is joined to the Lord is one spirit." There will be a most blessed union; a oneness, an interest, a life-giving, a life-strengthening principle, communicated continually from Christ to his members. For he saith himself, "Because I live, ye shall live also." Hast thou, my soul, these blessed testimonies? Moreover, where there is this union with Christ, and soul-communications from Christ, there will be not only life but fruitfulness; a perpetual verdure, a state of constant flourishing. Say, is it so with thee? Canst thou take up the language of this sweet scripture, and say, "But I am like a green olive-tree in the house of God?" — It is blessed so to be enabled to say; and blessed to ascribe all the glory to the one only source, even Jesus; and blessed to mark the distinguishing grace of the Lord in the appointment. For when the Lord Jesus took thee from among the olive-trees, which were all wild by nature, there were many there in the wilderness, apparently more promising, and surely none more undeserving! And yet, while others were left, thou wast taken. "Lord! (may I well and constantly cry out) how is it that thou hast manifested thyself unto me, and not unto the world?" Precious, bountiful Lord! fulfil in my soul that sweet promise; and cause "my branches to spread, and my beauty in thee to be as the olive-tree, and my smell as Lebanon," Hosea xiv. 6.

JULY 30.

MORNING.—" My grace is sufficient for thee."—2 Cor. xii. 9.

My soul, gather a rich cluster this morning of those precious fruits which hang upon the tree of life—even upon Jesus. Thou wilt find their taste more sweet and pleasant than all the branches of the vine. Consider the *fulness* in thy Lord. Such a fulness indeed, by virtue of the covenant engagements in Jehovah, is treasured up in Christ, that all the grace every individual of his seed could possibly want in time, and all the glory hereafter — all, all is lodged in him. What a thought is here! Consider also the *freeness* of this grace. Never, surely, did God give any gift more free than when he gave his Son. And as the apostle from hence justly reasons: " He that spared not his own Son, but delivered him up for us all, how shall he not with him also freely give us all things?" When, my soul, thou hast feasted thyself upon the *fulness* and *freeness* of the fruits of Jesus's salvation, gather another rich portion for thyself with the hand of faith, in the *suitableness* and *sufficiency* there is in him for *thee*. Take the sweet words spoken here to Paul, but not limited to Paul, as if personally addressed to thyself. It is Jesus now speaks and saith this day, " My grace is sufficient for thee." This is as if he had said, all the grace I have is for my people; and I have not only enough for all, but for every one; and I have it for thee. I have the very portion which I knew each would want every day, and all the day, through the whole of their pilgrimage state: from everlasting I knew their need; and from everlasting I have laid every individual child's portion by, and do keep it for him to the moment required: and each shall find a suited sufficiency exactly answering to all their wants, and corresponding to all their necessities. Precious thought! Henceforth, my soul, cast all thy care upon Jesus; for thou now seest how he careth for thee. Morning by morning hear his voice, speaking personally to thyself, "My grace is sufficient for thee."

EVENING.—"Why have I found grace in thine eyes, that thou shouldest take knowledge of me, seeing I am a stranger?"—Ruth ii. 10.

My soul! dost thou not find continual causes for sending forth the same inquiry as this poor Moabitess did, when thou art receiving some renewed instance of Jesus's favour? Her heart was overwhelmed with the kindness of Boaz, in permitting her to glean only in his fields, and to eat a morsel of food with his servants: but thy Boaz, thy Kinsman-Redeemer, hath opened to thee all his stores of grace and mercy; he bids thee come and take of the water of life freely; yea, he is to thee, himself, the bread of life, and the water of life; and is now, and will be for ever, thy portion, on which thou mayest feed to all eternity. When thou lookest back, and tracest the subject of his love from the beginning, in the springs and autumns of his grace; when thou takest a review of the distinguishing nature of these acts of grace; when thou bringest into the account thine ingratitude, under all the sunshine of his love and favour; will not the question again and again arise, at every review, "Why have I found grace in thine eyes, that thou shouldest take knowledge of me, seeing I am a stranger? Stranger indeed, by nature and by practice; living without God, and without Christ in the world. And, my soul, it might have been, long since, supposed, that, after such repeated unceasing acts of grace, as Jesus hath shewn, and even when thou hast caused him "to serve with thy sins, and wearied him with thy transgressions;" yet his compassions have failed not, but have been "new every morning;" it might have been supposed, that long and unceasing grace would at length have produced the blessed effect of living wholly to him, who hath so loved thee, as to give himself for thee. But, alas! the day that marks again his mercy, marks again thy rebellion. So that the heart is constrained every day to cry out, "Why have I found grace in thine eyes?" Precious Jesus! the only answer is, because thou art, thou wilt be Jesus. Lord! I bow down to the dust of the earth, in token of my vileness, and thy unspeakable glory! It is indeed the glorious attribute of thy grace to poor fallen men: "the Lord delighteth in mercy. He will perform the truth to Jacob, and the mercy to Abraham, which thou hast sworn unto our fathers from the days of old."

JULY 31.

MORNING.—"Watchman, what of the night? Watchman, what of the night?"—Isa. xxi. 11.

While this solemn inquiry may be supposed to have peculiar reference, as addressed to the servants of the Lord, whom he hath set as watchmen upon the walls of Zion, may it not be made personally to every man's bosom also, as it refers to himself? And the repeating of it twice should seem to imply the importance and earnestness with which it should be followed up. My soul, what is the night with thee? Art thou watching in it more than they that watch for the morning: yea, I say, more than they which watch for the morning? How art thou exercising this watchfulness? Is all safe respecting thine everlasting welfare? Art thou watching the approaches of the enemy? Art thou watchful in prayer; watchful for the gracious moment of the Spirit's helping thee in prayer; watchful in guiding thee in the exercise of it; watchful of the Lord's gracious answers to prayer; and, like the prophet on the watch tower, having given in thy petition to the heavenly court, into the hands of thy High Priest and Intercessor, art thou waiting to see what the Lord will say unto thee? Lord, make me eminently watchful in these things. Go on, my soul, in this heart-searching inquiry. Art thou waiting and watching thy Lord's return? What of the night is it now? May not Jesus come at even, or at midnight, or at cock-crowing, or in the morning? Pause, my soul. Suppose his chariot wheels were at the door, wouldest thou arise with holy joy, crying out, It is the voice of my beloved, saying, "Behold I come quickly?" And wouldest thou answer, "Even so come, Lord Jesus?" Oh for grace to be of that happy number, of whom the Lord himself saith, "Blessed are those servants whom, at his coming, he shall find so doing."

EVENING.—"Light is sown for the righteous, and gladness for the upright in heart."—Ps. xcvii. 11.

My soul! mark how blessedly the Holy Ghost speaks of the stores in Jesus laid up for his people. Light, in which is included all blessings in Christ Jesus, is sown, not reaped. This is not the harvest, but the seed-time of a believer. It is a life of faith, a life of trust, a life of dependence. Hence the apostle saith: "Let us not be weary in well doing; for in due season we shall reap, if we faint not;" Gal. vi. 9. Now this light is *sown for the righteous*; for the true believer in the righteousness of Jesus; and there shall be gladness in thee, and for truly regenerated in heart. My soul! it were exceedingly to be desired, that thou wouldest seek grace from the Holy Ghost to have a right apprehension of the promises. It is to the want of this, very frequently, that thy comforts are broken, and that thou walkest in darkness. Thy Lord Jesus doth indeed give thee many sweet love-tokens by the way, and handeth to thee many a blessed morsel of his bread in secret, to comfort thee on thy pilgrimage; but it never was his design, neither would it suit thy present state, nor his glory, to make the wilderness any other than a wilderness. The Lord forbid that ought should arise, to prompt thee to set up thy rest, like the Reubenites, on this side the land of promise. No. Light is sown: mark that: and the harvest is sure: here rest in full assurance of hope. Thy Jesus is thine: thy interest in him is not now to be called in question: let him then guide the way. And though clouds and darkness may rest upon it, yet he is bringing thee by a right way to a city of habitation. This is the minority of thine existence; and by and by thou wilt come of age. Thou and thy companions are all going home to thy Father's house, to thy Jesus, and his kingdom: and what will it signify, when thou gettest there, what accommodation thou hast had by the way? Nay, the poorer it hath been, the sweeter will be the refreshments that follow. And if thou art but little acquainted with the luxuries on which the carnal rejoice, the good things of the earth brought forth by the sun, and the precious things put forth by the moon; yet having "the good will of him that dwelt in the bush," thou hast a Benjamin's portion, and art most blessed indeed. Say then, as the Psalmist: "From men which are thy hand, O Lord, from men of the world, which have their portion in this life, and whose bellies are filled with thy hid treasure! But light is sown for the righteous and gladness for the upright in heart. As for me, I will behold thy face in righteousness, I shall be satisfied when I awake with thy likeness."

AUGUST 1.

MORNING.—" In thy name shall they rejoice all the day: and in thy righteousness shall they be exalted."—Ps. lxxxix. 16.

See, my soul, what a blessed cause is again before thee to begin the month, and to carry it on through every day, and all the day, and in every part of the day, for joy in the name and righteousness of Jesus. And mark it with peculiar emphasis, that it is Jesus, as Jesus, the Christ of God, and his righteousness as the righteousness of God, in which all thy rejoicing is, and not in the finest frames, or spiritual exercises of thine own. A daily sense of a need of Christ, and as constant a sense of acting faith upon Christ; these form the foundation of every true believer's joy, and make the savour of Christ's name like ointment poured forth. And whence is it, my soul, that all the redeemed are said to rejoice in the name of the Lord all the day, but because the Lord hath saved them and redeemed them for his name's sake? And whence is it said, that in his righteousness they shall be exalted, but because from their union with Christ, as their spiritual head, they are accepted in his righteousness, and are made the righteousness of God in him? Here's an exaltation indeed, enough to make the heart of the most sorrowful glad, let outward circumstances be what they may; when inward joy and peace in believing give such a blessedness to the believer's view of the name of Jesus. See to it then, my soul, that all thy fresh springs of joy are in him. Be very jealous over thyself, in the happiest moments of thy comfort, that Christ's name, and his righteousness and salvation, lie at the bottom of thy joy. Where is Jesus? I would ask my heart, when I am most at ease and happy. Is he in this happiness? And is this happiness enjoyed, and enjoyed purely, because Christ is in it? Trace this, my soul, through all the parts of salvation, and through all thy paths in grace, and see whether thou art bottoming every hope and every mercy, both for time and eternity, in the name and righteousness of Jesus only: for, depend upon it, as Jehovah hath said, in the pardoning and blotting out the transgressions of his people, " I, even I, am he that blotteth out thy transgressions for my name's sake;" so it is to the everlasting praise of his name, that all the glory of salvation is, and must be ascribed. Nevertheless, he saved them for his name's sake, that he might make his mighty power to be known.

EVENING.—" An anchor of the soul."—Heb. vi. 19.

In the opening of a new month, look, my soul, at thine anchor! Surely it is good and profitable for thee to see thy safety, that thou mayest ride out all the storms which arise, and never make " shipwreck of faith and a good conscience." And what is thine anchor? Nay, who, or what can it be, but Jesus, and his finished righteousness? He hath accomplished redemption by his blood, and hath entered within the veil to prove its all-sufficiency. On him, then, thou hast cast anchor; indeed, he is himself the anchor of all thine hopes, and the rock of ages, on which thou restest thine eternal security, " both sure and stedfast." True, it is unseen; and, like the sailor's anchor, thrown out into the deep. But, though unseen, it is not unenjoyed: for concerning him, who is the anchor of the soul, it is the blessed privilege of faith to say, " whom having not seen, we love: and in whom, though now we see him not, yet believing, we rejoice with joy unspeakable and full of glory, receiving the end of our faith, even the salvation of our souls." But the anchor of this world's mariner, and that of the spiritual navigator, differ most widely. His anchor is thrown forth at an uncertainty: it may break; it may find no anchorage; the cable may give way; the ship may drive; and one anchor after another be lost, and the vessel, after all, founder. Not so with him, whose hope and anchor of the soul is the Lord Jesus: " He is a rock; his work is perfect." His salvation is founded in the everlasting counsel, purpose, will, and good pleasure, of God our Father; it is secured in the perfect obedience, righteousness, blood-shedding, and death of our Lord Jesus Christ: and the soul who rests on this anchor of hope alone for redemption, hath been brought savingly acquainted with the Father's love and the Son's grace, through the blessed teaching, power, and application of God the Holy Ghost. My soul! is this thine anchor? Hast thou this glorious security, entered within the veil for thee; unseen, indeed, but not unknown; undeserved, but not unenjoyed? Oh! what unspeakable mercies are unceasingly arising out of this divine, this rapturous hope, to support my weather-beaten soul! Surely, precious Jesus! I may well look up to thee, in the opening and close of every day, and every month, as the anchor of my soul, both sure and stedfast; for thou hast been to me, and thou wilt still be, until I get into the haven of everlasting rest, what thou hast been to all thy redeemed; "a strength to the poor, a strength to the needy in his distress, a refuge from the storm, a shadow from the heat, when the blast of the terrible ones is as a storm against the wall;" Isa. xxv. 4.

AUGUST 2.

MORNING.—" My Father is the husbandman."—John xv. 1.

Blessed truth, and blessed assurance, to the true followers of Jesus. Yes, Almighty Father! I would pray for thy continual teaching, to behold thee as the husbandman of thy vineyard, the church, in which thou hast raised up the Plant of Renown, the Man whose name is the Branch, the true Vine, in whom, and upon whom, and through whom, all thy redeemed, taken from the olive-tree that is wild by nature, are grafted, and bring forth fruit unto God. Yes, Almighty Father! I would desire grace to behold thee, and while I behold, to love, to praise, to adore thee, that from everlasting thou hast graciously been the husbandman of thy church. It was in thee, and from thee, as the contriver and appointer of all that concerned redemption, we trace the fountain and source of all that grace, mercy, peace, and favour here, with all the unknown treasures of glory hereafter, which thou hast placed in his most blessed hands, who is the Lord our righteousness. In every renewed view of Jesus, as the true Vine, which thou hast planted; and in every renewed communication from his fulness, nourishment, and life-imparting influences; may it be my happy portion, Oh Lord, to eye thee, as the husbandman, while I feel and know my union in Jesus as the Vine. And do thou, most gracious God and Father, condescend to act the part of the kind husbandman still. Let thine eyes be upon me for good, as the husbandman visits his vineyard. Water, Lord, with the heavenly dew of thy word and Spirit, the dry and languishing plantation. Oh that the Lord may give showers of blessing, and that he may be to me as the latter, and as the former rain, upon the barrenness of my heart. Preserve me, Lord, from the wild boar of the wood, even Satan, that he may never tread me down. Weed out, Lord, the briers and thorns, even the corruptions of my own heart, which would twine themselves with the tender branches. And lop off, Oh Lord, all the superfluous shoots, even the world's enticements, which might prevent fruitfulness in Jesus. In all things, blessed God and Father, be thou the kind, the tender, the wise husbandman, in doing for me what thou seest to be needful, however painful to flesh and blood the pruning dispensations and wintry providences may be found. Do thou purge, as Jesus hath said, every branch that beareth fruit, that it may bring forth more fruit; and by thy gracious Spirit so cause me to abide in Christ, and that Christ may abide in me, that thou, my God and Father, mayest be glorified in my bearing much fruit, to the praise of thy grace, wherein thou hast made me accepted in the beloved.

EVENING.—" And he dreamed, and behold a ladder set up on the earth, and the top of it reached to heaven; and behold, the angels of God ascending and descending on it."—Gen. xxviii. 12.

Visions of the night, such as the patriarchs were

blessed with, serve to teach us how the Lord, in those early ages, watched over his people. And, my soul, I would have thee always take the sweet conclusion from the review of them, that if Jesus was thus mindful of his chosen then, depend upon it he is not less attentive now. There can be no difficulty, it should seem, interpreting this vision of the patriarch Jacob's ladder, after what Jesus told Nathaniel of the ascent and descent of the angels upon the Son of man, John i. 51. Under such an authority, we need not hesitate to consider Christ as the only communication, the only medium of intercourse between heaven and earth; John xiv. 6. And if the patriarch saw, in a vision, a ladder, with its foot on the earth, and its top reaching to heaven, thus uniting both; were not these representations of Jesus, as Emmanuel, his human nature and his divine: thus uniting such vast extremes, and forming in both, one glorious Mediator, to bring sinners to God, and bring down grace upon the earth? And as Jehovah stood above it, in the patriarch's view, what was this but to shew the authority of Christ, as the Christ of God? Precious addition to the vision indeed, for this is the warrant of faith in believing "the record that God hath given of his Son. God was in Christ, reconciling the world unto himself." Blessed Emmanuel! I hail thy glorious person! I bow down to the earth in humble adoration, love, and praise! I view thee, O Lord, as the only mediation for my precious soul; and desire to renounce every other! Witness for me, ye angels of light, who minister to the heirs of salvation, that on my bended knees, in transports of rejoicing, I bless God for having opened such a new and living way for poor sinners; and very humbly and earnestly do I beg of him, that my God will unceasingly make sweet communications of grace by Jesus, and call forth the suitable returns, in love, and praise and obedience, through Jesus, in my soul, until faith is swallowed up in absolute enjoyment, and that blessed hour, which Jesus promised, be fulfilled, when I shall see heaven open, and "the angels of God ascending and descending upon the Son of man."

AUGUST 3.

MORNING.—" Now I know that thou fearest God, seeing thou hast not withheld thy son, thine only son from me."—Gen. xxii. 12.

My soul, ponder these words. By whom were they spoken? It is said by the angel of the Lord; probably the messenger of the covenant; he, who in the fulness of time, was to make known, face to face, to all Abraham's seed, the whole revelation of Jehovah concerning redemption. It was a critical moment in Abraham's life, and a trying moment to his faith. It is said, "Now I know." Did not the Lord know before? Oh yes; but he that gave Abraham the faith, *now* afforded an opportunity for the exercise of it. My soul, how blessed is it to remark, that the largest gifts of grace are dispensed, when there is the largest occasion for them. "As thy days, so shall thy strength be." And, my soul, do not forget to remark also, that our Isaacs, our children, our earthly comforts, are most likely to be continued to us, when the Lord gives grace and faith to be most ready at his holy will to part with them. When I can say, Lord, all that thou hast given me is thine; and if thou art pleased to take all, or any part back again, still it is thine own—not mine, but lent. Oh, for grace, like Abraham, to bless a taking God, as well as a giving God, and to withhold nothing from him. Pause, my soul, one moment longer over this precious portion. Is there nothing more to be gathered from it? Look again; read it over once more. Pass beyond Abraham, and contemplate the God of Abraham, and see if thou canst not discover the infinite, unequalled, astonishing love of God the Father typified in this solemn transaction; and while we behold

Abraham, at the call of God, giving up his son, his only son; may we not behold God, uncalled, unsought, and without any one cause but his own free everlasting love, giving up his only begotten Son, as a sacrifice for the redemption of his people? The patriarch gave up his son but in intention; but God in reality. And, my soul, what oughtest thou now to say to God in the view of this transaction? Methinks I find authority, from these sweet words, to make a paraphrase upon them, and to make application of them, for all and every circumstance with which I may be exercised; and, looking up to God my Father in Christ Jesus, I would say, 'Now, O Lord and Father, I know thou dost love a poor, sinful, unworthy worm as I am, seeing thou hast not withheld thy Son, thine only Son from me.'

EVENING.—" A ringleader of the sect of the Nazarenes."—Acts xxiv. 5

My soul! hast thou arrived at that station of dignity, to be reproached for Christ's sake? If so, thou wilt enter into a proper sense and enjoyment of the title Paul was branded with; a ringleader, or a standard-bearer of the cross. One who, not content with receiving Christ into his own heart, determines, let the cost be what it may, the loss of reputation or of life, to proclaim Jesus upon the house-top. This is to be a ring-leader! An honourable station! and one that Jesus loves! Jesus himself was Jehovah's ringleader, for he saith, "In that day, there shall be a root of Jesse, which shall stand for an ensign of the people; to it shall the gentiles seek, and his rest shall be glorious." Isa. xi. 10. And elsewhere, Jehovah saith, "Behold, I have given him for a witness to the people, a leader and commander to the people." Isa. lv. 4. My soul, hast thou taken part in the reproaches of God's choicest servants? It is impossible to be a true follower of the despised Nazarene, unless thou hast followed him "without the camp, bearing his reproach." The world, from the days of Cain, in his persecution of Abel, hath, in all ages, branded the ringleaders of the Lord's cause. The servants were treated as the master. His prophets, "troublers of the land," Amos vii. 10. His city, always "a rebellious city," Ezra iv. 15. Yea, Jesus himself, as "one perverting the nation, and forbidding to give tribute to Cæsar," Luke xxiii. 2. Precious Lord! could not thy meek, harmless, and inoffensive conduct pass on without this censure; then who can hope to escape? I know, Lord, that to hold thee up, and proclaim thee as Jehovah's ensign to the nation, is to be indeed a ringleader of the cross, against which all hell must wage war, and all the powers of this world's customs will declare enmity. But be thou my standard, and I shall be more than conqueror, through thy grace helping me. Oh! let me unceasingly speak thy praise, and let the fathers to the children make known thy truth.

AUGUST 4.

MORNING.—"And he led them forth by the right way, that they might go to a city of habitation."—Ps. cvii. 7.

My soul, what are thy daily exercises concerning the way the Lord thy God is leading thee through a wilderness dispensation? Art thou convinced that it is the *right* way? What if it be a thorny way, a tempted way, frequently a dark way; yet art thou satisfied that it is the *right* way, because it is thorny, tempted, dark, and with numberless other exercises. This is the plan to judge by. And though, my soul, I trust thou hast grace enough given thee to see and know, in thy cool hours of thought, that whatever thy God appoints must be right, and his holy will must be done; yet there is an exercise of grace which goes much beyond these views of the subject, and which a believer is enabled to bring into practice, when he not only submits to a painful dispensation, but rejoiceth in it, because it is the right way. When he saith, I am afflicted; but afflictions are useful. I am in dark and trying circumstances; but these also are useful. I am buffeted by Satan; but this also I find to be right, because Christ is the more endeared thereby, and his strength is perfected in my weakness. My God is bringing me by a right way, to a city of habitation. Of this I am sure. And every step leading to the final attainment, is already marked by infinite wisdom, and provided for by infinite love; and Jesus himself is with me through all the pilgrimage. Hence then, I conclude, that if at any time I am at a loss to see my way, to find comfort in my way, or if I am obstructed in my way, still it is the *right* way, because Jesus himself is the way, and his unerring wisdom is in the appointment. Oh for grace in lively exercise, to be as satisfied now of all the despensations concerning the church and people, as when of old, in the wilderness! The Lord is leading forth by a right way, to bring to a city of habitation, whose builder and maker is God.

EVENING.—" But there is forgiveness with thee, that thou mayest be feared."—Ps. cxxx. 4.

My soul, this is a golden psalm, and every portion of it more ponderous in value than the choicest gold of Ophir; and this verse is as the tried gold, to ascertain the purity and value of all the rest. The cries of a truly broken heart, from the depth of sin to the depth of divine mercy, with which the psalm opens, prove the work of the Holy Ghost, imparting the words with which the humbled soul comes before the Lord. And the blessed consolations which this verse contains, in the view of the mercy-seat, and the mercy there (which is all-precious Jesus, the first-born in the womb of mercy; yea, mercy itself) as plainly prove the leadings of the Holy Ghost to him, who alone can say, "Oh Israel, thou hast destroyed thyself, but in me is thy help!" Ponder, my soul, these precious words: "But there is forgiveness with thee." Is it not as if thou wert to say to thy God and Father, when under deep searchings of heart by reason of conscious sin, 'There is Jesus with thee; he is my propitiation; he is my propitiatory, the mercy-seat, between the cherubim of glory; *in* whom, and *from* whom, thou hast promised to speak to thy people! And shall I doubt thy pardoning love and favour, as long as I behold Jesus with thee? Shall I for a moment question my acceptance in the beloved, while I behold "the man at thy right hand, even the Son of man, whom thou madest strong for thyself?" Shall I fear coming to a God in Christ for pardon, so long as I am interested in the forgiveness that is with thee, in God the Son's righteousness and atoning blood; and God the Father's covenant engagements in him, for the display of the glory of his grace?' Oh, how unanswerably strong, conclusive, and satisfactory, to a poor burdened conscience, is this view of Jesus, the propitiatory; Jesus the propitiation! But what is the meaning of the expression in the latter part of the verse; "there is forgiveness with thee, that thou mayest be feared?" Would not the verse read better if it were said, that thou mayest be *loved?* Oh no; "The fear of the Lord is the beginning of wisdom." And although "perfect love casteth out fear," that is, the fear of hell, the bondage fear of unpardoned sin; yet, the child-like fear, which a sense of pardoning love begets in the soul, is among the sweetest exercises of the renewed nature. Devils fear and tremble, and feel despair and horror; but the affectionate fear of a dutiful child is the reverse of this, and only manifests itself in the most earnest desire never to offend. And the sense of God's forgiving love, and of Jesus always on the propitiatory, becomes the great preservative from sin. Hence the Lord himself saith, "I will put my fear in their hearts, that they shall not depart from me," Jer. xxxii. 40. My soul, fold up this sweet portion, and take it with thee to thy pillow, that it may lie down with thee, and rest in thine heart; that Jesus, thy Jesus, thy propitiation, is with Jehovah, that thou mayest fear him; and he may be thy exceeding joy and confidence, both now and for ever. Amen.

AUGUST 5.

MORNING.—"Therefore, thus saith the Lord, I am returned to Jerusalem with mercies."—Zech. i. 16.

My soul, think what a sad state that land, that church, that family, that heart is in, where God withdraws but for a moment! This will be one way of rightly appreciating his presence. What a mercy, what an unspeakable mercy is it when God returns! For until he returns in grace, there will be no return to him in a way of seeking mercy. Pause, my soul, over the thought. Though a child of God loseth not the interest and favour of God in his covenant, because what unworthiness soever, as in ourselves, we must appear in before God, yet in Christ there is an everlasting worthiness, in which his people are accepted and beloved: yet if the Lord suspends his gracious influences on the soul; if Jesus speaks neither by Urim nor Thummim; if the Holy Ghost, though at home *in* the heart, manifests not himself *to* the heart; what shall the soul do? Ordinances are nothing if the God of ordinances be not in them. To look inward, the soul finds no peace. To look upward, there can be no comfort. For if the Lord commands the clouds to pour no rain upon his inheritance, their heaven is as brass, and their earth as iron. Hast thou, my soul, experienced trying seasons; and, though convinced of an interest in Jesus, hast thou languished after the sweet and blessed visits of his grace? Listen then to this precious scripture, " I am returned, saith the Lord unto Jerusalem with mercies." Welcome, Lord, to my soul, to my heart! Thy presence is better than life itself. And the mercies thou hast brought with thee, in pardoning, quickening, renewing, reviving, comforting, strengthening me, will put more joy in my heart than thousands of gold and silver. There will be no barren ordinances, no barren hearts, no barren land, where our God comes. Thou hast said, " I will be as the dew unto Israel." Oh what a revival in my poor heart; what a revival will thy presence make in my family; what a revival in thy churches; what a revival in this dear land of our nativity! Oh come, Lord Jesus, come in our midst; and let us hear thee say, " I am returned to Jerusalem with mercies." "Thou shalt no more be termed forsaken, neither shall thy land any more be termed desolate; but thou shalt be called Hephzibah, and thy land Beulah; for the Lord delighteth in thee, and thy land shall be married."

EVENING.—" To him that overcometh will I grant to sit with me in my throne, even as I also overcame, and am set down with my Father in his throne."—Rev. iii. 21.

My soul! let this evening's meditation be sacred, in contemplating Jesus, even thy Jesus, sitting down on the throne of his Father, having overcome all opposition, and triumphed by his cross, over death, sin, and hell! And in this contemplation, be sure that thou behold Jesus in *thy nature;* for it is in that nature the victory was obtained. The Son of God, as God, had no throne to obtain by overcoming; neither could a throne be *given* to him; for all things were his in common with the Father and the Holy Ghost, in the one glorious essence of the Godhead, from all eternity. So that it is in the human nature of Christ, these triumphs are set forth; and as the glory-man Mediator, thou art called upon to behold him, for his victories, and the merits of his redemption-work, as sat down in the throne. Sweet thought! cherish it my soul, as the first, and best, and most glorious of all thoughts! Thy Jesus, in thy nature, is on his throne. And now, when with an eye of faith thou art viewing him there, next hear the blessed and gracious words which come from him, on his throne: "To him that overcometh will I grant to sit with me." Blessed Lord! Is it possible, that my poor nature can ever arrive to such unspeakable felicity? Can I venture to cherish such a hope? What! shall this poor, feeble, trembling nature of mine, encompassed as it is with sin and temptation, and in the midst of a waste and howling wilderness; shall I one day sit down with my Lord, see him as he is, and dwell with him for ever? Oh! for faith to believe, and for grace in lively exercise, "to run with patience the race that is set before me, looking unto Jesus, the author and finisher, both of faith and salvation!" And shall I not, dearest Lord, be continually gathering new strength from thee? Will not Jesus, who hath taken my nature, undertaken my cause, and engaged as my surety, both for grace and for glory, be every thing I need, my light, and my life, my hope, and strength, and salvation? Yes! thou gracious Lord! thou wilt make me more than conqueror through thy grace upholding me; and, like the redeemed now in glory, I shall overcome "by the blood of the Lamb, and by the word of thy testimony;" and sit down with thee in thy throne, even as thou hast overcome, and art sat down in thy Father's throne. Hallelujah. Amen.

AUGUST 6.

MORNING.—"Set me as a seal upon thine heart, as a seal upon thine arm: for love is strong as death; jealousy is cruel as the grave: the coals thereof are coals of fire, which hath a most vehement flame."—Song viii. 6.

My soul, is this the language of thine heart to Jesus?

Yes, it is. Can any desire to be nearer Christ than thee? Can any long more to be worn as a signet upon his arm, and to lay nearer his heart than thee? And can any desire more than thou dost, to be sealed with his Holy Spirit unto the day of redemption? Surely, my soul, thou longest earnestly for these precious things, that that arm of Jesus, on which thou wouldest be set as a seal, may be ever clasping thee; and that heart of thy Redeemer's upon which thou art engraven, as the high priest bore the names of the people of Israel, may be always folding thee, and bearing both thy person and thy wants before the throne, and thus unceasing fellowship may abound with the Father and with his Son Jesus Christ. And canst thou not say, as the church did to Jesus, "For love is strong as death; jealousy is cruel as the grave?" For as death conquers all, and the grave admits of no rival, so thy love to Jesus, which he hath planted in thine heart hath conquered thee; and no rival, no partner, can divide the throne of thine heart with Jesus? Every thing in thee concerning Jesus, is as though on fire; and all the flames of thine affection burn with this language, "Whom have I in heaven but thee; and there is none upon earth I desire besides thee. My flesh and my heart faileth; thou art the strength of my heart, and thou art my portion for ever." But pause, my soul, is there not somewhat, in those precious words of the morning, in which Jesus may be supposed to say the same to thee? Surely, my soul, if thou lovest him, it is because he first loved thee! And if the real cry of thine heart is to be set as a seal upon his heart, and upon his arm, depend upon it, it is because he hath been before hand with thee in both. Precious Redeemer! and dost thou indeed bid me set thee in my heart, and on my arm? Lord Jesus, I would wear thee in my heart. I would never, never suffer thee to depart from my arms. I would feel thee *inward*, manifest thee by every *outward* testimony;

and as seals upon the arm and upon the breast are in sight, so would I set thee always before me, and tell the whole earth whose I am, and whom I love; that whither thou goest I would go, and where thou dwellest I would dwell: for I am no longer my own, but am bought with a price; therefore I would glorify God in my body, and in my spirit, which are his.

EVENING.—" (For many walk, of whom I have told you often, and now tell you even weeping, that they are the enemies of the cross of Christ: whose end is destruction, whose god is their belly, and whose glory is in their shame, who mind earthly things.)"—Phil. iii. 18, 19.

My soul! hast thou not felt somewhat of the affliction of the apostle, in beholding how the great mass of carnal men live, and for the most part die? Nay, who can look on and view it without tears? The apostle hath enclosed the view within parenthesis, and it were to be wished, that indeed it was no where to be found but in parenthesis. But, alas! the truth is too striking, too palpable, and meets the contemplative mind at too many entrances and passages through the world, not to shew that it is far more general than is imagined. By our apostacy from God, man, that was originally exalted above the whole creation, is sunk below the whole: for no creature of God, among the brutes that perish, ever arrived to such a proficiency in sensuality, as to *glory in* that which constitutes our disgrace and shame! Brutes may riot in gorging their corrupt passions: but it is the *human* brute alone that glories in the reflection! Hence, of all the creatures of God, none, by nature, can be more remote from God, devils excepted, than fallen man! None, in whose minds Satan could find a seat to rule and reign, but man! And while, by nature, thus exposed to perish, for any act of our own by which we could do aught to prevent it; yea, without even a desire to prevent it, or a knowledge of the awful depths of sin into which we are fallen, in order to send forth a cry for recovery: while thus living, and thus dying, at an everlasting distance from God, at once the scorn of angels, and the willing slaves of the devil. As in the delirium of a fever, so in the madness of the mind, the poor creature that is under the dominion of it, is unconscious of the whole, and glories in that which is his shame, and which melts every heart into pity, but the heart of fiends and the powers of darkness! My soul! hast thou duly considered these things? Dost thou behold, as Paul did, many around thee, that thus walk? Dost thou remember when thou didst so walk? Dost thou call to mind "the wormwood and the gall?" And canst thou ever overlook, or forget, who it was that brought thee out? Canst thou cease to remember when and where the Lord Jesus passed by, and took thee up in his arms, when thou wast loathsome in thy person to every eye but his; and when he, like the divine Samaritan to the wounded traveller, brought thee to the inn of his church, when thou wast left more than half dead by the enemy of souls? Oh! precious, precious Lord Jesus! the more I contemplate thy glorious person, and thy gracious mercy to our poor fallen nature, the more unceasingly lovely dost thou appear. There was indeed, and is, "a love that passeth knowledge!" Oh! for grace to reverence these bodies of ours, which thou hast redeemed; that while the carnal glory in their shame, all the redeemed may cry out, with the holy indignation of the apostle, and say, as he did, "God forbid that I should glory, save in the cross of our Lord Jesus Christ, by whom the world is crucified unto me and I unto the world," Gal. vi. 14.

AUGUST 7.

MORNING.—"A friend that sticketh closer than a brother."—Prov. xviii. 24.

And who is this, my soul; indeed, who can it be, but Jesus? None among the fallen race of Adam could ever redeem his brother; or, if he could, would have done it, at the expence of his own soul. But Jesus did all this, and more, when our cause was desperate, and gave himself a ransom for his redeemed. Oh for grace to mark the features of his love. It began in eternity, it runs through all time, and continues everlasting. As Jesus is himself, so is he in his love; the same yesterday, and to-day, and for ever. And how hath he shewn it? First, by engaging as our Surety; then paying all our debts; fulfilling the whole law; purchasing our persons; undertaking for our duty; nay, even to the conquering the stubbornness of our nature, and making us willing to be saved in the day of his power! And what is it now? Having accomplished redemption for us by his blood, he is gone to take possession of a kingdom in our name. There he still manifests "the friend that sticketh closer than a brother;" for he takes up all our causes, pleads our suits, and makes every case his own. And by and by he will come to take us to himself, that where he is, there we may be also. In the mean time he supplies all our wants, and this with a freeness, fulness, suitableness, and all-sufficiency, that knows no bounds, to manifest the unalterable friendship which he bears us. He visits us continually, sympathises with us in all our afflictions, and increases with his tender love the enjoyment of all our comforts; and all this, and a thousand other nameless, numberless tokens, Jesus is continually shewing, as proves that his whole heart and soul is our's. So that he is a faithful, loving, constant, powerful, kind, everlasting, unchanging Friend, that sticketh closer than a brother. My soul, what wilt thou say to such a Friend? How wilt thou love him? Oh precious Lord, when I think of thy love and my ingratitude—bu Lord, it is thine to love, thine to pity, thine to pardon. Lord, give me grace to appropriate thee to myself; and while thou art still saying to me, and to thy church, "I have called you friends,"—

may I say, "This is my Friend, and this is my Beloved, O daughters of Jerusalem!"

EVENING.—"But we see Jesus, who was made a little lower than the angels, for the suffering of death, crowned with glory and honour." —Heb. ii. 9.

Mark, my soul, the very sweet and peculiar manner in which God the Holy Ghost here speaks of Jesus. He was "made a little lower than the angels, for the suffering of death." Yes! a body, such as ours, was given him, for the express purpose of suffering. Our nature, by reason of sin, required a sacrifice for sin. It behoved him, therefore, to be in all things like unto his brethren. But when he had made his soul an offering for sin, he for ever sat down on the right hand of the Majesty on high. To none of the angels was it ever said, "Sit thou on my right hand until I make thine enemies thy footstool." Now ponder these blessed things, and then say, whether thou hast so seen Jesus? If so, thou hast seen thy nature, in the person of the Lord Jesus Christ, not only exalted above all principality and power, and might and dominion, and every name that is named, not only in this world, but also in that which is to come; but thou hast seen him "crowned with glory and honour," as the head of his body the church. I charge it upon thee, my soul, that in all thy views of the Lord Jesus, as a risen and exalted Saviour, thou for ever connect with it, and never lose sight of it, that it is Jesus, as Jesus in his human nature, that is so exalted, so honoured, and glorified. It would be no honour, but rather a degradation of the Son of God, as God, to say such things of him, as being *made*, or *receiving* a throne, or having glory *given* to him. All power, sovereignty, and might, were his before. But when we behold Jesus as "made a little lower than the angels," and becoming Mediator, he stands forth the *servant* of Jehovah, redeeming his church and people; and, as such, "for the suffering of death," is "crowned with glory and honour." And Oh! how blessed the view! For if he was thus crowned in our nature, then surely he will have respect to our nature in all the wants of his people. If he be exalted in our nature, surely he is exalted in that nature "as a Prince and a Saviour, to give repentance to Israel, and remission of sins." And if it be the same Lord Jesus, whose head is now crowned with glory, that was once crowned with thorns: Oh! with what humble confidence may a poor sinner, such as I am, look up, and tell him of the glories of his cross, now shining with tenfold lustre in the glories of his crown! Shall I not hope, dear Lord! by the sweet influences of thy blessed Spirit, to make every day a coronation day, when by faith I crown thee my true and lawful Sovereign, desiring to bring every thought and affection of my poor heart into obedience to thee, to bow the knee of my heart before thee, and with holy joy "confess that Jesus Christ is Lord, to the glory of God the Father?" Amen.

AUGUST 8.

MORNING.—"Henceforth there is laid up for me a crown of righteousness, which the Lord, the righteous Judge, shall give me at that day: and not to me only, but unto all them also that love his appearing."—2 Tim. iv. 8.

Pause, my soul, over this blessed verse, and mark the very weighty things contained in it. Many a soul is for deferring the thoughts of this great day of God, and conclude, that the justification of the sinner cannot be known until the day of judgment. But, my soul, see to it, that thou art for bringing the firm and unshaken belief of it into immediate possession and enjoyment now; for surely Jesus hath effectually and fully provided for it. "Whom he called, them he also justified; and whom he justified, them he also glorified." See to it then, my soul, that thou dost not suffer thyself to live a day, no, not an hour, in a state of uncertainty upon a point of such infinite consequence, in which the pardon of thy sins, and the justification of thy person before God, is so highly concerned. If Jesus be thy Surety, his righteousness and blood must be thy full justification before God, and his salvation as much now as it will ever be. Pause then, and ask thine heart, dost thou love his appearing? Suppose the trump of God was this moment to sound, wouldest thou love his appearing? No doubt the moment would be solemn, but would it not be glorious? Is Jesus thine; his righteousness thine; his blood thy ransom? Wouldest thou love his appearing if these things were sure? And what makes them not sure? Art thou looking to any other righteousness? Hast thou not disclaimed all other saviours? Ask thyself again; dost thou love his appearing, in the season of ordinances, providences, retirements; in his word, in the visits of his grace; at his table, his house of prayer, among his churches, his people? Dost thou love his appearing in the conversion of every poor sinner; and doth the same make thee to rejoice over the recovery of such as angels do, when one repents? My soul, let these things be among thy daily meditations concerning Jesus; for then will thy meditation of him be sweet. And by thus making the justification of thy person in the blood and righteousness of Jesus thy daily comfort, thou wilt be prepared to love his appearing, in death, and finally at judgment; that when the Master comes, and calleth for thee, thou mayest arise with holy joy, and mount up to meet the Lord in the air, and receive that crown of Jesus's righteousness which fadeth not away.

EVENING.—"And the Lord said unto Moses, is the Lord's hand waxed short? Thou shalt see now whether my word shall come to pass unto thee, or not."—Numb. xi. 23.

Is it not an extraordinary thing in the history of Moses, that he, who had seen the miracles in Egypt, should stagger at God's promises to feed his people with a new supply in the wilderness? Had Moses forgotten the rock which gave water, or the daily supply of manna? But pause, my soul! look not at Moses; look at home. What wonders hath thy God wrought for thee! and yet what doubts, and fears, and questionings, are continually arising in thy mind. Is there a child of God on earth, more apt to reason with flesh and blood than thou art? And is there a child of God, that hath less reason so to do? Dearest Lord! I blush to think how slender, at times, my faith is! When I read of the acts of those heroes in the gospel, who "through faith, subdued kingdoms, wrought righteousness, stopped the mouths of lions," and the like, I take shame and confusion of face, in the review of my unbelieving heart. Did Joshua bid the sun and moon to stand still; did Peter smite Ananias and Sapphira dead; yea, did he even call Tabitha from the dead, by virtue of faith in Jesus; and am I so much at a loss, at times, as to fear that I shall one day perish by the hand of the enemy? Oh, Lord! I beseech thee, strengthen my soul in this grace, that I may never more question the divine faithfulness. And do thou, blessed Jesus, pour in thy resources upon my poor forgetful and unbelieving heart, when doubts, and fears, and misgivings arise. Give me to see, that in all my journey past, thou hast brought me through difficulties and dangers, and that "thy strength is made perfect in my weakness." What are all intervening difficulties, when Jesus undertakes for his people? Nay, the very obstruction, be it what it may, is but the more for the display of thy glory, and the exercise of my faith. Help me then, O Lord, to look to thee, and not to the difficulty, with which I have nothing to do. It is enough for me, that my God hath promised, and my God can and will perform. How Jesus will accomplish it, is his concern, and not mine. He is faithful; he hath promised; and that is sufficient: the issue is not doubtful. Yea, Lord! I know thine hand is not shortened, and all that thou hast said must come to pass. "Faithful is he that hath promised, who also will do it!"

AUGUST 9.

MORNING.—"And the fire upon the altar shall be burning in it: it shall not be put out. The fire shall ever be burning upon the altar: it shall never go out."—Levit. vi. 12, 13.

Pause, my soul! behold the precept in one verse, and the promise in the other. The Israelites was not to put out this altar fire; and Jehovah promised that it should never go out. Neither did it, through all the Jewish church, until Christ came. And if it be true that it actually did expire (as it is said it did) the very year Christ died, what is this but a confirmation of the grand truth of God concerning the putting away of sin by the blood of Christ? For is not fire an emblem, through all the scriptures, of Jehovah's displeasure against sin? Is not God said to be a consuming fire? And by its burning, and that miraculously preserved under all the Jewish dispensation, is it not meant to manifest Jehovah's perpetual wrath, burning like fire against sin? And as the fire was never extinguished upon the altar, notwithstanding the numerous sacrifices offered, can any thing more decidedly prove the inefficacy of sacrifices under the law, how expensive soever they were, to take away sin? And is the fire now gone out? Hath God himself indeed put it out! Then hath he accepted that one offering of the body of Jesus Christ once for all, who came to put away sin, and hath for ever put it away by the sacrifice of himself. Hail, thou great, thou glorious, thou everlasting Redeemer! Thou art indeed both the High Priest and the altar, both the Sacrifice and the Sacrificer, whose one offering hath both put out the fire of divine wrath, and caused the holy flame of love and peace to burn in its stead, which hath kindled in every heart of thy people. Yes, yes, thou Lamb of God, it is thou which hast delivered us from the wrath to come! Thou hast made our peace in the blood of thy cross. Thou hast quenched, by thy blood the just fire of divine indignation against sin. Thou hast quenched no less all the fiery darts of Satan. Thou hast subdued the flaming enmity of our hearts, with all their fiery lusts and burning affections. What shall I say to thee, what shall I say of thee, what shall I proclaim concerning thee, Oh thou, the Lord our righteousness? Lord, help me to begin the song, and never suffer sin or Satan—nay, death itself, for a moment, to make an interruption in the heavenly note; but let thy name fill my whole soul, and vibrate on my dying lips, that I may open my eyes in eternity, while the words still hang there: "To him who hath loved us, and washed us from our sins in his own blood, and made us kings and priests unto God and the Father; to him be glory and dominion for ever and ever. Amen."

EVENING.—"And I, if I be lifted up from the earth, will draw all men unto me."—John xii. 32.

My soul! it is blessed, and refreshing to the faith of God's children, to behold, in their almighty Redeemer, the same properties as are ascribed to the Father and the Spirit; and more especially in the points which concern their personal salvation. Jesus told the Jews, that none could come to him, "except the Father, who had sent him, should draw them;" John vi. 44. And in the same chapter, he ascribes "the quickening power," which draws to Christ, unto the Holy Spirit, verse 63. But that his own sovereign power and God-head is also included in this act of grace, he here teacheth us, by describing whose love and grace it is that sinners are drawn by! Precious Lord Jesus! let mine eyes be ever unto thee for the quickening, reviving, restoring, comforting, and all healing graces, which thou now art exalted, as a Prince and a Saviour to give unto thy people. And dearest Lord! I beseech thee, let my views of thee, and my meditation of thee, in this most endearing character, be sweet in the consideration also, that thou, as the head of thy church and people, must be the head of all spiritual, life-giving influences. Surely, blessed Jesus, the head cannot be happy, if the members be not made blessed; the source and fountain of all goodness must needs send forth streams to impart of its overflowing fulness. And is it not for this very purpose, that as God-man Mediator, "the Father hath given thee power over all flesh, that thou shouldest give eternal life to as many as the Father hath given thee?" John xvii. 2. And will not Jesus delight to dispense all blessings to his people, to his chosen, that are the purchase of his blood, and the gift of his Father, and the conquests of his grace? I feel my soul warmed with the very thought! I say to myself, 'Did my Lord and Saviour say, when upon earth, that he was "anointed to preach the gospel to the poor, to heal the broken in heart, and to give out of his fulness grace for grace?" And did my Lord say, moreover, that when "he was lifted up, he would draw all men unto him?" And shall I not feel the drawing, the constraining graces of his Spirit, bringing my whole heart, and soul, and spirit into an unceasing desire after him, and unceasing longing for him, and an everlasting enjoyment of him?' Precious, blessed Lord Jesus! let the morning, noon-day, and evening cry of my heart be in the language of the church of old, and let the cry be awakened by thy grace, and answered in thy mercy: "Draw me, we will run after thee: the king hath brought me into his chambers: we will be glad and rejoice in thee; we will remember thy love more than wine;" Song i. 4.

AUGUST 10.

MORNING.—" Who hath saved us, and called us with an holy calling, not according to our works, but according to his own purpose and grace, which was given us in Christ Jesus, before the world began." —2 Timothy i. 9.

Mark, my soul, all the precious things, if thou hast power or time to do so, which are contained in this blessed scripture. Eternity itself will not be sufficient to allow space to enumerate them; neither will thy ripened faculties, even when full-blown and full-fruited, be found sufficient to enter into the complete apprehension of them all. Who is it that is here said to have saved us, and called us with an holy calling, but the holy, glorious, undivided Jehovah, existing in a threefold character of Persons—Father, Son, and Holy Ghost? For all have concurred in that blessed work; and all, in the essence of the One Jehovah, must have the joint praise and the joint glory to all eternity. Well, then, put thy salvation down to this glorious account: it is God who hath saved and called thee. Next, mark the order here set forth. Thou art said to be saved before thou art said to be called. Mark that! salvation precedes our knowledge of it. The covenant engagements of the Almighty Covenanters took place from everlasting. For so saith the apostle concerning the hopes of happiness founded on salvation: " In hope," saith he, " of eternal life, which God that cannot lie, promised before the world began." Next, my soul, take notice of the call itself. It is an holy call: for we are called to the fellowship and communion of Jesus Christ. " And as he who hath called us is holy, so are we called to be holy, in all manner of conversation and godliness." See to it, my soul, that thy fellowship and communion is in the holiness and sin-atoning blood of Jesus. Lastly, never, my soul, lose sight of the cause of these unspeakable mercies—no, not for a moment.

"We are saved and called, not according to our works, but accordinig to his purpose." Hence, what is God's gift, cannot be man's merit; and what resulted from infinite love, from all eternity, cannot flow from creature love in time. Blessed purpose, and blessed grace: and thrice-blessed, being given to us in God's dear Son, even Christ Jesus, before the world began!

EVENING.—"Are they not all ministering spirits, sent forth to minister for them who shall be heirs of salvation?"—Heb. i. 14.

My soul, art thou an heir of salvation? Think then of thy high privilege. "If," saith an apostle, "we are children, then heirs, yea, heirs of God, and joint-heirs with Christ," Rom. viii. 17. Though in this life, we be in a state of childhood, and, under age, yet by adoption and grace, we are made "heirs of God." Not like men of the world, in their earthly portions, where only one in a family can be the heir, and that the first-born; but all the church are included, for the church itself is called "the first-born which are written in heaven," Heb. xii. 23. And in this heaven-born inheritance, thou hast, my soul, if thou be a child of God, a portion in God thy Father; for all his people are a nation of spiritual priests, who, like Aaron of old, "have the Lord for their portion," Numb. xviii. 20. Yea, by virtue of thy union to Christ, who, as God-man Mediator, is "heir of all things," thou art interested in all things which are his, by virtue of his mediation. Oh, the rapturous thought! But do not stop here. By reason of this heirship, behold thy high dignity! Angels, who are high in intellect, disembodied spirits, and who excel in wisdom and in power, are servants in thine Emmanuel's kingdom, to minister unto thee, and to all thy brethren in Jesus who are heirs of salvation. Oh! couldest thou see how they watch over thee, how they guard thee from a thousand evils; didst thou but know how eternally safe thou art amidst a host of foes, which come against thee; then, like the prophet's servant, thou wouldest frequently see, by the eye of faith, "the mountain around thee full of horses and chariots of fire," 2 Kings vi. 17. And who shall say to what extent their ministry is exercised? If a single angel destroyed seventy thousand in the host of Israel, at the command of God, (2 Sam. xxiv. 15.) and a hundred and fourscore and five thousand of the Assyrians which came forth against Israel, (2 Kings xix. 35.) what may not the child of God hope for, who is an heir of salvation, from the perpetual ministry of these ministering spirits? Oh! thou dear Lord, cause thine holy angels thus, by night and day, to take their stand, and watch over my defenceless hours! And, yet more than this, my adored Redeemer! come thou, and bless me with the unceasing visits of thy love, and say to me, as to thy church of old; "Fear thou not, for I am with thee; be not dismayed, for I am thy God; I will strengthen thee, yea, I will uphold thee with the right hand of my righteousness," Isa. xli. 10.

AUGUST 11.

MORNING.—"By faith, Abel offered unto God a more excellent sacrifice than Cain."—Heb. xi. 4.

The Holy Ghost hath here marked down, by his servant the apostle, in the very first offerings which we read of in the bible, the vast importance of faith; by which it most decidedly proves, that it is faith which gives efficacy to all the offerings of his creatures. Faith in what? Nay—there can be but one view of faith throughout the word of God; namely, faith in the promised seed to bruise the serpent's head. This was the first promise which came in upon the fall. Every offering, therefore, offered unto God, unless it had an eye to this, became offensive. Cain did not offer the first-fruits of the ground with an eye of faith in Christ—hence, he was the first deist the world ever knew. Abel, by faith, offered the firstlings of his flock with an eye to Jesus—and hence the testimony that God respected his offering. What a striking evidence is here, my soul, of the vast and infinite importance of faith. Cain made an offering to God, and by so doing, he did, as the deists now do, acknowledge God to be his Creator; but not looking to him as a Redeemer, and thereby intimating that he needed none, both his person and his offering were rejected. Meditate on this, my soul, and learn by grace to mix faith in all that concerns thy soul. Oh keep an eye on Jesus, convinced that "there is no other name under heaven given among men whereby we must be saved." And if, through the gracious teachings of the Spirit, in taking of the things of Jesus, and shewing them unto thee, thou art able daily to apprehend by faith, and bring him (as the bee doth from the flower) his person, his work, his character, his relations, his grace, and righteousness, as the sent, and sealed, and anointed, of the Father, full of grace and truth; by thus living *upon* him, and living *to* him, and making him what he is to all his people, the Alpha and Omega of thy salvation; faith in him will give a sweet leaven to all thy poor prayers, and praises, and offerings, and thou wilt find favour with God, to the praise of the glory of his grace, who maketh thee accepted in the Beloved.

EVENING.—"Who, being in the form of God, thought it not robbery to be equal with God, but made himself of no reputation."—Phil. ii. 6, 7.

My soul, after all thy meditations upon the person of thy Lord, how very far short hast thou come in thy thoughts of the unequalled humility of the Son of God! Let thy present evening's contemplation be on this subject. But where, and at what part shall I enter upon it. Who shall speak, or what heart conceive the wonders contained in it! Blessed Spirit of all truth! do thou glorify the Lord Jesus to my evening meditation, in this interesting view of his person. He that, before all worlds, lay in the bosom of the Father, and was attended by the services of legions of angels, condescended to be made not only flesh, but in the likeness of *sinful* flesh; to be born in a stable, and to sleep in a manger; to advance in human intellect, and grow in wisdom and in stature; to labour for bread, and to gain that bread by the sweat of the brow; and, having spent an eternity in glory with the Father, to spend thirty years in poverty and want among men! Go on, my soul, in the meditation. Follow Jesus till thou hast beheld him, not only having no where to lay his head, but becoming the scorn and sport of the multitude; and he, who had been, and still was, and ever will be the delight and glory of the Father, branded by men, even by many of them he came to save, as a blasphemer, and one that had a devil! Sit down and ponder over these wonderful things; and then ask, what can raise affections in the soul, if such views of Jesus do not? Think what must have been the Father's love in giving his dear Son to such a purpose? and what must have been the Son's love in coming? Then ask thyself, what indignities oughtest thou not to submit to among men, if called upon to such an exercise, while contemplating the unequalled humility of thy Redeemer? Dearest Lord Jesus! I blush in the moment of recollection, while beholding thy real glory thus veiled under the cloud of humiliation, to think how often for trifles, yea, less than trifles, the false pride of my poor fallen nature hath felt hurt at some fancied inattention from men. Oh! for the same mind to be in me "which was in Christ Jesus!" He made himself of no reputation!

AUGUST 12.

MORNING.—"To the chief singer on my stringed instruments."—Hab. iii. 19.

My soul, take down thine harp from the willow; and now the night is past, let the first of the morn find thee going forth, in the matin of praise, to the chief singer on all the instruments of his grace, which he hath strung thine heart to use to his glory. And who is this chief singer, but Jesus? Doth not the prophet say, "The Lord God is my strength, and he will make my feet like hinds' feet, and he will make me to walk in mine high places?" Surely he that is the Lord God of my salvation, is the chief singer, and chief musician of my song. And he that will be my portion, my everlasting portion in the upper world, will be my strength and song in this. Surely David would not have directed, as he hath, in such numberless places, his psalms to a singer among men, in the temple service, when the whole scope of the psalm itself treats of the Lord, and of his Christ. The root of the word singer, or musician itself, means *the end.* And "Christ is the end of the law for righteousness to every one that believeth." Come then, my soul, strike up this morning this hymn of praise. God the Holy Ghost is exciting thee. It is he which points to Jesus. He shews the king in his beauty, and bids thee behold his suitableness, transcendent excellencies, grace, love, favour, glory. Carry, then, all thy concerns to this chief musician. Put forth all thy strength to praise him, that while Jesus is attentive to the hallelujahs of heaven, he may hear thy feeble note, amidst all the songs which are offered him, giving glory to his great name, from the uttermost parts of the earth. Follow the prophet's example, and let the goings forth of thy warmest desires be to the chief singer on thy stringed instruments:—"The Lord is my strength and my shield; my heart trusted in him, and I am helped; therefore my heart greatly rejoiceth, and in my song will I praise him."

EVENING.—"But were mingled among the heathen, and learned their works."—Ps. cvi. 35.

Pause, my soul, over this view of God's people of old. There is a natural disposition in the heart, to do and to live as others, in order to pass through life with as little reproach as possible; and, in the first face of things, what is called an *innocent* conformity to the world seems to be commendable and praiseworthy. But, alas! it is impossible to mingle with the carnal, and not to learn their works; and it is always dangerous to get on the confines of the enemy. In that blessed prayer, taught us by our Lord, we pray "not to be led into temptation;" and surely this implies, that we do not desire to lead ourselves into temptation. But this every child of God doth, that mingles unnecessarily with the world, or with the men of the world. The precept is positive to this purpose; "Come out from among them, and be ye separate, saith the Lord, and touch not the unclean thing." And the blessing is as positive of the gracious effects that shall follow: "And I will receive you, and will be a Father unto you, and ye shall be my sons and daughters, saith the Lord Almighty," 2 Cor. vi. 17, 18. My soul, do thou make a memorandum of this, for thou art too apt to forget it. How often hast thou been found in places and with persons, where the voice might have been heard speaking to thee, as unto the prophet, "What doest thou here, Elijah?" And often hast thou returned wounded from such society, where, to speak of him "whom thou lovest," forms no part in the conversation; but where the frivolous and unprofitable discourse too plainly testifies that "neither is God in all their thoughts." Precious Jesus! keep me, I beseech thee, from the heathen of every description and character, and suffer me "not to mingle with them, nor learn their works;" but let my whole heart be fixed on thee, considering how "thou didst endure such a contradiction of sinners against thyself," that I may be never weary nor faint in mind.

AUGUST 13.

MORNING.—"And every oblation of thy meat-offering shalt thou season with salt; neither shalt thou suffer the salt of the covenant of thy God to be lacking from thy meat-offering: with all thy offerings thou shalt offer salt."—Lev. ii. 13.

Ponder over these words, my soul, and looking up for grace, and the divine teachings, see whether Jesus is not sweetly typified here. Was not Jesus the whole sum and substance of every offering under the law? The Holy Ghost taught the church this, when he said, "the law was a shadow of good things to come, but the body is of Christ." And did not the church, by faith, behold him as the salt which seasoned and made savoury the whole? Moreover, as all the sacrifices were wholly directed to typify him who knew no sin, but became sin for his people; the seasoning the sacrifice with salt, which was also a type of Christ's purity and sinlessness, became a sweet representation, to denote that a sinner, when he came with his offering, came by faith; to intimate that he looked for acceptance in the Lord as his sacrifice, and for preservation in the salt of his grace, in Christ Jesus. And who then, among believers now, would ever approach without an eye to Jesus, and the seasoning with this salt all his poor offerings. Lord, grant that the salt of the covenant of my God may never be lacking; for where Jesus is not, there can be no acceptance. Lord, let me have this salt in myself, and may every renewed presentation of myself be there salted. Then shall I be as the salt of the earth, amidst not only the putrefaction of the world, but the corruptions of my own heart.

Lord, say to us, and impart the blessing of thyself in saying it, "Have salt in yourselves;" and then shall we have peace with thee, and with one another.

EVENING.—"And they shall say unto the elders of his city, this our son is stubborn and rebellious, he will not obey our voice; he is a glutton, and a drunkard. And all the men of his city shall stone him with stones, that he die."—Deut. xxi. 20, 21.

My soul, pause over this Jewish precept. What a thundering command must it have been to flesh and blood! Think, how agonizing to the feelings of tender parents, to have come forth as the accusers of rebellious children, and gluttons and drunkards! What comfort could such have concerning them in their welfare of the life that now is, and what hope for that which is to come? But, as if these distressing feelings were not enough, it is they, the very parents, which are here commanded to bring forward the charge to the elders against their own bowels, and they are to be the means of bringing them to death. But, painful as it must have been to flesh and blood, such were the triumphs of grace, that, by virtue of it, "all Israel was to hear and to fear;" and if God was honoured, and the evil of rebellion put away, the close was glorious. Better to follow a child to the grave, than follow that child to hell. Better to root out a noxious weed from Christ's garden, the church, than that it should live, and bring forth and spread its deadly fruit. And is there not a sweet spiritual lesson in all this? Look at it, my soul, and see. Hast thou a stubborn and rebellious lust warring against the law of thy mind, and bringing thee into captivity to the law of sin, which is in thy members? And dost thou groan, as Paul groaned under it? Is it like a child in thine affection, that to destroy it is like plucking out an eye, or cutting off an arm? Do by it as the Lord commanded the poor oppressed father to do by his son. Bring it, be it what it may, not before the elders of thy people indeed, but before the Lord of heaven and earth; bring it to Jesus, and tell him of thy burden, and shew to him thy sorrow. I venture to believe, that he will give grace to crush it, and strength, like so many stones of the people, to beat it down in thine heart, and it will be to his glory, and to thy joy. Oh! the blessedness of bringing all to Jesus! He can, he will subdue the stubborn heart, break the power of the rebellious heart, restrain the propensity of the gluttonous or sottish heart, and give suited help to the several necessities of his people, so as to make the soul cry out, under the blessed strength imparted to our weakness, "I can do all things through Christ, who strengtheneth me." Help me then, dear Lord, and help all thy children, under their several infirmities, by thy Spirit, "to mortify the deeds of the body, that we may live."

AUGUST 14.

MORNING.—"And shall not God avenge his own elect, which cry day and night unto him, though he bear long with them? I tell you that he will avenge them speedily."—Luke xviii. 7, 8.

My soul, mark for thy encouragement, in all thine approaches to a throne of grace, what Jesus here speaks, and never lose sight of it. Remember how well acquainted he, who came out of the bosom of the Father, must be with the Father's mind and will towards his people, over and above the gracious exercise of his priestly office in their behalf. Now, my soul, do mark down distinctly what blessed things are here promised. First—God's people are said in it to be his elect, his chosen, his jewels. "This people," saith God, "I have formed for myself; they shall shew forth my praise." Secondly—God's people are a praying people; "they cry day and night to him;" they are unceasing in their applications; and they wrestle, like their father Jacob in prayer: "Lord, I will not let thee go except thou bless me." Give me Jesus, and in him I shall have all things. He will subdue this corruption; he will soften this affliction; he will conquer Satan, and with him, all his temptations. Thirdly—God's people will and must be exercised. There will be sometimes long silence at the throne. The enemy will endeavour to improve this to strengthen his temptation; he will suggest, 'God hath forgotten thee; he will return no more; he hath cast thee off.' Lastly—mark what Jesus saith; "Shall not God avenge his own elect, who cry day and night unto him, though he bear long with them?" Yes, yes, he will, I tell you, saith one who could not be mistaken; "he will avenge them, and that speedily." When the hour of deliverance comes, it shall come so sudden, so sweet, so unexpected, that all their long waiting shall be forgotten; and it shall seem as if that promise of answering before they called was in it. And he will not only bless them, but avenge them of their foes. And whence all this, my soul, but because he is the Father of mercies, and God of all consolation. His people are his chosen, the gift of his love, the purchase of Jesus's blood, the conquests of his Holy Spirit. Lord, cause me ever to keep those precious things in remembrance, and to hang on, and hold out, and never, never to give over pleading in Jesus, until I hear that precious voice, "Be it unto thee, even as thou wilt."

EVENING.—"The word is nigh thee, even in thy mouth, and in thy heart; that is the word of faith which we preach, that if thou shalt confess with thy mouth, the Lord Jesus, and shalt believe in thine heart that God hath raised him from the dead, thou shalt be saved. For with the heart man believeth unto righteousness, and with the mouth confession is made unto salvation.—Rom. x. 8, 9, 10.

My soul, behold the tenderness of God the Holy Ghost to his people, in order to prevent the possibility of error, in their knowledge and enjoyment of Christ.

It is not difficult to attain a clear apprehension, whether a soul be in grace, or not; for here the point is most plainly set forth; "The word is nigh thee." What word? The word of faith. Christ in the word, Christ in the promise, Christ himself the salvation of the sinner. And when a poor sinner hath been led to see who Christ is, and what he hath wrought, what he hath done for sinners, and what he is to them; the infinite glories of his person, the infinite perfection and completeness of his work, and the infinite suitableness of Jesus in every possible way that a poor sinner can need, by way of justification before God, and acceptance with God; then these blessed truths are so sweetly brought home to the heart and conscience of the enlightened sinner, by God the Holy Ghost, that he rests *upon* Christ as one perfectly satisfied *with* Christ, and neither seeks nor desires any other. So that by the lively actings of faith, the soul beholds Christ in the word, and in the promise, and takes him with both into his very soul, until Christ is fully "formed there the hope of glory." Hence, both the outward confession of the mouth, and the inward enjoyment of the heart, have a beautiful correspondence; the one speaks what the other feels; "for out of the abundance of the heart the mouth speaketh." My soul, is not this faith? And if so, what can dispossess thee of it? What shall stop thy joy or confidence in Jesus a single hour? If Jesus, the uncreated word, the promised word, the sum and substance of all the written word, be nigh thee, yea, in thy mouth and in thine heart; not only thine understanding knows Jesus, but thine heart lives upon Jesus; surely salvation is secure; yea, heaven itself is begun in the soul; for "this is life eternal, to know the only true God, and Jesus Christ, whom he hath sent!"

AUGUST 15.

MORNING.—" The good will of him that dwelt in the bush."—Deut. xxxiii. 16.

And who is this, my soul; who indeed can it be but Jesus? Surely he is the glorious person. It was good will, in the highest possible instance of it, that prompted his infinite mind, from everlasting, to love his people, to engage for them in suretyship engagements, and to stand up and come forth, at the call of God the Father, as the head of his body the church. It was a continuation of the same good will which prompted him, in the fulness of time, to assume our nature for the purposes of fulfilling those engagements. Then it was, indeed, he dwelt in the bush; for what is our nature, at the best, but a poor dry bramble bush, fit for burning? But yet, by Christ in it, so sustained, and so preserved, that though the bush burns with fire, even the fiery lusts of our corruptions, and the fiery darts of the wicked, and all the fiery opposition of the world, it shall not be consumed. Precious Jesus! what good will hast thou shewn, dost thou shew, and everlastingly wilt shew, to our poor nature, since thou hast been in it, and art now, indeed, the dweller in it. And did Moses, when dying, thus connect the first views of thy love, when from the burning bush thou didst make thyself known to him, as God tabernacling in our flesh, for the purpose of salvation, with his last views as he was closing his eyes to this world, and looking up to thee as God-man Mediator, and thus pray for thy good will to the church? Oh then, let my every-day meditation do the same. Lord Jesus, I would seek thee and thy good will beyond all the riches of the earth, and all the enjoyments of the world. Lord, I would never forget that it was thy good will which brought thee down from heaven; thy good will which prompted thee to die, to rise again, for poor sinners; thy good will which makes thee wash them from all their sins in thy blood; all the visits of thy grace here, all the glories of redemption hereafter; all are the purchase and the result of thy good will. Precious Lord, do thou, day by day, grant me renewed tokens of thy good will; and let those visits be so gracious, so sweet, and so continual, that I may think of nothing else, speak of nothing else, but the good will of my dweller in the bush. I would pray for grace to spend all the moments of my life here in receiving from thee grace and love, and bringing to thee love and praise, until thou shalt take me home to live at the fountain of thy good will, and the whole happiness of eternity consists in the praises of God and the Lamb, and in enjoying "the good will of him that dwelt in the bush."

EVENING.—" Iniquities prevail against me: as for our transgressions, thou shalt purge them away."—Psalm lxv. 3.

My soul, ponder over this important verse. It is but short, but it is full of precious things. Blessed the man that can, from his heart, make use of what is here said as his own experience! He hath learned much of Christ, that can do so. In a time when a sense of sin abounds, when comforts run low, and the rebellion of the remains of indwelling corruptions riseth high; when the enemy cometh in like a flood, and no answers return from the sanctuary; yea, when the very spirit of prayer fails, and the heaven that is over the head, is as brass, and the earth that is under the feet, is as iron; then to rest simply upon Christ, and to say, "Iniquities prevail against me!" I feel the dreadful consequences of a fallen state; but all those transgressions Jesus will purge them away; though the Canaanites are yet in the land, my almighty Joshua will, by little and little, drive them out before me, until they are utterly destroyed;" to say these things, and to know them, and, by a firm reliance on Jesus, to depend upon the accomplishment of them, is to have faith in lively exercise indeed! This is to rest on God the Father's covenant engagement, and Jesus's person and righteousness only, and at a time, when, of all others, perhaps faith is hard put to it, to call Christ our own. Oh! the blessedness of this state of the soul, when a sense of prevailing iniquities, instead of damping the actings of faith, becomes a stimulus to look to Jesus, and to call in his powerful hand to restrain, when a man is driven out of himself, to lay hold on the blessed Jesus! My soul, hast thou thus far advanced in the school of grace? Happy, happy indeed, if a daily sense of thy nothingness tends more and more to endear the Lord's all-sufficiency! And blessed will be the final issue of that divine teaching which brings thee at last most low and humble at the feet of Jesus, content to be nothing, yea, worse than nothing, that Jesus may have all the glory, who is alone worthy of it, in the salvation of his people.

AUGUST 16.

MORNING.—" I am black, but comely."—Song i. 5.

See, my soul, whether thine experience corresponds to that of the church. Hast thou learnt from God the Spirit what thou art in thyself? Art thou truly sensible of the many sins and corruptions which lurk under fair appearances; and that, from carrying about with thee a body of sin and death, as the apostle said he did, in thee, that is, in thy flesh, dwelleth no good thing? Dost thou appear not only black in thine own view, but art thou despised for Christ's sake, and counted the offscouring of all things in the view of the world? Pause, my soul. Now look at the bright side. Art thou comely in Christ's righteousness, which he hath put upon thee? Comely in the sweet sanctifying grace of the Holy Ghost dwelling in thee? Comely in the eyes of God the Father, from being accepted in

Jesus the Beloved? Comely in church communion and fellowship, walking in the fear of God, and under the comforts of the Holy Ghost? What sayest thou, my soul, to these sweet but soul-searching testimonies? If thou canst now take up the language of the church: "I am black, but comely;" lowly in thine own eyes, self-loathing, self-despising, self-abhorring; but in Jesus rejoicing, and in his salvation triumphing all the day; think, my soul, what will it be when the King, in whose comeliness thou art comely, shall take thee home, as a bride adorned for her husband, and thou shalt then be found, "not having spot or wrinkle, or any such thing," but shalt be everlastingly holy, and without blame before him in love.

EVENING.—"Sing, O ye heavens; for the Lord hath done it: shout, ye lower parts of the earth: break forth into singing, ye mountains, O forest, and every tree therein: for the Lord hath redeemed Jacob, and glorified himself in Israel."—Isa. xliv. 23.

Come, my soul, and join this universal hymn of praise, this lovely evening. Surely, if the Lord, by his servant the prophet, calls upon all nature, both the animate and inanimate parts of creation, to join in the melody, well may "the redeemed of the Lord say so!" The heavens shall sing the song of redemption; for angels rejoice over converted sinners. The earth shall join the song; for the curse pronounced on the ground is taken away by redemption. Yea, the very trees of the desert, the most remote from the peopled city, in beholding the felicity of God's chosen, shall clap their hands also. And mark, my soul, what is the running verse and chorus of this blessed song? It is Jehovah's glory; "for the Lord hath redeemed Jacob, and glorified himself in Israel." Precious and principal feature in redemption! for what is God's work is God's glory. Think of this, when thou art contemplating the wonders and glories of redemption. And, moreover, let these views of divine glory, the first and ultimate end, in creation, providence, and grace, become the assurance, and security, and comfort of thy mind, under all the remaining points to be accomplished in thy personal circumstances, and interest in it. The Lord hath glorified himself, and will glorify himself in his people. Israel is the people of his purpose, the children of promise, the children of adoption, the objects of his choice, of his everlasting love; the seed of Christ; the purchase of his blood. "This people, (saith Jehovah) have I formed for myself, they shall shew forth my praise." Pause, my soul, and ask thy heart, what can shew forth God's praise in any way equal to all our conceptions of Jehovah's glory, more than by a way so gracious, so wonderful, and so passing all understanding, as that of taking them from nothing, yea, from worse than nothing, and constituting them a church, a people in Christ, his dear Son, to be the everlasting monument of his glory and praise, in the realms of eternity for ever? Well might the prophet exclaim, and well mayest thou join the song: "Sing, O ye heavens; for the Lord hath done it: shout, ye lower parts of the earth: break forth into singing, ye mountains, O forest, and every tree therein: for the Lord hath redeemed Jacob, and glorified himself in Israel."

AUGUST 17.

MORNING.—"The dead shall hear the voice of the Son of God: and they that hear shall live."—John v. 25.

What a promise is here, and what an encouragement for every dead sinner to hope, and for every living saint, who is interested for dead sinners, not to despair? Observe, my soul, the extensiveness of the mercy: it is the dead. Why, all are dead in trespasses and sins. Is there not hope then for all? "And they that hear shall live." Why, then, every sinner should ask his heart—do I hear? But, my soul, mark how this is done. It is by the voice of the Son of God. Yes; there is salvation in no other. He saith himself, "I am the resurrection and the life: he that believeth in me, though he were dead, yet shall he live; and whosoever liveth, and believeth in me, shall never die." But, my soul, while taking comfort from this blessed passage, as it concerns poor dead sinners, ask thine own heart whether thou hast been the happy partaker of it thyself. Hast thou heard the voice of the Son of God? Yes; if so be thou livest *in* him, and *upon* him, and walkest *with* him. Jesus's voice is a quickening voice, a life-giving voice, a soul-feeding, soul-strengthening, heart-warming, heart-breaking, heart-melting voice. What sayest thou, my soul, to these examinations? Oh if Jesus's voice hath been ever heard by thee, thou wilt be desiring the renewal of it from day to day, and thou wilt be saying, in the earnest language of the church: "let me hear thy voice, let me see thy countenance; for sweet is thy voice, and thy countenance is comely."

EVENING.—"Never man spake like this man."—John vii. 46.

What a decided testimony were even the enemies of Christ compelled, from their own consciences, to give to the Godhead and power of the Lord Jesus Christ! Think then, my soul, what an evidence thou wouldest bring, if called upon to tell what Jesus hath said to thee! From the first moment that Jesus revealed himself, *in* his word, and *by* his word, to thy heart, thou couldest truly say, as the Jewish officers did, "Never man spake like this man." Never any spake like this God-man, this Glory-man, thy Redeemer. All his words were, and are divine words; powerful, persuasive, tender, gracious words, and full of salvation. Say, also, how very blessed all that Jesus spake of salvation was to thy heart, when he made it personal, and spake it all to *thee*. When he said, I am *thy* salvation. I have pardon, I have peace, I have righteousness, I have grace here, and glory hereafter; and all I have is for *thee*. So that when reading the word, or hearing the word, and the question arose in thy heart, to whom speaketh my Lord thus? Oh! how unspeakably precious did the word become, when Jesus said by his servant, "To you is the word of this salvation sent." Precious Lord Jesus! how shall I express my soul's sense of thy love and grace, thy merey and favour? Since thou first manifested thyself to my heart, I am no longer my own. Thou hast taken all my affections with thee to heaven, and caused them to center every thing in thyself. And now, Lord, I still daily, yea, sometimes hourly, when I hear thy voice, am constrained to cry out, "Never man spake like this man!" How sweet and suitable are thy words to my weary soul; thou hast indeed "the tongue of the learned, and knowest how to speak in season to souls, (like mine) that are weary," Isa. i. 4. How truly blessed and seasonable is thy well-known voice to my soul, when a sense of my nothingness makes thy fulness yet more precious. Oh! when I hear thee say, "My grace is sufficient for thee, for my strength is made perfect in weakness;" surely, Lord, I feel a power that makes all my enemies seem as nothing. Like thy servant, I then truly "glory in my infirmities, that thy power may rest upon me." Be thou then, dearest Lord Jesus, all I need, and let me hear thy voice, and see thy countenance; for both in life and in death, in time, and to all eternity, the voice of my Lord Jesus will be my everlasting comfort, for none speaketh like thee!

AUGUST 18.

MORNING.—"Give strong drink unto him that is ready to perish, and wine unto those that be of heavy hearts. Let him drink and forget his poverty, and remember his misery no more."—Prov. xxxi. 6, 7.

What is the strong drink of the gospel but the covenant love, faithfulness, and grace of Jehovah? And what is the wine of the gospel but the love of Jesus, which the church saith is better than wine? Tell a poor sinner that is ready to perish, of God the Father's everlasting love towards his people, who were all by nature sinners ready to perish, when God passed by and bid them live; tell them that such was God's love that he gave his only begotten Son, to the end that all that believe in him should not perish, but have everlasting life; tell them of Jesus, his Godhead, his Manhood —both natures united in one person, forming one Christ; tell them, that faith in his blood will save the soul; that God the Father hath respect only to the person and worth of his dear Son; and that for his sake, and his sake alone, the greatest saint, and the greatest sinner, if believers, are alike saved. This is strong drink; and a poor perishing sinner needs the cordial. Neither will the heavy in heart be any more sad, that thus is made to drink of the wine of the gospel. My soul, hast thou tasted of this strong drink? Oh then, take the cup of salvation, and call upon the name of the Lord! Drink of this cup which Jesus puts into thine hand, and in his riches forget thy poverty, and in his free, and full, and finished redemption remember thine own misery no more. Live only to Jesus, and let him be thy strong drink, thy wine, and thy cordial for ever.

EVENING—" While he yet spake, behold, a bright cloud overshadowed them."—Matt. xvii. 5.

My soul! see here, how it fared with the disciples in the mount, in the moment of those blessed manifestations which Jesus was making to them; and when, to heighten their felicity, several of the inhabitants of glory came, and spake to Jesus in the view of his disciples; yet so sudden was the change, that, even while Jesus spake, a cloud intervened and obscured all. Somewhat of the same change thou hast thyself known. How often hast thou been made like the chariots of Amminadib, by the overpowering grace that Jesus hath shewn thee! And how often have those blessed moments been followed by a dark and long night! And what ought to be thy improvement of these dispensations? Look still to Jesus, under all. Whatever changes are induced, never forget that his person is the same, and his love the same. Mark this down. Next look up to Jesus, and tell him, that as his visits are so sweet, so gracious, and blessed, entreat the dear Lord to be often coming, often blessing thee with his love, and making his abode with thee. And see that thou art improving every occasion, and making the most of those hallowed seasons; for they are most blessed and precious; while thy Lord is with thee, and feasting thee with his love, and shewing thee his secret mark, the Bethel-places, made sacred by his presence, and the Bethel communications, made pleasant by coming from him. And do not forget to interest Jesus for Zion. Tell him that Zion is his own, and thou knowest that he loves her. Then, on the ground of this love, tell him how she languisheth, in the present awful day of much profession, with but little vital godliness. And while *the king is held* by thee *in the galleries* of his grace, bring in the arms of thy faith all thou wouldest seek a blessing for; thy children, if thou hast any, thy family, the church at large, the nation; and do, as did the patriarch, wrestle, plead, hold fast, and take no refusal, but say, 'Lord, thou comest to bless, and a blessing I must have; "neither will I let thee go, except thou bless me."'

AUGUST 19.

MORNING.—"My beloved is white and ruddy."—Song v. 10.

Pause, my soul, and contemplate thy Redeemer this morning under this engaging description of his person. It opens a delightful subject for meditation, in several points of view. Jesus is white and ruddy, if considered in his human nature only, He might be said to be white, in reference to the immaculate holiness of his body, underived as it was from a sinful stock like ours. He was born of the Virgin Mary by the miraculous conception of the Holy Ghost, and therefore emphatically called, that HOLY THING: agreeably to all which, his whole life was without sin or shadow of imperfection. "Such an High Priest become us, who is holy, harmless, undefiled, separate from sinners, and made higher than the heavens." Hence Jesus was truly white, as the Lamb of God, without blemish, and without spot. And was he not ruddy also, in his bloody sufferings, when his head was crowned with thorns, and his side pierced on the cross? Was he not ruddy in the garden, when his agony was so great as to force blood through all the pores of his sacred body, which fell in great drops on the ground. Behold, my soul, thy beloved in both these views, and say,—Is he not white and ruddy? But do not stop here. Look at him again, and contemplate the Lord Jesus as the Christ of God, in his two natures, divine and human, and say in the union of both,—Is he not white and ruddy? What can set forth the glories of the Godhead to our apprehension more lovely than the purity of whiteness, which, as in the mount of transfiguration, became a brightness too dazzling for mortal sight to behold? And what can represent the human nature more strikingly than the ruddiness of the countenance? Adam, the first man, takes his very name from hence; for Adam, or Adamah, signifies red earth. And such, then, was Jesus. And is he then, my soul, white and ruddy to thy view? And is he also thy beloved? Oh then, let him be thy morning, noon-day, evening, midnight meditation; and let him be sweet to thee, as he is to his church and people—the beloved who is white and ruddy?

EVENING.—" And Moses returned unto the Lord, and said, Lord, wherefore hast thou so evil intreated this people? Why is it that thou hast sent me? For since I came to Pharaoh to speak in thy name, he hath done evil to this people; neither hast thou delivered thy people at all."—Exod. v. 22, 23.

My soul! ponder over this scripture, and the history connected with it, and behold what a blessed volume of instruction it affords. The Lord sent Moses to deliver his people out of Egypt. He had heard their groanings, and graciously promised to redress them. The people believed the Lord, and bowed their heads, in token of their view of his love, and their own happiness, which was now to follow. But behold, the oppression under which they had groaned, instead of lessening, began to increase. In this state they grow desperate, and charge God foolishly. Yea, Moses himself, who had talked with God at the bush, and seen the miracles in confirmation of his commission there shewn, becomes tainted with the same spirit of unbelief, and returned to expostulate with Jehovah on the occasion.—Pause over this view of the human heart, even in God's own people. The sequel of Israel's history sheweth, that the Lord was pursuing one invariable plan for the deliverance of his people, as he had promised; and that there was no alteration in him. He was only laying his glorious scheme the deeper by seeming opposition, to make his people's emancipation more blessed, and his love of them more striking. But yet, while things appeared thus dark and unpromising, Israel forgot all that the Lord had promised.—And how is it, my soul, with thyself? When the promises of God seem to clash with his providences, and according to thy narrow views, seem impossible to be brought into agreement with each other, how dost thou act? Art thou not like Israel, much disposed to reason with flesh and blood? When the enemies of thy peace triumph, and carry things, as Pharaoh did in this instance with

Israel, with a high hand, saying, " Aha! so would we have it;" when unbelief creeps in, or a lust, which thou hadst hoped was subdued, breaks out afresh, like some peccant humour of the body; when no answers are heard to thy prayers; and though thou art falling under some renewed temptation, yet there appears no hand of Jesus stretched forth to bring thee off, and raise thee up: say, my soul! under such dark providences, how dost thou conduct thyself towards the Lord? Oh for grace to trace Jesus, more especially in trying seasons than even in prosperous moments; and to hear his voice in the whirlwind and the storm! It is blessed to wait, blessed to depend upon Jesus, blessed to believe in his promise, when all the ways to the fulfilment of that promise seem to be wholly shut. This is the crowning grace of faith, " against hope to believe in hope;" and amidst the most desperate circumstances, to cleave to Jesus as a sure friend, when, in his providences, he appears coming forth as a determined enemy, and to say, with the same well-grounded confidence as Job, " Though he slay me, yet will I trust in him."

AUGUST 20.

MORNING.—" Within the vail, whither the forerunner is for us entered, even Jesus."—Heb. vi. 19, 20.

Pause over these words, my soul, this morning. Is the vail removed? Was the vail rent in twain, from the top to the bottom, in the hour that Christ died? And did Jesus, as thy High Priest, with all his blood, then enter into the place not made with hands, having obtained eternal redemption for us? Did he enter too as thy forerunner? Pause over this thought—it is a sweet one. Is Jesus still there? Nay, my soul, look in and see. He calls thee to look unto him—nay, to follow him, " having boldness to enter into the holiest by his blood, in the new and living way which he hath consecrated for us through the vail, that is to say, his flesh." And what canst thou see there? Within the vail of the Jewish temple there was the golden censer, and the ark of the covenant, and the golden pot that had manna, and Aaron's rod that budded, and the tables of the covenant; and over it the cherubims of glory shadowing the mercy-seat. But within that vail, whither our forerunner is entered, look up, my soul, and see Jesus with the golden censer of his own merits and blood; and not the symbols of the covenant only, but he himself, the whole of the covenant, God the Father hath given him for the people; not merely manna, but himself the living bread, the bread of God, of which whosoever eateth shall live for ever; not the rod of Aaron, but the rod of his power, to make poor sinners willing in the day of his power; not the cherubims of glory, but himself the mercy-seat, the propitiatory, the sacrifice, high priest, and all in all. Look up, my soul; look in, my soul; go in, my soul, after him, by faith, and contemplate him as thy forerunner; and while all thy faculties, in grace and faith, are going forth in the most lively exercise, hear him say, and let his words sink deeper and deeper in thine unceasing remembrance: "I only go to prepare for you a place: I will come again, and receive you to myself, that where I am, there you may be also." Hail thou glorious Forerunner, who art made an high priest for ever, after the order of Melchisedec.

EVENING.—" A good man shall be satisfied from himself."—Prov. xiv. 14.

My soul! what is this scripture, and what is the design of the Holy Ghost in it? Art thou satisfied in thyself? Alas! every day makes me more and more dissatisfied with myself. How can I, indeed, be satisfied, who carry about with me such a body of sin and death, which is everlastingly fighting with, and opposing my better part? What satisfaction, then, is it, that is here meant? Scripture is best explained by scripture: hence the satisfaction that a believing soul finds from himself, is not from his own attaiments, nor his own righteousness, but from the witness of the Holy Ghost, that he is born of God, and brought out of nature's darkness into God's marvellous light. The apostle John hath given, in a single verse, a full illustration of what the wise man here saith, of a good man (that is, a child of God) being satisfied with himself: "He that believeth on the Son of God," saith the apostle John, "hath the witness in himself;" 1 John v. 10. Here is the grand source of all his satisfaction. The Holy Ghost witnesseth to the soul of the believer, that he is new born, that he is passed from death to life; that Jesus is precious, and his salvation very dear to him. The heart of such an one is brought to know and feel his own wants by reason of sin, and the infinite suitableness of Jesus to answer all those wants, and to be to him all he stands in need of. The poor creature, thus taught of God, is satisfied with the blessed discovery he hath made of Jesus, and his salvation; and rests wholly in it, as one perfectly satisfied, and desires no other; yea, renounceth every other. Hence he is satisfied from himself, and his own feelings, and not from what others have taught him, that Jesus is all he needs. My soul! hast thou arrived to this blessedness? If so, praise that distinguishing grace, by which, in the midst of self-loathing on account of thy sin, thou hast a self-satisfaction on account of having found Jesus and his righteousness. Let Jesus have all the praise, and do thou live as one eternally satisfied with his person and righteousness.

AUGUST 21.

MORNING.—"Fear not; for they that be with us, are more than they that be with them."—2 Kings vi. 16.

My soul, never lose sight of this which was shewn

to the prophet's servant in his fright. Though thou seest not, with bodily eyes, the mountain full of horses and chariots of fire in thy defence; yet with thy spiritual eyes, thou mayest see, infinitely beyond all this, as surrounding thee at all times and in all places, God thy Father, with all his divine attributes and perfections, all engaged, all made over, all pledged in covenant engagements, in Jesus, for thy defence, protection, comfort, security, and guiding thee in all things. There is more in that one assurance than in a thousand worlds, "I will be thy God"—and all in Jesus, yea and amen. Then, moreover, thou hast God thy Redeemer with thee, with all his fulness, all his grace, all his love—his whole heart, his whole soul thine. And thou hast God the Holy Ghost, with all his influences, gifts, teachings, quickenings, consolations, strengthenings. All these are with thee; to say nothing of angels, which are ministering spirits, sent forth to minister unto them which are heirs of salvation. Surely God's attributes, Jesus's graces, the Holy Ghost's comforts, being all thine own, and always with thee; let what armies of men, or legions of evil spirits assault thee—unbelief, or fear, or doubt, or misgiving; let nothing drive out the recollections nor remove thy confidence. "Fear not, for they that be with thee are more than all that can be against thee." Hallelujah. Amen.

EVENING.—"And it came to pass as they were eating of the pottage, that they cried out, and said, Oh thou man of God, there is death in the pot!"—2 Kings iv. 40.

It was at a time of great famine, that the prophet Elisha ministered among the sons of the prophets at Gilgal; no wonder, therefore, that their diet was reduced to a dinner of herbs. During the season of persecution in our kingdom, somewhat more than a century and half since, there was a spiritual famine, not of bread or of water, but of hearing the word of the Lord: and so precious was the word of the Lord in those days, that our good old fathers used to remark, " bread and water, with the gospel, was choice fare." We find, in the household of Elisha, that wild gourds by the ignorance of him that gathered the herbs, were served up in the pottage of the people, which, as soon as they were discovered, occasioned the cry to the prophet, " O thou man of God, there is death in the pot!" And is there not death in the pot, when any matters of a poisonous quality are mingled and served up to God's people with the word of his grace? Surely, the springs of all spiritual food and life are in Jesus: his blood, his righteousness, his finished salvation, the graces of his Holy Spirit, and the rest and dependence upon God the Father's covenant love and mercy in him; these are the only food of the soul by which it can be nourished. To drop these rich and savoury truths, whereby the soul is kept alive to God, and brought nigh to God in Christ; or, what is the same thing to mingle, like the wild gourds of the field, the righteousness of the creature, as being partly the means of salvation, with this only wholesome food of the soul; may surely cause the believing soul to cry out, " O thou man of God, there is death in the pot!" I charge it upon thee, my soul, this evening, in the view of this scripture, concerning the sons of the prophets, that thou take heed to receive not mingled things for the good old fare of the gospel. The smallest introduction to error is as one that letteth out water. Where the person of Jesus, his work, and glory, are neglected to be set forth, there will be death in the pot, whatever else be substituted in the place. A real believer cannot live in his soul's health a day, no more than a labouring man in his body, where the food suited to each is not given. And it surely were a pity, when there is such an infinite fulness in Christ, to substitute any thing for him. See to it then, my soul, that all thy food be Jesus, and let " all thy fresh springs be in him." Remember the promise, for in the saddest times of dearth, if Jesus be looked to, it never can fail: "They shall be abundantly satisfied with the fatness of thy house, and thou shalt make them drink of the river of thy pleasures: for with thee is the fountain of life;" Ps. xxxvi. 8, 9.

AUGUST 22.

MORNING.—"Seeking for Jesus."—John vi. 24.

This, my soul, should be thy constant employment, wherever thou art, however engaged; in going in, or out; at rising up, or lying down; whether in public or private, in the church or market-place; the closet, the family, the garden, the field, the house: the question ever arising in the heart should be—where is Jesus? Blessed Spirit! thou glorifier of my Lord, wilt thou constantly excite this seeking for Jesus in my heart? Wilt thou, Lord, give me every moment a sense of need, then a view of his fulness, suitableness, readiness to impart; then bring Him, whom my soul loveth, and me together; and then open a communication in leading me forth in desire, and giving me faith to receive from the infinite fulness of my Lord, and grace for grace? Lord Jesus! I would desire grace to seek thee, as for hidden treasure. I would seek thee, and thee only, O my God! I would separate myself from all other things. It is Jesus, my soul chooseth, my soul needs. I would trust in nothing beside. No duties, no works; neither prayers nor repentance; no, nor faith itself, considered as an act of my soul, shall be my comfort, but Jesus alone I would make my centre; and every thought, and every affection, and every desire, like so many streams meeting in one, should all pour themselves, as rivers, into the ocean of thy bosom! And the nearer, as a stream that draws near the sea is propelled to fall into it, so the more forcible and vehement let my soul be in desires after thee, as my soul draweth nearer the hour of seeing thee. Oh Lamb of God, give me to be seeking after thee through life, pressing after thee from one ordinance to another; and when ordinances cease, and all outward comforts fail, then, Lord, may I gather up (as the dying patriarch did his feet in the bed) all my strength, and pour my whole soul into thine arms, crying out, "I have waited for thy salvation, O Lord?"

EVENING.—"And there appeared a great wonder in heaven, a woman clothed with the sun, and the moon under her feet, and upon her head a crown of twelve stars."—Rev. xii. 1.

My soul! as the beloved apostle was invited to see those precious visions, which the Lord favoured him with, for the church's good, so do thou, this evening, attend his ministry, and gather, under divine teaching, instruction from this great wonder, which John saw. Surely, the woman here spoken of, means the church, the Lamb's wife, clothed in her husband's righteousness; and the moon, like that planet which ministers to our world, under her feet: and the crown, with which her head was adorned, sets forth how the church is made glorious by the ministry of the twelve apostles in the gospel of salvation: for what can be more suitable for the church to be crowned with, than the blessed truths contained in their writings? Now, my soul, as every representation of the church not only sets forth the whole body at large, but every individual member of that body, ask thyself, hath this wonder been wrought on thee, which John saw? Art thou clothed with the sun, even with Jesus, the sun of righteousness, in his garment of salvation? Hast thou mounted up, not in airy speculations, not in any fancied attainments of thine own, but in heavenly mindedness after Jesus, and devout communion with him; so that the earth, with all its perishing beauties, is got under thy feet? Hast thou such views of the blessedness and preciousness of the word of God, the gospel of thy salvation, that it is dearer to thee than gold, yea, than all the crowns of the earth? Pause, while these inquiries pass over thy mind; and surely, if the Lord, by the sovereignty of his grace, hath wrought such blessed effects upon thee, a great wonder is indeed wrought in earth, like that which John saw in heaven, and well mayest thou stand amazed at the greatness and the distinguishing nature of salvation. "Lord! what am I; and what is my father's house?"

AUGUST 23.

MORNING.—"The beloved physician."—Coloss. iv. 14.

My soul, catch a thought of what the apostle here speaks of the servants to think of the master! If Luke the physician was beloved, how much more so ought Jesus to be by thee in this sweet character. The Son of God came, as the great physician of the soul, to heal all that were diseased, to bind up the broken-heart, to give sight to the blind, to set at liberty them that are bruised, and to proclaim the acceptable year of the Lord. My soul, dost thou know Jesus in this tender and affectionate office? Hath he examined thy case, made thee sensible of thy disease; and art thou, through his mercy, restored to health? Though, through shame and fear at the first, you would never have made known your case to him, had he not first, of his own free accord, called upon you, yet hath he done so? Have you heard him ask the tender question, "Wilt thou be made whole?" And have you rejoiced to come under his care? Do you know what it is to have his blood applied to heal the wounds of sin, his righteousness to cover them, his grace to refresh under them, and his name as ointment poured forth, to make a fragrancy from all uncleanness? Moreover, hath Jesus shewn to thee the freeness of his remedies, without payment, without money, and without price? And doth he do all this, and a thousand affectionate offices beside, which belong to the physician, calling himself by that endearing name, Jehovah Rhophi, I am the Lord that healeth thee? No longer let it be said, then, "Is there no balm in Gilead; no physician there?" But tell to every poor sin-sick soul, Jesus is the beloved physician, who visits the poor and the needy, and heals all manner of sickness, and all manner of disease among the people, he hath healed me.

EVENING.—"For which of you intending to build a tower, sitteth not down first, and counteth the cost?"—Luke xiv. 28.

Ponder, my soul, over this very striking similitude of thy Lord's, respecting the divine life. The figure of a builder is most aptly chosen; for the christian builder is building for eternity. And the figure of a warrior, which our Lord also joins to it, is no less so, for the battle is for life, and that life is eternal. Hast thou counted the cost? Hast thou entered upon the work? Is the foundation-stone, which God hath laid in Zion, the rock on which thou art building? Pause and examine. Be the cost what it may; the loss of earthly friends; the parting with every worldly pursuit; the scorn, contempt, and derision of all mankind; yea, the loss of life itself: if these come in the way of competition, art thou ready to give them all up?—When thou hast answered these inquiries, go on, and see that thy foundation be really fixed on Christ. If so, it must have been previously sought for, by digging deep into the natural state in which thou wast born. Jesus must have been first discovered, as most essentially necessary, and most essentially precious, before the spiritual building of the soul was made to rest upon him. And, when found, unless the whole of the building rest entirely upon him, it will, as a column out of its centre, still totter. Oh! it is blessed to make Christ the all in all of the spiritual temple; blessed to make him the first in point of order; blessed to make him the first in point of strength, to support and bear the weight of the whole building; blessed to make him the grand cement, to unite and keep together, in one harmonious proportion and regularity, every part of the building; and blessed to bring forth the top-stone of the building, by his strength and glory, crying, " Grace, grace unto it." Precious Jesus! may it be found that I have so sat down, counted the cost, and formed my whole plan, in thy strength, and to thy praise; that whatever oppositions, like the Tobiahs and Sanballats of old, I may meet with in the work, I may feel the sweetness and encouragement of that blessed scripture, and exult with the prophet: " Who art thou, O great mountain? Before Zerubbabel thou shalt become a plain!" Zech. iv. 7.

AUGUST 24.

MORNING.—" God, according to his promise, hath raised unto Israel a Saviour, Jesus."—Acts xiii. 23.

Mark, my soul, the blessėdness of these words. Jesus is not only Israel's Saviour, and hath fully answered, in every point, to that glorious character, but here we are led to discover his credentials. This is faith's warrant. I believe in Jesus. Why? He brings with him the name, the authority, the commission of God the Father. Jesus is the appointment, the ordinance, the method Jehovah hath sent forth for salvation. Sweet thought! So that, added to all that I behold in the Lord Jesus, adapted to my case and circumstances, I here see that Jesus as the Father's gift, the Father's sent, the Father's anointed, full of grace and truth. Jesus is therefore the great promise of the bible; for in him are folded up and contained all the promises. And I see also, that God our Father was, and is, the great promiser. And I see that God not only gave this rich Soviour to poor sinners, but, according to his promise, raised him up also from the dead, when he had made his soul an offering for sin, to bless them: for it is said, "that he was delivered for our offences, and raised again for our justification. "My soul, pause over this blessed account, and look for thine own interest in it. If God hath raised up to Israel this Saviour, what knowest thou of him? Has thou felt thy need of a Saviour? Dost thou accept the Father's Saviour? Is Jesus thy Saviour? Art thou come to him for salvation? Now God the Father hath raised him up, doth he appear to thee in all his beauties, fulness, suitableness, and complete salvation?

EVENING.—"And God said, ask what I shall give thee?"—1 Kings iii. 5.

My honoured Lord! may I not, with all humbleness of soul, apply what was here said to Solomon, in the old testament dispensation, as said to all thy redeemed under the new testament grace? Didst thou not say, Lord! "whatsoever ye shall ask the Father in my name, he will give it you. Hitherto ye have asked nothing in my name; ask and ye shall receive, that your joy may be full?" John xvi. 23, 24. I feel encouraged by this saying of my Lord; and I am come up, this evening, to my Lord, to get large supplies of grace, mercy, pardon, peace; yea, Christ himself, with all his gifts, with all his fulness, and all his blessings. And sure I am, if my Lord will give me as large a hand to receive, as my Lord's hand is to give, I shall have a blessed time of it this evening. My soul, look to it, that thou take with thee all thy wants; yea, come as empty as the poorest beggar that ever appeared in the poverty and wretchedness of a fallen nature; for he that gives, "gives liberally, and upbraideth not." And knowest thou what thy wants are; and what the wants of Christ's church upon earth are, and thine household, thy family, thy children, thy friends? Let them tell thee, if thou dost not know; for say unto them, Jesus is upon the throne, and delighting to give out of his inexhaustible fulness; and there is an assurance of blessings, if asked in faith. Tell them that thou wilt faithfully lay their cases before him; yea, bring them with thee, and let all unite in prayer and supplication together, that every want may be supplied, and every poor sinner's heart made glad! Oh! what encouragement it is to consider, that every thing in Christ is for his people, and that he waits to be gracious, and delights in imparting blessings. The Father's gift of Christ is to this express purpose; for he so loved the world, as to give his only begotten Son; and therefore, with him, "he will freely give all things." And Jesus, who gave himself *for* his people, will surely give every thing that can be needed *to* his people. And it is the glory, grace, and love of the Holy Ghost, to give to the people views and enjoyments of both the Father's love and the Son's grace. Hear then, my soul, the voice from the mercy-seat, this evening, "ask what I shall give thee?" And see that thy petition, and the blessings thou prayest for, be great and large, suited to the glory of the great Giver, and the largeness and tenderness of the Lord's heart. And do mark this down, as an encouragement to take with thee, of the assurance of thy success: if he that bids thee ask, gives thee faith at the same time to believe; and if, while the Lord is stretching forth the sceptre of his grace, he enables thee to stretch forth thy withered hand to touch it; sure I am, that thou wilt not come empty away; for he hath said, "all things that ye ask believing, ye shall receive."

AUGUST 25.

MORNING.—"His servants shall serve him. And they shall see his face; and his name shall be in their foreheads."—Rev. xxii. 3, 4.

Mark these characters, my soul. Jesus hath servants, and they are distinguished from the world. They "serve him." What is it to serve Christ? The prophet hath described. Free grace hath made them servants, in bringing them from the bondage of corruption into the glorious liberty of the sons of God; and therefore he saith, in the Lord's name, " My servants shall eat, but ye shall be hungry; my servants shall drink, but ye shall be thirsty; my servants shall rejoice, but ye shall be ashamed; my servants shall sing for joy of heart, but ye shall cry for sorrow of heart." How distinguishing these characters! God's servants have the table of Jesus to sit down to; the bread of life, the bread of God, the living bread, which is Jesus himself, to feed upon. They shall drink also; for he that is their living bread is their living water also—even the water of life, of which whosoever drinketh shall thirst no more; " but it shall be in him a well of water, springing up into everlasting life." The servants of the Lord shall rejoice, and sing for joy of heart also. Yes, " the kingdom of God is not meat and drink, but righteousnes, and peace, and joy in the Holy Ghost." Neither is this all. The servants of the Lord shall " see his face." They do now, by faith in his word, in his ordinances, in his manifestations, visits, grace, providences. And, by and by, when this vail of covering, cast over all people, is totally taken down and removed at death, they shall have a glorious view of the King in his beauty by sight. Moreover, his name is said to be " in their foreheads." Yes, it is so; the image of Christ is impressed upon them, as " Holiness to the Lord" was engraven on the mitre of Aaron. " Beholding as in a glass, the glory of the Lord, they are changed into the same image from glory to glory, even as by the Spirit of the Lord." My soul, what sayest thou to these evidences? Are they thine? Canst thou take the comfort of them to thyself.

EVENING.—" And on the sabbath we went out of the city by a river-side, where prayer was wont to be made."—Acts xvi. 13.

What, had they no church, no synagogue, no prayer-house, in the city? Was it like another Athens, wholly given to idolatry? My soul, think of thy privileges, and learn rightly to prize them, and use them to the glory of the great Giver. It was "on the sabbath." What a mercy to poor fallen man is the sabbath? And yet what multitudes slight, despise, and never profit by it! My soul! think again, in this view also, of thy mercies; and bow down to the dust in the deepest humiliation of soul and body, that the sabbath is precious to thee. "Who made thee to differ from another?" By and by thou wilt enter into the everlasting sabbath of heaven. There is somewhat very interesting in what the apostle here saith of going out "by a river side." Probably it was in the recollection of the church, that in Babylon, where the people were captives, the Lord made the river Chebar famous for visions to one prophet, and Hiddekel to another. But, blessed be God! though our land is so sinful, we are not given up to captivity; and while many of the nations around have their churches turned into stables, amidst the din and horrors of war, our candlestick is not yet removed out of its place. Precious Jesus! wherever prayer is wont to be made by thy people, let my soul delight to be found. Let me hear thy voice inviting to communion: "Come with me from Lebanon, my spouse, with me from Lebanon." Yea, Lord, I would follow the Lamb whithersoever he goeth. I would follow thee to the assemblies of thy people. I would wait to see the goings of my God and King in his sanctuary. I would have my whole soul athirst for thee, as the hart for the cooling streams. And while I join thy people in the great congregation, where prayer is wont to be made, I pray thy grace, and the influences of thy blessed Spirit, to fire my soul with foretastes of that glorious assembly, which are keeping an eternal sabbath above, where the everlasting praises of God and of the Lamb will engage and fill my raptured soul with joy unspeakable and full of glory to all eternity.

AUGUST 26.

MORNING.—"The God of our fathers hath glorified his Son Jesus." —Acts iii. 13.

See, my soul, how every part and portion of scripture is directed to this one subject—to glorify the Lord Jesus. What is the very design of redemption but to glorify the Lord Jesus? What hath God constituted a church for, but to glorify the Lord Jesus? To what do all the precepts, promises, ordinances, sacrifices under the law, and institutions under the gospel, minister, but to this one end—to glorify the Lord Jesus? Talk they of promises? Why, all the promises of God are "in Christ Jesus, yea and amen, to the glory of God the Father by us." Talk they of the law? "Christ is the end of the law for righteousness to every one that believeth." Talk they of commandments? "This is the commandment, that ye believe in the name of the only begotten Son of God; and that believing, ye might have life through his name." And how hath the God of our fathers glorified his Son Jesus, in giving him as a covenant to the people. Hath he not constituted him the glorious Head, the Mediator, the Husband, the Lord, the Prophet, the Priest, the King of his people? How hath he glorified him in his person, offices, characters, relations! How hath he carried him through all the parts of redemption, in his incarnation, ministry, miracles, obedience, life, death, resurrection, ascension; and in all his triumphs over sin and Satan, death, hell, and the grave. And having constituted him the universal and eternal Lord of all, commands that "every knee should bow before him, and every tongue confess that Jesus Christ is Lord, to the glory of God the Father!" And is there any thing left, by which the God of our fathers might manifest that he hath glorified his Son Jesus? Yes, there is one thing more, my soul, by which the wonderful grace is shewn; and that is, when the God of our fathers hath glorified his Son Jesus in the heart of every poor sinner, who gives the glory of his salvation fully, heartily, completely to him, and puts the crown of redemption upon the head of Jesus. My soul, hast thou done this? Hast thou glorified Jesus in this way, the only way in which thou canst glorify him, and the Father in him? Then, if so, what a sweet thought is it, that the God of our fathers, and thou, a poor sinner, are both agreed in this one blessed work, to glorify Jesus. And here both meet in the only possible meeting-place for an holy God and unholy men to meet; and both are engaged in one and the same deed—to glorify Jesus! Oh thou Lamb of God, be thou eternally glorified in my salvation!

EVENING.—"And all king Solomon's drinking-vessels were of gold, and all the vessels of the house of the forest of Lebanon were of pure gold, none were of silver; it was nothing accounted of in the days of Solomon."—1 Kings x. 21.

Behold, my soul! the splendour of Solomon, and figure to thyself what a court and people his must have been, with whom silver was as nothing; and then turn thy thoughts to Jesus, and ask thyself, whether it be possible to suppose that he, with whom are hid all "the treasures of wisdom and knowledge," can be otherwise than rich himself, and abundantly gracious to enrich his people? Thy Solomon, thy Jesus, hath all things, and all things richly to dispense. He is the universal Lord and proprietor of all. In him dwelleth all fulness; "yea, durable riches and righteousness." And what endears Jesus, and marks the superiority of his kingdom is, that every thing in it is everlasting. Solomon's splendour was great, but it was limited to the period of his life; yea, less than life. But Jesus is everlasting; the riches and the blessings he hath, and which he gives, are everlasting. Jesus maketh both gold and silver, yea, the riches of grace and wisdom, as the stones of the street for abundance; and their blessedness is, like him, eternal. So that here we find an eternity of blessings. All beside is hollow, transitory, fading. But with Jesus it is solid and substantial. "I will cause them," he saith, "that love me to inherit substance, and I will fill their treasure." Precious Lord! may I never contemplate earthly pageantry, without taking into the view thy glory; and while I behold human grandeur, however splendid, or however shining, which is but for the day, may my soul hasten to the consideration of thy glory, which is a portion for thy redeemed to live upon to all eternity!

AUGUST 27.

MORNING.—"I have exalted one chosen out of the people."—Ps. lxxxix. 19.

My soul, wert thou refreshed on the past day with the precious meditation of the God of our fathers glorifying his Son Jesus? Suffer not, then, the blessed subject to pass away from thy thoughts this day, or any day, but look at the same delightful meditation proposed in the words which God spake to his Holy One in vision—"I have exalted one chosen out of the people." Yes, the Lord Jesus, as man and Mediator, was chosen in the infinite mind of Jehovah, Father, Son, and Holy Ghost, from everlasting. And before that God went forth in the immediate acts of creation, when that vast mass of beings the Lord determined to call into existence arose in his own infinite mind at his command, this blessed one, this glorious, this distinguished, this precious individual which was to become one with the uncreated Word, in order to constitute the Wisdom-man, Mediator, was from everlasting chosen. This was the glorious act—this was the great appointment. Then Christ Jesus, our glorious Head, our Surety, Redeemer, Saviour, was then set up from everlasting! And my soul, hadst thou been present, had there been a possibility of such a thing, had the whole church been there, would not every heart, every soul of his redeemed, have shouted aloud in the contemplation of such a Saviour, and cried out, "He is the altogether lovely, the chiefest among ten thousand!" Precious Jesus, thou art indeed lovely in thyself, lovely in thy cross, lovely in thy crown, lovely in all thy gracious acts, victories, triumphs, grace, and mercy. Every thing in thee is lovely; and thou communicatest loveliness to all thy people. Thou hast chosen our inheritance for us; reign and rule over us, and in us; for thou art "The Lord our righteousness."

EVENING.—"Then will I sprinkle clean water upon you, and ye shall be clean; from all your filthiness, and from all your idols, will I cleanse you."—Ezek. xxxvi. 25.

Was there ever a more precious scripture? And was there ever a poor sinner needed it more than thou, my soul? And what a thousand beauties are contained in it? Who is the great promiser, but the Lord Jehovah, the Father of mercies, and the God of all consolation? And what is the clean water here spoken of, but the blood of Christ? Christ, with all his redemption, all his fulness, all his suitableness, and his all-sufficiency? And what doth this sweet promise imply? Every thing, in one, is folded up in it. It is all of God; all in himself, and all to be wrought by himself. He provides the clean water; he cleanseth the sinners; he sprinkles, he applies, he promiseth the sure efficacy; for they "shall be clean;" and he makes the blessings most comprehensive, and full, and complete; for it shall be a cleansing from *all* their filthiness, and from *all* their idols. See then, my soul, what a portion thou hast here found, in the word of God's grace, for thine evening's meditation! Evening, did I say? yea, for the meditation of thy whole life, and to form the foundation of a song of praise to all eternity!

Here is every thing in it thou canst possibly need, to encourage thee to come for cleansing, under all thy pollutions, in thy daily walk through life. Here is God the Father fully engaged, and as fully promising. Here is Jesus, in his blood of sprinkling, as the Father's gift for cleansing, in all his divine offices and suited mercy. And here is the purity wrought by the Holy Ghost, in his gracious application of the whole; and which he doth most graciously and most fully testify, when he shews thee thy need, and the suitableness of Jesus, and inclines thee to believe the efficacy of this blood of Christ to cleanse from all sin. Now, my soul, muse over the blessedness and fulness of this sweet scripture, and see how suited it is, in every point, to thy wants, and to thy Lord's glory. And when thou hast gathered from it, like the bee from the flower, all the honey it contains, take it home to thy inmost affections, as the bee doth what he gathers to the hive, and live upon it for thy daily food. The promise is absolute; for God saith, "I will do it." And the certainty of its effect is as fixed; for God saith, "Ye shall be clean." And the extent of it is as sure; for God saith, "From all your filthiness, and from all your idols, will I cleanse you." My soul, ask the most daring heart of unbelief, what shall arise to unsay what God hath said, or to counteract what God hath promised?

AUGUST 28.

MORNING.—"The creditor is come to take unto him my two sons to be bondmen."—2 Kings iv. 1.

My soul, how doth this affect thee? Art thou in debt? By nature and by practice thou wast miserably so, unless the debt be cancelled. As a creature, and as a sinful creature, thou art in thyself for ever insolvent. Thou hast nothing to pay, and art shut up in a total impossibility ever to pay. And how much owest thou unto my Lord? Alas, my soul, thou owest millions of debts to thy Almighty Creditor. The law thou hast broken; justice demands retribution; conscience condemns; Satan accuses; and the creditor is come to take not thy two sons only, but both thy two parts, soul and body, to the prison of death and hell, unless some almighty Surety hath stept in and paid the dreadful debt, that thou mayest be free. At death, and at judgment that follows, the everlasting release, or the everlasting imprisonment, will take place. And who knows whether the decision may not be to-morrow? nay, whether the same sentence as went forth to the rich man in the gospel, is not already gone forth concerning thee—"This night thy soul shall be required of thee!" Pause, my soul! Is it not high time to flee to the prophet, even the Prince of the prophets, the Lord Jesus, to tell him thy case, and to seek his deliverance? Hark, doth he say, as the prophet did to the poor woman, "What shall I do for thee? Tell me what hast thou in the house?" Is not Jesus with thee? Is not his fulness suited to thy emptiness? Hast thou him with thee in the house? Shut then the door; bring, bring, my soul, all thy empty vessels—Jesus will fill them all. Nor will his bounty stay until that all thy vessels be filled; nay, every vessel will fail, before that his grace fails. And when thou art full of Jesus, live on Jesus, and see that Jesus hath paid thy Almighty Creditor, and left enough for thee to live on for ever. Oh the rapture and the joy, when the Almighty Creditor comes, at midnight, or at cock-crowing, or in the morning, to know the dreadful debt is paid, and to hear him say, "Deliver him from going down into the pit; I have found a ransom."

EVENING.—"The word which ye hear is not mine, but the Father's which sent me."—John xiv. 24.

My soul, hast thou ever fully and thoroughly considered that sweet and precious teaching of thy Lord, which, as Mediator, when upon earth, in all his discourses and conversations with his disciples, he was perpetually shewing them? I mean, that all he was, and all he had, and all he dispensed, were the blessings and gifts of his Father, in him, to his people. If thou hast been meditating upon this most blessed point of the gospel ever so fully and closely, it will still afford new glories for every renewed attention to it; and therefore, sit down this delightful summer's evening, and take another view of it. Jesus comes to his people in his Father's name, and he saith in this charming scripture, that his very words are not his, but the Father's; so much of the heart of the Father is in Christ, and in all of Christ, in all he saith, and in all he hath done. So that what is Jesus doing, in all his ministry upon earth, yea, in all his sovereignty now in heaven, but shewing to his redeemed, the Father, and the Father's love, and grace, and mercy, towards his people in him? Did he not then come forth from the bosom of the Father full of grace and truth, as if to unfold to us what passed in the heart of the Father, of love and mercy towards his people, in the wonders of redemption? And is not Jesus now, in every renewed manifestation, teaching his redeemed the same? If all that the Father hath are our Jesus's, and all the fulness of the Godhead bodily dwelleth in him; surely we ought never to receive any of his good and blessed gifts without acknowledging the Father's love in them. And would not this make every blessing doubly sweet and increasingly precious? If Jesus himself be the gift of the Father, shall I not enjoy the Father in all that Jesus bestows? And as I can have no immediate communion with the Father but by him, will not the mercies gather a blessedness, and a value, in coming to my poor soul through Jesus's hands, as the bountiful dispenser of them? Yea, shall I not find a savour, which otherwise could never have been known, in receiving them in and from Jesus; convinced, as I am, that none cometh to the Father, but by him; and but for his opening a new and living way by his blood, never should I have known the Father's love, or the Redeemer's grace? Dear Lord Jesus! do thou give me, by thy blessed Spirit, ever to keep in remembrance these most precious things. So shall I truly enjoy both thy person and thy gifts. And then I shall not, like the apostle, pray for a sight of the Father distinct from thee; for I shall then be perfectly satisfied and convinced, that in seeing thee, I see the Father also; and from henceforth, that I know him, and have seen him. " Thanks be unto God for his unspeakable gift."

AUGUST 29.

MORNING.—" Have I been so long time with you, and yet hast thou not known me?"—John xiv. 9.

Pause, my soul, over this question of the Lord Jesus which he put to Philip—figure to thyself that the Lord saith the same to thee; and now see what answer thou wilt give him. It is a great question: and if thou art able to answer it with a —" Yea, Lord;" and from the blessed Spirit's teaching thou truly knowest Jesus to be what the scripture saith he is, and canst as truly, from the receiving that testimony which God hath given of his dear and ever-blessed Son, set to thy seal that God is true; then art thou truly happy, and mayest humbly take to thyself a portion in that blessedness which the Lord Jesus pronounced upon Peter, from the same grace manifested: " Flesh and blood hath not revealed it unto thee, but my Father which is in heaven." Pause then, and inquire: dost thou know who Christ is? Art thou perfectly satisfied, my soul, of the oneness in nature, in essence, in glory, in will, in worship, in work, in design, in attributes, perfections, power, sovereignty; in short, in all and every thing which constitutes the Godhead between the Father, and the Son, and the Spirit? Oh yes, my soul cries out, I do, through the teaching of my God, most firmly, heartily, and cordially believe, that Jesus is one with the Father over all, God blessed for ever! Amen. Pause again, my soul, and say, dost thou as firmly and heartily believe that thy Jesus, who, in the divine nature, is one with the Father, is no less in the human nature, which he united to the Godhead for the purposes of salvation, one with thee, bone of thy bone, and flesh of thy flesh? Doth this make an equal article in thy creed? Oh yes, I am, through the same divine teaching, as fully and perfectly convinced that he who is and was, and ever will be, the uncreated Word, was made flesh, and thereby became the true Immanuel, God with us, God in our nature. Pause, once more, my soul, and say, dost thou believe that, by this union of God and man, Jesus became the true, the only, the blessed Mediator, the Christ of God, the Sent of God, the Sealed of God, the Anointed of God, the Lamb of God, the Word of God, the Wisdom of God, and the power of God for salvation to every one that believeth? Bow down, my soul, with unceasing thanksgivings and praise to the Author and Giver of faith, for the stupendous discoveries he hath made to thee of himself, while thou criest out in transports of rejoicing — Lord, all this I believe; and am perfectly satisfied that thou art one with the Father, and art in the Father, and the Father in thee. And while thou thus givest in thy testimony of the Lord Jesus, wilt thou not, my soul, at the same time, under a conscious sense of the distinguishing mercy, cry out also with the astonished disciple—"Lord, how is it that thou hast thus manifested thyself unto me, and not unto the world."

EVENING.—" Thus saith the Lord, the Holy One of Israel, and his Maker, ask me of things to come concerning my sons, and concerning the work of my hands command ye me."—Isa. xlv. 11.

Nothing can give a higher proof of the love of God, than what the scriptures reveal concerning him. He opened a way of access to himself, when man by sin had lost the way; and in his dear Son he has made every provision for bringing us nigh by his blood. The throne of grace he hath opened for their approach; the assurance he hath given of accepting them in the beloved; the very tender and kind expressions which issue from the throne; and the answers which have been given to thousands, and are continually given to thousands who come there; yea, the promises with which they are surrounded, that " before they call, he will answer, and while they are speaking, he will hear:" all these are full of endearments, to shew forth the love of God in Jesus Christ to all his people. But still, if possible, beyond all these, this portion from the writings of the prophet is most wonderful, and is confirmed by Jehovah's own saying, " Ask me of things to come concerning my sons, and concerning the work of my hands command ye me." What! doth the Lord indeed allow himself to be commanded? Hath he thrown, as it were, the reins of government into the hands of his people; and, if the object of their petition be for his glory and their welfare, may they command him? My soul! what an astonishing, what an unparalleled instance of condescension is this!—But are there any instances upon record of the kind? Yes! When Jacob wrestled with God in prayer, he boldly told the Lord, that he would not let him go without a blessing: and the blessing he had. And God himself, a thousand years after, noted it down by the prophet, that " by his strength, he had power with God," Gen. xxxii. 26, 28. Hosea xii. 3, 4. When Joshua was pursuing the enemies of God, and of his Christ, he bade the sun stand still; and it did so; Joshua x. 12—14. When the Lord Jesus went with the disciples to Emmaus, and they constrained him to abide, he was entreated of them, and went in with them; Luke xxiv. 29. And who shall say, what instances of wonder, grace, and love, in a thousand and ten thousand cases, both public and private, in the history of the church and the Lord's people, have been accomplished, of the same kind, and are every day going on in their experiences? My soul! look at Moses, stopping the Lord's hand, when coming forth to destroy Israel; Exod. xxxii. 9—14. Look how Elias shut up, and again opened, the windows of heaven, by the prevalency of prayer; and read the apostle's comment upon it; 1 Kings xvii. 1. James v. 16—18. And when thou hast duly pondered the wonderful subject, say, what is there thy God and Father can or will deny thee, when thou comest to him in the name, and blood, and intercession of his dear and ever blessed Son? Read the inscription on his cross, in connection with this blessed scripture of the prophet, and then say, with the apostle: "He that spared not his own Son, but delivered him up for us all, how shall he not with him freely give us all things?" Romans viii. 32.

AUGUST 30.

MORNING.—"And thou shalt remember that thou wast a bondman in the land of Egypt, and the Lord thy God redeemed thee."—Deut. xv. 15.

Say, my soul, canst thou ever forget the wormwood and the gall of that state of nature, from which the Lord thy God brought thee? Figure to thyself the most horrid state of captivity which the world ever knew; and what could the whole be, bounded, as it must be, by the short period of human life, compared to the everlasting vassalage of sin and Satan, in which thou didst lay when Jesus passed by and brought thee out? No galley-slave, chained to the oar, could equal thy misery, bound with the chain of sin. No duration of misery, bounded by time, equals that endless state of woe to which thou wast exposed. Thou wert a bondman to the power of sin, to the love of sin, to the desire of sin, to the punishment of sin; a bondman to the law of God, to the justice of God, to the displeasure of God, to the threatenings of God; a bondman to thine own guilty conscience; a bondman to thine own corrupt lusts, not one lust, but many, serving, as the apostle saith, "divers lusts and pleasures, hateful, and hating one another;" a bondman to Satan, a willing drudge, wearing his livery, delighted in his service, though full of sorrow, vexation, and disappointment, and his wages sure death; a bondman to the fear of many creatures among the inferior creation, many of whom had continual power to vex and distress thee; a bondman to the fear of death, hell, and a judgment to come! Was this thy state, my soul, by nature and by practice? And hath one like the Son of Man brought thee out? Precious Jesus, what shall I say *to* thee, what shall I say *for* thee? What shall I render to the Lord for all the mercies he hath done to me, and for me? And dost thou say, Lord, that I may remember that bondage and thy redemption! Oh may my tongue cleave to the roof of my mouth, if I forget thee, thou Author of all my joy, and all my happiness! Nay, if I do not remember thee, and prefer thy love more than wine. In life, in death, and to all eternity, may my soul hang upon thee, as the bee upon the flower; and let the fragrancy of thy name be as ointment poured forth.

EVENING.—"Return, return, O Shulamite, return, return, that we may look upon thee. What will ye see in the Shulamite? As it were the company of two armies."—Song vi. 13.

It is the church that is here called upon to return, and most likely by the daughters of Jerusalem. Some have thought the church is so called, as being of Salem, or Shulem, the shortened word for Jeru-salem. And some have thought that Salem is the same with Solomon, as the feminine of Solomon, the wife. And others have supposed, that as Jerusalem means peace, the church is called so, on account of her loveliness. And no doubt, in each sense, the church may well be called so, being married to Christ; being of the "Jerusalem that is above, which is the mother of us all;" and being beautiful, peaceful, and lovely in Jesus, as Jerusalem is the praise of the whole earth, Psalm xlviii. 2. But wherefore is the Shulamite called upon to return, to be looked upon, and with such earnestness, as to cause the request to be so often repeated? The answer is very plain. If it be the inquiry immediately on a soul's conversion, the change from death to life, from sin to salvation, is so great, that every one may be supposed anxious to behold. If it be the return of the poor believer, after a state of backsliding, the blushing face of a poor soul might also be well considered as a grateful sight to all that love to behold the blessed fruits of the Holy Ghost. And if it be in the after-stages of a life of grace, when a believer, from long knowing Jesus, and long living upon him, is become most beautiful and comely in his profession, no object upon earth can be an equal object of delight, or more worthy universal attention. So that in either sense, the earnest and repeated call for her return, to be looked upon, may be well accounted for. And the church's answer is equally engaging. What would you see in me? As if she had said, "In my best and highest attainment, I am but a poor creature in myself. All my beauty is derived from Jesus. I am indeed comely in him; and he is my glory, and the lifter-up of my head. But in myself I am no other but as one contending with two armies. I feel corruption rising continually against grace; and "when I would do good, evil is present with me."' My soul! is not this thy very state? Art thou not perpetually exercised in this struggle? Precious Lord Jesus! let this view of thy church comfort me in a consciousness of a family likeness. And Oh, Lord! while I thus groan under the remains of indwelling corruption, give me to see that they are but *remains*. Jesus will at length, and by little and little, drive these Canaanites out of the land.

AUGUST 31.

MORNING.—" One thing I know, that, whereas I was blind, now I see."—John ix. 25.

This is a great thing to say, my soul: on what foundation dost thou rest this knowledge? If the Lord Jesus hath opened thine eyes, then indeed thou canst not but discover thy former blindness; for during that state of nature thou literally couldst discern nothing. And if thy former blindness be discovered, then thy present sight hath brought thee acquainted with new objects. Pause over the review of both this morning. The blindness of nature to spiritual things is marked in scripture in strong characters. A poor blind sinner sees nothing of the light of life. The Sun of Righteousness is not risen upon him. He discerns nothing of the love of God in Christ. If he reads the scripture, the vail is upon his heart. If he hears of Jesus, he sees no beauty in him. Nothing is nearer to him than the Lord, and nothing further from his thoughts. To tell him of the sweetness of the word of God, is strange to him; for he tastes nothing of sweetness in it. To tell him of the loveliness of ordinances and the sabbaths; these are strange things in his esteem. My soul, if indeed thine eyes be opened, thou wilt know that thou wast once indeed blind, in the fullest sense of the word, to all these delightful views of sacred things, which now are thy supreme pleasure and thy joy. Say, then, what hast thou seen to justify this saying: "One thing I know, that, whereas I was blind, now I see?" Hast thou seen the king in his beauty? Hast thou seen with the eye of faith the glories of Jesus? Yes, if so be all other objects are obscured. The sight of Jesus, as the Christ of God, hath darkened the glory and excellency of all beside, Jesus, as he is in himself, as he is in his offices, characters, relations; as he is to thee and thy happiness; is the one, the only one thing needful; and thou must count all things but dung and dross to win Christ. These, my soul, are blessed tokens that Jesus hath opened thine eyes, and brought thee out of darkness into his marvellous light. By and by thou shalt see him as he is, and dwell with him for ever.

EVENING.—"O Lord, what shall I say, when Israel turneth their backs before their enemies? For the Canaanites, and all the inhabitants of the land shall hear of it, and shall environ us round, and cut off our name from the earth: and what wilt thou do unto thy great name?"—Joshua vii. 8, 9.

My soul, learn a most blessed lesson here, such as will be an unanswerable argument for thee at all times, and upon all occasions, to make use of at a mercy-seat, and among the strongest pleas in prayer. Israel had sinned, and had fallen before the enemy in consequence of it. Joshua confesseth that all that was come upon Israel was just, and had that been all the event included in Israel's destruction, it would have been no more than what was right. But God had promised to bring Israel into Canaan; and therefore the honour of God was concerned that this should be accomplished. Now, saith Joshua, if for our sins thou sufferest us to fall before our enemies, what will the nations of the earth say of it? How will the promise be fulfilled, and thy faithfulness and honour be secured? "O Lord, what shall I say? What wilt thou do unto thy great name?" Pause, my soul, and apply the sweet truth. God will magnify his name above all his word. He saith himself,

" I wrought for my name's sake, that the land should not be polluted before the heathen, in whose sight they dwelt." And the Lord repeats it three times, to the same purpose, in one chapter, Ezek. xx. 9, 14, 22. Now, my soul, under all thy straights and difficulties, do thou adopt the plan of Joshua, and be assured that this is the great argument to ensure success. His name is engaged *in* and *to* Jesus, to give him to see the travail of his soul, now he hath made his soul an offering for sin, and to be satisfied. Hence, therefore, the name of Jehovah is pledged to this. " Once have I sworn," he saith, " by my holiness, that I will not lie unto David;" Psalm lxxxix. 35. Every believer in Christ should be for ever pleading this in the blood and righteousness of Jesus. Dost thou want pardon? Ask it for his name's sake. Dost thou want grace? Here again let the Lord's name's sake be the plea. To interest the name of the Lord in every petition, is the sure way to obtain it. To plead duties, or ordinances, or, in short, any thing but Jesus, and God the Father's covenant engagements to Jesus, is to go off the ground. No reason, or shadow of a reason can be found, but God's own name, and this engaged in a way of redemption by Jesus, wherefore the Lord should be merciful to pardon and bless a poor sinner. Do not forget this, but for ever plead with the Lord for his name's sake, and for his glory in Christ; and the event will surely be that Jehovah must work, and, as he hath said himself, have pity for his holy name, " that it be not profaned among the heathen:" and answer thy petition for grace. And Oh! how blessed that scripture in which the Lord sums up and confirms the whole, on this one account: " Not for your sakes do I this, saith the Lord God, be it known unto you: be ashamed, and confounded for your own ways, O house of Israel;" Ezekiel xxxvi. 22, 32.

SEPTEMBER 1.

MORNING.—" And his name, through faith in his name, hath made this man strong."—Acts iii. 16.

My soul, begin this month as the Lord in mercy hath enabled thee to begin some that are past, in taking the name of Jesus for thy theme. Let his name be as ointment poured forth, whose fragrancy shall make thee strong, as it made the poor man whole. And as the Lord hath opened a new month to thee in grace, do thou take up his name, through faith in his name, in praise and prayer. And see to it, my soul, that through the month, and indeed the whole of life, improve his name in every case, in every want, in every need. Depend upon it, his name will answer all. Whatever thy necessities are, in Jesus's name there is a supply for all. Art thou poor, he is rich: sick, he is thy health; weak, he is strong; sinful, he is the Lord thy righteousness. Every thing, and in every way, upon all accounts, and upon all occasions—his name, through faith in his name, is the universal charm, the everlasting remedy, supply, comfort, strength of all. Jesus hath every thing, and all things; and he hath them all for his people. Oh then, my soul, look to Him and his name, for the suited grace in every time of need! He will, as the Psalmist sweetly reasons—he will, nevertheless, (notwithstanding all thy undeservings, this *nevertheless* is still in the covenant,) he will save for his name's sake, that he might make his mighty power to be known.

EVENING.—" Say not ye, there are yet four months, and then cometh harvest? Behold, I say unto you, lift up your eyes, and look on the fields; for they are white already to harvest."—John iv. 35.

My soul, the month hath opened most graciously; the season of the year is very interesting; all the reapers of the fruits of the earth are now busy in the fields to gather in the food that perisheth. Oh! let it never be said of thee, "The harvest is past, the summer is ended, and thou art not saved!" Jerem. viii. 20. Pause, my soul, over the sweet words of Jesus, in the evening and cool of the day, and consider their import. As in nature there is a seed time and harvest, so is there in grace. And we are told, that the Lord hath given "the appointed weeks of harvest." At what season dost thou now stand? Surely, thou art advanced to the time of ripening. How wilt thou discover this? Is there not a similarity here also between nature and grace? As the ripened corn becomes more full and ponderous, and golden and weighty, and, in proportion to ripeness, bends nearer to the earth; so the child of God, the better he is prepared for the garner of heaven, the more is he filled with spiritual attainments; becoming lower in his own eyes, and Jesus increasingly precious and exalted. And when the Lord gives the signal for his harvest-time, he cometh to the grave "like a shock of corn in full season." Precious Lord of the harvest! I beseech thee, carry on thy work in my heart, and let thy kingdom there be as thou hast described it, where the good seed is cast into the ground, and it springeth up and groweth, men know not how. Oh! prepare me for the harvest, that when, at thy command, the angel of death shall put in the sickle, I may be gathered to thy garner in heaven! Amen.

SEPTEMBER 2.

MORNING.—"The Lord, the God of Hosts, shall be with you, as ye have spoken."—Amos v. 14.

My soul, pause over this precious scripture, and ask thyself, is it indeed confirmed to thy experience? And do remark how the promise of the old testament scripture is confirmed in the new. Jesus assured the same, when he said, "If a man love me, he will keep my words; and my Father will love him, and we will come and make our abode with him." Pause, my soul, again, and see whether both testaments concurring in the same, and the Holy Ghost ever abiding with the Lord's people, to confirm his word in the heart; are not these promises thine, and art thou not everlastingly enjoying them? Precious Jesus, morning by morning would I besiege thy mercy-seat, to put thee in mind of this promise, which in this blessedness, comprehends every other. If the Lord, the God of Hosts, be with me; if the Father graciously come; if the Son himself come, both to make their abode, not as a wayfaring man that turneth in to tarry for a night, but to make their abode; and if the Holy Ghost abide with me for ever — Oh the blessedness of such a state, the glory of such company! Lord, I pray, be it unto me according to thy word.

EVENING.—" Come, my beloved, let us go forth into the field: let us lodge in the villages. Let us get up early to the vineyards, let us see if the vine flourish, whether the tender grape appear, and the pomegranates bud forth: there will I give thee my loves."—Song vii. 11, 12.

My soul! wilt thou do as the church here hath done, and invite Jesus to come with thee into retirement, to enjoy sweet fellowship and communion, and to tell him how exceedingly thou lovest him, or desirest so to do? Jesus invites thee repeatedly to this, and why shouldest not thou invite him? It is blessed to catch the gracious words of thy Lord from his mouth, and to say to him what he first saith to thee. See Isa. xxvi. 20. Song ii. 10. Matt. xi. 28. Rev. xxii. 17. And where wouldest thou have thy Lord to go with thee? Surely thou wilt say, to the field of his own scriptures, and to the villages of his own people, and to the vineyards of his own church; that Jesus may open to thee his own blessed word, and that thou mayest not barely visit, with Jesus, his people, but lie down with him, and he with thee, and arise early to visit the vineyards of his church, as the blessed place, where his honour dwelleth. And what is thy motive for this divine society with thy Lord? Is it not to take delight in Jesus, and in all that concerns him? His vine is his church, Isa. v. 7. And Oh! how refreshing is it to thee, to behold the church of Jesus flourishing in the earth? How truly blessed to behold the first dawnings of grace in young believers, which are not unlike the appearance of the tender grape; and the more confirmed faith of old saints, which the buddings of the strong fruit of the pomegranate shadow forth. Is this thy motive, and dost thou really, truly, and heartily invite thy honoured Lord to this communion? And wilt thou there shew him thy loves, and tell him how truly lovely and truly loving he is; that "his love is better than wine;" and that thou desirest to love him, who hath first loved thee; and that thou longest to see more, and to know more of that love of Jesus, "which passeth knowledge, that thou mayest be filled with all the fulness of God?" —If these be thy longings, and thou communicatest them to Jesus, he will be found of them that seek him; yea, "before thou callest, he will answer, and while thou art speaking, he will hear." And, precious blessed husband of thy church and people! may I not consider this invitation as given also by thee to thy church and to thy people, yea, to my poor soul? Methinks I hear thee saying to me, personally to me, 'Come, my beloved; come, let us go forth into the field of my word alone; let us go together also to the villages of my people, and dwell in my house and vineyards: both in private and in public will I manifest myself unto thee, and shew thee my loves.' Oh, thou bountiful Lord! thy whole heart is love. All is grace, and mercy, and kindness in Jesus; and all thou art, and all thou hast, is for thy people, thy redeemed, thy Segullah, thy chosen! Lord, give me but grace in the lively actings of faith, and my soul shall follow thee "whithersoever thou goest!"

SEPTEMBER 3.

MORNING.—" Let not the wise man glory in his wisdom, neither let the mighty man glory in his might; let not the rich man glory in his riches; but let him that glorieth glory in this, that he understandeth and knoweth me, that I am the Lord."—Jer. ix. 23, 24.

And didst thou, my poor, proud, vain, sinful heart, after so much as hath been said to thee of Jesus, and so much as thou hast been feelingly taught thy want of Jesus, didst thou need this precept? Oh yes, my soul; every day it had need be sounded in thy ears, and wrote over again by the Holy Ghost upon thine heart. Now it is, Lord Jesus, I learn from hence why thou art so suited to a poor convinced sinner. Thou, and thou only, art the Lord our righteousness: and therefore let those that know not their own worthlessness, nor thy glory, boast in what they may; let others talk of what they will, I see plain enough there s nothing out of thee for a poor soul to rejoice in. The wise men hath no wisdom, but in thee; nor the mighty man strength, nor the rich man riches, but if thou art my portion, thou art made of God to me both wisdom, righteousness, sanctification, and redemption; and then indeed I shall glory in the Lord!

EVENING.—" Hold thy peace at the presence of the Lord God: for the day of the Lord is at hand: for the Lord hath prepared a sacrifice, he hath bid his guests."—Zephan. i. 7.

My soul, here is a portion of God's word, which, like the pillar of the cloud in the camp of Israel, hath a double aspect; it becomes a cloud of trembling indeed, of darkness, dread, and fear, to all who, spiritually considered, are yet in Egyptian bondage, but a glorious refreshing light to the people of God. The presence of the Lord God is a solemn presence to all, and will command silence, yea, a trembling. " The Lord is in his holy temple; let all the earth keep silence before him."

And is the day of the Lord at hand? Yea, verily, every day brings it nearer; every breath, every pulse that beats, shortens the distance. There is, there must be, a day, in which " the Lord will judge the world in righteousness, and minister true judgment unto the people." And observe, my soul, what this blessed scripture adds: " The Lord hath prepared a sacrifice, he hath bid his guests." God hath set forth his dear Son as a propitiation, for " without shedding of blood, there is no remission." He hath bid his guests. Yes! the Lord that hath made this rich feast of salvation, hath also invited the people he will have to partake of it. He hath sent out his word, his servants, into the highways, and lanes, and hedges of the city, to call them in. And their characters are marked: they are " the poor, and the needy, and the halt, and the blind." Thousands, answering to this character, are come; have partaken of the rich feast, and called it blessed; " and yet there is room." My soul! art thou come? Hast thou accepted the invitation, and come under this character? Hast thou found it blessed? Pause over the inquiry. The reverse of this will be a cup of trembling, and astonishment, and madness, to all that reject the counsel of God against their own souls, who are too proud to accept the bidding to the feast of Jesus's blood, to cleanse them, and too rich, in their own eyes, to look for salvation in his righteousness to justify them.

SEPTEMBER 4.

MORNING.—" A just God, and a Saviour."—Isa. xlv. 21.

My soul, hast thou learnt, from the teaching of God the Holy Ghost, to contemplate him, with whom thou hast to do, under these blessed united characters? If thou hast, thou hast found it a blessed and an approved way of opening communion with God, and maintaining that communion alive in the soul. Thou knowest, then, that God, as a just God, can admit of no pardon to sin, but upon the footing of a complete satisfaction; for, without this, his truth and justice would still be violated by unatoned sin. But if thou beholdest God in Christ, reconciling the world to himself, and hast been taught by the Spirit that Christ hath redeemed thee from the curse of the law, being made a curse for thee; that, as thy surety and thy representative he hath paid thy debt, and restored that which he took not away; here thou beholdest indeed "a just God, and a Saviour," and hast learnt that precious, blessed truth, how God can be just, and the justifier of every poor sinner that believeth in Jesus. See to it then, my soul, that thou keepest this precious thought always in view. Always blend together, in all thy approaches to a mercy-seat, that thou art approaching "a just God, and a Saviour." Never lose sight of the high demands of God's righteous law; neither the perfect worth and efficacy of Jesus in his blood and righteousness: and connect always with the blessed view thine own personal interest in that obedience, by thy union with him. Then wilt thou as much delight in God's justice as his mercy; and his holiness will be as dear to thee as his love. Then wilt thou understand that blessed truth, and join issue with it in every part: "Surely shall one say, in the Lord have I righteousness and strength; even to him shall men come; and all that believe in him shall not be ashamed nor confounded, world without end."

EVENING.—"Wherefore, the king hearkened not unto the people; for the cause was from the Lord."—1 Kings xii. 15.

What a light doth this one verse throw upon the whole of this history, and upon ten thousand of a similar kind, which are perpetually going on through life! The event recorded in this chapter that the king should listen to the counsel of fools, and disregard the advice of wise men, would have appeared incredible, the thing itself being so very obvious. But when we understand the latent cause, and are told that it was "from the Lord," how strikingly doth it set forth the wonderful government of God in bringing about the sacred purposes of his holy will! My soul, sit down this evening, and ponder well the subject. Think how truly blessed it is, and how truly sanctified, to behold this almighty hand in every dispensation. And bring home the doctrine itself, for it is a very blessed one, if well studied and well followed up, to thine own concerns and circumstances. When, in any of the providential or gracious appointments of thy Jesus, thou art exercised and afflicted, what can be thy relief, but seeing the cause as from the Lord? The sin and transgression that induceth it, indeed, are all thine own. But the over-ruling of it to thy future welfare and the divine glory is the Lord's. Thus the man of Uz was grievously afflicted in every direction; but we are told that the Lord's permission was in the whole; and the sequel fully proved the Lord's design. Thus "the man after God's own heart" was cursed by Shimei, in the moment when his life was sought after by his own unnatural son; but what said David under the heavy trial?—"Let him alone, for the Lord hath bidden him." And what a gracious and sanctified improvement did he make of it, in proof that the Lord, who was smiting, was also upholding: "It may be," said he, "that the Lord will look on mine affliction, and that the Lord will requite me good for his cursing this day," 2 Sam. xvi. 5—12. My soul, behold every cause, every event, and every dispensation, as from the Lord; "He ruleth in the armies of heaven, and among the inhabitants of the earth." If he afflict his children, still they are his children; the relationship never lessens, neither is his love abated; "Whom the Lord loveth, he chasteneth, and scourgeth every son whom he receiveth." Doth he raise up bad men to persecute them? Still they are but the sword; the government of it is the Lord's. Doth Jesus speak in frowning providences, or hide himself from giving out his accustomed gracious visits of love? Still he is and must be Jesus. There is no change in him, whatever outward dispensations seem to say. He saith himself, "I know the thoughts I think towards you, thoughts of peace and not of evil, to give you an expected end," Jer. xxix. 11. Precious Lord Jesus, give me the seeing eye, and the understanding heart, to behold thy hand in all, to rest upon thy love and faithfulness in all, and to be for ever looking unto thee under all; so shall I bless thee for all; and, sure I am, the issue will be to thy glory, and my everlasting happiness.

SEPTEMBER 5.

MORNING.—" The praise of all his saints."—Ps. cxlviii. 14.

And who is this, my soul, but Jesus? Is he not indeed both the praise and the glory, the delight and the joy, the portion and the happiness of all his people? His saints, doth it say? Yes, saints, made so by his righteousness and salvation, when taken from among sinners; and when themselves sinners, he hath washed them in his blood, clothed them with his garment of salvation, and granted them an inheritance among the saints in light. And is he not their praise? Indeed, is there any other the object of their praise, to whom they look up, in whom they delight, but Him, in whom God their Father hath made them accepted in Him, the Beloved? Say then, my soul, is he not thy praise this day; and will he not be thine everlasting, unceasing praise, every day, and all the day, and through the endless day of eternity? Who shall be thy praise but Jesus; his beauty, his glory, his excellency; in whom all divine perfections centre? Who shall be thy praise but Jesus, the Mediator, the Christ of God, whose glory it is to redeem poor sinners and make them saints; to give out of his fulness, and grace for grace? Who shall be thy praise, but he that hath made thy peace, in the blood of his cross, and ever liveth to make intercession for thee? Oh thou fair and lovely one, the chiefest among ten thousand, thou art my praise, my glory, my song, my rejoicing! Every day will I praise thee; morning by morning will I hail thy name, and night by night testify thy faithfulness. Here, while upon earth, will I unceasingly speak of thy praise; and, ere long, I shall join the happy multitude above, in that song—"To him that hath loved us, and washed us from our sins in his own blood!" Oh thou that art the praise of all the saints.

EVENING.—"While the earth remaineth, seed-time and harvest, and cold and heat, and summer and winter, and day and night, shall not cease."—Gen. viii. 22.

My soul, look at this gracious covenant promise of God, which was made more than four thousand years since, and is as faithfully confirmed to thy experience this night, as in the first hour wherein the Lord delivered it. How hath the seed-time and harvest, the cold and heat, the summer and winter, and day and night, through every generation, proclaimed the unfailing truth! And although we are taught to expect, and by faith both to look and to long for the "new heavens and the new earth, wherein dwelleth righteousness;" yet is this blessed promise not less sure, or less to be depended upon, while the present earth remaineth. And do not overlook that special feature of divine faithfulness, in the fulfilment of this gracious promise; I mean that amidst all the unworthiness of man, God's bounty continues the same. Were the sun to cease its beneficial influence, or the clouds to withhold their fatness, until man deserved those blessings, the sun would rise no more, neither would the bottles of heaven pour down their fruitfulness. Sweet thought to the heart of a poor sinner! The Lord's goodness is all in himself, and from himself, and to himself for his own glory. Indeed, so abundantly gracious and compassionate is the Lord, that he very frequently takes occasion from our misery, to magnify the riches of his mercy; and "where sin hath abounded, grace doth much more abound; that as sin hath reigned unto death, even so might grace reign through righteousness unto eternal life, by Jesus Christ our Lord." There is one delightful thought more arising out of this blessed scripture, in the confirmation which the regular return of day and night gives to the faithfulness of the almighty Promiser, namely, that the Lord himself appealeth to this fulfilment of his covenant in nature, as the confirmation that he will fulfil his covenant in grace. "Thus saith the Lord, if ye can break my covenant of the day, and my covenant of the night, that there should not be day and night in their season; then also may my covenant be broken with David my servant," Jer. xxxiii. 20, 21. Oh! precious words of a gracious covenant God in Christ! Lord, I bow down before thee, under a deep sense of thy grace and love! Thou hast indeed "sworn once in thy holiness, that thou wilt not lie unto David;" even the David of thy people, thy dear and ever blessed Son! Oh! grant that, each night and morning, as well as through all the changing, but sure seasons of nature, all may be sweetly sanctified in their regular visits to my soul, while remaining on earth; that I may have a double relish and enjoyment in a sanctified use of them; and accept thy daily faithfulness in nature, as a sure pledge of thy everlasting faithfulness in grace, that "in Jesus all the seed of Israel shall be justified, and shall glory."

SEPTEMBER 6.

MORNING.—"And the Lord turned, and looked upon Peter."—Luke xxii. 61.

My soul, hath that eye that looked so graciously

upon Peter, looked graciously upon thee? Pause and determine the point by the effects. "Peter went out and wept bitterly." Hath such impressions of grace been upon thee, my soul? Hast thou wept over the recollection of sin and a ruined nature, which is continually manifesting itself in the same faithlessness and worthlessness as in the apostle? Moreover, hast thou ever looked with an eye of faith and love to Jesus? If so, it must have been wrought by this eye of Christ upon thee, my soul: for, mark it, we never look to him with an eye of faith, until Jesus hath first looked on us with an eye of love. If we love him, it is because he first loved us. Sweet testimony this, if so be thou hast it in thine experience, that he that turned and looked upon Peter, hath looked on thee also. Moreover, any thing short of this glance of Jesus's eye, is short of all to induce true repentance. Peter heard, unmoved, again and again, the crowing of the cock; just as we hear, unmoved, the warnings of God's holy word in his scriptures; until Jesus accompanied the crowing of the cock, which he had admonished the apostle concerning, with his tender and remonstrating look: then, and not before, the blessed effects were wrought. Oh precious Master! turn, I beseech thee, and look on me; and let that look enter my very soul, that I may "look on thee whom I have pierced, and mourn as one that mourneth for his only son, and be in bitterness as one that is in bitterness for his first-born." Let all my soul's affection be continually going out after the look of Jesus, until eye-strings and heart-strings break and give way; and when they close in the sleep of death, may I, with the eyes of the soul, behold thy face in righteousness, that I may be satisfied when I awake with thy likeness.

EVENING.—"Ready to be revealed in the last time."—1 Pet. i. 5.

My soul, hast thou ever considered the very great and blessed things contained in these few words? Sit down, this evening, and look them over. Dost thou ask, what is ready to be revealed in the last time? The answer is direct. All the fulness, glory, grace, provision, peace, and everlasting happiness, that are in the covenant of redemption, and all centered in the person and finished work of the Lord Jesus Christ. Thou hast now but obscure views of Jesus, and his fulness, suitableness, and all-sufficiency. Thou hast believed indeed unto salvation, and art resting upon Christ for thy justification, and sanctification, and comfort; but of the fulness in which believers stand complete in Christ, no saint upon earth hath ever had a conception equal to what it really is. "Beloved, (saith John) now are we the sons of God! and it doth not yet appear what we shall be: but we know that when he shall appear we shall be like him, for we shall see him as he is," 1 John iii. 2. Now the blessedness of these things, in all their fulness, and in all their glory, are reserved to "be revealed in the last time:" and they are now all ready. Angels are always upon the wing, and are waiting to bring the heirs of the kingdom into the immediate possession, and immediate enjoyment of them. And although clouds here rise between, to obscure those bright and glorious objects, yet the heirs of promise ought to enjoy them now by faith; for they are eternally secure, and, through the Lord of them, eternally their own. Now, my soul, what sayest thou to these things? Are they ready to be revealed in the last time? Are they thine now? Hast thou Jesus, and with him all things? Is the last time approaching? Are angels waiting? Is Jesus waiting to unfold all to thy ravished view; and every thing ready? What sayest thou, my soul? Art thou ready also? Lord Jesus! give me grace to be always on the look out for thy coming, and to be as delighted with thy approach as they that wait for the morning!

SEPTEMBER 7.

MORNING.—" For the Lord the God of Israel saith, that he hateth putting away."—Malachi ii. 16.

And well is it for thee, my soul, that he doth: for if the Lord God of Israel had dealt by thee *once*, as thou hast been dealing with him *always*, thou wouldest have been ruined for ever. But what is the cause of thy mercies? Is it not the covenant faithfulness of God thy Father, founded in his own everlasting love, engaged in his promise and his oath, to Jesus, and secured in his blood and righteousness? And is this the cause why the Lord God of Israel hateth putting away? Is this the cause why God resteth in his love? Oh for grace to see the cause, to adore the mercy; and where the Lord God of Israel rests, there, my soul, do thou rest also. See to it, my soul, that thy life of faith, and thy life of hope, are both founded in Jesus, and not in the sense thou hast of these precious things. The things are the same, how different soever, at different times, thy view of them may be. The everlasting worth, the everlasting efficacy, of Jesus's blood and righteousness, is always the same; and his people's interest in it the same, although, from the different view we have of it, at different times, it seems as if sometimes it were lost, and our own state was worse and worse. My soul, upon such occasions call to mind this sweet scripture: " The Lord God of Israel saith, that he hateth putting away." Observe, the Lord not only doth hate putting away, but he saith it, that his people may know it, and properly esteem his unchanging love. Oh to cry out under the assurance of this precious truth, and to feel the blessedness of what the Lord said by his servant the prophet: " The Lord thy God in the midst of thee is mighty: he will save: he will rejoice over thee with joy, he will rest in his love, he will joy over thee with singing."

EVENING—" For the people will not eat until he come, because he doth bless the sacrifice; and afterwards they eat that be bidden."—1 Sam. ix. 13.

I know not how scrupulous the Israelites were of not partaking of the sacrifice, until the prophet Samuel had blessed it in the name of the Lord; but well I know, no offering, under the gospel dispensation, can be profitable or blessed, until Jesus be first seen in it, and first enjoyed in it too. Surely, thou dear Lord! thou art the all in all of every thing that is sacred, blessed, and interesting. Thou art the altar, the sacrificer, and the sacrifice! And it can only be from thy blessing upon our poor ordinances, when we hold a feast upon thy one all-sufficient sacrifice, that any real enjoyment of a spiritual nature can be found in them. Neither, Lord, till I hear thy bidding, can I venture to eat. If Jesus indeed say, " Eat, O friends, drink, yea drink abundantly, O beloved;" then I feel a confidence in thy welcome to every gospel feast, and " sit down under thy shadow with great delight, and thy fruit is sweet to my taste." Come then, thou dear Lord! come to thine own banquet; to thy church, thy table, thine house of prayer, thine ordinances! Come and bless thy people, and command a blessing upon all thine own appointments, and all will be blessed indeed!

SEPTEMBER 8.

MORNING.—" Ye have dwelt long enough in this mount."—Deut. i. 6.

Pause, my soul, and remark the gracious words of God to Israel. They were just entering the border of Canaan at that time. Forty years long had they been in a wilderness state; many ups and downs, battles and restings, conflicts and trials. God graciously said, " It is long enough." " There is a rest that remaineth for the people of God." Hark, my soul, doth Jesus speak to thee to the same amount? Hast thou indeed *dwelt* long enough in this mount of exercises, sin, sorrow, and temptation? Hast thou *seen* enough of the emptiness of all creature comforts to satisfy thee? Hast thou *felt* enough of a body of sin and death, which drags down the soul, to make thee groan under it, being burdened? Is there any thing now worth *living* for? Are not the glories above worth *dying* for? Doth Jesus call thee, invite thee, allure thee, to come up to the Canaan which he hath taken possession of in the name of his redeemed; and wilt thou not mount up upon the wings of faith, love, and longing desire, to be for ever with the Lord? Doth Jesus say, thou hast dwelt long enough here below? And wilt thou not say the same? Doth Jesus call thee to his arms; and wilt thou say, not yet, Lord? Ah my soul, art thou indeed in love with this prison? Dost thou wish to wear thy chains a little longer? And is this thy kindness to thy friend? Precious Lord, break down every intervening thought or passion that would rob thee of thy glory, and my soul of thy presence, and give me to cry out—"Hasten, my beloved! and be thou as a young hart upon the mountains of Bether."

EVENING.—"He is near that justifieth me.' —Isaiah l. 8.

My soul, hast thou ever considered one of the sweet properties of justification; not only in the fulness and completeness of it, and in all the several blessings connected with it, as it ariseth out of Jehovah in his own threefold character of persons; all and each taking part in it; but also in that which this portion points out, the *nearness* in which Jesus, the glorious justifier, always stands to thee, and surrounds thee? Sit down, this evening, and contemplate the subject of justification in this point of view, for it is indeed most blessed. All the persons of the Godhead have, and are engaged in making it effectual to every poor sinner, so as to give the mind always somewhat to rest upon, in the assurance of it. God the Father is the source and fountain of it, not only in having provided it in his dear Son, but also as having by the justification of all the Redeemer's work, to all intents and purposes, justified the poor believer in Jesus. Hence the apostle, with rapture, exclaims: "It is God that justifieth; who is he that condemneth?" Rom. viii. 33, 34. And it is Jesus that justifieth all his redeemed, by his blood and righteousness; "for he was delivered for our offences, and was raised again for our justification;" Rom. iv. 25. And that the hand of God the Holy Ghost was in all this, is equally evident; for it is as expressly said, that Christ was "justified in the Spirit;" which would never have been the case, had not both God's law and God's justice been satisfied, and thus justified Jesus, as the sinner's surety. 1 Tim. iii. 16. Rom. i. 4. But, over and above these glorious truths, as the foundation of every poor believer's hope, I charge thee to mark it down, my soul, in the memorandums of thine inmost thoughts, that as God the Father, who justified Jesus, thy surety, was always near to him, so he that justifieth thee is always near to thee. The charter of grace, and thy pardon written down in it in letters of blood, even the blood of Christ, is always near and at hand. Here it stands on eternal record, "that God is just and the justifier of him that believeth in Jesus." And he is near that justifieth, both as thine advocate to plead, that if any doubts should arise in thy poor timid mind concerning it, Jesus might open the volume of record, and there, by his Holy Spirit, shew it unto thee; and also, by the same almighty power, incline thy heart to the perfect belief of it, to thy joy and peace in believing. Now I again charge it upon thee, this night, that thou from henceforth never lose sight of the soul-reviving truth contained in this blessed scripture. But when Satan accuseth, and fears arise, and doubts would creep in, and both law and justice seem to be reviving their claims, look not at thyself, but look to all-precious Jesus. Behold him in all his fulness, suitableness, and all-sufficiency, as thy law-fulfiller and sin-atoning surety, and cry out in those divine words which the Holy Ghost hath given thee, " He is near that justifieth me!"

SEPTEMBER 9.

MORNING.—" In those days, and in that time, saith the Lord, the iniquity of Israel shall be sought for, and there shall be none; and the sins of Judah, and they shall not be found; for I will pardon them whom I reserve."—Jeremiah l. 20.

What those days and that time refer to is very plain; namely, the day when the great trumpet shall be blown, and when they shall come which were ready to perish; the glorious day of gospel grace by Jesus. For God the Father, having appointed and accepted a Surety for poor sinners, in the blood and righteousness of his dear Son, beholds no iniquity in Jacob, nor perverseness in Israel. Blessed thought to comfort a poor soul—that, seen in Christ, and accepted in the beloved, " there is no condemnation to them that are in Christ Jesus, who walk not after the flesh, but after the Spirit!" Pause, my soul, over this precious scripture, and take to thyself the comfort of it. If thou art in Christ, thou art beheld righteous in his righteousness; and, as thy Surety, what he wrought, and what he suffered, was for thee. So that, in this sense, thou art, as Christ tells the church, all fair, and there is no spot in thee. So that, amidst all thy groans for the remains of indwelling sin, (and groan thou dost daily,) and as thou sometimes art prompted to think, there is growing imperfection in thee; yet, in Jesus, as thou art found and beheld in him, sin is pardoned, and thy person accepted, and thou art in a state of justification before God in the righteousness of God thy Saviour. And, as this is so essential to be known and enjoyed, see to it, my soul, that thou livest upon it. Go in the strength of Christ's righteousness every day to the throne, pleading that righteousness, and that only. And, under a perfect conviction that not a single sin of thine was left out when Jesus bore the sins of his people on the tree, beg for grace to exercise faith, and to know that in Jesus thou art justified before God, and that God hath cast all thy sins into the depths of the sea. "Oh the depth of the riches both of the wisdom and goodness of God!" What shall separate from the love of Christ?—surely not sin. For Jesus hath put away sin by the sacrifice of himself! The law of God cannot: for that law, Jesus, as the sinner's Surety, hath satisfied. And justice, so far from condemning, now approves. God is just to his dear Son, as our Surety, who hath answered all the demands of sin, and therefore hath forgiven sin, and cleansed from all unrighteousness. Blessed thought! in this day sin is pardoned in Christ: and in that day, when God shall arise to judgment, the sin of Judah, and the inquity of Israel cannot be found.

EVENING.—"Then is the offence of the cross ceased."—Gal. v. 11.

The cross of Jesus was, of old, the great offence both to Jews and Greeks; and, in the present day, we may add, it is so to every one, who, by a perversion of language, calls himself christian, but yet denies the Godhead of him whom he presumes to call Maker. And if the believer would but relinquish this distinguishing feature in his Lord's person and atonement for his sins by the blood of his cross, then indeed would the offence of the cross cease. But, my soul, ask thyself, whether the offence of the cross be ceased in thy view? Yea, rather, whether, like Paul, not only the reproach of the cross is taken away for ever; but thou art crying out with an holy indignation against all rejoicings but in Jesus and his cross? Say, is it not thy daily, hourly song: "God forbid that I should glory, save in the cross of our Lord Jesus Christ, by whom the world is crucified unto me, and I unto the world?" Gal. vi. 14. Is all thy glory in him, whom, in reproach, the world called "The man hanged upon the tree?" Art thou for ever looking on him there, and for ever rejoicing in the view? There, sayest thou, there hangs all my confidence, all my joy, my security, my victories, my triumphs! Offence, do they say? Witness for me, I would say, all ye angels of light, that "this is all my salvation, and all my desire!" My soul utterly renounceth, utterly despiseth every idea of any other Saviour, but my Lord Jesus, and him crucified. Lead me, thou blessed Holy Spirit, lead me to the continued celebration of my Lord's cross, in my Lord's supper. There let Jesus Christ be evidently set forth crucified for me; and there may I receive the bread and wine, the representations of his body and blood, in token that I seek redemption in no other, but am heartily, fully, completely satisfied and convinced, that "there is no other name under heaven given among men, whereby we must be saved."

SEPTEMBER 10.

MORNING.—"While the king sitteth at his table, my spikenard sendeth forth the smell thereof."—Song i. 12.

That was a precious testimony Mary gave of her love to Jesus; and Jesus himself hath given his approbation of it, when she anointed Jesus's feet with the spikenard. God our Father hath anointed his dear Son; and so ought we. Surely God's anointed should be our anointed; and if Mary poured forth the best of her offerings, my soul, do thou the same. Indeed, while the king sitteth at his table, and reigneth in thine heart, the graces will flow. Yes, thou heavenly

King! when thou spreadest thy table, and callest thy redeemed as thy guests, while thou suppest with them, and they with thee, the humble spikenard, in the heart of a sinner, awakened by thy grace, and brought forth into exercise, will send forth all that shall testify love, and praise, and affection, and duty, and regard. Do thou then, dearest Lord, sit as a king frequently at thy table. Let me hear thy gracious invitation: "Eat, O friends; yea, drink abundantly, O beloved!" And, O thou heavenly Master! as all at the table is thine; the bread of life, the water of life, the wine of thy banquet —and all is thine own, and of thine own do thy redeemed give thee; "let me hear thy voice, let me see thy countenance." And while thou givest forth thyself with all thy fulness, O let my poor spikenard send forth faith and grace in lively exercise, that I may eat of thy flesh, and drink of thy blood, and have eternal life abiding in me.

EVENING.—"Thou hast avouched the Lord this day to be thy God. —And the Lord hath avouched thee this day to be his peculiar people." —Deut. xxvi. 17, 18.

What a most lovely view doth this scripture hold forth of the solemn transaction between God and his people! What an amazing thought, that the High and Holy One, who inhabiteth eternity, should condescend to propose and confirm such a covenant! and, my soul, dost thou think that, in the charter of grace, sealed as it is in the blood of God's dear Son, this covenant is less blessed or less sure? Doth not God confirm it in every promise? Is it not read and ratified in every ordinance? And doth not that Holy Spirit of promise set his seal to the whole, "whereby we are sealed unto the day of redemption?" Pause over the blissful subject! Ponder it well, this solemn evening! Surely, every service, every ordinance in the church of Jesus, becomes a confirmation of the blessed truth. What, indeed, is the gospel itself, but God's covenant in

Christ, avouching himself to be our God, and addressed to the ear? And what is the institution of the supper, but the same thing addressed to the eye? And when received by faith, both become seals of the covenant, to certify that the Lord this day, by this service, avouches himself that he is, and ever will be our God; and we avouch, by the same, that we are, and ever will be his people. Oh! it is sweet and refreshing at an ordinance, yea, without ordinances, to be looking over, and reviewing continually, those bonds of the covenant. Dost thou not feel an inexpressible joy, and rapture, and delight, to look back on those gracious transactions, which have passed between thee and thy God in Christ? From the first Bethel visits of the divine love, through the numberless renewals of it, in which thou hast heard his lovely voice speaking to thee again, and saying to thee, as to Jacob of old, "I am the God of Bethel, where thou anointedst the pillar, and where thou vowedst a vow unto me;" Gen. xxxi. 13. Yea, Lord! I have done, and still do, and desire everlastingly to be found doing it. It is my daily prayer to avouch thee to be my gracious Lord God in covenant, in the blood and righteousness of Christ? And do thou, my glorious Lord God, avouch me to be among the redeemed of thy people. Surely, Lord, in this charter of grace, thou hast made over thyself, in all thy divine perfections, to be thy people's. In this royal grant, as the God and Father of our Lord Jesus Christ, "of whom the whole family in heaven and earth is named," all thine attributes are pledged for the fulfilment of thy covenant promises to thy dear Son, and his church in him. Thy very name, Lord, gives a being to thy engagements, and an assurance of their being fulfilled. Yea, Lord, thou hast given thyself to thy people in Christ, and commanded them to call thee theirs. Begin thy song, my soul, and say, "The

Lord is the portion of mine inheritance and of my cup; he will maintain my lot;" Psalm xvi. 5.

SEPTEMBER 11.

MORNING.—" For thou hast been a strength to the poor, a strength to the needy in his distress, a refuge from the storm, a shadow from the heat, when the blast of the terrible ones is as a storm against the wall." —Isaiah xxv. 4.

Who so poor as Jesus's poor? Who so needy as the needy of the Redeemer? The world knoweth them not, because it knew him not. And as the master was, so are his servants in this world. But, my soul, observe how sweetly Jesus is all this. A strength to the poor in his distress, by taking all the storm himself. He is a shadow from the heat, the heat of the wrath of a broken law, which Jesus bore himself, when he died to expiate the breaches of it. His blood and righteousness cool the heat of sin, and quench all the fiery darts of the wicked: these terrible ones which beat upon a poor sinner like a storm against the wall. Moreover, when the showers of wrath shall fall at the last day on the wicked, when that horrible tempest of fire and brimstone, the Psalmist speaks of, shall come down on the ungodly, Jesus will be an hiding-place from the storm, and a covert from the tempest: not a drop can fall on those that are under him, and sheltered by his blood and righteousness. As the church is now said to sit under his shadow with great delight in this wilderness state, and his fruit is sweet to her taste; so when she is fairly come up out of it, having all along leaned upon her beloved, and having entered with him into his glory; there will be both security and delight, everlasting safety and joy. Precious Jesus, thou hast been a strength indeed to my poor soul, and thou wilt be my portion for ever. Oh give me to see my daily need of thee, to feel my poverty and weakness; the exercises of persecution, both without and within; that from all the terrors of the law, the alarms of guilt in the conscience, the remains of in-dwelling sin in a body of death, which is virtually all sin—the accusations of Satan, the just judgments of God; in thee, thou one glorious ordinance of heaven, precious Lord Jesus, I may behold myself secure in thee, and continually cry out, in the language of thy servant the prophet, "Surely shall one say, in the Lord have I righteousness and strength; even to thee do I come; and never shall I be ashamed or confounded, world without end."

EVENING.—"And they said among themselves, who shall roll us away the stone from the door of th esepulchre? (And when they looked, they saw that the stone was rolled away) for it was very great."—Mark xvi. 3, 4.

My soul, how very often, like these poor women at the door of our Lord's sepulchre, hast thou been at a loss to think whence help should arise to succour thee in the needed moment? And how often, like them, hast thou found, when looking again, all the difficulties which thou hadst figured to thyself removed! And with thee the mercy hath been, if possible, yet more striking. For thou not only needest the stone to be rolled away from the door of the sepulchre, that thou mightest see Jesus, but to have the stone taken away out of thine heart, that thou mightest love and believe in Jesus to the salvation of thy soul. Is it so then, that whilst, at any time, thou art putting forth the question and inquiry, full of doubt, and fear, and misgiving, who shall help in this or that difficulty; and when thou lookest again, behold the Lord hath been better to thee than all thy fears, and "every mountain before thy great Zerubbabel is become a plain?" Wilt thou not learn hence, that thy Lord Jesus, with all his benefits, is not only set before thee, and revealed to thee, but made over to thee, to be received, and to be enjoyed, and to be made use of, by thee, for all and every purpose in which his glory and thy salvation are concerned? The stone is indeed very great in every heart by nature, and unmoveable by natural strength. But look again. He that arose from the dead, and broke open the sepulchre, can and will take it away, according to that sweet promise, Ezek. xxxvi. 26. And if the stone be removed, and the fountain of life broken up, in the person, and glory, and triumphs of Jesus, come then, my soul, "and draw water out of those wells of salvation." Oh! how truly blessed is it to see Jesus in all; and to enjoy Jesus in all; for then, whatever great obstructions seem to lie in the way, the Lord himself doth and will remove them. "He brings the blind by a way they knew not. He causeth them to walk in places that they have not known. Crooked things are made straight, and rough places plain: and all his redeemed then see the salvation of our God!"

SEPTEMBER 12.

MORNING.—"And as Moses lifted up the serpent in the wilderness, even so must the Son of man be lifted up; that whosoever believeth in him should not perish but have eternal life."—John iii. 14, 15.

Pause, my soul, over these words, and remember that they are the words of Jesus. Call to mind the wonderful event to which Christ refers, in the church's history in the wilderness, as related, Numb. xxi. 5—9. Israel had sinned; and the Lord sent fiery flying serpents among the people, which bit them, and they died. In their distress they cried unto the Lord, and the Lord appointed this method of cure. A figure of a serpent was made in brass, to which Israel was commanded to look only, and be healed. They who did so, lived. If any refused, he died. This was the ordinance of God. "Now," saith Jesus, "as Moses, at the command of God, lifted up the serpent, so must I be lifted up; that whosoever believeth in me shall never perish, but have eternal life." Now, my soul, mark what the Saviour saith, and see the blessedness contained in his precious assurance. It was a serpent, that stung the Israelites. It was the old serpent, the devil, which poisoned our nature at the fall. All his temptations, assaults, and poisons, are fiery. And when the dreadful effects of sin are felt in the awakened conscience, how do they burn with terrors in the soul! What could the dying Israelite do to heal those venomous bites? Nothing. Would medicine cure? No. Was there no remedy within the power of man? No; it baffled all art, it resisted all attempts to heal. Such is sin. No prayers, no tears, no endeavours, no repentance can wash away sin. If the sinner be restored, it must be by the interposition and mercy of God alone. Now observe the method God took with Israel—a figure of brass. And if, as some men tell us, any thing shining like brass, to look upon, when the head and brain is diseased, would make the person mad; so far was this serpent of brass likely to cure, that it was the most unpromising thing in the world to accomplish it. But yet it was God's command; and that was enough. It infallibly cured. Look now to Christ. Here also is God's appointment, God's command, God's authority. Christ was made in the likeness of sinful flesh: and though holy in himself, yet becoming sin for us, that we might be made the righteousness of God in him. The single precept is, "Look unto me, and be ye saved." What, must I do nothing, bring nothing, take nothing? No. The answer is, "look unto me." This is the appointed way. Christ is the One only ordinance; Christ is the Altar, Offering, High Priest. "If thou liftest up thy tool upon it, thou hast polluted it." Christ is the Father's gift for healing. In Jesus there is a fulness to heal. Faith then hath a double plea—the authority of God the Father, and the fulness of salvation in God the Son. Lord, I take this for my warrant. Help me, thou blessed Spirit, so to look, so to depend, so to fix my whole soul on this complete remedy for all my need, that heaven and earth may witness for me, I seek salvation in no other, being most fully convinced that there is salvation in no other; "neither is there any other name under heaven, given among men, whereby we must be saved."

EVENING.—"And have been all made to drink into one Spirit."—1 Cor. xii. 13.

What a most lovely and endearing representation is here given of the several members of Christ's mystical body, as all united to their one glorious and common head, and, like so many branches of the vine, deriving every thing of life, and grace, and fruitfulness, from him! "They have been all made to drink into one Spirit." Yes; the Lord the Spirit, the Holy Ghost the Comforter, whose gracious influence first unites them to Jesus, unites them also, in him, to one another. Hence, though distant and remote from each other; divided and separated by distant climes, and countries, and languages; though unknown by face to each other, yea, in language, and manners, and customs wholly dissimilar; and of different degrees of knowledge, and apprehension, and attainment in the divine life; yet, from being one with Christ, they are also one with each other, and "are members of his body, of his flesh, and of his bones;" part of the universal church, and constituting one complete whole, of which Christ is the head: "whether one member suffer, all the members suffer with it: or one member be honoured, all the members rejoice with it." My soul, couldest thou ask the native of any country or climate, who is a real member of Christ's body, what are his feelings of sin, and what his views of Jesus, thou wouldest find a complete correspondence with thine own. He hath groaned for sin, as thou hast groaned; and he hath found Jesus precious, as thou hast found him. And whence all this, but because one and the same almighty Teacher hath been the instructor of both? "We have been all made to drink into one Spirit!" He is the source and fountain of spiritual life, and sustenance, and strength in all! And as the first quickenings of grace arise from his divine influences, so is it from his blessed impressions that believers are sealed and secured unto the day of eternal redemption. Hail! thou holy and almighty Lord! cause the whole church of Jesus to be for ever living at the fountain-head of mercies, "who have been all made to drink into one Spirit!"

SEPTEMBER 13.

MORNING.—"And thou shalt write them upon the posts of thy house, and on thy gates."—Deut. vi. 9.

See, my soul, what a gracious provision the Lord made for the glory and honour of his Israel, that every traveller passing by might say, 'Here dwelleth an Israelite indeed; he hath the name of the Lord of Hosts upon his house.' And did it please the Lord God of Israel so to have his people known, and shall it be not my desire to have thy name, Lord, upon the gates of my house. Shall any pass by my door, ignorant that a lover of the Lord Jesus dwelleth there? Nay, shall I not esteem it my highest honour to have it known whose I am, and whom I serve, in the gospel of his dear Son? Shall I be ashamed of that name before which every knee bows in heaven and in earth? Oh Lord Jesus, not only write thy name upon the gates of my house, but engrave it in the centre of my heart, my affections, my first, and last, and earliest, and latest thoughts! Let it be my rapture and my joy, to speak out of the abundance of my heart concerning thee and thy great salvation. In all I say, in all I do, let it be manifest that I am in pursuit of him whom my soul loveth. Let every action tend to recommend thy dear name; and whether at home or abroad, in my house or family, when lying down or when rising up, let all creation witness for me, that the love, the service, the interest, the glory, of my God in Christ, is the one only object of my soul's desire; and let every thing speak this language; "Whom have I in heaven but thee, and there is none upon earth I desire but thee; and though my flesh and heart fail, yet thou art the strength of my heart, and my portion for ever."

EVENING.—"But which of you having a servant plowing, or feeding cattle, will say unto him by and by, when he is come from the field, go and sit down to meat? And will not rather say unto him, make ready wherewith I may sup, and gird thyself, and serve me till I have eaten and drunken; and afterward thou shalt eat and drink?"—Luke xvii. 7, 8.

I have often thought that the Lord Jesus, the bountiful Lord of all his servants, and who giveth largely to the supply of all his household, hath a more special and suited food for his servants in the ministry, who are employed by him to set forth his table for others. They are, as the servant here described, in the field, plowing, and engaged in every branch of the spiritual husbandry. But when they return, their peculiar privilege is to wait upon their Master. And well is it for them; for in the faithful discharge of their labours, so great and constant are their engagements in following up the several departments of it, that, while keeping the vineyard, the church, their own interests would be sadly neglected and forgotten. Yet it is a most certain truth, that no servant in a family can be faithful to his Lord's interest, who is not faithful to himself. No minister of the Lord Jesus can be concerned for other men's souls, who hath no concern for his own. How very blessed is it then, that the Lord Jesus hath made suitable provision in this particular, that when the public service of the day is over, he opens to the private enjoyment of his people in himself alone. My soul, hath not Jesus, in this delightful scripture, taught thee this sweet lesson? Public ordinances will be doubly blessed, when, in the after-retirement, we wait upon Jesus in private. And in the most busy life, there will be always some moment found to do this. Jesus himself, "when he had sent the multitudes away, went up into the mountain, apart, to pray." The night opened to him the pleasures of communion, when the public services had engaged him all the day. And will not thou, dear Lord, while thy servant is waiting upon thee at thy table, bless him with some glimpse of thy glory? Shall he not find himself, refreshed in hearing the gracious words which drop from thy sacred lips? Will he not indeed esteem "thy words more than his necessary food?" Yea, Lord, thou wilt thyself be both his meat and his drink; and to wait on thee at thy table will be found more blessed than all the unsanctified tables of those who fare sumptuously every day!

SEPTEMBER 14.

MORNING.—"And he must needs go through Samaria."—John iv. 4.

And what was there, blessed Jesus, that constrained thee to this necessity? Was it because there was a poor adulterous woman there, that needed thy grace, and the hour was come for her conversion? Sweet thought! let me cherish it this morning. Was there not the same *needs be* for the Father setting thee up, from everlasting, for the head of thy church and people? Could there have been a church without thee? And when thy church had fallen by sin, what archangel could have recovered her but thee? Why then there was a *needs be* that thou shouldest take the nature of thy people upon thee, and come to seek and save that which was lost. And as it is said of thee concerning this poor woman, that "he must needs go through Samaria," so must it be equally said, Jesus must needs go to Jerusalem, to save Jerusalem sinners by his blood. Oh yes, there was a blessed necessity upon thee, thou Lamb of God, that thou shouldest do all this. "Ought not Christ to have suffered these things, and to enter into his glory?" My soul, indulge this precious thought yet further, and see if there be not a *needs be* in thy Jesus for numberless other occasions. Is there not a blessed necessity that Jesus should give out of his fulness to his people? Is there not a *needs be*, when his blessed gospel is preached, that he should be present to give virtue and efficacy to the word delivered? Might not every poor, waiting, needy sinner say, there is a blessed necessity Christ should be here? Surely he is constrained by his promise, that where two or three are met in his name, he is in the midst of them; and therefore he will come, he will bless his word, he will give out of his fulness; for he knows my need, and the need of all his people present. Nay, is not the glory of our Jesus depending upon the receiving of his poor, and making them rich by his bounty? Go one step further, my soul, this morning, as it concerns thyself. Doth not Jesus know now thy state, thy want, thy circumstances, and that thou art waiting for thy morning alms before that thou canst leave his gate? Then is there not a *needs be* that he, who was constrained to pass through Samaria, should come to thee? Precious, precious Jesus! I wait thy coming; I long to hear thy voice. What I need thou knowest. And as thy glory and my salvation are both blended, do for me, Lord, as shall best conduce to this one end, and all will be well. Jesus will be glorified, and my soul made happy. Amen.

EVENING.—"Which things the angels desire to look into."—1 Pet. i. 12.

My soul, what an argument ariseth out of this view, of the angels of light being inquisitive about man's redemption, to stir thee up to the same most blessed contemplation! If in the apprehension of those intelligent and exalted beings of light, the subject is so glorious, what ought it to be to thee? If, as the words represent, they fix their closest attention, and are lost in admiration, wonder, love, and praise; how is it that thou, who art so deeply interested in the blissful theme, shouldest forget it, as thou dost for hours together, and, even when thou thinkest of it, contemplate it so very coolly? Oh for grace more and more to study Jesus and his love, Jesus and his grace, Jesus and his great salvation! But among the wonders of redemption, is there not one point (and as it concerns thee, my soul, a marvellous one indeed it is) which may well be supposed to call forth the greater astonishment of the holy angels as they behold it; I mean, as they behold the glory of thy Jesus advanced, not only when poor sinners praise him for what he is in himself, and what he is to them, but when their emptiness, poverty, wants, and wretchedness, afford the rich opportunity for the Lord Jesus to get to himself glory in giving out of his fulness? Here, surely, angels may well desire to pry into the cause, and be lost in the contemplation. And, as it concerns thee, my soul, how must the angels, "that are ministering spirits, sent forth to minister unto them that are heirs of salvation;" how must they stand amazed, when they see thy Lord waiting to be gracious unto *thee*, even in the very time when thou wouldest tire every patience but his, "in wearying with thine iniquities?" And how must their angelic minds feel amazed that Jesus should get glory from such a poor worthless worm as thou art, in making the riches of his grace to shine upon thee, while thousands, not more undeserving, know him not, and are unacquainted with his grace and mercy! Oh! gracious Lord! how is it that thou thus dost manifest thyself to me otherwise than thou dost unto the world? Ye angels of light! ye ministering spirits of my God! join with me in praise for my Lord's graciousness to such a sinner; for, surely, your high intelligent minds cannot but be lost in admiration, when beholding the aboundings of grace exceeding even the aboundings of sin, and, in my instance, as far surpassing "as the heavens are higher than the earth."

SEPTEMBER 15.

MORNING.—"As for me I am poor and needy, yet the Lord thinketh upon me."—Ps. xl. 17.

My soul, sit down, and reckon up thy true riches. See what are thine *outward* circumstances, and take an inventory of all thine *inward* wealth. Thou art, by nature and by practice, one of the children of a bankrupt father, even Adam, who lived insolvent, and died wretchedly poor in himself, having entailed only an inheritance of sin, misery, and death, with the loss of divine favour, upon the whole race of his children. By nature and by practice thou art poor in the sight of God, despised by angels on account of thy loathsome disease of sin; thine understanding darkened; thy will corrupt; passions impetuous, proud, self-willed; all in opposition to the law of God; exposed to all present evil, everlasting evil; a slave to Satan, a willing captive in his drudgery; hastening daily to death, to the *second* death, and with an insensibility which is enough to make every heart mourn that beholds thee. Such, my soul, was thy state by nature; and such, and far worse, would have been thy state for ever, had not Jesus interposed, and looked upon thee, and loved thee, when thou wast cast out to perish, and no eye to pity thee, nor help thee from thy ruin. My soul, canst thou now say, though poor and needy, the Lord thinketh upon thee? Oh blessed Jesus! thou dost indeed think upon me, and provide for me, and hast given me to see, to feel, my poverty, need, and misery; and to live wholly upon thee and thy alms from day to day. Yes, Jesus! I would be poor, I would be needy; I would feel yet more and more my nothingness, worthlessness, poverty, wretchedness, that Jesus may be increasingly precious, and thy salvation increasingly dear. Oh for grace, as a poor needy debtor, daily to swell my debt account, that my consciousness of need may make thee and thy fulness increasingly blessed. Let it be my daily motto —"As for me, I am poor and needy; but the Lord thinketh upon me."

EVENING.—"A door-keeper in the house of my God."—Ps. lxxxiv. 10.

My soul, hast thou ever considered the blessedness of such an appointment, of such an office, when truly followed up? If Jesus indeed appoint, and both teach the nature of it, and give grace to the faithful discharge of it, then is it most honourable, and truly blessed. A door-keeper is supposed to know the several apartments of the house, and to be well acquainted with his Lord and Master, in whose service he ministers. He is supposed also to know who goeth out, and who cometh in; whether his Lord be at home, and how his fellow-servants are employed in their ministry. And if he be a faithful door-keeper, he will willingly open to none but such as his Lord approves, but most gladly shew all that come in his Lord's name, and are welcome to his Lord, the way to his Lord's presence and his Lord's table. What sayest thou, my soul, to such an office? Surely, to be "an hewer of wood, and a drawer of water, in the service of the sanctuary," is an honourable employment; and how much more to be "a door-keeper in the house of God!" The man after God's own heart was so much delighted with the thought of God's house, that he seemed to grudge the constant abode of the birds that made their nests at the altar. Poor David, though a king in Israel, could only now and then go up to the house of God, but these birds rested there. And under the full impression of the happiness resulting from a constant residence, he broke out in an hymn of praise: "Blessed are they that dwell in thy house," whose home, whose abode, whose constant employment is there; for "they will be still praising thee." Pause, my soul! hast thou the same views as David? Consider wherein this blessedness consists: the servants of the Lord, who dwell in their Lord's house, are blessed, not because they are in the receipt of wages; not because their bountiful Lord provides a table for them; but because he gives them employment, and his praises are their meat and drink: "they will be still praising thee," saith David. Yes! the house of God is then an heaven below, where the servants of the Lord find their joy and happiness from the everlasting praises of God and the Lamb! But, alas! if the servants of the Lord's house, in any or all of the departments, from the highest to the lowest, dwell there, not to glorify the Lord and promote his honour, but to serve their own bellies, and, like the finger-post to the traveller, stand to direct him in his way, but move not a step themselves; so far from a blessedness, they will find in the end of their labours, that the heaviest of all condemnations will follow! Blessed Lord Jesus! thou wert a door-keeper indeed to thine own house, that in all things thou mightest have the pre-eminence! Thou, for the love thou hadst to thy Master, to thy church, thy wife, and thy children, didst, like the Jewish servant, submit to have thine ear bored at the door-post, to go out no more free, but to remain for ever. Oh! for grace to cry out, in the review of such love as passeth knowledge, " I had rather be a door-keeper in the house of my God, than to dwell in the tents of wickedness." See Exod. xxi. 5, 6.

SEPTEMBER 16.

MORNING.—" I will strengthen them in the Lord, and they shall walk up and down in his name, saith the Lord."—Zech. x. 12.

My soul, mark these words, how precious they are; and mark the Speaker and Promiser, and consider how sure they are. Is not this God the Father speaking of the church, and most graciously assuring the church that he will strengthen the church in Jesus, the church's glorious Head? Is not this said with an eye to Christ, who is represented in another part of this blessed prophecy as calling upon the church to attend to him, who is come to build the temple of the Lord, and to bear all the glory, and who expressly saith that the church shall know that he, the Lord of Hosts, is sent by the Lord of Hosts unto his people? Who but the Lord of Hosts could build the temple of the Lord of Hosts; or who but him bear all the glory? Zech. vi. 12. So then, my soul, observe that Christ is the strength, as well as the righteousness of his redeemed. And do observe further, that when at any time thou art strengthened in Jesus, it is the Father's gracious hand and office which is manifested in this merciful act. If thou art drawn at any time to Jesus, it is the Father's sweet constraining love that thus works upon the soul. John vi. 44. If thou enjoyest at any time some new and delightful revelation of Jesus, which lifts thee up with a joy unspeakable, remember, my soul, from whom the blessing comes; and learn to ascribe the mercy, the distinguishing mercy, as the apostle did, to the Father's grace, when it pleased him to separate thee from thy mother's womb, and called thee by his grace to reveal his Son in thee, Gal. i. 15, 16. Yes, Almighty Father, it is thy special mercy, both to give thy Son, and with him all things, to the higly favoured objects of thine everlasting love. It was he who, from all eternity, didst contrive, order, will, appoint, and prepare the great salvation of the gospel, and choose Christ as the head, and the church as the body of this stupendous work of redemption. It is thou which hast carried on and executed all the great designs; and it is thou who dost strengthen and complete the whole in the final salvation of all the members of it, in grace here, and glory hereafter. Blessed, holy compassionate Lord God! for Jesus's sake fulfil this promise daily in my soul; bear me up, carry me through, and strengthen me in the Lord my God, that I may indeed walk up and down in his name, until thou bring me in to see his face in thine eternal home, and dwell under the light of his countenance for ever.

EVENING.—" And Isaac went out to meditate in the field at the even-tide."—Gen. xxiv. 63.

My soul, every season is suited for meditation, if the Lord the Holy Ghost suit the mind for the employment. But unless he prepare the heart, no preparation will be found in any season. What multitudes are there, to whose unthinking minds neither the morning breath nor the evening call, in the Lord's mercies in providence and in grace, have any hearing? They arise, as they lay down, unconscious and unconcerned as to whom they are indebted for keeping their persons and their dwelling-places in safety. They put on the garment to cover and adorn the body, but are ignorant that their souls are without clothing! They wash and refresh the body, but the pollution of the soul they see not! They are anxious to preserve the casket, but the jewel it contains, falls under their feet, as an object of no value! My soul, do thou look at the patriarch Isaac, and take him for thy pattern. He went out " to meditate in the field at the even-tide!" He turned his back upon the house and family, and sought, in the solitude of the field, to have his mind disengaged from men, that he might be wholly engaged in devout communion with God. And is not the present evening suited to thee for this purpose. It is a calm and serene season, and every thing invites thee to the employment. Thy wants and necessities; the solemn inquiry how thou art advancing in grace, and in the knowledge of thy Lord and Saviour Jesus Christ; the consciousness that another day of thy pilgrimage is ended, and thou art by so much the nearer thine eternal home; every momentous interest belonging to a dying creature in a dying world, presses the matter upon thee, to ponder the path of thy feet, which, in every step, is leading thee to eternity. Go then, if not to the field of nature, yet to the field of grace, and if thou hast no closet to retire to, yet retire to thine own heart, and there meditate on all those interesting subjects which belong to an immortal soul. Jesus waits to meet thee, to be gracious to thee, and he will shew thee his secret. Oh, thou dear Lord of thy people! cause me to delight in those sweet and sacred interviews! Let every evening toll the bell of recollection to call home my poor wandering heart; and when the tumult of a busy, unsatisfying, and troublesome world is over, Oh! for grace to do as my Lord did; "send the multitude away, and get up apart into the holy mountain" of faith and love in the Lord Jesus, "to meditate and pray!"

SEPTEMBER 17.

MORNING.—"Brethren, pray for us."—1 Thess. v. 25.

My soul, mark how earnestly the apostle sought an interest in the prayers of the faithful. And if so eminent a servant in the church of Jesus thus entreated to be remembered by the brethren at the mercy-seat, how needful must it be that the brethren should remember one another; not only ministers to pray for the people, but the people for their ministers. "Brethren, pray for us," should be the constant request of every lover of Jesus. Methinks I would ask every one that I knew to be a constant attendant at the heavenly court, to speak for me to the king when he was most near, and in the enjoyment of his presence. Tell the Lord, I would say, that his poor prisoner needs his alms, longs for his grace, and is waiting the anxious expectations of his visits. Beg for me, that I may live always under the blessed tokens of his love, that I may be ever living near the Lord, and strong in the grace which is in Christ Jesus. And do tell his Sovereign Majesty that the one great object of my soul's desire is, that I may have increasing views of the infinite dignity of his person, work, merit, offices, relations, characters, and in short, every thing that relates to one so dear, so lovely, so glorious, and so suited to a poor sinner, as the Lord Jesus Christ is in all things. And do add for me, that my humble suit is, that after he hath given me all in gifts and graces that he sees needful for me in my pilgrimage state, that Jesus will give me yet more than all, by giving me himself, and causing my heart to be dissatisfied with all but himself; for until Jesus himself be my portion, I still have not what I want. It is not enough to give me life; but he himself must be my life. It is not enough to give me rest, unless he himself is my rest, and I rest in him. Precious Jesus! I would say, in thyself is all I need: all to pardon, all to justify, all to sanctify, all to glorify, all to satisfy, all to make happy here and for ever. Brethren, let this be your prayer for me, and it shall be mine for you; that Jesus be the all in all of our souls, and our portion for ever.

EVENING.—"A seed shall serve him; it shall be accounted to the Lord for a generation. They shall come, and shall declare his righteousness unto a people that shall be born, that he hath done this."—Ps. xxii. 30, 31.

It is precious, yea, truly blessed also, to discover the

happy correspondence subsisting between the several parts of scripture, in their testimony concerning the features of God's people. Jehovah, in his threefold character of person, is always found as engaged in it; and each One in the holy and undivided Three gives assurance to it. "I will pour my Spirit, (saith God the Father speaking to the person of his dear Son, as the Israel of his people) upon thy seed, and my blessing upon thine offspring," Isa. xliv. 3. "A seed, (saith Christ, or, as it might be rendered, and indeed is rendered in the version of the psalms read in the churches, *my seed*) shall serve him." This is the very seed which the Lord hath blessed, and which all that see shall acknowledge; Isa. lxi. 9. "the people which Jehovah formed for himself," which he gave unto his Son, and "which shall shew forth his praise," Isa. xliii. 21. And as both the Father and the Son have thus marked them with these striking particularities, so the Holy Ghost as plainly sets his seal to the great truth, and confirms who they are, by making them "willing in the day of his power." Now, my soul! behold, in this most blessed scripture, how decidedly the characters of the seed of Christ are marked, and trace thine own features in them. The seed of Christ, his offspring, his people, his redeemed, more or less delight in the Lord; they serve the Lord; and they are numbered, accounted to the Lord as his people, his generation. And they are as truly his by the new generation in grace, as they are by the old generation in nature, the seed of Adam after the flesh. So they are accounted, accepted, and received, in God's sight. Mark also another blessed property by which they are known: "They shall come, and shall declare his righteousness." Yes! for the language of every one of them is, "I will make mention of thy righteousness, even of thine own," Ps. lxxi. 16. Yea, the name by which they call their Holy One their Redeemer is, "The LORD OUR RIGH-

TEOUSNESS!" Neither is this all: for they shall not only renounce every thing in themselves, as in any way a procuring cause to this blessedness; but, both in original design, and in actual possession, they shall refer all unto the unsearchable goodness, and mercy, and grace of God. The work, and glory, and praise, are all the Lord's, and all the declarations of it shall be to this amount: that the Lord "hath done it!" What sayest thou, my soul, to this precious and blessed testimony of Jehovah? Surely, thou canst, and wilt set to thy seal, "that God is true!"

SEPTEMBER 18.

MORNING.—"The king is held in the galleries."—Song vii. 5.

And who but Jesus is King in Zion? As one with the Father over all, God blessed for ever, he is indeed the King eternal, immortal, invisible. And as Mediator God-man, he is my God and King, both by his conquest of my heart, and the voluntary surrender of my soul. Yes, blessed Jesus, I not only hail thee my God and King, but I would have every knee bow before thee, and every tongue confess that thou art Lord and King, to the glory of God the Father. But, my soul, what are those galleries where thy King is held? Are they the scriptures of truth, where Jesus is held and retained, adored and admired? Or are they the public ordinances of thine house, or the place where thine honour dwelleth; or the secret chamber, or the closet of retirement and meditation; when thou comest to visit thy people, and when thou knockest at the door of their hearts, when thou comest in to sup with them, and they with thee? Well, my gracious, condescending Lord, be they what they may, or where they may; methinks, like the patriarch, when thou comest to wrestle with my poor, heedless and sleepy heart, I will hold thee in the galleries, and say, as he did, "I will not let thee go, except thou bless me." I would say, as another famous patriarch did, " My Lord, if I have found favour in thy sight, pass not away from thy servant. Rest yourself under the tree; and I will fetch a morsel of thine own bread, and of thine own giving, and comfort ye your hearts: for therefore are ye come to your servant," Gen. xviii. 3 – 5. I would entreat thee, Lord, not to be as the wayfaring man, that turneth in to tarry but for the night: but I would hold thee in the galleries of thine own graces, and thine own strength, imparted to my poor soul; and I would beg of thee, and entreat thee to tarry until the dawn of day, and make thyself fully known unto me, in breaking of bread, and in prayer. Yes, my adorable King, my Lord and my God! I would detain thee in the galleries, I would hold thee fast, I would not let thee go, until that I had brought thee into my mother's house, the church—and until thou hadst brought me home to thine eternal habitation which is above; and there to sit down at thy feet to go out no more, but at the fountain head of joy to drink of the spiced wine of the juice of the pomegranate in everlasting felicity.

EVENING.—" He that saith he abideth in him, ought himself also so to walk, even as he walked."—1 John ii. 6.

Sweet testimony to the truth as it is in Jesus, when, from being *in* Christ, we are walking *with* Christ; and one and the same spirit runs through both. As a man never walks as Christ walked, before he is first united to Christ; so when truly united to Christ, the evidence is made to appear by loving what Jesus loves, and hating what Jesus hates. As Ruth said to Naomi, so the believer saith to the Lord Jesus: " Where thou goest, I would go, and where thou lodgest, I would lodge; thy people shall be my people, and thy God my God!" And, my soul, think what a blessed unanswerable proof doth it afford, both to thyself and to the world around, when, from abiding in Christ, we live as Christ; that is, his Holy Spirit moves in us, speaks in us, walks in us, yea, doth all in us; and as the soul of man gives life and action to the body, so Christ, who is the soul of the believer, gives life and action to the soul. Hence Paul considered himself so wholly actuated, in every part of the spiritual life, by the in-dwelling residence of the Spirit of Christ, that he said, it was not he that lived, but Christ that lived in him: "The life," saith he, "which I now live in the flesh, I live by the faith of the Son of God, who loved me, and gave himself for me:" Gal. ii. 20. My soul, canst thou subscribe to the same? "If Christ be in thee, the body is dead because of sin, but the Spirit is life because of righteousness;" Rom. viii. 10. Oh! for grace so to abide in Jesus, that every act of my life may testify "whose I am, and whom I serve;" and like that martyr, who to every question put to him, only answered, "I am a christian;" so, my soul, may every act, every word, yea, every thought of thine, so proclaim Jesus, and thy union and oneness with him, that all with whom thou hast to do may plainly discover thou art no longer thine own, but that, "being bought with a price, thou dost glorify God in thy body, and in thy spirit, which are both his."

SEPTEMBER 19.

MORNING.—"I have set before thee an open door, and no man can shut it."—Rev. iii. 8.

Blessed Jesus! thou hast indeed done all this, and more. Thou art thyself the door into thy fold here below, and to thy courts above; for thou hast said, by thee, "whosoever entereth in, shall go in, and find pasture:" and it is thou that hast opened a new and living way by thy blood. Thou art the only possible way of access to the Father. And because thou hast opened it, no man can shut it; for thou ever livest to keep the way, which thou hast once opened, still open, by thy all-prevailing intercession. Yes, thou heavenly Lord, the gate is never shut, day nor night, in the preaching of thine everlasting gospel, all the ends of the earth shall see this salvation of our God. And, as thou hast graciously said, all that come to God by thee, shall never be shut out. The word, the authority, the warrant of Jehovah, is gone forth to this purpose. Thy blood and righteousness secure it. The Spirit sets his seal to it. Thou wilt receive, thou wilt bless, thou wilt cause all the Father hath given thee to come to thee; and thou wilt keep the door always open for all comers. Oh heavenly way! Oh precious, endless salvation! My soul, see to it that thou art entered in, and there abidest securely. Oh ye! my fellow sinners, yet without, rouse up from your carnal security and sloth, before the master of the house hath arisen and shut to the door; and ye then, too late, cry out, " Lord, Lord, open to us. Now is the accepted time; now is the day of salvation."

EVENING.—" An hireling his day."—Job xiv. 6.

The sufferings of Job are proverbial; but the sermons of this exercised believer, though delivered from a dunghill, were sweet sermons. The figure of *an hireling* accomplishing his day (and that a day, both on account of original sin and actual transgression, fleeting and full of labour and sorrow) forms a just, though sad representation of human life. But this, like all the other circumstances of our fallen state, when read through the medium of the gospel, and softened and sweetened with the blood of Christ, puts on a different aspect. It is then found in its shortness to be the better, and in its crosses to be the more sanctified; and, like Samson's riddle, " out of the eater to come forth meat, and out of the strong to bring forth sweetness;" Judges xiv. 14. It is the blessed property of grace, to work by contraries; so that the cross of Jesus, like the tree cast into the waters of Marah, put into our hireling life, sweetens all. My soul, if thou art taken from the rubbish of nature, into the house and service of Jesus as an hireling, it is not until the day of the hireling be accomplished, that the Lord of the vineyard bids the steward to call the labourers, and give them their hire. It was only "in the end of the world," that Jesus himself appeared, "to put away sin by the sacrifice of himself." Is the hireling's life to be regretted, because it is short, when every portion of it is marked with sin, and consequently is unsatisfying? Yea, is not rather its shortness rendered blessed? And if all the comforts and blessedness of God's house are treasured up for the labourers of his house, when the evening is come, and the steward is commanded to call them home to be paid; doth it not comfort thee, my soul, in the thought that thy life here is but as that of an hireling? Hath Jesus passed by, and employed thee, and sent thee into his vineyard, when thou wert standing idle at the market-place? Hast thou been doing the work of the day in the day, according to the Lord's appointment? Hath thy Lord's eye been upon thee, and, like another Boaz, come from Bethlehem, hath Jesus often visited thee, blessed thee, held up thine hands, refreshed thy soul, and made thee glad with the light of his countenance? Ruth ii. 4. Oh! then bless him, that thy continuance here is but as "an hireling in his day." The evening will come; the hour is at hand, when Jesus will call thee home to his "house, not made with hands, eternal in the heavens;" when all the blessings of the everlasting covenant will be given to Jesus's labourers, and the supper of the Lord will be spread, and all his redeemed shall sit down with him, to go out no more for ever! Amen.

SEPTEMBER 20.

MORNING.—" Behold the man whose name is the Branch."—Zech. vi. 12.

My soul, listen to the call, and behold this wonderful Man, whose name is the Branch. Mark the wonderful features of his person. This is one of the prophetical names of Him, in the faith of whom, as the Redeemer of Israel, all the old testament saints died. The branch of the Lord—the branch of righteousness; or, as he is elsewhere called, the Nazarene. But observe how very descriptive of his nature is this title. He grows up out of his place. And where is that?—In the eternal counsel of Jehovah. Who shall declare his generation? He is indeed a rod out of the stem of Jesse, and a branch out of his roots. But all this as the root himself of David; planted in the eternal purpose of God's own sovereign decree, and budding forth as a branch in all the periods of his incarnation, death, resurrection, ascension, glory. And what a branch of never-failing loveliness, and everlasting verdure and fruitfulness, in all the proclamations of his gospel, converting sinners, and comforting saints. And what an eternal perennial branch to all his redeemed in grace and glory. Hail, thou glorious, wonderful Man, whose name is the Branch! Thou art indeed, as the prophet described thee, beautiful and glorious in the eyes of all thy redeemed. On thee, Lord, would I hang all the glory of thy Father's house, and all the glory of my salvation. May it be my portion to sit under thy shadow with great delight here, until thou bring me home to sit under thee, the tree of life, in the Paradise of God, in the fulness of enjoyment of thee for ever.

EVENING.—" The true vine."—John xv. 1.

Dearest Jesus, how shall I ever be able sufficiently to admire, much less adore thee, for thy wonderful and unequalled condescension? What image, what similitude in nature, hast thou made use of here, in that of the vine, to mark the lowliness and meekness of thy person; and in the same moment, thy fruitfulness, and love, and usefulness to thy people! It was truly prophesied of thee, my Lord, that thou shouldest be "as a root out of a dry ground." And what so apparently dry and unpromising, before the budding season, as the vine? It was said that thou wouldest have "no form nor comeliness, nor any beauty, that we should desire thee." And here when thou callest thyself "the true vine," surely, Lord, thou couldest have chosen no image more unsightly. It was said, that thou shouldest be "lowly and meek, when coming with salvation." And what so low as the vine, that sends forth her branches upon the ground? What so weak and feeble as the vine, that needs always some prop or stay to cast her feeble arms upon? Thy extent, O Lord, in the spreading of thy gospel, was prophesied to be "from sea to sea, and from the river unto the ends of the earth." And truly, Lord, in the wide-spreading branches of the vine, thou art the fruitful bough of Joseph, "even a fruitful bough by a well, whose branches run over the wall." And when we see the multitude of thy people all hanging on thee, all united to thee, and all drawing sap, and moisture, and life, and strength, and fruitfulness from thee; what can more beautifully represent Jesus and his people than the rich vine and her branches, on which grow the fullest clusters of the pure blood of the grape? Precious Lord Jesus, thou art indeed "the true vine," and "the plant of renown," which, for wholesomeness, verdure, nourishment, and delight, surpasseth the whole creation of God. Lord, let me sit under thy shadow, let me taste of thy fruit, "for they that dwell under thy shadow shall return, they shall revive as the corn, and grow as the vine, the scent thereof shall be as the wine of Lebanon!"

SEPTEMBER 21.

MORNING.—"Ye shall be baptized with the Holy Ghost."—Acts xi. 16.

Blessed promise! realize it, Oh thou Holy Spirit, day by day, in and upon my soul. Bring me under the continued baptisms of thy sovereign influence, and cause me to feel all the sweet anointings of the Spirit sent down upon the hearts and minds of thy redeemed, as the fruits and effects of Jesus's exaltation, and the promise of God the Father. Yes, blessed Spirit, cause me to know thee in thy person, work, and power; in all thy offices, characters, and relations. I need thee day by day, as my Comforter. I need thee, as the Spirit of truth, to guide me into all truth. I need thee, as the Remembrancer of the Lord Jesus, to bring to my forgetful heart all the blessed things he hath revealed to me. I need thee, as the witness of my Jesus, to testify of my wants, and his fulness to supply. I need thee, as my advocate and helper, in all my infirmities in prayer. I need thee, as the earnest of the promised inheritance, that I may not faint, nor want faith to hold on and hold out in all dark seasons. I need thee, Lord; nay, I cannot do a moment without thee, nor act faith, nor believe a promise, nor exercise a grace, without thy constant, thine unceasing agency upon my poor soul. Come then, Lord, I beseech thee, and let me be brought under thine unceasing baptisms. Shed abroad the love of God my Father in my heart, and direct me into the patient waiting for Jesus Christ.

EVENING.—"He made a feast unto all his princes, and his servants; the power of Persia and Media, the nobles and princes of the provinces being before him. When he shewed the riches of his glorious kingdom, and the honour of his excellent majesty, many days, even an hundred and fourscore days."—Esther i. 3, 4.

Who can read the account here given of the royalty and liberality of the Persian monarch, without having the mind immediately directed to look at the Lord

Jesus, in his royalty and grace, and to consider both the extent of his bounty, and the honour of his excellent majesty, compared to which this earthly potentate sinks to nothing? What though his kingdom reached over a hundred and seven and twenty provinces, from India to Æthiopia; what is this to Him, whose dominion is "from sea to sea, and from the river even unto the ends of the earth;" yea, who hath "all power in heaven and in earth," and hath "the keys of hell and the grave?" And what a day, in point of duration, was that feast, which, though extended to a hundred and fourscore, yet, when ended, left nothing to follow, but perhaps induced sickness and sorrow; when we contemplate that eternal and everlasting day, to which Jesus invites, and in which he entertains all his people, whom he hath made "kings and priests unto God and the Father," and where they shall not only feast with him, and he with them, but shall sit down with him on his throne, as he hath overcome, and is sat down with his Father, on his throne? And in this one eternal and never-ending feast of the Lord Jesus, from which the guests shall go out no more, there is nothing to nauseate, nothing unpleasant to mingle, but all is light, and joy, and peace, and unspeakable felicity. Here Jesus openly sheweth the riches of his glorious kingdom, and the honour of his excellent majesty! Here he brings his redeemed into a perfect acquaintance with himself, and opens to their astonished unceasing contemplation and delight, the wonders of his person, and the wonders of his love; and fills their ravished souls "with joy unspeakable and full of glory," in the knowledge of "the mystery of God, and of the Father, and of Christ." Hail, thou glorious King of kings, and Lord of lords! Here thou art making a feast of grace in thine holy mountain, for all thy poor and needy, and halt, and blind, whom thou hast made the princes of thy kingdom, and whom thou wilt bring, in thine own good time, to the everlasting feast of glory in thy kingdom above! Grant me, blessed Jesus, to be one of the happy number who partake of thy bounties of grace here, and sure I am, that I shall then one day sit down to the everlasting enjoyment of thyself in the glories of heaven for ever!

SEPTEMBER 22.

MORNING.—"The justifier of him which believeth in Jesus."—Romans iii. 26.

And who is this, indeed who can it be, but Jehovah? "It is God that justifieth. Who is he that condemneth?" But, my soul, mark how each person of the Godhead is revealed in scripture under this character; as if to convince every poor sinner that is looking for redemption in Israel only in Jesus, that God can be just, and yet the justifier of him that believeth in Jesus. God the Father justifieth the poor believing sinner: for he manifests that he is faithful and just to forgive us our sins, having found a ransom in the blood of his Son for sin, whereby he is faithful to all his covenant promises in pardoning us, having received at our Lord's hand double for all our sins. God the Son justifieth also his redeemed: for it is expressly said by the prophet, "In the Lord shall all the seed of Israel be justified, and shall glory." And that God the Holy Ghost justifieth, is as evident also; because it was through the eternal Spirit the offering of the body of Jesus Christ was offered, by which Christ is said to have been justified in the Spirit; and believers are said to be justified by virtue of it in the name of the Lord Jesus, and by the Spirit of our God. Hence all the persons of the Godhead concur in the act of justifying every believer in Jesus; by whom we have peace with God, fellowship with the Father, and with his Son Jesus Christ. Here then is a portion to live upon through life, in death, and to all eternity.

EVENING.—"Who maketh thee to differ from another?"—1 Cor. iv. 7.

My soul, sit down, in the cool of this lovely evening, and in the recollection of *distinguishing* mercies look up and behold the gracious hand that "maketh thee to differ from another; until thine heart overflow, in a view of the wonderful subject, with thanksgiving, love, and praise. If thou wilt open the volume of thine own life (and surely, of all volumes, when explained by the word of God, it is the most interesting to read) thou wilt behold such a multitude of instances, in all the departments of "nature, providence, and grace," as under divine teaching, will bring home the question with the most awakened earnestness to the heart, and cause thee frequently to exclaim, as thou passest on, "Who maketh thee to differ from another?" Every defect of nature in others, every poor cripple, or the blind, or deaf, which thou meetest with; the want of intellect, or the want of understanding, yea, that thou wert not born among the reptiles of the earth, but among them who are created in the image of God, may, and ought to direct thy heart to the contemplation of him and his distinguishing favour, "in whose book all thy members were written!" And when, from the kingdom of *nature,* in the appointments of the Lord, thou followest the tract of thine own history into the kingdoms of *providence* and *grace,* and beholdest through all, and in all the distinguishing mercies with which thy life hath been marked, the question will arise all around, and in every direction, "Who maketh thee to differ from another?" What a mercy to be born in this land of thy nativity, and not among the dark places of the earth, where the name of Jesus was never heard, nor the sound of the church-going bell invites sinners to salvation! What a mercy to have had praying parents, who sought blessings for us before we had power to ask for ourselves! Or, on the other hand, if sprung from ungodly parents, who never, by advice or example, led us to the throne of grace, what a mercy, that under all such unpromising circumstances, without advice and without example, the word of God, and the ordinances of Jesus, are dear to us! Surely the apostle's words enter with a strength of inquiry under these views, "Who maketh thee to differ from another?" And, my soul, if now, as from a rising ground, thou lookest back, and tracest "all the way which the Lord thy God hath brought thee these many years, to humble thee, and to prove thee, and to shew thee what was in thine heart," thou beholdest thy Lord's gracious dealings with thee, compared to others: how many with whom, in thy boyish days, thou enteredst the field of life together, that are now no more; how many that still survive, but know not the Lord; how many, in circumstances far more promising than thine, and yet have come short of the grace of God! Views like these, and all the thousand, and ten thousand incidents connected with them, instead of lifting the mind with pride, are enough to humble the soul to the dust before God, and melt all the finer affections into the most heartfelt sense of the apostle's question, "Who maketh thee to differ from another?" Jesus, my Lord, behold me at thy feet! How shall I dare lift mine eyes to thee, while in the moment of recollection of thy distinguishing mercy towards me, I call to remembrance my baseness towards thee? Lord, is it possible, that in a life where so much grace hath abounded, sin should so much abound? That in every spot where my God hath erected a monument of his love, my sinful and ungrateful heart should have left an inscription of my unworthiness! What others feel, I know not; but blessed, for ever blessed be the unwearied patience and goodness of my God, that through his distinguishing grace alone, I am what I am; and while my soul desires to refer all and every part of divine mercy, in all the departments of nature, providence, and grace, into the Lord's own free, and rich, and sovereign pleasure; I praise him for having given me that precious testimony in my soul, which the Lord himself said should be the consequence, inwrought by his divine teaching in the heart: "I will establish my covenant with thee, and thou shalt know that I am the Lord; that thou mayest remember and be confounded, and never open thy mouth any more, because of thy shame, when I am pacified toward thee for all that thou hast done, saith the Lord God." Ezek. xvi. 62, 63.

SEPTEMBER 23.

MORNING.—"Is there no balm in Gilead? Is there no physician there? Why then is not the health of the daughter of my people recovered?"—Jer. viii. 22.

Yes, there is both balm in Gilead, and a physician there. For the blood and righteousness of Jesus is the truest balm; and Jesus himself a Sovereign and an Almighty Physician. But if that blood be not applied, if Jesus be not known nor consulted, how shall health be obtained? My soul, hast thou known thy disease, felt thy disorder? Art thou convinced that it is incurable by all human means—no medicine, no earthly physician, can administer relief? Hast thou known these things? And convinced of the infinite importance of seeking elsewhere, art thou come to Jesus? What sayest thou, my soul, to the enquiry? Art thou acquainted with Jesus? Hast thou made known thy case to him? And hath he told thee all that is in thine heart? Hath he taken thee under his care? Is he administering to thee the balm of Gilead? Oh my soul, see to it that nothing satisfieth thy mind, until that thou hast heard his soul-reviving voice, saying, "I am the Lord that healeth thee," Exod. xv. 26. Seek it for thy life. Say unto the Son of God, "Speak but the word, Lord, and my soul shall be healed."

EVENING.—"And the earth helped the woman."—Rev. xii. 16.

How blessed is it to see the hand of the Lord, when no hand beside can be near to help! and that when our situation is as lonely and forlorn as that of the pelican in the wilderness, Jesus is still near; and we are never less alone than when alone! When the church brought forth her offspring, and hell stood ready to devour it, God sheltered it from his jaws. And when he cast forth a flood to sweep the church away, the earth helped the woman, by opening its mouth, and swallowing it up. My soul! look into thine own circumstances, and trace the Lord's dealings, and thou wilt find a great multitude of corresponding instances. It is from the inattentive minds of the Lord's people, that mercies so often pass and repass, and they see them not. There are thousands of them in every believer's life, that he is as unconscious of, as the world are of the sweet-blowing flower of the desert, which sheds her rich perfumes to the air, and her beauties to the heath, and hath no beholder. The Lord's dealings with his people, as well in the kingdom of providence as of grace, will form a huge volume to read over in eternity, in which, like the earth helping the woman, we shall find wonders to call forth love and praise to God and the Lamb. The timing of mercies, the unexpected coming of them, the instruments by which they have been brought, the means by which they have been accomplished, and, what above all must endear them, the cause whence they come, the medium through which they flow in the person of Jesus, and the covenant of redemption in his blood; all these bring them home to the heart, with "a joy unspeakable and full of glory," and richly fulfil that precious promise of a covenant God in Christ, "Yea, I will rejoice over them to do them good; and I will plant them in this land assuredly, with my whole heart, and with my whole soul," Jer. xxxii. 41.

SEPTEMBER 24.

MORNING.—"How much owest thou unto my lord?"—Luke xvi. 5.

My soul, if this question, which the unjust steward put to his lord's debtors, was put to thee concerning that immense debt which hath made thee insolvent for ever, what wouldest thou answer? Never couldest thou conceive the extent of it, much less think of paying the vast amount. A debtor to free grace for thy very being; a debtor to free grace for thy well-being; ten thousand talents, which the man in the parable owed his master, would not be sufficient to reckon up what thou in reality owest thy Lord, for even the common gifts of nature and of providence. But when the calculation goeth on in grace, what archangel shall write down the sum total? To the broken law of God, a bankrupt exposed to the justice of God; to the dreadful penalty of everlasting death; to the fears and alarms of a guilty conscience; to the worm that dieth not; to the accusations of Satan, unable to answer one in a thousand! My soul, how much owest thou unto thy Lord? Are there yet any other outstanding debts? Oh yes, infinitely and beyond all these! What thinkest thou, my soul, of Jesus? How much owest thou to the Father's love in giving; to the Redeemer's love in coming; and to the Holy Ghost in making the whole effectual to thy soul's joy; by which Jesus hath paid all thy debts, cancelled all the demands of God's righteous law, silenced Satan, answered justice; and not only redeemed thee out of the hands of everlasting bondage, misery, and eternal death, but brought thee into his everlasting kingdom of freedom, joy, and glory! Say, say, my soul, how much owest thou unto thy Lord? Oh precious debt! ever increasing, and yet everlastingly making happy in owing. Lord Jesus! I am thine, and thy servant for ever; thou hast loosed my bonds.

EVENING.—" Should not a people seek unto their God?"—Isaiah viii. 19.

To be sure they should. My soul, what would become of thee, in thine exercises, hadst thou not had a God in Christ to fly to, and a God in Christ to depend upon? Where wouldest thou find a bosom to pour all thy griefs into, did not Jesus say to thee, as to the sorrowful father, concerning his child, " Bring him hither to me?" Thou knowest, dearest Lord, that there are circumstances into which I am cast, where none but thyself can help; and even if help could be derived from man, yet who is there to whom I could seek with a certainty of success? " My friends," saith Job, " have dealt deceitfully, like a brook;" like a brook which, dried up by the summer heat, disappoints the traveller when he most needs supply to slake his thirst. Oh for grace to centre all my desires in thee, and to seek unto thee with all my concerns! Blessed Lord! let that devout frame of David, in the wilderness, be the frame of my soul in every wilderness dispensation, until I shall have passed through the whole of the valley of Baca, and have attained to the everlasting enjoyment of thee in heaven! " O God, thou art my God, early will I seek thee; my soul thirsteth for thee, my flesh longeth for thee, in a dry and thirsty land, where no water is," Psalm lxiii. 1.

SEPTEMBER 25.

MORNING.—" Thou shalt prepare thee a way, and divide the coasts of thy land which the Lord thy God giveth thee to inherit, into three parts, that every slayer may flee thither."—Deut. xix. 3.

Sweet thought to my soul, that He who is the *refuge*

is also the *way* to every poor soul-slayer, who hath murdered his own soul by sin. And who, my soul, could prepare thee this way, but God thy Father, who gave both Jesus for the way, and Jesus for the refuge? And how hath God the Spirit pointed to the way, cast up and prepared it, by taking up the stumbling-blocks out of the way, as God saith of his people? Isa. lvii. 14. Is it not God the Holy Ghost that sets Jesus up, as Moses did the serpent; points to his person, to his blood, to his righteousness, as the sanctuary and the city of refuge to every poor sinner that is the man-slayer of his own soul? And if what the Jews have said be true, that magistrates once a year made it their duty to have the roads examined, lest any obstructions should arise to block the path of the poor fugitive; and that they were obliged to set up a post at every turning and avenue, with the word *miklat—refuge*, upon it, to direct the murderer in his flight; well may ministers, every day, and all the day, stand in the gates of the city, and in the high places of concourse, pointing to Jesus, and crying out, "Behold the Lamb of God, which taketh away the sin of the world!" Precious Lord Jesus! lo, I come to thee; thou art my city of refuge—thou art the *miklat* of my soul! Under thee, and in thee, I shall be safe. Cease, ye avengers of blood, your vain pursuit; Christ hath taken me in. Thou shalt answer for me, Oh Lord my God.

EVENING.—"For I, saith the Lord, will be unto her a wall of fire round about, and will be the glory in the midst of her."—Zech. ii. 5.

Precious promises these, my soul! and, like all the other promises of our God, are "Yea and amen in Christ Jesus!" Is the church, in this wilderness-state, exposed to the ravages of Satan, who goeth about as a roaring lion, seeking whom he may devour? then will God "be unto her a wall," and that "of fire," which (like travellers in the desert, who encircle themselves with fire against the attacks of wild beasts by night) will keep her secure from all approaches. Doth the church, in her poor circumstances, need comfort within? then will God in Christ be " the glory in the midst of her." And hence, all around, within and without, in every direction, and in every way, Jesus will be " the hiding-place from the storm, and a covert from the tempest; and upon all the glory shall be a defence." Look up then, my soul! What hast thou to fear? What though the rains beat without, and poverty be felt within; he that is " the wall of fire" can never be extinguished, and he that is " the glory in the midst" will still shine upon thee, and fully satisfy all thy need. Precious Lord Jesus! While thou art my defence, what host of foes can I fear? And while thou art my glory, surely I shall never consider my own humble circumstances. I will therefore say, with an exercised believer of old, " At what time I am afraid, I will trust in thee!" Ps. lvi. 3. To whom shall a child run, but to his father, in a season of distress? And to whom shall a poor ransomed soul of Jesus look, but to his Redeemer? And he will be both a shield and sun, " when the blast of the terrible ones is as a storm against a wall." Sweet thought to hush the soul asleep! And thou, my soul, take it with thee to thy bed, this night: Jesus is unto thee as " a wall of fire round about," and he that is in the midst of thee is " thy God, thy glory!"

SEPTEMBER 26.

MORNING.—" And they shall hang upon him all the glory of his father's house."—Isa. xxii. 24.

And who is this but Jesus, the true Eliakim and Governor of heaven and earth? Jesus sweetly explained it himself, when declaring himself possessing the key of David. Rev. iii. 7. And hath not God the Father literally given all things into his hands? Is there any thing which Jehovah hath kept back? Hath it not pleased the Father, that in him should all fulness dwell? Is not Jesus the head over all things to the church, which is his body? Is he not the Almighty Lord and Treasurer of all things—grace here, glory hereafter? And is not our Jesus the administrator of all things in the world, both of providence and grace? My soul, is there aught remaining to hang upon Jesus? Pause, hast thou hung upon him all the glory of thy salvation? Pause again, my soul. Is *all* and every title given? Is there aught kept back? Is there any Achan in the camp of thine heart? Forbid it, Lord. See to it, my soul, (for it is thy life,) that thou art "hanging all the glory of the Father's house upon Jesus?" Make him not only the Alpha, but the Omega also of thy salvation. And as the Father loveth the Son, aud hath given all things into his hands; so do thou come to him for all things, receive from him all things, and ascribe to him all things, in the receipt of grace here, and glory hereafter—that Christ may be all, and in all, to the glory of God the Father. Amen.

EVENING.—" Jesus—wearied with his journey."—John iv. 6.

My soul, art thou wearied with the labours of the day, and glad that the evening of rest is come? Look unto thy Lord! Behold Jesus wearied with *his* journey. As part of the curse, this, among other consequences, seized upon the Lord of life and glory, from the moment he became flesh: "It behoved him in all things to be made like unto his brethren." All the sinful frailties and infirmities of our poor nature; all the calamities to which human life is exposed, in the thorns and thistles which the earth is made to bring forth to man, and the dust of death, into which, as Jesus spake by the spirit of prophecy, he knew Jehovah would bring him (Ps. xxii. 15.) these were the very conditions to which the Redeemer subjected himself, in the days of his flesh, when "he was made sin for us who knew no sin, that we might be made the righteousness of God in him:" and hence his whole life was a life of weariness, sorrows, and affliction. And he not only felt in himself the common wants, and was exposed to the common miseries of nature; but, living as in an hospital of woe, amidst the sick and wounded, he participated in every groan he heard, and, as the prophet spake of him, " himself bare our sicknesses, and carried our sorrows." And what can bring relief to the pilgrimage tears of the redeemed, or so sweetly soothe the wearied frames of his people both in body and soul, as looking unto Jesus? Precious Lord! Do I see thee wearied with thy journey; and shall I repine at mine? Hadst thou not where to lay thine head; and shall I feel hurt if the world refuse me a lodging? Was the Son of God, though rich, yet condescending to be poor: and though the Lord of life and glory, yet " a man of sorrows, and acquainted with grief;" subjecting himself to hunger, and thirst, and weariness, and affliction; tempted, and buffeted, and despised; yea, " a worm, and no man, a reproach of men, and the outcast of the people?" Oh Lord! how sweetly accommodating is thy blessed example to all the tried and trying circumstances of life! Grant me, dear Lord, as oft as sorrow, weariness, disappointment, and any of the afflicting dispensations incident to human life come upon me, grant me to be looking unto thee; and I would say, " Jesus was wearied with his journey!"

SEPTEMBER 27.

MORNING.—" He hath not despised nor abhorred the affliction of the afflicted: neither hath he hid his face from him: but when he cried unto him he heard him."—Ps. xxii. 24.

My soul, behold Jesus, the Lamb of God, in this sweet scripture. Is it not said of him, that in the days of his flesh " he offered up strong crying and tears, and was heard in that he feared? Though he were a Son, yet learned he obedience by the things which he suffered." And was Jesus the Holy One, the afflicted One, also? Was he truly so, when he bore thy sins? And was this the time to which the scripture refers, when God the Father had respect to the sufferings of Jesus, and neither despised nor abhorred them? Did the Father behold him then through the whole as the sinner's Surety, and graciously accept Jesus and the church in him? Oh then, my soul, think of this in all thy trials and afflictions. Carry all thy sins and sorrows to the throne. Jesus knows them all, sees them all, nay, appoints them all. He is always looking upon thee, and presenting thee in himself to the Father. And depend upon it, as thy afflictions are not only known by him, but appointed by him, he will measure out no more to thee than he will sanctify. And so far from abhorring or despising thy affliction, he will with every sorrow grant support, and with every temptation make a way to escape. Go then, my soul, cast all thy care upon him; for he careth for thee.

EVENING.—"For Demas hath forsaken me, having loved this present world."—2 Tim. iv. 10.

Was this the same Demas of whom the apostle spake, Coloss. iv. 14.? I should hope not. But if it was, it becomes no proof of a man's falling from grace. The apostle no where speaks of this man as being a partaker of grace. And a man cannot fall *from* grace, who never *possessed* grace. Professors there may be, who follow the means of grace, as Demas followed Paul; but the world, as in his instance, is still in their heart. But, my soul, what the apostle hath said of *him*, may well serve for an instruction to *thee*. If Jesus, and the love of Jesus, with all his sweetness, beauty, suitableness, and delight, be come into thine heart, then will the love of this present world be gone out. Both cannot dwell nor live together in the same heart. A believer in Christ Jesus will carry with him his affection to Jesus even into the world, wherever the business or duties of life, in the honest maintenance of himself and family, necessarily call him. Is he constrained to go to the market-place, or engaged in the labours of his hands at home, still the savour of Jesus's name is upon his soul; and fellowship with heaven is carried on, while intercourse with the earth and earthly things engage his hands. " Holiness unto the Lord shall be upon the bells of the horses," Zech. xiv. 20. that is, every thing shall carry with it a memorandum for the sanctified use of all providences. When a soul hath once made Jesus his portion, his desires are to trace Jesus in every thing, and to enjoy Jesus in every thing; and to say, with one of old, " Nevertheless I am continually with thee; thou hast holden me by my right hand," Ps. lxxiii. 23. My soul, what saith thine experience to this statement? If, Demas-like, thou lovest this present world, thine enjoyments, even in religion, will rise or fall, and be as the world countenanceth or frowneth upon it, like those springs of water which have a subterraneous communication with the sea; if the tide flow, they rise high; if the tide be at ebb, they will ebb also. But if Jesus, the living water, be the source and fountain of all thy love and enjoyments, the tides of this world will have no effect upon the streams of thy delight; " the water (which Jesus hath given thee) will be in thee a well of water springing up to everlasting life!"

SEPTEMBER 28.

MORNING.—" And there was a rainbow round about the throne." —Rev. iv. 3.

Mark this, my soul, and connect with it what God said after the destruction of the old world by water: " I do set my bow in the cloud, and it shall be for a token of a covenant between me and the earth. And I will look upon it, that I may remember the everlasting covenant between God and every living creature of all flesh." And was not this rainbow round the throne which John saw, to tell the church of Jesus, on whom the Father is always looking, to remember his everlasting covenant of grace? And what doth it say but this, there shall be no more a deluge, nor floods of vengeance poured out upon the sinner that believes in Jesus. He looks to Christ, while the Father beholds Christ: he trusts in Jesus, whom the Father hath trusted with his honour: he accepts Jesus as the whole of the covenant, in whom the Father beholds the whole of the covenant fulfilled. Help me, Lord, in the view of every renewed token of the rainbow in the heavens, to connect with it the promise of Jehovah to his poor redeemed upon earth. Yes, blessed Lord, there is a rainbow round about the throne; and Christ is the bow which Jehovah hath set in the cloud. On him, my soul, gaze and feast thy ravished eyes. On him thy God and Father looks, and is well pleased.

EVENING.—" Thou art more glorious and excellent than the mountains of prey."—Psalm lxxvi. 4.

My soul, the more thou turnest over the word of God in inquiries after thy beloved, the more wilt thou be astonished at the relation given of him in his excellency and glory. By every thing that can represent the adorable Redeemer, in his beauty, loveliness, grace, fulness, and all-sufficiency, whether considered in his absolute, his comparative, his relative, or his official glory, or in his glory as the head of his body, the church, the fulness of Him that filleth all in all; thou art constrained, with the church to cry out at every view, " Yea, he is altogether lovely; the chief among ten thousand." There is somewhat particularly striking to this amount in this verse for thine evening portion: " Thou art more glorious and excellent than the mountains of prey." Yes! it must be so: for when the soul hath found Jesus, like the merchant-man seeking goodly pearls, having found this one of immense and incalculable value, the soul gladly parts with every thing beside, to attain it. Hence one of old, having got possession of Jesus, cries out with holy joy and rapture, " I rejoice at thy word as one that findeth great spoil;" Psalm cxix. 162. In life men become mountains of prey to one another; and too frequently find, to their sorrow, that the pursuit and chase is folly, and the end of the game, vanity and vexation of spirit. But in following thee, thou blessed Jesus, every renewed discovery of thee is glorious, and every new attainment most excellent indeed. In thy person, offices, character, relations, thou art most glorious and excellent. Thou art a glorious Redeemer, a glorious head of thy church and people; a glorious husband, brother, friend; a glorious prophet, priest, and king, in thy Zion. And when I behold thee in all these relative excellencies, and can and do know thee, and enjoy thee, and call thee mine, under every one of them, surely I may well take up the language of this sweet scripture, and say, " Thou art more glorious and excellent than the mountains of prey?"

SEPTEMBER 29.

MORNING.—" And it came to pass, when the vessels were full, that she said unto her son, bring me yet a vessel. And he said unto her, there is not a vessel more. And the oil stayed."—2 Kings iv. 6.

Do I not see Jesus and his fulness here? His giving out never ceaseth, until we have no more empty vessels to receive. And surely it is but proper the oil of grace should stay, when there are no more souls to be supplied. Pity indeed would it be, that any thing so precious should be spilt on the ground. My soul, art thou not poor as this poor woman? Is the creditor come to take thee for bondage? Cry mightily to Jesus, the Lord God of the prophets. And wilt thou borrow vessels to receive his bounty? Borrow not a few; for every vessel must fail before that Jesus fails. Hast thou filled all? See then that thy Almighty Creditor is paid from Jesus's bounty; for he hath paid all thy debt: and see that thou live henceforth on Jesus's fulness. Oh bountiful Lord, let me learn from hence sweet lessons of faith. There is no narrowness in thee, but all fulness. All thou hast, moreover, is for sinners. And, precious Lord, art thou not glorified in giving out to sinners? Is it not thy glory, thy delight so to do? Art thou not pleased when sinners come to thee? Oh for grace to come to thee, and to know and believe that it is thy glory and thy pleasure to receive them. Indeed, indeed thou keepest open house, an open hand, an open heart. Lord, give me daily, hourly, to come empty to thee to be filled; with grace here, and glory hereafter.

EVENING.—" Yet they seek me daily, and delight to know my ways, as a nation that did righteousness, and forsook not the ordinance of their God: they ask of me the ordinances of justice: they take delight in approaching to God."—Isaiah lviii. 2.

My soul, when thou readest a scripture like this, which, as far as the outward observance of religion goes, seems to carry a fair face, it may be well to consider the wretched delusion under which such men labour. The world, indeed, calls them very good sort of people; but the Lord speaks most awfully concerning them. Persons of this complexion do not venture to say, that they hope to be found before God without sin: for they will tell you, that they know " we have all sinned and come short of God's glory:" but their faith is, that for their sins they have endeavoured to repent, and made amends; and they hope Christ will make up the deficiency. They have not been so bad as many others; and in point of doing, they have done a great deal more: so that if they do not go to heaven, they know not who will. As to ordinances, as this scripture represents, they profess to seek the Lord daily, as a nation that does righteousness, and that takes delight in approaching to God. "Wherefore have we fasted, say they, and thou seest not? Wherefore have we afflicted our soul, and thou takest no knowledge?" Mark, my soul, the awful feature of such characters, and behold what is the leading principle in the religion of many who are not openly profane. Here are no cries for sin, no concern for the sufferings of Jesus; no inquiries for redemption in his blood; neither any heart-felt acquaintance with the teachings and humblings of the soul by the Holy Ghost. Doth God bid his sent servants to cry aloud, and spare not, in shewing *his people* their transgressions, and "the house of Jacob" their sins? And can such as these be found righteous in his sight? Oh! for the warning voice, to bid them flee from the wrath to come! Had I the power of persuasion, I should say, 'My poor deluded, self-righteous brother! rouse from this carnal security and vain confidence. If salvation be of works, then is it no more of faith. And if any thing but the blood of Christ can cleanse from sin, or any thing but the righteousness of Christ justify the sinner, then must all the threatenings of the gospel be void, and all the promises be altered.' Blessed be the Lord that teacheth thee, my soul, to profit, and hath fully, finally, and completely established thee in this decisive truth, that "there is salvation in no other but in Jesus only: neither is there any other name under heaven given among men whereby we must be saved."

SEPTEMBER 30.

MORNING.—"And this day shall be unto you for a memorial."—Exodus xii. 14.

It is blessed to end the month, and end every day, as we would wish and desire to end life, blessing and praising God in Christ; rising from the table of divine bounties, and thanking the great Master of the feast. Pause, my soul, and see whether, in the past month, such hath been thine experience of sovereign grace and unmerited mercies, that thou canst now set up thine Ebenezer, and mark this day for a memorial. What visits hath Jesus made to thee, my soul; and how hath thine heart been drawn out after him? Hath the Father, as well as the Son, come and made his abode with thee? Hath the Holy Ghost, the glorious inhabitant in the souls and bodies of his people, manifested his continued presence to thee? This day is indeed a memorial, if, in summing up the wonderful account of divine manifestations of divine love in providence and grace, during the month now nearly closed, and the years already passed, thou canst mark down the blessed enumeration. And will not my Lord, while the day is not passed, and yet remains to be added to the month, will he not make it memorable by some renewed favour? Oh, for some new visits from Father, Son, and Spirit—this morning, this day, and all the day! As long as I live I would have my soul going forth in exercises of faith and love upon the person of Emanuel, that I may carefully mark down the numberless instances of it. Here, I would say, Jesus visited me; here it was he met me, here he shewed me his loves, and made the place and day ever memorable by his grace.

EVENING.—"I must work the works of him that sent me, while it is day: the night cometh, when no man can work."—John ix. 4.

Pause, my soul, over this sweet scripture, and these sweet words of thy Lord! Look at Jesus, even *thy* Jesus, who, in the service of Mediator, as God's servant, had work to do in his day, as thou hast in thine. And Oh! what a day was his! Every portion of it filled with good! Now, my soul, the night of this present day is come; and the night of the whole day of thy life upon earth will shortly follow; it may come this very night; for nearly as the month is ended, thy life may end before it: and though death come not this very night, it cannot be far off, and may be near indeed. How then stands thy great account? Take down thy memorandums, as merchants do their ledger at certain seasons, to ascertain their stock; and review thine experience. Hath Jesus filled up every page? Hast thou the several *items* of his grace, and love, and bounty? Canst thou tell of Him that sent *thee* into the world, as he saith his Father *sent* him? John xvii. 18. Canst thou call to mind, from the first Bethel visit of his love, to the present hour, how he hath borne thee, and carried thee as on eagle's wings? And though it would tire the arm of an angel to write down the vast account of his mercy and grace, and though in thy poor forgetful heart, thousands, and ten thousands of instances have passed away, like traces on the water, and thou canst remember them no more; yet in looking back upon the whole, canst thou say, "Jesus is mine, and I am his?" Oh! the unspeakable felicity of thy summing up months, and days, and years, when the night cometh that no man can work. Precious Lord Jesus! thou hast indeed done all *for* me, and wrought all *in* me; thou hast made, and thou dost bear. It is thou that formed me from the womb, and now hast made me in thyself: thou hast redeemed me, and washed me from my sins in thy blood; borne with me in all my unworthiness, and carried me in all my sorrows! Into thy gracious hands, Lord, I desire to fall this night, and every night, and in the night of death; under the blessed assurance, that "when my heart shall faint, and my strength shall fail, thou wilt be the strength of my heart, and my portion for ever." Amen.

OCTOBER 1.

MORNING.—"Shiloh."—Gen. xlix 10.

Precious name of the Lord Jesus! how blessed hath

it been in all ages to thy people. Oh Lord, make it as ointment poured forth this morning to my soul! Both Jews and Christians alike agree in it, that it belongs only to the Messiah. And how then is it that they do not see Christ in it, even our Jesus, who suffered under Pontius Pilate, and died, as Caiaphas predicted the expediency, that one man should die for the people, and that he should fulfil the dying patriarch's prediction, by gathering together in one the children of God which were scattered abroad? That Jesus answered to Jacob's prediction, and none but Jesus ever did, is evident from their own testimony:—" We have a law," said they to Pilate, " and by that law he ought to die." Now, then, they themselves hereby confessed that as Jacob prophesied, the Lawgiver was not departed from Israel when Christ came. And when they added, " We have no king but Cæsar," certain it was, from their own testimony, the sceptre was gone out of the family of Judah, when the heathen emperor was king. Think of these evidences, my soul, and feast thyself upon the precious name of thy Shiloh. Thy Jesus, thy Shiloh, thy Almighty Deliverer, is come. He is both thy Lawgiver and thy Law-fulfiller; thy God and thy King, who sprang out of Judah. Oh thou glorious Shiloh! let my soul be gathered to thee, to live upon thee and to thee; and do thou, Lord, arise out of Zion, and when the fulness of the gentiles is completed, let both Jew and gentile be gathered into one fold, of which be thou the ever-living, ever-loving, ever-governing Shiloh, to bless them in thyself for ever. Amen.

EVENING.—" Although the fig-tree shall not blossom, neither shall fruit be in the vines, the labour of the olive shall fail, and the field shall yield no meat, the flocks shall be cut off from the fold, and there shall be no herd in the stalls: yet I will rejoice in the Lord, I will joy in the God of my salvation!"—Habakkuk iii. 17, 18.

See, my soul, in the prophet's example, the blessedness

of living *above* creature enjoyments, by living *upon* Creator fulness. Here is a sun, which never goes down! Here is a fountain, whose streams can never dry up! He that lives upon creature excellency, will want both food and comfort when that excellency dies, for they must die with it, when the period of its flourishing is over. But the soul that draws all from Jesus, the God of his salvation, will have Jesus and his salvation to live upon, and to be an everlasting source, when nature, in all its varieties, ceases to supply. My soul, what are thy resources for a day of famine? Canst thou join issue with the prophet? If blasting, or mildew, or frost, shall nip the fig-tree of its blossom; if both the vine and the olive fail; yea, if the staff of life, as well as the sweets of life, should all be gone; hast thou Jesus to live upon; canst thou rejoice in him, when there is nothing else left to rejoice in; and call him thine, and the God of thy salvation, when none will own thee, and thou hast none beside him to own? They say that music upon the waters always sounds best. Be this so or not, yet the melody of the soul is certainly sweetest when nature is out of tune, if the believer can take his harp from the willow, and sing aloud on the tribulated waters of sorrow, to the God of his salvation. And this is a song never out of season, but has peculiar joy in the note, when from a new-strung heart, the believer sings it *of* the God of his salvation, and addresses it *to* the God of his salvation. Blessed Lord Jesus! give me grace, like the prophet, so to sing and so to triumph, that since, lose what I may, I cannot lose thee, while thy creature comforts remain, I may enjoy them, from enjoying thee in them: and when all are taken away, still, having thee for my portion, may I sing aloud with the prophet, though all earthly enjoyments cease, "I will still rejoice in the Lord, I will joy in the God of my salvation."

OCTOBER 2.

MORNING.—"By night on my bed I sought him whom my soul loveth."—Song iii. 1.

Pause, my soul, over this account which the church gives of herself, and see whether such be thine exercises. It is night indeed in the soul whenever Christ is absent, or his presence not enjoyed. And though, blessed be God, the believer's interest in Christ varies not, yet his joy in the sense of safety is not always the same. Though it be the bed of affliction, or the bed of sickness, it is not the bed of carnal security, when the soul seeks Jesus. We cannot be said to be in a cold, lifeless, and indifferent state, while Jesus is sought for. It may be night indeed, it may be a dark season; yet, nevertheless, when we can say, "With my soul have I sought thee in the night, yea, with my spirit within me will I seek thee early:" surely, this earnestness implies grace, and love, and desire, in lively exercise. However dull, stupid, and unprofitable, at times, ordinances and means of grace may seem; still grace, like the live coal under the embers, is not gone out nor extinguished. Him whom my soul loveth frequently breaks out, and plainly shews that Jesus still lives and reigns within. Oh precious Lord, thou art still the lovely one, the chief one, and the fairest among ten thousand. Be thou all in all, the hope of glory.

EVENING.—"And when they had nothing to pay he frankly forgave them both."—Luke vii. 42.

My soul, nothing can be more grateful, and commendatory to the state of thine insolvency, than the recollection of what thy God and Saviour hath taught in this beautiful parable; that the debtor of five hundred pence, and the debtor of fifty, being both equally incapable of discharging the respective claims upon them, are equally considered as objects of mercy, and are therefore both alike forgiven. And this, indeed, is the distinguishing property of grace. It is totally distinct from merit; yea, in direct opposition to it. Hadst thou the least pretensions to divine favour, or couldest thou have put forth the least helping hand towards thine own salvation; grace then would have been no more grace. The frank forgiveness of all debt, carries with it the plainest testimony of man's total helplessness, and the sovereign freedom of divine love. And hence, when the sinner, of every description and character, is brought into this glorious privilege of redemption, the whole result is "to the praise of the glory of his grace, who hath made us accepted in the Beloved." What a beautiful and interesting view is this of the gospel of Jesus! It is full, and free, and suited to every case, and answering to the state and circumstances of every poor sinner. For as all have sinned and come short of God's glory; so all, being unable to make the smallest restitution, are equally objects suited to divine mercy: and, whatever other causes operate, certain it is, that the greatness or smallness of the debt, in a state of total insolvency, becomes no bar to pardon. So runs the charter of grace, and the proclamation from the court of heaven. Let all that are poor, and insolvent, and helpless, and conscious of their lost state, come alike to the footstool of the mercy-seat. The Son of God will have his court surrounded with such; and every one to whom his free salvation is welcome, that poor creature, be his circumstances what they may, shall be welcome to take it; whether him that oweth ten thousand talents, or whether him that oweth fifty: having nothing, either of them, to pay, the Lord frankly forgives both! Oh! the unsearchable riches of grace! Thanks be unto God for his unspeakable gift!

OCTOBER 3.

MORNING.—" Even the righteousness of God, which is by faith of Jesus Christ unto all, and upon all them that believe; for there is no difference."—Romans iii. 22.

Here, my soul, is a morning portion for thee! Surely here is enough for a morning portion for poor believing souls to live upon to all eternity. Mark, my soul, what is here said. That righteousness of the Lord Jesus Christ, which he wrought out for his church, is the righteousness of God: for, as he was God as well as man, his righteousness was, to all intents and purposes, the righteousness of God. Now the sin of Adam, and the sins of all Adam's children, put the whole together, form but the sins of *creatures;* consequently the righteousness of the Lord Jesus Christ is more than an equivalent, a more full payment than their debt can demand, because it is the righteousness of the *Creator*. Sweet thought! for God is more honoured by Christ's obedience, than dishonoured by our disobedience. And observe, my soul, how this righteousness is the church of Christ's, namely, by faith; " it is unto all, and upon all them that believe." It is received by faith. The scripture language of this unspeakable mercy is, that as it was imputed to Abraham for righteousness, so it shall be imputed unto us also, if we believe on Him that raised up our Lord Jesus from the dead. This is another delightful portion of this precious verse. Neither is this all—for, as if to encourage the poorest, weakest, and most timid believer, this righteousness of God, which is by faith of Jesus Christ unto all, and upon all that believe, " hath no difference" in its blessed effect. All partakers of it are alike partakers. By him, that is by Christ, the scripture saith, " all that believe are justified from all things." Acts xiii. 39. So that, though the faith of an Abraham or of a Peter might have been vastly greater than that of the timid

Ananias, or the poor man that came to Christ for his son, saying, "Lord, I believe, help thou mine unbelief;" yet the justification by Christ, to all, is one and the same—"it is to all, and upon all that believe; for there is no difference." Oh precious righteousness of the God-man Christ Jesus.

EVENING.—"For a testament is of force after men are dead; otherwise it is of no strength at all whilst the testator liveth."—Heb. ix. 17.

Precious Lord Jesus! and was it needful that thou shouldest die, that the rich legacies of thy will might be paid thy children, and thy spouse, the church? Was the testament in thy blood of no force until thou hadst finished redemption by expiring on the cross? And hast thou now confirmed the whole, by this gracious act of thine, when dying "the just for the unjust, to bring us to God?" Sit down, my soul, this evening, and ponder over the unequalled love of thy dear Redeemer. Jesus died, and thereby gave validity and efficacy to his will. Now therefore it is of force. Now the large estate of "an inheritance, incorruptible, and undefiled, and which fadeth not away," which Jesus hath purchased by his blood, is eternally and everlastingly secured. Yea, the will hath since his death, been proved in the court of heaven, and Jesus is gone thither to see every legacy paid; yea, Jesus becomes the executor and administrator of the whole, and ever liveth for this express purpose. So that it is impossible for any of his poor relations, and their claims through him, ever to be forgotten or overlooked. Pause over this view of this most interesting subject. Shall the great ones of the earth, the rich and the mighty, be so anxious over their legacies from one another, as never to lose an estate for want of enquiry, when their rich relations die; and wilt not thou, my soul, now thy rich relation is dead, and liveth again, and hath left thee the most blessed of all inheritances, wilt not thou seek after it, and be anxious for the full possession of it? Dost thou know thyself to be indeed a part of Christ's body, the church, the Lamb's wife, and, by adoption and grace, a child of God, and a joint-heir with Christ; and wilt thou not see that thy legacy be fully paid? Surely, thou hast already taken out a probate of thy Lord's will from the chancery of heaven, the book of life, and therefore mayest well look for all the testamentary effects. Precious Lord Jesus! I hear thee speak, and well do I remember the words; "Peace I leave with you; my peace I give unto you; not as the world giveth, give I unto you!" Oh the unspeakable mercy of being thus related to the Lord Jesus Christ! by which, my soul, thou hast every legacy needful for thy present peace paid in part; and the whole reversionary interest of that immense estate in heaven shall be fully paid when thou comest of age, and thou shalt enter upon the possession of it, in the presence of thy Lord, and sit down with him in the everlasting enjoyment of it for ever!

OCTOBER 4.

MORNING.—"Behold, I am with thee, and will keep thee in all places whither thou goest; for I will not leave thee, until I have done that which I have spoken to thee of."—Gen. xxviii. 15.

Here is a promise to Jacob, and not to Jacob only, personally considered, but to Jacob's seed. For the apostle Paul was commissioned by the Holy Ghost to tell the church of Jesus, that we, as Isaac was, are the children of promise. Hence this, like all other promises in Christ Jesus, is yea and amen. Pause, then, my soul, and ask thyself what hath the Lord spoken to thee of? Hath he met with thee in Bethel, as he found Jacob? And hath he there spoken unto thee? How wilt thou know? Very plainly. Jesus hath met with thee, hath indeed spoken unto thee, if so be thou hast seen thine own unworthiness and sinfulness by nature and by practice; and if thou hast seen the King in his beauty, even Jesus in his own glory, suitableness, and all-sufficiency, as a Saviour; and inclined thine heart by his grace to believe in him, to depend upon him, and to live to him and his glory. What sayest thou, my soul, to these things? Is this promise made to Jacob and his seed thine? If so, live upon Jesus, and plead the fulfilment of it daily, hourly. Say to him, my soul, Lord, what hast thou spoken to me of, but mercy, pardon, peace, and grace, with all spiritual blessings in Christ Jesus? And what have I to depend upon, or what indeed can I need more, but thy promise and the great Promiser? Yes, Lord Jesus, I do depend, I do believe. Surely thou wilt never leave whom thou hast once loved; and therefore thou wilt not leave me, until thou hast done that which thou hast spoken of in grace here, and wilt complete in glory hereafter.

EVENING.—" Man did eat angels' food."—Psalm lxxviii. 25.

Yes, so he did, when the Lord rained down manna upon the people in the wilderness. But, my soul, what hast thou eaten, now thou hast been at the table of thy Lord? What did Jesus there entertain thee with? "Wonder, O heavens, and be astonished, O earth!" Thou hast feasted upon the body and blood of Christ! and this is food which angels never ate, neither was such a feast ever prepared for them. Pause over this blessed subject, for it is enough to call up the wonder, praise, and love of all thine intellectual faculties for ever! When man fell, the earth was made to bring forth thorns and thistles; this was all the inheritance then left us; man was to eat bread in the sweat of the brow. But Jesus interposeth, and removes the curse, in being made a "curse for us." The curse being removed by him and his cross, the earth is made to bring forth its blessings, and "wine that maketh glad the heart of man, and oil to make his face to shine, and bread which strengtheneth man's heart." But after this, who should have thought, yea, what imagination could have conceived an idea so wonderful and surpassingly rich in mercy, that Jesus should become the bread of life, and the water of life, to his people; and feed them, as an heavenly pelican, with his own blood! Think, my soul, of thy privileges; thou art unworthy of the most common blessings of thine own table, which thy Lord hath provided; and yet Jesus feasts thee with the choicest of blessings of *his*. Thou hast merited nothing but "the cup of trembling;" but Jesus giveth thee the "cup of salvation." Thou art unworthy to gather up the crumbs that fall from thy Lord's table; but Jesus seats thee at his table with himself, and bids thee eat and drink, "yea, drink abundantly, O beloved." Lord, I fall down under the deepest self-abasement at the recollection of thy grace and my undeservings. Oh thou precious, precious Jesus! this is not angels' food indeed, but above angels' food; yea, divine food; thy body and blood! "Lord! evermore give me this bread!"

OCTOBER 5.

MORNING.—"He goeth before you into Galilee; there shall ye see him."—Mark xvi. 7.

Mark this, my soul, in all thy goings forth; look out for thy gracious, glorious Forerunner, and see whether the same going before thee of thy Lord hath not been from everlasting. Was it not Jesus that was set up as the Head of his people from everlasting? Did he not then go before them, when he went forth for the salvation of his people? In the council of peace did he not go before them; not only before we knew our need, but before we had a being? In all his covenant engagements, as the Surety of his people, he went before them. And in all his offices, characters, and relations, he was preventing us with the blessings of his goodness. And in the personal salvation of every individual of his redeemed, was not Jesus beforehand in quickening, illuminating, redeeming mercy? "If we love him, is it not because he first loved us?" And what is it now? Do not his mercies go before our prayers? and before we call, doth not Jesus answer? And will it not be so during the whole day of grace, even to the eternal day of glory? Precious Jesus, surely thou art going before me into Galilee. Oh for grace to follow the Lamb whithersoever he goeth. And do thou, Lord, walk with me, and talk with me, as thou didst to the disciples in the way, and make thyself known unto me in continual manifestations, and in breaking of bread, and in prayer.

EVENING.—"They made me keeper of the vineyards, but mine own vineyard have I not kept."—Song i. 6.

My soul, now the day is over, sit down, and look back on the employments of it. What a day hath it been? What portion of it hath been engaged in the service of thy Lord, and the improvement of thy soul? How wholly occupied in the busy and imperious demands of the world, the care of the body, and in procuring the bread that perisheth! Surely the complaint of the church is thine also. Keeper of the vineyards of others, thine own goeth to waste! And of what avail, in the path of grace, if though occupied by a thousand things in the aid of others, thou art making no progress in the heavenly road by thine own soul? Are not the peace of thy life, and the glorious expectation of a better, to be advanced in the knowledge and enjoyment of Jesus? If I lose sight of thee, thou dear Immanuel; if the lively actings of faith upon thee be remitted, will the recollection of attention to others give assurance or comfort? If I lose all that sweet personal communion and fellowship with thee, which is the very life of the soul, and receive none of thy private visits, what signifies the best and most successful public usefulness in thy church, and among thy people? I do indeed rejoice to say or do any thing which may minister to others in the knowledge of my Lord; but God forbid, that, like the post to the traveller, I be found merely to direct, but never move a step myself. Rather, blessed Jesus, be it my portion to be like the star to the wise men, which not only lighted to Christ, but went with them, and before them, until it came and stood over where the young child was. Oh! then, with the church, under the same complaint, let me cry out, as she did: "Tell me, O thou whom my soul loveth, where thou feedest; where thou makest thy flock to rest at noon; for why should I be as one that turneth aside by the flocks of thy companions?"

OCTOBER 6.

MORNING.—"Trust in him at all times; ye people, pour out your heart before him. God is a refuge for us. Selah."—Ps. lxii. 8.

My soul, the Holy Ghost hath marked this verse with Selah; therefore, pray observe it. You see the argument for trust, because God, that is, the Elohim, is a refuge. Yes, God the Father is a refuge, in his covenant engagements, word, oath, promises. God the Son is a refuge, in his suretyship engagements, in his perfect righteousness, in his blood-cleansing, sin-atoning death and salvation, and in all his securities of grace here, and glory hereafter. God the Holy Ghost is a refuge, in all his blessed offices, characters, and relations; by which he undertakes and fulfils all the purposes of salvation, in the glorifying of the Father and the Son, to every poor believer's joy and comfort. And wilt thou not, my soul, then trust in this glorious Elohim? Wilt thou not pour out thyself before him, and trust in him at *all* times, at *any* time, at *every* time? Nay, wilt thou not call upon all the people to this soul-rewarding service, and tell them of his grace and glory? "Come hither, I would say, and hearken, all ye that fear God, and I will tell you what he hath done for my soul." Oh let us magnify his name together; for he is a rock, and his work is perfect.

EVENING.—"By faith, Joseph, when he died, made mention of the departing of the children of Israel; and gave commandment concerning his bones."—Heb. xi. 22.

See, my soul, the triumphs of faith in this lively instance of the patriarch Joseph! How many have I known, who, though they have given up their souls, with full assurance of faith, into the hands of Jesus, conscious of an interest in him, and of redemption in his blood; have, nevertheless, felt fears and alarms for the moment in which the soul separates from the body, and have wanted faith "concerning their bones!" Look at the patriarch when dying, and learn from him whence to derive strength and comfort for every emergency, and for every concern. "By faith:" is the one universal charm. Jesus is *in* every thing, and *for* every thing the believer can possibly need or require, all the way home; in death, as in life; concerning the bones, or concerning the soul. In him the soul goes forth boldly from the body at the hour of death; and in him the body as safely and securely reposeth in the grave. The believer hears, or may hear, the voice of Jesus, in terms like those he spake to Jacob: "Fear not to go down into Egypt; I will go down with thee:" so Jesus speaks to his people: 'Fear not to go down into the grave; I will go down with thee!' Hence, by faith, like the patriarch, the believer feels a holy confidence in Jesus concerning his bones. And who can feel concern, when, by faith, all is committed unto Jesus? Who would fear concerning their bones, if Jesus make the grave, and appoint the sepulchre where, and when they are to be deposited; yea, inters the remains, visits and watches over the dust of his saints with more care than the goldsmith doth the golden particles, which he suffereth not the least air to blow away? Precious Jesus! be it my portion like Joseph, when dying, to have the same lively actings of faith as he had in thee, (and sure I am, he had not greater cause for the full exercise of this principle than believers now,) and may I then enjoy with equal, yea, with increasing strength, this blessed assurance in thee, and by the same faith that hath carried me through many sharp trials in the past, be carried through this last and trying conflict. Lord! let me die, as I have lived, *believing;* yea, triumphing in believing. And when the earth gives way under my feet, and every object of sense is sinking also, then may my soul go forth as the jewel from the casket, in all the joy which a soul in Christ must find; and in the last act of the holy triumph of faith leave all with thee "concerning my bones!"

OCTOBER 7.

MORNING.—"Looking for that blessed hope, and the glorious appearing of the great God, and our Saviour Jesus Christ."—Titus ii. 13.

Pause, my soul, over these sweet and solemn words. Is Jesus my hope? Surely then it is a blessed hope; for all blessings are in him. Art thou looking for his appearing? Pause, for the thought is solemn. How shall I know? Suppose this moment the trumpet of the archangel was to sound, "Arise, ye dead, and come to judgment;" my soul, art thou ready? Pause once more. Do I long for Jesus's appearing now, in the conversion of every poor sinner? Do I rejoice to hear, at any time, that a soul is born to God? If so, is not this looking for his appearing? Again—Do I long for Jesus appearing in the after-manifestations of his grace to the souls of the people?—for this is to rejoice with them that do rejoice, and to prove a family interest.

Again—Is Jesus precious to me, and do I long for the renewal of his visits, as the earth longeth for the rising sun? When I read his word, sing his praise, call upon his name, mingle in the congregation, go to his table; is his appearing upon all these occasions precious now, and are his love-tokens sweeter to my soul than honey, and the honey-comb? If, my soul, thou canst bear a cheerful testimony to these things, and canst truly call them blessed *now;* surely the hope of Jesus's *second* coming is blessed also, and thou canst well subscribe to the apostle's words; for his appearing being now *gracious,* will then be *glorious,* in the appearing of the great God, and our Saviour Jesus Christ.

EVENING.—" For the vision is yet for an appointed time, but at the end it shall speak, and not lie : though it tarry, wait for it, because it will surely come, it will not tarry."—Hab. ii. 3.

My soul, there is always a set time to favour Zion. It may not be so early as we could wish; it may not come at the time we look for it; yea, it may be deferred until our impatience hath given over the very expectation of it; nevertheless, " it will surely come; it will not tarry." We are like children, who wish to gather the fruit before it is ripe; but there is no haste with God. He stops until the mercy, intended to be given us, is fully prepared, and our souls as fully ready to receive it. And what endears the mercy (be it what it may) yet more, is, that from everlasting it hath been appointed. " The vision is for an appointed time." So that, however tedious it may seem in coming, it will neither go a moment beyond the appointment, nor come a moment before: and when it arrives, it will explain wherefore it came not sooner, by shewing how suited and seasonable it is now in its coming. My soul, let this sweet scripture be ever uppermost in thy recollection, to help thee on in seasons of exercise. God's appointments are sure; never shall his people be disappointed in them, nor of them; come they will, and at the very hour. Israel was to be a certain time in Egypt; when that time was accomplished, we are told, "The self-same night the Lord brought them out, with their armies." Exactly the same in Babylon, and exactly the same deliverance. So, my soul, in all thine exercises, the hour is marked: "The vision is for an appointed time." Though it tarry much beyond thy expectation, it cannot tarry beyond the Lord's appointment. Oh! for grace, upon every occasion, to follow the advice of David: "Wait on the Lord, be of good courage, and he shall strengthen thine heart: wait, I say, on the Lord," Ps. xxvii. 14.

OCTOBER 8.

MORNING.—"But him they saw not."—Luke xxiv. 24.

Mark, my soul, what is here said. Though Jesus sought out his disciples in the morning of his resurrection, and was found of them that sought him not; yet many saw him not, while he was thus gracious to many that looked not for him. So is it now. Many, like those women, have seen the sepulchre, as it were, of Jesus, heard his word; nay, many saw his body when on earth, yet saw not God in Christ in him. "The grace of God," saith the apostle, "hath appeared unto all men;" that is, the gospel grace is preached in common before believers and unbelievers; but believers only see Jesus as the wisdom and the power of God for salvation; of others it may be said, as here, "but him they see not." Oh precious Jesus, give me to see thee as the Sent and Sealed of the Father, that my soul may have such a saving sight and knowledge of thee as the apostle had, which flesh and blood cannot reveal, but the Father only which is in heaven. Oh heavenly Father! give me the Spirit of wisdom and revelation in the knowledge of thy dear Son; and do by me as by Paul, reveal thy Son in me.

EVENING.—" The house of the Rechabites."—Jer. xxxv. 2.

My soul, as the prophet had his commission from the Lord, to go unto the house of the Rechabites, and the Holy Ghost hath been pleased to have the event of the visit recorded ; do thou go down to it also, and see what instructions thou canst gather there, under his gracious teachings, for thine evening meditation. The house of the Rechabites drank no wine. And was not this to intimate the law of the Nazarites? Surely there was a reference, in this prohibition, to the one glorious Nazarite, even Jesus! The Rechabites had no fixed dwelling-place, but lived in moveable tents; and believers in Jesus, like their Lord himself, have " here no abiding city, but are seeking one to come." Hence, when the King of Babylon came into the land where the Rechabites had no fixed abode, they had no attachment to the place, and therefore the more readily took their departure. Such, my soul, will be the case with thee, in the land where thou art but a stranger, if, as a stranger and a pilgrim, " thou abstain from fleshly lusts, which war against the soul; and set thine affections upon things above, and not on things of the earth." Oh! how truly blessed to have no ties, no clogs, no impediments, to fasten down the soul; but " when the Assyrian cometh up into the land, this man, (this Glory-man, Christ Jesus,) is our peace," Micah v. 5. My soul, ponder well this sweet view of the house of the Rechabites, and mark the Lord's observation concerning them: they obeyed Jonadab their father, in all their abstinence and movements. The precept for this obedience, it should seem, was but once given, and the motive to it had no reward, either in dwelling-places here or hereafter. But with thee, my soul, all that thy God and Father hath enjoined thee concerning his dear Son, he hath again and again held forth; as he saith himself, " rising early and speaking, he hath sent all his servants, the prophets," as if intreating an attention to what must make for thy present peace and everlasting happiness. Oh! how truly blessed, like the house of the Rechabites, to sit loose and detached from earth and earthly things, and to be tracing Jesus in all, and enjoying Jesus in all. Go, my soul, go down frequently to the house of the Rechabites, that there the Lord may cause thee to hear his word!

OCTOBER 9.

MORNING.—" And all mine are thine, and thine are mine; and I am glorified in them."—John xvii. 10.

Precious testimony of a precious truth. See to it, my soul, that thou suffer not these blessed words of Jesus to drop from thy remembrance; but make them the everlasting meditation, not only of this morning, but every morning, and every day, and all the day; and mark thine interest in them. All Jesus's treasures in his people and his grace, are still the Father's; for, as Jesus and the Father are one in essence and in will, so also in property. And the Father's giving the church to Jesus, with all blessings in him, doth not alienate the Father's right: so in like manner, all that Jesus hath are the Father's, and Christ is glorified in them. It is a blessed order in the work and purpose of redemption, to trace the Father as the original Giver, Fountain, and Source of all; and then to trace them as Jesus's by virtue of his being the glorious Mediator. And hence the Holy Ghost is said to take them as Jesus's and shew unto the people. The Holy Ghost doth not take them immediately from the Father, but mediately from Christ; because, without the person and work of Jesus, they never could have been communicated to us. So that Christ is glorified by the Holy Spirit in the hearts of his people, when that blessed Spirit takes them, and gives them, and shews them, not immediately as the Father's, but as the fruit and consequence of Christ's merits and death, and thus shewing the common interest both of Father and Son, in all the blessed things of salvation. My soul, dost thou understand these precious things? Oh then, live in the enjoyment of them, and see that Jesus is glorified, and the Father glorified in his dear and ever blessed Son.

EVENING.—"But we are bound to give thanks alway to God for you, brethren, beloved of the Lord, because God hath from the beginning chosen you to salvation, through sanctification of the Spirit, and belief of the truth."—2 Thess. ii. 13.

Some of the sweetest enjoyments in grace, are the freeness and undeserved nature of that grace towards the happy objects of its distinguishing favour: and as the first and ultimate design of all, for which grace is given, is the glory of Jehovah; so the promotion of that glory, in the redemption and sanctification of the church of Jesus, is the means and end. Now, my soul, sit down, this evening, and mark well, in the blessed effects wrought in thine own heart, what the apostle hath here said, that if *thou* art chosen, it must have been from the beginning thou art chosen to salvation, through sanctification of the Spirit, and belief of the truth. Pause, and ask thyself: art thou chosen? Hath this sovereign act of grace passed upon thee? How shall I know? Look at the effects. Art thou humbled to the very dust before God, under the impression of the distinguishing nature of it? Dost thou know, dost thou feel, dost thou stand as one most fully convinced, that the eternal choice of thee was not for aught wherein thou differedst from others, but wholly of the Lord's own free and sovereign grace? And in the recollection that such love was shewn to thee, when meriting it no more than others; yea, when meriting wrath, instead of receiving grace, as much as others; dost thou lie yet lower in the dust on this account? And in proportion to the astonishing goodness of the Lord, do thine own conscious undeservings make thee continually yet more acquainted with thine own vileness? And as the views of grace rise higher, does the sense of sin make thee fall lower; that where "sin hath abounded, grace should much more abound?" Look at the subject under another point of view, but which leads to the same conclusion. As the consciousness of being chosen, from the beginning, to salvation, through the sanctification of the Spirit, becomes the highest and strongest of all possible motives to hide pride from the eyes, and to lay the soul down in the deepest self-abasement before God; so in the same breast, and from the same source, through the sanctification of the Spirit, there will be a most ardent affection towards the gracious author of such distinguishing mercy! Say then, my soul, should Jesus put the question to thee, as he did to Peter, "Lovest thou me more than these?" couldest thou appeal to him, who reads hearts, that he would find love in thine heart, because he himself had put it there? Pause over this great volume of inquiry, and follow up the question, in the numberless methods by which it might be sought and discovered. And, to add no more, if to those *two* great branches, under which God from the beginning makes choice of all the beloved of the Lord, through sanctification of the Spirit, thou canst add a satisfactory conclusion, in a *third* instance also, of sovereign power; and discover that since God called thee by his grace, and revealed his Son in thee, thou hast been conferring less and less "with flesh and blood," and by the Spirit hast been "mortifying the deeds of the body, and crucifying the flesh with its affections and lusts: Oh! what cause wilt thou find also for holy joy in the distinguishing grace of God, and to cry out with the apostle, "I am crucified with Christ:" and, "I am bound to give thanks alway to God, because from the beginning he hath chosen me to salvation, through the sanctification of the Spirit and belief of the truth!"

OCTOBER 10.

MORNING.—" That ye may know how that the Lord doth put a difference between the Egyptians and Israel."—Exod. xi. 7.

Who shall mark down all the properties of distinguishing grace? What a vast difference doth grace make, in this life, between him that serveth God, and him that serveth him not! And what an everlasting difference will be made in the life which is to come. My soul, make this thought the subject of thine unceasing meditation. Thou canst not walk the street, nor go to public worship, nor watch the Lord's dealings in all the vast and numberless dispensations going on in life, in the wide world of providence and grace, but what every thing speaks, in the language of the morning portion, of the difference there is still put between the Egyptians and Israel. Every thing proclaims it, every event confirms it. And do not overlook the great point of all—it is the Lord that doth all this. "Who maketh thee to differ from another?" Oh for grace to be always on the watch-tower to mark this, and for grace to acknowledge it! Precious Jesus, thou art the Source, the Fountain, the Author, the Finisher, of all. " Oh the depth of the riches both of the wisdom and knowledge of God! How unsearchable are thy judgments, and thy ways past finding out."

EVENING.—" As obedient children, not fashioning yourselves according to the former lusts, in your ignorance."—1 Pet. i. 14.

There is somewhat very striking in these words of the apostle; and they certainly mean more than not being found in actual transgression. The very *fashion* of a new-born child of God is supposed to distinguish his obedience; and his whole *appearance*, as well as his whole *conduct*, marks that the former lusts of his ignorant state, when unregenerated, are done away. And though the believer is not called upon to a singularity of dress or apparel, yet a singularity against customs leading to the confines of sin, and unsuited to the manners of a soul walking with Jesus, should certainly distinguish the Redeemer's people. It was said, as one among the characters by which they should be known; that "they should dwell alone, and should not be reckoned among the nations," Numb. xxiii. 9. And surely a total diversity of character, pursuit, and conduct, ought to distinguish them from the world. For, even among men, different nations have their diversity of character and occupation; and if there be a subject of contention between them, the ports and garrisons of one kingdom are shut against the admission of the people of another; there will be a total disconformity in this case, and nothing of harmony between them. My soul, see to it, that thy path and walk of life bear not the fashion of the world. Thou hast given thy name unto Jesus: his thou art, and the subject of his kingdom; professing to be guided by another Spirit, directed by another rule, walking by another faith, and looking forward to another world. See then, that every thing in and about thee mark this character of Jesus's pilgrim. Let thy dress be the robe of Jesus's righteousness; thine armour, the sword of the Spirit; thy conversation always "such as becometh the gospel of Christ." And as the Redeemer, long before he came, by the spirit of prophecy, pointed out the singularity of himself and followers, "as for signs and wonders in Israel," Isa. viii. 18. so let the character be thine, as "Joshua and his fellows, men wondered at," Zech. iii. 8. Precious Jesus! keep me always near thyself, and let my soul be always exercising a holy jealousy over all the parts of my conduct. Lord, I would pray, that where-ever I am, or however engaged, all who behold me may know that "I have been with Jesus!"

OCTOBER 11.

MORNING.—"He wakeneth morning by morning: he wakeneth mine ear to hear as the learned."—Isaiah l. 4.

Who is this but Jesus in his human nature, of whom

the prophet speaks? Eminently to him doth it refer, to whom was given the tongue of the learned, that he might know how to speak a word to him that is weary. Precious Lord, it is indeed thy province, and thine only, to speak a word to weary souls, and to be the rest wherewith thou causeth the weary to rest, and to be their refreshing. Not only to give them rest, but thyself to be their rest. Not only to give them salvation, but thyself to be their salvation.—But, blessed Lord! may not a poor soul like myself say of thee also, that thou wakenest me morning by morning?—for who is it but Jesus, that, by the sweet influences of the Spirit, wakens his people morning by morning, and openeth the ear to hear, and the eye to see, and the heart to feel the blessed tokens of his coming? Have I not found thee, Lord, wakening my soul sometimes before the dawn of day, and calling my soul up in gracious meditation, to attend to the soft whispers of thy love? Have I not heard thee saying, as to the church of old, "Rise up, my love, my fair one, and come away?" And hast thou not made my soul, or ever I was aware, like the chariots of Aminadab? Do thou, Lord, waken me, I beseech thee, morning by morning, and while thou art thus speaking to my soul, let mine answer be, "My voice shalt thou hear betimes, Oh Lord, in the morning; early will I direct my prayer unto thee, and will look up. My soul shall wait for thee, more than they that watch for the morning, yea, I say, more than they that watch for the morning."

EVENING.—"And the king said unto Esther at the banquet of wine, what is thy petition? and it shall be granted thee: and what is thy request? even to the half of the kingdom it shall be performed."—Esther v. 6.

My soul, thou hast lately been at the banquet of wine indeed, even of the Redeemer's blood, which Jesus holds at his table; and didst thou not behold the numberless petitioners who attended there with thyself? Surely, if the Persian king made so generous an offer to Esther, to perform her petition, be it what it might, to the half of his kingdom; thy Jesus, thy heavenly King, with whom are all the treasures, and the unsearchable riches of grace and glory, did not suffer a poor humble petitioner to go empty away. Tell me, ye that attended there, did ye not find the King most gracious? How went the matter with you? I pray you tell me. Did the poor man find Jesus indeed rich; and did the trembling sinner, under the apprehensions of wrath, find himself delivered by him "from the wrath to come?" Surely, Jesus had a suited mercy for every case. And, sure I am, that whatever heart was prompted by his grace to look to him, the eye and heart of Jesus were looking with mercy upon that poor sinner. Oh! what gifts, what graces, what pardons, doth every renewed banquet of Jesus scatter among the people! At his table the doors are thrown open, and nothing is needed to ensure welcome, but a sense of need and an hungering to partake. How often, my soul, hast thou seen the people made joyful in the Lord's house of prayer, and returning, as they did after the feast of the dedication of Solomon's temple, to their tents, "joyful and glad in heart?" Yea, how often hast thou returned thyself, and left all thy sorrows, sins, and wants behind thee, when the King hath held forth his sceptre of grace, and given thee faith to touch it! Come, ye polluted, poor, exercised, distressed souls; ye wandering, weary, backsliding people; come to Jesus: he holds a feast, and every case and every need, he can, and will supply. Let but a sense of need be inwrought by the blessed Spirit in the heart, and the language of our Jesus is to this amount: "What is thy petition, and what is thy request? and it shall be granted thee."

OCTOBER 12.

MORNING.—" And this man shall be the peace, when the Assyrian shall come into our land."—Mic. v. 5.

What man is this but the Glory-man, the Mediator between God and men, the man Christ Jesus? And what peace, when all enemies oppose the soul, but peace in the blood of his cross? Yes, my soul, Jesus is the wonderful man, who alone could make thy peace. " For as it was by one man's disobedience many were made sinners; so by the obedience of one shall many be made righteous." And none but one in our own nature could redeem that nature; for the right of redemption belonged only to him. Levit. xxv. 25. And none but one in our nature could atone, could bleed, could die, and rise again, that he might be the Judge, both of the dead and living. Oh precious Jesus, how suited wert thou by the union of thy two natures, as God and man, and God-man, both in one, to be our glorious Mediator, and to be the Lord our Righteousness! Yes, precious Lord, God hath said it, and my soul evermore rejoiceth in the blessed truth: this man, Christ Jesus, shall be my peace, my glory, my salvation, my refuge, when the Assyrian shall come into our land.

EVENING.—" The day-dawn, and the day-star."—2 Peter i. 19.

And what is " the day-dawn, and day-star," arising in the hearts of God's people, but Jesus, " the day-spring from on high, visiting us?" Is not Jesus " the bright and morning star, the light and the life of men?" Yea, is he not " the Sun of righteousness arising with healing in his wings?" And when he ariseth on our benighted minds, may he not be called, " the day-dawn, and the day-star?" Pause, my soul, over the sweet thought. It was all darkness in the creation of God, until Jesus arose. And his coming was as the breaking forth of the morning, the sure harbinger of day. Indeed,

Jesus was "the day-dawn, and the day-star," in the light of redemption, before the world was formed: for in the council of peace, as man's light and salvation, he came up, at the call of God, from all eternity. And in time, during all his eventful ministry upon earth, was not Jesus "a light to lighten the gentiles, and to be the glory of his people Israel?" And what is Jesus now, but "the day-dawn, and day-star" of all the promises? Until we see Christ in them, they are nothing. It is he that makes them all "yea and amen;" and is "the day-dawn, and day-star" of all dispensations. His word, his providences, his grace, his ordinances; all are dark, until Jesus ariseth, as "the day-dawn, and day-star," to enlighten them. When he shines in upon them, then are they blessed and clear. When he withdraws his light, not one of them can be read. And what is "the day-dawn, and day-star," in the hearts of his people, converting them from darkness to light, and from the power of sin and Satan to the living God, but Jesus, shining by his Holy Spirit within, and bringing them to the knowledge, love, and enjoyment of himself? Say, my soul, what was the day, the ever blessed, ever-to-be-remembered day, when God, who commanded the light to shine out of darkness, shined in upon thine heart; and Jesus, "the day-dawn, and the day-star," arose, to give thee "the light of the knowledge of the glory of the Lord, in the face of Jesus Christ?" Hail, thou glorious light and life of my soul! Oh! continue thy sweet influences, morning by morning, and in the day-dawn, and evening-star of thy grace; until, after many dark dispensations, and wintry days of my blindness, ignorance, and senseless state, in which thou wilt renew me, in the precious discoveries of thy love, I am carried through all the twilight of this poor dying state of things below: for then shall I awake up to the full enjoyment of thyself in glory, to see thee in one full open day, and to be made like unto thee in thy kingdom of light, and life, and happiness, for ever and ever.

OCTOBER 13.

MORNING.—" Jesus made a surety."—Heb. vii. 22.

My soul, look at Jesus as a Surety, and as " made thy Surety" this morning! Blessed view, if so be the Holy Ghost will enlighten thine eyes to see him under all these characters. First; a Surety. " We are all ruined by a debt incapable of ever being paid by any, or by all, the fallen sons of Adam. Jesus steps in, becomes a Surety for our debt, and pays the whole by his obedience and death. But we owe a duty also, as well as a debt. Jesus becomes here again the Surety. He will put his Spirit in us, and we shall live. He becomes also a Surety for promises, that all God hath promised for his sake, shall be fulfilled in him, and in us for him. But he is not only a Surety, but *made* a Surety; for the Father's name, and the Father's authority, is in him. It is God the Father which saith, I have given him for a covenant. Precious thought for faith to act upon! And, my soul, is not Jesus *thy* Surety? Yes, if while the Father thus freely gives, thou as fully receivest, and art looking to no other. Say then, my soul, is it not so with thee? Is not Jesus thy all in all, thy Surety, thy Sponsor, thy Redeemer? And dost thou not say, Thou shalt answer for me, Oh Lord my God! Oh comprehensive word, Jesus made a Surety.

EVENING.—" I am doing a great work, so that I cannot come down: why should the work cease, whilst I leave it and come down to you?"—Nehem. vi. 3.

My soul, a very blessed instruction is held forth to thee, in these words. Nehemiah met with sad interruptions in his service, while building the Lord's house. Various were the attempts made by the enemies of God and his cause, to call him off from his labours. But this was his answer to all. Now, my soul, thou hast many enemies also, both from within and without; the world, and the powers of darkness, and thine own corruptions, are all in league to interrupt thy pursuit of divine things. When, therefore, the Sanballats and the Geshems of the day invite thee to the villages, in the plain of *Ono*, here is thine answer: "Why should the work of the Lord cease, when the King's business requires dispatch?" Wherefore should the body, with all its corrupt affections, drag down the soul? Is it reasonable, is it proper to be concerned for the things of a day, while regardless of eternity? Wilt thou for ever be as little children, amused with toys, and taken up with playthings, when Jesus is calling thee, and proposing himself to thee, for thy constant, unceasing, present, and everlasting delight? Oh! for grace and strength from the Lord, to be able, like Abraham, to fray away those fowls which come down upon the sacrifice! Oh! do thou, Lord, drive both the buyers and the sellers from thy temple! Take my whole heart and soul, and all my affections, and fix and centre them all on thyself! Every vanity, every robber, like Barabbas of old, will be preferred to thee, thou dear Emanuel, unless thy grace restrain and keep under, what thy grace hath taught me to know and feel that I carry about with me, a body of sin and death, which is for ever calling me aside from thee. Oh! let thy grace make its way through all the swarms of vain thoughts and interruptions which surround me, and make my soul "as the chariots of Aminadab!" Let no longer these "dead flies spoil the excellent ointment," made fragrant by the rich spices of thy blessed Spirit; but when saluted even by the most innocent call, like that made to Jesus himself, of his mother and his brethren being without, desiring to speak to him, Oh! for grace, that, like my Lord, even then, I may not suffer the higher claims of my God and Saviour to pass by, nor the work of the Lord and the concern of my soul to cease, whilst I come down to them!

OCTOBER 14.

MORNING.—"Behold I give unto you power to tread on serpents and scorpions, and over all the power of the enemy."—Luke x. 19.

Astonishing the mercy, and wonderful the privilege manifested to the followers of the Lamb! Poor, and weak, and helpless, as they are in themselves, yet how strong in the grace which is in Christ Jesus! My soul, never lose sight of these blessed things. In Jesus thou art not only a conqueror, but more than conqueror. As the armies in heaven overcame by the blood of the Lamb, so here below, it is all in him, and by him, the victory is obtained. God will bruise Satan under our feet shortly; but it is God that must bruise him, and it is he that must put him under our feet. Oh for grace to see where our strength is, and as cheerfully to ascribe all to him; that He, in whom we are made to tread on serpents and scorpions, may have the glory due to his name, that He who gives the strength may have the praise.

EVENING.—"Neither be ye of doubtful mind."—Luke xii. 29.

My soul, it is a blessed thing to arrive at a fixed point, on the momentous concern of "the one thing needful." As long as there remains any doubt or uncertainty whether Christ be the soul's portion or not, there is always a proportioned degree of doubt and uncertainty in the soul's comfort. What the dying patriarch said to his son, may with equal truth be said of every one of this description: "Unstable as water, thou shalt not excel," Gen. xlix. 4. For as long as the soul forms conclusions of safety, not from what Jesus is, but from what the soul's views of Jesus are, there will be always an unstable, unsettled state. And how many have I known, who are of doubtful mind, whether they really do believe to the salvation of the soul, and yet have no doubt whether they be sinners, and both need and earnestly desire that salvation. They will tell you that Jesus is more precious than the golden wedge of Ophir; but they tell you at the same time, they dare not say that they have an interest in his blood and righteousness. They see a loveliness in his person, and a suitableness to their necessities, in every point of view; but they cannot presume to hope that they are welcome to enjoy either. They can and do cry out, under the thirst of the soul for Jesus, as David did for the waters of Bethlehem; but still, like David, they do not make use of the blessing, though it be procured them. My soul, it is blessed to live above doubts and fears, by living upon Jesus. The assurance of faith is founded in what Jesus is, and not what his people feel; in what view God the Father beholds Christ as the sinner's surety, and not what our apprehensions are concerning our present feelings. Faith is most strong where sense is most weak; and the glory given to Jesus is greater, when, like Abraham, "against hope, we believe in hope." Blessed Lord Jesus! let the faith of my soul be the one fixed unalterable faith, that admits of no doubt nor change. Let me, with full purpose of heart, cleave unto the Lord. And while I can and do behold, through thy Spirit's teaching me, the Father's appointment and approbation, in all thy work and finished salvation; here let me fix, and never be of doubtful mind, but live and die in the full assurance of faith, well pleased with what my God and Father is well pleased with, and always "rejoicing in hope of the glory of God!"

OCTOBER 15.

MORNING.—"Whose names are in the book of life."—Phil. iv. 3.

How is this known? It must be a blessed privilege

this, and highly desirable to attain, if there be a truly scriptural testimony to it. That there is a book of life, in which the record is made of the people of the Lamb, is without all dispute, from many parts of scripture. The church of the first-born are said to have their names written in heaven; such as are chosen of God in Christ before the world began. But these are secret things which belong to the Lord our God. Yet it is said, " the secret of the Lord is with them that fear him, and he will shew them his covenant." Hence therefore, is not the bible a copy of this book of life? Are there not scriptural marks and characters given, by which the correspondence is proved? In both, they are distinguished by one and the same name and character. They are called the *people*, the *seed*, the *offspring* of Jesus. They are his, by gift, by purchase, by conquest, by a voluntary surrender. They are known by the character as well as by name. They seek salvation only in Jesus. God is their Father, Jesus their Redeemer, the Holy Ghost their sanctifier. My soul, see thy name in bible characters answering to this persuasion, and be assured that the original writing of the book of life in heaven, and the book of God for life upon earth, is his written word, is in exact correspondence. Blessed Jesus! give me in this way to know whose I am and to whom I belong, and then assured shall I be that my name is in the book of life.

EVENING.—" And I will deliver thee out of the hand of the wicked, and I will redeem thee out of the hand of the terrible."—Jer. xv. 21.

My soul, hast thou ever considered some of the many ways of softening trouble? Sit down, and learn it from this sweet scripture. Here is a general promise, which may be suited to particular circumstances, and such as will hold good in all. But first remember, that he who promiseth to deliver from the sorrow, is the same that appointeth the sorrow: " Hear ye the rod, and who hath appointed it." The Lord's rod hath a voice that *speaks*, as well as *corrects*; and it is a mark of wisdom to *listen*, as well as *feel*. Hence, if we mark the hand that appoints, we shall observe also all the other interesting particulars, both of the instruments by which the Lord works, the time and place, the means and end, and then discern love and grace, yea, Jesus himself, in all. Suppose it be the world that crosses, or Satan that tempts, or false friends that oppose, or our mother's children that be angry with us; yet all are but the Lord's ministers; they are the sword, but the hand is the Lord's; and though they mean ill, he will bring good; if they even cast into prison, Jesus will be there. All things, and all means, and all times, shall, at his command, minister to his own purpose. If there be a storm without, Jesus hath chambers to take them into; if the affliction be within, Jesus can help them out. Yea, the very "earth shall help the woman," when the enemy casts forth a flood after her to swallow her up. Be the storm what it may, Jesus is at the helm. Like Joseph's afflictions, they shall minister to good, and the end bring the proof, that the whole had the appointment in love. Hence, my soul, though the direction is short, it is very sweet; never look at the trial, without looking also at the Appointer; never allow thyself to view the affliction, without looking through it to One that stands behind, regulating and moving all. It matters not in this case, what the storm threatens, but what the Lord Jesus means; not what the instrument intends, but what Jesus hath appointed. And by thus looking to Christ, the greatest troubles will give thee but little concern. He saith, (blessed be his name) "I will deliver thee out of the hand of the wicked; and I will redeem thee out of the hand of the terrible." How it is to be accomplished, is *his* concern, and not *mine*. All I have to do is to rest in the certainty of the promise, by giving credit to the great Promiser; and the end will shew, that with him it is to make "darkness light, and crooked things straight."

OCTOBER 16.

MORNING.—"We will make thee borders of gold, with studs of silver."—Song i. 11.

My soul, ponder over these words. What borders of gold shall be made for the believer, but the robe of Jesus's righteousness? And what silver, but the garment of his salvation? If thou art clothed with this, my soul, thou wilt shine indeed with more lustre than all the embroidery of gold and precious stones, which perish with using. But mark, my soul, who it is that makes them, and who puts them on thee—surely none but God. And observe how all the persons of the Godhead are engaged in this work. "*We* will make thee," is the language. Yes, Jehovah, Elohim, who said, "Let *us* make man," at the original creation; the same now saith, at the new creation, "*We* will make thee borders of gold, with studs of silver." And is it not the hand of God the Father in this blessed, gracious act, in the gift of his Son to the poor sinner? Is it not Jesus who hath wrought out a robe of salvation for the poor sinner? And is it not the Holy Ghost who puts on the blessed adorning upon the poor sinner, in taking of the things of Jesus, and shewing unto him? Oh precious testimony of a precious God in Christ! Be it unto me, Lord, according to thy word. Let me be thus clothed and adorned, and I shall be happy now, and happy to all eternity.

EVENING.—"Wherefore Jesus also, that he might sanctify the people with his own blood."—Heb. xiii. 12.

My soul, I would have thee this evening, take a view of thy Jesus in his own blood, under the special and particular act in which this scripture holds him forth; sanctifying the people by the application of it, as the great object and design for which he suffered. There is somewhat uncommonly interesting in this view, though not so commonly considered. That this is the only laver for sin, is unquestionable; and that it is infinitely meritorious, and of eternal efficacy, is also equally true. But when we consider farther, the infinite purity of it, flowing, as it did, from an holy heart, in a nature that was altogether holy, harmless, undefiled, separate from sinners, and made higher than the heavens; there is somewhat which, though too deeply founded in mystery to be perfectly apprehended by us, may yet serve to intimate the immense preciousness of it, and its immense importance and value. But we must not stop here. The union of the Godhead with the human nature, giving both dignity and validity to the sacrifice which Jesus once offered, that he might sanctify the people; here angels, as well as men, find their faculties unable to ascertain the extent of the wonderful subject; and, perhaps, through all eternity, none among the creation of God, will fully be competent to explain it. But, my soul, though unable to explain, or unable to conceive the infinitely precious nature of thy Jesus's blood, yet do thou gather this sweet and soul-reviving thought from the contemplation; it must be in itself so incalculable in value, and so infinitely powerful in its pardoning and cleansing properties, that no sin, no, not all the sin of finite creatures taken in the aggregate, can stand before it. Oh precious, precious Jesus! precious, precious blood of Jesus, which cleanseth from all sin! Oh, let me hear, and feel, and know my personal interest in that sweet promise of my God in Christ, and my happiness is made for ever; "I will sprinkle clean water upon you, and ye shall be clean; from all filthiness, and from all your idols, will I cleanse you." Amen! Amen! So be it.

OCTOBER 17.

MORNING.—" And in the cities of Judah shall the flocks pass again under the hands of him that telleth them, saith the Lord."—Jer. xxxiii. 13.

See, my soul, what a blessed scripture is here. Meditate upon it, this morning. Whose hands can these be but Jesus's? For whose are the flocks but his? Is he not in all the scripture said to be a Shepherd, and the good Shepherd that giveth his life for the sheep? And would he give his life for sheep he knew not? Surely that is impossible. Moreover, did not the Father give them to him? Did he not receive them from the Father? And did he not know them and count them over, when he received them? " I know my sheep," saith Jesus, " and am known of mine." And observe, the flocks are said to pass *again* under his hands. A plain proof that they have all passed before. Nay, is it not said, that he *telleth* them? Yes, " He calleth them all by name, and leadeth them forth, and goeth before them." And he saith himself, " Of all thou hast given me, I have lost none." Precious scripture of a most precious Saviour! How then can any be lost? If Jesus knew them when he received them, counted them over, set his seal upon them, and they must all pass again under his Almighty hand, how shall one, even one, be found wanting, when he maketh up his jewels? Poor weather-beaten shorn lamb of Jesus's fold, whosoever thou art, think of these things, when wandering, or cold, or in darkness, or on the mountains. Jesus will seek thee out in the dark and cloudy day. He will bring thee home, and thou shalt lie in his bosom, and by and by dwell with him for ever; for he is, he must, he will still be, Jesus.

EVENING.—" As the girdle cleaveth to the loins of a man, so have I caused to cleave unto me the whole house of Israel, and the whole house of Judah, saith the Lord; that they might be unto me for a people, and for a name, and for a praise, and for a glory."—Jer. xiii. 11.

See, my soul, the blessedness of witnessing *to* God,

and witnessing *for* God. His people, the Lord saith, are called, and are, in the midst of a crooked and perverse generation, as lights in the world. Both Israel and Judah are included in what is here said; and by the figure of a girdle cleaving to the loins of a man, so close, so strongly bound, and extending all around, is shewn the nearness, and firmness, and the security in every way, and by every direction, in which the Lord's people are brought into relation with him. Such, then, were the Lord's people of old, a people near to himself; and as they were the Lord's own choice, so were they dear to the Lord; and as he had made the whole of the nation a kingdom of priests to the Lord, so were they wholly designed for the divine glory: "This people have I formed for myself; they shall shew forth my praise." Now pause, my soul, over this blessed scripture, and contemplate with what holy rapture and delight a child of God, under the new testament dispensation, may look up and behold his nearness and dearness to God in Christ, by virtue of his union with Jesus. Here the figure, beautiful as it is, of a girdle encircling the loins, doth not come up to the full idea of that oneness and union which the believer stands in with Jesus. For the soul not only is made by the Lord himself to cleave unto Christ, as the ivy clings to the oak; but being part of Christ's mystical body, is, like the branch in the vine, one with Christ, and Christ with him. The believer in Jesus is interested in all that is in Jesus; and not only cleaves to him, but is part of himself, and is blessed in his blessedness, and beheld and accepted, and loved by God the Father, as the Father loveth Jesus. And think, my soul, what unspeakable felicity ariseth out of this one consideration, that, amidst all thy coldness, and wanderings, and departures, still the Lord causeth his Judah and Israel to cleave to him. However the poor senseless child in arms lets go his holdfast, when hanging round the neck of its nurse and protector, yet the little creature falls not, because he is upheld by his support from her. So the one only cause that thou art supported and preserved from falling is, because "the eternal God is thy refuge, and underneath are the everlasting arms." It is the Lord that saith, "I have caused to cleave unto me the whole house of Israel, and the whole house of Judah." And Oh! what a name, and a praise, and a glory, will be the whole redeemed church of God in Christ, when Jesus brings them all home, and presents them to himself and Father, as "a glorious church, not having spot or wrinkle, or any such thing, but that it should be holy and without blemish before him in love!"

OCTOBER 18.

MORNING.—"And God heard their groaning, and God remembered his covenant."—Exod. ii. 24.

This is a precious scripture. My soul, put a note upon it. No sigh, no groan, no tear of God's people can pass unobserved. He putteth the tears of his people in his bottle. Surely then he can never overlook what gives vent to those tears, the sorrows of the soul. Our spiritual afflictions Jesus knows, and numbers all. How sweet the thought! the Spirit maketh intercession for the saints with the groanings which they cannot utter. And do, my soul, observe the cause of deliverance. Not our sighs, nor our groanings, nor our brokenness of heart; not these, for what benefit can these render to an holy God? But God hath respect in all to his own everlasting covenant. Yes, Jesus is the all in all of the covenant. God the Father hath respect to him. For his sake, for his righteousness, for his atoning blood, the groanings of his people find audience at the mercy-seat and redress. And God hath respect to his own word, his oath, his promises to his dear Son. Oh blessed assurance—Oh precious security! How shall any poor groaning child of God go unheard, unpardoned, unrelieved, who hath double security in the glory of God the Father's sovereign grace, and covenant word and oath to depend upon; and the everlasting covenant righteousness, and atoning blood of God the Son, to be found in? Here, my soul, rest, for ever rest, thy sure claim to grace and glory.

EVENING.—" Be sober, be vigilant; because your adversary the devil, as a roaring lion, walketh about, seeking whom he may devour, whom resist stedfast in the faith, knowing that the same afflictions are accomplished in your brethren that are in the world."—1 Pet. v. 8, 9.

My soul, thou knowest, and hast long known, from the many wounds given thee by Satan, what a cruel, insidious, and powerful enemy thou hast to contend with; and thou too truly knowest, also, how sadly unequal thou art in thyself to resist his wiles. He is a prince of the power of the air: he is by nature, a spirit, and therefore invisible; thou seest not his approaches; he is a tremendous foe, full of envy, malignity, subtilty, craft, and design: and what renders him yet more formidable is, that in the corruptions and unbelief of thy fallen nature, he hath but too many confederates in thine own heart, to aid him in his diabolical designs. Where then is thy strength to resist him? It cannot be in thyself, nor in thy best exertions. The devil would laugh at these, and all would be but as feathers to the breath of his temptations. Hear what the apostle saith: " Whom resist stedfast in the faith." See here, where thy strength is. Faith in Jesus is the only, and it is an infallible defence against all the fiery darts of the wicked. There is nothing that Satan dreads, but the blood of the cross. There is nothing that conquers him, but faith in Jesus's blood. Tell him of the blood which cleanseth from all sin, and he will flee from thee. This was the sole power by which the holy armies in heaven cast down the accuser which accused them before our God, day and night: " they overcame by the blood of the Lamb," Rev. xii. 9—11. and the same will give thee the victory now. Faith in the blood of the cross, is the grace by which we have access to God. It is by faith the soul looks to Jesus; by faith the soul is kept stedfastly resting on Jesus; by faith the devil is stedfastly resisted, in taking confidence in the full and complete redemption that Jesus accomplished on the cross. Look then, my soul, for ever to the cross, and while thy faith honours Jesus, Jesus will honour thee; and this will be the standard which the Spirit of Jehovah will lift up, when at any time the enemy cometh in like a flood; Isa. lix. 19. Oh! the triumphs of the cross! "They overcame by the blood of the Lamb."

OCTOBER 19.

MORNING.—"There shall be no more thence an infant of days, nor an old man that hath not filled his days: for the child shall die an hundred years old, but the sinner being an hundred years old shall be accursed."—Isa. lxv. 20.

My soul, contemplate this morning the auspicious and blessed effects brought into the circumstances of mankind by the gospel. Not only shall there be new heavens, and a new earth, but new hearts, new minds, new dispositions to enjoy them. "If any man be in Christ, he is a new creature. Old things are passed away, and all things are become new." And among the many blessed changes that shall take place in consequence of Jesus's salvation, all untimely deaths are done away. Indeed, there can be no such thing as an untimely death to those who are in Christ: for a voice from heaven pronounces all blessed that die in the Lord. A child new born, if born also in Christ, an infant of a day, if a gracious day, is as ripe for glory as if an hundred years had passed over him. Indeed, he is an hundred years old in Jesus. Sweet thought! what a blessedness, dearest Jesus, hath thy great salvation introduced into the circumstances of thy people. But what an awful thought — the life of an unawakened, unregenerated sinner, though protracted to an hundred years, is lengthened only to misery. As he came into the world, so he goes through it, and so he goes out of it—an unrenewed sinner. Oh distinguishing grace! Oh great salvation!

EVENING.—" He shall choose our inheritance for us, the excellency of Jacob, whom he loved. Selah."—Ps. xlvii. 4.

My soul, to whom, but to the all-lovely and all-loving Jesus, couldest thou have thought this blessed verse referred, even had this little word Selah not been placed at the end, by way of marking the emphasis of the Holy Ghost? Who couldest thou have considered suitable to have chosen the inheritance of his people, but he who is the Lord of his people, and himself their inheritance and their portion for ever? It was God thy Father that chose him to be the excellency of Jacob, when he gave him for a covenant to the people; and when to the infinite mind of Jehovah, this One glorious Person, in the holiness and purity of his nature, came up before him here, on him the Lord placed his choice. And had all his people been present; had it been possible for the whole of the chosen of Zion to have been consulted in the choice, would not every soul have fixed its longing eyes upon him, and from the millions of tongues resounding his blessed and blissful name from every heart, the universal voice would have been heard in the delightful words of this scripture: " He shall choose our inheritance for us; the excellency of Jacob, whom he loved!" Hail! thou dear and blessed Lord! thou art indeed our inheritance, and our portion for ever! And hail, thou glorious, gracious, and almighty Father! thy choice, and thy gift, and thine appointment, gives and confirms, sweetens and sanctifies the eternal and unspeakable mercy. And hail, thou holy and blessed Spirit! do thou cause my poor soul to live by grace here, and in glory to all eternity, upon this excellency of Jacob, whom Jehovah loved!

OCTOBER 20.

MORNING.—" Christ is all, and in all."—Colos. iii. 11.

Hail, thou great, thou glorious, thou universal Lord. To thee, blessed Jesus, every knee shall bow. Thou art all in all in creation, redemption, providence, grace, glory. Thou art all in all in thy church, and in the hearts of thy people: in all their joys, all their happiness, all their exercises, all their privileges. Thou art the all in all in thy word, ordinances, means of grace, the sum and substance of the whole bible. Speak we of promises?—Thou art the first promise in the sacred word, and the whole of every promise that follows—for all in thee are yea and amen. Speak we of the law? " Thou art the end of the law for righteousness to every one that believeth." Speak we of sacrifices? " By thy one sacrifice thou hast for ever perfected them that are sanctified." Speak we of the prophecies? " To thee give all the prophets witness, that whosoever believeth in thee shall receive remission of sins." Yes, blessed, blessed Jesus, thou art the all in all. Be thou to me, Lord, the all in all I need in time, and then surely thou wilt be my all in all to all eternity.

EVENING.—" His glory is great in thy salvation; honour and majesty hast thou laid upon him; for thou hast made him most blessed for ever."—Ps. xxi. 5, 6.

My soul, it is the most delightful of all thoughts, when at any time thou art solacing thyself in the glories of thy Redeemer, to call to mind that God the Father is glorified, while thou art made happy in the salvation thy Jesus hath accomplished by his blood and righteousness. It is indeed God the Father which called Jesus to the office and character of the Redeemer, and furnished him with all suitable requisites for the vast work he called him to do. But the glory and honour of Jehovah were the first and great object of the Redeemer's work; and hence Jesus, in the days of his flesh, never speaks of his own glory, but as in connection with, and leading to the glory of Jehovah. "Now is the Son of man glorified, and God is glorified in him! Father! glorify thy Son, that thy Son also may glorify thee." Hence, therefore, when Jehovah laid honour and majesty upon the blessed Jesus, and made him most blessed for ever; all these things were to the Father's honour and glory: and never was God the Father's glory more great than in and by the salvation of his dear Son Christ Jesus. See, my soul! I charge it upon thee, that thou never lose sight of this precious view of God thy Father's glory, in thy redemption by thy adorable Redeemer. Say continually, and dwell with rapture on the blessed subject: 'My God, my Father in Christ Jesus, is glorified, yea, greatly glorified in his dear Son, in that he hath wrought out such a salvation as brings more glory to God the Father than all the works of his creation; and it is to the honour and glory of Jehovah, that poor sinners should be saved in this blessed way of his own appointing. And shall I not then come to him in and through Jesus? Shall I not delight to tell my God and Father how great his glory is in the salvation by Jesus? Shall I not bless and glorify my God and Father in being the Author and Giver of such great salvation? Yea, most blessed God and Father! I do bless thee, I do praise thee, I desire to love thee, in and through Jesus. And while my whole soul is going out in enjoyments on the person, and work, and offices, and relations of Jesus; always would I keep in view, and connect with it, in the enjoyment, that it is thou, most gracious and almighty Father, that hast made him most blessed for ever. Surely then, thy glory is great in *his* salvation! And the glory of the Son of God is great in *thy* salvation!'

OCTOBER 21.

MORNING.—" All are your's; and ye are Christ's, and Christ is God's."—1 Cor. iii. 22, 23.

Oh what a rich inventory is here. All things, all blessings, all gifts, all grace, all mercy; all, all the the christian's. And observe, my soul, on what it is suspended—" If ye are Christ's." And whose art thou, my soul, but his? Hath not the Father given thee to him? And hath not the Son of God bought thee with a price? Hast thou not made a voluntary surrender of thyself to Jesus, and given thyself to him in an everlasting covenant which cannot be broken? Oh yes, yes, all this is certain. Lord, grant me grace and faith in lively exercise, that I may now take to myself all the blessedness of it by anticipation; until I come to realize the whole in absolute enjoyment in glory. Christ is mine, and with him, heaven is mine. God the Father is mine, the Holy Ghost is mine, all covenant blessings are mine; ordinances, means of grace, the holy book of God, all are mine here, and will be my portion for evermore. Hallelujah.

EVENING.—" Thy plants are an orchard of pomegranates, with pleasant fruits, camphor with spikenard, spikenard and saffron, calamus and cinnamon, with all trees of frankincense, myrrh, and aloes, with all the chief spices."—Song iv. 13, 14.

Hear, my soul, what Christ, thy Husband and thy Saviour, saith to the church! and as thou art a part of it in him, take it to thyself. Surely the church of Jesus is his garden, and every plant in it, which the heavenly Father hath planted, must flourish, with all the increase of God, as trees of the Lord's right-hand planting. Even the tenderest plants, the youngest of his people, form a part in this orchard of pomegranates; for every one hath been taken out of nature's wild wilderness, and brought, by sovereign and distinguishing grace, into the Lord's garden, his church; and, like pomegranates, a large and full-bearing fruit, sweet and delicious, they are in Jesus's eye most pleasant, from the beauty and comeliness he hath put upon them. And do observe how very gracious thy Lord is, in enumerating not only "the pleasant fruits," but "the chief spices;" meaning, no doubt, that as in him they partake of all that is his, and derive beauty, and fragrancy, and fruitfulness, from their Lord, as the branch from the vine; so do the various graces of his blessed Spirit appear in them, as the sweet fruits under his creating and ripening influence. See to it, my soul, that these things do appear in thee; and that faith, and love, and hope, and joy, and peace in believing, abound in thee, through the Holy Ghost. Oh! the blessedness of knowing these things, and enjoying them. And Oh! the blessedness of being thus distinguished, as the rare spices of the east, with such love-tokens of Jesus. Thou knowest that if thou art as an orchard of pomegranates with pleasant fruits, thou art wholly so from Jesus. Nature never produceth them, neither can bring them forth, or cause them to flourish. Oh! then, thou dear Lord! if I am by sovereign grace, precious and pleasant in thy view, be thou eternally praised, and eternally glorified for the distinguishing mercy: for *of* thee, and *from* thee, and *by* thee, I am what I am; and Oh! let thy grace live in me, to thy praise, and to the glory of his grace, "who hath made me accepted in the Beloved!"

OCTOBER 22.

MORNING.—"The Lord will command his loving-kindness in the day-time, and in the night his song shall be with me, and my prayer unto the God of my life."—Psalm xlii. 8.

Both night and day open sources of comfort, when Jesus is present, and when Jesus sanctifies. How, indeed, my soul, canst thou be otherwise than comfortable, while Jesus is with thee, and manifesting himself unto thee? And do observe, my soul, the sweet expression in this verse. Thy Lord, thy Jesus, will both create blessings and command them. His loving-kindness, which is better than life itself will make daylight in the soul, when otherwise it is night. And his love will shine, as the stars in the darkest night sparkle with more lustre, with increasing brightness, when dark providences are around. Nay, Jesus will give songs in the night, when all things else are out of tune. Do thou, Lord, do thou, my Lord, command then thy loving-kindness both by day and night, and my prayer and praise shall both go forth to thee, the God of my life; and " It shall put more gladness in my heart, than when corn, and wine, and oil increase."

EVENING.—" Thy holy child Jesus."—Acts iv. 30.

There is somewhat so very sweet and precious in this expression, that, my soul, I would have thee to meditate upon it. Surely the apostles had a special meaning in calling the Lord Jesus, " the holy child Jesus:" and no doubt the Holy Ghost did not cause his servants thus to express themselves for nought. It will be thy wisdom, therefore, to inquire. I do not find a similar phrase in all the word of God. The Redeemer is spoken of, in the days of his infancy, as " the child Jesus;" and when twelve years of age, he is still called " the child;" see Luke ii. 27, 34, 43; but no where, that I recollect, does he receive the blessed appellation that he is here distinguished by, of " the holy child Jesus." It would be presumption in thee, to determine the cause of this distinction; but it can be none to inquire. Sit down then, this evening, favourable as it is to solemn meditation, and ponder well the subject. *Child* and *servant*, in scripture language, we are told, have the same meaning: hence the apostle observes, in his epistle to the church of the Galatians, that " the heir, as long as he is a child, differeth nothing from a servant, though he be Lord of all," Gal. iv. 1. The phrase, therefore, may be accepted under this view, and it will be agreeable to the whole tenor of the bible. See Isaiah xlii. 1. compared with Matt. xii. 18. Nevertheless, I am inclined to think, that somewhat more is intended by it, in this place of the apostles' prayer, when they called Christ "the holy child Jesus." Perhaps in allusion to his *holy* nature, contrasted to the *unholy* hands by whom he was crucified and slain; and in this view the subject is truly lovely and interesting. Christ was to be crucified by the determinate counsel and foreknowledge of God; but none but unholy hands were to be embrued in the blood of God's "holy child Jesus." And doth not the expression, "holy child Jesus," serve, in a very striking manner, and with peculiar emphasis, to bring home to thy thoughts the holiness of that nature, which, in the childhood of Jesus, and from the womb, was altogether "holy, harmless, undefiled, separate from sinners, and made higher than the heavens?" Hence, before his incarnation, the angel called him by a peculiar name, "that holy thing;" not that holy man, but that "holy thing;" Luke i. 35. And doth not the expression bring home, in a yet more endearing manner, if possible, the blessedness of all this in the cause. For "the holy child Jesus," that "holy thing," became the one holy representative of all his church and people; he was, and is, and ever will be, "the head of his body, the church;" and hence, in the sight of Jehovah, Christ and his members are one. Now, my soul, considering the phrase in this point of view, what a fulness of light, and life, and glory, and joy, doth it hold forth, and pour in, upon the believer's mind! Lamb of God! I would say, "holy child Jesus!" in thy holiness, cause me to behold myself always appearing before God, and my Father; for, sure I am, if the Lord Jehovah made thee to be sin for thy people, when thou knewest no sin, it was with the express design, in his holy purpose, counsel, and will, that "they should be made the righteousness of God in thee."

OCTOBER 23.

MORNING.—"Now therefore go, and I will be with thy mouth, and teach thee what thou shalt say."—Exod. iv. 12.

My soul, pause over this sweet promise which the Lord gave to Moses; for surely the same is in effect said to every minister, every child of God, and every believer. He that made man's mouth, will give every thing suitable to the mouth, and proportion every thing to the necessity of his people. And do, my soul, remark the comprehensiveness of the promise. Will not He who undertakes to be with the mouth, be also with all the renewed faculties of the soul? Jesus gives the tongue of the learned. Jesus gives grace to the lips, understanding to the heart, eyes to the blind, feet to the lame: the bread shall be given, and the water shall be sure, and the defence shall be the munition of rocks. Go then, my soul, go wheresoever the Lord leads: for he saith, "Be not afraid, I am with thee, I am thy God." Learn, my soul, then to eye Jesus in all, and depend upon it, Jesus will bless thee in the use of all. Make his glory thy aim, and thy happiness will be his glory.

EVENING.—"Afterward shall the children of Israel return, and seek the Lord their God, and David their king."—Hosea iii. 5.

What a sweet scripture is this, and what abundant gospel contained in the bosom of it? "*Afterward* shall the children of Israel return." After having been long scattered on every high mountain, wandering over the face of the whole earth, the Lord will bring them back; "he that hath scattered Israel will gather him." There shall be abounding grace, for abounding transgression; and what sin hath ruined, grace shall restore. But to whom shall they return? To seek the Lord their God!

Yes! this *may* be done, and this *will* be done, if the Lord incline their hearts; the same that gives the grace to seek, will give the mercy to find. "He hath never said to the praying seed of Jacob, seek ye my face in vain!" But it is said also, that they shall return to "David their king." Alas! David king of Israel, had been dead many a year, when this promise was made, and his sepulchre, as Peter afterwards remarked, was with the people unto this day; how then could they return to David their king? Oh! the blessedness to see David's Lord thus preached in days before the gospel. Though David king of Israel be dead; Christ, the seed of David after the flesh, ever liveth, and to him shall Israel seek; after all their rebellion, and after all the pursuit of their idols. Oh! precious Lord Jesus! be it my portion also to seek unto thee in all thy covenant relations and characters; "for where should a people seek, but unto their God?" Let my soul feel the same longings as David himself felt, when he cried out, "O God, thou art my God, early will I seek thee; my soul thirsteth for thee, my flesh longeth for thee, in this dry and thirsty land where no water is!"

OCTOBER 24.

MORNING.—"And the remnant of Jacob shall be in the midst of many people, as a dew from the Lord, as the showers upon the grass, that tarrieth not for man, nor waiteth for the sons of men."—Micah v. 7.

Observe, my soul, the character given of Jacob's seed, and bless the Lord for being included in the number.—For so saith the apostle, "If ye be Christ's, then are ye Abraham's seed, and heirs according to the promise." Mark then their characters. They are a *remnant*. But they are God's remnant, being in covenant with God in Christ, and as such, distinguished and separated from the world. "They are a people that dwell alone, and not reckoned among the nations." They are in the midst of many people, but belong to none of them. For though living in the world, they are not of the world, but chosen out of the world. They are, moreover, as a dew from the Lord. Beautiful resemblance! For as the dew is from heaven, so believers in Christ are born from above: not of the will of the flesh, nor of the will of man, but of God. Moreover, they are as showers upon the grass; meaning, that as Jesus is promised to come down as showers upon the mown grass to refresh his people, so his people live in a constant dependence upon Jesus, and receive out of his fulness, while all the earth is dry as stubble around them. Moreover, as the rain waiteth not for man, but wholly falls from God's appointment, so grace is not dispensed for man's desert, but the Lord's free bounty. Oh precious promise, or rather precious cluster of promises, and all in Jesus.

EVENING.—" I am a woman of a sorrowful spirit."—1 Sam. i. 15.

My soul, look at Hannah at the mercy-seat, and mark the sorrowful spirit with which she there appeared. Blushing and sorrow, at the feet of Jesus, are among the highest tokens of real heartfelt communion. Perhaps there never was a moment in the life of Hannah, in which faith was in more lively exercise, than in that memorable season. And, perhaps, never did she speed with more success than then; for it is said, that when she arose from before the throne, " she went her way, and her countenance was no more sad." Now, my soul, take a precious instruction from her example. Do thou go to the throne, and present thyself at the feet of thy Jesus. Let grace have a full and lively exercise in thine heart. See that thy prayers be really and truly heart prayers, and not lip-service. Tell thy Lord how greatly thou needest his grace and mercy; and tell him, also, how much thy Lord Jesus will get glory in being gracious. Let him see that thou art indeed in earnest. And let the offering of a broken and contrite heart decidedly shew that thou art also of a sorrowful spirit. And when thou hast done this, do as Hannah did; leave thy sorrow with Jesus. She went her way and was no more sad. To be sure not; for if she really left her concerns with Jesus, she could not take them home to her own heart again. Here, my soul, is thy mistake; thou dost as Hannah did only in part; a throne of grace can witness for thee, that thou hast, times without number, brought thy burdens, both of sin and sorrow, and laid them down at the feet of thy Lord; but, alas! the same throne can witness against thee, that, shortly after, through distrust, and fear, and unbelief, thou hast fetched them away again, and taken the whole upon thyself. Dearest Jesus, undertake for me. Oh, for grace, not only to *bring* all my burdens to thee, but to *leave* them all with thee: for this is the only way to make a sorrowful spirit glad, when I make thee as God the Father hath made thee, the Almighty Burden bearer of all the sins and sorrows of thy people!

OCTOBER 25.

MORNING.—"My beloved is unto me as a cluster of camphire in the vineyards of Engedi."—Song i. 14.

How full, indeed how infinitely full, abundant, and soul-satisfying is Jesus, in all that concerns life, light, grace, glory! A cluster of all is Christ; whether the *copher* of medicine to heal, or of sweetness to satisfy, or of riches to enlarge, or salvation to impart. Every way, and in every thing that is lovely or desirable, Jesus is a cluster indeed to his people. And whether we meet him in the valley or in the mount, in the plains of Jericho, or in the vineyards of Engedi, neither place nor situation, neither state nor circumstances, make any alteration in our Beloved; he is, he must be, Jesus, and that is always lovely.

EVENING.—"For whosoever shall give you a cup of water to drink, in my name, because ye belong to Christ, verily, I say unto you, he shall not lose his reward."—Mark ix. 41.

How little is this attended to in the charities of life! I fear, that even the soul which loveth Jesus most, doth not regulate his alms, whether of this world's goods, or of prayer, or of good wishes, when he giveth them, by this blessed standard. Dost thou not, my soul, plead guilty to this charge? Heavenly Lord! enlighten mine eyes to see thee in all thy representatives. And when I have only the cup of cold water to bestow upon any poor needy creature, yet let me give *that* in thy name! 'Do you belong to Christ?' should be the only question. This is a claim which carries every thing before it. Is it Jesus, who, in the person of his poor members, asketh the alms? Doth the Lord of life and glory condescend to be beholden to the poor creatures of his bounty; and of his own absolutely receives as a loan or debt? Surely the most selfish heart might here covet to be liberal. But, alas! love to Jesus is at too low an ebb to swell the tides for pouring into the parched ground of our neighbour's vineyard, from such principles. My soul, let this charming scripture be henceforth much upon thy mind. Take it about thee whithersoever thou goest. Look out for the Lord's poor, and so far read their characters, as to see that they belong to Christ. And if thy Lord hath made thee his almoner, if it be no farther than to minister the cup of cold water; yet let that cup be given in his name, and because they belong to Christ. Methinks, had it pleased my heavenly Father, to have entrusted me with ample circumstances, I should rejoice to follow the plan of his bounties, "who maketh his sun to rise upon the evil and upon the good; and sendeth the blessings of his rain both upon the just and the unjust." But even then, amidst the indiscriminate scattering of temporal blessings all around, the given cup of cold water to one of thine, thou blessed Jesus, because he belonged to thee, would be a cordial to my own heart, that needed no higher joy than the inexpressible felicity of testifying that myself as well as the receiver were both the Lord's poor, and the Lord's property.

OCTOBER 26.

MORNING.—" He went on frowardly in the way of his heart; I have seen his ways, and will heal him."—Isa. lvii. 17, 18.

Pause, my soul, over this sweet scripture; and while thou readest it, wilt thou not cry out with David, in the contemplation of the overwhelming mercy: "And is this the manner of man, Oh Lord God!" 2 Sam. vii. 19. Think, Oh my soul, how it was with thee, when in the days of thy unregeneracy thou wentest on frowardly in the way of thy perverse heart. Who could have stopped thee, had not sovereign grace? And how justly might the Lord have said, I have seen thy ways, and will punish thee; I will give thee over to a reprobate mind, and forsake thee for ever!—Oh the riches of grace, when, from my very unworthiness, the Lord took occasion to magnify his love and mercy. Oh Lord Jesus, do thou incline the heart that thou hast healed to live to thy praise, and let the life thou hast saved from destruction, be spent in thy service.

EVENING.—" And his feet shall stand in that day upon the mount of Olives, which is before Jerusalem."—Zech. xiv. 4.

My soul, pause over this blessed promise. To whom could it refer, but to Jesus? "That day," through all the old testament dispensation, meant the gospel church of the new testament dispensation. And when the Son of God came, the day was come also. And did not Jesus stand often, during this day of his grace, in his own ministry, teaching the people on the mount of Olives? Yea, was it not the very last sacred spot on which his holy feet stood, when from thence he ascended to heaven, having finished redemption-work upon earth? My soul, do thou often, by faith, visit the hallowed ground, and from thence let thy meditation take wing, after thine ascended and exalted Saviour. And while, like the wondering disciples, looking after Jesus as he went up, thou art contemplating the glory of thy Lord, who is now above, carrying on all the blessed designs of his love, for which he came below; recollect the assurance, that the angels, who attended their Lord to grace his triumph, gave of his return: His feet shall again stand at the last day upon the earth. "He shall come to be glorified in his saints, and to be admired in all them that believe." Oh! for grace to be always on the look out for my Lord's return! Give me, blessed Jesus, to know thee as my Kinsman-Redeemer; to know thee as the Lord my righteousness; to be living upon thee now by faith, that then I may enjoy thee by living upon thy fulness, as in grace here, so in glory to all eternity. Amen.

OCTOBER 27.

MORNING.—"I have chosen thee, and not cast thee away."—Isa. xli. 9.

Is this thy portion, my soul? Hath the Lord thy God indeed chosen thee? Hath he manifested his love to thee in so distinguishing a way? Take comfort, then, in all thine exercises, when seasons of darkness and discouragement are around; think of God's choice, and venture on God's love. Art thou distressed, exercised, afflicted? Dost thou call on God, and find no answer? Doth the enemy tempt thee to doubt? Doth thine own unbelieving heart misgive thee? Still recollect, Jesus knows all. He chose thee —and he that chose thee knows all thine exercises; nay, he himself hath appointed them. And remember, thou wast not forced upon him. It was his own free choice first made thee his; and his own love will be the security of thy present dependence. Jesus resteth in his love; he hateth putting away. Cast down as thou art, thou art not cast off. Though fallen, he can raise. Though dejected, he can and will comfort. Sweet thought! He will turn again; he will have compassion upon us, and he will cast all our sins into the depths of the sea. Hallelujah.

EVENING.—" And when they had prayed, the place was shaken where they were assembled."—Acts iv. 31.

Think, my soul, what a blessed testimony this must have been, in confirmation to the disciples, that their God was a prayer-hearing, and a prayer-answering God! And what a full reply to all they had been praying for! The enemies of God, and of his Christ, had threatened the poor disciples what they would do to them, if they persisted in preaching Jesus to the people. The purport, therefore, of the apostles prayer was, not that the Lord would stop their malice, and silence all their opposition: this they sought not to avoid. But the single prayer was, that their souls might be animated to go on, let the malice of their foes manifest itself as it might. In answer, " the place is shaken." As if the Lord had said, " He that shakes the place, can make your enemies hearts tremble." And so it proved. Now, my soul, take thine improvement from it. Jesus sees all, knows all, hears all, as well of thine exercises, as of thine enemies attempts upon thee. Carry all complaints therefore to him. Depend upon it, that it is blessed to be exercised; blessed for thee, that the enemies of God, and of his Christ, threaten thee; blessed to be opposed, that thou mayest not recline upon thine arms, or, like stagnant waters, become corrupt for want of running. The hatred of the foes of Jesus affords occasion yet more for Jesus to manifest his love; and though the place be not shaken whence thy cries go up, the word of his grace gives the same sure answer. Jesus looks on, Jesus upholds, Jesus supports. Do thou call every Bethel place as Abraham's handmaid did: "Thou, Lord, seest me." No weapon formed against God's people can prosper; and every tongue that riseth against them in judgment, the Lord will condemn. "This is the heritage of the servants of the Lord, and their righteousness is of me, saith the Lord."

OCTOBER 28.

MORNING.—"Casting all your care upon him; for he careth for you."—1 Pet. v. 7.

Yes, blessed Jesus, I would cast all upon thee: sins, sorrows, trials, temptations. Thou art the Almighty Burden-bearer of thy people; for the Lord Jehovah hath laid on thee the iniquity of us all. And as thou bearest all our sins, so thou carriest all our sorrows. And dost thou not bear all the persons of thy redeemed? Dost thou not bear all our troubles, all our exercises, all our temptations, trials, difficulties? The government is upon thy shoulder; the care of the churches is all with thee. And shall I not cast all my care upon thee? Shall I be careful for many things, while Jesus saith, "Cast thy burden upon the Lord, and he shall sustain thee?" Oh for grace to sit loose to all things, and to leave all things with thee. Lord, do thou bear me up when I am falling, support me when weak, uphold me against all mine enemies, carry me safe through a life of grace here—and, finally, bring me home to thy glory, to behold thee, and dwell with thee for ever.

EVENING.—"O the hope of Israel, the Saviour thereof in time of trouble, why shouldest thou be as a stranger in the land, and as a way-faring man that turneth aside to tarry for a night?"—Jer. xiv. 8.

My soul, follow up these holy pleadings with thy

Lord. Jesus loves boldness, and not bondage frames. Remember, when thou goest to him, thou goest to a tried friend, a long-proved, a faithful friend, and one that loveth at all times; and he that was and is the hope of Israel, hath ever been, and will be thy hope, thy Saviour, the Rock of Ages; yea, "Jesus Christ, the same yesterday, to-day, and for ever." Is then thy Jesus as a stranger to thee? Are his visits short, and but as the wayfaring man that is hastening on his journey, who, though he stops at the inn for the night, stops only to refresh himself, and takes no account of what passeth in the house? Pause, my soul, it is time to enquire. I hope no shyness has crept in between thy Lord and thee! When did he last visit thee? When did he last manifest himself unto thee, otherwise than he doth to the world? What precious Bethel visits hast thou lately had? When did he shew thee all his secrets, and thou didst tell him all that was in thine heart? When was his well-known voice last heard by thee, saying, "Come with me from Lebanon, my spouse, with me from Lebanon: look from the top of Amana, from the top of Shenir and Hermon, from the lions' den, from the mountains of the leopards?" And when didst thou answer the gracious invitation, crying out, with joy unspeakable, "It is the voice of my beloved! Behold, he cometh leaping upon the mountains, and skipping upon the hills!" Oh, my soul, my soul! I charge it upon thee, to be very chary of the Lord's visits! See to it, that thou art always upon the alert, waiting for them, and going forth in holy longings and vehement desires after them. Depend upon it, Jesus is no stranger in his visits, but it is thou who art a stranger to the consciousness of his coming. Never is thy Lord as a wayfaring man, that tarrieth but for a night with his people; but it is through thy sleepy, slothful, forgetful frame, that, while Jesus is standing and knocking at the door, saying, "Open to me," thou art regardless of his coming, and having put off thy coat, feelest not inclined to put it on. Jesus, Master, suffer not a coldness to arise, no, not for a moment, in my poor heart, towards thee. · Oh! give me a holy jealousy to be always on the look-out for thy sweet visits. Do thou, my beloved, put in thy hand by the hole of the door of my heart, that my bowels may be moved in earnest desires for thy coming. For then, thou sweet Lord, thou that art the hope of Israel and the Saviour thereof, then when thou comest, and I shall find thee without, I will lead thee, and bring thee into my mother's house, who would instruct me; and I would cause thee to drink of spiced wine of the juice of my pomegranate; yea, I would constrain thee, and hold thee fast, that thou shouldest not be as a wayfaring man of the night, but I would keep thee until the break of day, and thou shouldest make thyself known to me in breaking of bread and in prayer!

OCTOBER 29.

MORNING.—" He sent his word and healed them."—Ps. cvii. 20.

Of all the subjects to comfort our minds in the recollection of the mercies in Jesus, the authority and name of Jehovah in the appointment comes home with the greatest comfort to the heart. This is faith's warrant —this is faith's confidence. Who sent Jesus; who sent his word; who is it that gives validity and efficacy to salvation? Jehovah. " Beware of him," saith the Lord, " my name is in him." And how then can my soul fail, or any promise in Christ pass unfulfilled, when Jehovah sends and Christ completes the work the Father gave him to do? Blessed Jesus! may I always look to thee under this precious character; and may I hear thee speaking under that solemn, but blessed title, " I am the Lord that healeth thee."

EVENING.—"I have said to corruption, thou art my father; to the worm, thou art my mother, and my sister."—Job xvii. 14.

My soul, take a turn now and then to the grave. It will be profitable to look at the bed where thou art shortly to take up thy residence, before thou art sent there to remain. Nothing so profitable to allay all that heat and folly which keep men in a continual ferment, as a solemn view of "the house appointed for all living." To be sure, nothing can be more humbling than what Job here speaks of his relations: great men and nobles will not be very fond of the alliance; but in reality, all the other affinities of life are imaginary. Corruption is the common father of all. In this we all are formed; for corruption when dried, becomes the original dust it was before it was animated. And as corruption is the father, so the worm is both mother and sister; for here they burrow, and this is their proper element. But, my soul, while thou knowest these things, art thou living as one under the influence of them? Every man may say, as Job said, and call corruption his father, and the worm his mother and sister; but thousands while they say it, do not live as though they believed it. To say to corruption, "Thou art my father," in a scriptural sense, implies a heartfelt knowledge of a man's own corrupt, fallen, and sinful state; and under a sense of sin, and a consciousness of salvation by the Lord Jesus Christ, that soul hath attained a self-loathing and abhorrence, so as to look to corruption and the worms of the earth with complacency, as the blessed asylum where will be deposited a vile body that shall harass the soul no more. Art thou, my soul, so looking at the grave? Dost thou so view it, as to love it for the blessed property contained in it? Precious Jesus! thou didst take pleasure in thy relationship with our nature, though thy holy body, untainted by sin, was liable to no corruption; yet, in the affinities of humanity, thou calledst thyself " a worm, and no man, a reproach of men, and despised of the people!" Oh, the transporting thought! to know, like Job, that thou my Kinsman-Redeemer liveth! And to know also, from a well-founded hope and assurance in thee, that " though after my skin, worms destroy this body, yet in my flesh shall I see God: whom I shall see for myself, and mine eyes shall behold for myself, and not another for me!"

OCTOBER 30.

MORNING.—" Thy shoes shall be iron and brass; and as thy days, so shall thy strength be."—Deut. xxxiii. 25.

What a thought that is which the word of God furnisheth, in the view of everlasting engagements, that a suitable strength is laid up for every emergency. God's love hath provided adequate supplies to the wants of all his people. What strength of enemies shall be equal to the everlasting strength of God? What shall drain the resources of everlasting love? What shall dry up the streams which flow from an everlasting fountain? Jesus therefore will proportion the back of his people to the burden. His grace shall be sufficient for all: it shall be sufficient for you, it shall be sufficient for me, for every one, for all. Sweet thought! Oh for grace to keep it always in remembrance!

EVENING.—" For I know that this shall turn to my salvation, through your prayer, and the supply of the Spirit of Jesus Christ."—Philip. i. 19.

Blessed frame of mind! when, like Paul, however unpromising circumstances are, to be able to say, ' I know that this exercise, be it what it may, is among *the all things* which work together for good to them that love God, and are the called according to his purpose!' My soul, do thou, once for all, mark down this one certain and never-to-be-questioned truth: that thy God, thy Jesus, hath but one end in view from all the providences he appoints to his people, and is invariably and everlastingly promoting it, however to thy apprehension at times, things seem to run counter. And when thou hast settled this in thy mind, as a certain fixed principle, next take into the account all, or (at least as thou canst not know all,) some of the many foundations on which the certainty, for the accomplishment of a final issue of good to the people of God, rests. Think of the ability, power, wisdom, and purpose of thy Lord. Call to mind the grace, the love, the fixed affection, Jesus bears, and from everlasting hath always borne to his people. Then recollect the plentiful means in his own almighty hand, which he hath, to make all purposes minister to his will, and all creatures to become instruments of his pleasure. And when thou hast studied, and well studied these blessed things in Christ's school, under the supply of the Spirit's teaching, make application of the doctrine to every event in the dispensations of thy Lord's providences and grace, which thou meetest with through life. Art thou afflicted in soul; in sickness of body; in want or weakness; with inward trials, or outward evils; tempted by sin, or tempted by Satan; Jesus knows all, appoints all, is carrying thee through all, and will finally bless thee in all. The enjoyment of ordinances, or interruption of ordinances; heart-straitenings in prayer, or enlargement in prayer; in short, all things, past, present, and future; all circumstances, times, and occasions; the blessings of heaven, yea, the very malice of hell, Jesus will over-rule, arrange, direct, and order; that, like the hidden springs of a machine, a beautiful design is in the whole, and not a pin could be left out without injury to the work. Learn these things, my soul, and get, through grace, into the practical use of those lessons, and then thou wilt be able to say, and with the same degree of assurance as Paul did, let thy trials be what they may, under every one of them; "I know that this shall turn to my salvation, through the prayer of the faithful, and the supply of the Spirit of Jesus Christ."

OCTOBER 31.

MORNING.—" There remaineth therefore a rest to the people of God."—Heb. iv. 9.

Blessed motto for the close of the month, or the day, or year; after being fatigued with the thoughts, and cares, and anxieties of life. My soul, delight thyself in the thought of it, look forward to the speedy enjoyment of it. Like the prophet's vision, it will come; wait for it. No sorrow you have gone through will ever come over again. No persecution already felt shall exactly be again practised. The same trial shall not be again known, Every day, every hour of the day, we are nearer home. Precious consideration. And Jesus is the rest of his people. Lord, in thee alone I find rest; be thou my hope, and be thou my portion for ever.

EVENING.—" At my first answer no man stood with me, but all men forsook me.—Notwithstanding, the Lord stood with me, and strengthened me."—2 Tim. iv. 16, 17.

My soul, think of the apostle's situation, when brought as a prisoner, for Jesus's sake, before the council, and deserted by all. Nay, look to an infinitely greater than Paul, when hurried away to Pilate, and when all his disciples forsook him and fled. Make improvement of the view of both, as it may be profitable to thyself and thine own circumstances. There is a period coming, and, for aught thou knowest, may be near indeed, in which no man *can* stand with thee; in which the kindest earthly friend, if thou hast any, or the tenderest-hearted neighbour, *cannot* minister to thy safety. When thou art going down to the valley of the shadow of death, and the Lord is undressing thee for Jordan's river, think of that season, and how blessed must it then be to say, with Paul, ' Though no man hath stood with me, or can stand, yet Jesus will be with me to strengthen me.' Oh! what blessedness is in this sweet word, *notwithstanding!* Though all friends fail, though creatures of every description, and every degree, stand aloof, unable to help; though in thyself thou hast nothing, thou art nothing, yea, by reason of sin and unworthiness, art worse than nothing, and can merit nothing; *notwithstanding* all these, the Lord will be there, and he will stand by thee, and strengthen thee. Precious Jesus! I need no more, I desire no other; nay, I pray every other to depart, and leave a dying man alone: for humbly shall I say, as my Lord hath said before me, "I am not alone, because the Father is with me." And who shall say, how Jesus may bless me in these solemn seasons? Who shall describe what passeth between Jesus and my soul then? May there not be many sweet love-tokens then given by Jesus to his people, which before, to have shewn, would have lessened the exercise of faith? Will not then some more enlarged views of divine love and faithfulness break out to lighten up the passage of death? Oh! for grace, until the hour arrives, to walk by faith in this soul-supporting and soul-refreshing hope! And when the moment comes, who shall speak, or even conceive the blessedness of realizing the sweet promise of Jesus, which all the redeemed rejoice in, but none below have ever fully apprehended equal to its vast extent: "At that day ye shall know that I am in my Father, and ye in me, and I in you!" John xiv. 20.

NOVEMBER 1.

MORNING.—"For thou wilt light my candle."—Ps. xviii. 28.

Precious consideration! It is the Lord that lighteth the candle of his people. And if the Lord light it, what power can put it out? Cherish, my soul, the faith this thought awakens, amidst all the darkness around thee and in thee. Hath the Lord, indeed, given thee light? Dost thou in his light see light? In the light of God the Father, dost thou behold God the Son, and, by the enlightening of the Holy Ghost, hast thou the light of the knowledge of the glory of God in the face of Jesus Christ? Oh the blessedness of such a state of light, and life, and knowledge; how is it possible then any more to be in darkness, when the Lord himself is my everlasting light, and my God my glory? Now consider the reverse of this in creature-enlightening. "How oft," saith Job, "is the candle of the wicked put out!" And how exposed it is to be every moment put out; for it is not of God's kindling. A *fleeting* of its own oil will do it. What is called a *thief* in the candle will do it. It may be *blown* out; it may be *snuffed* out; or if none of these causes occur, yet of itself it must shortly *burn* out. "For what is our life but a vapour?" My soul, ponder these things. Hath the Lord lighted thy candle? Is Jesus thy light, thy life, thy joy, thy sunshine, thy morning star, thy all in all? And hath he risen upon thee, never more to go down? Oh then, though all thou knowest, all thou beholdest now, is but as the faint taper of the night, compared to the glory of that day which shall be revealed, yet take to thyself by faith all the sweet comforts of thy state of grace, and say, it is the Lord that hath lighted my candle. The Lord my God will enlighten all remaining darkness: I shall see thy face in glory, and shortly awake up after thy likeness.

EVENING.—"The curse causeless shall not come."—Prov. xxvi. 2.

It is a sweet thought, that the prayer of the wicked is an abomination in the sight of the Lord. And surely the curse of the wicked cannot injure the righteous. But it is doubly blessed when a child of God finds a promising God, a performing God, in making their curses fall to the ground; yea, converting their very curses into blessings. Had not Joseph's brethren sold their brother, humanly speaking, how would he have arrived to the government of Egypt? Had not Haman planned the destruction of Mordecai, and for this purpose erected the gallows, though means would not have been wanting for his own destruction, yet the idea of hanging might not have entered the breast of the king. Yea, had not the Jews crucified the Lord Jesus, where would have been the triumph of the cross to his redeemed? Learn, my soul, to be looking at these things; not by mere outward appearances, not by the event of the moment, but by the final issue and termination of things. "The curse causeless shall not come." This is quite enough for every believer. Jesus will prevent, or over-rule, or make it minister the very reverse of what the enemy designed. It shall be frustrated, or it shall be sanctified, or it shall be productive of salutary effects, like medicated waters, that by running over certain properties of the earth, have their nature changed, and become wholesome and healing. Lord! cause me to repose in thee, and if the enemy curse, do thou but bless, and all his causeless anger will then be as nothing.

NOVEMBER 2.

MORNING.—"But the Comforter, which is the Holy Ghost, whom the Father will send in my name, he shall teach you all things, and bring all things to your remembrance, whatsoever I have said unto you." —John xiv. 26.

Oh blessed Spirit, to whom I owe such unspeakable mercies, let me, Lord, contemplate thee this day under this gracious, kind, compassionate office of the Comforter. Thou art indeed the Holy Ghost the Comforter. And how mercifully dost thou sympathize with all the followers of Jesus in their various afflictions, both of soul and body. How tenderly dost thou shew us our sins, and lead to Jesus's blood to wash them away. How sweetly dost thou visit, encourage, strengthen, instruct, lead, and guide, into all truth. And how powerfully at times, by thy restraining grace, dost thou enable us to mortify the deeds of the body, that we may live. Hail, thou holy, blessed, almighty Comforter! Oh let thy visits be continual. Come, Lord, and abide with me, and be with me for ever. Manifest that thou art the Sent of the Father, and of the Son, in coming to me in Jesus's name, in teaching me of all the precious things concerning Jesus, and acting as the Remembrancer of Jesus; that in thee, by thy blessed office-work, I may know, and live in the sweet enjoyment of fellowship with the Father, and with his Son Jesus Christ, through the influence of the Holy Ghost, the Comforter.

EVENING.—" I said in my haste, all men are liars."—Ps. cxvi. 11.

Hasty words, for the most part, are not wise words. But, as the apostle remarks,' " Let God be true, and every man a liar." It should seem that this hasty expression of David was at a time when he was greatly afflicted. Alas! what exercises, for want of the proper use of them, in their sanctifying properties, are men brought into! But if, from long experience, the heart be led to a just conclusion, that man, in his best friendship, and best intention, is too fickle and helpless a creature to trust in, or depend upon; and from a full conviction of the hollow and deceitful nature of the human heart, the soul is led unto God in Christ, as the only stable and permanent security; thus changing the reeds of Egypt, for the Rock of Israel: here it becomes not the subject of haste, but the deliberate conclusion formed by grace, to consider every being fallacious but the faithful Jehovah. My soul, take thy stand, this evening, under Jesus's banner: and though thou hast been deceived by man, yea, by every man; though thine own heart be deceitful, and desperately wicked, so much so, that though, since grace brought thee first acquainted with it, thou hast been making discoveries more and more that have astonished thee, and thou hast not yet, nor ever will in this life get to the bottom in exploring the depths of deception; though the world and the great enemy of souls be all in league to deceive thee; yet shall not the whole of these deceivers prevail, nor separate thee from the love of Christ. Jesus will make thee more than conqueror through his grace supporting thee. As the armies in heaven, so his faithful upon earth, " overcome by the blood of the Lamb, and by the word of their testimony, and have loved not their lives unto death."

NOVEMBER 3.

MORNING.—" And in that day there shall be no more the Canaanite in the house of the Lord of Hosts."—Zech. xiv. 21.

Oh precious day of God, when will it arrive? Shall the house of Jesus be indeed delivered from all false pastors, all corrupt worship, and the Lord have turned to the people a pure language, that they may all call upon the name of the Lord, to serve him with one consent? Shall my soul indeed be freed, not only from all the sorrows, pains, evils, and afflictions of sin around me; but what is infinitely better than all, from the very being and indwelling of sin within me? Shall the fountain of corruption, both of original and actual sin, be dried up, so that I shall never think a vain thought, nor speak an idle sinful word any more? Is there such a day, in which the Canaanite shall be wholly driven out? Oh blessed thought: precious, precious promise! Oh dearest Jesus, to what a blessed state hast thou begotten poor sinners of the earth by thy blood and righteousness! Hasten it, Lord. Cut short thy work, thou that art mighty to save, and take thy willing captive home from myself, and all the remaining Canaanites yet in the land, which are the very tyrants of my soul.

EVENING. — "For my thoughts are not your thoughts, neither are your ways my ways, saith the Lord."—Isa. lv. 8.

My soul, hast thou ever considered the blessedness in this verse, as it concerns the great work of salvation? Ponder over it, this evening. There is nothing, perhaps, in which there is a greater and more striking difference than there is between our crude and contracted notions of redemption, and the perfect and unerring thoughts of Jehovah on this point. Our conduct towards each other is so limited on the score of pardon, that though we may forgive a first or second offence, yet if it be repeated too many, nature revolts at the offender, and seems to take a kind of justification in withholding any farther acts of clemency. Hence we frame the same standard to judge by, concerning God. But with God, abounding sin calls forth abounding grace, and, like the tide, riseth above high water-mark, yea, overflows all the banks and surrounding ground; so much so, indeed, that it covers the mountains, and "If the sin of Judah be looked for, it shall not be found." Hence the prophet, in a transport of holy joy and triumph in the contemplation, cries out, "Who is a God like unto thee, that pardoneth iniquity, and passeth by the transgression of the remnant of his heritage? He retaineth not his anger for ever, because he delighteth in mercy. He will turn again: he will have compassion upon us: he will subdue our iniquities; and thou will cast all our sins into the depths of the sea," Micah vii. 18, 19. How truly blessed, then, must it be, to carry the same kind of reasoning concerning God into all the departments of thinking, in relation to himself and his dealings with us. Think as highly as I may be able concerning him, I must fall infinitely short of what he really is, both in the nature of his existence, and in all his dealings with his creatures. In those points where he hath been pleased to reveal himself, I cannot err. But if I attempt to go farther, the bar to inquiry stops my way, and this sweet verse stand for a memorandum to inform me: "For my thoughts are not your thoughts, neither are your ways my ways, saith the Lord." Now grace rejoiceth in this discovery, while proud unhumbled nature revolts at it. Say, my soul, dost thou feel delight in such views of Jehovah? Is it blessed to thee, that in all thy Jesus hath taught thee, he hath brought thee to see more and more thy nothingness, thy littleness, and the Lord's all-sufficiency? Surely it must be divine teaching alone that can create joy in the heart, when such discoveries are made which tend to humble the creature and exalt the Creator. Blessed be the Lord, who teacheth me to profit!

NOVEMBER 4.

MORNING.—"For I know that ye seek Jesus which was crucified."—Matt. xxviii. 5.

Is it indeed known unto my Lord that I seek him? Doth Jesus know that I desire him more than my necessary food? Ye angels of light that watched over his sepulchre, do ye witness for me that he is more precious to me than gold, yea, than the golden wedge of Ophir. And can I, do I, humbly appeal to him that readeth the heart, and knoweth all things, and say, "Thou knowest, Lord, that I love thee!" Be comforted, then, my soul: he whom thou seekest will soon be found of thee. He is near at hand. He hath never been a wilderness to his people; neither hath he ever said to the praying seed of Jacob, "Seek ye my face in vain." While thou art seeking him, he is looking on thee. And the very desire in thine heart of seeking him, it is Jesus hath kindled. And nothing can be more sure than that he who kindled them in thine heart, did not kindle them in vain. Sweet thought; I bless thee for it, thou gracious Lord.

EVENING.—"I counsel thee to buy of me gold tried in the fire, that thou mayest be rich; and white raiment, that thou mayest be clothed, and that the shame of thy nakedness do not appear; and anoint thine eyes with eye-salve, that thou mayest see."—Rev. iii. 18.

My soul, take advice of thy Lord, for he is a Wonderful Counsellor, and all these blessings will be thine. He will cause thee to inherit substance, and fill all thy treasures; yea, he will give thee durable riches and righteousness. If Jesus clothe thee with the robe of his salvation, thy nakedness will be indeed covered; but no fig-leaves of thine own gathering and sewing together will do this for thee. If Jesus but anoint thine eyes with the precious anointing of his Holy Spirit, thou wilt both see and know the way to buy this tried gold. Now, pause over this sweet verse, and ask thyself, how thou shalt buy this golden treasure? What is the treasure, but faith? For the Holy Ghost calls it *precious* faith; "Yea, more precious than gold that perisheth, though it be tried with fire," 1 Pet. i. 7. And if thy Lord, who gives thee counsel to buy, will sell this article to thee, as he sells it to all his people, "Without money and without price," it will get for thee every thing thou needest, to cover and to clothe, to give sight, and to gain substance. It will become both meat and drink, and house and home; it will keep thee from every danger; yea, and preserve thee to his heavenly kingdom. It will form a complete livelihood, for "The just live by faith;" and as to riches, there are none, properly speaking, that deserve to be called so, but "The rich in faith, and heirs of the kingdom." So that if thou make this purchase, here is a title to all that God in Christ is to his people. God himself, thy Father, is thine; Christ, with all his fulness, is thine; the Holy Ghost, with all his blessed influences, is thine. The promises are all thine; all the blessings of grace are thine; and all the inheritance of glory is thine. And let Satan vent whatever rage he may, as thou art going home to thy Father's house, yet, by following the counsel of Jesus, and buying of him gold tried in the fire, by thus taking the " Shield of faith, this will quench all the fiery darts of the wicked." Precious Jesus! give me, Lord, I pray thee, grace to follow thy counsel, and to buy of thee this gold tried in the fire, and bless both the counsel and the Wonderful Counsellor, who both counsels and inclines my soul to follow what my Lord hath said, and to enjoy in him all things which make for my present peace and everlasting happiness.

NOVEMBER 5.

MORNING.—" The king hath brought me into his chambers." —Song i. 4.

Yes, he who is King of nations, King of saints, is my God and King also; for he hath an universal empire, being one with the Father over all, blessed for ever. Amen. To him I bow the knee, and humbly and gratefully desire to put the crown of my salvation on his adorable head. And what hath this Sovereign done for thee, my soul? Oh record his praise; tell it to saints and sinners all around. This great, and glorious, and condescending King, hath not only brought thee out of darkness and the shadow of death, but hath brought thee into his chambers. What chambers? Chambers of sweet communion and fellowship; chambers of love, of grace, of mercy, of redemption, of ordinances, and of all covenant blessings. He hath taught me of his love, and my privileges in him, and so assured me of my everlasting safety in him and his finished salvation, that by and by, when from those outward chambers of grace, he hath accomplished all his blessed purposes concerning me, he will bring me home into his inner chambers of light and glory, from whence I shall go out no more, but dwell in them, and in the presence of God and the Lamb, for ever and ever. Hallelujah.

EVENING.—" And lo, the heavens were opened unto him, and he saw the Spirit of God descending like a dove, and lighting upon him. And lo, a voice from heaven, saying, this is my beloved Son, in whom I am well pleased."—Matt. iii. 16, 17.

Take thy stand, my soul, this evening by the river Jordan, and by faith behold the wonders displayed in the hour thy Jesus entered upon his public ministry. Behold a decisive proof of the distinct personality in the threefold character, which all the sacred volume of the scriptures gives to the revelation of the Godhead. Behold Jesus, the uncreated word, on the bank of Jordan! Behold the Holy Spirit, hovering as a dove on his sacred person! And hear the voice of God coming from heaven, proclaiming who Jesus was, his relationship to him, and his approbation of him. And when thou hast duly pondered the precious testimony, bend thy knee in adoration, love, and praise, to the sacred Three in One, for so condescending an act of grace, in confirmation of the faith once delivered to the saints. Nor quit the hallowed spot until thou hast well and duly considered the blessedness of the proclamation given from heaven by the Father, to the person and character of the Lord Jesus. John the Baptist was taught to form his conclusion of Christ by this very evidence. He that sent John to baptize, had said unto him, " Upon whom thou shalt see the Spirit descending, and remaining on him, the same is he which baptizeth with the Holy Ghost. And I saw," said John, " and bare record, that this is the Son of God." And do thou, my soul, take thy confidence from the same precious testimony; and then ask thyself another question: Is he whom the Father declared to be his beloved Son, thy beloved Saviour? And while God declares himself well pleased with him as thy Saviour, art thou well pleased with him also in this precious character? If to these questions thou canst truly say, yes, yes; thou wilt find a blessed testimony indeed, and a soul refreshing consolation in this view of Jesus. Go then, in all thy holy exercises of faith and prayer, go to thy God and Father in Christ Jesus, and plead for all thou standest in need of, for the life that now is, and that which is to come, upon this footing: that in Him, in whom God hath declared himself well pleased, thou art well pleased; and for his blood and righteousness sake, thou seekest every supply of grace here, and glory hereafter. This will be a sure plea, and such as can never fail. And he that proclaimed, by a voice from heaven, his perfect approbation of Jesus, as a Saviour for poor sinners, will give, for his sake, every thing that poor sinners can need during a life of grace, until consummated in glory.

NOVEMBER 6.

MORNING.—"For the Father himself loveth you, because ye have loved me, and have believed that I came out from God."—John xvi. 27.

See, my soul, how thy Jesus hath endeared to thee the Father in the assurance of his love. And wilt thou not feel thine whole affections going forth in continual love after him? Was it not thy Father which, from everlasting, gave thee Jesus as thy Saviour, and gave thee to Jesus that he might redeem thee? Was it not from the same precious source that Jesus came as a Saviour, and a great one, to redeem thee and other great sinners? Is it not thy Father that hath adopted thee into his family in Jesus, and given thee the Spirit of adoption, whereby thou criest, Abba, Father? And doth he not accept thee in Jesus, bless thee in Jesus, nourish thee with the body and blood of Jesus, clothe thee with the righteousness of Jesus, and give thee all temporal, spiritual, and, by and by, will give thee all eternal blessings in Christ Jesus! Nay, even his chastisements have nothing in them of wrathful punishment, but fatherly love and mercy in Jesus. Oh my soul, pause, and behold what manner of love the Father hath bestowed upon thee, that thou shouldest be called a child of God. And wilt thou not then from henceforth and for ever say unto him in Jesus,—" My Father, thou art the guide of my youth; for thou hast commanded me so to call thee." Jeremiah iii. 19.

EVENING.—" In that day, sing ye unto her, a vineyard of red wine. I the Lord do keep it, I will water it every moment; lest any hurt it, I will keep it night and day."—Isaiah xxvii. 2, 3.

And in what day, but the gospel day, could this song be sung with greater justness? Christ's church is indeed a vineyard, hedged in, and fenced round, from the world's wilderness; so that all within it may well sing this song in Judah, when God hath made it like a strong city, and appointed " salvation for walls and bulwarks." Yea, God himself hath sung to his well beloved Son, this song of his beloved, touching his vineyard. But what is the red wine of the vineyard? Red wine of Judæa, was of the choicest grapes; and surely the blood of Christ is the choicest of all blessings to the sinner's view. Now, my soul, mark the sweetness of Jesus's promise; it is he who engageth to keep it; yea, to have his eye upon it night and day, lest any hurt it; yea, not only to keep it, but water it, and that every moment: so that he is both a fence and a refreshing, a covert from the storm and as rivers of water in a dry place; and, like some rich luxuriant tree in a sultry land, not only forms a shade to shelter the poor sun-burnt traveller from the heat, but also affords fruit to slake his thirst, and to feed him; so that while he is strengthened in his journey, in resting under its branches from his fatigue, he may find occasion also to bless God, both for protection and support. And art thou, blessed Jesus, all this, and infinitely more, to thy people? Art thou the tree of life in the paradise of God? Dost thou keep thy church, thy vineyard, night and day, that none shall hurt it; yea, and water it every moment, and every individual soul of thine, of the plants of thy

Father's planting? Help me, then, thou blessed, gracious Lord! Help me to feel all that confidence which is suited to an entire dependence upon thee! Sit down, my soul, under "the shadow of thy Lord, with great delight, and his fruit will be sweet to thy taste."

NOVEMBER 7.

MORNING.—"And yet there is room."—Luke xiv. 22.

Room! where, and for whom? Room in the gospel of salvation, and for poor perishing sinners, in the blood and righteousness of Jesus Christ. Room in the heart of God the Father, in the love, grace, mercy, and peace of God the Son, and in the teachings, influences, and fellowship of God the Holy Ghost. Room in the plentiful provisions of grace, the calls of the gospel, the ministration of the word and ordinances in the house of prayer. "Whosoever will," is the gracious invitation; whosever feels his heart made willing in the day of God's power, "let him come and take of the water of life freely." Lord, is there room for me? Thousands, and tens of thousands have found room through thy grace inclining them to come; and yet the scripture sweetly saith again this day, "And yet there is room." Oh give me grace to see that I am one of the invited, one of the happy number that hath found room; and from experiencing the blessed fulness, riches, grace, suitableness, and all-sufficiency in the blood and righteousness of Jesus for poor sinners, I may proclaim every where around that others may find the same, that yet there is room. And Oh Lord! grant, that while yet there is room, multitudes that are ready to perish may come. And then all thy royal guests whom thou bringest to thy banquet, and who find room in all the mercies of Jehovah for redemption here below, will find room in the house not made with hands, eternal in the heavens.

EVENING.—"And they feared as they entered into the cloud."—Luke ix. 34.

My soul, here is much instruction for thine evening thoughts to be employed upon. Sit down, and take a leisurely view of the situation of the disciples of Jesus, at this hallowed season, on the mount. The Lord Jesus was about to manifest to them somewhat of his glory. But the prelude to it was infinitely solemn. "They feared as they entered into the cloud;" though, when there, Jesus was going to open to their souls the richest enjoyment of himself. And is it not so with all the sweetest manifestations which the Lord makes to his people? Seasons of sickness, bereaving providences, afflictions from the world, disappointments, crosses, and the like; these are like the cloud to the disciples, as we enter them; but what gracious events have we found folded up in them, and when opened to our view, how much of Jesus's love, and grace, and glory, have come out of them, which, but for the dispensation, we must have lost. And recollect, my soul, as thou lookest back, and tracest the divine hand leading thee through dark and trying providences, in how many cases, and in how many instances, though the cloud was frowning as thou didst enter, the most blessed sunshine soon after broke in upon thee. Precious Jesus! choose for me in every circumstance yet remaining to be accomplished. I know not what is in thy sovereign appointments concerning me; but sure I am that both love and wisdom are at the bottom of all. Give me grace to enter the cloud, be it what it may, without fear, because I know Jesus is with me; and though, in this my day, it be neither clear nor dark, yet well I know all shall be well in thee and from thee; "and at evening-time it shall be light."

NOVEMBER 8.

MORNING.—" The people shall dwell alone, and shall not be reckoned among the nations."—Numb. xxiii. 9.

Mark, my soul, the character of God's Israel, and remember that they are the same in all ages. Distinguishing mercies are sweet mercies. God's people dwell alone, in the everlasting appointment of the Father, by whom they were set apart, and formed for his glory, and given to his Son. They dwell alone, in being brought into the church of Jesus as the redeemed and purchased by his blood. They dwell alone, under the sweet influences of the Spirit, by whom they are known, distinguished, regenerated, and sealed unto the day of redemption. Thus set apart, thus formed, thus given, thus redeemed, thus purchased, thus sealed, surely they are not reckoned among the nations, but are supposed to shew forth God's praises, who hath called them out of darkness into his marvellous light. My soul, what sayeth thy experience to these things? Oh how different the state, the circumstances, the new birth, the fellowship, pursuits, way, life, and work of God's people from the world! Blessed Jesus, cause me to dwell alone from the nations around; but let me not dwell a moment without thee; but do thou come with thy Father and the Holy Spirit, according to thy sweet promises, and make constant abode with me.

EVENING.—" Verily, verily, I say unto you, whatsoever ye shall ask the Father in my name, he will give it you."—John xvi. 23.

My soul, do not fail to remark, in this blessed promise of thy Lord, how he hath secured the accomplishment of it. Here is a double verily if one will not do. And this is said by the faithfnl witness, and the amen of heaven. Had Jesus said but the words themselves, without a single verily, his bare word was enough to give confirmation to faith; but when he says, " verily,

verily," repeating it twice over, how gracious and condescending, as well as comforting and confirming, ought it to be to our dependance upon what he hath said. But the promise itself comes in with a blessed *shall* and *will;* and that not to any limited request or petition, but extended to a *whatsoever;* as if Jesus threw the reins of government into his people's hand. In some parts of scripture we find a *may be* for our encouragement. "It may be," said the prophet, "that the Lord of Hosts will be gracious," Amos v. 15. and this ought to encourage a child of God in the exercise of faith, under every trial. But when God saith, "It *shall* be," and confirms it with a double asseveration of "Verily, verily I say unto you;" this sums up, all in one, every assurance that can be desired. Pause, my soul, over the subject, and then say, what shall be thy requests to thy God and Father, in the name of his dear Son? Nay, do not ask for small things, while the King of heaven hath given thee two verilies, that whatsoever thou shalt ask shall be granted. Jesus himself doth as it were put into thine hand a blank paper for thee to fill in, having signed and set his own blessed and holy name at the bottom. Now what wilt thou write down? Thou hast nothing more to do, than to follow thy Lord's example, and as he hath written his name in the promise, do thou also write Jesus, and Jesus only, on the whole paper. Ask of God thy Father to give thee Jesus; for in giving him, in him and with him, he giveth all things. Lord, I would say, give me thine own dear Son, and I need nothing more; Christ is all, and in all.

NOVEMBER 9.

MORNING.—"And many of them that sleep in the dust of the earth shall awake, some to everlasting life, and some to shame and everlasting contempt."—Dan. xii. 2.

What a morning will this be!—how distinguished

from every other! Lord, how often do I now awake with thoughts of earth, and sin, and trifles, and vanity! How have I opened mine eyes this morning?—was it, dearest Jesus, with thoughts of thee? In that solemn morning there will be no longer dreams, as now, even in our waking hours — for all childish imaginations, shadows, doubts, and fears, will be done away. Precious, blessed Lord Jesus! cause me morning by morning, while upon earth, to awaken with sweet thoughts of thee. Let the close of night, and the opening of the day, be with thy dear name in my heart, on my thoughts, and on my lips; and in that everlasting morning, after having dropped asleep in Jesus, and in thy arms by faith, may I awake up in thy embraces, and after thy likeness, to be everlastingly and eternally satisfied with thee.

EVENING.—"And such were some of you: but ye are washed, but ye are sanctified, but ye are justified in the name of the Lord Jesus, and by the Spirit of our God."—1 Cor. vi. 11.

It is profitable at times to see our mercies, and to trace them to their source, by considering what we once were, the better to apprehend what we now are. "Such," the apostle saith, when speaking of the vilest of the vile, "were some of you:" dead in trespasses and sins, hateful, and hating one another. But now, being washed from all your filthiness, and from all your idols, there is a justification *by* Christ, and a sanctification *in* Christ; and by the effectual work of God the Spirit in the heart, the believer stands complete before God, in the name of the Lord Jesus. This is a blessed testimony to the soul of the poor sinner, whom the Holy Ghost hath convinced of sin, of righteousness, and of judgment. For God the Father gave the promise, in the old testament scripture, that he would sprinkle clean water upon the people, and they should be clean. And here, in the new testament dispensation, the fountain is opened, by which it is to be accomplished, and they are said to be clean; yea, "both washed, and justified, and sanctified, in the name of the Lord Jesus, and by the Spirit of our God." So that all the persons of the Godhead are engaged in this glorious act, to render it secure and certain to the believing soul. See to it then, my soul, that this be thy privilege, and that from long-tried and approved experience thou canst take home this sweet scripture to thyself, as both "washed, justified, and sanctified," and set to thy seal that God is true. Oh! for grace to live in the daily exercise of faith upon it, until faith be swallowed up, and lost in sight, and amidst the throng of the redeemed in glory, thou shalt live at the fountain-head of enjoyment, with those that have "washed their robes, and made them white in the blood of the Lamb!"

NOVEMBER 10.

MORNING.—"For such an High Priest became us, who is holy, harmless, undefiled, separate from sinners, and made higher than the heavens."—Heb. vii. 26.

What a sweet thought!—surely, as a poor sinner, I need an High Priest to act for me. I cannot, I dare not, approach in myself, and with my poor polluted offerings, without one. But he that intercedes for me must be himself holy, free from sin; his sacrifice holy, his obedience holy, and in all points suited to his office and my necessities. Cherish, then, the thought, my soul—He that is thine High Priest is all this, and infinitely more. So holy in himself, that not the shadow of sin was in him. So harmless, that in his mouth was found no guile. So undefiled, that though he took all the sins of his people upon him, yet in himself he was free from all sin. So separate from sinners, that though he took the nature of man, yet wholly underived from man. And so much higher than the heavens, that his own personal holiness infinitely transcended the holiness of angels; for, while they are said to be charged with folly, Jesus is the Holy One in whom the Father declared himself well pleased. Meditate, my soul, on these precious features in thy Jesus, at all times, and upon all occasions; and more especially when thou drawest nigh the throne of grace, in and through this glorious Mediator. And moreover, for thy further comfort and encouragement to come boldly to the mercy-seat, forget not to recollect the still further blessed thought, that this holiness of Jesus is the righteousness of all his people; for he was made sin, when he knew no sin, that they might be made the righteousness of God in him. And as if this was not enough, Christ glorified not himself to be made thy High Priest, but was called to it, as was Aaron. Go then, my soul, go to the precious, the holy, the harmless, the undefiled High Priest, Christ Jesus, in whom, and in whose righteousness and atoning blood thou mayest always have boldness to draw nigh, to find grace and mercy to help in all time of need.

EVENING.—"Thou dumb and deaf spirit, I charge thee come out of him, and enter no more into him."—Mark ix. 25.

Oh! that the Lord Jesus, in a spiritual healing, would frame my powers anew in himself, that neither dumbness nor deafness might ever more stop my voice of praise for the cure of my soul, as the Lord healed the poor man's son in his body! One should suppose that after the song of salvation had been once chanted in the renewed heart, that heart would never more be out of tune, nor feel a dumbness or deafness in the Lord's praise. But, alas! so much of unbelief lies lurking within, and so much of exercises come from without, that the harp is often hanging on the willow, and we seldom sing to the Lord's praise, or proclaim abroad his glory. Whereas the promise of Jehovah, in allusion to gospel-days, was, that his Israel should, even from the valley of Achor, find a door of hope; and the Lord added, that he would cause his church to sing there, "as in the days of her youth, and as in the day when she came up out of the land of Egypt," Hosea ii. 15. Surely God is glorified when, from the depth of exercises, songs of redemption still go on, and even in the fire the believer sings his morning and evening hymn to the praise of Jesus. Say, my soul, hath Jesus cured thee of this dumb and deaf spirit? Art thou daily shewing forth his praises, who hath called thee out of darkness into his marvellous light? Dost thou delight thyself in the Lord, and delight to sing in the ways of the Lord, that "great is the glory of the Lord?" See to it, that this be among the evidences of a spiritual healing; for the Lord promised, in allusion to Israel's recovery, that the ears of the deaf should be unstopped, and the tongue of the dumb should sing. Hence all the way through the pilgrimage state, the song of salvation should be heard from the mouth of Zion's travellers, until they arrive in glory, where "songs of everlasting joy shall be upon their heads, and sorrow and sighing be done away for ever."

NOVEMBER 11.

MORNING.—" And in that day there shall be a root of Jesse, which shall stand for an ensign of the people; to it shall the gentiles seek, and his rest shall be glorious."—Isa. xi. 10.

Jesus is both the root and the offspring of David, and the bright and morning star; and therefore, is not this the day, the very day, the joyful day, in which he who was set up, as God the Father's ensign from everlasting, for salvation in the council of peace? And was he not brought forth, and set up, and proclaimed as God's salvation to us poor gentiles in the fulness of time, as well as the light of his people Israel? Surely it can have reference to no other. Precious Jesus, I do indeed behold thee as set up from everlasting. Thou wert so exhibited in the council of peace, and thy goings forth were from everlasting, when thou wentest forth for the salvation of thy people. In the bible thou art the great promise, and the whole of the promises. Thou art the whole of the law and the prophets. Both the old testament dispensation, and the new testament grace, all pointed to thee, and in thee they had their completion. Thou art the Father's ensign of redemption, the signal of war with sin, with Satan, and all the powers of hell and corruption. Lord, to thee do I seek; under thy banner, and in thy strength, would I enjoy a rest which indeed must be glorious. And Oh thou blessed Spirit of all truth! when at any time the enemy cometh in like a flood, do thou lift up thy ensign, even Jesus, as a standard against him.

EVENING.—" And his commandments are not grievous."—1 John v. 3.

Is it so, my soul, that the commandments of thy Lord are not grievous unto thee? Surely it is; for though thou carriest about with thee a body of sin and death, which is everlastingly harassing thee, yet thou canst, and dost say, " I delight in the law of God after the inward man :" yea, in the very moment that thine old unrenewed nature, when evil is present with thee, is tempting thee to break through the hedge of divine precepts, in thy regenerated part thou truly lovest and delightest in the holiness of thy Lord's commandments. And are there not seasons in thine experience, when, in spite of sin, and Satan, and the world, thou canst adopt the language of one of old, and say, " Oh, how I love thy law; it is my meditation all the day!" And is it not joy to thy heart, and a blessed part of thy faith, that the law of thy God was so pure and so strict, that rather than a jot of it should pass unfulfilled, or the smallest breach of it go unatoned for, Jesus must and did die? And is it not one of the sweetest and most satisfying principles to thee in the gospel, that Jehovah did not, and would not clear the guilty, but by an equivalent; so that, both in obedience and by sacrifice, the law is magnified by thy great Surety, and made honourable? Precious Jesus! it is wholly by thee, and in thee, that my soul finds the commandments of my God to be not grievous. By faith I behold them all fulfilled in thee, as my glorious Head; and by virtue of my union with thee, I feel the gracious principle of thy quickening Spirit inclining my soul both to love thy commandments, and most earnestly desiring to fulfil them. "Lord! enable me to run the way of thy commandments, now thou hast set my soul at liberty!"

NOVEMBER 12.

MORNING.—"And they shall come which were ready to perish." —Isa. xxvii. 13.

What a blessed promise is this to a poor sinner, that is conscious of his being in perishing circumstances? My soul, pause over it this morning. Art thou not, if considered out of Christ, in perishing circumstances, by reason of the captivity of sin? Art thou not perishing under the sentence of God's broken law; under the just judgment of God, the alarms of thine own guilty conscience, the accusations of Satan, the fear of death, and the prospect of judgment and eternity? And doth this sweet scripture hold forth a provision for such perishing circumstances? Doth it really say that such shall come; nay, that they *shall* come, whatever obstructions, either from within or without, shall block up the way? Will the Lord enable them, lead them, help them; nay, constrain them to come, in defiance of all impediments? Oh precious, precious Jesus! may the blessing of him that is ready to perish come upon thee; for thou dost indeed make the widowed heart, and the sorrowful heart, to sing for joy. Blessed be thy name, for that thou hast made me willing in the day of thy power.

EVENING.—" Then shalt thou call, and the Lord shall answer; thou shalt cry, and he shall say, here I am !"—Isa. lviii. 9.

Mark the graciousness of thy God, my soul, in the readiness of his answers to thy cries. He hath said, indeed, in another sweet promise, " It shall come to pass, that before my people call, I will answer; and while they are yet speaking, I will hear," Isa. lxv. 24. But in addition to this, Jesus here throws in another precious assurance; for when we call, he will not only answer, but to our cry, he will say, " Here I am !" As if, and which is indeed really the case, the Lord would have his children know, that he is always present with them; nearer to support, than any of their foes can be to hurt. Now, my soul, I charge it upon thee, this evening, that this view, and the recollection of the everlasting presence of thy Lord, be never more from thy thoughts. How full to the same purport is that blessed scripture: " As the mountains are round about Jerusalem, so the Lord is round about his people from henceforth even for ever," Ps. cxxv. 2. And if Jesus encircle them in his arms, what power shall break through to wound? If Jesus himself be their shield, what weapon shall penetrate through him to come at them? Lie down, my soul, this night, and for ever, under these blessed impressions. Jesus doth by thee as one whom his mother comforteth. When the timid child is put to bed, the tender parent will sit by her darling until he is gone to sleep. But if the child be fearful that the mother hath left the room, frequently the child sends forth a cry, until by her voice she quiets him again. Jesus doth this, and more: for when new fears arise, and darkness adds to the distress, " Then shalt thou call, (saith he,) and the Lord shall answer; thou shalt cry, and he shall say, here I am." Oh! how blessed is the thought! I AM is always I AM; and always here!

NOVEMBER 13.

MORNING.—" Christ hath given himself for us, an offering and a sacrifice to God, for a sweet-smelling savour."—Eph. v. 2.

If, when Noah offered by faith his sacrifice at the coming forth from the ark, the Lord smelled a sweet savour in it, because both the ark and sacrifice were a type of his dear Son, how fragrant and acceptable must have been the substance, when Jesus offered himself without spot to God? Behold him by faith, my soul, in that hour, in the full incense of his own merit, the censer of his own offering, and the golden altar of his own nature. And while God, even the everlasting Father, accepts Jesus as thy Surety, in the fragrancy of his offering, wilt thou not by faith so apprehend the sweet influence of his person, work, and righteousness, as to rejoice before God in the sure acceptance of thyself and all thy poor offerings in the Beloved? Oh let a throne of grace be a daily, hourly, testimony for thee, that all thy approaches here are under the incense and intercession of Jesus; and all thine hopes and expectations of glory hereafter, are all founded in him and his finished salvation. Yes, thou Lamb of God! let all witness for me, that thou and thou alone, art the Lord my righteousness, and that I seek salvation in no other; most perfectly assured from thine own Spirit's teaching, that there is no other name under heaven, given among men, whereby we must be saved. Hallelujah.

EVENING.—" O taste and see that the Lord is good!"—Ps. xxxiv. 8.

Those views of Jesus are blessed, which not only take in his loveliness, but his usefulness; which tend both to commend him to our regard, as fair and beautiful, and at the same time full and bountiful; that, like some rich and wide-spreading tree, yea, like the tree of life in the paradise of God, is at once both for shelter and fruit. My soul, look at thy Jesus thus, and thou wilt then enter into the sense of this delightful verse of scripture: "O taste and see that the Lord is good!" In this experience of Christ consists the proper knowledge and apprehension of him. An hearsay account of Jesus is but a poor account. By hearing sermons, reading the scriptures, attending ordinances, and the like, men may acquire some knowledge of him; but until the Holy Ghost form him in the heart, "The hope of glory," we never taste and see that the Lord is good. It was this which distinguished the church's enjoyment of her Lord, and which enabled her to make a suitable answer to that question of the daughters of Jerusalem: "What is thy beloved more than another beloved?" For when we can say, "Of his fulness have all we received, and grace for grace;" then, and not before, can we say also, as he did from whom this testimony was given, "I saw and bare record, that this is the Son of God." My soul, see to it, that in your commendation of Jesus, you can add to the account your own personal enjoyment of him. And think what a blessedness must accompany that recommendation of the Lord, when, like the beloved apostle, you can hold forth Christ upon the same principles, and for the same cause as he did: "That (said he) which was from the beginning, which we have heard, which we have seen with our eyes, which we have looked upon, and our hands have handled of the word of life—declare we unto you; that ye also may have fellowship with us: and truly our fellowship is with the Father, and with his Son Jesus Christ," 1 John i. 1, 3.

NOVEMBER 14.

MORNING.—"And the parched ground shall become a pool, and the thirsty land springs of water."—Isa. xxxv. 7.

Oh how refreshing is this promise to my poor, dry, barren, thirsty soul! Surely every poor sinner, like me, that knows his own leanness and poverty, will feel the blessedness of it; for whether it be in the sapless state of unawakened nature, or whether in a scorched or languishing state from the want of the renewings of grace, nothing can be more refreshing than such a promise. Precious Jesus, do thou revive the languishing frame of thy people; do thou "pour water upon him that is thirsty, and floods upon the dry ground." Oh what a fulness, blessed Lord, there is in thyself to supply all. Surely thou art, as the church said, "A fountain of gardens, a well of living waters, and streams from Lebanon." Do thou then, Oh Lord, send forth this day, this blessed day, such copious streams from thyself, as may cleanse, revive, comfort, satisfy, and strengthen all thy churches. Lord, cause me to drink of the rivers of thy pleasure; for with thee is the fountain of life.

EVENING.—"This is he that came by water and blood, even Jesus Christ; not by water only, but by water and blood."—1 John v. 6.

My soul, ponder this weighty scripture well. There is much in it. When the soldier pierced the sacred side of Jesus, John recorded the act and its effects, as most significant and important. That it penetrated the heart, is most evident, because from no other part of the body could blood and water, in a full stream, flow together: and as both, in the purposes of redemption, strikingly set forth the great object of Christ's mission; so John is here impressing the great truth on the minds of the church, as a matter most essentially necessary to be regarded. He repeats it, that it might not be overlooked or forgotten. It was not by water only, that Christ came, but by water and blood. Both represented the necessity of that redemption our nature universally required for the purpose of salvation, and therefore Christ came by both. The water administered by the various washings under the law, and the blood shed in the innumerable sacrifices; as Jesus came to sum up and fulfil all in one, it was needful that he should come with both. And hence, as by the washing of regeneration, and renewing of the Holy Ghost, shed on us abundantly through Jesus Christ our Saviour, the Lord accomplisheth that which the typical representations of the law set forth; so by his blood he completes that also in the full price of redemption which the numberless sacrifices on the Jewish altar were uniformly intended to shadow. Behold, my soul, the vast and infinite importance of the thing itself, and look, this evening, with an eye of faith unto Jesus, who thus came, until by faith thou also not only enter into a full apprehension of the great design of his coming, but art perfectly assured that thou hast a personal interest therein, and that Jesus hath presented thee, among his redeemed, to himself, a glorious church, "not having spot or wrinkle, or any such thing, but that thou shouldest be without blame before him in love."

NOVEMBER 15.

MORNING.—"At our gates are all manner of pleasant fruits, new and old, which I have laid up for thee, Oh my beloved."—Song vii. 13.

Yes, blessed Jesus! at the gates of ordinances, and the word of thy gospel, all the pleasant and precious fruits of the Spirit, which come in new and in fresh supplies from thee, are indeed laid up. And Oh how sweet and refreshing are they brought home and laid up in my heart by thy divine power, when thou enablest me by faith, and in thy leadings and strength, to go forth and bring them home, and to live upon them, and feed upon them from day to day! And shall I not then, blessed Jesus, by the endearing name of my Beloved, call upon thee to command the north wind and the south wind to blow upon thy garden in my heart and in my soul, that the spices may flow; and that then my Beloved may come into his garden, and eat of his own pleasant fruits which his grace alone planted, and which his Spirit bringeth forth and ripens?

EVENING.—"To remember the words of the Lord Jesus, how he said, it is more blessed to give than to receive."—Acts xx. 35.

My soul, do not forget these words of thy Lord, after the Holy Ghost had been pleased thus sweetly to give them to the church. It is extremely probable, that Jesus had more than once expressed himself in those gracious words to his disciples, though none of the evangelists have recorded them. But God the Holy Ghost would have them communicated to the church, and therefore the apostle Paul folds up his parting sermon to the church at Ephesus with them. And blessed be that eternal Spirit for this, among a thousand other instances of glorifying the Lord Jesus! And now, my soul, do not forget the words of thy Lord, but bind them as frontlets between thine eyes, and beg of the Holy Ghost to engrave them on thine heart. Is it, my Lord, more blessed to give than to receive? With Jesus, indeed, it hath been for ever thus: for thou canst receive nothing but broken hearts; and we have nothing else to give thee. Hast thou found it so, my Lord, that it is more blessed to give than to receive? And doth thy blessedness consist in giving instead of receiving? Yea, Lord, it is indeed thy blessedness, thy glory, thy joy, to give pardon to guilty sinners, and grace to needy sinners. Thou art most blessed in this barter, in giving out of thy fulness, to supply the emptiness of thy poor pensioners, and to shed thy blood on purpose that there might be an open and everlasting fountain for sin and for uncleanness. Lord! may I always remember this, and so remember it as to see, that while it is thy blessedness to give and not to receive, it is my blessedness to have to do with One who cannot receive, but hath all to give. Yea, thou ever blessed, ever lovely, ever gracious Jesus! let me so remember those sweet words of thine, that I may see that it is part of the blessedness of my Lord to give to his poor creature, and that Jesus is made blessed and glorious by laying out his grace upon such a poor worm as I am. Let me say, and let my faith be strengthened while I say it, through thy grace teaching me; 'my God, my Saviour, my Lord Jesus will get glory in the everlasting praises of heaven, from my poor soul, and from every poor sinner whom he hath saved like me, in having laid out the riches of his grace, and in saving, by his blood and righteousness, souls that were dead in trespasses and sins.' Henceforth may I always remember the words of my Lord. It is Jesus that hath found it "more blessed to give than to receive."

NOVEMBER 16.

MORNING.—" Thou shalt weep no more; he will be very gracious unto thee, at the voice of thy cry; when he shall hear it, he will answer thee."—Isaiah xxx. 19.

Listen to this, my soul. Ponder over every precious word in it. Are not all tears dried from thine eyes, when beholding that complete salvation in which thou art interested in Christ Jesus? Believers are commanded to sorrow no more, as others without hope. And doth Jesus indeed wait to be gracious, nay, very gracious? Is it possible to consider that He, who hath all power in heaven and in earth, waits upon a poor worm of the dust, and this in order to be gracious? Come then, my soul, unto the mercy-seat. Do thou wait for him, who thus waits for thee. And as soon as thy Lord hath heard, and answered one prayer, do thou follow it up with another. Remember that he waits to be gracious; and Jesus is glorified, in giving out of his fulness to supply the wants of his people. And what petitions, my soul, hast thou now before the throne? What mercies art thou waiting for? Lord, help me to know my need, and thy fulness to supply. Help me to be for ever bartering my poverty for thy riches, and my sins for thy righteousness; that while thou art coming forth to me in mercy, my soul may be going forth to meet thee in prayer; and while Jesus is loading me with benefits, my poor heart may for ever be proclaiming his praise.

EVENING.—"Shall I bring to the birth, and not cause to bring forth? saith the Lord. Shall I cause to bring forth, and shut the womb? saith thy God."—Isa. lxvi. 9.

Observe, my soul, not only how readily the Lord undertakes to bless his people, and makes good his promises, but the gracious manner in which he confirms his word unto his servants, "wherein he causeth them to hope." All the promises of God in Christ Jesus are sweet, and sure, and amen; but methinks there is a double blessedness in those, which, from their seeming to come to us with difficulty, the Lord recommends yet more by bringing in the sovereignty of his power to their accomplishment. It is as if the Lord said by every one, "Because it be marvellous in your eyes, should it be also marvellous in mine eyes? saith the Lord of Hosts," Zech. viii. 6. My soul, if thou wilt read once more, this blessed evening, the gracious verse of the prophet in this view, the beauty and glory of it will more abundantly appear. Did God ever, in nature or in grace, fill the womb with expectation, and in the end cause a disappointment? Look through the whole compass of creation, and observe the appointed weeks through all his works. And will he restrain in the new creation? Is he not pledged in covenant engagements to people Zion with men as a flock? Is not the travail of the Redeemer's soul to be as incalculable as the dew-drops of the morning? And shall Jehovah cease to be Jehovah here? Shall he bring to the birth, and not cause to bring forth? Shall he restrain or shut the womb? saith thy God. My soul, while thou art looking at the divine faithfulness, and the divine power, as the everlasting security for the fulfilment of all the promises of God in Christ to Zion at large, take home the same strength of argument (for it is the same) to thine own security in particular. Hath the Lord thy God brought forth to thy new birth in Jesus, all the blessed hopes of salvation in his blood and righteousness; and will he not go on to the accomplishment of every thing needful in grace here, and glory hereafter to all eternity? Is any thing too hard for God? Shall thy cold and unbelieving heart make the word of God, and the oath of his promise of none effect? Dost thou not see that all thy security is in God's faithfulness, and not dependent upon man's improvement? Oh, the blessedness of ceasing from man, and resting upon God. Give me, blessed Jesus, give me grace to look off from myself, and to be wholly looking to thee; to live off from myself, and to live wholly upon thy fulness!

NOVEMBER 17.

MORNING.—"And he was clothed with a vesture dipped in blood." —Rev. xix. 13.

Oh thou bleeding Lamb of God! didst thou thus appear to thy servant John, to tell him, and the church through him, that thy priesthood and thy sacrifice are of the same everlasting nature and efficacy as thy person and thy finished work—"the same yesterday, and to-day, and for ever?" And didst thou thus manifest thyself by way of assuring thy poor needy followers that thou delightest in thine office, and lovest to be employed? Was it not, dearest Jesus, to this end, and as much in effect, as if thou hadst said, 'see, I wear these priestly garments: behold my vesture still fresh with the blood which I offered in the day of my sacrifice on the cross, for my redeemed, and for whom I still appear in the bloody robe, as a proof of the everlasting efficacy. For whom, but for my people, do I wear this vesture?' My soul, art thou looking now, with an eye of faith, within the veil? Hast thou a blessing to ask at the court of heaven, this day? Fly then to Jesus. Behold him still, as John beheld him, and hear what he saith. Remember, his blood speaks; for so the Holy Ghost declares—"it speaks better things than that of Abel;" for Abel's blood cried for vengeance. Jesus pleads for mercy. And doth it not speak *to* God for pardon, and *from* God in covenant promises of pardon? Oh the blessedness to behold Jesus clothed with a vesture dipped in blood, in confirmation that "we have redemption through his blood, the forgiveness of sins, according to the riches of his grace."

EVENING.—"The night-watches."—Psalm lxiii. 6.

The night-watches afford blessed seasons to the soul, when those who know Jesus, and can and do enjoy him, wait more for his coming than they that wait for the dawn of the morning. My soul, what saith thine experience to the visits of Jesus in the night-watches? Hast thou ever known any thing like the Bethel visit of Jacob, in those silent hours of the night? When no eye hath seen thee but his, that seeth in secret, and no ear heard but his, that wakeneth thee morning by morning; canst thou say what hath passed between thy Lord and thee, giving refreshments of soul, infinitely more satisfying than all the sleep of the body? Hast thou known somewhat of these inexpressibly sweet visits of thy Lord? Hath Jesus at times manifested himself in those hallowed hours, otherwise than he doth to the world? Yea, hath he not sometimes awakened thee to the call of his visit, and graciously prepared thee to the enjoyment; and hath he not come in the communication by his word and grace in such a way and manner, that, like the patriarch, thou hast been constrained to consider it as the very gate of heaven? These visits of Jesus are blessed visits. Many a child of God is so straitened in the necessary and unavoidable labours of the day, that the cares and concerns of himself, and perhaps of a family, or of service, too much interrupt the life of communion with God in the soul: but the night-watches afford many an hour, when no interruption can arise, for the enjoyment of fellowship with the Father, and with his Son Jesus Christ. My soul, be always on the look-out for a visit from thy Lord in the night-watches. If thou art listening, thou wilt hear his voice, as the church of old did, saying, "Open to me! for my head is filled with dew, and my locks with the drops of the night;" Song v. 2. And Oh! with what refreshing dews of grace, and love, and favour doth he come! All the drops of the night, and the dew of the morning, are not so grateful to the thirsty earth, as the visits of Jesus, when coming as rain upon the mown grass, to the languishing souls of his people. Come, Lord! and visit my soul in the night-watches; and do thou tarry with me until the break of day, and make thyself known unto me, as thou didst to thy disciples, while talking of thyself, and opening to me thy scriptures!

NOVEMBER 18.

MORNING.—"Good news from a far country."—Prov. xxv. 25.

From a far country, indeed; for it is no less distance than from heaven to earth, and from beings as opposite as holiness and sin could make—even from God to man, from a rich Saviour to poor sinners! And so remote that had not this good news been sent, heaven must have remained at an eternal distance, as an inaccessible region! And what is the good news itself? The angels who were first sent to proclaim it, called it glad tidings of good things, of great joy to all people.

And indeed, such glad tidings it contains, as language fails to describe. It is pardon, mercy, and peace to poor rebels. It holds forth joy, happiness, and everlasting felicity to poor sinners, enemies, and the fallen race of men. God revealed; sin atoned; Satan conquered; death destroyed; hell vanquished; heaven opened! And these not all. This good news informs also of the stupendous way by which the blessings are given, and everlasting happiness secured. Jesus, the Son of God, the author, the finisher, the source, cause, sum, substance, beginning, end, and portion of all his people. These, among an infinite and endless volume of mercies, are contained in the good news from a far country: but we must enter upon that country, to which indeed we are invited by the proclamation of the gospel, before that we shall fully know, or even conceive, the thousandth part of what God hath laid up for them that love him. My soul, hast thou heard this good news? Dost thou know the joyful sound? Art thou truly alive to the blessed things contained in it, and anxious to be interested therein? Oh then, meditate upon them; give thyself wholly to them. And while men of the world, from the world are seeking their chief good, and asking one another, what news? do thou turn a deaf ear to every other relation of a dying world, from which thou art dying daily, and let thy meditation be all the day, and let thine eyes prevent the night-watches to dwell upon this good news, and this only, which cometh from a far country.

EVENING.—"Then a lord, on whose hand the king leaned, answered the man of God, and said, behold, if the Lord would make windows in heaven, might this thing be? And he said, behold, thou shalt see it with thine eyes, but thou shalt not eat thereof."—2 Kings vii. 2.

My soul, do not fail to remark, from the numberless instances given upon record in scripture, how the sin of unbelief is bound up in our very nature. Every man is of himself disposed to it. The subtilty of Satan induced this among the master-pieces of his devilish art. Hence nothing but an act of sovereign grace can bring a cure. What the prophet promised, in the midst of dearth, of so sudden and so great a supply of bread, appeared so incredible to human reason, that this unbelieving lord, on whose hand the king of Israel leaned, and perhaps in whose judgment he had great confidence, brake out into the indecent expression, that nothing less than the Lord's making windows in heaven could accomplish it. But the event, to Israel's joy, and his punishment, literally took place: and such was the pressure of the people for bread, at the gate of the city, that the unbelieving lord was trodden to death. And what is thine instruction, my soul, in the spiritual illustration of this scripture history? The Lord need not make windows in heaven, to rain down the bread of life for the famine of thy soul. Jesus himself, the true bread of God, is come down, that "whosoever believeth on him may eat and live for ever." Oh! for faith to give credit to God's testimony of his dear Son: and both to see, and to eat of him, and to live for ever. Lord! I would say, "Evermore give me this bread!"

NOVEMBER 19.

MORNING.—"The strength of sin is the law. But thanks be to God which giveth us the victory, through our Lord Jesus Christ."—1 Cor. xv. 56, 57.

Pause, my soul, over this solemn, but yet sweet verse. "The strength of sin is the law." Doth sin derive strength from the law? Yes, for the motions of sin, which is in our members, gather strength from the precepts in God's holy law, just as pent-up waters, that are increasing from various sources, will swell and rage the more because they are restrained. And this is what the apostle means, when he saith, "Sin, taking occasion by the commandment, wrought in me all manner of concupiscence." For the mass of indwelling corruption is stirred up, and excited into action by the law. The Lord, in rich mercy, teaching us by this very process, that so totally corrupt is our nature, that we do not know the whole workings of sin, until, by the holiness of his commandment, we are led to see, and feel a disposition to break it; like the first transgressors in the garden of Eden, who lusted to eat of the forbidden fruit, because it was forbidden, so that the very precepts of God, by the sin of our nature, become the means of giving strength to that sin of our nature. The law of God, in this instance, acts upon the heart, as when the gardener's spade uncovers the surface of the earth, and the worms, which before lay concealed, appear. The worms were there before; but they did not appear before. In like manner, the law turns up the heart, and then appears the sin which, though there before, lay undiscovered. Is this thy case, my soul? And dost thou still carry about with thee such a body of sin and death! Well might Paul call it the mystery of iniquity; and well might Paul, from his deeper knowledge in the anatomy of the heart, cry out so greatly under the burden of it. Oh precious, precious, precious Lamb of God! how little understood, and less regarded, even by those that know somewhat of thee in the riches and greatness of thy salvation, is it considered, in ten thousand instances which pass away in the gulph of forgetfulness over our unthinking minds. Lord, give me to see and feel, yet more and more, that in myself I am virtually all sin. And, Oh Lord, give me to see and feel, yet more and more, that thou, and thou alone, art my righteousness. And let the apostle's hymn of praise be henceforth daily and hourly mine: "Thanks be to God which giveth us the victory, through our Lord Jesus Christ."

EVENING.—" The eyes of all wait upon thee, and thou givest them their meat in due season. Thou openest thine hand, and satisfieth the desire of every living thing."—Psalm cxlv. 15, 16.

What a full and comprehensive scripture is here! and what a view doth it open to the mind in the contemplation of God, in all his works of nature, providence, and grace! Pause over it, my soul, and as thou meditatest, apply it to the several circumstances of thine own wants, and the wants of Jesus's church in Zion. Remember, that as all eyes of the redeemed wait upon thy God, as well as thine; so it is Jesus, and Jesus only, that can satisfy the desire of all. Figure to thyself, at this moment, the court of Jesus thronged with waiting petitioners! and behold Jesus coming forth to supply, and answer all, and every one. Think, how many, how great, how diversified their cases. And then behold Jesus as not only having the suited blessing for all; but that when the desire of every living thing is satisfied, Jesus is no less full than before; neither is an atom of the riches of his grace abated. Oh! could this great truth but be once thoroughly impressed upon the minds of sinners, yea, not only the needy, but wretched, worthless sinners, how would the heavenly court be crowded day and night to watch for, and to partake of his bounty. My soul, hasten with thy petition, for the King is on his throne, and waiting to be gracious. And as thou goest, invite every poor creature whom thou seest, to go with thee. Tell him there is enough for thee, enough for him, enough for all. And tell him to accompany thee with full confidence: for however ready and earnest his soul is to seek, Jesus is infinitely more ready to bestow. Tell him, moreover, that while Jesus will be making him blessed in receiving, Jesus himself will be abundantly more glorious in giving: for it is on such poor sinners that he makes his grace to shine. Say, dear Lord! art thou not more blessed to the view and love of thy church in proportion as they receive of thy grace? and the happier thy people are made in thee, the more glorious art thou in them. And whence all this, thou dearest Lord, but because thou art, hast been, and will be, from everlasting to everlasting, Jesus?

NOVEMBER 20.

MORNING.—"Christ the wisdom of God."—1 Cor. i. 24.

Think, my soul, what wisdom is contained in that one word, and that one person, Christ. An whole eternity will not be sufficient to read over the immense volume. Wisdom in planning, wisdom in executing, wisdom in completing the great salvation. And what a world of wisdom, in the two natures united in one person—the God-man, the Glory-man, the Wisdom-man, Christ Jesus! And Oh what wisdom, in making sin, which strikes at God's sovereignty, the very means of manifesting God's power and love. Such is the wisdom of God in Christ, that sin, which in its nature becomes productive of the greatest dishonour to God, should be rendered subservient to produce the greatest glory. My soul, ponder these things; then ask thyself, is there not a wisdom in this vast subject, as far as it concerns thee, yet more wonderful than all? Yes, for surely the greatest of all mysteries in this wonderful volume, to thy view, is, that thou, even thou, shouldest be made the subject for the exercise of such wisdom, as Christ, the wisdom of God, and the power of God, for thy salvation. And all this even against thy determined resolution to ruin thyself. Well mayest thou join the apostle in his overwhelming song of praise, and cry out, "Oh the depth of the riches, both of the wisdom and goodness of God."

EVENING.—"And when Jesus came to the place, he looked up and saw him, and said unto him, Zaccheus, make haste, and come down; for to-day I must abide at thine house."—Luke xix. 5.

Precious Jesus! what an instance is here of the

freeness, fulness, and sovereignty of thy grace! And was there "a needs be," O Lord, that thou shouldest go to the place where this publican was? "a needs be" to look up and see him? "a needs be" to call him? and "a needs be" to abide at his house? Is this thy manner, O Lord, in calling sinners? So then it was not Zaccheus seeking Jesus, but Jesus seeking Zaccheus. His curiosity, as he thought, led him thither; but it was the prevenient grace of Jesus in the poor man's heart, that first awakened that curiosity in him. And did Jesus seek Zaccheus, call Zaccheus, incline Zaccheus to receive him, and bring salvation to his heart and house that blessed day? Oh! then for grace to see, and enjoy Jesus in all. Yea, I see, Lord, now, plain enough, that all is thine; and of thine own, all we give is from thee. When first my heart felt inclined to seek Jesus, it was Jesus who inclined my heart to this Christ seeking. Never should I have looked on thee, nor felt an inclination to see thee, hadst thou not first looked on me, and given me that desire. And what it was first, so is it now, in all the after enjoyments of thy sight and of thy presence. If I am at any time looking after thee, I may cry out with Abraham's handmaid, "Thou, Lord, seest me," and art looking after me. For never, even after all my knowledge of thee, should I look to thee with an eye of desire, except the eye of Jesus glance on me, as it did on Peter, in quickening and awakening grace. Oh! then, thou dear Lord! let me daily, hourly, hear thy voice calling me down from all creature concerns, and creature confidences, to receive my Lord; and be thou constrained by thy love to come, not as the wayfaring man, to tarry but for the night, but to abide, and dwell, and never more depart from me. Be thou my God, and make me thy servant for ever.

NOVEMBER 21.

MORNING.—" And righteousness shall be the girdle of his loins, and faithfulness the girdle of his reins."—Isaiah xi. 5.

Mark these expressions, my soul, concerning thy covenant God in Christ. The Lord condescends by them to represent both his righteousness and faithfulness, as they are engaged to make good the purposes of redemption, in the Father and the Son. Jehovah's righteousness, and Jehovah's faithfulness, are blessed securities for this purpose; for so saith the Holy Ghost. " God is faithful and just to forgive us our sins." Wherefore? Because " Christ is the end of the law for righteousness to every one that believeth." And do not overlook the striking figure of the girdle, which is chosen to represent it by; for as a man binds on the girdle round his loins, as a strengthener; so Jehovah takes to himself the righteousness of his dear Son. " Let him take hold," saith Jehovah, " of my strength, to make peace with me, and he shall make peace with me," Isaiah xxvii. 5. This is the girdle of Jehovah, which compasseth him about, and cleaveth to him all around; so that his people, whether they are behind or before, may lay hold of the girdle of his perfections, and hang upon them, and depend upon them, and even when God's providences seem to frown, or the Lord seemeth to have turned his back upon them. Oh for grace and faith both in Jehovah's covenant faithfulness, and Christ's righteousness, thus to trust, and thus to stay; for he is faithful that hath promised.

EVENING.—" Let him kiss me with the kisses of his mouth; for thy love is better than wine."—Song i. 2.

And what are the kisses of Jesus, but the manifestation of himself to his people? Old testament saints longed for this blessing; and new testament believers live by the same faith in the enjoyment of it. The cause is most evident indeed; for the love of Jesus passeth knowledge. Nothing of the nether-springs in comforts can even describe the blessedness of it; for corn, and wine, and oil, when they increase, cannot satisfy those desires, which Jesus in himself and his upper-spring mercies, can alone fulfil. Wine indeed may act as a temporary cordial to the body's weakness, and it may for the moment relieve worldly sorrow; but in both cases, the maladies will return, sometimes with double violence, and baffle all its powers; nay, if wine be used too freely, so far from affording relief, it will add drunkenness to thirst. But thy love, blessed Jesus, never fails of its gracious end and design. Its power and efficacy is not confined to the relief of bodily distresses, but extends to those of the soul; yea, it raiseth the sinner, who is dead in trespasses and sins, and infallibly saves him from the second death. And such is its cordial and refreshing nature, that it not only gives the body ease, but cheers and gladdens the soul; and, unlike the juice of the grape, where large draughts injure both; he that drinks deepest into thy love, thou blessed Jesus, can never find an excess of injury, but delight. Every one that hath only tasted of thy love, is constrained to cry out with the church: " Stay me with flagons, comfort me with apples; for I am sick of love," Song ii. 5. Shall I not then join in this sweet scripture, and say, as she did: " Let Jesus kiss me with the kisses of his mouth; for thy love is better than wine!"

NOVEMBER 22.

MORNING.—" Come, buy wine and milk, without money, and without price."—Isa. lv. 1.

Surely, no man can plead poverty as an excuse for not buying, when the things sold are not only without money, but without even the proposals for money; not only without ready money, but without any money.

Here is not even a price given. My soul, remember this. The poorer the wretch, the more welcome to this market. But what are the things sold? Both wine and milk. A blessed variety in the gospel feast—wine to cheer, and milk to nourish. Yes, blessed Jesus, thy love is better than wine, and thy salvation more healing than milk. Besides, it comes free, it comes pure, it comes in plenty. And it far, very far, exceeds the strongest wine, and the richest milk. For though wine may remove a temporary heaviness, yet was it never known to raise the dead; but thy love, blessed Jesus, hath raised, and will keep alive for ever, sinners dead in trespasses and sins, and preserve the languishing graces of thy saints. Come then, my soul, obey the gospel invitation of this day, and every day; come, buy these precious things without money, and without price. Come, ye poor, needy, perishing, sinners; come, every one of you, and buy, there is enough in Jesus for us all; and depend upon it, not one of you will be sent empty away, if you come empty to be filled, and hungry to be satisfied. This is the only mark and evidence of every real purchaser. If Jesus, with all his blessings, be welcome to your heart, you are welcome to take of his free salvation. Lord, I am come this day, and every day. Now let me hear thy voice; "Eat, O friends; yea, drink abundantly, O beloved."

EVENING.—"The Lord's free-man.'—1 Cor. vii. 22.

And who is the Lord's free-man? Jesus himself hath given a decided answer to this enquiry. "Whosoever committeth sin (saith Jesus) is the servant of sin." Now as by nature we were all born in this state of bondage to sin, and by practice have fully manifested the stock of servitude to which by nature we belong; we are vassals and slaves to sin, and in bondage to all the dreadful consequences. "But (saith Jesus) if the Son shall make you free, you shall be free indeed!" John viii. 34—36. Hence then, my soul, learn what it is to be the Lord's free-man, and the blessed effects resulting from this freedom. If this be thy portion thou art no longer in bondage to " the curse of God's broken law." Jesus hath freed thee from this; having " redeemed thee from the curse of the law, in being made himself a curse." Thou art no longer under " the penalty of sin :" Jesus delivered thee from the wrath to come, when " He, who knew no sin, became sin for his people, that they might be made the righteousness of God in him." Thou art no longer under " the dominion of sin :" Jesus hath taken away this power also; for " the law of the Spirit of life which is in Christ Jesus, hath made his people free from the law of sin and death." Thou art loosed from " the yoke of Satan :" for by the conquest of Christ on the cross, thou art " delivered irom the power of darkness, and translated into the kingdom of God's dear Son." Thou art freed from " the slavish fears of death:" for through death Jesus hath destroyed him that had the power of death, that is the devil, and hath delivered them, " who, through fear of death, were all their life-time subject to bondage." Are these among the privileges of the Lord's free-man? Is it thus to be a citizen of the Jerusalem above, which is free, and the mother of us all? Hail then, thou almighty Lord of thy people! It is thou who hast redeemed them to God by thy blood! And therefore to thee we wave the palm of victory, ascribing all our salvation to God and the Lamb!

NOVEMBER 23.

MORNING.—" If the Lord were pleased to kill us, he would not have received a burnt-offering and a meat-offering at our hands; neither would he have shewed us all these things."—Judges xiii. 23.

Precious faith this of the wife of Manoah, and sound and conclusive reasoning. My soul, hath the Father, who gave thee Jesus for a Saviour, accepted thee in Jesus? Hath the Father, who sent his dear Son to be the Saviour of the world, accepted Jesus for thy Saviour? Hath the Holy Ghost shewed thee the glorious things of redemption in his blood, the forgiveness of sins according to the riches of his grace? And hath he given thee to believe in the record that "God hath given eternal life, and that this life is in his Son?" Oh then say, with the wife of Manoah, surely the Lord would never have done all this, neither would he have shewed me all these things, had he not intended my salvation! Treasure up, then, these past tokens of favour: consider present evidences of mercy, and say, is not Jesus still precious? Are not my desires after him? And small as you sometimes think your hope, yet would you, my soul, relinquish it for a thousand worlds? Oh then, my soul, hang upon Jesus, cleave to Jesus, hold fast on Jesus. Never would the Lord have shewed me the beauty, glory, fulness, suitableness, and all-sufficiency of Jesus, nor enabled my soul to hold up Jesus in the arms of my faith for acceptance, if the Lord had been pleased to kill me.

EVENING.—"While we look not at the things which are seen, but at the things which are not seen."—2 Cor. iv. 18.

This was the blessed plan of old testament believers, under present exercises; to look off from the objects of sight, and to substantiate and realize the objects of faith. They saw "the day of Christ afar off;" and in that view, "rejoiced and were glad." By this means they brought into present enjoyment things which were distant; their faith acting like those glasses which magnify and bring home whatever is remote, as though it were nigh. Now, my soul, take instruction from those eminent worthies of the old testament school, that "through patience and comfort of the scriptures, thou also mayest have hope." By virtue of thine interest in Jesus, thou hast a large property in the world to come. If Christ be thine, all is thine. And certainly it is an extensive domain which thou hast in Christ's bond promises, and God's covenant securities: yea, thy right is confirmed beyond all earthly charters whatever. God thy Father hath promised and confirmed the whole with an oath; Jesus hath written, as well as bought it with his blood; and God the Holy Ghost hath sealed it with the great seal of heaven. Now whenever thou art at any time put to it, by reason of difficulties and exercises below; look off from all those things which are but temporal, and take a view of those which are eternal. And while thou lookest upon them as thine own, with a sure right of a reversionary interest after the death of an old life, which is consuming daily, enter by faith upon the enjoyment of them now. Do as men of the world do by their estates and their property: the husbandman values his crops, and counts up what the harvest, when it comes, will bring in; whereas he may be disappointed with a blasting, or mildew, or storms, or canker-worms: but no such events can happen to thee. The merchantman will borrow money upon the credit of his ships returning from a foreign market; notwithstanding many peradventures are between him and his vessels' return: but this is not thy case. Thine inheritance is certain, perfect, sure. Hence, therefore, live by present faith upon the enjoyment of it, and thou wilt find that this is the grand secret of all the happiness of life. This is what the apostle declared to be the profitableness of being godly; for it "hath the promise of the life that now is, and of that which is to come." So that if men oppress thee, devils tempt thee, the plague of thine own heart be daily making thy pilgrimage troublesome; turn from the things which are seen, and feast upon those to which thou art hastening, which are not seen: and, like those valiant heroes gone before, "take joyfully the spoiling of thy goods, knowing that in heaven thou hast a better and an enduring substance." For if the Lord break up thine housekeeping, and remove thy furniture from thee, he will shortly take thee home to his own house: and if he cause thy bed to be taken from under thee, it will be no loss to exchange it for Jesus's bosom. This is the cause why the old saints fainted not. Lord Jesus! give me the same Spirit!

NOVEMBER 24.

MORNING.—"Behold, I send an angel before thee, to keep thee in the way, and to bring thee into the place which I have prepared. Beware of him, and obey his voice, for my Name is in him."—Exod. xxiii. 20, 21.

Who can this be, my soul, but Jesus? He, and He only, who is the whole of the covenant, is also the Messenger and the Angel of the covenant. Jehovah hath never put his name in any other; neither given his honour to any other. But in Jesus he is eternally well pleased, and hath given all things into his hand. Pause then, my soul, and contemplate this holy, this blessed, this only-begotten of the Father, full of grace and truth. I see in Him all the glory, the sovereignty, the wisdom, grace and goodness of the Father, and he is Jehovah's salvation to the ends of the earth. And wilt thou then, my gracious God and Father, send Jesus before me in all my way, to keep me, to guide me, and to bring me in, to behold thy glory in the face of Jesus Christ, and to dwell with thee for ever? Oh Lord Jesus! I would desire grace so to beware of thee, so to love thee, so to obey thee, so to adore thee, so to make thee my all in all, my life, my love, my joy, my present, my everlasting hope and portion, that in life and death, in time and to all eternity, Jesus may be my glory and salvation for ever and ever.

EVENING.—"But I have a baptism to be baptized with, and how am I straitened till it be accomplished!"—Luke xii. 50.

My soul, look at Jesus under his straitenings, and thou wilt find it the best support and encouragement under thine. He had in view, when he thus expressed himself, the water-spouts, and the billows of divine wrath against sin, which, as the sinner's surety, were to be poured upon him. Jesus calls it a baptism. I cannot sufficiently admire the word, because it is my Lord's, and because it is so applicable. Afflictions, then, are baptisms to his people, when commissioned by his grace, and when blessed by his Holy Spirit. Never lose sight of them, my soul, in this view; they will be always sacred: and from the straitenings of Jesus, until his were accomplished, do thou at all times fetch relief and encouragement under thine. He that felt straitening for himself, well knew how to enlarge thine heart: and he that knew the baptism he had to go through, knows, and hath laid in all proper enlargements and support for thine. One look at Jesus in the priestly vestment which he still wears, will give more comfort to thine heart under all straitenings, be they what they may, than all thine own laboured attempts, that without an eye to Jesus, thou canst set up: and surely, He, who in the days of his flesh felt straitenings, will not forget thine. Lord! bring my poor soul under the continual baptisms of thy Spirit.

NOVEMBER 25.

MORNING.—"Once have I sworn by my holiness, that I will not lie unto David."—Psalm lxxxix. 35.

Wonderful condescension! Was it not enough, that Jehovah gave his Son to poor sinners; gave his word, his promise, that all that believe in him should not perish, but have everlasting life? But, as if consulting the weakness of our faith, confirmed it with an oath; pledged his holiness to Jesus, and to poor sinners in Jesus, for the sure accomplishment of all covenant engagements, in the blood and righteousness of his dear Son. Oh my soul, never, never more call in question the truth of thy gracious God. Say with Job, "Though he slay me, yet will I trust in him." What are afflictions, trials, darkness, poverty? These are in me, and about me, but no obstructions to the efficacy of Jesus's righteousness, or the Father's faithfulness. Read under every one of them the charter of rich sovereign grace; hear what God hath said, what God hath sworn: and believe the record that God hath given of his dear Son:—" Men shall be blessed in him." Jesus shall see the travail of his soul, and be satisfied. Here then rest, my soul. God hath sworn once by his holiness: Jesus hath once died, the Just for the unjust, to bring sinners unto God. Return to thy rest; the Lord hath dealt, my soul, bountifully by thee.

EVENING.—" For every creature of God is good, and nothing to be refused, if it be received with thanksgiving: for it is sanctified by the word of God and prayer."—1 Tim. iv. 4, 5.

I have often thought that there is somewhat in our ordinary meals, and especially the evening meal, which hath a tendency to call up the exercise of grace. Surely our family refreshments should remind us of the Lord's family; and our own supper, of the Lord's supper. The thing itself might well be supposed to call up our attention, and to create holy conversation concerning Him and his table, and of that supper of the Lamb in heaven, at which believers hope very shortly to meet as one family, to rise up no more for ever. And, as at the Lord's table, so at our own, every thing is sanctified by the word of God and prayer. My soul, mark what this scripture saith, concerning our food; " Every creature of God is good, and nothing to be refused, if received with thanksgiving, and sanctified." God's word over it, and the prayer of the faithful offered up with it, gives a sanctified use to all our comforts, and brings with them a double sweetness. And if, while receiving them, we look to him; so that while the body feeds on his bounties, the soul is fed on his grace; surely the heart feeds with thanksgiving, and every creature is good. Many a poor man, by these means, hath found more of Jesus at his own table, than thousands who perceive not Jesus, do at the Lord's. And to be thus feasted night and morning, every service becomes sacramental; for Christ is still the passover. Lord, make my whole use of the creatures of thy bounty thus sanctified to me, that I may behold and enjoy Jesus in every one!

NOVEMBER 26.

MORNING.—" And it shall come to pass, that every thing that liveth, which moveth, whithersoever the rivers shall come, shall live."—Ezek. xlvii. 9.

Listen to this promise, my soul, and make it the subject of this morning's meditation, of this day, and every day. See how rich, how extensive it is in the life-promising power. And the river of life in Jesus possesseth all these blessed effects. To every poor sinner, brought into this rich stream, it gives life, spiritual life, eternal life. And who shall describe the length, the breadth, the heights, the depths of it? Not only extending over all the continent of the earth, but from the borders of hell to heaven, and from one eternity to another. And its sovereignty is such that it bears down all before it—washing away sin, and guilt, and misery; diffusing streams of life, and grace, and mercy; opening sources of joy, and peace, and happiness, for ever and for ever. Oh precious, precious Jesus, make glad my soul with the streams of this river; be thou the fountain of all my happiness, and let all my springs be in thee.

EVENING.—" The King's daughter is all glorious within."—Psalm xlv. 13.

As the Redeemer is known to his church under a great variety of names and characters, and is blessed to the church in every one, whether of brother, or husband, or friend; so Jesus condescends to call his church by a variety of names also, all descriptive of the unbounded love he bears towards her. She is his fair one, his spouse, his chosen, his sister; and in this song of loves, she is called "the King's daughter." But it is most blessed to observe that by whatever name she is known, it is all in allusion to Jesus, for from him, and in him, she derives the whole of her beauty and excellency. Her glory is in her Lord, and she is wholly spiritual, all derived, like the shining of the moon, from the sun. If the church be comely, it is from the comeliness the Lord Jesus hath put upon her. For as the whole perfection of beauty is in Christ, as a rich and complete constellation, so every perfection in his people is from their union with him. It is Jesus who gives a loveliness to every object that is lovely. My soul, what saith thy experience to this statement? Thou art indeed "all glorious within," if Christ be formed there "the hope of glory." And if thy God be thy glory, then wilt thou feel what the church felt, and, taking up her language, thou wilt say, "I am black as the tents of Kedar but comely as the curtains of Solomon," Song i. 5. Oh! the felicity of knowing the total unworthiness of the human heart, which, like the spots and swarthiness of the Æthiopian, makes the church truly black and deformed: and Oh! the felicity also of knowing our comeliness, from the beauty Christ hath put upon us, and the sanctifying and regenerating influences of the Holy Spirit. Precious Lord Jesus! be it my portion always to appear in the spotless robe of thy righteousness, and then shall I be indeed "all glorious within!"

NOVEMBER 27.

MORNING.—"For lo, I will command, and I will sift the house of Israel among all nations, like as corn is sifted in a sieve; yet shall not the least grain fall upon the earth."—Amos ix. 9.

Blessed promise to my poor soul; sifted, blown about by temptation. Look then to Jesus with it, and plead it under every new sifting time. Corn must be sifted, for it is much covered at times with tares and chaff. And so must the seed of Jesus, that the precious may be known and separated; "for what is the chaff to the wheat?" saith the Lord. Oh Lord, if it please thee, for thou knowest the necessity of it, sift me, try me, separate me, not only from the ungodly, with whom I am constrained to dwell, but from myself, from my own trifling, vain conversation, from the corruption of indwelling sin in my fallen nature, from the vain thoughts which lodge within me. Yes, precious Jesus, sift all, and every thing which is unsuitable to thee, and let the whole fall through the sieve, that thou alone mayest remain with me, for sure I know my God hath said, though his Israel be sifted, yet not the least grain of the true wheat shall be lost.

EVENING.—"For he loveth our nation, and he hath built us a synagogue."—Luke vii. 5.

What a very interesting character is given, though but in few words, of this honest centurion. Though unconnected with Israel, and a Gentile, yet he loved the Jews. Was he, like another Rahab, partaker of the faith, and though unconscious of it, had a part in Jesus? It is most blessed to behold such rich provisions in grace, making way for the calling of the people, both Jew and Gentile, in that plan of redemption, "given in Christ Jesus before the world began!" But we must not stop here, in our view of the centurion. He not only *loved* the Jewish nation, but gave proofs of that love in building them a synagogue. Surely nothing short of grace in the heart could have wrought such acts of love and affection to Israel, and to Israel's God, in a Gentile mind! But, while admiring this gracious conduct in the centurion, and admiring still more the blessed author and giver of that grace which wrought it in his mind; is it possible not to have the affections instantly and irresistibly directed to thee, thou blessed Lord Jesus, who, as far as light transcends darkness, or the heaven is higher than the earth, surpassest every other pattern of excelling charity? Of thee, thou dear Redeemer, it must be truly said, "thou lovest our nation," and hast built us indeed, not a synagogue only, but art thyself our dwelling-place for ever! For thy love brought thee from heaven, prompted thee to live for us, to die for us, to rise again for us, and to take possession for us of the glorious tabernacle, not made with hands, eternal in the heavens. Yea, Lord Jesus, thou so lovedst us, as to accomplish this vast, this wonderful, this never before heard of undertaking, and never more to be undertaken, of laying the foundation in thy blood! My soul, what wilt thou render to the Lord for all his benefits? Oh take the cup of salvation, and call upon his name. Tell the whole world how he hath loved, and how he hath founded Zion, and is and will be her King for ever!

NOVEMBER 28.

MORNING.—" For when we were yet without strength, in due time Christ died for the ungodly."—Rom. v. 6.

My soul fold up this sweet and precious scripture, and carry it about with thee in thy bosom, and in thine heart, that it may help thee on at any time, and at all times, when thy strength seems gone, and there is no power left. Was it not when the whole nature of man was without strength, that Christ was given of the Father? And was it not equally so, when Christ came to seek and save that which was lost? And was it not in due time when Christ died for the ungodly; due time in his resurrection, due time in his ascension, " when he ascended up on high, led captivity captive, and received gifts for men, yea, even for the rebellious, that the Lord God might dwell among them?" Go further yet, my soul, as it concerns thyself—was it not due time indeed, when Jesus passed by and saw thee in thy loathsome state of sin, cast out to perish, and when no eye pitied thee, that then his eye compassioned thee, and bid thee live? Who more ungodly than thee? Who more weak? Who more undeserving? Did Jesus then look upon thee, call thee, strengthen thee when thou wast without strength, and hath helped thee to this hour? Oh then, trust him now, trust him for ever. "His strength is made perfect in thy weakness." And depend upon it, when thou art most weak in thyself, then is the hour to be most strong in the Lord, and in the power of his might. He that in due time died for the ungodly, will be thy strength in due time of need.

EVENING.—"Thy words were found, and I did eat them, and thy word was unto me the joy and rejoicing of mine heart."—Jer. xv. 16.

Yea, Lord, I have indeed found thy words most precious, and, through thy grace, I have eaten them, and they are as honey and the honey-comb to my soul. In them I find my God and Father in his covenant engagements, all pledged in faithfulness to his dear Son, to be the everlasting and unchanging portion of his redeemed. Oh! what unknown, what unspeakable blessedness do I find in that one promise; "I will be their God, and they shall be my people!" Here also I find Christ and his fulness; the Holy Ghost and his graces; the whole covenant and its rich promises: all, all secured, made over, and co-operating to the assurance of salvation! And how then can thy word, Lord, wherein thou hast caused me to hope, be otherwise than "the joy and rejoicing of mine heart?" I have Jesus in all, and his promises in all, and therefore can never fail of all that is here engaged, since all the promises of God in Christ "are yea and amen!" Oh then, let thy word continue "as a lamp unto my feet, and a light unto my path;" which will shine all the way through, even to lighten up the dark valley of the shadow of death, until I come "to dwell in the house of my God for ever!"

NOVEMBER 29.

MORNING.—"Until the day break, and the shadows flee away, I will get me to the mountain of myrrh, and to the hill of frankincense."—Song iv. 6.

Methinks I would have every poor sinner, until the day dawn of awakening grace breaks in upon his soul, get away to the ordinances of God in the mountain of the Lord's house: there he should live, there wait, until the Lord speaks to his soul. And methinks I would have every poor sinner that is awakened, until the day of glory breaks in with an everlasting light upon him, get away to the gospel mountain, where the odour of Jesus's incense, and the savour of his blood and righteousness, become sweeter than myrrh, and more fragrant than frankincense. Here, Lord, cause me to get away from all surrounding impediments, and to be constantly found waiting, that my soul may drink in the fresh, reviving, renewing streams, until Jesus himself, the morning star, breaks in upon my soul, to lead me home to his everlasting glory, in his bosom for ever.

EVENING.—"And he looked up and said, I see men as trees, walking."—Mark viii. 24.

I have often considered the case of this man as holding forth a sweet and comfortable lesson of instruction, to the small attainments of the followers of Jesus. Perhaps our gracious Lord, in the method he was pleased to adopt, in the opening of this man's eyes by gradual means, intended so to instruct his people. My soul, look at it in this point of view; it may be profitable to thee. When the Son of God, who came to give light to the spiritually blind, as well as to restore vision to the eye of the body, first touched this poor man's eyes, the effect was that when he looked up, the men he saw were only like "trees, walking;" the sight was imperfect, and the objects obscure. And such is it very frequently in our apprehension of spiritual things; but then it should be remembered, and remembered with great thankfulness, that this imperfection of our sight differs altogether from total darkness. Objects we certainly see, though we do not clearly see them as we desire. If I see "men as trees, walking," it is past a doubt that men I see; and by a parity of reasoning, if, in a spiritual sense, I see Jesus in his suitableness, fulness, and all-sufficiency, for a poor sinner; though I long to see more of him, and to see him more plainly, yet the sight I now have is blessed, and being wrought by his own gracious hands, it begets a lively hope that he who hath begun the cure will perfect it. The way to ascertain the reality of *spiritual* life, is not unsimilar to what is done in doubtful cases in respect to *animal* life. It is a sure sign of life if the body *feel*, however the other symptoms of health may be suspended. There is a vast difference between deadness and death. If a man cannot *speak*, yet is he conscious of what others say? If he cannot make *signs*, yet can he take *food*? If he cannot take *food*, doth he *move*? If he doth not *move*, doth he *breathe*? Still then there is life. And, in like manner, the soul that is breathing after Jesus, though he doth not move, hath life. He is looking up, like this poor creature, and all he seeth is imperfect. But Jesus will do by him as by this blind man; he will put his hand upon him again, and at length he will make him to behold every object clearly. Lord, give me grace to bless thee for all attainments, and never "to despise the day of small things!"

NOVEMBER 30.

MORNING.—"It is high time to awake out of sleep; for now is our salvation nearer than when we believed."—Rom. xiii. 11.

Solemn consideration! What time is it with thee, my soul? Let me ask, with the prophet, "Watchman, what of the night? The morning cometh, and also the night." Perhaps there may be but a step between me and death. Am I really awakened from the sleep of carnal security? Am I alive from spiritual death? Am I dead to the world, but alive unto God through Jesus Christ our Lord? Oh Lord Jesus, impress these solemn enquiries upon my soul yet more and more, since everlasting happiness, or everlasting misery hangs upon the decision. My beating pulse is hastening to fulfil the appointed number. Even while I think of these things the account is increased. Every fleeting breath is one the less to take. Lord, make me wise to remember my latter end!

EVENING.—"Clouds and darkness are round about him; righteousness and judgment are the habitation of his throne."—Psalm xcvii. 2.

What a blessed scripture is here! And what a satisfying answer is given in it to the endless questions which are for ever arising in the human mind, for explaining the ways and works of God towards his creatures! The words are as if the sacred writer had been answering such inquiries, and had therefore made this conclusion; there must be much darkness, which the dim view of short-sighted creatures cannot see through, in carrying on the purposes of Jehovah: but here is an everlasting rule to go by; righteousness and judgment are the habitation of his throne, who is "wonderful in counsel, and excellent in working." Oh, my soul! couldest thou call to remembrance this blessed scripture every day, and all the day, in the several exercises of thy warfare, how many anxieties would it save thee? I know as well as can be, in the perfect and clear conviction of my heart, the blessed truth; but when it comes to be put into practice, I am for ever calling it in question. I know that Jesus is pleased very frequently to work by contrary means; it is his province and his prerogative to quicken the dead, and to call "things that are not, as though they were:" his strength is perfected in weakness; and he sometimes kills to make alive, and wounds in order to heal. But in a killing time, I am so apt to reason with flesh and blood, that I forget the quickening time; and when the wounds are bleeding, so that life seems running out of them, I judge it impossible that they ever can again be healed; and hastily conclude, with the church, "My strength and my hope is perished from the Lord;" Lament. iii. 18. Oh! for grace to view the righteousness and judgment of my God and Saviour as the habitation of his throne, and to rest for ever unshaken and fixed in this most perfect assurance! Jesus cannot mistake in ordering what shall be for my welfare; neither can he appoint any thing but what carries the mark of his love upon it. Let me, thou dear Lord! let me hear thy sweet voice through all the clouds and darkness which are round about thy dispensations, and whisper to me, as thou didst to thine astonished apostle, and then in every one, how mysterious soever it may be, it will silence my fears: "What I do thou knowest not how, but thou shalt know hereafter."

DECEMBER 1.

MORNING.—"Praise waiteth for thee, Oh God, in Zion."—Psalm lxv. 1.

Is this the language of my heart? Am I indeed waiting until that Jesus be ready to receive my poor praise? Hath God the Holy Ghost prepared my heart? Oh then, hasten to him, my soul, with thy morning offerings, poor as they are; for sure I am, Jesus is waiting to be gracious. God will accept both thee and thy offering in him the Beloved. Go forth to meet him as early and as often as thine heart can wish: depend upon it, thy Redeemer will be beforehand with thee, and is waiting thy coming. Neither thy praise nor thy prayer can outrun his love; for both are the blessed effects of his grace, and of his own quickenings. Precious Jesus, grant me to come as often as I need thee. And, Lord, if thou wilt grant me this blessing, I shall never be from thee, for I need thee every moment.

EVENING.—"And they continuing daily with one accord in the temple, and breaking bread from house to house, did eat their meat with gladness, and singleness of heart, praising God, and having favour with all the people."—Acts ii. 46, 47.

What a beautiful picture is here given of the primitive church! My soul, think of the happiness of the saints of God in those days, when, instead of that idle and unprofitable conversation, which, for the most part, fills up the employment of christians professing godliness in the present day, believers never met without celebrating the Lord's supper (for so the expression of eating bread from house to house means); and their ordinary meals were conducted with a single eye to God's glory! What a sad change hath taken place in the circumstances of christians! "They were daily with one accord in the temple:" and thousands who would be very highly offended, were their religious profession to be called in question, think one part of the Lord's day sufficient to be found there. They conversed "from house to house" of the great things of salvation: but what parlour, what place of meeting, what house or family must we go into, to hear of Jesus and his gospel? They were daily setting forth the broken body of Christ, in the action "of breaking of bread and of prayer:" but how many are there, who think the observance of monthly communions of Christ's body and blood too frequent, and only attend now and then, lest the frequency of the service should lessen the reverence due to it! My soul, look to it, that thy life be upon the plan of those venerable followers of the Lord! Oh! for grace to make every day a sabbath day; and every table the Lord's table! Precious Jesus! I would pray to keep up a constant remembrance of thee, that "whether I eat or drink, or whatever I do, I may do all to the glory of God!"

DECEMBER 2.

MORNING.—"It is written in the prophets, and they shall be all taught of God. Every man therefore that hath heard, and hath learned of the Father, cometh unto me."—John vi. 45.

Mark, my soul, these precious words of thy Jesus. It was one of the old testament promises, that all God's children should be taught of him. And as this condescension of God, in teaching, implied the Father, so the blessed consequence and effect of it should be, that every one thus taught proved his being a child, and inclined his heart to come to God in Christ as a Father. My soul, art thou come? Art thou looking to, leaning upon, trusting in, walking with, and seeking for Jesus? Is he the Lord thy righteousness, thine only righteousness, thine only hope, thine only confidence? Dost thou, like the apostle, count all things else but dung and dross to win Christ, and to be found in him? Courage then, my soul! These are blessed tokens of thine adoption character. None but God the Father, by his Holy Spirit, could have taught thee these things. None but He, that revealed his Son in the heart of the apostle, could have been thy teacher. Thou hast both heard and learned of the Father, and in proof thereof thou art come to Christ for life and salvation. Fold up then this precious scripture in thy bosom for thy daily use, and examine thine interest in Christ continually, by a mark so sure and infallible. And remember what the Lord Jesus hath said, as a collateral testimony to the same blessed truth: "All that the Father giveth me (saith Jesus) shall come to me: and him that cometh I will in no wise cast out."

EVENING.—"I sleep, but my heart waketh."—Song v. 2.

My soul, behold the church fallen into a sleepy state, after having been at the banquet of her Lord; and view in her the resemblance of thyself. How often art thou in this cold and lifeless situation; and instead of seeking increasing communion and fellowship with Jesus, falling asleep, as one insensible to past enjoyments and present need! It is not indeed the sleep of death; for, through the sovereignty of almighty grace, thou hast been quickened to a new and spiritual life in Christ Jesus; and thine heart waketh to the knowledge of thy Lord. But how unsuitable and unbecoming is it, for one who hath tasted that the Lord is gracious, to be indifferent to the farther enjoyment of him! Time was, when, if thou didst miss Jesus in the ordinance, or hadst not a visit from thy Lord for a short space, thou wert on the wing of love, going forth in every way, and in every direction, in the inquiry, "Saw ye him whom my soul loveth?" And canst thou, my soul, be contented to live in this sleepy frame, and without the visits of thy Lord? Look up to Jesus, he is near at hand, and waiting to be gracious! Listen to his voice, in his word, in his ordinances, in all the means of his grace; hasten to the awakening ministry of some one of his faithful servants. These methods the Lord will bless. Jesus will come again: he will do by thee, as he did by the church, "He will put in his hand by the hole of the door, until that thy bowels are moved for him." Precious Lord Jesus! keep from me all sleepy lifeless frames! Give me day by day, to be pressing after some renewed tokens of thy love; and let each mercy quicken my poor soul to desire farther manifestations: that in greater degrees, and more frequent enjoyment of thee, I may, like thy servant the apostle, "forget those things which are behind, and, reaching forth unto those which are before, press toward the mark for the prize of the high calling of God in Christ Jesus?" Amen.

DECEMBER 3.

MORNING.—"Whether our brethren be inquired of, they are the messengers of the churches, and the glory of Christ."—2 Cor. viii. 23.

What a blessed account is here given of the children of God to all inquiries concerning them. See, my soul, whether thy experience corresponds to it, and mark their character. They are not only brethren to one another, but to Christ also; for we are told that he is not ashamed to call them brethren. Precious condescending Saviour! Moreover, they are the messengers of the churches. What is that? A messenger, in scripture, is called also an angel. And if the brethren of Jesus do know, and can speak of him as his people should, then are they like angels come down from the court of heaven, to relate what they have seen and known, of the King in his beauty, and their hearts glow with a warmth of earnestness to proclaim his glory, and his love to poor sinful creatures here below. Neither is this all. For they are the glory of Christ. Mark this, my soul, and dwell with rapture upon it. A true believer in Jesus is the glory of Jesus. Not only because he gives glory to the Redeemer for his grace; but because Jesus derives glory from his redemption. Not only because the poor sinner hath everlasting happiness from Jesus; but Jesus hath everlasting glory from that poor sinner's salvation. Never lose sight of this, my soul, when thou goest to Jesus. Indeed, indeed, Jesus is glorified in receiving thee, in pardoning thee, in blessing thee, in giving to thee of his fulness. And the Father is glorified in this great salvation by his Son. Oh what encouragement is this to faith; what inducement to come to Jesus! Lord, how ought I to blush when I think how little glory I give to thee in not seeing that thy church and thy people are thy glory, in being saved and redeemed by thee.

EVENING.—" And the angel of the Lord came again the second time, and touched him, and said, arise and eat, because the journey is too great for thee. And he arose, and did eat and drink, and went in the strength of that meat forty days and forty nights, unto Horeb the mount of God."—1 Kings xix. 7, 8.

How blessed is it to observe, in the several instances of God's people, that the Lord measures out strength in proportion to their wants, and fits every back for the burden. The prophet was obliged to flee from the king's court, but the King of kings will give him a table in the wilderness. Elijah shall be taught at one time, how to live by faith, when fed by ravens; and at another, how to go forty days and forty nights without food, when sustained by grace in going to Horeb. My soul, canst not thou find in thy experience, similar exercises of faith; if not so splendid, yet at least no less profitable? Hath not Jesus many a time fed thee at his banqueting house, and made thy cup run over, when telling thee, in some sweet communion visit, either at his table or thine own, either in the church or in the closet, how suited his grace is for thee, and that his strength is perfected in thy weakness? And hath not Jesus, as in the instance of Elijah, touched thee a second time, yea, and a third, and many a time, and laid in refreshments for thee, against the coming hour of trial, when the journey of spiritual exercises, that were to follow, would otherwise have been too great for thee? Knowest thou nothing of these things? Surely, in such trainings as these, the Lord is as much leading on his people now, as he did of old. Doth he come in a full tide of glory, and shew himself to be Jesus, and open to our spiritual sight his pierced hands, and his side? Doth he come into the soul as the King of glory, openly manifesting his refreshing, his comforting, his strengthening, his loving presence; and at the same time, opening our eyes and hearts to receive him; so that the soul is made joyful, and brought as into the very suburbs of heaven?—Mark what follows: perhaps, as in the case of the prophet, a long abstinence is to follow. Jesus hath therefore laid in a store of comforts. He hath victualled the ship. He hath fortified the garrison. "The just shall live by faith." Precious Jesus! give me to live on thee, when all outward comforts fail. In fulness or in famine, in life or death, if I have thee, I have enough to live upon, and in thy strength to go forty days and forty nights; yea, for ever, to the mount of God in glory!

DECEMBER 4.

MORNING.—"Come, see the place where the Lord lay."—Matt. xxviii. 6.

Lord, I would desire grace to accept the call, for it is always profitable to have faith in lively exercise. I would pray that my meditation might frequently take wing, and view the memorable sepulchre of my Lord. Did Jesus once lay in the grave? Surely death never had such a prisoner before! But did Jesus lay so low for me? Am I shortly to lay there? Sweet consoling thought! The grave is now softened, and the chambers of death are perfumed with the fragrancy contracted from his holy incorruptible body. But is there not another place where the Lord lay? And doth not the angel invite his people to see him there also? Yes, Jesus lay in the bosom of the Father from all eternity. And doth he not lay there now, and will he not through all eternity? But can I see him there? Yes;—for if by faith I behold Jesus as the Christ, the Sent, the Sealed of the Father; in seeing him, I see the Father also. He saith this himself, John xiv. 9. And again, John xiv. 20. "At that day ye shall know that I am in my Father, and you in me, and I in you." Blessed assurance! Jesus is one with the Father, and all his people one with him. And as he is in the bosom of the Father, so are they in his, and there shall dwell for ever and ever. Hallelujah. Amen.

EVENING.—"Wherefore glorify ye the Lord in the fires, even the name of the Lord God of Israel in the isles of the sea."—Isa. xxiv. 15.

My soul, hast thou ever considered, in how many ways, and by what a variety of means, every poor sinner called by grace, is furnished with ability to glorify God in Christ? It is blessed to see this, and doubly blessed to be employed in such a service. The poor sinner not only glorifies Jesus, actively, when he is praising him; but passively also, when his wants and necessities afford occasion for Jesus to be glorified in giving out of his fulness to his relief. And how is the Lord glorified in the fires? Evidently when in the furnace of affliction, or in the fire of temptation, the poor exercised soul glories in his infirmities, that the power of Christ may rest upon him! when he can, and when he doth receive all, and take all, and feel happy under all, from the consciousness that the Lord's hand is in it, and the Lord's blessing will be upon it. "I was dumb, (said one of old) and opened not my mouth, for it was thy doing." And another ancient sufferer cried out, "Why should a living man complain, a man for the punishment of his sins?" Oh! it is most blessed to see a child of God, thus engaged for God, when matters are most dark and discouraging! It is easy, comparatively speaking, for a man to praise and give glory to the Lord, when all things around him are gay and smiling: but when songs are heard from the fires, and when the soul feels its own wretchedness, and cries out under it, "My leanness, my leanness!" and is looking to a God in Christ; here is a frame of mind suited to the divine glory. My soul, see that all thy glory be centered in Jesus, and on God in Jesus, as the name of the Lord God of Israel. And Oh! for grace to give him both the praises and the glory, in whom "all the seed of Israel shall be justified, and shall glory!"

DECEMBER 5.

MORNING.—"It pleased the Lord to bruise him; he hath put him to grief."—Isa. liii. 10.

The depths of wisdom were explored to furnish redemption, and to find a person competent to accomplish it; and when found, the depths of love were broken up, to make it complete. My soul, read over the mysterious volume which the Lord hath in part opened before thee. It cost the Father his thoughts from all eternity, to appoint a plan, by which, consistently with his holiness and his justice, thou mightest be saved. It cost the Father his Son, his dear Son, his only Son, before that thou couldest be redeemed. Jesus must die ere thou canst live. Pause over the subject as it is here expressed. "It pleased the Father to bruise him." Jesus, who was in himself holy, harmless, undefiled, separate from sinners, and made higher than the heavens; he, who knew no sin, must be made sin; he who never merited wrath, must be made a curse. Read on; Jesus must die! and by whom? Not by Jews, nor Gentiles only; not simply by high priests and governors among men; but by God the Father. He must bruise him, and put him to grief; for though Jesus was taken, and by wicked hands crucified and slain, yet all this, we are told, was "by the determinate counsel and foreknowledge of God." And is there yet another chapter of wonders in this mysterious volume? Yes;—what can it be? Namely,—that all this was for sinners, for rebels, for enemies; nay, my soul, for *thee*. Wonder, O heavens, and be astonished, O earth! Had our whole nature been bruised to all eternity in the mortar of divine wrath, for the sin of our nature; what would all this have been to the sufferings, agonies, and death of the Lamb of God? And didst thou die for me, O thou unequalled pattern of love and mercy, and by thy stripes is my soul healed? Precious Jesus!

EVENING.—" Weeping may endure for a night, but joy cometh in the morning."—Ps. xxx. 5.

It is most profitable, yea, blessed, to have right conceptions of the Lord's dealings with his people. Jesus is everlastingly pursuing one plan of love; and never, in a single instance, departs from it. But as we see only part of his ways, until the result come, exercises by the way much perplex our poor short-sighted view of things. Jesus, for the most part, brings his people into the wilderness, in order to speak comfortably to them there. But while in the wilderness, we are at a loss to trace the footsteps of his love. And when, after some sweet love-tokens of his favour, new trials arise, though Jesus, it should seem, designed by the mercy to prepare for trouble, yet, by our false interpretation of it, we aggravate the trouble, and make it greater. My soul, do learn from the precious thoughts suggested by the scripture of the evening, to form a right estimate of the Lord's dealings with thee. " Weeping may endure for a night." It may appear a long night, a wearisome night: but, remember, it is but a night. Every hour, yea, every moment is shortening it, and when the morning comes, joy will come with it. And in proportion to the darkness or the sorrow of the night, the daylight will be more delightful. The most blessed discoveries Jesus makes of himself, are generally those after a sorrowful night. Precious Lord! be thou thyself the " day-dawn, and the day-star" to my soul, after a night of painful exercise; yea, be thou " the Sun of righteousness" with healing in thy wings! And then neither the night of sleep, nor the night of death will be more than the passing hour. And, Lord,

"When I awake up from both, I shall be still with thee!"

DECEMBER 6.

MORNING.—"If ye shall ask any thing in my name, I will do it." —John xiv. 14.

Is it so, blessed Jesus, that if I go to the Father in thy precious name, my petitions shall be certainly heard, and answered? Lo, then, I come. I feel my faith and confidence emboldened in this gracious assurance. And as thou knowest, Lord, this day, what is most suited for me, let thy wisdom choose, and let thy love bestow, that very grace and mercy, be it what it may. And let a throne of grace witness for me, that I seek it wholly on Christ's account. I consider it as good as given, from the high love my God and Father bears towards his dear Son, as my Surety and Saviour. And although in the moment that I ask with this boldness of faith, I see and know in myself, that I have nothing to recommend me to thy favour, as in the least meriting that favour, but much, very much, to make me an object in meriting thy displeasure; yet looking up in Jesus, depending upon his blood and righteousness, and wholly asking in his name, and for his righteousness sake only, I am encouraged to hope that I shall not ask in vain. Oh then, Lord, hear for Jesus's sake, and let my petition and prayer be answered, that the Father may be glorified in his Son.

EVENING.—"I saw in the visions of my head upon my bed, and behold, a Watcher, and an Holy One came down from heaven."—Dan. iv. 13.

My soul, that which terrified the impious monarch in his visions of the night, ought to be to thee a subject of holy joy! When Jesus proclaims "the day of vengeance which is in his heart;" he adds also, "the year of my redeemed is come!" *A day* is enough for destruction; *a year*, yea, an everlasting year, will not be too long to make his people happy. But what a striking character is this of " a Watcher, and an Holy One!" To whom but to Jesus can it possibly refer? Jesus, at the call of God his Father, stood up from everlasting, to watch over his church, to water it every moment; yea, to keep it night and day least any hurt it. And who shall describe in how many ways the Lord Jesus is for ever performing this blessed office, and hath been, and will be to all eternity? Is he not for ever in the midst of them, to do all that is needful for them: to protect, to comfort, to lead out, to bring home, until he brings in and houseth them in his temple for ever? Yea, he saith himself, " I will rejoice over them to do them good, and I will plant them in this land, assuredly with my whole heart, and with my whole soul," Jer. xxvii. 41. But Oh! ye despisers of my God! tremble at the approach of this almighty Watcher, this Holy One coming down from heaven! For he comes, armed with zeal and with wrath, " To take vengeance on them that know not God, and obey not the gospel of Christ." Oh! kiss the Son, lest he be angry, and ye perish from the way, when his wrath is kindled but a little. " Blessed are they that put their trust in him!"

DECEMBER 7.

MORNING.—" And we have known and believed the love that God hath to us."—1 John iv. 16.

Who hath known, and believed, in terms equal to the greatness of the mercy itself, the love of God to the poor sinner! God's love must be an infinite love, and consequently the display of it must be infinite also. God, we are told, " Commendeth his love to us, in that while we were yet sinners, Christ died for us." Had God loved and delighted in saints that loved him, this would have been love. Had God taken the holy angels into a nearer acquaintance with him, this would have been love. But when he raised beggars from the dunghill, and took rebels from the prison to sit upon his throne, and at a time when his justice would have been magnified in their destruction; to prefer sinners, haters of God, and despisers of his grace; to bring them into the closest and nearest connection with him, in the person of his dear Son; and all this by such a wonderful plan of mercy, as the incarnation and death of Jesus; who hath ever calculated the extent of such grace? Who hath thoroughly known or considered, or believed, in any degree proportioned to the unspeakableness of the salvation, the love that God hath to us? Oh Lord, add one blessing more. Cause my cold heart to grow warm in the contemplation of it; and let it be my happiness to be daily studying the breadth, and length, and depth, and height, and to know the love of God, which passeth knowledge, that I may be filled with all the fulness of God.

EVENING.—"For he hath said, I will never leave thee, nor forsake thee. So that we may boldly say, the Lord is my helper, and I will not fear what man shall do unto me."—Heb. xiii. 5, 6.

Sweet thought! Blessed promise of a covenant promiser, whose name is I AM! Indeed, the whole covenant of grace is made up of God's *wills*, and his engaging for our *shalls:* and the whole is founded in the purposes of God's love, and faithfulness, and immutability; secured in the blood and righteousness of Christ; and stamped with the broad seal of heaven, by God the Holy Ghost. Hence, therefore, the covenant runs, "I WILL be their God, and they SHALL be my people." Hence, also, Jesus with all his fulness is in the covenant. And hence, also, the Holy Ghost is engaged to abide with them for ever, to lead them into all truth, and to glorify the Lord Christ in their hearts. How is it possible for them to do otherwise than rejoice, and boldly to say, "the Lord is my helper!" for the fear of man is driven out by the fear of God? My soul! what saith thine experience to this? Surely, thou wilt take up the same confident language, and from the same cause, as the church. If the Lord hath said it, he will confirm it: he will never leave, neither forsake the redeemed of Jesus. So that I never shall be left hopeless, helpless, comfortless! Precious Jesus! in thee I set up the Ebenezer afresh this evening: thou, Lord, art my helper: "I will not fear what man shall do unto me!"

DECEMBER 8.

MORNING.—"Gad, a troop shall overcome him; but he shall overcome at the last."—Gen. xlix. 19.

Is there nothing, my soul, in this sweet promise, that suits thy case and circumstances? Was not Gad one of the children of Israel? And are not all the seed of Israel interested in the promises? Was the tribe of Gad for a time brought down, and brought under, by a troop of foes? And are not all the seed of Israel oppressed and brought into subjection? Was not that glorious Israelite, the great Captain of our salvation, made perfect through suffering? Think, my soul, what troops of hell assaulted him. But was the issue of the battle with him doubtful? Neither is it now. In his blood and righteousness all the seed of Israel shall be justified and overcome by the blood of the Lamb. What then, though there be troops of lusts within, and legions of foes without? Troops from earth, and troops from hell, may, and will, assault thee; but look unto Jesus. It is said of his people of old, that they had an eye unto him, and were enlightened, and their faces were not ashamed. So now, Jesus undertakes for thee, and for thy faith, He saith, I will be an enemy to thy enemies, and an adversary to thine adversaries. God the Father is looking on: angels are beholding; all heaven is interested. Nay, hadst thou but eyes to see, thou wouldest behold, like the prophet's servant, mountains around thee, full of horses and chariots of fire, all engaged for thy defence. Shout, then, for the battle is already obtained by Jesus for all his people. Though a troop may overcome the Gadites of the Lord, yet shall they overcome at the last. " Thanks be to God who giveth us the victory through our Lord Jesus Christ."

EVENING.—" Thus shalt thou say unto him, the Lord saith thus, behold, that which I have built, will I break down; and that which I have planted, I will pluck up."—Jer. xlv. 4.

My soul, ponder well these words; and when thou hast duly meditated, behold and see, in the instance of the church at large, and in thine own circumstances in particular, whether the powerful operations of the Lord's grace be not thus frequently carried on, by seemingly opposite means? Doth not the Lord appear to be often breaking down what his own right hand hath built, and withering what he hath planted, when providences appear to run counter to his promises, and the way to their accomplishment seems impossible? Thus the gourd of Jonah was blasted when the prophet needed most a covering: thus the poor man's child, in the gospel, when in the view of Christ, was thrown down by the devil, and torn more than ever he had been before; Mark ix. 26. thus the children of Israel felt Pharaoh's oppression the more called forth, because the Lord had promised them deliverance;" Exod. v. 22, 23. Look at home, my soul, and see how matters are there. Since the Lord called thee by his grace, to reveal his Son in thee, hadst thou conferred with flesh and blood, how often to thy view would it have appeared, that things were worse with thee than before? Surely thy corruptions never strove for the mastery with equal strength, as since grace put a restraint upon them: like the swelling waters, which become more violent in proportion as the bank is thrown up to keep them back. Never did Satan so rage in his temptations, as since Jesus blessed thee with the visits of his love. And how often, when the enemies of thy salvation have for a season seemed to prevail, hath it appeared to thy view, as if the Lord had broken down that which he had built, and plucked up that which he had planted? And how often, in the distress of soul occasioned by it, hast thou cried out, "Hath the Lord forgotten to be gracious: and will he shut up his loving-kindness in displeasure?" Precious Jesus! how infinitely precious, in these instances, as in every other, is the view of thee, and of the ways of thy grace! I see, Lord, by this process of thine, that both building and planting, both beginning and ending, are of the Lord. That sweet scripture is confirmed: "The hands of Zerubbabel have laid the foundation of this house: his hands shall also finish it," Zech. iv. 9. In thee, and upon thee, O Lord, is all founded. It is Jehovah hath said it, and Jehovah will confirm it: "I have said, (saith the Lord) mercy shall be built up for ever!" Ps. lxxxix. 2.

DECEMBER 9.

MORNING.—"For he said, surely they are my people, children that will not lie: so he was their Saviour."—Isa. lxiii. 8.

Oh what a tenderness of expression is contained in these words! Jesus not only takes his people into relationship with him, but undertakes for their faithfulness. In the birth of God's everlasting purpose, this was done from everlasting; so that in one and the same moment, we are his people, his children, his brethren, his wife, his redeemed, his fair one, made comely in his comeliness, and in his blood cleansed, and in his righteousness justified before God. And observe, my soul, the grounds of this relationship: surely, he saith, they are my people. Not only as God's workmanship and property, but as his purchase. Not only in first giving them being, but in giving them new being in Christ Jesus. The Lord hath taken them into covenant with him in Christ, and granted them a charter of grace and salvation in Jesus. Sweet and precious thought. God the Father, whose right they are by creation, hath given them to his Son. And Jesus hath made them his, both by his own purchase, and the conquests of his grace: therefore he hath an interest in them, and in all that concerns them. Surely, saith Jesus, they are my people, my jewels, my treasure, my hidden one. And observe further, how he speaks *for* them as well as *of* them: they will not lie. How is this? Why, they are children of the covenant. And because he hath undertaken for them, therefore he was their Saviour. Oh the preciousness of such a Saviour, to every circumstance, to every state, in every way, and upon every occasion in life, in death, in time, and to all eternity. Jesus, thou art indeed a Saviour, thou art truly called Jesus, for thou hast saved, and thou wilt save, thy people from their sins.

EVENING.—"For whatsoever is not of faith, is sin."—Rom. xiv. 23.

My soul, thou hast long known, and I hope in a great measure felt, the vast importance of that blessed principle, faith, without the possession of which, "it is impossible to please God." But hast thou also considered what the Holy Ghost here saith, by the apostle, that "whatsoever is not of faith, is sin? Pause over the expression: "whatsoever is not of faith, is sin!" Why then it will follow, that whatever is undertaken without an eye to God in Christ, and for God's glory in Christ, is sin. All the acts of creatures, as sinful creatures, must partake of sin. It is by faith in Christ, that the iniquity of our most holy things is taken away. Hence, love to our neighbour, is no love, unless it be a stream from the love of God: for what doth not begin in God, will never end in God. Such views of faith are striking; and this portion of God's word certainly opens to them, and the reason is obvious: it is by faith only that we hear what God saith, or regard what God appoints. We never can glorify God, till we hear and believe in God. All God's promises are in Christ: but without faith in Christ, there can be no belief in the promises of God in Christ. My soul, this is a striking view of faith, and serves to shew its vast and infinite importance. If all I undertake, all I say, all I do, the whole, without an eye to God in Christ, partake of sin; it is high time to see that I make Jesus the bottom, the cementing principle, and the top-stone of the whole building. And as "whatsoever is not of faith, is sin," so the humble offerings in faith, humble and poor as they are in themselves, if offered in and through Jesus, come up with acceptance upon that altar which sanctifieth both gift and giver. Hence saving faith gives glory to God, because it brings nothing, it offers nothing, but seeks all from God in Christ, and desires that God in all things may be glorified in Christ. Oh! for the continual outpourings of the blessed Spirit, to be strong in this grace which is in Christ Jesus. "Lord! increase our faith!"

DECEMBER 10.

MORNING.—"But there the glorious Lord will be unto us a place of broad rivers and streams; wherein shall go no galley with oars, neither shall gallant ships pass thereby."—Isa. xxxiii. 21.

See, my soul, how thy God condescends to represent himself to thee as thy God, under various similitudes, so as to strengthen thy faith and thy confidence in him. He that is thy gracious Lord, is also thy glorious Lord; for he is both a sun and a shield; and he that gives grace, will give glory; one is the earnest of the other. Well, then, this glorious Lord will be there. Where? Why in Jesus, in *thy* Jesus, God in covenant with him. "He will be unto thee a place of broad rivers and streams." What is that? Why as

Jerusalem had no navigable rivers, or seas, to defend her from the approach of enemies all around; so God's people are unprotected by nature, or by art, and lie open to their foes. But what they want in nature, shall be abundantly made up to them in grace. And as they have no art nor contrivance in themselves, God's wisdom and love will provide true counsel for them. Since they have no sea for their frontier, God in covenant love will himself be their sea, their ocean, their bulwark. And what galley or ship shall pass God to attack his people? Surely none can. And observe, my soul, as God himself will be rivers, and broad rivers too, to defend, so will he be streams to provide, and full streams to provide plentifully all possible blessings. Hallelujah. Shout, my soul, as the church of old, and say, "A fountain of gardens, a well of living waters, and streams from Lebanon, is my Beloved."

EVENING.—"Behold, his reward is with him, and his work before him."—Isa. xl. 10.

The whole scope of prophecy, as referring to the person and offices of Christ, was comprised in the two great branches of "the sufferings of Christ, and the glory that should follow." From everlasting, the work of Jesus was before him. To his infinite and comprehensive mind, all that he had to do and to suffer for his church, was always in his view. He saw his church in all the glory and beauty that, in his comeliness, he would one day put upon her; he saw this before creation took place, when "his delights were with the sons of men;" and he saw his church also, in all the depths of guilt and pollution, into which, by apostacy, she would fall, and from whence he undertook to redeem her with his blood. Hence, "for the joy that was set before him," it is said, "he endured the cross, and despised the shame;" and having, as well by his active as his passive obedience, both by doing and dying, finished the work in the fulness of time, which the Father gave him to do, Jesus entered upon his reward. But who shall describe it, or what heart fully conceive it? Who shall say, what is the reward of Jesus in our nature, united to the Godhead, in beholding his Father's holy law thus magnified and honoured; the robbery done to God's honour completely restored; the loss man had sustained, more than repaired; and salvation bestowed upon millions of souls, by virtue of his blood and righteousness? Who shall describe it, in beholding the human nature of Jesus advanced above all created intelligence, either of angels or of powers? Who shall speak of the reward of Jesus, in giving out, day by day, grace to the infinite cases and wants of his church here below, and of glory, in all its varieties, to the church above? Precious Jesus! let such views ever encourage my poor soul to come to thee for all I need; since it is thy glory, and a part of thy reward, thou dearest Lord, to give out of thy fulness, as the blessed Head of thy church, to the wants of thy people; and thou wilt be more glorious to my view, the more thou givest, and the more I receive from thee. Jesus, I will say, loveth to give; may my soul delight to receive; that while I am receiving everlasting life from thee, the Lord Jesus may be everlastingly glorified by me, and both Father and Son glorified in my salvation!

DECEMBER 11.

MORNING.—" And he shall sit as a refiner and purifier of silver. And he shall purify the sons of Levi, and purge them as gold and silver, that they may offer unto the Lord an offering in righteousness."—Malachi iii. 3.

My soul, contemplate this gracious office of thy Jesus, and then see, whether he hath as graciously wrought it on thee. Jesus found our whole nature, when he came to save it, wanting refining and purifying indeed. By the operation of his holy word, and by the influences of his blessed Spirit, he brings the souls of his people into the furnace of purification. By the fire of troubles, of afflictions, of persecutions, he melts down their stubborn nature there. By the Spirit of judgment, and by the Spirit of burning, he purgeth their dross, taketh away their tin, and forms all his people into vessels of mercy and sanctification; that he may at length present them unto himself, a glorious church, not having spot or wrinkle, or any such thing, but that they may be without blame before him in love. And what endears him to his people under this blessed character as their Refiner is this, that all the while the process is going on, Jesus sits by, watches over them, tempers the fire in exact proportion to what it should be, and suffers not the enemy to fan it a jot more than his love and wisdom see it fit to be. Is this the case, my soul, with thee? Are all the fiery trials thou hast gone through, regulated, kept under, and blessed, by thy Jesus, to so much good? Oh my foolish heart, how have I repined in my affliction, because I saw not Jesus's hand in the appointment, nor discerned his love carrying me through it. Blessed Refiner, henceforth give me to see thee. And do thou sit in this most needful office over my soul, that as all true believers are of the royal priesthood, being sons of Levi, and made kings and priests to God and the Father, never may my soul come out of the furnace of thy purification, until that I am enabled, by thy grace, to offer to the Lord an offering in the blood and righteousness of Jesus, whereby alone I can find acceptance with God in grace here, and glory hereafter.

EVENING.—" If there be among you a poor man of one of thy brethren, within any of thy gates, in thy land which the Lord thy God giveth thee, thou shalt not harden thine heart, nor shut thine hand from thy poor brother; but thou shalt open thine hand wide unto him, and shalt surely lend him sufficient for his need, in that which he wanteth." —Deut. xv. 7, 8.

How is it possible, dearest Lord Jesus, that I can

read this scripture, and call to mind thy obedience for me, in fulfilling the whole law, without connecting with it all the blessedness of looking up to thee under every circumstance, and in every case, for thy favour and thy love? When Jesus became circumcised for his people, he made himself a debtor to the whole law. And is not this delightful precept of my evening meditation a part of it? Surely, Lord, this precept speaks to thee. Not that my glorious Surety needed a command to the love of any of his poor brethren; for, blessed Jesus, thy love brought thee down from heaven, and it was thine own free voluntary love that, at the call of God thy Father, prompted thine infinite mind to stand up as thy brethren's law-fulfiller from all eternity. But though thou needest not to be put in mind of mercy to any poor brother of thine, yet is it precious to my soul to see that this command of God my Father forms a part in the obedience of Jesus to the whole law; and doubly blessed is it to my soul to see, that in all the blessings wherewith Jesus, the Head of his body the church, blesseth his people, the hand of God my Father is in it. How hath God the Father manifested his love to his church in the gift of his dear Son, and in all those blessed commands given to Jesus for the church's welfare! And how hath Jesus manifested his love in giving himself, yea, and becoming sin and a curse for his church, that all his redeemed might be made the righteousness of God in him! Look up then, my soul, to thy Jesus, thy Brother, thy Law-fulfiller! He will not overlook, nor forget this sweet precept. Thou art waxen poor indeed, but Jesus knoweth all thy poverty and all thy need; and though thou hast been a transgressor from the womb, and hast forgotten, times without number, thy relationship, Jesus will never forget his. He hath so loved thee as to die for thee; so loved thee as to shed his blood for thee; so loved thee as to plead for thee, and is for ever appearing in the presence of God for thee. And therefore, he will never harden his heart against thee, nor shut up his hand, nor his heart, nor his loving-kindness, in displeasure. Precious Lord! thou art indeed a brother born for adversity, and one that loveth at all times; yea, "thou stickest closer than a brother."

DECEMBER 12.

MORNING.—"Take this and divide it among yourselves."—Luke xxii. 17.

Precious Lord, such was thine unbounded love to thy people that thou gavest all to them! And, dearest Jesus, what didst thou reserve for thyself? And how wisely was thy love manifested! To every one grace according to the measure of the gift of Christ; for the purchase of redemption, in the case of all, cost thee the same. If, indeed, a lamb of thine be weak, or diseased, or torn, or scattered, thou wilt take it to thy bosom, while thou wilt gently lead those that are with young. But every one, and all, shall have thy care; all, as their several wants may be. Here then, Lord, to thy table I would come. Thy death hath confirmed all thy purchased blessings. And in the holy supper I would seek grace, that my right may be confirmed in them. Before God, and angels, and men, I would take the seal of thy gift. In thy blood thou hast signed them: in the word of thy gospel thou hast recorded them: in the ordinances of thy church they are published and brought forth: and by thy Spirit thou givest the tokens and the pledges of them to thy redeemed. Witness for me, then, ye angels of light, that I accept of all in Jesus and in his free gift, the purchase of his blood, and the tokens of his love. Sweeter are they to my mouth than honey and the honeycomb. Blessed Jesus, thy love is better than wine.

EVENING.—" For thus saith the Lord, ye have sold yourselves for nought: and ye shall be redeemed without money."—Isaiah lii. 3.

Sweet thought, arising from this gracious promise of a most gracious covenant God in Christ! It is indeed for nought that every poor sinner hath sold himself, and mortgaged his inheritance; for sin produceth no wages but death, and Satan gives nothing but misery to his captives. The world holds out great promises indeed, but never fulfils them. Vanity and vexation of spirit are all that we receive in the close of the account. So that what Jehovah saith, every man finds to be true; we have sold ourselves for nought. But, blessed Lord! when at any time, for our sin and rebellion, thou sufferest our enemies to lead us captive, what profit doth our Lord gain by it? May we not say, in the language of the church, " Thou sellest thy people for nought, and dost not increase thy wealth by thy price?" Psalm xliv. 12. If, Lord, it would be to thy glory, that our shame, and the triumph of our enemies ministered to thy praise, it would be enough to make thy church say, " Let us suffer, so Jesus be but glorified." But, Lord, this is so far from being the case, that when Jesus's members suffer, the glorious Head is injured, and the triumph of the foe becomes an insult to our God. How very blessed is it then to know, that though we are soul destroyers by ministering to our own ruin, Jesus is our soul restorer by redeeming us without money. Oh! for grace to keep in view the vast, the immense price Jesus hath given for our redemption! Oh! for grace to give him all the glory of our recovery, who alone hath accomplished it! And, Lord! I would pray, that as " the redemption of the soul is precious, and it ceaseth for ever," my soul may everlastingly rejoice in the assurance, that being bought with such a price, not of silver and gold, but by thy blood, I may henceforth glorify God in my body and in my spirit, which are his! Remember, my soul, it is the Lord that saith this: "Ye have sold yourselves for nought; and ye shall be redeemed without money!"

DECEMBER 13.

MORNING.—"The tree of life."—Rev. xxii. 2.

Lead me, O Holy Ghost, by the hand of faith, this morning, into the paradise of God, and cause me to sit down under the tree of life; and for a while, before the world breaks in upon me, enable me to meditate on its beauties, its loveliness, and its fruit. Is it not Jesus which I behold in this charming similitude? Surely Jesus is to me the tree of life, for I have no life but in him! And it is not only he which gave me life at the first, but preserves it, maintains it, and will preserve it for ever. He saith himself, "Because I live, ye shall live also." And as he is himself the life of my soul, so every thing in him is the promoter of my life. His fruit also is all my sustenance, all I want, all I desire, all I can truly enjoy. He bears twelve manner of fruits. Yes, for there is in him both fulness and variety: pardon, mercy, and peace, in the blood of his cross; favour with God, affection with men; the Spirit's gifts, graces, influences; comfort in this life, happiness and joy in that which is to come. And every month these fruits abound. Yes, he saith himself, "My fruit is better than gold, yea, than fine gold: and my revenue than choice silver." "I will cause them that love me to inherit substance; yea, I will fill all their treasures." Nay, the very leaves of this tree of life are for the healing of the nations. And how healing indeed is Jesus, in his word, his ordinances, his providences, his promises, his dispensations! Neither is this all: the tree of life grows in the midst of the street, and is open in every gospel ordinance, both to Jews and Gentiles, both to bond and free. He is also on either side the river. The church above, though sitting under the full enjoyment of him, doth not keep him wholly to herself. Blessed be his name, he is as much for the glory and happiness of his church here below, on this side the river of death. And is this tree of life, this Jesus, mine? Oh the vast privilege! I bless thee, Oh thou Holy Spirit, for giving me the knowledge of him now by faith: and ere long, I hope to sit down for ever in the paradise of God, in the unceasing enjoyment of him, from whence I shall arise no more, but dwell under his branches for ever.

EVENING.—"And at midnight there was a cry made, behold, the bridegroom cometh, go ye out to meet him."—Matt. xxv. 6.

When Jesus, the bridegroom of his church, first came, it was in a moment sudden and unexpected, like the surprise at a midnight hour. And when Jesus cometh to any of his people, it is unlooked for. Indeed, it is always midnight in the soul of a sinner, when the cry is made! But how blessed is the cry, when a poor lost perishing sinner is advanced to the midnight of death, on the verge of an approaching eternity, and in that season hears the voice of the Son of God, and lives! How many, like the thief on the cross, or like the jailor at Philippi, have been surprised into grace at such seasons, by the sovereignty of Him, "who calleth things that are not, as though they were?" Precious Jesus! in all the circumstances of life, in the midnight of nature, the midnight of carnal security, the midnight of sleep, in which even thy dear children are so liable to be found; Oh! that we may hear thy voice, and go forth to meet thee! And, Lord! let the going forth of thy redeemed be, not with the lamp of a profession, but with the enlightened oil of grace, that we may meet thee with all our affections alive, to hail and welcome thy coming; so that "at midnight, or cock-crowing, or in the morning," when Jesus saith, "Behold, I come quickly," our souls may cry out, in joyful reply, "Even so; come, Lord Jesus!"

DECEMBER 14.

MORNING.—" Nevertheless, he saved them for his name's sake, that he might make his mighty power to be known."—Psalm cvi. 8.

Pause, my soul, over this verse, and observe how thy gracious God took occasion, from the misery of Israel, and even from their unworthiness, to magnify the riches of his grace. Israel had highly sinned: they had provoked the Lord; and their provocations were aggravated, from the spot where they were committed, for it was at the sea, even at the Red Sea, that memorable sea where the Lord had made a path for their deliverance. And wherefore, then, did he save them? Wherefore did not the Lord drown them in the depths of the sea, for their unbelief and hardness of heart? This sweet scripture gives the reason. " He saved them for his name's sake." His name was engaged in covenant promises, and his glory was magnified in making good his engagements, notwithstanding all their undeservings. And what saith this doctrine to thee, my soul? There is a *nevertheless* with thee also, from God's covenant engagement *in* Christ and *to* Christ, thy glorious covenant head, notwithstanding all thy unworthiness and provocations. Though I fail in all, God's covenant fails in none. Though my unbelief breaks out like Israel's, even at the red sea of Christ's blood; yet the efficacy of that blood is still the same, and the Father's engagement to his dear Son, by virtue of it, never can fail. His own love is the standard of his grace, and not my deservings; his name's sake, and not my merit, the rule of his favour towards his people; and all in Jesus. Fold up, then, this blessed scripture, my soul, for thy daily meditation, and learn to bless the freeness of that grace which hath for its object the glory of God's name, and no motive for thy salvation, but God's glory in Christ Jesus.

EVENING.—" In that day, saith the Lord, will I assemble her that halteth."—Micah iv. 6.

Mark, my soul, the graciousness of thy God! Jesus is not only blessing his people when they follow him, but he will bless them by recovering them when they halt. And of all the tokens of grace, that is the most endearing which is manifested over the aboundings of transgression. We have a passage similar to this in the writings of Isaiah, in which the Lord complains of the baseness of his people: " But thou hast not called upon me, O Jacob; but thou hast been weary of me, O Israel. Thou hast made me to serve with thy sins, and thou hast wearied me with thine iniquities." One might suppose, after such a charge, and such instances of ingratitude, that the next account would be, that the Lord had given up Jacob to the curse, and Israel to reproaches: but, no! what saith the Lord? " I, even I, am he that blotteth out thy transgressions, for mine own sake, and will not remember thy sins;" Isaiah xliii. 22, &c. How doubly refreshing is grace, when it comes over all our unworthiness, rebellions, and sins! See, my soul, how the Lord graciously overrules thine haltings, and makes a falling time to become a rising time, to his praise, and to thy comfort! Lord! confirm thy word unto thy servant, wherein thou hast caused me to hope! Do thou, Lord, in this day, thine own day, the gospel day, fulfil thy promise, and let all our haltings be healed, and " give us to run the way of thy commandments, when thou hast set our souls at liberty."

DECEMBER 15.

MORNING.—" Knowing that tribulation worketh patience."—Rom. v. 3.

Have former trials been blessed to thee, my soul? Why then depend upon it, this, be it what it may, will be also. The covenant love and faithfulness of God in Christ are both the same now, as they ever were. If the Lord hath hitherto been making all things work together for good, so will he now. Only pause and consider why it must be so. Thy God is the same God as ever: is he not? And his love to thee the same, because it is in Jesus; his covenant the same, his promises the same; the blood and righteousness of the Lord Jesus in efficacy the same. Well then, as all the perfections of God are engaged for God's people, certain it is, that no trial to his people can arise which he knew not, nay, which he appointed not, and for which he hath not made a suitable provision. Well then, what trouble of thine can be so great, as to counteract and overcome divine strength? What burden so heavy that Jesus cannot bear? What afflictions so painful that Jesus cannot soften? What grief so scorching as to dry up the streams of God's love? Hear then his words: "In your patience possess ye your souls." My soul, rest in this. Let past experience bring thee present confidence. See that all the fresh springs of patience flow from Jesus. Wait patiently for the Lord, by believing in him; and, depend upon it, thy present tribulation, of what sort or kind soever it is, will terminate, like every former, in bringing glory to God and comfort to thy soul.

EVENING.—"They did eat manna, until they came unto the borders of the land of Canaan."—Exod. xvi. 35.

How graciously did God the Holy Ghost teach Israel, by type and shadow, concerning good things to come! It must be our duty, and it will prove our happiness, to read in every event, as far as the Holy Ghost teacheth, our new testament blessings dressed up in the old testament figures. The feeding of the church in the wilderness with manna forty years, was a standing miracle, and, as such, became a most suitable type of Jesus. My soul, look at it, this evening, in this point of view, and behold what the Spirit holds forth in it, concerning the Lord Jesus. The continuance of this supply from heaven became a beautiful resemblance of the state of believers in all ages. The rebellion of Israel occasioned not any suspension of the mercy; for though they murmured and rebelled, the manna was sent the same, " new and pure every morning." Sweet thought to the poor timid believer! Though we fail in our duty, Jesus will not diminish in his love; and though we neglect him, yet will he not forget us. Moreover, morning by morning, the blessing came; not a day, not an hour omitted. Jesus is all this, and more: " For it shall come to pass, that before my people call, (saith Jehovah) I will answer; and while they are speaking, I will hear;" Isaiah lxv. 24. There is another precious thought suggested in the view of the type, and the thing signified; all the people partook of the rich mercy. There was enough manna for every one; for each and for all. Such is Jesus to his people. Every state and every circumstance he is able to supply, and he doth and will supply; and therefore, between the old church of the old testament believers, and the new church of new testament saints, there is a great analogy and agreement. Christ is the sum and substance of all and every one of the people. One thing more: As Israel had no other sustenance until they came to the borders of Canaan, so the people of God now have no other, yea, they desire no other, until they come to the Canaan above. In Jesus there is a fulness of grace, and life, and glory. Hail, thou heavenly bread! thou word of God! Be thou my portion, the bread of life, until I am brought down to the waters of Jordan. Help me, Lord, by faith, to feed on thee and on thy great salvation; and " may my meditation of thee be sweet!"

DECEMBER 16.

MORNING.—" He that is surety for a stranger shall smart for it: and he that hateth suretyship is sure."—Prov. xi. 15.

Blessed Jesus, well is it for me that thou didst not hate to become a Surety; for hadst thou so done, and refused the vast undertaking, I must have perished for ever. And hadst thou consented to have become a Surety only for friends, and those only that loved thee, still here again I should have been lost: but when thou condescendedst to become Surety for me, Oh Lord, it was not simply for a stranger, but for a rebel, a hater and despiser of thee, and of thy great salvation. Oh the love of God that passeth knowledge! And how, blessed Jesus, didst thou indeed smart, and wert crushed and broken, when for my dreadful debt of sin, which surpassed all the angels of light to pay, it pleased the Father to bruise thee, and to put thee to grief. Oh matchless love of a most compassionate Saviour! Methinks I still see thee taking my place under the angry eye of God's broken law. Methinks I see thee striking my worthless name out of the bond of the covenant of the law of works, and putting thine own in. Methinks I still hear thee, like another Judah, who in this was evidently thy type, saying to God and the Father, " I will be Surety for him: at my hands thou shalt require him." Oh Lamb of God! I bless thee as my Surety. I acknowledge thee as my glorious Sponsor. I was a stranger, indeed, and thou hast owned me, and brought me home. I was in debt and insolvent, and thou hast cancelled the whole in the blood of thy cross. " I was naked, and thou hast clothed me; sick, and in prison, and thou hast visited, healed me, and brought me out." I was lost, and thou hast redeemed and saved me. " Oh what shall I render unto the Lord for all the benefits he hath done unto me? Bless the Lord, Oh my soul, and all that is within me, bless his holy name."

EVENING.—" God shall enlarge Japheth, and he shall dwell in the tents of Shem."—Gen. ix. 27.

None but God himself could do either. Who but God could enlarge the one, or persuade and overrule the other? Of Japheth came the Gentiles, Gen. x. 5; and Shem is the father of Israel. But Jesus, and Jesus only, can bring both Jew and Gentile into one fold, under one Shepherd. And when the fulness of the Gentiles shall be completed, then shall all Israel be saved. Then will the Deliverer arise out of Zion, to turn away ungodliness from Jacob. My soul, art thou, night by night, and morning by morning, besieging a throne of grace, that the Lord would hasten the latter day of glory? Surely, if thou feelest due concern for the Redeemer's glory, this must form a part in thy daily petition. Who indeed can be indifferent to the interests of Christ's kingdom? "In the multitude of the people," saith Solomon, "is the king's honour;" Prov. xiv. 28; and in the multitude of redeemed souls, is the glory of Christ Jesus. Lord! I would pray, fulfil this blessed promise. Enlarge Japheth, and cause him to dwell in the tents of Shem. Let the heathen be given to our God and Saviour for his inheritance, and the utmost parts of the earth for his possession. "Oh! that the salvation were given unto Israel out of Zion! Oh! that the Lord would deliver his people out of captivity! then shall Jacob rejoice, and Israel shall be glad!"

DECEMBER 17.

MORNING.—" Fear not: I have the keys of hell and of death."—Rev. i. 17, 18.

Is it Jesus, all precious, all lovely, all powerful Jesus, that saith this? He who hath redeemed my soul from hell, mine eyes from tears, and my feet from falling? And hath Jesus, my Husband, my Brother, my Redeemer, the keys both of hell and of death? Why then it is impossible for any to open death's door one moment before that he gives the appointment. And doth he command me to fear not? Oh then, my soul, dismiss all anxiety about thy departure. Thy time is in Jesus's hands; the keys are hanging at thy Redeemer's girdle. Never fear, neither to die as thou hast lived, and art living, in a believing frame in Jesus. This is as much suited to a dying time, as it is to a living time; for with this thou mayest go out of the world, as safe as living in it. "To live is Christ, and to die is gain." God's covenant love, and God's covenant promises in Jesus, are the same. They are, both in death and life, fixed and sure. When Jesus therefore comes, when the Master calls for thee, wilt thou feel reluctant? What, reluctant to go to Jesus? Is this thy love, thy kindness to thy friend? Forbid it, dearest Lord! No, my precious, blessed Jesus, open the gate of death to me *when* thou pleasest, *where* thou pleasest, and *how* thou pleasest. Sure I am thou wilt be present, and that is enough for me; and when the ground of all sensible comforts is sinking under me, Oh for a vigorous effort of faith communicated by thee, that I may drop the body, and leap at once into thy arms, with the last cry of faith, "Lord Jesus, receive my spirit, for thou hast redeemed me, Oh Lord, thou God of truth."

EVENING.—"All my springs are in thee." -Psalm lxxxvii. 7.

Sweet thought! And this, as Solomon saith upon another occasion, forms the conclusion of the whole matter. Jesus is the source, the fountain, the author, the finisher of all our mercies; for every thing of life and salvation, of grace and glory, flow from him, centre in him; and therefore in him and from him, as the source of blessedness, all our springs must flow. In him dwelleth all the fulness of the Godhead bodily! All glories are in him: the glory of the church above; the glory of the church below; yea, the glory of angels and of God himself; for the Father hath given all his glory into his almighty hands. Hence, my soul, from whom should thy springs flow, but from Jesus? If all divine attributes, all divine perfections are in him; if grace be no where but in Jesus; no blessing, no redemption but in his blood; if all gifts, and graces flow from him, and can no where else be found, to whom shall the gathering of the people be, or from whom shall all blessings come? And what a refreshing consideration is this, under all the barren, dry, and withering frames of the believer's heart. See to it, my soul, that thou art coming to Jesus, day by day, for suitable supplies; and let not thine emptiness discourage thee, or keep thee away, but rather let a sense of thy poverty endear to thee Jesus's riches. Thou art as exactly suited for him, as he is suited to thee; and as much as thou needest his fulness, Jesus no less needs vessels to fill into, and to pour out upon, of his blessings. Precious Lord Jesus! behold then I am come to thee; I find, in every thing beside thee, sin, death, and misery. Oh, the rapturous thought! "All my springs are in thee!"

DECEMBER 18.

MORNING.—"For through him we both have access by one Spirit unto the Father."—Eph. ii. 18.

Who would have thought that so short a verse should contain so much sweetness? And who would have conceived that in it the gracious offices of all the Persons of the Godhead, as they are mercifully exercised towards a poor sinner, are described? Is not the access to a throne of grace the work, the leading of God the Holy Ghost? Surely, he is the Spirit here spoken of. And through whom can a poor sinner have access to the mercy-seat but in him, and by him, and through him, whom the Father heareth always? And of whom should the regenerated, adopted child of God have access, but unto his God and Father in Christ Jesus? Are then all the glorious persons of the God-head thus revealed, as engaged in every poor sinner's approach to the heavenly throne? Oh for grace to give to each, and to all, the praise, and glory, and love, due to such transcendent mercy; and in a conscious sense of being interested in this great salvation, to cry out with the apostle: "Now thanks be unto God, who always causeth us to tiumph in Christ."

EVENING.—"The daughters saw her, and blessed her."—Song vi. 9.

These are the words of Jesus, in commendation of his church. He holds her forth as lovely not only in his view, but in the eyes of others. The *daughters* probably, mean true believers, in whose esteem Christ and his church are most engaging; and it is more than probable that by *daughters, young believers* are particularly meant, whose first love, like the blossom of the apple-tree, is most beautiful in its first opening. Pause, my soul, and behold, from what Jesus himself saith of his church, how truly lovely she must be in the Redeemer's view; and indeed without a proper apprehension of the infinite value of the human soul, it is not possible to conceive of the exalted light wherein the church must appear to Jesus. We may form some faint idea of its value, from the vast price it cost Jesus in the redemption. None but the Son of God could make the purchase; and even Jesus only by blood. Who shall say how infinitely precious then must the church at large, composed of an innumerable host of redeemed souls as it is, appear in Jesus's eyes? The soul washed in his blood, and clothed in his spotless robe of righteousness, must be lovely indeed! And in that day, when Jesus brings the church home finally and fully, to present her to himself and Father, a glorious church, not having spot or wrinkle, or any such thing; and when the church shall appear amidst a congregated world of men and angels, the purchase of Jesus's blood, the gift of his Father's grace, and the conquest of the Holy Ghost; how will the daughters who see her, then bless her, and bless him, who is the author of all her unspeakable glory and felicity! Precious Lord Jesus! if such be the beauty of thy church, what must thy glory be, in whose comeliness alone she is made lovely? Oh! for grace to view Jesus in all, and to love Jesus in all! Thou, Lord, art the source and fountain of blessedness to thy church and people, for grace here, and glory to all eternity.

DECEMBER 19.

MORNING.—" God is faithful by whom ye were called unto the fellowship of his Son Jesus Christ our Lord."—1 Cor. i. 9.

Think, my soul, what a dignity believers in Jesus are called unto, when brought into a nearness of communion with their glorious head, in any exercise of trial or affliction for his sake. God is faithful in the appointment. How?—In that it proves God's fulfilment of his covenant promises, when Jesus and his members are considered by him as one. God is faithful in manifesting this oneness and fellowship, in making the members conformable to their glorious head, by trials or sufferings. God is faithful in sending the affliction. And God manifests his faithfulness in guiding through it, and supporting under it. The trial itself, be it what it may, is a discovery of the covenant love and faithfulness of Jehovah. Nay, God would not have manifested his faithfulness to a believer without it. What a sweet consoling thought this is to the afflicted exercised followers of the Lamb under their trials! My soul, do thou look at the subject, and learn from it to consider all tribulations in this view; and what a blessedness will pour in upon thee from so doing. Hath the Lord called thee to exercises? Hath the progress of them led thee more to Jesus? Hath the issue of them tended to endear Jesus?—Oh then, proclaim God's faithfulness. I know, Lord, said one of old under trials, "that thy judgments are right, and that thou in very faithfulness hast afflicted me." Precious Jesus, what a dignified path is tribulation, when we are enabled to see thy footsteps going before marked with blood.

EVENING.—" And they shall see his face; and his name shall be in their foreheads."—Rev. xxii. 4.

My soul, thy morning thoughts were directed to the sweet subject of being called to fellowship with thy Lord Jesus Christ in grace. Do thou, this evening, beg of God the Holy Ghost to enable thee to connect with it the transporting subject of the everlasting enjoyment of Jesus in glory This is the great end and final consummation of all. This blessed scripture leads immediately to the contemplation: "They shall see his face;" and on "their foreheads shall be his name:" that is, the token of their oneness, union, and relationship in and with Jesus; so that he will be their glory, their supreme happiness and joy; and thus he will never cease to be the immediate head of all his body, the church, "the fulness that filleth all in all;" yea, the only and everlasting medium of communication in glory, as he is of grace in this life. Pause, my soul, over this vast thought! when soul and body, after the long separation by death, shall be again united, and both, as the redeemed of the Lord, be formed one in him in glory; both then equally made capable of enjoying Christ, and both equally disposed for that enjoyment; then will the blessedness of seeing his face be complete. No doubt but that at death the sight and enjoyment of Jesus will be a joy unspeakable and full of glory; but the full, complete, and eternal enjoyment of God in Christ must be reserved to the consummation of all things, when the Lord hath brought home all his redeemed, and the mediatorial kingdom of Jesus in grace here is swallowed up in glory, and God, in his threefold character of person, Father, Son, and Holy Ghost, shall be "all in all!" Pause, again, my soul, over the vast thought! The glorious head of his church will then have brought home every individual of his body! He will fill all his members with glory. All their glory shall be in God in Christ! And God in Christ will be the life, the light, the everlasting happiness, and glory in them all. Ponder well the glorious thought! Take it with thee to thy chamber! Drop asleep with it! And, Oh! may it be the sweet thought in death, when thou droppest asleep in Jesus; then may Jesus be the last of thy dying thoughts, and the first of thy everlasting enjoyment, when, waking from the sleep of death, thou shalt open thine eyes to the glories of eternity, "to see his face, and his name in thy forehead!"

DECEMBER 20.

MORNING.—"The blood of Jesus Christ his Son, cleanseth us from all sin."—1 John i. 7.

My soul, sit down for a while, by this crimson fountain, and duly ponder over this glorious property of thy Redeemer's blood. Oh the sovereign efficacy of it! For it not only cleanseth sin, but all sin: not only other's sins, but our sins: not only the present evil of sin, but the everlasting evil of it: not only now, but for ever. It cleanseth from all sin. Pause, my soul. Is there any other laver to wash away sin; can prayers, or tears, or repentance, or ordinances, or communions, or duties, or alms? Oh no. We must say of every thing, and of all things, out of Christ, and void of Christ, as Job did concerning his friends, "Miserable comforters are ye all; physicians of no value." Here then, my soul, seek thy cleansing, and here only. And while to this fountain thou art daily brought by the Holy Ghost, look up and behold the whole assembly of the redeemed above, who are now standing around the throne, owing their bliss and their cleansing to the same source. Listen to their songs of joy, and catch the notes, to sing even now the same song of rejoicing. "They have washed their robes, and made them white in the blood of the Lamb." And *therefore* it is, and for no other cause, that they are now before the throne, and serve the Lord in his temple day and night.

EVENING.—"Them also which sleep in Jesus, will God bring with him."—1 Thess. iv. 14.

My soul, thy last night's thoughts, with which thou fell asleep, were upon a subject so truly connected with Jesus, that I hope thou couldest and didst say, "My meditation of him was sweet!" There is another blessed thought, connected both with Jesus and it, that may be proper to take along with it. Seek of God the Spirit to unfold its beauties in Jesus to thy view, this evening, and lead thee with it to fall asleep, this night, as on the former, in the Lord. The apostle opens it to thy meditation in these words; "They which sleep in Jesus, God will bring with him." The bodies, as well as the souls of the redeemed, are alike the purchase of Christ's blood, and Jesus will have them all with him. They are his jewels, his treasure, his *segullah*. He suffers them to lie among the dust, it is true; but he saith himself, though they have so lain, yet shall they be "as the wings of a dove covered with silver, and her feathers with yellow gold," Ps. lxviii. 13. How will Jesus accomplish this at the last day? He explains it himself; "And I, if I be lifted up, will draw all unto me;" John xii. 32. And if the magnetic powers of the loadstone be such that it will separate the smallest particles of steel from every thing of earth or dust around, so that they shall fly to the touch of the loadstone in every direction; can his powers be doubted, who hath constituted such principles in nature so to act and so to be governed? Oh, my soul, how sure is it, that Jesus will at the last day open the graves of his people, and cause them to come up out of them! Heaven would not be complete without this; neither the Lord Jesus fully rewarded, to see "the travail of his soul." This final consummation of all things, is the blessedness Paul speaks of, when, "in the dispensation of the fulness of time, Jehovah might gather together in one, all things in Christ, both which are in heaven and which are on earth, even in him," Eph. i. 10. Sweet thought, my soul, take it with thee to thy bed. This glory, this triumph of thy Jesus, as Mediator, the head of his body the church, remains to be accomplished; neither will it be accomplished until "the last trumpet shall sound, and the dead shall be raised incorruptible, and we shall be changed!" The patriarchs, the prophets, and holy saints of God, who died in Christ, before his incarnation, felt, no doubt, an accession to their glory and happiness, and joy in their souls, when the Son of God, after he had finished redemption-work, returned to heaven. The sight they had of Christ in his human nature opened a new source of joy unspeakable. Oh, the unknown rapture of feasting their eyes upon him. And "the spirits of just men made perfect (some of whom, my soul, thou hast seen, and known, and enjoyed sweet communion with in the church below) who are now before the throne, and serve him in his temple night and day:" they are at the fountain-head of bliss, in "seeing Jesus as he is, and knowing, even as they are known." Nevertheless, their present enjoyments are the enjoyments of the soul only; their felicity is not complete, until, at the restitution of all things, their bodies shall be raised to the triumphs of eternity. Take, my soul, these thoughts with thee to bed; and be as ready to give thy body to thy Jesus for the grave, that he, in his own time, which is the best time, may undress thee for it, as thou takest off thy garments for nightly rest; for most certain it is, that as "Jesus died and rose again, even them also which sleep in Jesus, will God bring with him."

DECEMBER 21.

MORNING.—"Then I restored that which I took not away."—Psalm lxix. 4.

Whose words are these? They can be none but the words of Jesus; for none ever made restoration but he; and none but he could say, I took nothing away. And what was taken away? God's glory was taken away by sin; and consequently, man's happiness also. For when Adam sinned, he robbed God of his glory, and robbed himself and all his posterity of God's image, and with it all happiness. Nay, my soul, thou hast done the same, in every renewed act of disobedience. And in breaking the divine law thou hast justly lost the divine favour. And hath Jesus, all precious Jesus, restored all these? Yes, blessings on his name, he hath! And what renders it ten-fold more gracious, he hath so done it as never to be lost any more. By his finished work of salvation he hath restored to God his glory. And by his obedience and death, as our Surety, he hath restored to man his happiness. The favour of God we lost by sin; Jesus hath restored it, by justifying us in his righteousness. The image of God we lost by rebellion; Jesus hath restored to us this image, in sanctifying us by his holiness. So that every way, and in all things, Jesus hath made up the breach; and the poor sinner who is led by grace to believe in Jesus, stands more complete and secure now, than before the fall. For if Adam had never sinned, nor his children in him, yet, after all, their righteousness before God would have been but the righteousness of creatures. Whereas now, in Jesus, the believer stands accepted and secured in the righteousness of the Creator.

Hail, then, thou Almighty Restorer of our fallen nature! In thee, Lord, would my poor soul triumphantly say, "have I righteousness and strength; even to thee shall men come; and all that believe in thee shall never be ashamed nor confounded, world without end."

EVENING.—"Who planteth a vineyard, and eateth not of the fruit thereof? Or who feedeth a flock, and eateth not of the milk of the flock?"—1 Cor. ix. 7.

Surely Jesus will not! Is not Jesus's church his vineyard? Did he not purchase it with his blood; and does he not water it every moment with the same? And will he not eat of the fruit of his own vine, of his own planting, and what cost him so dear? Or doth Jesus buy a flock; daily, hourly, feed his flock; carry the lambs in his arms, and cause them to lie down in his bosom; and will he not eat of the milk of his flock? Lord Jesus, when I contemplate thy love to our poor nature; when I behold all things, by thine ordination, ministering to our nature; when I see such a profusion of grace, and love, and mercy bestowed for our accommodation; all things prepared for man; both worlds engaged for him; yea, man himself as if a world in himself, and another prepared for him; the sacred word designed wholly for him; angels, ministering spirits sent forth to minister to the heirs of salvation; God, his Father; Jesus, his Brother, Surety, Redeemer; the Holy Ghost, his Comforter! When I look around, above, below, in every way, and in every direction, and behold man like some palace, built by thee, O Lord, the great architect! surely, I cry out, Jesus would never have prepared such a temple but for his own glory! O come then, Lord; come and inhabit what is thine own! Having created it, and by a new creation made it again thine; bought it, washed it with thy blood, and prepared it by thy Spirit; Oh come, and dwell in it, and take the full, the entire, the everlasting possession of it. Lord, who ever planted a vineyard, and did not eat of the fruit thereof? Who ever fed a flock, and did not eat of the milk of the flock? Surely not Jesus!

DECEMBER 22.

MORNING.—"Having made known unto us the mystery of his will, according to his good pleasure, which he hath purposed in himself."—Eph. i. 9.

My soul, pause over these volumes of divine truth: for they are not as so many simple words, but contain vast volumes indeed, and such as a whole eternity will not afford space to read over and finish. The first is a large one indeed—even the mystery of God's will: namely, the mystery of redemption, originating in the divine mind, before all worlds. And this is not the smallest part of it, that it should be made known in any degree or measure to thee, my soul, a poor creature of a day, and that day, a day of nothing but sin. The *second* volume in this vast subject is another precious part of the same glorious truth; namely, that this mercy of God in Christ is the sole result of God's good pleasure. No foresight, no merit, no pretensions of thine, my soul; no, nor the merits of arch-angels, becoming in the least the cause. For though a gracious God hath taken occasion to make a glorious display of the depths of his grace, from the depths of man's ruin; yet it was not our state, but his good pleasure, which laid the foundation of our recovery by Jesus Christ. And the *third* volume in this stupendous subject is, that he that planned, executed and finished it. As none but infinite wisdom could purpose, so none but infinite power could accomplish. Pause, my soul, and contemplate the vast mercy! It comes from God in Christ, as the first cause; and reverts back again to God in Christ, as the final end. Hallelujah.

EVENING.—"The promise of life which is in Christ Jesus."—2 Timothy i. 1.

Here is a short portion, but it is a full one. Life, and the promise of life, are great things, and both in Christ Jesus. Observe it, my soul; "life in Christ Jesus," and "the promise of life in Christ Jesus." What wouldest thou have more? Nay, what canst thou have more? Life, with all its eventful consequences; grace here, and glory to all eternity, in Christ, as thine head, everlastingly secured by God the Father's promise in Christ. So that as God the Father is the almighty promiser, and Christ comprehensively so in himself, and all his fulness the promise; so the Holy Ghost, the Spirit of promise, in all his manifold influences, confirms and seals the same to the heart of all true believers, in a life of grace, leading to a life of glory. Say, my soul, what a portion hast thou then to live upon, and to rejoice in for ever!

DECEMBER 23.

MORNING.—"Lo, I come."—Ps. xl. 7.

What a longing had old testament saints for the Lord Jesus's coming! And what an earnest wish and prayer it is among new testament believers, for Jesus's coming by the visits of his grace, and the sweet influences of his Holy Spirit, from day to day! My soul, methinks I would realize by faith this day, even this very day, these words of thy Redeemer, as if he were now standing at the door of thine heart, and asking for admission. And shall I not say, under this sweet impression, "Come in, thou blessed of the Lord, wherefore standest thou without?" Oh blessed Jesus, when I consider the many precious instances of thy coming, set up from everlasting in thy goings forth for the salvation of thy chosen, thy anticipation, in thy visits before the season of thy tabernacling in our flesh; thy visits to the patriarchs and prophets; thy manifestation openly to the people; thy secret, sweet, and inexpressibly gracious visits now, and thy promised return in the clouds at the final consummation of all things; Oh Lamb of God, dost thou say, "Lo, I come?" Oh for the earnestness of faith, in all her devout longings, to cry out with the church of old, and say, "Make haste, my Beloved, and come! Oh come quickly, Lord Jesus!"

EVENING.—"The day-spring from on high."—Luke i. 78.

Truly it was so when Jesus came; for a long night of Jewish darkness and ignorance had covered the earth, and gross darkness the people. Look, my soul, at Jesus under this blessed similitude. Though it be evening with thee, this day-spring will give light, and the promise will be fulfilled, "at even-time it shall be light." Jesus was the day-spring in the everlasting council and purpose of Jehovah, when he stood up the light of his people from all eternity. And when, in the fulness of time, he came, it was to fulfil all the shadows of ordinances concerning him. And what is it now, in every individual instance of his visiting his people, but as "the day-spring" on their souls? When first, from a state of nature, he calls them to a state of grace, is it not "the day-spring from on high?" And in all the after-stages, during a life of grace leading to glory, is not every renewed manifestation of his love as "the day-spring from on high?" And what will it be after the night of death, when Jesus shall come "to be glorified in his saints, and admired in all that believe," but the same? Jesus will then be "the day-spring," and "the morning-star" of that everlasting day, whose sun shall go down no more. Precious day-spring of my God! arise daily on my poor soul, and fill my heart with light and glory.

DECEMBER 24.

MORNING.—" God sent forth his Son, made of a woman."—Gal. iv. 4.

How little did Adam suppose, when he charged God foolishly, as by the way it may be observed all sinners do by this plan, in attempting to palm off his sin upon God, that the Lord in after ages would put distinguishing honour upon the woman, in which the man should bear no part. " The woman," said Adam, " whom thou gavest to be with me, she tempted me, and I did eat." Thus endeavouring to throw the whole blame of his transgression upon his gracious Benefactor. It is as if he had said, hadst thou not given me this woman, I should not have disobeyed thy command. Now observe, my soul, God's benignity and grace upon this occasion. " The seed of the woman," said God, " shall bruise the serpent's head." Not the seed of the man, but of the woman. And when the fulness of the time was come for this promise to be accomplished, " God sent forth his Son made of a woman," without the intervention of an human father, but by the miraculous impregnation only of the Holy Ghost, as if to honour the weaker vessel, and to open a source of peculiar comfort in the female breast. As if God had said, in answer to Adam's daring impiety, though all the redeemed among men shall partake in this great salvation, yet the woman shall have in it an eminent token of divine favour. And as the accursed enemy of God and man did first beguile the woman; from the woman shall arise him that shall destroy the devil. The blessings of redemption shall begin with the woman, to her peculiar honour, and to the serpent's everlasting shame. For he that in after ages shall do away more than all the evil of sin and the fall, by the sacrifice of himself, shall be born of a woman. And thus the Lord manifested forth his grace in silencing Adam's unbecoming expostulation. Oh the wonderful way and method of our wonder-working God!

EVENING.—" Shepherds abiding in the field, keeping watch over their flock by night."—Luke ii. 8.

My soul, think what a memorable night was that, which ushered in the wondrous day, the most momentous ever marked in the annals of time, since reckoning of days or years was made. The unconscious shepherds in the fields had no other thought but of their flock. But what a morning did the angels call them to celebrate! Now, my soul, sit down and take a leisurely survey of the wonderful story of Jesus's birth. Mark the several volumes in it; for a night, yea, for a whole eternity must end before the subject of God incarnate can be exhausted in the meditation. Let thy evening thoughts on this, be followed by the night contemplation; and let thy midnight only be broken in upon, by the same call that the heavenly host gave to the shepherds. Arise but to sing as they sang, and to go in quest of Jesus, as they went. God and man in one person, one Christ; and God in Christ coming for the purposes of salvation, will furnish out an hymn, which, though begun in life, will never end in eternity; " Glory to God in the highest, and on earth peace, good-will towards men!"

DECEMBER 25.

MORNING.—" And the Word was made flesh, and dwelt among us."—John i. 14.

Turn aside, my soul, this day, from every vain and worldly thought, as Moses did at the bush, and behold by faith the accomplishment of what he then saw in type and figure, of this great sight which the Lord hath made known unto thee. The Word, the uncreated Word, even the eternal Son of God, taking upon him the nature of man, and uniting both in one Person, that by the union he might be a suitable Saviour for his people. As God, he was mighty to save, and fully competent to the wonderful act. As man, he was a suitable Saviour, for the right of redemption belonged to him. And as both, he, and he alone, could become a proper Mediator, to reconcile and bring together God and man, which by sin were at variance. This was the glorious news angels posted down from heaven to proclaim. This was the song of heaven, for which they sung "glory to God in the highest, and on earth peace, good will to men." My soul, canst thou join in the song? Yes, if so be thou hast received Christ in those glorious characters; if, as for this divine purpose he was born in our streets, he is born in thy heart also, and formed there the hope of glory. Oh it is a blessed thing to have true scriptural views of the Lord Jesus, and so to receive him, as Jehovah hath sent him forth, the Christ of God. Amen.

EVENING.—" And without controversy, great is the mystery of godliness: God was manifest in the flesh, justified in the Spirit, seen of angels, preached unto the Gentiles, believed on in the world, received up into glory."—1 Tim. iii. 16.

My soul, sit down this memorable evening, and in commemorating the great event of Christ's nativity, listen to what the Holy Ghost here speaks, by his servant the apostle, concerning the mystery of godliness! Here are so many wonders branched out into so many chapters: they hang like a rich and full cluster upon the vine. Gather them one by one, mark their beauties, and taste their sweetness. The *first* is, "God manifest in the flesh:" here is a meditation for thee to live upon, and to feast upon for ever. Thy God, thy Jesus, thy Holy One, the Son of God, was made flesh! Go on to the *second:* He was "justified in the Spirit:" a matter that would never have taken place, had he not fully, by his righteousness and death, satisfied his Father's law, and brought in an everlasting righteousness for his people. Take down the *third* blessed character: He was " seen of angels." Yes! they worshipped him also: for angels, principalities, and powers, were made subject unto him. Look, my soul, at thy Lord, under the *fourth* description which the Holy Ghost hath here given of him: He was " preached unto the Gentiles:" and this was as great a mystery to the Jewish church, as any; that God should " grant to the Gentiles also, through Christ, repentance unto life." And how dear this part of Jesus's character should be to thee, my soul, who wast by nature a poor Gentile, an alien to the commonwealth of Israel, having no hope, and without God in the world, thou needest not to be told. Mark another, and the *fifth*, particularity of thy Jesus; he is said to be " believed on in the world:" and how should this have been done, even in a single instance, but for the sovereignty of God's grace? Surely this is no less a mystery also. Remark, my soul, how great, how very great in thy case. *Lastly*, the account closeth: " Jesus was received up into glory:" and there, my soul, do thou follow him, by faith, until the Lord come to take thee home with him in absolute enjoyment, that " where he is, there thou mayest be also." Amen.

DECEMBER 26.

MORNING.—" Jesus Christ of the seed of David."—2 Tim. ii. 8.

Sweet thought! Jesus will have regard to both sexes in his incarnation. He will be of the seed of the woman. He will be also truly and properly man. As both the man and woman had sinned, so redemption shall be for both. But in the holy nature, in which as Redeemer he will come, he will partake of none of their sins. The man shall have no hand in his generation. And the womb of the woman shall be but the deposit of that holy thing so called, (Luke i. 35.) by the miraculous conception of the Holy Ghost. So that the body which God the Father prepared him, belonged to both, but was unconnected with either. He must be truly man; for the law had said, "Every male that openeth the womb shall be called holy unto the Lord." He must be a priest; and no woman could minister in that office. He must be a prophet; and no woman could exercise that province, for it is not permitted for a woman to speak in the church. He must be a king; and the kingly office belongeth not to the weaker vessel. But both sexes shall be equally at the same time concerned in the blessed event of his incarnation. The woman is saved in the child-bearing of this Redeemer, and the man brought into favour and reconciliation; "for as by man came death, by man came also the resurrection of the dead. So that, as the apostle strongly and satisfactorily concludes, "there is neither Jew nor Greek, there is neither bond nor free, there is neither male nor female, but ye are all one in Christ Jesus."

EVENING.—"A stone of stumbling, and a rock of offence."—1 Peter ii. 8.

O my Lord! how wonderful is it, that thy coming should have given such offence to thy people? The prophet, indeed, said it should be so, and thereby gave one among the many testimonies to thy character. "He," saith the prophet (Isaiah viii. 14.) "that shall be for a sanctuary, shall be but for a stone of stumbling, and for a rock of offence to both the houses of Israel." But what was there, my Lord, in thee, and the gracious purpose for which thou came, that could have furnished occasion for stumbling? Thy birth, indeed, was humble, thy life marked with sorrow, thy death ignominious, and every thing about thee debased. But under all these things, did not the Godhead burst forth in acts which none but God could perform? And is the offence of the cross ceased in the present hour? Alas! what multitudes of sinners now, as much as then, still live to despise salvation by thy blood and righteousness? Precious Jesus! who made me to differ from another? Why was I constrained to look unto thee as the Rock of Ages, the precious stone that Jehovah hath laid in Zion for salvation, while thousands refuse that thou shouldest reign over them? Oh! for grace to praise thee, and to love thee! Now, Lord, do I discover a preciousness in that divine scripture, and thank thee for it as my own; "Blessed is he (thou hast said) whosoever is not offended in thee!"

DECEMBER 27.

MORNING.—"For the mountains shall depart, and the hills be removed: but my kindness shall not depart from thee, neither shall the covenant of my peace be removed, saith the Lord, that hath mercy on thee."—Isaiah liv. 10.

What a rest is here for a poor redeemed sinner to stand firm upon, in time, and to all eternity! Well may he cry out concerning Jesus, and his great salvation in him, "He is a rock, and his work is perfect." Yes, yes, thou Lord God of my salvation: thou art my dwelling-place in all generations. My soul, look all around thee, look within thee, look every where about thee. Search, behold, examine diligently, what else will or can afford thee any security. And think what a dying world it is in which thou art dwelling, or rather travelling through. What friend, what brother, what child, what relation, can give thee help of soul, or even of body, when thou most shalt need it? Think what a day, a week, an hour, may bring forth! Amidst all these changes, is Jesus thine? Doth he tell thee, "that though mountains depart, and hills be removed, his salvation and the Father's covenant of peace is the same?" Shout, shout, my soul, and begin the song, which in a dying hour will only swell louder, "Salvation to God and the Lamb!"

EVENING.—" For he that is entered into his rest, he also hath ceased from his own works, as God did from his."—Hebrews iv. 10.

My soul, see to it, that among other blessed evidences of thine union and rest in Christ, thou hast this also: " We which have believed," the apostle saith, " do enter into rest." Our dependence on, and knowledge of Jesus, are such, that we really and truly enjoy the blessings of redemption. And as God the Father, when he had finished creation, rested from all his works which he had made; and as Jesus, when he had finished redemption, entered into his glory; so true believers, when they have once found Christ, and redemption in his blood, no longer weary themselves in the works of sin, or the works of self-righteousness, by way of justification before God; but cease from every thing in self, and rest with complacency and delight in the rich, free, and full salvation that is by Christ. My soul, what sayest thou to this blessed testimony of thine interest in Jesus? Is Jesus to thee the resting-place from sin, from sorrow, from guilt, and the wrath to come? As God the Father rests in him, well pleased for his righteousness sake, dost thou rest in him? Oh! the felicity of such a rest! Jesus is indeed the rest, wherewith the Lord causeth the weary to rest: and this is the refreshing! " Return to thy rest, O my soul, for the Lord hath dealt bountifully with thee!"

DECEMBER 28.

MORNING.—" The eyes of the Lord thy God are always upon it, from the beginning of the year even unto the end of the year."—Deut. xi. 12.

Oh for grace, to live always under an abiding sense of this most blessed truth. My soul, never forget it, if possible, but always possess in recollection an abiding apprehension of Jesus's gracious presence. And do thou, dearest Lord, when thou art coming forth in mercies, give me grace to be going forth to meet thee with praises: and while thou art bartering thy riches for my poverty, let all thy bounties be doubly sweetened in coming from thine own hand, and being sanctified by thy blessing, that I may receive all to my soul's joy, and to the praise of the Father's grace in Christ Jesus. Amen.

EVENING.—"The end of all things is at hand: be ye therefore sober, and watch unto prayer."—1 Peter iv. 7.

My soul, how hath the year been hastening from thee, and thou hastening in it from the world! Where are the days fled? They are gone to be numbered with the years beyond the flood; and thou art now standing as on the isthmus of time. "The end of all things is at hand." Friends are dying around thee, thou art dying thyself; yea, the world is dying: and the end of all things is at hand. In this state, my Lord, well may I look up to thee! Circumstances so very solemn may well induce soberness, and watchfulness unto prayer. Yes! blessed Jesus! I would pray thee to induce in me every suited state, that every faculty may be on the watch tower, waiting my Lord's coming. Thou hast said: "Yet a little while, and he that shall come, will come, and will not tarry." Oh! then for grace to live by faith on thee; and so to live, that when I change worlds, I may not change my company. For if in time I live with Christ, and enjoy Christ; I shall not live less with Christ, nor enjoy Christ less, when I exchange time for eternity! Lord Jesus! be thou my watchfulness unto prayer, and thou wilt be, both now and then, in life and death, my portion for ever.

DECEMBER 29.

MORNING.—"Not one thing hath failed of all the good things which the Lord your God spake concerning you."—Joshua xxiii. 14.

Say, my soul, in looking back the past year, canst

thou set thy seal to this truth? Is there a promise which thy God hath not fulfilled? Is there an instance in which God hath forfeited his word? Canst thou point to the time, or place, in any one trial, or under any one affliction, in which thou hast not found God faithful? Give then the Lord the honour due unto his name. If not one thing hath failed, proclaim his glory, set forth his praise, declare his truth, let the father to the children make known that God is faithful. And Oh let thine heart bear testimony to what must be said of all his Israel, in all ages, " What hath God wrought."

EVENING.—" Few and evil have the days of the years of my life been."—Gen. xlvii. 9.

My soul, in looking back upon thy life, mayest thou not well take up the same languge as the patriarch, and confess that " few and evil have thy days been?" Surely the review appears like the heath of a desert, " that knoweth not when good cometh!" Out of Jesus, and considered without an eye to him, there is not a single circumstance of real merit, or of real happiness to be seen. The whole of life, from the days of childhood, through all its intermediate stages, presents but one view " of vanity and vexation of spirit? Precious Jesus! what would the arithmetic of life have been in the now departing year, or in the departure of myself from the world, but for thee? Hadst thou not graciously sought me, when I sought not thee: hadst thou not opened to me " the good old way, trodden by the patriarchs, and guided and held up my feet in following them; had not Jesus been my way, and truth, and life; what a sad conclusion should I now have had to make of the " few and evil days of my pilgrimage?" Blessed Lord! go before me all the remainder of the untrodden paths, and be thou to me " the pillar of cloud by day, and the pillar of fire by night." Bring me, Lord, to the inns of thine ordinances, and to thine house of prayer, and cause me to drink out of " the wells of salvation." Oh! for increasing knowledge of thee, my Lord, and for the increasing enjoyment of thee, that I may "go from strength to strength, until my pilgrimage be over, and I come to appear before my God in Zion!"

DECEMBER 30.

MORNING.—"Then Samuel took a stone, and set it between Mispeh and Shen, and called the name of it Eben-ezer, saying, hitherto hath the Lord helped us."—1 Sam. vii. 12.

Did Samuel do this? Was that servant of the Lord, who lived not to see Christ in the flesh, so full of faith in the coming Saviour, and in the experience of Jehovah's faithfulness in what was past, that he set up his Ebenezer? Surely, my soul, thou wilt blush to be outdone by the prophet, when thou hast not only seen the day of the Son of man completed, but felt his power. Oh my soul, let thine Ebenezer be Jesus! Let the stone thou settest up, be indeed the Rock of Ages. Yes, my soul, set up Jesus indeed, in all places, at all times, upon all occasions. And Oh Lord, do thou by thy blessed Spirit set up thyself in my heart, and enthrone thyself there, and reign and rule there for ever. Surely, my soul, Jesus is thine every-day Ebenezer; for he not only hath hitherto helped, but he doth help, and will help, and be himself thine help, thy God, thy Portion, thy Jesus, for evermore.

EVENING.—"A building of God, an house not made with hands, eternal in the heavens."—2 Cor. v. 1.

My soul, after thy last evening's meditation on the shortness and unsatisfying nature of life, let thy present thoughts be occupied in beholding, with steady faith, the great contrast to it: and see whether thy confidence be as strong, and well founded, as the apostle's. His was not a mere hope only, but an assurance in Jesus. "We know, (saith he) that if this tabernrcle were dissolved, we have a building of God, an house not made with hands, eternal in the heavens." Dost thou know this? Is Jesus thy foundation? Hath God thy Father built for thee? And doth the Holy Ghost set his almighty hand to the work, in sweetly witnessing to the writings, and sealing the deed, that it is thine? Oh! the blessedness to know this, to live already in the enjoyment of it; and while the pins of thy earthly tabernacle are daily loosening, and taking out, to be looking with full assurance of an entrance into this house "not made with hands, eternal in the heavens!"

DECEMBER 31.

MORNING.—"And the Lord spake unto Moses, saying, speak unto Aaron, and unto his sons, saying, on this wise ye shall bless the children of Israel, saying unto them, the Lord bless thee, and keep thee. The Lord make his face to shine upon thee, and be gracious unto thee. The Lord lift up his countenance upon thee, and give thee peace. And they shall put my name upon the children of Israel, and I will bless them.' —Numb. vi. 22—27.

Pause, my soul, and in these sweet words behold thine almighty Aaron, even Jesus, in his everlasting priesthood, day by day, thus blessing his people. Observe, the blessing in the name of the Lord Jehovah is thrice pronounced, as if to teach the plurality of Persons in the Godhead. And observe also, after this blessing thrice pronounced, Jehovah, as if to intimate the unity of the divine essence, declares, I will bless them. My soul, mark each. The *first* may be considered as the personal blessing of God the Father, whose gracious office it is in the work of redemption to bless and keep his people. The *second* is the peculiar mercy of Jesus, whose face is always upon his people, and his grace their portion. And the *third* is the work of God the Holy Ghost, when his blessed influences are shed abroad upon the soul, in the light of his divine countenance. And, my soul, observe further, how personally this blessing from the Holy Three in One is, to each individual; it is to *thee*, even to *thee*. And, my soul, do not forget nor overlook this vast privilege in the blessing: Aaron, the great high priest of the church, could only *pray* for the people that these mercies *might* be upon them; but thy great High Priest, the Lord Jesus, *confirms* them. His language is, Father, *I will.* And God having raised up his Son Jesus, hath sent him to bless us. Here then, blessed, precious Jesus, thou great High Priest of my soul! close the day, every day, close the year, close my life, whenever thou shalt be pleased to call me home, in thus blessing me. Lord, put thy name upon me, and upon all thy church and people, and we shall be most blessed indeed, in life, in death, and for evermore. Amen. Hallelujah: Amen.

EVENING.—"The grace of the Lord Jesus Christ, and the love of God, and the communion of the Holy Ghost, be with you all. Amen." —2 Cor. xiii. 14.

Here, my soul, set up thy pillar. Baptised as thou hast been into the joint name, love, praise, and adoration, of the Holy Three in One; and blessed as thou hast been, and art, in their joint mercies, grace, and favour; here every day, and all the day, seek thy portion and blessing, as the united source of all thy salvation. End the year, and begin the year, under those precious tokens of God in Christ; and daily keep up a lively communion and friendship with each, as the blessed cause of all thine happiness. Jehovah, in his threefold character of person, is engaged to perfect what he hath begun: and it is, and should be thy happiness to be for ever viewing the testimonies of it, in the holy scriptures of truth. God thy Father hath so loved the church in Jesus, as to give him to the church, and the church to him; and God the Son hath so loved the church, as to give himself for it; zeal for his Father's honour, and longing for the salvation of his people, led him through all the work of redemption, and now engageth his heart, until he hath brought home all his redeemed to glory: and God the Holy Ghost is unceasingly engaged to render the whole effectual, by taking of the things of Christ, and shewing them to his people. See to it then, my soul, that every day, and all the day, thou hast the love-tokens of each person of the Godhead; for this will make thee blessed upon earth, and blessed to all eternity. Hail! holy, holy, holy, Lord God Almighty! Bless both him that writes, and him that reads, with thy grace: and open and close the year with grace, until grace be consummated in everlasting glory. Amen and Amen.

PASSAGES OF SCRIPTURE

ILLUSTRATED IN THIS VOLUME.

PASSAGES OF SCRIPTURE

ILLUSTRATED IN THIS VOLUME.

PASSAGES OF SCRIPTURE

ILLUSTRATED IN THIS VOLUME.

END OF VOL. VIII.

E. Justins and Son, Printers, 41, Brick Lane, Spitalfields.